Hybrid Algorithms for Service, Computing and Manufacturing Systems:

Routing and Scheduling Solutions

Jairo R. Montoya-Torres
Universidad de La Sabana, Colombia

Angel A. Juan
Open University of Catalonia, Spain

Luisa Huaccho Huatuco
University of Leeds, UK

Javier Faulin
Public University of Navarre, Spain

Gloria L. Rodriguez-Verjan
Ecole Nationale Supérieure des Mines de Saint-Étienne, France

Information Science
REFERENCE

Senior Editorial Director:	Kristin Klinger
Director of Book Publications:	Julia Mosemann
Editorial Director:	Lindsay Johnston
Acquisitions Editor:	Erika Carter
Development Editor:	Michael Killian
Production Editor:	Sean Woznicki
Typesetters:	Milan Vracarich, Jr.
Print Coordinator:	Jamie Snavely
Cover Design:	Nick Newcomer

Published in the United States of America by
Information Science Reference (an imprint of IGI Global)
701 E. Chocolate Avenue
Hershey PA 17033
Tel: 717-533-8845
Fax: 717-533-8661
E-mail: cust@igi-global.com
Web site: http://www.igi-global.com

Library of Congress Cataloging-in-Publication Data

Hybrid algorithms for service, computing and manufacturing systems: routing and scheduling solutions / Jairo R. Montoya-Torres ... [et al.]
    p. cm.
  Includes bibliographical references and index.
  Summary: "This book explores research developments and applications from an interdisciplinary perspective that combines approaches from operations research, computer science, artificial intelligence, and applied computational mathematics"--Provided by publisher.
  ISBN 978-1-61350-086-6 (hardcover) -- ISBN 978-1-61350-087-3 (ebook) -- ISBN 978-1-61350-088-0 (print & perpetual access) 1. Operations research. 2. Artificial intelligence. 3. Computer science--Mathematics. I. Montoya-Torres, Jairo R., 1977-
  T57.6.H93 2012
  658.5'3--dc23
                    2011023571

British Cataloguing in Publication Data
A Cataloguing in Publication record for this book is available from the British Library.

All work contributed to this book is new, previously-unpublished material. The views expressed in this book are those of the authors, but not necessarily of the publisher.

Table of Contents

Section 1
Hybrid Algorithms for Routing Problems

Chapter 1

Luca Bertazzi, University of Brescia, Italy
M. Grazia Speranza, University of Brescia, Italy

Chapter 2

Nathalie Perrier, École Polytechnique de Montréal, Canada
James F. Campbell, University of Missouri-St. Louis, USA
Michel Gendreau, École Polytechnique de Montréal, Canada
André Langevin, École Polytechnique de Montréal, Canada

Chapter 3

Burcin Bozkaya, Sabanci University, Turkey
Buyang Cao, Tongji University, China
Kaan Aktolug, Aktolug Consultancy Ltd., Turkey

Chapter 4

Gülfem Tuzkaya, Yildiz Technical University, Turkey
Bahadır Gülsün, Yildiz Technical University, Turkey
Ender Bildik, Yildiz Technical University, Turkey
E. Gözde Çağlar, Yildiz Technical University, Turkey

Section 2
Hybrid Algorithms for Scheduling Problems

Section 3
Other Applications of Hybrid Algorithms

Foreword

Most fundamental problems in combinatorial optimization field have been proven to be computationally hard to solve to optimality and are known as NP-hard problems in the literature. Knowing that a problem of interest is NP-hard implies, on the one hand, that the problem is unlikely to be solved within a reasonable amount of computation time and, on the other, that one has to be satisfied with solving the problem approximately or near-optimally.

An important class of algorithms that have shown their usefulness in solving many computationally hard optimization problems is that of meta-heuristics. This is by no chance –meta-heuristics methods possess many good features, among which we could distinguish: they are able to find high quality solutions in a reasonable amount of computation time, are robust, generic, flexible and easy to implement on sequential, parallel and networked computer systems. This, together with the fact that for most practical applications in industry and businesses high quality solution would suffice, have converted meta-heuristics into *de facto* approaches to cope in practice with the computationally hard optimization problems. In fact, even when a polynomial time algorithm is known for a certain problem, solving large-size/real-life instances (e.g. instances at enterprise scale) calls again for the application of meta-heuristics methods. Not less importantly, meta-heuristic approaches can tackle with efficacy both single and multi-objective optimization problems.

Meta-heuristics methods have been applied for decades now. Besides using them as stand alone approaches, during the last years, the attention of researchers has shifted to consider another type of high level algorithms, namely hybrid algorithms. These algorithms do not follow any concrete meta-heuristic, but rather combine meta-heuristics with meta-heuristics and/or other methods (e.g. divide-and-conquer, linear programming, dynamic programming, constraint programming or other AI techniques) yielding thus *hybrid meta-heuristics*. One fundamental question here is how can be achieved for hybrid approaches to outperform stand alone approaches? The hybridization aims at exploring the synergies among stand alone methods in order to achieve better results for the optimization problem under study. For instance, using hybrid approaches one can explore the synergies between *exploration* of solution space (through population based meta-heuristics, such as Genetic Algorithms—GAs) with the *exploitation* of the solution space (through local search methods, such as Tabu Search –TS); the GA could them be used as a main search method while TS can improve locally the individuals of the population.

The rationale behind the hybridization resides in the ``no free lunch theorem'' stating that ``*... all algorithms that search for an extremum of a cost function perform exactly the same, when averaged over all possible cost functions. In particular, if algorithm A outperforms algorithm B on some cost functions, then loosely speaking there must exist exactly as many other functions where B outperforms A.*'' Based on this theorem, existing algorithms can be used as components for designing new efficient search algorithms and expect improved performance of the newly obtained algorithm for some cost functions.

Naturally, there are major issues in designing hybrid meta-heuristics for a given optimization problem, such as: (a) how to choose heuristic and/or meta-heuristic methods to be combined (within the same family or from different families of existing algorithms), and, (b) how to combine the chosen methods into new hybrid approaches. Unfortunately, there are no theoretical foundations for these issues, yet there are interesting evidences, experiences and reports on the literature. For the former, different classes of search algorithms can be considered for the purposes of hybridization, such as exact methods, simple deterministic or random heuristic methods and meta-heuristics. Moreover, meta-heuristics themselves are classified into local search based methods, population based methods and other classes of nature inspired meta-heuristics. Therefore, in principle, one could combine any methods from the same class or methods from different classes. Regarding the later, there are some attempts for taxonomies of hybrid meta-heuristics; in fact, the common approach is to try out in smart ways, based on domain knowledge of problem at hand and characteristics of heuristics methods, different hybrid approaches and shed light on the performance of the resulting hybrid approach. The level of hybridization here plays an important role, namely the degree of coupling between the meta-heuristics (e.g. coercive *vs.* cooperative). It should as well be noted that frameworks that facilitate fast prototyping have been also provided in the hybrid meta-heuristics literature.

This book brings excellent contributions to the field of hybrid algorithms, their design, implementation and experimental evaluation. The proposed hybrid approaches tackle fundamental problems in the domain of logistics, industry services, commercial distribution and manufacturing systems. The studied problems include routing, different forms of scheduling, such as permutation scheduling and shop scheduling problems, service allocation problems, etc. The proposed approaches include hybridization of meta-heuristic methods with other meta-heuristic methods such as Genetic Algorithms (GA) and Simulated Annealing (SA) or the hybridization of meta-heuristics with the exact solution of one or several mathematical programming models.

Besides advancing in the design of more sophisticated hybrid solution strategies for routing and scheduling problems, the contributions of the book have a practical focus for solving real life problems. The aim is to support decision processes in companies and thus to enable achieving better business objectives by solving the problems at company scale. Also, the use of benchmarks and software packages are good examples of best practices in the field.

The editors of this volume bring together experts and researchers from the field whose contributions explore new research findings, developments and future directions in the hybrid approaches for routing and scheduling problems arising in service, computing and manufacturing systems. Finally, although focused on the concrete field of the routing and scheduling for service, computing and manufacturing systems, most of the conclusions provided in the volume could be extended to routing and scheduling in other research fields.

Fatos Xhafa
Technical University of Catalonia, Spain

Fatos Xhafa *holds a PhD in Computer Science from the Department of Languages and Informatics Systems (LSI) of the Technical University of Catalonia (UPC), Barcelona, Spain. He was a Visiting Professor at the Department of Computer Science and Information Systems, Birkbeck, University of London, UK (academic year 2009-2010) and a Research Associate at College of Information Science and Technology, Drexel University, Philly, USA (Sept.2004-Feb.2005). Dr Xhafa holds a permanent position of Professor Titular at the Department of LSI, UPC (Spain). His research interests include parallel and distributed algorithms, combinatorial optimization, approximation and meta-heuristics, networking and distributed computing, Grid and P2P computing. Dr. Xhafa has widely published in peer reviewed international journals, conferences/workshops proceedings, book chapters and edited books in the field. Dr. Xhafa has an extensive editorial and reviewing service. He is Editor in Chief of the International Journal of Space-based and Situated Computing, Inderscience (http://www.inderscience.com/browse/index. php?journalCODE=ijssc) and of International Journal of Grid and Utility Computing, Inderscience (http://www.inderscience. com/browse/index.php?journalCODE=ijguc). He is also an associate/member of Editorial Board of several international peer-reviewed scientific journals and has guest co-edited several special issues of international journals.*

Preface

PURPOSE OF THE BOOK

In a global and highly-competitive world, organizations face an increasingly difficult environment, with increasing economic pressure and customer demands for more complex products and services that are inexpensive and that can be provided at short notice. In relation to this, hybrid algorithms could play an important role in helping organizations achieve current imperative costs reduction and fast product development.

This book deals with the study of Hybrid Algorithms for Service, Computing and Manufacturing Systems. Solutions to current real-life problems, such as supply chain management require more than an individual algorithm. Hybrid algorithms take advantage of each individual algorithm and help find solutions which are stronger/faster or more efficient than those provided by individual algorithms. Recently, the use of hybrid algorithms has increased in popularity in different research areas and industries. One of the indicators of this situation is the number of sessions, workshops, and conferences dealing with the design and application of hybrid algorithms. In practice, hybrid algorithms have proved to be efficient in solving a wide range of complex real-life application problems in different domains, including: Logistics, Bioinformatics and Computational Biology, Engineering Design, Networking, Environmental Management, Transportation, Finance and Business.

This book aims at exploring state-of-the-art research developments and applications in these research areas from an interdisciplinary perspective that combines approaches from Operations Research, Computer Science, Artificial Intelligence and Applied Computational Mathematics.

The interest in hybrid algorithms has risen considerably among academics in order to improve both the behavior and the performance of meta-heuristics. Meta-heuristics are a branch of optimization in Computer Science, Operations Research and Applied Computational Mathematics that are related to algorithms and computational complexity theory. The past few years have witnessed the development of numerous meta-heuristics in various communities that sit at the intersection of several fields, including Artificial Intelligence, Computational Intelligence, Soft Computing, and Mathematical Programming. Most of the meta-heuristics mimic natural metaphors to solve complex optimization problems (e.g. evolution of species, annealing process, behavior of ant colonies, particle swarm, immune system, bee colony, wasp swarm, or bacterial behavior).

Some results of many real-life application problems are presented in this book. As reported in the literature, hybrid algorithms could result from one of the following, by:

- Combining meta-heuristics with complementary meta-heuristics,
- Combining meta-heuristics with exact methods from mathematical programming,
- Combining meta-heuristics with constraint programming approaches developed in the artificial intelligence community,
- Combining meta-heuristics with machine learning and data mining techniques,
- Combining meta-heuristics or exact methods with simulation techniques (optimization through simulation).

TARGET AUDIENCE

This book is a valuable tool for Researchers, Practitioners and Managers, Master and PhD students, Consultants, Government officials and Policy makers, as explained below:

1. Researchers: Since this book presents cutting-edge research on hybrid algorithms for routing, scheduling and other real-life application of hybrid algorithms. As shown by the chapters included in this book, researchers in Operations Research, Management Science, and Computer Science are developing new hybrid algorithms to solve problems in Logistics (to a large extend), Supply Chain Management and Design, Production and Operations Management, Applied Operations Research and Applied Combinatorial Optimization.
2. Practitioners and Managers: Logistics and Operations Managers, Supply Chain Managers, Production Managers and Control Engineers are dealing with real-life problems on a daily basis. The hybrid algorithms presented in this book provide a valuable resource to draw upon to inform their daily practice.
3. Master and PhD students: The book can be of interest for lecturers and students in Operations Research, Computer Science, Applied Computational Mathematics, Discrete Mathematics, Logistics and Operations Management, Industrial Engineering and Systems Engineering. Especially useful for the teaching and learning of the following topics: vehicle routing, scheduling, applied and discrete mathematics and artificial intelligence.
4. Consultants: this book provides off-the-shelf hybrid algorithms that have been tried and tested which can be used by consultants and further applied to their clients.
5. Government officials and Policy makers: In general, decision-makers in both private and public sectors could benefit from this book by tailoring and assessing the hybrid algorithms according to their decision-making criteria.

OVERVIEW OF THE BOOK

The chapters published in this book are authored by a total of 38 researchers affiliated to Higher Education Institutions based in 13 countries, as follows (in alphabetical order): Brazil, Canada, Chile, Colombia, France, Germany, Italy, Mexico, Portugal, Spain, Turkey, United Kingdom and United States of America. These manuscripts cover a range of hybrid algorithms theory and practice in three main areas: Routing, Scheduling, and Other real-life application problems. These areas correspond to the three sections of the book, as explained in detail below.

The first section contains six chapters and it is devoted to the application of hybrid algorithms for solving complex realistic Routing problems.

Chapter 1 is written by Bertazzi and Speranza. This invited chapter reviews the main heuristic approaches for the solution of Inventory Routing Problems (IRP) by presenting the most recent and novel ideas for the design of a new class of heuristics called matheuristics. This class of heuristic algorithms embeds, in a heuristic or meta-heuristic scheme, the exact solution of one or several mathematical programming models.

Chapter 2 is authored by Perrier, Campbell, Gendreau, and Langevin. It provides a survey of recent optimization models and solution methodologies for the vehicle routing problem for spreading operations. The chapter presents a detailed classification scheme of models developed over the past 40 years. It highlights some factors that may be limiting the application of Operations Research models in practice and discuss promising future research trends.

The Vehicle Routing Problem with Time Windows (VRPTW) is dealt with in chapters 3 and 4, respectively. VRPTW consists on finding routes for the vehicles to serve all the customers at a minimal cost without violating the capacity and travel time constraints of the vehicles and the time window constraints set by the customers. **Chapter 3** is written by Bozkaya, Cao and Aktolug. It provides the reader with the background, mathematical models and various solution approaches for the Vehicle Routing Problem with Time Windows (VRPTW). Three case studies are presented as "success stories" of implementation of decision-aid tools for solving the VRPTW at an enterprise scale. **Chapter 4** is authored by Tuzkaya, Gülsün, Bildik, and Çağlar. The chapter considers a multiple objective Vehicle Routing Problem subject to Time Windows deliveries. A hybrid meta-heuristic algorithm based on Genetic Algorithm (GA) and Simulated Annealing (SA) is proposed.

Chapter 5 is written by Lourenço and Ribeiro. It studies the problem of designing market-efficient and cost-effective product distribution routes. This chapter explores three different distribution routing strategies: (i) the classical vehicle routing problem where total distance or cost is minimized, responding to the classical objective functions of a Logistics Department in a company, (ii) a master route strategy with daily adaptations with maximization of customer's loyalty, as intended by Marketing Departments, and (iii) a strategy that takes into account the cross-functional planning between the logistics (cost-based objective) and the marketing (customer-oriented objective) objectives through a multi-objective model. All strategies are analyzed in a multi-period scenario through a meta-heuristic algorithm based on the iterated local search scheme.

Chapter 6 is authored by Juan, Faulin, Bektaş and Grasman, discusses how simulation can be efficiently integrated with a classical heuristic in order to solve Vehicle Routing Problems with route length constraints and customer service costs. The strategy behind the hybrid solution procedure is to combine Monte Carlo Simulation with the classical Clarke & Wright Savings (CWS) algorithm and a divide-and-conquer technique. Authors also discuss the advantages and disadvantages of the procedures in relation to other existing approaches from literature.

The second section of the book is composed of four chapters and it is devoted to the presentation of hybrid algorithms for the solution of various Scheduling problems.

Chapter 7 is authored by Czogalla and Fink, and proposes a Particle Swarm Optimization (PSO) approach for the Resource-Constrained Project Scheduling Problem (RCPSP). It incorporates well-known procedures such as the serial Schedule Generation Scheme (SGS) and is hybridized with forward-backward improvement. The proposed procedure is compared against state-of-the-art methods from the literature through an extensive computational experiment using a benchmark instances.

Chapter 8 is written by Palominos, Parada, Gatica, and Vejar. It provides an exploratory analysis of the marriage of honey-bees optimization (MBO) algorithm to solve scheduling problems. The chapter also evaluates the potential utility and adaptability of this method. Two scheduling problems are considered: minimization of earliness-tardiness penalties under single machine scheduling environment with a common due date constraint and the permutation flow shop problem.

Chapter 9 is written by Solano-Charris, Gómez-Vizcaíno, Montoya-Torres and Paternina-Arboleda. It proposes the use of a novel bio-inspired algorithm to solve hard combinatorial optimization problems. The procedure is called Global Bacteria Optimization (GBO) algorithm and emulates the movement of microscopic organisms (bacteria) in response to stimulus from light. Applications are considered to solve hard mono-objective and bi-objective jobshop scheduling problems, with makespan and due date-based objective functions.

Chapter 10 is authored by Huaccho Huatuco and Calinescu. In this chapter, manufacturing rescheduling of customized production versus commodity production is investigated. Five hybrid rescheduling algorithms are presented. These are obtained by combining two key rescheduling-related elements found in the literature: rescheduling criteria and level of disruption transmitted to the shop-floor due to rescheduling. The main advantage of the proposed hybrid rescheduling algorithm over individual rescheduling algorithms consists of their ability to combine the main features of two different algorithms in order to achieve enhanced performance, depending on the objective of the organization. The practical impact of the hybrid algorithms is analyzed in the context of three manufacturing companies.

The third section is composed of three chapters and it is devoted to the presentation of hybrid algorithms for solving Other real-life application problems.

The Territory Design and Alignment Problems are considered in chapters 11 and 12, respectively. The Territory Design Problem (TDP) consists on grouping small geographic Basic Units (BU) into larger geographic territories. **Chapter 11** is written by Lopez. It considers a real-life case study from a large soft drinks distribution company that operates in the city of Monterrey, Mexico. The chapter proposes a new strategy based on a hybrid-mixed integer programming method (HMIP). By taking advantage from territory centers obtained through a relaxation of the p-median model, the procedure requires a small number of iterations to find connected solutions. The chapter highlights that the model is currently being used by the large beverage bottler in Latin America.

Chapter 12 is authored by Freire de Sousa, Barros-Basto and Lima Júnior. It briefly updates the review of the existing literature on the territory alignment problem, its applications and solution approaches. The chapter also illustrates the most recent tendencies by proposing a hybrid resolution approach based on the Greedy Randomized Adaptive Search Procedure (GRASP) and Tabu Search meta-heuristics that is integrated to an interactive and user-friendly Geographic Information System (GIS) application.

Chapter 13 is authored by Xie, Turnquist and Waller. It presents a hybrid Lagrangean relaxation and Tabu Search procedure for a class of discrete network design problems with complex interdependent-choice constraints. The algorithm is implemented on the solution of a network design problem with lane reversal and crossing elimination strategies, arising from urban evacuation planning.

In such a context, the reader will gain full exposure to some of the latest research models and frameworks with hybrid algorithms to solve practical real-life application problems. In addition, the literature is enriched by the discovery of current and future trends due to evolution of the research in the field.

Jairo R. Montoya-Torres
Universidad de La Sabana, Colombia

Angel A. Juan
Open University of Catalonia, Spain

Luisa Huaccho Huatuco
University of Leeds, UK

Javier Faulin
Public University of Navarre, Spain

Gloria L. Rodriguez-Verjan
Ecole Nationale Supérieure des Mines de Saint-Étienne, France

Acknowledgment

The completion of this book has involved the efforts by several people in addition to the Authors of the chapters. The Editors are grateful to the members of the Editorial Advisory Board, who are well-recognized academics in their fields, for supporting and overseeing the development of this Editorial project. We also want to express our gratitude to Professor Fatos Xhafa for writing the foreword of this book.

The chapter submissions for this book were subjected to double-blind refereeing process which engaged up to three reviewers per chapter. The Editors thank the reviewers for reviewing, proposing improvements, and advising the status of the chapters considered for publication in this book, their names are provided in a list of reviewers elsewhere in this book. Without their efforts, this book could not have been completed according to schedule. We are also would like to extent our appreciation to those authors who considered publishing in this book, but whose chapters could not be included for a variety of reasons. We trust that their work will eventually appear elsewhere in the literature.

The Editors would like to express their recognition to their respective organizations and colleagues for the moral support and encouragement that have proved to be indispensable during the preparation and execution of this editorial project. This book is part of the CYTED IN3-HAROSA Network. Jairo R. Montoya-Torres wishes to thank the financial support of Universidad de La Sabana under grants CEA-24-2008, CEA-46-2008 and CEA-53-2010. Javier Faulin and Angel Juan wish also to thank the financial aid of "VERTEVALLÉE" research network (funded by the Working Community of the Pyrenees by means of the grant IIQ13172.RI1-CTP09-R2), the "Sustainable TransMET" research network (funded by the program Jerónimo de Ayanz from the Government of Navarre, Spain), and the project TRA2010-21644-C03 (funded by the Spanish Ministry of Science and Technology). Luisa Huaccho Huatuco would like to acknowledge the financial support provided by the UK Engineering and Physical Sciences Research Council (EPSRC) "Complexity in the Supply Chain" project led by Principal Investigators: Dr Janet Efstathiou & Mr Gerry Frizelle (EPSRC Grant No. GR/M57842) and Leeds University Business School (LUBS) Seedcorn "Rescheduling and Complexity for Customised Products" project (Grant No. 54010803). Luisa would also like to thank the following colleagues for their help with this Editorial project: Dr Thomas F. Burgess (Leeds University Business School, University of Leeds), Dr Janet Smart (Saïd Business School, University of Oxford) and Dr Ani Calinescu (Computing Laboratory, University of Oxford). Gloria L. Rodríguez-Verjan wishes to acknowledge Dr. Claude Yugma for his collaboration, remarks and help during this editorial process, and Carlos Fernando Rodríguez for his moral support.

Last, but not least, the editors would like to acknowledge the relentless support of the IGI Global team, and in particular to Michael Killian, as their help and patience have been infinite and significant. More importantly, the editors would like to extend their sincere appreciation to their respective families for their love, support, and patience.

Section 1
Hybrid Algorithms for Routing Problems

Chapter 1
Matheuristics for Inventory Routing Problems

Luca Bertazzi
University of Brescia, Italy

M. Grazia Speranza
University of Brescia, Italy

ABSTRACT

In this chapter the authors review the main heuristic approaches for the solution of inventory routing problems and present the most recent and interesting ideas for the design of a new class of heuristics, that they call matheuristics. A matheuristic embeds, in a heuristic or metaheuristic scheme, the exact solution of one or several mathematical programming models and rely on the power of commercial software.

INTRODUCTION

The class of Inventory Routing Problems (IRPs) includes a variety of different optimization problems that may have very different characteristics but all simultaneously consider a routing and an inventory management component of an optimization problem. Time may be discrete or continuous, demand may be deterministic or stochastic, specific application-dependent characteristics may be considered, inventory holding costs may be accounted for in the objective function or not. When in an IRP the holding costs are not included in the

objective function, a limited inventory capacity at the customers is available and cannot be exceeded. IRPs have received little attention, if compared to plain vehicle routing problems (VRPs). However, the interest in this class of problems has been increasing from the beginning of the eighties. We refer for an overview of the available literature to the surveys Bertazzi et al (2008), Campbell et al (1998), Cordeau et al (2007), Federgruen and Simchi-Levi (1995), Moin and Salhi (2007). In this chapter we will focus on deterministic inventory routing problems.

IRPs model the simultaneous optimization of inventory management and routing that are traditionally optimized separately and independently.

DOI: 10.4018/978-1-61350-086-6.ch001

Clearly, the traditional separate optimization may lead to a global sub-optimum. The efforts invested in the optimization of the routing side of the problem may be vanished because the optimization ignores the relations between the routing and the inventory management sides of the problem. In VRPs usually the quantities to be delivered to the customers in a specific day by a fleet of capacitated vehicles are given. In a IRP, whereas the demands of the customers are known, the quantities to be delivered have to be decided. An optimal solution of a IRP may suggest that customers located close to each other should be served the same days, that customers close to the factory should be served more frequently, while customers far from the factory should be served more rarely.

Obviously, IRPs are more complex to solve than VRPs. A time dimension is present in the IRPs that is rarely considered in the VRPs. Whereas the value of IRPs in supply chain optimization is widely accepted, the class of the studied IRPs is still quite limited and relatively little is known in terms of solution techniques. The plain VRPs are known to be computationally very hard to solve. The IRPs are even harder. Few attempts to find the optimal solution to IRPs have been proposed in the literature. In most cases heuristic algorithms have been presented.

In this chapter we will illustrate traditional and new ideas for the design of effective heuristics by making use of a simple instance of a basic IRP. We will also review the use of heuristics for IRPs in the literature in a separate section. A set of customers have to be served by a factory (or a warehouse) over a discrete time horizon, measured for example in days, by using a fleet of capacitated vehicles. The factory and the customers have an initial inventory and limited inventory capacity. The production rate of the factory and the consumption rate of the customers are known and are time-dependent. The problem consists in deciding which customers to serve each day of the time horizon and which routes the vehicles

travel to serve the customers of each day in such a way that a cost function is minimized. The cost function includes the routing costs and possibly the inventory costs at the factory and/or at the customers. We call this problem the basic IRP.

The scope of this chapter is to present and motivate the study of a new class of heuristics, the so-called matheuristics, that make use of mathematical programming models, typically Mixed Integer Linear Programming Problems (MILPs), inside a heuristic scheme. The computational effectiveness of commercial optimization software makes it interesting and promising the design of heuristic solution approaches that make use of the optimal solution of MILPs. We will present different ways to embed MILPs in a heuristic scheme. Some of these are straightforward evolutions of traditional heuristics, others are based on more recent ideas that have recently appeared in the literature. An optimal solution approach has been proposed for the basic IRP in Archetti et al (2007) for the case of one vehicle and the optimal solution of benchmark instances with up to 3 days and 50 customers and 6 days and 30 customers is known. This will allow us to test the different heuristic solutions against the optimum and calculate the exact errors. Recent ideas for a matheuristic have been proposed for the basic IRP in Archetti et al (2010), where a tabu search heuristic includes, as an improvement step, the solution of two different mixed integer linear programming (MILP) models. The MILP models are run whenever a new best solution is obtained in the tabu search. The computational results show that this hybrid approach is more effective than the plain tabu search. Although the MILP models are shown to be NP-hard, CPLEX can solve the models to optimality in a short computational time for instances with up to 200 customers.

We will complete the chapter with a review of the literature on heuristic approaches for IRPs.

The chapter is organized as follows. In Section 1 we describe and formally define the basic IRP we consider. In Section 2 we discuss the evolution of heuristics used to solve VRPs and IRPs. In Section 3 we discuss several matheuristics for the IRP, most of them inspired by traditional heuristics, and show how they behave on a simple instance of the basic IRP. Finally, in Section 4 we review the literature.

1. PROBLEM DESCRIPTION

We define here the basic IRP we consider in this chapter. A graph $G=(V,E)$ is considered, where V is the set of vertices and E is the set of edges. The set of vertices V includes a depot, denoted by 0, and a set of customers $M=\{1,2,\ldots,n\}$. An edge (i,j), where $i,j\in V$, represents the possibility to travel directly between vertices i and j. A length or traveling cost c_{ij} is associated to each edge $i,j\in E$. We assume $c_{ij}=c_{ji}$, $i,j\in V$. A time horizon of length H is considered. At each discrete time $t\in T=\{1,\ldots,H\}$ a quantity r_{0t} is made available in 0 and a quantity r_{it} is consumed at customer $i\in M$. A starting inventory level B_0 in 0 is given. Each customer i has a maximum capacity U_i and a given starting inventory I_{i0}. Obviously, $I_{i0}\leq U_i$. We denote by h_0 the unit inventory cost of the depot 0 and by h_i the unit inventory cost of customer $i\in M$. Shipments from the depot to the customers can be performed at each time $t\in T$ by a vehicle of capacity C. We denote by T' the set $T\cup\{H+1\}$.

We will make use of the following variables:

- x_{it} is the quantity shipped from 0 to i, $i\in M$, at time $t\in T$;
- B_t is the inventory level at the depot 0 at time $t\in T'$;
- I_{it} is the inventory level at the customer $i\in M$ at time $t\in T'$;
- z_{it} is a binary variable equal to 1 if $i\in V$ is visited at time t and 0 otherwise. Note that $z_{0t}=1$ means that the depot is "visited" at time t, that is a route is traveled at time t;

- y_{ij}^t is a binary variable equal to 1 if $j\in M$ immediately follows $i\in M$, $j<i$, in the route traveled at time $t\in T$ and 0 otherwise;
- y_{i0}^t is an integer variable not greater than 2 for each customer $i\in M$ at time $t\in T$. It is equal to 0 if the customer i is not the last customer visited in the route traveled at time t, equal to 1 if it is the last one and equal to 2 if it is the only customer visited in this route.

The objective of the problem is to find a feasible solution that minimizes the overall cost. A feasible solution is a solution that does not cause stock-out at the depot (i.e. $B_t\geq 0 \;\forall t$) and at the customers (i.e. $I_{it}\geq 0$, $\forall i,t$), such that the level of the inventory of any customer i is never greater than U_i and the total quantity delivered at any given time does not exceed the vehicle capacity C. The overall cost is the sum of the routing cost and of the inventory cost, at the depot and at the customers, over the time horizon. The time $H+1$ is included in the computation of the inventory cost in order to take into account the consequences of the operations performed at time H.

We now recall the mixed-integer linear programming formulation of this problem introduced in Archetti et al (2007). The objective function expresses the minimization of the inventory cost at the depot, the inventory cost at the customers and the routing cost:

$$\min \sum_{t\in T'}h_0 B_t + \sum_{i\in M}\sum_{t\in T'}h_i I_{it} + \sum_{i\in V}\sum_{j\in V,j<i}\sum_{t\in T}c_{ij}y_{ij}^t.$$

(1)

The constraints of the problem are the following:

1. **Inventory definition at the depot:** The inventory level of the depot at time t is given by the level at time $t-1$, plus the product quantity r_{0t-1} made available at time

$t-1$, minus the total quantity shipped to the customers at time $t-1$, that is

$$B_t = B_{t-1} + r_{0t-1} - \sum_{i \in M} x_{it-1} \qquad t \in T',$$
(2)

where $r_{00}=0$ and $x_{i0}=0$, $i \in M$.

2. **Stock-out constraints at the depot:** These constraints guarantee that for each time $t \in T$ the inventory level at the depot is sufficient to ship the total quantity delivered to the customers:

$$B_t \geq \sum_{i \in M} x_{it} \qquad t \in T.$$
(3)

3. **Inventory definition at the customers:** The inventory level at time t is given by the level at time $t-1$, plus the quantity x_{it-1} shipped from the depot to the customer i at time $t-1$, minus the quantity r_{it-1} consumed at time $t-1$, that is

$$I_{it} = I_{it-1} + x_{it-1} - r_{it-1} \qquad i \in M \quad t \in T',$$
(4)

where $x_{i0}=r_{i0}=0$, $i \in M$.

4. **Stock-out constraints at the customers:** These constraints guarantee that for each customer $i \in M$ the inventory level I_{it} at each time $t \in T$ is non-negative:

$$I_{it} \geq 0 \qquad i \in M \quad t \in T.$$
(5)

5. Capacity constraints at the customers: These constraints guarantee that for each customer $i \in M$ the maximum quantity U_i is never exceeded:

$$x_{it} \leq U_i - I_{it} \qquad i \in M \quad t \in T.$$
(6)

6. **Routing constraints:** These constraints guarantee that, for each time $t \in T$, a feasible route is determined to visit all customers served at time t. They can be formulated as follows:

    a. The total quantity loaded on the vehicle at each time $t \in T$ does not exceed the transportation capacity:

$$\sum_{i \in M} x_{it} \leq C z_{0t} \qquad t \in T.$$
(7)

    b. If a positive quantity is delivered to customer i at time t, the customer i has to be visited:

$$x_{it} \leq C z_{it} \qquad i \in M \quad t \in T.$$
(8)

    c. If deliveries are made at time t (i.e. z_{it} is equal to 1 for some $i \in V$), then the route traveled at time t has to contain one arc entering every vertex i of the route and one arc leaving every i:

$$\sum_{j \in V, j < i} y_{ij}^t + \sum_{j \in V, j > i} y_{ji}^t = 2 z_{it} \qquad i \in V \quad t \in T.$$
(9)

    d. Subtours elimination constraints (see Fischetti et al, 1998, and Gendreau et al, 1998):

$$\sum_{i \in S} \sum_{j \in S, j < i} y_{ij}^t \leq \sum_{i \in S} z_{it} - z_{kt} \qquad S \subseteq M \quad t \in T$$
(10)

for some $k \in S$.

7. **Non-negativity and integrality constraints:**

$$x_{it} \geq 0 \qquad t \in T \quad i \in M \qquad (11)$$

$$B_t \geq 0 \qquad t \in T' \qquad (12)$$

$$z_{it} \in \{0,1\} \qquad i \in V \qquad t \in T \qquad (13)$$

$$y_{ij}^t \in \{0,1\} \qquad i \in M \quad j \in M, j < i \quad t \in T \qquad (14)$$

$$y_{i0}^t \in \{0,1,2\} \qquad i \in M \quad t \in T. \qquad (15)$$

We refer to this problem as Problem P.

2. EVOLUTION OF HEURISTICS

Over the last decades the increasing computational power of computers and the advancement in algorithms design has made it possible to solve exactly instances of hard problems of increasing size. Commercial software for linear and mixed integer linear mathematical programming models has become extremely powerful, incorporating the most recent algorithmic advancement. At the same time, more and more research efforts have been devoted to the design of heuristics for problems of increasing complexity.

Although it is out of the scope of this chapter to overview the evolution of heuristics, if we restrict the attention to the area of routing problems, we may summarize such evolution as follows:

- greedy heuristics;
- local search heuristics;
- metaheuristics;
- hybrid heuristics and matheuristics.

The nearest neighbor is a classical example of greedy heuristic for the Traveling Salesman Problem (TSP). The tour is built starting from the origin. The next visited vertex is the vertex closest to an extreme of the partial tour. The cheapest insertion heuristic for the TSP is another classical example of greedy heuristic. At each iteration, given a partial tour (at the beginning the tour contains the depot only), for any vertex not yet included in the partial tour the cheapest way to insert it into the partial tour is identified. The vertex with the minimum cheapest insertion cost is chosen and inserted.

The 2-opt heuristic is a well known example of a local search heuristic for the Vehicle Routing Problem (VRP). Given any solution, however built for the VRP, a local search is performed by evaluating all the solutions where two vertices, belonging to two different tours, are exchanged. If the best of the evaluated solutions improves the previous solution, a new solution is obtained and a new local search is performed. A sequence of better and better solutions is built until no more improvement is achieved.

Local search heuristics can be very effective but in many cases they end up in a local minimum where they remain trapped. Different so called metaheuristics have been designed to escape from local minima. Simulated annealing, tabu search, genetic and evolutionary are the most successful metaheuristics proposed.

The most recent heuristics for routing problems explore new directions and take new names, hybrid heuristics, optimization-based heuristics, matheuristics. We believe that an extremely interesting direction for the design of new classes of heuristics is related to the use of the power of commercial software. As a commercial software can be used to solve instances of complex problems up to a certain size, a commercial software can be used to solve sub-problems, but also to solve different problems that are embedded in a heuristic scheme and are used to effectively explore promising parts of the solution space.

At present, the word hybrid is used to indicate a solution approach that combines ideas or techniques that are typically used separately. A matheuristic is a heuristic that embeds a mathematical programming model. An optimization-based heuristic is a heuristic that is based on the solution of an optimization problem. In this chapter we will use the term matheuristic to identify any heuristic that embeds a step where a mathematical programming model is solved. A hybrid heuristic may be seen as more general than a matheuristic.

There exist several ways to embed a mathematical programming model in a heuristic scheme:

1. **To solve sub-problems:** The IRP jointly considers a routing problem and an inventory management problem. A natural decomposition approach consists in treating the two problems separately. In the inventory management sub-problem we will determine the days of service and the quantities to be delivered to the customers, whereas in the routing sub-problem we will determine the routes of the vehicles, given the days of service and the quantities. We will solve the two sub-problems of the basic IRP optimally to evaluate the impact of the decomposition on the quality of the solution.

2. **To solve parts of an instance:** A direct way to reduce the complexity of an instance to be solved is to decompose the instance and solve the same problem on sub-instances of smaller size. In the case of the IRP, when the customers are geographically distributed in clusters, it may be possible to decompose the instance and solve the IRP on different sub-instances of smaller size, one for each cluster.

3. **To restrict the search space:** Restricting the search space is another way to reduce the complexity. While what discussed in the previous two points may be seen as special case of restricting the solution space, there are also different ways to do it. In IRPs the space can be restricted by focusing the search of specific policies that are, for different reasons, attractive.

4. **To explore neighborhoods:** Some of the most innovative and recently proposed heuristics belong to this class. Promising neighborhoods are explored in depth by means of a mathematical programming model. The challenge consists in identifying the neighborhoods that contain a high density of high quality solutions and to design an appropriate mathematical programming model that finds the best solution of each neighborhood.

3. OLD AND NEW IDEAS FOR MATHEURISTICS TO SOLVE THE BASIC IRP

In this section we discuss several matheuristics. Most of them are inspired by traditional heuristics. The difference here is that some operations, usually executed heuristically, are now executed more accurately by means of MILPs that are solved with a commercial software. Some new ideas for matheuristics are also discussed.

The matheuristics for IRPs that we will illustrate through an example for the basic IRP are:

*   minimizing the routing cost (Routing-based matheuristic);
*   first solving the inventory part of the problem without routing and then finding the best routes to serve the customers (Inventory-first Routing-second matheuristic);
*   first cluster the customers into sets and then solve the inventory routing problem for each set separately (Cluster-first Inventory Routing-second matheuristic);
*   by iteratively inserting in the partial solution the optimal solution of the subprob-

lem of a single customer (Customer-based matheuristic);

- restricting the search space to simplifying policies (Policy-based matheuristic);
- MILPs in a tabu search scheme (Intensified tabu search matheuristic).

The Routing-based and the Inventory-first Routing-second matheuristics belong to the class 1 of the previous section, whereas the Cluster-first Inventory Routing-second and the Customer-based matheuristics belong to the class 2. The Policy-based matheuristic belongs to class 3 and the last one to the class 4.

We now describe an instance of the basic IRP that we will use as an example to illustrate the matheuristics and also to show that the design of a good matheuristic is not trivial, as the most natural or traditional ideas may generate poor or infeasible solutions.

A set $M=\{1,2,3,4\}$ of customers is served by the depot 0 over a time horizon $H=3$. The depot is located at (50,50), while the customers are located at (0,0), (0,100), (100,100) and (100,0), respectively. The traveling costs c_{ij}, $i,j \in V$, are:

c_{ij}	0	1	2	3	4
0	0	71	71	71	71
1	71	0	100	141	100
2	71	100	0	100	141
3	71	141	100	0	100
4	71	100	141	100	0

and correspond to the rounded off Euclidean distances. The quantity r_{0t} made available at the depot 0 at each time $t \in T$ is equal to 100, while the quantity r_{it} consumed at each customer $i \in M$ at each time $t \in T$ is 25. The starting inventory level B_0 at the depot is 100, while the starting inventory level I_{i0} at each customer $i \in M$ is 25. The unit inventory cost h_0 at the depot is 0.01, while the inventory cost at the customers are $h_1=h_2=1$

and $h_3=h_4=10$. The maximum capacity U_i of each customer $i \in M$ is 50 and the transportation capacity C is 70. Note that, since for each customer $i \in M$ the initial inventory level I_{i0} is equal to 25 and the total demand is 75, then in any feasible solution at least 50 units have to be delivered to each customer during the time horizon. Moreover, due to the initial inventory and the maximum capacity $U_i=50$, at most 25 units can be delivered to each customer i at time 1.

Let us first show the optimal solution obtained by solving exactly Problem P in which the total cost is minimized. The optimal solution has been obtained with CPLEX. The following table shows the quantity x_{it} sent to each customer $i \in M$ at each time $t \in T$ and the route traveled by the vehicle at each time $t \in T$:

t	x_{1t}	x_{2t}	x_{3t}	x_{4t}	Route	Routing Cost
1	25	25	10	0	$0 \to 1 \to 2 \to 3 \to 0$	342
2	25	0	15	30	$0 \to 1 \to 4 \to 3 \to 0$	342
3	0	25	25	20	$0 \to 2 \to 3 \to 4 \to 0$	342
Total Quantity	50	50	50	50	Total Routing Cost	1026

A total quantity of exactly 50 units is delivered to each customer. The vehicles used at times 2 and 3 have a full load. On the basis of the values of these decision variables, the corresponding values of the inventory levels B_t and I_{it} and the inventory cost can be easily computed as follows:

t	B_t	I_{1t}	I_{2t}	I_{3t}	I_{4t}
1	100	25	25	25	25
2	140	25	25	10	0
3	170	25	0	0	5
4	200	0	0	0	0
Total Inventory	610	75	50	35	30
Inventory Cost	6.1	75	50	350	300

Therefore, the total cost is 1807.1, given by the sum of the routing cost (1026), the inventory cost at the depot (6.1) and the inventory cost at the customers (75+50+350+300=775).

Routing-Based Matheuristic

We first consider a matheuristic based on the minimization of the routing cost. The rationale of this type of matheuristics is two-fold. The first is based on the fact that, since the inventory costs are not explicitly paid, it is common from the operational point of view to solve the problem by simply focusing on the routing cost. The second is that several heuristics are known for the solution of routing problems. We show that, if the routing cost only is taken into account, bad solutions may be obtained, even if the routing part of the problem is optimally solved.

Consider our instance. We solve with CPLEX the model (1)-(15) where in (1) we only consider the third term, that is the routing cost only.

The following table shows the quantity x_{it} sent to each customer $i \in M$ at each time $t \in T$ and the route traveled by the vehicle at each time $t \in T$, when the objective function of Problem P is replaced by the routing cost only:

t	x_{1t}	x_{2t}	x_{3t}	x_{4t}	Route	Routing Cost
1	25	25	0	20	$0 \to 2 \to 1 \to 4 \to 0$	342
2	0	0	50	10	$0 \to 3 \to 4 \to 0$	242
3	25	25	0	20	$0 \to 2 \to 1 \to 4 \to 0$	342
Total Quantity	50	50	50	50	Total Routing Cost	926

A total quantity of 50 is delivered to each customer. The vehicles used at times 1 and 3 have a full load. On the basis of the values of these decision variables, the corresponding values of the inventory levels B_t and I_{it} and the inventory cost can be easily computed as follows:

t	B_t	I_{1t}	I_{2t}	I_{3t}	I_{4t}
1	100	25	25	25	25
2	130	25	25	0	20
3	170	0	0	25	5
4	200	0	0	0	0
Total Inventory	600	50	50	50	50
Inventory Cost	6	50	50	500	500

Therefore, the total cost is 2032, given by the sum of the routing cost (926), the inventory cost at the depot (6) and the inventory cost at the customers (50+50+500+500=1100). Although the routing cost has been significantly reduced, the percent increase of the total cost is about 12.5% with respect to the total cost of the optimal solution of Problem P.

Inventory-First Route-Second Matheuristic

The Inventory-first Route-second matheuristic is a two phase algorithm. In the first phase the inventory cost is minimized, while in the second phase the optimal routes are found, given the quantities to be delivered at each time.

In the first phase the following Problem *Inv* is solved.

Problem *Inv*:

$$\min \sum_{t \in T'} h_0 B_t + \sum_{i \in M} \sum_{t \in T'} h_i I_{it} \tag{16}$$

$$B_t = B_{t-1} + r_{0t-1} - \sum_{i \in M} x_{it-1} \qquad t \in T' \tag{17}$$

$$B_t \geq \sum_{i \in M} x_{it} \qquad t \in T \tag{18}$$

$$I_{it} = I_{it-1} + x_{it-1} - r_{it-1} \qquad i \in M \qquad t \in T' \tag{19}$$

$$I_{it} \geq 0 \qquad i \in M \qquad t \in T \tag{20}$$

$$x_{it} \leq U_i - I_{it} \qquad i \in M \qquad t \in T \tag{21}$$

$$\sum_{i \in M} x_{it} \leq C \qquad t \in T \tag{22}$$

$$x_{it} \geq 0 \qquad t \in T \qquad i \in M \tag{23}$$

$$B_t \geq 0 \qquad t \in T'. \tag{24}$$

The optimal solution of Problem *Inv* is obtained with CPLEX, that provides the following values of the variables x_{it}:

t	x_{1t}	x_{2t}	x_{3t}	x_{4t}
1	25	25	10	0
2	25	5	15	25
3	0	20	25	25
Total Quantity	50	50	50	50

On the basis of the values of these decision variables, the corresponding values of the inventory levels B_t and I_{it} and the inventory cost can be easily computed as follows:

t	B_t	I_{1t}	I_{2t}	I_{3t}	I_{4t}
1	100	25	25	25	25
2	140	25	25	10	0
3	170	25	5	0	0
4	200	0	0	0	0
Total Inventory	610	75	55	35	25
Inventory Cost	6.1	75	55	350	250

Then, in the second phase a minimum cost tour is found for each time $t \in T$. This means that a Traveling Salesman Problem has to be solved for each t. The optimal routes are again obtained through the use of CPLEX.

t	Route	Routing Cost
1	$0 \to 1 \to 2 \to 3 \to 0$	342
2	$0 \to 1 \to 2 \to 3 \to 4 \to 0$	442
3	$0 \to 2 \to 3 \to 4 \to 0$	342
	Total Routing Cost	1126

Therefore, the total cost is 1862.1, given by the sum of the routing cost (1126), the inventory cost at the depot (6.1) and the inventory cost at the customers (75+55+350+250=730). Although the total inventory cost has been significantly reduced, the percent increase of the total cost is about 3% with respect to the total cost of the optimal solution of Problem *P*.

Cluster-First Inventory Routing-Second Matheuristic

In the Cluster-first Inventory Routing-second matheuristic we first group the customers into sets in such a way that customers that belong to the same set are geographically close and then each set is optimized separately. The rationale of this type of heuristics is two-fold. First, this approach is often used by practitioners. Second, it allows us to reduce the complexity of the problem as several smaller instances have to be solved instead of a single large instance. We show that clustering the customers may even cause infeasibility.

Consider our instance. Let j be the index of the clusters and S_j the j-th cluster. We first note that if the cardinality of each cluster is 1, a feasible solution does not exist. The reason is very simple. Since we have 4 clusters, we need four routes to serve them. However, since the time horizon H is equal to 3 and at most one route can be used at each time instant, there is no way to find a feasible solution of the problem.

Consider now clusters with cardinality 2, say $S_1 = \{c_1, c_2\}$ and $S_2 = \{c_3, c_4\}$, where c_i is a customer in the set M. Since at least 50 units have to be delivered to each customer, even if exactly 50 units are delivered, four routes are needed, as the transportation capacity is 70 and at most 3 routes can be traveled during the time horizon.

Finally, consider the case with one cluster of cardinality 3 and one cluster of cardinality 1, say $S_1 = \{c_1, c_2, c_3\}$ and $S_2 = \{c_4\}$. One route is needed to serve S_2. Since the transportation capacity is 70 and the total demand of three customers in S_1 is at least 150, the remaining two routes do not have enough transportation capacity to serve the demand of three customers. Therefore, a feasible solution does not exist.

In general, a Cluster-first Inventory Routing-second matheuristic can be implemented by clustering customers according to some logic and then using CPLEX to solve the basic IRP on each cluster. As an alternative, the optimal method presented in Archetti et al (2007) can be used on each cluster. Obviously, to make the problem solvable exactly on each cluster the clusters should be created accordingly, that is they should be of relatively small size.

Customer-Based Matheuristic

We now consider a matheuristic in which the solution is obtained by iteratively solving a subproblem where a single customer is considered at a time. The rationale is to decompose the problem into subproblems that are in principle simpler to be solved. We show that this type of heuristics may generate infeasibility, even if the subproblem each customer is optimally solved through CPLEX.

Consider our instance. Since one customer is inserted at each iteration, the first step is to order the customers according to a criterion. Since all customers have the same distance from the depot, we order the customers according to the non-increasing unit inventory cost h_i. Consider the first iteration. Since customers 3 and 4 have the same unit inventory cost, we insert customer 3. Therefore, we set $r_{it}=0$ for $i=1,2,4$ and $t \in T$ and solve Problem P. We compute the corresponding optimal solution with CPLEX and capture the value of the variables x.

t	x_{1t}	x_{2t}	x_{3t}	x_{4t}
1	0	0	0	0
2	0	0	25	0
3	0	0	25	0
Total Quantity	0	0	50	0

At the second iteration, we try to insert customer 4. To do that, we first set $x_{31}=0$, $x_{32}=x_{33}=25$ and $r_{3t}=r_{4t}=25$ for $t \in T$ and then solve Problem P.

Note that the routes selected in the first iteration can be completely modified. We compute the corresponding optimal solution and capture the values of the variables x.

t	x_{1t}	x_{2t}	x_{3t}	x_{4t}
1	0	0	0	0
2	0	0	25	25
3	0	0	25	25
Total Quantity	0	0	50	50

At the third iteration, since customers 1 and 2 have the same unit inventory cost, we try to insert customer 1. To do that, we first set $x_{31}=0$, $x_{32}=x_{33}=25$, $x_{41}=0$, $x_{42}=x_{43}=25$ and $r_{1t}=r_{3t}=r_{4t}=25$ for $t \in T$ and then solve Problem P. We compute the corresponding optimal solution and capture the values of the variables x.

t	x_{1t}	x_{2t}	x_{3t}	x_{4t}
1	10	0	0	0
2	20	0	25	25
3	20	0	25	25
Total Quantity	50	0	50	50

Finally, at the fourth iteration, we try to insert customer 2. To do that, we first set $x_{11}=10$, $x_{12}=x_{13}=20$, $x_{31}=0$, $x_{32}=x_{33}=25$, $x_{41}=0$, $x_{42}=x_{43}=25$ and $r_{it}=25$ for $i \in M$ and $t \in T$ and then solve Problem P. Unfortunately, Problem P is infeasible. This is due to the fact that the routes at times 2 and 3 have already a full load. Therefore, customer 2 could be served only at time 1 by delivering to it a quantity of 50 units. However, this is not feasible due to the maximum capacity $U_2=50$ and the initial inventory level $I_{20}=25$.

Policy-Based Matheuristic

We now consider a matheuristic in which only particular types of solutions are admitted. In other words, a simplified structure of the possible solutions is defined (policy) and the matheuristic has to determine a solution that satisfies this policy.

A typical example for the IRP is the so called Order-up-to Level policy, in which the quantity x_{it} shipped to each customer $i \in M$ at each time $t \in T$ is either U_i-I_{it} if i is served at time t, and 0 otherwise. Let z_{it} be a binary variable equal to 1 if the customer i is served at time t and 0 otherwise. Then, this policy is defined by adding the following constraints to Problem P:

$$x_{it} \geq U_i z_{it} - I_{it} \qquad i \in M \quad t \in T \qquad (25)$$

$$x_{it} \leq U_i z_{it} \qquad i \in M \quad t \in T. \qquad (26)$$

In fact, if the customer i is served at time t, that is z_{it}=1, then constraints (6) and (25) imply that x_{it}=U_i-I_{it}, while if z_{it}=0 then constraints (26) imply that x_{it}=0.

Consider our instance. We use CPLEX to find the optimal solution for this policy. Unfortunately, Problem P with the addition of these constraints is infeasible.

Intensified Tabu Search Matheuristic

In Archetti et al (2010) a new matheuristic for the solution of the basic IRP has been presented. Although the heuristic is presented in the paper as a hybrid heuristic, it should be more specifically called a matheuristic, according to the logic presented in this chapter, as it makes use of MILP models embedded in a metaheuristic scheme.

The algorithm combines a tabu search scheme with ad hoc designed MILP models whose scope is to intensify the search in some promising parts of the solution space. We provide here the main ideas of this matheuristic, called HAIR (Hybrid Approach to Inventory Routing), and refer to Archetti et al (2010) for more details. The general structure of this algorithm is shown in Algorithm 1.

In HAIR an initial solution s is generated by means of a procedure Initialization. The solution s' is the best solution found in the neighborhood $N(s)$ of s, identified by means of the procedure Move. The solution s_{best} is the currently best found solution. HAIR starts from the initial solution s, explores the neighborhood $N(s)$, identifies the

Algorithm 1. HAIR

```
Apply the Initialization procedure to generate an initial solution s. Set
s_best ← s.
While the number of iterations without improvement of s_best ≤ MaxIter do
   Apply the Move procedure to find the best solution s' in the neighborhood
N(s) of s.
            If s' is better than s_best then
                  Apply the Improvement procedure to possibly improve s' and set
s_best ← s'.
            end if
      Set s ← s'.
      If the number of iterations without improvement of s_best is a multiple of
JumpIter then
            Apply the Jump procedure to modify the current solution s.
      end if
end while
```

best solution of $N(s)$, s', replaces s with s'. HAIR repeats this cycle of operations until a maximum number of iterations without improvement, *Max-Iter*, is reached. Moreover, to diversify the search, if the number of iterations without improvement of the current s_{best} is a multiple of a parameter *JumpIter*, the procedure Jump is run to modify the current solution s.

The innovative feature of HAIR consists in the intensification phase carried out through the procedure Improvement. Whenever a new best solution is identified, that is s_{best} is updated, Improvement is run. This procedure intensifies the search by means of two MILP models. In the first MILP, called the Route-Assignment problem, a solution s', characterized by a route for each time and the associated quantities delivered to the customers, is considered. The first MILP attempts to improve s' by assuming that the structure of the routes, independent of the time each route is used in s', is good and that by assigning the routes of s' to different times a better solution may be identified. No customer can be inserted in the routes and the sequence of the customers in a route cannot be modified. However, customers may be removed from a route because, by changing the time where the routes are used, it may become unnecessary to serve some customers. For the same reason, we let the quantities delivered to the customers be modified by the Route-Assignment problem. As a matter of fact, the Route-Assignment problem explores in an systematic way a neighborhood of s' and generates a new solution s''. If s'' is better than s_{best}, it will become the new best found solution.

The second MILP run in the procedure Improvement is called Customer-Assignment problem. The underlying idea in this case is that, given a solution s', the routes of s' have been assigned to the right times but their structure requires to be adjusted in order to hopefully improve s'. Thus, the Customer-Assignment problem allows the removal or insertion of customers into

routes and obviously a change of the delivered quantities.

In Archetti et al (2010) it is shown that the matheuristic HAIR is extremely effective with errors that are systematically below 1% with respect to the optimum, whenever the optimum can be found, and with a much smaller average error. HAIR also finds a high percentage of optimal solutions. Moreover, the use of the intensification phase based on the MILP models, is shown to be computational effective. This is shown by means of the comparison between the algorithm run with and without the intensification phase for the same amount of time.

On the instance that we used as an example HAIR finds the optimal solution. Finally, one can note that the structure of the algorithm is very general and can be seen as a basis for the design of matheuristics for the solution of other inventory routing, or other NP-hard, problems.

4. REVIEW OF HEURISTICS FOR IRPS

In this section we review the literature on heuristics for inventory routing problems. While most of the heuristics have a traditional nature and cannot be classified as matheuristics, we believe that several of them could be improved by means of appropriate MILP models and result in more effective solution approaches.

Whereas it is out of the scope of this paper to review in detail the state of the art, we intend to provide here references that may be interesting to develop new matheuristics for inventory routing problems. The inventory routing problems studied in these papers are often very different from each other. We organize this concise review by characteristics of the heuristics proposed.

Constructive and improvement heuristics have been proposed by Bertazzi et al. (1997, 2002) and by Abdelmaguid et al. (2009). Incremental cost approximations to be used in a rolling horizon framework are proposed by Jaillet et al (2002).

Heuristics based on the decomposition of the problem in sub-problems are presented by Christiansen (1999) and by Campbell and Savelsbergh (2004).

Policy-based heuristics have been proposed by Herer and Roundy (1997), where power-of-two policies are investigated. A different policy-based heuristic is proposed by Viswanathan and Mathur (1997). A fixed partition policy and a tabu search algorithm to find the partition regions are presented by Qiu-Hong Zhao et al (2007). Abdelmaguid and Dessouky (2006) have presented a genetic algorithm.

Combining exact and heuristic search techniques in a matheuristic has received some attention recently. Besides the already cited Archetti et al (2010), this kind of approach has been adopted Savelsbergh and Song (2008). A Lagrangian relaxation method in which the relaxed problem is decomposed into an inventory problem and a routing problem that are solved by a linear programming algorithm and a minimum cost flow algorithm, respectively, is proposed by Yu et al. (2008).

CONCLUSION

In this chapter we have reviewed the main heuristic approaches for the solution of inventory routing problems and emphasized the advantages of combining exact and heuristic techniques in a new kind of hybrid approaches that we called matheuristics.

We believe that the design of matheuristics for inventory routing and other classes of hard problems, relying on the availability of powerful commercial software for the solution of MILP problems, will attract much interest in the near future.

REFERENCES

Abdelmaguid, T. F., & Dessouky, M. M. (2006). A genetic algorithm approach to the integrated inventory-distribution problem. *International Journal of Production Research, 44*, 4445–4464. doi:10.1080/00207540600597138

Abdelmaguid, T. F., Dessouky, M. M., & Ordónez, F. (2009). Heuristic approaches for the inventory-routing problem with backlogging. *Computers & Industrial Engineering, 56*, 1519–1534. doi:10.1016/j.cie.2008.09.032

Archetti, C., Bertazzi, L., Hertz, A., & Speranza, M. G. (2010). (to appear). A hybrid heuristic for an inventory-routing problem. *INFORMS Journal on Computing.*

Archetti, C., Bertazzi, L., Laporte, G., & Speranza, M. G. (2007). A branch-and-cut algorithm for a Vendor Managed Inventory routing problem. *Transportation Science, 41*, 382–391. doi:10.1287/trsc.1060.0188

Bertazzi, L., Paletta, G., & Speranza, M. G. (2002). Deterministic order-up-to level policies in an inventory routing problem. *Transportation Science, 36*, 119–132. doi:10.1287/trsc.36.1.119.573

Bertazzi, L., Speranza, M. G., & Savelsbergh, M. W. P. (2008). Inventory routing. In Golden, B., Raghavan, R., & Wasil, E. (Eds.), *Vehicle routing: Latest advances and new challenges* (pp. 49–72). New York: Springer. doi:10.1007/978-0-387-77778-8_3

Bertazzi, L., Speranza, M. G., & Ukovich, W. (1997). Minimization of logistic costs with given frequencies. *Transportation Research, 31B*, 327–340.

Campbell, A. M., Clarke, L., Kleywegt, A., & Savelsbergh, M. W. P. (1998). The inventory routing problem.In Crainic, T.G., Laporte, G. (eds.) *Fleet Management and Logistics*, 95-113, Boston: Kluwer.

Campbell, A. M., & Savelsbergh, M. W. P. (2004). A decomposition approach for the inventory-routing problem. *Transportation Science, 38*, 488–502. doi:10.1287/trsc.1030.0054

Christiansen, M. (1999). Decomposition of a combined inventory and time constrained ship routing problem. *Transportation Science, 33*, 3–16. doi:10.1287/trsc.33.1.3

Cordeau, J.-F., Laporte, G., Savelsbergh, M. W. P., & Vigo, D. (2007). Vehicle routing. In Barnhart, C., Laporte, G. (eds.) *Handbooks in Operations Research and Management Science: Transportation, 14*, 367-428.

Federgruen, A., & Simchi-Levi, D. (1995). Analysis of vehicle routing and inventory-routing problems. In Ball, M.O., Magnanti, T.L., Monma, C.L., Nemhauser, G.L. (eds.) *Handbooks in Operations Research and Management Science, 8*, 297-373, North-Holland.

Fischetti, M., Salazar-González, J. J., & Toth, P. (1998). Solving the Orienteering Problem through Branch-and-Cut. *INFORMS Journal on Computing, 10*, 133–148. doi:10.1287/ijoc.10.2.133

Gendreau, M., Laporte, G., & Semet, F. (1998). A Branch-and-Cut Algorithm for the Undirected Selective Traveling Salesman Problem. *Networks, 32*, 263–273. doi:10.1002/(SICI)1097-0037(199812)32:4<263::AID-NET3>3.0.CO;2-Q

Herer, Y., & Roundy, R. (1997). Heuristic for one-warehouse multiretailer distribution problem with performance bounds. *Operations Research, 45*, 102–115. doi:10.1287/opre.45.1.102

Jaillet, P., Bard, J., Huang, L., & Dror, M. (2002). Delivery costs approximations for inventory routing problems in rolling horizon framework. *Transportation Science, 36*, 292–300. doi:10.1287/trsc.36.3.292.7829

Moin, N. H., & Salhi, S. (2007). Inventory routing problems: a logistical overview. *The Journal of the Operational Research Society, 58*, 1185–1194. doi:10.1057/palgrave.jors.2602264

Qiu-Hong Zhao, Q.-H., Wang, S.-Y., & Lai, K. K. (2007). A partition approach to the inventory/routing problem. *European Journal of Operational Research, 177*, 786–802. doi:10.1016/j.ejor.2005.11.030

Savelsbergh, M. W. P., & Song, J.-H. (2008). An optimization algorithm for inventory routing with continuous moves. *Computers & Operations Research, 35*, 2266–2282. doi:10.1016/j.cor.2006.10.020

Viswanathan, S., & Mathur, K. (1997). Integrating routing and inventory decisions in one warehouse multiretailer multiproduct distribution system. *Management Science, 43*, 294–312. doi:10.1287/mnsc.43.3.294

Yu, Y., Chen, H., & Chu, F. (2008). A new model and hybrid approach for large scale inventory routing problems. *European Journal of Operational Research, 189*, 1022–1040. doi:10.1016/j.ejor.2007.02.061

Chapter 2
Vehicle Routing Models and Algorithms for Winter Road Spreading Operations

Nathalie Perrier
École Polytechnique de Montréal, Canada

James F. Campbell
University of Missouri-St. Louis, USA

Michel Gendreau
École Polytechnique de Montréal, Canada

André Langevin
École Polytechnique de Montréal, Canada

ABSTRACT

Winter road maintenance operations involve challenging vehicle routing problems that can be addressed using operations research (OR) techniques. Three key problems involve routing trucks and specialized vehicles for spreading chemicals and abrasives on roadways, snow plowing, and snow disposal, all of which are undertaken in a very difficult and dynamic operating environment with stringent level of service constraints. This chapter provides a survey of recent optimization models and solution methodologies for the routing of vehicles for spreading operations. The authors also present a detailed classification scheme for spreader routing models developed over the past 40 years. Key trends in recent model developments include the inclusion of more details of the practical operating constraints, the use of more sophisticated hybrid solution strategies and consideration of more comprehensive models that integrate vehicle routing with models for other related strategic winter maintenance problems. They highlight some factors that may be limiting the application of OR models in practice and discuss promising future research trends.

DOI: 10.4018/978-1-61350-086-6.ch002

1. INTRODUCTION

There are many challenging and expensive winter road maintenance decision problems that can be addressed using operations research techniques. A key operation is spreading of chemicals and abrasives on the road network, which is conducted on a regular basis in almost all rural and urban regions that experience significant snowfall or roadway icing. The importance of winter road maintenance operations is obvious from the magnitude of the expenditures required to conduct winter road maintenance operations, as well as the indirect costs from both the lost productivity due to decreased mobility and from the effects of chemicals (especially salt) and abrasives on infrastructure, vehicles and the environment. In the US alone, 70% of the population and 74% of the roads are in snowy regions and state and local government agencies spend over US $2.3 billion (US) per year for snow and ice control activities (Federal Highway Administration [FHWA], 2010; Pisano, Goodwin, & Stern, 2002). Indirect costs (e.g., for environmental degradation, economic losses and mobility reductions) are thought to be several times larger; for example, the costs for weather-related freight delays in the US have been estimated at US $3.4 billion (US) per year (Nixon, 2009).

Recent developments in winter road maintenance technologies and operations improve efficiency, reduce resource (materials, equipment and personnel) usage, and minimize environmental impacts (Shi et al., 2006; Transportation Research Board [TRB], 2005, 2008; Venner Consulting and Parsons Brinkerhoff, 2004). These developments include use of alternative deicing materials, anti-icing methods, improved snow removal equipment, more accurate spreaders, better weather forecasting models and services, road weather information systems, vehicle-based environmental and pavement sensors, etc. These new technologies, and their growing use by state and local government agencies, have improved the

effectiveness and efficiency of winter maintenance operations, benefiting government agencies, users, and the general public.

While new winter road maintenance technologies are being developed and deployed on a broad basis, implementations of optimization models for winter road maintenance vehicle routing remain very limited. Most agencies continue to design vehicle routes based on manual approaches derived from field experiences and most agencies rely on static weather forecasts (Fu, Trudel, & Kim, 2009; Perrier, Langevin, & Campbell, 2007a, 2007b). As Handa, Chapman, and Yao (2005) note, "In practice [route] optimization has traditionally been a manual task and is heavily reliant on local knowledge and experience" (p. 158). The limited deployment of optimization models for winter road maintenance vehicle routing is especially surprising given the documented successes in other areas of arc routing, perhaps most notably for waste management (Sahoo, Kim, Kim, Kraas, & Popov, 2005). Thus, winter road maintenance vehicle routing optimization would appear to offer the promise of significant cost savings, along with a reduction in negative environmental and societal impacts.

There are probably many reasons for the limited field use of vehicle routing optimization. In large part, this has been due to the complexity of the problems studied, which in turn is derived from the difficult operating environment. However, it also results from the unique organizational characteristics of the winter road maintenance agencies. Winter road maintenance decisions problem, including vehicle routing for spreading (and plowing), are more complex than most other arc routing problems because of unique characteristics of each site and agency, and the tremendous diversity in operating conditions such as geographical location, climatic and weather conditions, demographics, economics, technological innovations (for materials application, mechanical removal, and weather monitoring), legislative requirements, interagency agreements, variations of traffic rate, and information on the status of personnel, equipment and materials. Also, real-life vehicle routing problems facing winter road maintenance planners should be studied in a dynamic context, where the arrival of new information, such as meteorological forecasts received in real time, can lead to dynamic modifications to the current vehicle routes. Furthermore, political and operational constraints and policies depend on the specific level of service policies and expectations, the characteristics of the transportation network, the strategic and tactical decisions related to design of the operational sectors, choice of chemicals and abrasives, depot and material stockpile locations, vehicle fleet compositions, and driver rules. Differences in these conditions and constraints necessitate differences in the planning and operation of winter road maintenance across agencies.

One important theme in recent winter road maintenance modeling efforts is the inclusion of more real-world characteristics of the problems arising in applications. These models offer greater potential for implementation as they better capture more of the complexities from the field. These improved models, together with the increasing budget pressures on state and local agencies, continuing expectations for high levels of service, and desires for reduced environmental impacts, all motivate a greater role for vehicle routing optimization in winter road maintenance.

The aim of this chapter is to provide a review of recent contributions dealing with the routing of vehicles for winter road spreading operations. The authors will cover models and solution algorithms developed over the last decade or so. Earlier models will not be treated here but the interested reader is referred to recent work by Perrier, Langevin, and Campbell (2007a). In this chapter, the authors describe the important characteristics, model structure and algorithmic aspects for vehicle routing models in spreading operations. In addition to extending the earlier review, the contributions of this chapter include a detailed classification scheme for spreader routing models developed over the past 40 years, discussion of application issues, and identification of key opportunities and needs in future research.

The chapter is organized as follows. The operations of spreading chemicals and abrasives and the vehicle routing problems related to those operations are presented in Section 2. Recent models dealing with the routing of vehicles for spreading operations are reviewed in Section 3. An analysis of existing research on vehicle routing problems for spreading operations is presented in Section 4. Conclusions along with some promising future research opportunities are presented in the last section.

2. OPERATIONS CONTEXT AND DECISION PROBLEMS

This section contains a brief description of spreading operations for winter maintenance and a discussion of associated problems of vehicle routing. More detailed information on the state of the practice in managing winter road maintenance operations is presented in the Transportation Research Board reports (TRB, 2005, 2008).

2.1 Spreading Operations

Spreading operations for winter maintenance are directed at achieving three specific goals: anti-icing, deicing, and traction enhancement. Anti-icing is the timely application of a chemical freezing-point depressant before or during the initial stages of a precipitation event, to attempt to prevent the bonding of snow and ice to the pavement. Deicing is a similar process used to remove snow and ice from the pavement, often requiring destruction of bond between pavement and snow/ice to eliminate the frozen layer. Traction enhancement is the spreading of abrasive materials, such as sand, cinders, ash, tailings, or crushed stone and rock, to improve traction on thick snow-packed and ice-covered roadways. The selection of the appropriate spreading operation is based on economics, environmental constraints, climate, desired level of service, material availability, and application equipment availability. The level of service policies determine the extent of the resource investment. The environmental constraints (e.g., current and forecast weather conditions) influence the choice of a chemical or nonchemical material to spread.

2.2 Vehicle Routing Problems for Spreading

The routing of vehicles for spreading operations is the problem of designing a set of routes such that all required road segments of a transportation network are serviced by a fleet of spreaders, which may be heterogeneous vehicles (e.g., trucks of different capacities) based at multiple depots. The transportation network is generally described through a graph, whose arcs and edges represent the one-way streets and two-way streets to be serviced, respectively, and whose nodes correspond to the road junctions and to vehicle and materials depot locations. Not every road segment may need to be serviced, and road segments with positive demands (amounts of chemicals and abrasives) are called *required* road segments.

This section presents a comprehensive classification scheme for vehicle routing models in winter road spreading operations (see Table 1). The first level of the classification is composed of six categories: (1) Problem type, (2) Planning level, (3) Problem characteristics, (4) Model structure, (5) Solution method, and (6) Instance data. The first category, Problem type, identifies whether the model is limited to vehicle routing only, or includes vehicle routing along with another problem such as facility location or sector design. The second category, Planning level, taken from the work of Perrier et al. (2007a), classifies vehicle routing models for spreading operations according to the planning horizon considered.

Decisions concerning the location of vehicle or materials depots may be viewed as strategic or tactical, while decisions relating to the routing of vehicles for spreading operations usually belong to the operational planning level. In "static" models, all inputs required to solve the problem are known in advance for the duration of the period covered by the routing process, such as a winter (although the input may vary over time, as in the time-dependent variant of the spreader routing problem). In "dynamic" models, the input (that is, which road segments actually require service) varies over time in a fashion that is revealed to the router very shortly before the routes are constructed. This may occur when new routes are created for each storm or precipitation event based on each unique forecast and weather conditions. The authors distinguish "real-time" routing from dynamic routing, by using real-time routing to refer to cases where the routes are (re)computed during the vehicle's traversal of the route, because of new inputs received in real-time.

The third category, Problem characteristics, includes numerous factors that are part of the problem environment or constraints embedded into the solution. This category is an extended version of the work of Perrier et al. (2007a). Typical characteristics of this category include:

- road network characteristics;
- service hierarchy constraints, including linear precedence relations between classes of road segments in a route that require higher level roadways (e.g., based on level of traffic) to be served prior to lower level roadways, and class upgrading, which allow servicing of lower-class roads in a route servicing higher-class roads (in order to reduce the service completion time of this class and/or the total completion time);
- service costs associated with each road segment, possibly dependent on the time of beginning of service;

Table 1. Characteristics of vehicle routing problems for spreading

1. Problem type	3.12. Number of routes per spreader
1.1. Spreader routing only	3.12.1. One route
1.2. Combined spreader routing + other problem(s)	3.12.2. Multiple routes
1.2.1. Combined routing and sector design	3.13. Route configuration
1.2.2. Combined routing and depot location	3.13.1. Load balancing imposed
2. Planning level	3.13.2. Class continuity imposed
2.1. Strategic	3.13.3. Both-sides service imposed
2.2. Tactical	3.13.4. Turn restrictions imposed
2.3. Operational	3.13.5. Service connectivity or route continuity imposed
2.3.1. Static routing	3.13.6. Sector boundaries imposed
2.3.2. Dynamic routing	3.14. Objectives
2.3.3. Real-time routing	3.14.1. Min variable or routing costs
3. Problem characteristics	3.14.2. Min sum of fixed and variable costs
3.1. Transportation network	3.14.3. Min time-dependent service costs
3.1.1. Undirected network	3.14.4. Min fleet size
3.1.2. Directed network	3.14.5. Min alternations between deadheading and servicing
3.1.3. Mixed network	3.14.6. Min operational constraints violations
3.1.4. Rural network	4. Model structure
3.2. Service hierarchy	4.1. Integer programming models
3.2.1. Linear precedence relation imposed	4.1.1. Linear 0-1 IP model
3.2.2. Class upgrading allowed	4.1.2. Linear MIP model
3.3. Time (or distance) limit for service completion	4.1.3. Nonlinear MIP model
3.3.1. Restriction on routes	4.2. Arc routing problems
3.3.2. Restriction on road classes	4.2.1. Directed Chinese postman problem
3.3.3. Restriction on road segments	4.2.2. Capacitated arc routing problem
3.4. Road segment service costs	4.2.3. Location-arc routing problem
3.4.1. Independent of service start time	4.3. Capacitated vehicle routing problem
3.4.2. Dependent on service start time	4.4. Spanning tree problems
3.5. Service time window type	4.4.1. Capacitated minimum spanning tree problem
3.5.1. Restriction on road classes	5. Solution method
3.5.2. Restriction on road segments	5.1. Exact methods
3.6. Service frequency type	5.1.1. Column generation
3.6.1. Restriction on road classes	5.2. Constructive methods
3.6.2. Restriction on road segments	5.2.1. Sequential constructive methods
3.7. Number of passes per road segment	5.2.2. Parallel constructive methods
3.7.1. One pass	5.2.3. Cluster first, route second methods
3.7.2. Multiple passes	5.2.4. Optimization-based methods
3.8. Number of lanes in a single pass	5.3. Composite methods
3.8.1. One lane	5.4. Adaptation of metaheuristics
3.8.2. Two lanes	5.4.1. Simulated annealing
3.9. Sectors	5.4.2. Tabu search
3.9.1. Compactness or shape	5.4.3. Elite route pool
3.9.2. Balance in sector size or workload imposed	5.4.4. Genetic algorithms
3.9.3. Basic units defined	5.4.5. Memetic algorithms
3.10. Vehicle and materials depots	5.4.6. Variable neighborhood descent
3.10.1. Single depot	5.5. Simulation used
3.10.2. Multiple depots	5.6. Solution method implemented
3.10.3. Centrally located depots relative to sectors	6. Instance data
3.11. Vehicle (capacities)	6.1. Real world instances
3.11.1. Similar vehicles	6.2. Randomly generated instances
3.11.2. Road segment-specific vehicles	6.3. No instance used
3.11.3. Heterogeneous vehicles	

- limits on the maximum time or distance of routes and of service completion;
- time windows for servicing road segments, possibly by road class or road segment;

- minimum road service frequencies, possibly by road class or road segment;
- basic units of analysis used to design sectors (for example, small geographic zones);

- operational constraints regarding the number of lanes covered in a single pass and the number of passes per road segment;
- road segment-specific vehicles, which require that a road segment be serviced by a specific type of vehicle (for instance, because of possible access limitations);
- route constraints to ensure load balancing (approximately equal workloads, lengths or durations across routes), class continuity (each route services road segments with the same priority class), turn restrictions, etc.;
- vehicle and materials depot characteristics;
- service connectivity or route continuity, which requires that the subgraph induced by the set of road segments serviced by a spreader be connected; and
- the objective (e.g., minimize route costs, fleet size, constraint violations, etc.

The fourth category describes the basic mathematical model structure and the fifth category provides the solution method. The last category, Instance data, classifies the type of instances solved. In Section 4, the categories presented in Table 1 are applied to classify the spreader routing models developed during the last four decades.

3. VEHICLE ROUTING MODELS FOR SPREADING

Vehicle routing problems related to spreading operations are generally formulated as arc routing problems. Corberán and Prins (2010) presented an annotated bibliography on recent results on arc routing problems. In this section, our purpose is to survey the more recent solution approaches for the routing of vehicles for spreading operations. The authors first discuss the exact algorithm proposed by Tagmouti, Gendreau, and Potvin (2007), followed by metaheuristics applied to

the routing of vehicles for spreading operations during the last decade. Earlier models for the routing of vehicles for spreading operations will not be treated in this section; the authors instead refer the interested reader to the recent survey by Perrier et al. (2007a).

3.1 Exact Algorithms

In the classical version of the problem, the cost associated with servicing each road segment is fixed. However, in the *time-dependent* variant of the vehicle routing problem for spreading operations, the timing of each service pass is of prime importance. That is, the cost to service a road segment depends on the time of beginning service. Recently, Tagmouti et al. (2007) proposed a nonlinear, mixed integer program and a column generation algorithm for a salt spreader routing problem with capacity constraints and time-dependent service costs. In this problem, the service cost on each required road segment is a piecewise linear function of the time of beginning of service. The authors clarify here that all of the problem inputs are known in advance. Hence, the problem studied is a static problem, even though the term "time-dependent" might be interpreted as synonymous to "dynamic". To present the formulation, let $G = (V, A)$ be a directed graph where V is the vertex set and A is the arc set. First, the arc routing problem in graph $G = (V, A)$ is transformed into an equivalent node routing problem in a transformed graph $G' = (V', A')$. The depot is duplicated into an origin depot o and a destination depot d in V'. Let also N' be the set of nodes that must be serviced ($N' = V' \setminus \{o, d\}$). Each required arc in graph G corresponds to a node i in graph G' with demand d_i, service time st_i and time-dependent service cost $sc_i(T_i)$, where T_i is time of beginning of service on node i. Each pair of distinct nodes i and j in G' is connected by an arc $(i, j) \in A'$ with travel time tt_{ij} and travel cost tc_{ij}. Let K be the set of identical spreader trucks with capacity Q. For each arc $(i, j) \in A'$ and for each spreader truck $k \in K$, let x_{ij}^k be a binary variable equal to 1 if and only if spreader k travels on arc (i, j) to service node j. For every node $i \in V'$ and for every spreader truck $k \in K$, let Q_i^k be a nonnegative real variable representing the load of spreader k just after servicing node i and let also T_i^k be a nonnegative real variable specifying the time of beginning of service of spreader k at node i. The formulation is given next.

Minimize

$$\sum_{k \in K} \left(\sum_{(i,j) \in A'} tc_{ij} x_{ij}^k + \sum_{i \in N'} sc_i \left(T_i^k \right) \sum_{j \in N' \cup \{o\}} x_{ji}^k \right) \tag{1}$$

subject to

$$\sum_{k \in K} \sum_{i \in N' \cup \{o\}} x_{ij}^k = 1 \tag{2}$$
$$(j \in N')$$

$$\sum_{k \in K} \sum_{j \in N'} x_{oj}^k \leq m \tag{3}$$

$$\sum_{j \in N' \cup \{d\}} x_{oj}^k = 1 \tag{4}$$
$$(k \in K)$$

$$\sum_{j \in N' \cup \{d\}} x_{ij}^k - \sum_{j \in N' \cup \{o\}} x_{ji}^k = 0 \tag{5}$$
$$(k \in K, j \in N')$$

$$\sum_{i \in N' \cup \{o\}} x_{id}^k = 1 \tag{6}$$
$$(k \in K)$$

$$x_{ij}^k \left(T_i^k + st_i + tt_{ij} - T_j^k \right) \leq 0 \tag{7}$$
$$(k \in K, (i, j) \in A')$$

$$x_{ij}^k \left(Q_i^k - d_j - Q_j^k \right) \leq 0$$
$$(k \in K, (i, j) \in A') \tag{8}$$

$$0 \leq T_i^k \leq T$$
$$(k \in K, i \in V') \tag{9}$$

$$0 \leq Q_i^k \leq Q$$
$$(k \in K, i \in V') \tag{10}$$

$$0 \leq x_{ij}^k \leq 1$$
$$(k \in K, (i, j) \in A') \tag{11}$$

$$x_{ij}^k \in \{0, 1\}$$
$$(k \in K, (i, j) \in A') \tag{12}$$

The objective function (1) minimizes the sum of travel costs and time-dependent service costs. Constraint set (2) requires that each node (except the depot node) be serviced exactly once. Constraint set (3) imposes an upper bound m on the number of spreader trucks. Flow conservation is guaranteed by constraint sets (4)-(6). Constraint sets (7) and (8) ensure the feasibility of the time schedule and loads, respectively. Constraint set (9) ensures that the time that service begins at every node is a nonnegative value that does not exceed the deadline T. Similarly, constraint set (10) requires nonnegative load values that do not exceed the spreader salting capacity Q. Tagmouti et al. (2007) proposed to decompose the model into a master problem and a set of $|K|$ different independent subproblems. The master problem corresponds to constraints (2) and (3) in the original formulation (1)-(12). Let Ω be the set of all feasible paths from the origin depot o to the destination depot d. For each path $p \in \Omega$, let u_p be a binary variable equal to 1 if and only if path p is selected and define C_p as the total cost of path p (sum of travel costs and service costs on all arcs and nodes along the path). The model for the master problem can be stated as follows:

Minimize

$$\sum_{p \in \Omega} C_p u_p \tag{13}$$

subject to

$$\sum_{p \in \Omega} a_{ip} u_p = 1 \tag{14}$$
$$(i \in N')$$

$$\sum_{p \in \Omega} u_p \leq m \tag{15}$$

$$u_p \geq 0 \tag{16}$$
$$(p \in \Omega)$$

where the binary constant a_{ip} is equal to 1 if and only if node i is in path p. Moreover, for every spreader truck $k \in K$, the subproblem is of the following form:

Minimize

$$\sum_{(i,j) \in A'} \overline{tc}_{ij} x_{ij}^k + \sum_{i \in N'} sc_i \left(T_i^k \right) \sum_{j \in N' \cup \{o\}} x_{ji}^k \tag{17}$$

subject to

$$(4) - (12)$$

where $\overline{tc}_{ij}$ is the reduced travel cost on arc $(i, j) \in A'$. The master problem, solved with CPLEX, is a linear relaxation of a set covering problem with an additional constraint on the total number of spreader trucks. Columns (paths) of the master problem are generated by solving, for each spreader truck $k \in K$, the corresponding subprob-

lem with an objective that is iteratively updated to reflect the new values of the dual variables. The subproblem for each spreader truck is an elementary shortest path problem with resource constraints that is solved using an extension of the algorithm of Feillet, Dejax, Gendreau, and Gueguen (2004) to take into account the time-dependent service costs. The resource constraints are the capacity constraint and the time deadline for the return of the spreader to the depot. To obtain an integer solution, the column generation approach is embedded in a previously reported branch-and-bound algorithm (Feillet, Dejax, Gendreau, & Gueguen, 2004). Computational results were presented on problems derived from a set of instances of the vehicle routing problem with time windows (Solomon, 1987). The largest instances solved contained 40 customers.

3.2 Metaheuristics

In a previous survey, Perrier et al. (2007a) described a linear, mixed integer programming model developed by Qiao (2002) for routing salt spreader trucks. The model, which is an extension of a previous formulation proposed by Haghani and Qiao (2002), incorporates service connectivity and vehicle capacity. The model will not be presented here but the authors instead refer the reader to the work by Perrier et al. (2007a). The model is solved with a classical tabu search algorithm and an elite route pool procedure. The elite route pool procedure is similar to the technique of genetic algorithms. The population is formed by a pool of good routes found in the best solutions, called the elite route pool. Associated with every route in the elite route pool is a weight corresponding to the frequency with which the route appears in the best solutions. New offspring routes are produced by selecting the routes with the highest weights in the elite route pool while avoiding duplications of serviced required arcs. Mutations are then obtained by applying the multiroute improvement methods developed by Haghani and Qiao (2002).

Qiao (2002) provided an interesting comparison of the various multiroute improvement methods, the tabu search algorithm, the elite route pool procedure and four popular constructive methods for the capacitated arc routing problem from Pearn (1984), Golden, DeArmon, and Baker (1983) and Christofides (1973). Computational tests on 23 networks derived from the test problems used by Pearn (1984) showed that the elite route pool procedure obtained the largest number of best solutions on sparse networks with $7 \leq |V| \leq 27$ and arc densities between 13% and 40%. On dense networks, the algorithm in Pearn (1984) produced the best solutions in most cases.

Toobaie and Haghani (2004) studied the problem of designing spreader routes in a multi-depot network so as to minimize the number of vehicles and the deadhead distance, while satisfying vehicle capacities (all the same), route continuity and workload balance. Also, some two-lane highways require servicing in both directions (one lane in a single pass), whereas others can be serviced in a single pass. The problem is solved using a three-stage procedure. The first stage decomposes the road network into subnetworks, one for each vehicle, by solving a minimal arc partitioning problem with vehicle capacities and service connectivity constraints. The objective of the first stage is to minimize the number of subnetworks (vehicles). Given a connected network in which costs are associated with links, the minimal arc partitioning problem consists of partitioning the network into a minimum number of connected subnetworks so that the overall cost of each subnetwork does not exceed the budget limit for the subnetwork. In the salt spreader routing problem, the link cost corresponds to the link salt requirement and budget corresponds to the spreader's salt capacity. The minimal arc partitioning problem is similar to the arc partitioning problem studied by Bodin and Levy (1991) in the context of postal delivery. To solve the minimal arc partitioning problem, Toobaie and Haghani (2004) developed a genetic algorithm in which each solution, or collection of subnetworks, is represented as a string of n real numbers (a chromosome with n genes), where n is the number of links in the network. The genetic algorithm can be described as follows.

1. *Initialization.* Generate the initial population by assigning a random real number to each gene from a uniform distribution between 0 and 1.
2. Generate initial routes using the first-fit heuristic.
3. *Evaluation.* Evaluate the population and update the best solution on the basis of the maximization of the fitness function $F = k \times e^{\alpha \times N + \beta}$, where α and β are coefficients, α is negative, N is the number of subnetworks, and k is a positive number.
4. *Selection.* Apply the roulette wheel selection method to generate a new population.
5. *Elitism.* Randomly replace a chromosome with the best solution.
6. *Crossover.* Apply two-point crossover on the basis of crossover probability.
7. *Mutation.* Select and replace genes with random numbers between 0 and 1 on the basis of the mutation probability.
8. Repeat Steps 2 to 7 until the convergence criteria are met (elitism guarantees the convergence of the algorithm).

In Step 1, if each chromosome consists of n genes and each population consists of P chromosomes, then $n \times P$ random real numbers are generated. In Step 2, the first-fit heuristic is a greedy procedure that starts by sorting the links in a given order, and then constructs subnetworks one at a time by repeatedly adding the next unassigned link that preserves the route continuity and vehicle capacity constraints to the current subnetwork. In Step 4, the roulette wheel mechanism is adopted for the selection procedure. In this method, the cumulative fitness ratio f_j for chromosome j is computed as

$$f_j = \frac{\sum_{i=1}^{j} F_i}{\sum_{i=1}^{P} F_i}$$

where F_i is the fitness value of chromosome i. To select P chromosomes for the new generation, P random numbers between 0 and 1 are chosen from a uniform distribution. For each random number r, chromosome j is selected such that $f_{j-1} < r < f_j$. After the selection process, elitism is applied in Step 5 to migrate the best individual to the new generation. Elitism consists of randomly selecting and replacing one chromosome with the best chromosome. In Steps 6 and 7, the two classical genetic algorithm operators, crossover and mutation are adapted for the reproduction phase. The two-point crossover is adapted for the crossover step, while the mutation operation is achieved by randomly selecting a gene and changing its value to another random real number. Once the network is partitioned into connected subnetworks, the second stage of the procedure tries to balance the subnetwork workloads (salt demands) by swapping links between neighboring subnetworks so as to reduce the imbalance between the two subnetworks, while satisfying the route continuity and vehicle capacity constraints. The following conditions must be satisfied to move a link l_i from subnetwork S_1 to subnetwork S_2:

1. Link l_i has common nodes with at least a link in subnetwork S_2.
2. Link l_i can be removed from subnetwork S_1 without violating the route continuity constraint.
3. The salt demand criteria, $D(S_1) - D(l_i) < D(S_2)$, is satisfied, where $D(S_1)$, $D(l_i)$ and $D(S_2)$ are the salt demands for subnetwork S_1, link l_i and subnetwork S_2, respectively.

Finally, in the last stage, spreader routes are obtained by solving a Chinese postman problem for each subnetwork using Edmonds and Johnson's algorithm (Edmonds & Johnson, 1973). The three-stage procedure was tested on data from Calvert County, Maryland. The instance contained 42 nodes, including 2 depots, and 52 edges grouped into four subnetworks. The procedure reduced the number of vehicles, the distance covered by deadheading trips and the workload imbalance by 14%, 27% and 67%, respectively, over the solution in use by the County with short computing times (in the order of seconds).

Spreader routing problems are often studied in a static context, where all data input are assumed to be given in advance. However, in real-life applications, some information might not be readily available when the vehicles start their routes. In an attempt to address the dynamic nature of the problem in which road surface temperature data and condition across the road network are revealed over a 24 hour period, Handa et al. (2005) developed a prototype system that combines a memetic algorithm with Road Weather Information Systems (RWIS) to solve a dynamic salt spreader routing problem. The problem is modeled as a dynamic capacitated arc routing problem where the set of required road segments and their demands (amount of salt) are defined based on the predicted temperature provided by the RWIS. Typically, a road segment is defined as required if there is at least one RWIS point with a predicted temperature less than a predefined threshold. Thus, the amount of required salt on the same required road segment for two days can be different. Moreover, the amount of salt required can vary with road width (type), e.g. motorway, high-class road segments, medium-class road segments, etc. The memetic algorithm is based on a hybrid algorithm of evolutionary algorithms and local search methods. The main steps of the memetic algorithm include: selecting parents, reproducing offspring, applying local search to offspring, and replacing the resultant offspring if the offspring is better than the worst individual in the population. The permutation representation of a chromosome details the order of required edges in which a vehicle must spread salt. Symbols are also used in the chromosome to indicate the beginning of the route for each vehicle. The authors used the edge assembly crossover operator proposed by Nagata and Kobayashi (1997) and Nagata (2004). However, since this operator is designed for solving traveling salesman problems, it can yield infeasible solutions where the vehicle capacity is exceeded. In order to fix these infeasible solutions, a repair operator for offspring individuals is incorporated in the memetic algorithm. As with the memetic algorithms presented by Lacomme, Prins, and Ramdane-Cherif(2004), some initial individuals are generated using the path-scanning algorithm developed by Golden et al. (1983) for the capacitated arc routing problem. Also, three local search methods are used in the memetic algorithm: move one or two edges from one route to another and swap two edges among two routes. Finally, the following fitness function is used to evaluate a set of routes:

$$F = \sum_{i=0}^{m} \left[C_i + \left(p \times E_i \right) \right]$$

where C_i denotes the total distance traveled by vehicle i, E_i is the amount of salt by which vehicle i is above its capacity and p is the corresponding penalty parameter. Results on two instances (two nights) of the South Gloucestershire network, UK, with 385 and 97 required road segments, respectively, showed that the proposed system is effective at finding dynamic salting routes. In a follow-up paper, Handa, Lin, Chapman, and Yao (2006) discussed extensions to the case where a robust solution is required. This is an important practical consideration since it may confuse the highway agency and truck drivers if every different road temperature gave rise to a different set of salting routes. Therefore, a robust solution is desirable. The memetic algorithm is adapted to address this version of the problem by placing

emphasis on "thermally ranking" salting routes so that the "warmer" routes could be left untreated on marginal nights. Comparisons on real data from the South Gloucestershire Council, UK, for various values of environmental parameters showed that the memetic algorithm reduced the total distance traveled by the vehicles by more than 10% over the routes in use by the Council.

Omer (2007) proposed a model for a salt spreader truck routing problem in which maximum route length and duration, fleet size, vehicle capacity, and service frequency constraints are considered, with an objective of minimizing the total distance traveled. The model is based on the formulation proposed by Golden and Wong (1981) for the undirected capacitated arc routing problem (later modified by Haghani & Qiao, 2001). Let $G = (V, A)$ be a directed graph where $V = \{v_1, \ldots, v_n\}$ is the vertex set and $A = \{(v_i, v_j): v_i, v_j \in V$ and $i \neq j\}$ is the arc set. The depot is represented by the node v_1. With every arc $(v_i, v_j) \in A$ are associated a nonnegative length c_{ij} and a deadheading time t_{ij}. Define $R \subseteq A$ as the set of required arcs. With each arc $(v_i, v_j) \in R$ are associated a demand q_{ij}, expressed as the total amount of chemicals required for servicing the arc, and a time g_{ij} corresponding to the difference between the time for servicing arc (v_i, v_j) and the time for deadheading arc (v_i, v_j). Define also $A_1 \subseteq R$ as the set of counterpart arcs in opposite directions between intersection nodes that can be serviced only once from one direction. Associated with every arc $(v_i, v_j) \in R \setminus A_1$ is a positive number of times n_{ij} arc (v_i, v_j) should be spread. Let K be the set of vehicles. For every arc $(v_i, v_j) \in A$ and for every vehicle $k \in K$, let x_{ijk} be a binary variable equal to 1 if and only if arc (v_i, v_j) is either serviced or traversed while deadheading by vehicle k and let f_{ijk} be a nonnegative real variable representing the flow on arc (v_i, v_j) in the route associated with vehicle k. For every arc $(v_i, v_j) \in R$ and for every vehicle $k \in K$, let y_{ijk} be a binary variable equal to 1 if and only if arc (v_i, v_j) is serviced by vehicle k. Finally, let D, T and W be the maximum distance a vehicle can cover in a route, the maximum time a vehicle can take to cover a route, and the vehicle capacity, respectively. The formulation is then as follows.

Minimize

$$\sum_{k \in K} \sum_{(v_i, v_j) \in A} c_{ij} x_{ijk} \tag{18}$$

subject to

$$\sum_{v_j \in V, v_j \neq v_i} x_{jik} - \sum_{v_j \in V, v_j \neq v_i} x_{ijk} = 0$$
$$(v_i \in V, k \in K) \tag{19}$$

$$\sum_{k \in K} y_{ijk} + y_{jik} = 1$$
$$((v_i, v_j) \in A_1) \tag{20}$$

$$\sum_{k \in K} y_{ijk} = n_{ij}$$
$$((v_i, v_j) \in R \setminus A_1) \tag{21}$$

$$\sum_{(v_i, v_j) \in A} c_{ij} x_{ijk} \leq D$$
$$(k \in K) \tag{22}$$

$$\sum_{(v_i, v_j) \in A} t_{ij} x_{ijk} + \sum_{(v_i, v_j) \in R} g_{ij} y_{ijk} \leq T$$
$$(k \in K) \tag{23}$$

$$\sum_{(v_i, v_j) \in R} q_{ij} y_{ijk} \leq W$$
$$(k \in K) \tag{24}$$

$$x_{ijk} \geq y_{ijk}$$
$$((v_i, v_j) \in R, k \in K) \tag{25}$$

$$\sum_{v_r \in V, v_r \neq v_i} f_{irk} - \sum_{v_r \in V, v_r \neq v_i} f_{rik} = \sum_{v_j \in V} y_{ijk}$$
$$(v_i \in V \setminus \{v_1\}, k \in K) \tag{26}$$

$$f_{ijk} \leq |V|^2 \cdot x_{ijk}$$
$$((v_i, v_j) \in A, k \in K) \tag{27}$$

$$f_{ijk} \geq 0$$
$$((v_i, v_j) \in A, k \in K) \tag{28}$$

$$x_{ijk} \in \{0, 1\}$$
$$((v_i, v_j) \in A, k \in K) \tag{29}$$

$$y_{ijk} \in \{0, 1\}$$
$$((v_i, v_j) \in R, k \in K) \tag{30}$$

The objective function (18) minimizes total distance traveled. Constraints (19) ensure route continuity. Constraints (20) and (21) state that each arc is serviced as required. Maximum route length, maximum route duration and vehicle capacity are not violated on account of constraints (22), (23) and (24), respectively. Constraints (25) guarantee that an arc can be serviced by a vehicle only if the vehicle covers that arc. Constraints (26)-(28) prohibit the formation of illegal subtours. The flow variable f_{ijk} can take on positive values only if $x_{ijk} = 1$. For details, see Golden and Wong (1981). The problem is solved using a Greedy Randomized Adaptive Search Procedure (GRASP) heuristic. In each iteration of the GRASP, an initial solution is built using a constructive method, and local search is performed on the solution obtained using simulated annealing. The best overall solution obtained from several iterations of the GRASP is considered as the final solution. The constructive method builds a route starting at the depot node and incrementally inserts an arc until a feasible route is completed. At each iteration of the constructive method, a list of candidate arcs is created by considering all possible arcs that satisfy a greedy evaluation function and that can be added to the current partial solution without violating operational constraints. The greedy evaluation function calculates the incremental increase in total cost due to addition of the candidate arc to the partial solution and considers only the candidate arcs whose incremental cost lies below a threshold value. A candidate arc is randomly selected from the list and inserted into the current partial solution. The simulated annealing algorithm starts with the solution obtained from the constructive method and searches for better solutions by moving arcs between pairs of routes. Two types of moves can be performed: one-arc move and *m-n* exchange. The one-arc move involves moving a single arc from one route to another. The *m-n* exchange consists in moving *m* arcs from one route A to another route B and moving *n* arcs from route B to route A, without exceeding the vehicle capacity. Arcs that are removed or inserted in a route may separate the route into disconnected components. The author proposed an improvement algorithm to combine these disconnected components into a new feasible low cost route. The algorithm first builds a route starting and ending at the depot and connecting all the disconnected components in the route. The route is then again divided into multiple disconnected components and the sequence of disconnected components in the route is modified by interchanging the disconnected components within the route. This results in multiple sequences or routes. Finally, the route (sequence of disconnected components) with the lowest cost among the evaluated sequences of disconnected components is chosen. Comparisons with both the CARPET heuristic (Hertz, Laporte, & Mittaz, 2000), and memetic algorithm (Lacomme, Prins, & Ramdane-Cherif, 2004) on four sets of problem instances (total of 115 instances) obtained from the literature (DeArmon, 1981; Belenguer & Benavent, 2003; Prins, Belenguer, Benavent, & Lacomme, 2006) showed that the proposed GRASP heuristic improved the best-known solution on 18 of the 115 instances, and matched the results on 89 of those instances.

The location of depots related to spreading operations is usually given as an input in spreader routing models (Haghani & Qiao, 2002). Since the quality of the vehicle routes is highly dependent on the location of the depots, this sequential approach obviously leads to suboptimal decisions, at both the strategic and operational levels. A better approach consists in treating simultaneously the vehicle routing problem and the depot location problem. Cai, Liu, and Cao (2009) used this approach for designing routes for spreading operations. The author proposed a tabu search algorithm to help planners in constructing combined depot location and spreader routing plans. The algorithm takes into account the materials depot capacities, spreader capacities (all the same) and the maximum number of routes. The tabu search algorithm first finds an initial solution to the depot location problem and then tries to improve this solution by applying two types of moves. The first move involves opening a depot and closing another depot, while the second move consists in increasing the number of depots. After every move, the current vehicle routes are optimized. The author did not, however, provide a detailed description of the tabu search algorithm. Computational experiments carried out on real-data from the central part of the Changchun city, China, involving 321 road sections, 20 candidate depots and 13 spreaders allowed an improvement of 6% over the solution obtained from the traditional sequential approach.

Tagmouti, Gendreau, and Potvin (2010) studied a salt spreader truck routing problem with capacity constraints and time-dependent service costs. The problem is modeled as a variant of the capacitated arc routing problem, where a time-dependent piecewise linear service cost is associated with each required arc in a directed graph. The authors proposed a variable neighborhood descent heuristic for solving the problem. An initial solution is first obtained by means of either the parallel version of the Clarke and Wright (1964) savings procedure for the capacitated vehicle routing problem, or a sequential insertion heuristic, where the routes are constructed one by one. Then, a variable neighborhood descent is applied to the initial solution to improve it. During a local descent, three different neighborhoods are explored: arc move, cross exchange and block exchange. Each neighborhood is explored using a first-improvement local descent. The arc move neighborhood structure removes a required arc from one route and inserts it between two other required arcs in the same route or in another route. Given a pair of routes in the current solution, the cross exchange neighborhood structure exchanges two sequences of arcs. Each sequence must contain the same number of required arcs, with up to five required arcs, plus the arcs on the shortest path between them in the route. Similarly, the block exchange neighborhood structure identifies sequences made of consecutive required arcs with no deadhead arcs in-between, called blocks, and exchanges them between two routes. However, the number of required arcs in a block is not limited and two blocks can be exchanged even if they do not contain the same number of required arcs. An improvement procedure, called *shorten* (Hertz et al., 2000), is also used for attempting to reduce the total travel cost of the routes by inverting the service and travel on a given arc, when this arc is crossed twice. The variable neighborhood descent heuristic proposed by Tagmouti et al. (2010) can be summarized as follows:

1. *Initialization.* Let M be the maximum number of required arcs in a sequence of arcs in a route. Define N_1, N_2 to N_{M+1} and N_{M+2} as the arc move neighborhood, the M cross exchange neighborhoods, and the block exchange neighborhood, respectively. Define also $s(N_j)$ as a local optimum solution based on neighborhood N_j, $j = 1,\ldots, M + 2$. Find an initial solution $s(N_0)$.
2. Set $j = 1$. Until $j = M + 2$, repeat the following steps:
   a. *Exploration of neighborhood.* Perform a local descent based on neighborhood N_j with $s(N_{j-1})$ as initial solution. Denote with $s(N_j)$ the local optimum obtained.

   b. *Move or not.* If the solution thus obtained $s(N_j)$ is different from $s(N_{j-1})$, set $s(N_0) := s(N_j)$ and go to Step 2.
3. Apply the *shorten* procedure to $s(N_{M+2})$ to obtain $s(short)$. If $s(short)$ is better than $s(N_{M+2})$, then set $s(N_0) := s(short)$ and go to Step 2. Otherwise, the best solution is $s(N_{M+2})$.

In this procedure, Step 3 is reached and the *shorten* procedure is applied only when the $M + 2$ neighborhoods are explored without any improvement to the starting solution. If the *shorten* procedure improves the solution, Step 2 is restarted with the improved solution. Otherwise the best solution found is returned. The variable neighborhood descent algorithm is executed twice, using the savings and the insertion heuristics to generate an initial solution, and the best solution is returned at the end. Tested on problems derived from classical capacitated arc routing problem instances (Golden et al., 1983; Li, 1992; Li & Eglese, 1996), the algorithm appeared to be fast and competitive when compared with the recent adaptive multi-start local search algorithm of Ibaraki et al. (2005) for solving vehicle routing problems with soft time window constraints.

In a follow-up paper, Tagmouti, Gendreau, and Potvin (2011) adapted the variable neighborhood descent heuristic to address the dynamic version of the problem where weather report updates lead to real-time modifications to the current routes. In this dynamic variant, a starting solution is first computed with the variable neighborhood descent heuristic using service time cost functions based on some initial forecast. As spreader trucks execute their routes, regular weather report updates lead to modifications to the optimal service time interval associated with each required arc. Basically, each time a weather report is received, the variable neighborhood descent heuristic is applied on a new problem, called the *static problem*, defined with updated service time functions for unserved required arcs based on the new storm location and speed. Since the computation times with the heuristic are not negligible, when a new report is received, the current solution is followed for an additional Δt time units using the updated service time functions. During that time, the solution is optimized with the heuristic based on the projected state of the system at time $t + \Delta t$. The new solution obtained can then be implemented as soon as it is available. Computational results were presented for three types of generated instances with 25, 49 and 100 vertices and with 36, 76, and 162 required arcs, respectively. Comparisons with both the *a priori* solutions obtained with the initial service cost functions (based on some initial storm speed forecast), but evaluated in the dynamic setting, and the *a posteriori* solutions computed with the true service cost functions (namely those obtained at the end of the dynamic process when everything is known), showed that the dynamic solutions lie within 10% of the *a posteriori* solutions on the instances with 25 vertices. However, on the 49-vertex instances, the gap jumps to 50%. This gap stabilizes on the largest 100-vertex instances, due to a smaller time step between two updates on these instances, which leads to more frequent calls to the reoptimization procedure.

4. ANALYSIS OF EXISTING RESEARCH ON VEHICLE ROUTING PROBLEMS FOR SPREADING OPERATIONS

In this section, the authors provide a classification of important optimization models developed over the past 40 years for the routing of vehicles for spreading operations. They utilize the categories and characteristics presented in Table 1 as a basis to classify the research works in Tables 2 and 3 at the end of the section. These tables are arranged chronologically with the oldest works near the top. The categories from Table 1 are listed across the top of Tables 2 and 3 and are included in parentheses where appropriate throughout this section. The remainder of this section follows the classification categories in Tables 1-3 to highlight key research contributions and gaps.

The vast majority of the operations research literature on vehicle routing for spreading considers the routing problems alone (1.1). Only a few works combine vehicle routing and other tactical or strategic problems in winter road maintenance, such as sector design or the location of depots for vehicles or materials (1.2). Typically, these different problems are treated sequentially in a hierarchy with the lower level more operational problems subject to the conditions resulting from solving the higher level more strategic problems. The integrated models that combine routing and other problems generally adopt a longer-term perspective at the strategic or tactical level (2.1 and 2.2), although some pure routing models also incorporate a more strategic view (Evans, 1990; Evans & Weant, 1990). The dominance of static routing models (2.3.1) is clear in Table 2, with dynamic or real-time routing models being quite rare. An example of dynamic spreader routing (2.3.2) is Handa et al. (2005), which allows new routes to be developed each day as conditions change. This is in contrast to the real-time routing (2.3.3) in Tagmouti et al. (2011), where vehicle routes may change during the traversal of the route as new information (e.g., weather conditions) becomes available. Recent technological developments, such as road weather information systems, weather forecasting services, geographic information systems, global positioning systems, electronic data interchange, and intelligent vehicle-highway systems, enhance the possibilities for efficient dynamic and real-time vehicle routing for spreading operations by providing new instructions directly to vehicle operators in response to sudden changes in weather and road surface conditions.

Tables 2 and 3 link the many and varied problem characteristics (category 3 of Table 1) to the key research. Some very rarely observed attributes are: service hierarchy (3.2), service time

Table 2. Summary of the classifications of spreader routing problems (attributes 1 to 3.12)

Authors	1.1.	1.2.1.	1.2.2.	2.1.	2.2.	2.3.1.	2.3.2.	2.3.3.	3.1.1.	3.1.2.	3.1.3.	3.1.4.	3.2.1.	3.2.2.	3.3.1.	3.3.2.	3.3.3.
Liebling (1973)		X								X							
Soyster (1974)	X					X			X						X		
Cook and Alprin (1976)	X			X		X			X								
England (1982a, 1982b)		X			X	X			X								
Reinert, Miller, and Dickerson (1985)			X		X	X											
Ungerer (1989)	X					X			X						X		
Xin and Eglese (1989)	X					X			X			X			X		X
Evans (1990), Evans and Weant (1990)	X			X		X			X			X			X		
Eglese (1994)	X					X			X			X	X	X	X		
Li and Eglese (1996)	X			X		X					X	X	X		X	X	
Lotan, Cattrysse, Oudheusden, and Leuven (1996)			X	X		X			X		X		X			X	
Benson, Bander, and White (1998)	X					X				X		X			X		
Haghani and Qiao (2001)	X					X			X			X	X		X		
Haghani and Qiao (2002)	X					X				X		X					
Qiao (2002)	X					X			X			X					
Toobaie and Haghani (2004)	X					X			X								
Handa et al. (2005, 2006)	X						X		X			X					
Omer (2007)	X					X			X			X			X		
Tagmouti et al. (2007)	X					X				X		X					X
Cai et al. (2009)			X	X		X				X							X
Gabor (2010)	X					X				X		X	X		X		
Tagmouti et al. (2010)	X					X				X		X					
Tagmouti et al. (2011)	X							X		X		X					

continued on the following page

Table 2. Continued

	1	2	3	4	5	6	7	8	9	10	11	12	13	14	15	16	17	18	19	20	21	22
3.12.2.										X												
3.12.1.	X	X	X	X	X	X		X	X	X	X	X	X	X	X	X	X	X	X	X	X	X
3.11.3.		X	X				X	X	X	X	X		X	X		X				X	X	
3.11.2.																						
3.11.1.	X								X			X		X	X	X	X				X	X
3.10.3												X										
3.10.2	X			X	X		X	X	X	X	X	X			X	X				X	X	
3.10.1		X	X			X			X	X	X		X	X	X					X	X	
3.9.3	X				X		X															
3.9.2	X			X																		
3.9.1				X																		
3.8.2.		X				X	X	X	X		X	X	X	X								
3.8.1.			X			X			X		X			X								
3.7.2.									X	X		X										
3.7.1.									X			X										
3.6.2.	X			X					X		X	X										
3.6.1.																						
3.5.2.					X				X	X												
3.5.1.						X			X													
3.4.2.																X				X	X	
3.4.1.	X	X	X	X		X	X	X	X	X	X	X	X	X	X	X	X		X	X		

Table 3. Summary of the classifications of spreader routing problems (attributes 3.13 to 6)

Authors	3.13.1.	3.13.2.	3.13.3.	3.13.4.	3.13.5.	3.13.6.	3.14.1.	3.14.2.	3.14.3.	3.14.4.	3.14.5.	3.14.6.	4.1.1.	4.1.2.	4.1.3.	4.2.
Liebling (1973)	X					X	X									
Soyster (1974)						X	X					X	X			
Cook and Alprin (1976)	X		X				X									
England (1982a, 1982b)				X		X	X				X					X
Reinert, Miller, and Dickerson (1985)[1]							X						X			
Ungerer (1989)							X									
Xin and Eglese (1989)							X			X						
Evans (1990), Evans and Weant (1990)							X									
Eglese (1994)										X						
Li and Eglese (1996)						X		X								
Lotan, Cattrysse, Oudheusden, and Leuven (1996)		X					X			X						
Benson, Bander, and White (1998)							X					X			X	
Haghani and Qiao (2001)							X							X		
Haghani and Qiao (2002)			X		X		X			X						
Qiao (2002)	X				X		X							X		
Toobaie and Haghani (2004)	X				X		X			X						
Handa et al. (2005, 2006)							X									
Omer (2007)					X		X							X		
Tagmouti et al (2007)							X		X						X	
Cai et al. (2009)								X	X							
Gabor (2010)							X			X						
Tagmouti et al. (2010)							X		X							
Tagmouti et al. (2011)							X		X							

continued on the following page

Table 3. Continued

	4.2.1.	4.2.2.	4.2.3.	4.3.	4.4.	4.4.1.	5.1.	5.1.1.	5.2.	5.2.1.	5.2.2.	5.2.3.	5.2.4.	5.3.	5.4.1.	5.4.2.	5.4.3.	5.4.4.	5.4.5.	5.4.6.	5.5.	5.6.	6.1.	6.2.	6.3.
	X										X	X	X									X	X	X	
		X								X	X		X	X	X						X				
		X														X					X				X
				X																			X		
					X																		X		
						X																	X		
							a																X		
								X															X		
									X																
										X			X								X		X	X	
											X												X		
												X											X		
														X									X		
													X			X	X				X		X		X
														X	X	X									
																X	X						X		
																	X						X		
																		X							
																			X						
																				X	X				
		X	X	X																		X	X		
	X			X																		X			

windows (3.5), number of passes per road segment (3.7), load balancing (3.13.1), class continuity (3.13.2), both-sides service (3.13.3), turn restrictions (3.13.4), service connectivity (3.13.5), and sector boundaries (3.13.6). These problem characteristics appear less than six times in Tables 2 and 3. Also, one empty column related to problem characteristics denotes "road segment-specific vehicles" (3.11.2), which was not addressed by any contribution. Not surprisingly, the earlier works considered relatively few, more straightforward characteristics, and it was only after introduction of faster heuristics that more complex and realistic arc routing problems with a larger variety of constraints and possibilities were considered. Examples include modeling of service hierarchy constraints (Dror, Stern, & Trudeau, 1987), time windows (Labadi, Prins, & Reghioui, 2008), and turn penalties (Corberán, Martí, Martínez, & Soler, 2002). Note that routing with both-sides service constraints and multiple passes per road segment usually arises in plowing operations, which are limited to one lane at a time. In spreading operations, chemicals and abrasives are often spread onto the road segment through a spinner which can be adjusted so that two lanes are treated on a single pass. Also, the impact of undesirable turns, such as U-turns and turns across traffic lanes, is generally lower in routing spreaders as compared to plowing operations.

The model structures in Tables 2 and 3 (category 4 of Table 1) show that vehicle routing problems for spreading operations are generally formulated as capacitated arc routing problems, where the capacity of the spreader is expressed as the maximum quantity of chemicals or abrasives the spreader can discharge. Vehicle capacities can also be taken into consideration during the sector design process (Liebling, 1973; England, 1982a, 1982b), where the service region (e.g., city) is first divided into a number of geographically disjoint sectors, so that a route satisfying the vehicle capacity can be constructed for each sector. The capacities of the vehicles can also be given

as time limits (Soyster, 1974; Gabor, 2010) or as maximum distances which can be spread in one route (Soyster, 1974; Eglese, 1994; Li & Eglese, 1996). Very little work has been reported concerning the possibility for spreader vehicles to refill with materials at intermediate facilities (materials depots) without returning to the original starting point. Hayman and Howard (1972) proposed a model to determine the spreader truck fleet size based at each depot with this condition. Li and Eglese (1996) proposed a three-stage heuristic with decision rules to determine if the spreader should head back towards the vehicle depot or the nearest materials depot to refill with salt. Qiao (2002) showed how multiple salt depots can be taken into account. One interesting line of research would be the further development of more realistic models where vehicles may refill at materials depots by exploiting the research on arc routing problems with intermediate facilities (Ghiani, Improta, & Laporte, 2001; Zhu, Li, Xia, Deng, & Liu, 2009; Ghiani, Laganà, Laporte, & Mari, 2010).

Because of the inherent difficulties of vehicle routing problems for spreading operations, most solution methods that have been developed are heuristics. Much early work (1970-1990) adapted or extended simple capacitated arc routing models with little consideration of operational constraints. These simplified models were generally solved with simple constructive heuristics (5.2), such as sequential constructive methods (5.2.1), parallel constructive methods (5.2.2), cluster first, route second methods (5.2.3), or optimization-based methods (5.2.4), for undirected networks (3.1.1). These constructive heuristics gradually build a feasible solution while giving attention to solution cost, but they do not contain an improvement phase. Some of these heuristics were embedded into discrete event simulation models (5.5) to evaluate benefits and to model spreader movements and interactions (Soyster, 1974; Cook & Alprin, 1976; England, 1982a, 1982b). Recently proposed models are solved with more sophisticated local search techniques, such as composite methods (5.3), which blend route construction and improvement algorithms, and metaheuristics (5.4), which have proven to be very effective for several classes of discrete optimization problems. However, even though recent models tend to incorporate a larger variety of practical characteristics, very few implemented solution methods can be found in the literature (Evans, 1990; Evans & Weant, 1990; Li & Eglese, 1996; Benson, Bander, & White, 1998). In fact, implementation details are rarely considered. This contrasts with the frequency of papers with real world data (6.1), which seems relatively high (see Table 3).

5. CONCLUSION AND FUTURE RESEARCH DIRECTIONS

The research described in this chapter for optimizing the routing of spreader vehicles builds on earlier, more idealized, operations research models by better addressing a variety of practical considerations. While the new models demonstrate impressive capabilities to include more issues important to the operating agencies, there is still a large gap between state-of-the-art models and actual implementations. Some reasons for this gap include the difficulty of the problems, the unfamiliarity in the practitioner community with the advantages and benefits of OR models, and problems of technology transfer to a decentralized area such as winter maintenance.

Arc routing research remains a rich area within OR, and winter road maintenance vehicle routing problems will likely remain an important subarea of arc routing. However, vehicle routing for winter road maintenance is different than other arc routing applications for a variety of reasons. First, the demand for service (i.e., the current and forecast road conditions) can vary dramatically over small geographic regions and change quickly over time. Second, the timing of operations is crucial to achieve the desired level of service: spreading a roadway too early is ineffective, and spreading a roadway too late increases costs and reduces the level of service achieved. Third, winter road spreading operations are often conducted in a very difficult and dynamic operational environment characterized by limited visibility, poor traction, and unexpected obstacles (e.g., parked, stalled or abandoned vehicles), all of which can change very rapidly.

In spite of the wealth of theoretical research in winter road maintenance, and the prominent contributions from OR to practice in seemingly similar areas such as emergency services and waste removal (Green & Kolesar, 2004; Sahoo et al., 2005), OR has not yet reached its potential in winter road maintenance operations. A recent "synthesis report on winter highway operations" (Transportation Research Board [TRB], 2005) surveyed 22 prominent winter road maintenance agencies in North America including 19 US states or Canadian provinces and three municipalities. They found a widespread and increasing level of technology being deployed, with all but two agencies using pavement temperature sensors and all but a single agency using computerized spreader controls on vehicles. However, the report includes only a short paragraph on "route optimization" with one mention of using sensor data and automatic vehicle location (AVL) to "optimize plowing and spreading activities". There is no mention of route optimization as commonly used in OR (e.g,. arc routing models), and it seems that a somewhat different language is being spoken regarding route optimization in the practitioner and OR communities.

Another reason for the limited linkages between OR and public works agencies may be the decentralized nature of winter maintenance operations, where individual regional and local agencies have responsibility for snow and ice control over small regions (cities or towns). This differs from some other public works and emergency service systems (e.g., waste removal or fire protection) that have become more centralized on regional or national levels across political jurisdictions, in part to exploit efficiencies of scale and standardization. It may be that winter road maintenance operations are less amenable to standardization and consolidation of neighboring regions with the potential benefits from improved routings.

There remain a number of important areas for future research on vehicle routing for winter maintenance operations, including: (1) the development of new models, especially dynamic routing models, that exploit the availability of more accurate and timely information from new technologies, (2) the development of better models that integrate vehicle route optimization with other winter maintenance decision problems, (3) studies that use optimized routing to quantify the tradeoffs between cost and level of service, especially in light of rising environmental concerns, and (4) implementations of OR models in the field. Each of these areas is briefly described below.

1. *Models that exploit the availability of more accurate and timely information from new technologies.*

An impressive array of technologies are in use and in development to provide better information for winter maintenance operations. Two major categories of technologies involve improved weather forecasting tools, such as RWIS and now-casting, and fixed or vehicle-based sensors. The availability of better weather data that is more accurate, more timely, and at a finer geographic scale is important for improved winter maintenance operations and in case studies has been show to generate a very favourable benefit-cost ratio (Ye, Shi, & Strong, 2009b). A recent scan for the "best practices" in winter road maintenance describes the range of technologies to sense road and environmental conditions, improve safety and effectiveness of spreading operations, and reduce environmental impacts (Pletan, 2009).

Sensor technologies for winter maintenance may be mobile (on vehicles) or fixed, and include automatic vehicle location (AVL), roadway surface sensors (for temperature, freezing, and ice-presence), salinity measuring devices, radar, other visual and multi-spectral sensors, etc. (See Shi et al., 2006 and Transportation Research Board [TRB], 2008, for details.) Some agencies also deploy a variety of fixed assets for roadway snow and ice control, such as FAST (fixed automated spray technology), road warming, snow fences, etc. While such technologies are expensive, they can be used at selected critical locations on roadways. Naturally, this affects vehicle routing plans and research is needed to assess the integration of such fixed technologies into optimal vehicle routes.

One challenging opportunity for vehicle routing research is to develop real-time routing models that can exploit real-time winter maintenance information. Real-time routing may be needed to respond dynamically not just to changing ice and snow conditions and forecasts, but also to equipment breakdowns, traffic congestion and accidents, all of which are more common in winter driving. Real-time route changes can also be used to respond to citizen complaints (e.g., streets not cleared) in a more timely manner, thereby increasing customer service. The survey from the "synthesis report" mentioned above (Transportation Research Board [TRB], 2005) highlighted the use of dynamic routes in practice as 72% of the agencies responding indicated that they dynamically change routes. A few researchers have begun to address some dynamic and real-time issues in winter road maintenance as noted earlier in the chapter, but more research is needed on dynamic, real-time, and stochastic winter maintenance arc routing problems. One avenue for this research may be to exploit the growing research on challenging dynamic *node* routing problems (Ghiani, Guerriero, Laporte, & Musmanno, 2003; Ichoua, Gendreau, & Potvin, 2000; Psaraftis, 1995).

2. *Models that integrate vehicle route optimization with other winter maintenance decision problems.*

There are a range of winter maintenance problems beyond vehicle routing that are amenable to operations research approaches, such as depot and materials stockpile locations, fleet sizing, sector design, personnel and vehicle scheduling, etc. (Perrier, Langevin, & Campbell, 2006a, 2006b). The traditional approach has been to solve these problems separately and sequentially, which is likely to be suboptimal. Noble, Jang, Klein, and Nemmers (2006) adopt a broad perspective and consider sector design, depot location and route design in an iterative sequential approach – along with fleet assignment. This more integrative perspective is promising and it may provide new opportunities for implementing route optimization in conjunction with strategic or tactical planning activities. However, coupling a very difficult arc routing (operational) problem with other difficult more strategic OR problems creates a host of challenges for researchers. The recent effort by Cai et al. (2009) is also a step in this direction, though a truly integrated model that optimizes several decision areas simultaneously remains a promising area for future research.

3. *Studies that use optimized vehicle routing to quantify the tradeoffs between cost and level of service.*

Vehicle routes play an important role in determining the cost and the level of service provided by winter road maintenance and it is essential to have a good routing model to assess accurately the tradeoff between cost and level of service. Improved vehicle routes could lead to higher levels of service at the same cost, or lower costs to achieve the same level of service. Tradeoff analysis can be at a strategic level to determine the level of service for a whole season – or more dynamic, as to assess different levels of service that may be deployed in response to individual storms. Furthermore, because improved vehicle routing provides environmental benefits from reduced materials (especially chemicals) usage and

broader social benefits from improved mobility, along with the direct cost benefits from reduced use of vehicles and drivers, winter maintenance routing models that incorporate environmental and social costs and benefits are an important area of future research. Tradeoff analyses are also needed to assess the benefits from different weather and sensor technologies, many of which have proven difficult and expensive to implement and to integrate into the winter maintenance decision-making process (Shi et al., 2006; Ye, Shi, & Strong, 2009a).

4. *Implementation of OR tools to optimize vehicle routing.*

While engineers from several disciplines have long played a prominent role in working with public works agencies to develop, test and deploy new technologies for winter road maintenance, operations researchers have been much less successful and reported implementations of sophisticated OR models for winter road maintenance remain rare. Campbell and Langevin (2000) describe in detail three implementations of sophisticated OR models (in the US, Canada and the UK). There is certainly interest from many operating agencies in optimizing the vehicle routes, and the authors are aware of a variety of projects funded by state, provincial or municipal agencies that include vehicle routing. These projects generally develop models for "optimizing" vehicle routing and then test the models with real-world data from the associated agency. However, subsequent actual implementations of the new optimized routing approach seem very rare, in spite of the generally positive results from testing with "real" data.

There are likely a variety of reasons for the lack of implementation success stories, including those noted earlier, but it does *not* seem that the slow pace of adoption of vehicle routing optimization is due to ineffective models or an inability to generate timely results. Nor is a "fear" of technology a likely reason, as agencies are becoming increasingly reliant of sophisticated technologies and computerized controls for operations (and communications). One approach to increase implementation successes might be to integrate vehicle routing optimization with other technologies being implemented, such as the ongoing development and deployment of the winter MDSS (maintenance decision support system) in the US (Pisano, Hoffman, & Stern, 2009; Ye et al., 2009a). This is a multistate effort to develop a system that can "provide weather and road condition forecasts and real-time treatment recommendations (e.g., treatment locations, types, times, and rates) for specific road segments, tailored for winter road maintenance decision makers." (Ye et al., 2009a). Although the MDSS includes real-time treatment recommendations, it does not include real-time routing optimization at this point.

In summary, there remain many challenging research opportunities (theoretical and applied) in winter road maintenance vehicle routing. One strong trend in practice has been to exploit technological advances and move away from traditional *reactive* static snow and ice control such as de-icing, to more *proactive* approaches, such as anti-icing and dynamic operations based on localized, accurate and timely forecasts. As the technology and operations continue to evolve, rich opportunities for applied arc routing research will continue to emerge – and the authors hope that optimized vehicle routing will become a "best practice" for winter road maintenance.

REFERENCES

Belenguer, J. M., & Benavent, E. (2003). A cutting plane algorithm for the capacitated arc routing problem. *Computers & Operations Research*, *30*(5), 705–728. doi:10.1016/S0305-0548(02)00046-1

Benson, D. E., Bander, J. L., & White, C. C. (1998). A planning and operational decision support system for winter storm maintenance in an ITS environment. In *Proceedings of the 1998 IEEE International Conference on Intelligent Vehicles* (pp. 673-675). Ann Arbor: The University of Michigan.

Bodin, L., & Levy, L. (1991). The arc partitioning problem. *European Journal of Operational Research*, *53*(3), 393–401. doi:10.1016/0377-2217(91)90072-4

Cai, W. P., Liu, G., & Cao, W. S. (2009). A study of vehicle and materials depot location problems for winter road maintenance. In *Proceedings of the 9th International Conference of Chinese Transportation Professionals, ICCTP 2009: Vol. 358. Critical Issues in Transportation System Planning, Development, and Management* (pp.1530-1535). Reston, VA: American Society of Civil Engineers.

Campbell, J. F., & Langevin, A. (2000). Roadway snow and ice control. In Dror, M. (Ed.), *Arc Routing: Theory, Solutions and Applications* (pp. 389–418). Boston, MA: Kluwer.

Christofides, N. (1973). The optimal traversal of a graph. *Omega*, *1*(6), 719–732. doi:10.1016/0305-0483(73)90089-3

Clarke, G., & Wright, J. (1964). Scheduling of vehicles from a central depot to a number of delivery points. *Operations Research*, *12*(4), 568–581. doi:10.1287/opre.12.4.568

Cook, T. M., & Alprin, B. S. (1976). Snow and ice removal in an urban environment. *Management Science*, *23*(3), 227–234. doi:10.1287/mnsc.23.3.227

Corberán, A., Martí, R., Martínez, E., & Soler, D. (2002). The rural postman problem on mixed graphs with turn penalties. *Computers & Operations Research*, *29*(7), 887–903. doi:10.1016/S0305-0548(00)00091-5

Corberán, A., & Prins, C. (2010). Recent results on arc routing problems: an annotated bibliography. *Networks*, *56*(1), 50–69.

DeArmon, J. S. (1981). *A Comparison of Heuristics for the Capacitated Chinese Postman Problem*. Master dissertation, University of Maryland at College Park, Maryland.

Dror, M., Stern, H., & Trudeau, P. (1987). Postman tour on a graph with precedence relation on arcs. *Networks*, *17*(3), 283–294. doi:10.1002/net.3230170304

Edmonds, J., & Johnson, E. L. (1973). Matching, Euler tours and the Chinese postman. *Mathematical Programming*, *5*(1), 88–124. doi:10.1007/BF01580113

Eglese, R. W. (1994). Routeing winter gritting vehicles. *Discrete Applied Mathematics*, *48*(3), 231–244. doi:10.1016/0166-218X(92)00003-5

England, R. (1982a). Computer analysis ensures a clean sweep. *Surveyor*, *6*(May), 15–16.

England, R. (1982b). Cluster analysis and your roads. *Surveyor*, *7*(January), 10–11.

Evans, J. R. (1990). *Design and implementation of a vehicle routing and planning system for snow and ice control*. Working paper QA-1990-002, College of Business Administration, University of Cincinnati, Cincinnati, Ohio.

Evans, J. R., & Weant, M. (1990). Strategic planning for snow and ice control using computer-based routing software. *Public Works*, *121*(April), 60–64.

Federal Highway Administration. (2010). *How do weather events impact roads*. Retrieved August 13, 2010, from http://ops.fhwa.dot.gov /Weather /q1_roadimpact.htm.

Feillet, D., Dejax, P., Gendreau, M., & Gueguen, C. (2004). An exact algorithm for the elementary shortest path problem with resource constraints: Application to some vehicle routing problems. *Networks*, *44*(3), 216–229. doi:10.1002/net.20033

Fu, L., Trudel, M., & Kim, V. (2009). Optimizing winter road maintenance operations under real-time information. *European Journal of Operational Research*, *196*(1), 332–341. doi:10.1016/j.ejor.2008.03.001

Gabor, M. (2010). Proposal for the size of the fleet to provide winter road maintenance. *Komunikacie*, *12*(3A), 46–49.

Ghiani, G., Guerriero, F., Laporte, G., & Musmanno, R. (2003). Real-time vehicle routing: solution concepts, algorithms and parallel computing strategies. *European Journal of Operational Research*, *151*(1), 1–11. doi:10.1016/S0377-2217(02)00915-3

Ghiani, G., Improta, G., & Laporte, G. (2001). The capacitated arc routing problem with intermediate facilities. *Networks*, *37*(3), 134–143. doi:10.1002/net.3

Ghiani, G., Laganà, D., Laporte, G., & Mari, F. (2010). Ant colony optimization for the arc routing problem with intermediate facilities under capacity and length restrictions. *Journal of Heuristics*, *16*(2), 211–233. doi:10.1007/s10732-008-9097-8

Golden, B. L., DeArmon, J. S., & Baker, E. K. (1983). Computational experiments with algorithms for a class of routing problems. *Computers & Operations Research*, *10*(1), 47–59. doi:10.1016/0305-0548(83)90026-6

Golden, B. L., & Wong, R. T. (1981). Capacitated arc routing problems. *Networks*, *11*(3), 305–315. doi:10.1002/net.3230110308

Green, L. V., & Kolesar, P. J. (2004). Improving emergency responsiveness with management science. *Management Science*, *50*(8), 1001–1014. doi:10.1287/mnsc.1040.0253

Haghani, A., & Qiao, H. (2001). Decision support system for snow emergency vehicle routing. *Transportation Research Record, 1771*, 172–178. doi:10.3141/1771-22

Haghani, A., & Qiao, H. (2002). Snow emergency vehicle routing with route continuity constraints. *Transportation Research Record, 1783*, 119–124. doi:10.3141/1783-15

Handa, H., Chapman, L., & Yao, X. (2005). Dynamic salting route optimization using evolutionary computation. In *Proceedings of the 2005 IEEE Congress on Evolutionary Computation* (pp.158-165). Piscataway, NJ: Institute of Electrical and Electronics Engineers Computer Society.

Handa, H., Lin, D., Chapman, L., & Yao, X. (2006). Robust solution of salting route optimisation using evolutionary algorithms. In *2006 IEEE Congress on Evolutionary Computation* (pp. 3098-3105). Piscataway, NJ: Institute of Electrical and Electronics Engineers Computer Society.

Hayman, R. W., & Howard, C. A. (1972). Maintenance station location through operations research at the Wyoming State Highway Department. *Highway Research Record, 391*, 17–30.

Hertz, A., Laporte, G., & Mittaz, M. (2000). A tabu search heuristic for the capacitated arc routing problem. *Operations Research, 48*(1), 129–135. doi:10.1287/opre.48.1.129.12455

Ibaraki, T., Imahori, S., Kudo, M., Masuda, T., Uno, T., & Yagiura, M. (2005). Effective local search algorithms for routing and scheduling problems with general time-window constraints. *Transportation Science, 39*(2), 206–232. doi:10.1287/trsc.1030.0085

Ichoua, S., Gendreau, M., & Potvin, J. Y. (2000). Diversion issues in real-time vehicle dispatching. *Transportation Science, 34*(4), 426–438. doi:10.1287/trsc.34.4.426.12325

Labadi, N., Prins, C., & Reghioui, M. (2008). GRASP with path relinking for the capacitated arc routing problem with time windows. In A. Fink & F. Rothlauf (Eds.), *Studies in Computational Intelligence: Vol. 144. Advances in Computational Intelligence* (pp.111-135). Berlin, Germany: Springer-Verlag.

Lacomme, P., Prins, C., & Ramdane-Cherif, W. (2004). Competitive memetic algorithms for arc routing problems. *Annals of Operations Research, 131*(1-4), 159–185. doi:10.1023/B:ANOR.0000039517.35989.6d

Li, L., & Eglese, R. W. (1996). An interactive algorithm for vehicle routeing for winter gritting. *The Journal of the Operational Research Society, 47*(2), 217–228.

Liebling, T. M. (1973). Routing problems for street cleaning and snow removal. In Deininger, R. (Ed.), *Models for environmental pollution control* (pp. 363–374). Ann Arbor: The University of Michigan.

Lotan, T., Cattrysse, D., Oudheusden, V., & Leuven, K. U. (1996). Winter gritting in the province of Antwerp: a combined location and routing problem. *Belgian Journal of Operations Research. Statistics and Computer Science, 36*(3), 141–157.

Nagata, Y. (2004). The EAX algorithms considering diversity loss. In *Proceedings of the 8th International Conference on Parallel Problem Solving from Nature – PPSN VII* (pp. 332-341).

Nagata, Y., & Kobayashi, S. (1997). Edge assembly crossover: a high-power genetic algorithm for the traveling salesman problem. In *Proceedings of the 7th International Conference on Genetic Algorithms* (pp. 450-457).

Nixon, W. (2009, February). *National advances in winter maintenance.* Paper presented at the 8th Annual Road Salt Symposium, Minneapolis, MN.

Noble, J. S., Jang, W., Klein, C. M., & Nemmers, C. (2006). An integrated systems approach to the development of winter maintenance/management systems. Final Report MTC Project 2005-03, Midwest Transportation Consortium, Iowa State University.

Omer, M. (2007). *Efficient routing of snow removal vehicles*. Master dissertation, College of Engineering and Mineral Resources, West Virginia University.

Pearn, W. L. (1984). *The capacitated Chinese postman problem*. Doctoral dissertation, University of Maryland, College Park, MD.

Perrier, N., Langevin, A., & Campbell, J. F. (2006a). A survey of models and algorithms for winter road maintenance Part I: system design for spreading and plowing. *Computers & Operations Research, 33*(1), 209–238. doi:10.1016/j.cor.2004.07.006

Perrier, N., Langevin, A., & Campbell, J. F. (2006b). A survey of models and algorithms for winter road maintenance Part II: system design for snow disposal. *Computers & Operations Research, 33*(1), 239–262. doi:10.1016/j.cor.2004.07.007

Perrier, N., Langevin, A., & Campbell, J. F. (2007a). A survey of models and algorithms for winter road maintenance Part III: vehicle routing and depot location for spreading. *Computers & Operations Research, 34*(1), 211–257. doi:10.1016/j.cor.2005.05.007

Perrier, N., Langevin, A., & Campbell, J. F. (2007b). A survey of models and algorithms for winter road maintenance Part IV: vehicle routing and fleet sizing for plowing and snow disposal. *Computers & Operations Research, 34*(1), 258–294. doi:10.1016/j.cor.2005.05.008

Pisano, P., Goodwin, L., & Stern, A. (2002). Surface transportation safety and operations: The impacts of weather within the context of climate change. In *The potential impacts of climate change on transportation. Federal Research Partnership Workshop, October 1-2, 2002, Summary and Discussion Papers* (pp. 165-184). U.S. Department of Transportation.

Pisano, P. A., Hoffman, W. H., & Stern, A. D. (2009). Integrating maintenance management systems with maintenance decision support systems, Maintenance management 2009. *Transportation Research Circular. E (Norwalk, Conn.), C135,* 245–254.

Pletan, R. A. (2009). *Best practices in winter maintenance*, Summary Report. NCHRP 20-68A, US Domestic Scan Program, Scan 07-03. Retrieved August 16, 2010, from http://sicop.net/?siteid=88&pageid=2173

Prins, C., Belenguer, J. M., Benavent, E., & Lacomme, P. (2006). Lower and upper bounds for the mixed capacitated arc routing problem. *Computers & Operations Research, 33*(12), 3363–3383. doi:10.1016/j.cor.2005.02.009

Psaraftis, H. N. (1995). Dynamic vehicle routing: status and prospects. *Annals of Operations Research, 61*(1), 143–164. doi:10.1007/BF02098286

Qiao, H. (2002). *Capacitated arc routing problem: formulations, algorithms and application.* Doctoral dissertation, University of Maryland, College Park.

Reinert, K. A., Miller, T. R., & Dickerson, H. G. (1985). A location-assignment model for urban snow and ice control operations. *Urban Analysis, 8,* 175–191.

Sahoo, S., Kim, S., Kim, B. I., Kraas, B., & Popov, A. (2005). Routing optimization for waste management. *Interfaces, 35*(1), 24–36. doi:10.1287/inte.1040.0109

Shi, X., Strong, C., Larson, R. E., Kack, D. W., Cuelho, E. V., El Ferradi, N., et al. (2006). *Vehicle-based technologies for winter maintenance: The state of the practice*. Final Report Project No. 20-7(200). Western Transportation Institute, College of Engineering, Montana State University, Bozeman, MT.

Solomon, M. M. (1987). Algorithms for the vehicle routing and scheduling problem with time window constraints. *Operations Research, 35*(2), 254–265. doi:10.1287/opre.35.2.254

Soyster, A. L. (1974). Examination of alternative models for routing winter maintenance trucks. In *Cost-effectiveness studies of antiskid and deicing programs in Pennsylvania*. (pp. 11-24). Report No 7408, Pennsylvania Transportation Institute.

Tagmouti, M., Gendreau, M., & Potvin, J. Y. (2007). Arc routing problems with time-dependent service costs. *European Journal of Operational Research, 181*(1), 30–39. doi:10.1016/j.ejor.2006.06.028

Tagmouti, M., Gendreau, M., & Potvin, J. Y. (2010). A variable neighborhood descent heuristic for arc routing problems with time-dependent service costs. *Computers & Industrial Engineering, 59*(4), 954–963. doi:10.1016/j.cie.2010.09.006

Tagmouti, M., Gendreau, M., & Potvin, J. Y. (2011). A dynamic capacitated arc routing problem with time-dependent service costs. *Transportation Research Part C, Emerging Technologies, 19*(1), 20–28. doi:10.1016/j.trc.2010.02.003

Toobaie, S., & Haghani, A. (2004). Minimal arc partitioning problem. *Transportation Research Record, 1882*, 167–175. doi:10.3141/1882-20

Transportation Research Board. (2005). *Winter highway operations, A synthesis of highway practice. NCHRP Synthesis, 344*. Washington, DC: Transportation Research Board.

Transportation Research Board. (2008). *Surface transportation weather and snow and ice control technology. Transportation Research Circular, E-C126*. Washington, DC: Transportation Research Board.

Ungerer, R. P. (1989). *Decision models for winter highway maintenance. Report No FHWA/NY/SR-89/95*. New York State Department of Transportation.

(2004). Winter operations and salt, sand and chemical management. In *Compendium of Environmental Stewardship Practices in Highway Construction and Maintenance. NCHRP 25-25(04), Transportation Research Board*. Washington, DC: Venner Consulting and Parsons Brinckerhoff.

Xin, Z., & Eglese, R. W. (1989). *The road gritting problem and its heuristic solution*. Working paper, Lancaster University, Lancaster.

Ye, Z., Shi, X., & Strong, C. K. (2009a). Cost-benefit analysis of the pooled-fund maintenance decision support system - Case studies. Maintenance Management 2009. *Transportation Research Circular. E (Norwalk, Conn.), C135*, 229–243.

Ye, Z., Shi, X., & Strong, C. K. (2009b). Use and cost–benefit of weather information in winter maintenance. Maintenance Management 2009. *Transportation Research Circular. E (Norwalk, Conn.), C135*, 255–266.

Zhu, Z., Li, X., Xia, M., Deng, X., & Liu, L. (2009). A hybrid genetic algorithm for the arc routing problem with intermediate facilities under capacity and length restrictions. *Journal of Computer Information Systems, 5*(4), 1297–1304.

ADDITIONAL READING

Anderson, E., Metzger, H., & Burt, W. (2000). *Snow and ice removal monitoring and management system (SIRMMS). Final Report for ITS-IDEA Project 56.* Washington, DC: Transportation Research Board.

Assad, A. A., & Golden, B. L. (1995). Arc routing methods and applications. In Ball, M. O., Magnanti, T. L., Monma, C. L., & Nemhauser, G. L. (Eds.), *Network routing. Handbooks in Operations Research and Management Science* (pp. 375–483). Amsterdam: North-Holland.

Belenguer, J. M., Benavent, E., Labadi, N., Prins, C., & Reghioui, M. (2010). Split-delivery capacitated arc-routing problem: Lower bound and metaheuristic. *Transportation Science, 44*(2), 206–220. doi:10.1287/trsc.1090.0305

Blackburn, R. R., Bauer, K. M., Amsler, D. E., Boselly, S. E., & McElroy, A. D. (2004). *Snow and ice control: guidelines for materials and methods.* NCHRP Report 526, Washington, DC.

Blesik, K. H. (1994). Optimization in winter maintenance. In *Ninth PIARC International Winter Road Congress* (pp. 440-446). Vienna, Austria: Bundesministerium fur Wirtschaftliche Angelegenheiten.

Corberán, A., & Prins, C. (2010). Recent results on arc routing problems: an annotated bibliography. *Networks, 56*(1), 50–69.

Dror, M. (Ed.). (2000). *Arc routing: theory, solutions and applications.* Boston, MA: Kluwer.

Durth, W., & Hanke, H. (1983). Optimization of winter road service. *Straße und Autobahn, 34*(2), 63–71.

Eglese, R. W., & Li, L. Y. O. (1992). Efficient routeing for winter gritting. *The Journal of the Operational Research Society, 43*(11), 1031–1034.

Eiselt, H. A., Gendreau, M., & Laporte, G. (1995). Arc routing problems, part I: the Chinese postman problem. *Operations Research, 43*(2), 231–242. doi:10.1287/opre.43.2.231

Eiselt, H. A., Gendreau, M., & Laporte, G. (1995). Arc routing problems, part II: the rural postman problem. *Operations Research, 43*(3), 399–414. doi:10.1287/opre.43.3.399

Gini, M., & Zhao, Y. (1997). *Automated route planning and optimizing software.* St. Paul, Minnesota: Final Report, Minnesota Department of Transportation.

Gupta, J. D. (1998). *Development of a model to assess costs of opening a new or closing an existing outpost or county garage. Report No FHWA/OH-99/003.* Ohio: University of Toledo.

Hertz, A., Laporte, G., & Nanchen, P. (1999). Improvement procedures for the undirected rural postman problem. *INFORMS Journal on Computing, 11*(1), 53–62. doi:10.1287/ijoc.11.1.53

Jaquet, J. (1994). Winter maintenance by Vinterman. In *Ninth PIARC International Winter Road Congress* (pp. 8-15). Vienna, Austria: Bundesministerium fur Wirtschaftliche Angelegenheiten.

Kandula, L. N. P. (1996). *Network partitioning for edge-oriented route design.* Doctoral dissertation, Purdue University, West Lafayette, IN.

Ketcham, S. D., Minsk, R., Blackburn, R., & Fleege, E. (1995). *Manual of practice for an effective anti-icing program. Report No FHWA-RD-95-202.* US: Federal Highway Administration.

Korhonen, P., Teppo, M., Rahja, J., & Lappalainen, H. (1992). Determining maintenance truck station network and snow plow routes in Finland. In *International Symposium on Snow Removal and Ice Control Technology.* Washington, DC: National Research Council.

Kuemmel, D. E. (1994). *Managing roadway snow and ice control operations*. NCHRP Synthesis of Highway Practice No 207, Washington, DC.

Ljungberg, M. (2000). Expert system for winter road maintenance. In *Ninth AASHTO/TRB Maintenance Management Conference* (pp. 167-175). Washington, DC: American Association of State Highway and Transportation Officials.

Malmberg, Å., & Axelson, L. (1991). *Expertsystm: En Förstudie och Prototyp*. Högskolan, Östersund.

McDonald, A. (1998). Managing the elements. *Traffic Technology International*, Annual review, 152-154.

Ministry of Transportation, St. Catharines, Ontario, Canada,.

Ministry of Transportation of Ontario. (1999). *Maintenance manual*. Ontario: Maintenance Office.

Minsk, L. D. (1998). *Snow and ice control manual for transportation facilities*. New York: McGraw-Hill.

Perchanok, M., Comfort, G., & Wahlgren, R. (2000). *Decision support system for winter maintenance: feasibility demonstration*. Retrieved August 18, 2010, from http://www.aurora program. org/projectdetail.cfm?projectID=6.

Prins, C., Labadi, N., & Reghioui, M. (2009). Tour splitting algorithms for vehicle routing problems. *International Journal of Production Research*, *47*(2), 507–535. doi:10.1080/00207540802426599

Qiao, H. (1998). *Capacitated rural directed arc routing problem: algorithm and applications*. Master dissertation, University of Maryland, College Park.

Rahja, J., & Korhonen, P. (1994). Total optimizing of the storage and transportation process for salt and sand. In *Ninth PIARC International Winter Road Congress* (pp. 413-420). Vienna, Austria: Bundesministerium fur Wirtschaftliche Angelegenheiten.

Turchi, J. R. (2002). *A taxonomy of winter maintenance decision support systems. Master project*. University of Minnesota Duluth.

Waddell, B. (1994). Snow and ice control excellence with routing software. *Public Works*, *125*(September), 72–74.

KEY TERMS AND DEFINITIONS

Arc Routing: Arc routing problems determine a set of tours that covers a predefined subset of edges or arcs of a transportation network at minimum cost, while satisfying some side constraints. Arc routing problems arise in contexts where road segments require treatments. Practical examples include the routing of street sweepers, snow plowing, salt spreading, postal delivery, meter reading, school bus routing, garbage collection and road maintenance.

Capacitated Arc Routing Problem: The capacitated arc routing problem consists of designing a set of routes performed by vehicles of restricted capacity such that a set customers represented by the edges or arcs of a network are serviced and the total cost is minimized.

Chinese Postman Problem: The Chinese postman problem consists of determining a minimum cost tour that traverses every edge or arc of a network at least once.

Snow Disposal: Physical removal of snow and ice to designated disposal sites following plowing operations. This is usually accomplished by loading the snow in-to trucks and hauling it to disposal sites that may be vacant land, waterways, or openings into a sewer system.

Snow Plowing: Mechanical removal of snow and ice from pavement, generally using a truck or other maintenance vehicle equipped with a metal blade.

Snow Removal: Clearing of a roadway of snow and ice by chemical (e.g., spreading salt to melt snow and ice), mechanical (e.g., plowing), or thermal (e.g., roadway warming) means.

Spreading Operations: Dispersal of chemical or abrasive materials onto a roadway (or sidewalk) usually by means of spreader equipment on trucks for winter maintenance operations. The materials may be in dry form, liquids or brines. Chemicals, commonly salt (sodium chloride) or calcium magnesium acetate, are used to lower freezing-points and change the chemical properties of snow and ice, while abrasives, such as sand, crushed stone, or cinders, are used to improve traction on roadways.

Winter Road Maintenance: Operations conducted to create safe roadways (and sometimes sidewalks) for winter travel. The primary operations include: spreading of chemicals and abrasives to melt snow and ice or to prevent snow and ice from bonding to the pavement, snow plowing to mechanically remove snow and ice from roadways, and snow disposal to load snow into trucks and haul it to disposal sites.

Chapter 3
Routing Solutions for the Service Industry

Burcin Bozkaya
Sabanci University, Turkey

Buyang Cao
Tongji University, China

Kaan Aktolug
Aktolug Consultancy Ltd., Turkey

ABSTRACT

First introduced by Dantzig and Ramser over 50 years ago, vehicle routing problems (VRP) have drawn the attention of both academic researchers and practitioners due to its difficult-to-solve nature and hence its attractiveness in theoretical research as well as wide applicability in real-world settings. Today VRP is probably one of the most widely encountered types of problems for routing and distribution in the service industry. Examples include furniture delivery to a customer's address, scheduling of bus service pick-up/drop-off for students or company personnel, or service technician routing. The goal of this chapter is to provide a background, mathematical model and various solution approaches on a more commonly encountered variant of the problem, namely the VRP with Time Windows (VRPTW). The authors also present three case studies from their experience in the service industry that are real applications of VRPTW. For each study, they describe the overall approach and methodology, and the positive contributions to the respective company which has implemented enterprise-scale GIS-based systems around the distribution problem of interest.

INTRODUCTION

Vehicle routing problems (VRP) are difficult-to-solve combinatorial optimization problems. At the same time, a VRP addresses an important fact that the distribution costs of many firms in the service industry may account for a major portion of the total logistics costs of the firm. Ever since the problem was introduced by Dantzig and Ramser (1959) over 50 years ago, it has drawn the attention of academic researchers and practitioners due to its attractiveness in theoretical research as well as the potential to apply it in real-world settings.

DOI: 10.4018/978-1-61350-086-6.ch003

The goal of the VRP is to determine how to deploy a fleet of vehicles to distribute products or provide services to customers in the most economic way. The cost of such an operation can be a function of different criteria such as time, distance, or service quality. The VRP is a generalization of the well-known traveling salesman problem (TSP), but is more difficult to solve than the same. The VRP is also one of the most widely encountered types of problems in practice; various problems can be modeled as one form of VRP though some problems might not involve transportation of physical goods at all.

The VRP can be extended to a vehicle routing problem with time windows (VRPTW) as time window commitments may be required by customers. Given a fleet of homogeneous vehicles each with a certain capacity, a common depot location where these vehicles start and end their daily operation, and a set of customers with demands for certain products and imposed delivery time windows, the VRPTW attempts to find the most economic way to deliver products to these customers within their required time windows. Each customer is serviced by one and only one vehicle, and each vehicle may have its own working hours defined by a start time and an end time. The total amount of the product loaded on a vehicle cannot exceed the vehicle's capacity. Finally, at each customer location, the assigned vehicle spends a predefined amount of time to complete the delivery or service.

The VRP has many variants; we, however, focus on VRPTW in this chapter because we find that this version of VRP represents a majority of routing problems found in practice. VRPTW-type problems have many different and interesting versions and they are unarguably one of the most widely studied types of routing problems in the academic literature. Many different models along with exact and heuristic solution techniques have been proposed by scholars, leading to a rich literature on VRPTW.

In public and private service industry, where efficient product pickup/delivery or service person dispatching is sought in order to provide the best service at the lowest possible cost, it is not surprising that the VRPTW is the most suitable model to employ. Note that some industrial applications of VRPTW are indeed another specific version of VRP, which is known as VRP with simultaneous pickup and delivery (VRPPD). In this version, vehicles can have a mixture of pickup and delivery visits to customer sites, such as the case for picking up or delivering cash to ATMs and bank branches. This problem, however, is structurally a different type of problem requiring somewhat different problem solving techniques and hence is considered outside the scope of this chapter.

The service industry nowadays is faced with increased challenges such as offering better services while keeping the overall costs at bay. Higher gasoline and personnel costs put more pressure on providing services efficiently. This economic issues have motivated researchers and practitioners to actively seek the use of state-of-the-art optimization and information technologies. As is the trend in the service industry, it is typically necessary to solve real problems with thousands of customers instead of hundreds, using hundreds of vehicles instead of tens. Furthermore, companies request that VRPTW solutions be more realistic and feasible rather than optimal. In order to provide certain real-time services (e.g. processing a service order over the web), it is required that the solution for a VRPTW be obtained in a matter of seconds, and be as realistic and implementable as it can be. To this end, modern information technologies such as GIS (Geographic Information Systems), GPS (Global Positioning Systems), and/or RFID (radio frequency identification) have been incorporated to solve real-world VRPTW problems.

This chapter has a practice-oriented focus. Instead of an extensive coverage on the theory behind various VRPTW models and their associated solvers, which has been done in numerous papers, we have chosen to focus on existing

VRPTW solution reviews and real applications of VRPTW based upon our practical experiences.

We state the objectives of this chapter as two-fold: first, to provide a review of the mainstream models and solution techniques along with a comprehensive set of examples from the service industry in such contexts as:

- products distribution routing,
- maintenance operations routing,
- e-delivery operations routing with and without dynamic service requests,
- student and personnel bus scheduling,
- service personnel dispatching and routing.

The second goal of this chapter is to present the reader with interesting real applications of the VRPTW: one from service personnel dispatching and scheduling, one from the energy sector, and the third one from the food services sector. These applications are presented as case studies in the chapter. For each case study, we describe the special solver development considerations in accordance with the particular business needs. In order to achieve results that are acceptable to practitioners, certain real-world features also need to be incorporated in a VRPTW solution procedure. In all three cases, we consider such features as the speed limits on roads, different road types, different kinds of restrictions (one-ways, turns, etc.), and geographic obstacles such as rivers, mountains, and coastal lines. We further discuss how to combine GIS and optimization techniques to solve large-scale VRPTW problem instances with thousands of nodes (customers) in the service industry. This, we believe, provides the reader with a more realistic and operationally acceptable view of the available solution alternatives. In all three case studies, we also present the economic benefits of applying GIS integrated with optimization, to demonstrate excellent ROI (return on investment) realizations for such deployed systems.

The rest of this chapter is organized as follows. In the next section, we provide a background on VRPTW and present a literature review. Next, we present the basic VRPTW model in mathematical terms and the mainstream solution approaches. The next section contains three case studies in which the authors of this chapter were directly involved. The chapter ends with concluding remarks and ideas for future studies.

BACKGROUND

There are many documented applications of VRPTW in the service industry. For instance, Weigel and Cao (1999) describe a VRPTW solution approach to address the problem of delivering products including furniture, appliances, and related services to customer homes. Kim et al. (2006) present a methodology to solve the VRPTW problem found in a waste collection operation. Spada et al. (2005) discuss the problem of scheduling bus service pick-up/drop-off for students or company personnel. In order to maintain the best condition of elevators in use, service personnel must check elevators and conduct necessary repairs on them periodically. Therefore, an elevator company has the challenge to plan efficient service routes over a planning period. Blakeley et al. (2003) present a system that is able to generate periodical routes for service technicians.

In addition to a common set of rules found in the studies mentioned above, real VRPTW instances in the service industry usually contain other business rules or constraints such as:

- Multiple objectives: it is quite often the case that a VRPTW objective function may consider more than one factor. For instance, one goal might be to minimize the number of vehicles used, while another might be to minimize the total travel time or total travel distance measured by the fleet of vehicles. At times, a firm may seek to build routes that minimize the total time window violation (in case time window violations are allowed) in addition to those mentioned above.

- Non-homogeneous vehicles: vehicles in a fleet can have different characteristics in terms of capacities, cost parameters, maintenance fees, skill(s) required to operate each vehicle, road traversal restrictions due to size, weight or height of vehicle, etc.
- Customer-vehicle/personnel compatibility: also known as the specialty-matching requirement, a vehicle may be restricted on the type of customers it can feasibly serve. This situation is quite common in the service industry. For instance, a service person may have the skill to fix a computer but not a refrigerator, in which case this person cannot be dispatched to a customer requiring a refrigerator repair service.
- Multiple depots: there may be more than one depot in a service territory where vehicles start and end their day. In the service industry, a depot can be a service office. Service personnel can report to one office in the morning but sign off his working day at another one. In some VRPTW cases, a vehicle may start the day at a customer location but end at the depot.
- Return and reload: in urban delivery services, a vehicle may have to run more than one trip in a day within its working hours, due to the limitation on fleet size. For each trip, a vehicle is loaded up to capacity to deliver products to customers on that trip. More trips may be required, for which the vehicle returns to the depot and re-loads products for the next trip as long as there are available working hours left.
- Special time window considerations: although the basic VRPTW model includes time windows as constraints, it treats the time window concept as black-and-white. This means if the time window of a customer cannot be met, this customer is not served in the final solution. In practice,

customers may accept some degree of time window violation; a concept which is captured in a "soft" time window constraint. As a result, many application systems let their users enter a penalty for time window violations (Blakeley et al., 2003; Muller, 2010, Weigel and Cao, 1999). A user is able to adjust the penalty for the time window violation upon his/her business needs.

- Multiple time windows: service companies might have to deal with multiple time windows such as the case for restaurants, where a delivery can only be accepted between 9 AM and 11 AM and between 2 PM and 4 PM (excluding the busy lunch hour). If these time windows are also soft constraints, further complexity is added to the VRPTW as a new type of decision is now under consideration: violating a time window versus waiting at the customer doorstep.
- Customer visiting precedence: a partial ordering may be imposed on the customer service or delivery sequence. A common example is for home delivery service, when a vehicle has to go to a particular store to pick up a merchandise before delivering it to the customer who purchased it. In a backhaul-type problem, all pickup stops must be visited before the delivery stops.
- Service priority: at times, a fleet of vehicles may be unable to meet all customer required services due to capacity or time limits of the vehicles. In such cases, companies often require that services for "high-priority" customers be completed first.
- Periodic visit requirement: periodic VRPTW problems arise in the distribution of products such as soft drinks, snacks, etc. Certain equipments such as elevators request periodic maintenance services as well. In such cases, a service-providing company is interested in building a series of day-routes over a planning period (such

as a week or month) so that each customer receives the required service at a desirable frequency.

- Customer preference: a customer might require a specific service person or type of vehicle to service his/her request.
- Curb approach requirement: a customer might ask the driver to drop off or pick up products on the pre-defined side of his/her street only, or on either side of a street segment.
- Service person or vehicle service area preference: quite often companies want to generate service routes that are relatively stable, where each route is committed to a certain part of the service region. In this case, the service efficiency may be increased as each service person gets more knowledgeable about his/her service area and customers. The company may also designate a "seed point" for each vehicle in order to confine the route to the area around the seed point.
- Grouping of visit points: service companies may have a requirement that no more than one vehicle be dispatched to multiple customer orders located in the same facility or nearby facilities. This typically results in the grouping of the corresponding locations and routing them as if they were a single visit point.

To solve VRPTW more efficiently and to create more realistic solutions, it is necessary to collect and use accurate data. Thanks to the progress in information technologies, we are now able to access all kinds of data from corporate databases and/or enterprise application systems such as ERP, CRM, TMS, etc. The data required for a routing application may include vehicle properties such as the number of available vehicles and their characteristics (e.g. capacities, costs, specialties, working hours). Customer related data typically include quantities to be delivered or pickup, spe-

cialty or skill requirements, time windows, and service priorities, if any. A VRPTW problem solution cannot be obtained without geographic data on travel times and costs between any possible pair of stops. Due to the deployment of GIS applications in many companies, the data on travel times and costs are readily used. Furthermore, with the development of intelligent transportation systems, other useful data such as real time traffic information can be obtained and utilized to solve a VRPTW. The deployment of such systems in route planning activities helps greatly in offering more realistic and implementable solutions for the VRPTW.

Another issue in solving VRPTW efficiently is related to the concept known as territory planning or districting. When a VRPTW instance involves an extensive number of customer visit locations in a large geography, one had better implement a "divide-and-conquer" approach. This means clustering visit locations into smaller subsets using a territory optimization algorithm, and solving the VRPTW on each subset. There is extensive literature on territory optimization, however this topic is also outside the scope of this chapter, and hence the reader is referred to the recent studies by Kalcsics et al. (2005) and Rios-Mercado and Fernandez (2009) for further details.

As mentioned above, VRPTW is a difficult problem and large instances of VRPTW cannot be solved in reasonable time unless one uses a heuristic approach. In what follows, we discuss some general guidelines in solving a classical VRPTW based on heuristic and metaheuristic approaches.

Review of Solution Techniques

Since first introduction of the problem, the research on VRP or VRPTW has been closely tied to practice. The paper by Dantzig and Ramser (1959) describes a practical problem of delivering gasoline to gas stations and presents the first mathematical formulation of the vehicle routing problem. Motivated by another practical problem, the delivery of consumer nondurable products, Clarke and Wright (1964) thereafter published a paper outlining a greedy heuristic that improved the Dantzig-Ramser solver; their algorithm based on a "savings" criterion is still being the basis for numerous solution methods due to its efficiency and ease of implementation. In another paper, Kallenhauge (2008) presents a review of the mathematical formulations and exact algorithms developed for the VRPTW in the past several decades. An even more recent study is by Azi et al. (2010) who also provide an exact algorithmic approach. On the 50th anniversary of VRP, Laporte (2009) published a paper providing a brief account of the historical development of VRP. His paper describes the basic model of a VRP, and presents a survey on exact algorithms, classical heuristics and metaheuristics that have been widely applied and that are still attracting significant attention.

It is well known that a VRP is an NP-hard problem (Lenstra and Kan, 1981); that is, large instances of the problem, say those with thousands of nodes and one hundred vehicles or more, generally cannot be solved to optimality in reasonable computational times. For this reason and because of the problem's relevance in real-world applications, the VRPTW has gained a lot of attention from researchers who seek practical solutions to the problem. More than two decades ago, Bodin et al. (1983) published a survey paper on heuristic and exact algorithms for the VRPTW. Braysy and Gendreau (2005) gave a comprehensive survey on algorithms for solving the VRPTW. The first part of their paper presents route construction and local search algorithms. Several route construction methods such as the Clarke and Wright (1964) savings heuristic and the Solomon (1987) insertion heuristic, and their performances are reviewed in this paper.

Although some scholars attempted to develop exact algorithms most of which are branch-and-bound based (e.g., Ropke and Cordeau, 2009), heuristics are usually the best choice for solving

real VRPTW instances. In order to obtain better solutions for the VRPTW, one needs to figure out effective steps to improve the initial solutions yielded by a route construction procedure. The classical local search is a strategy employed by most scholars for obtaining reasonable solutions to VRPTW in short computational times. A classical local search method is greedy heuristic that iteratively improves an initial solution to the problem by exploring neighborhood solutions. The neighborhood of a solution can be created by obtaining new solutions after changing one or more of its attributes. For instance, a VRPTW neighborhood can be generated by changing some arcs linking stop pairs. During local search, a member solution of the neighborhood is compared against the incumbent best solution. If it is better than the current best solution, the neighborhood solution is accepted as the incumbent solution and the search continues with new neighborhoods. The search stops when no neighborhood solution can be found to be better than the incumbent solution.

The local search heuristic has three main advantages: ease of implementation, being able to deal with various business constraints that may be hard to model mathematically, and being capable of generating a solution in short computational time. However, it has a major weakness in that the search process can be trapped at a local optimum. This can be overcome through the use of metaheuristics in solving the VRPTW, which results in more satisfactory solution outcomes. In the second part of their paper, Braysy and Gendreau (2005) provide a survey on metaheuristics for the VRPTW. Unlike classical heuristics, metaheuristics allow deteriorating and/or infeasible solutions in order to explore more of the solution space. Metaheuristics act as general guidelines for search procedures that explore the solution space seeking better solutions. Many algorithms for the VRPTW are developed based upon three well known metaheuristics—Tabu Search (Glover, 1986), Genetic Algorithm (Holland, 1975), and Simulated Annealing (Kirkpatrick et al., 1983).

Recently, algorithms using other metaheuristics such as ant colony optimization, particle swarm optimization, hybrid-search, and scatter search also offer high quality solutions to the VRPTW (see Ahmmed et al., 2008; Yu et al, 2009; Bent and van Hentenryck, 2004; Zheng and Zhang, 2009; Russell and Chiang, 2006). The current technology in computer hardware allows researchers to utilize higher capacity and computational power to solve larger and more complicated optimization problems in acceptable computational times.

Among the common metaheuristics, Tabu Search (TS) selects the best solution contained in the solution space that does not violate certain restrictions to prevent the solution process from cycling. Usually, for a VRPTW these restrictions prevent for the next t (also called tabu length or tabu tenure) iterations a movement of stops that might cause an "undo" of a previous movement (i.e. re-visiting a previous solution). During this process, TS allows deteriorating and/or infeasible solutions. Intensification and diversification strategies are employed to guide the search process, and oscillation strategy is employed to accept infeasible solutions. TS stops when one of the stopping criteria is met. We describe how the TS technique is applied to solve real instances of the VRPTW in the next section..

Simulated Annealing (SA) is a metaheuristic that attempts to achieve global or near global optimum for an optimization problem. Analogous to the annealing process in metallurgy, each step of a SA algorithm replaces the current solution by a randomly selected solution from its neighborhood, chosen with a probability that depends on the difference between the corresponding function values and on a global parameter T (called the temperature), that is gradually decreased during the process. The principle is that the current solution changes almost randomly when T is large, but goes increasingly "downhill" as T goes to zero. SA allows "uphill" (i.e. non-improving) moves in a minimization problem to prevent the process from getting stuck at local optima.

Genetic Algorithm (GA) is a metaheuristic inspired by population genetics, and is a special case of evolutionary algorithms (EA) that use techniques to simulate biological processes such as inheritance, mutation, natural selection and crossover. GA evolves a population of individuals (i.e. solution pool) encoded as chromosomes by iteratively generating new offspring until a stopping criterion is met. The best solution is decoded to represent the solution for the corresponding problem. Based upon a genetic representation of the solution space and a fitness function to evaluate each solution, GA continuously produces new solutions to the pool. A new member of the solution pool is created by mating two parent solutions selected upon probabilities that are proportional to each parent's respective fitness value. The mutation operator is then applied to finalize the two new child solutions for the pool. The child solutions replace their parents according to a replacement rule. All parameters of this process depend on the problem under consideration and are highly customizable.

Based on the published papers and the survey conducted by Braysy and Gendreau, we find that the solutions for the VRPTW obtained through metaheuristics are much better than those yielded by classical heuristics. Furthermore, although metaheuristics may require longer computational times, researchers have invented many implementation strategies such as parallel processing or utilization of multi-core hardware to speed up the solution procedures significantly. Because of that, solving a complicated real-instance VRPTW more effectively has become a reality.

In a recent paper, Mendoza et al. (2009) present an evolutionary-based decision support system for vehicle routing problems. Their application background is the customer-related processes in a public utility such as meter replacement. The purpose of the decision support system is to assist operation managers to plan site visits in a most efficient way. The system integrates the commercial SAP/R3™ and ArcGIS™ software in addition to the custom routing component. To solve the vehicle routing problems, they introduce an evolutionary-based algorithm similar to the genetic algorithm. The system built on this algorithm was tested on real world applications with problem sizes ranging from 323 to 601 nodes.

In another example of a real life service application, Kim et al. (2006) present a paper dealing with a VRPTW in a waste collection operation. The main goal of this VRPTW is to minimize the number of vehicles used and the total travel time of the fleet. The time windows are introduced due to the commercial nature of the problem. When a vehicle is full, it travels to a disposal site to unload and come back to re-join the waste collection operation if permitted. The authors use Solomon (1987) insertion algorithms to generate initial routes and further employ a Simulated Annealing based local search algorithm called CROSS (Taillard et al., 1997) to improve routes. The system employing the algorithms combined with GIS technology was implemented at Waste Management. The estimate savings are reported as $44 million.

While most of the literature deals with the single-depot VRPTW, Zheng and Zhang (2009) present a paper on solving the multi-depot VRPTW, where the number and locations of depots are predetermined and the vehicles have limited capacities. The authors solve the problem in three phases: grouping, assignment and sequencing. In the grouping phase, customers are clustered with each cluster being serviced from a single depot. In assignment and sequencing phases, a standard VRPTW is solved for each depot independently. To obtain better solutions, the authors introduce a hybrid Ant Colony-based metaheuristic. The computational experiments, however, are performed on small instances (up to 100 customers, 10 depots, and 8 vehicles), and no real world implementation is presented.

In their paper, Goel and Gruhn (2010) study the so called general vehicle routing problems that generalize the vehicle routing with pickup and de-livery operations. The business considerations for this kind of problems may include time windows, heterogeneous fleet with different vehicle traveling speeds, different capacities and dimensions, and order/vehicle compatibilities. In this problem setting, it is also decided whether self-operating vehicles are to be deployed or not. The authors propose a heuristic based on two neighborhood search schemes due to computational time limits. The impact of combining these two schemes is focusing on good solutions while exploring a larger solution space to avoid local optima.

Ibaraki et al (2005) discuss a VRPTW where the service start time for each customer is a non-negative, piecewise linear penalty function. They treat time windows and vehicle capacities as soft constraints, and use a weighted objective function that includes total travel distance, start time penalty, and capacity violation. The authors propose a "cyclic-exchange" neighborhood search procedure in addition to the standard 2-opt and Or-opt procedures for VRP problems. Computational results suggest that the proposed algorithm is effective in getting satisfactory results for the VRPTW as well as parallel machine scheduling problems.

Gutierrez et al (2010) present an interesting VRP that may be found in the service industry, particularly in reverse logistics, where vehicles may selectively satisfy pickup requests in addition to meeting delivery requests. Furthermore, there is revenue associated with each pickup. Both pickup and delivery customers have imposed time windows. The goal of this type of problem is to find a solution with minimal net cost (travel cost minus revenue). An exact branch-and-price algorithm is proposed to solve this kind of problem, and it is applied to problems up to 50 customers.

Many vehicle routing problems take into account a single criterion such as travel time. In certain contexts, road segments may have other attributes for consideration such as road class and road restrictions. Very often the transportation activity takes place on a multi-modal transportation network. To deal with these extensions, Garaix et al (2010) propose a dynamic programming based algorithm that is able to solve the VRP on a multigraph. This algorithm can yield alternative paths for the VRP, which makes a compromise between different attributes of road segments.

In service industry, customers may also require periodic services. For instance, restaurants may request periodic delivery of beverages; high-rise buildings need periodic maintenance of their elevators. Unlike the standard VRPTW where single day-routes are built, periodic VRPTW involves building routes for multiple days of a predefined planning period. A service request in a periodic VRPTW generally has multiple visit requirements during this period, such as once a week, twice a week, once a month, twice a month, etc. A solution to the problem assigns service orders to individual vehicles or service persons on multiple days over the planning period with a route built for each vehicle on each day. While the day-routes are built, standard VRP routing constraints apply. It is conceivable that the introduction of time horizon increases the complexity and computational time. Because of this, solution approaches for the periodic VRPTW differ from those for the standard VRPTW. Typically, the periodic route planning calculations are not performed daily, which provides computational time flexibility for solving larger instances of the problem.

Francis et al. (2006) present an algorithm to solve such a periodic vehicle routing problem (PVRP). In their model, a full visit schedule must be determined by the solver. A service request may ask for visits twice a week, for instance on either Mon-Tue, Mon-Wed or Wed-Fri days. The solver must honor one of these options taking into account the cost aspect. Furthermore, a customer may be willing to accept higher visit frequency at a premium service fee. In this case, the algorithm needs to determine the frequency as well as the visit day combination. The goal is to build routes for the entire planning period with the lowest objective value that consists of total travel time and

service benefits while meeting other constraints such as vehicle capacity and visit requirements. The authors propose Lagrangian relaxation and branch-and-bound approaches to solve the corresponding model. They apply their algorithms to solve a number of problem sets (ranging from 12 to 44 libraries) derived from real applications.

Blakeley et al. (2003) present an application where the optimization problem can be modeled as a periodic VRPTW. The business background is related to the Schindler technician operations that involve thousands of employees that visit elevator and escalator installations every day for maintenance, repair and sometimes emergency services. Each visit location has a preferred service frequency and the service routes are built while considering geographic proximity, technician workload, required skill sets, and customer relationship/preference. The authors describe an interactive GIS-based route planning and optimization system named PASS, where they propose a set of heuristics to address the underlying periodic VRPTW problem. The solution procedure is carried out in two phases: assignment and sequencing. The assignment phase assigns service requests to individual technicians considering factors such as workload balance, expected travel time and distance, and expected overtime. The sequencing procedure schedules visits for all service requests over the entire planning period and builds individual day-routes. A tabu search metaheuristic is implemented to guide the local search in order to obtain good quality solutions. The authors report that PASS has been deployed at many Schindler service centers, and the system is able to create, in a matter of minutes, 65 day-routes of 700 service requests with 15 to 20 service technicians. The system brings economic benefits of over $1 million savings annually and an investment payback period of less than a year.

MATHEMATICAL MODEL AND ALGORITHM

The Vehicle Routing Problem with Time Windows is widely studied in the literature and various models have been proposed and used. What we provide below as the mathematical model that forms the basis of our case studies we describe later is known as the 3-index model and appears in many past studies such as Kohl and Madsen (1997). While we have introduced additional features to this model in our case studies (to account for various additional business rules discussed above), we nevertheless provide the basic model and our corresponding solution methodology below.

Mathematical Model

Before we formally present our VRPTW mathematical model, let us introduce first our decision variables and related notation. Let $i, j \in I$ represent indices of customers from a customer index set I and $k \in K$ be indices of vehicles from set K. The customer index set I, with $|I| = n$, is further extended to $I^+ = I \bigcup \{0, n+1\}$ to include the single depot location index that marks the start and end point of each route. Furthermore, let:

x_{ijk} : 1, if vehicle k drives from customer i to customer j, 0 otherwise

s_{ik} : the time vehicle k starts service at customer i

r_k : total route time (in minutes) of vehicle k

o_k : total overtime (in minutes) of vehicle k

where x_{ijk} is defined only for $i, j \in I^+$; s_{ik} is defined for $i \in I^+$; and y_{ik}, z_i, u_i are defined for $i \in I$. The rest of the notation is as follows:

c_k^d : travel cost per unit distance for vehicle k

c_k^r : regular labor cost per minute for vehicle k

c_k^o : overtime labor cost per minute for vehicle k, assuming $c_k^o > c_k^r$

w_i : amount of capacity use by customer i on any vehicle it is assigned to

p_i : duration of service at customer i location

d_{ij} : travel distance between customer i and customer j

t_{ij} : travel time in minutes between customer i and customer j

a_i, b_i : time window limits for customer i

R_k : allowable total route time, including any possible overtime, for vehicle k

O_k : allowable overtime for vehicle k

l_k : regular work time for vehicle k beyond which overtime will accumulate

Q_k : maximum capacity of vehicle k

The objective function of our basic model is the sum of the following cost items: travel cost, route labor cost and route overtime cost. This objective function, however, may be revised to accommodate other specific business rules and logic in service industry applications, which we do in the following sections.

Formally, we state our mathematical model as shown in Table 1.

In this model, constraints (1) indicate that each customer must be assigned to a vehicle, constraints (2) ensure that vehicle capacities are not exceeded, constraints (3)-(5) maintain flow balance at each node of the transportation network, constraints (6) correctly calculate the arrival time of a vehicle at each customer location it visits, constraints (7) and (8) calculate the total route time (including overtime, if any) and total route overtime, respectively, constraints (9) and (10) set the corresponding time limits on route time and route overtime, constraints (11) make sure the hard time window limitations are not violated, and finally constraints (12)-(14) enforce the integrality and non-negativity requirements.

Table 1.

$$\min F = \sum_{k \in K} \sum_{i,j \in I^+} x_{ijk} c_k^d d_{ij} + \sum_{k \in K} [c_k^r r_k + \left(c_k^o - c_k^r\right) o_k]$$

subject to

$$\sum_{k \in K} \sum_{j \in I^+} x_{ijk} = 1 \qquad\qquad \forall i \in I \qquad\qquad (1)$$

$$\sum_{i \in I} w_i \sum_{j \in I^+} x_{ijk} \le Q_k \qquad\qquad \forall k \in K \qquad\qquad (2)$$

$$\sum_{j \in I^+} x_{0jk} = 1 \qquad\qquad \forall k \in K \qquad\qquad (3)$$

$$\sum_{i \in I^+} x_{ihk} = \sum_{j \in I^+} x_{hjk} \qquad\qquad \forall h \in I, \forall k \in K \qquad\qquad (4)$$

$$\sum_{i \in I^+} x_{i,n+1,k} = 1 \qquad\qquad \forall k \in K \qquad\qquad (5)$$

$$s_{ik} + p_i + t_{ij} \le s_{jk} + M(1 - x_{ijk}) \qquad \forall i,j \in I^+, \forall k \in K \qquad (6)$$

$$r_k = s_{n+1,k} + p_{n+1} - s_{0k} \qquad\qquad \forall k \in K \qquad\qquad (7)$$

$$o_k \ge r_k - l_k \qquad\qquad \forall k \in K \qquad\qquad (8)$$

$$r_k \le R_k \qquad\qquad \forall k \in K \qquad\qquad (9)$$

$$o_k \le O_k \qquad\qquad \forall k \in K \qquad\qquad (10)$$

$$a_i \le s_{ik} \le b_i \qquad\qquad \forall i \in I, \forall k \in K \qquad\qquad (11)$$

$$x_{ijk} \in \{0,1\} \qquad\qquad \forall i,j \in I^+, \forall k \in K \qquad\qquad (12)$$

$$s_{ik} \ge 0 \qquad\qquad \forall i \in I^+, \forall k \in K \qquad\qquad (13)$$

$$r_k, o_k \ge 0 \qquad\qquad \forall k \in K \qquad\qquad (14)$$

Note that, the model presented above is a capacitated VRPTW model where time windows are hard, and there are limits on the route time, overtime and capacity. Furthermore, all vehicles start at and return to the same common depot location. We discuss extensions to this model as necessary while we present our case studies.

Algorithm

The VRPTW is known to be NP-Hard (Lenstra and Kan, 1981), which suggests that polynomial-time algorithms for finding solutions to large problem instances with thousands of nodes or customers are only possible through heuristic approaches. This is also our experience with the real-world instances of the VRPTW including the three case studies we present later in this chapter. The solution methodology we present here is essentially a heuristic neighborhood search algorithm tailored according to the business rules dictated by the problem at hand.

To solve the capacitated VRPTW, we take a two-phase approach where in the first phase we "assign" customers to vehicles to come up with a complete feasible initial solution, and in the second phase, we "improve" the routing solution iteratively until no more improvements can be found or another stopping condition is met. We discuss these two phases in detail below:

Assignment

In the assignment phase, our primary goal is to produce a complete initial solution that satisfies all constraints of the VRPTW including vehicle capacities, hard time windows, limits on total route time and total route overtime. While doing so, the assignment procedure attempts to minimize the total operational costs (i.e. travel costs and labor costs) when it assigns stops to routes. We further take the liberty to attach weights to different cost components of the objective function, essentially making it a weighted objective function. Although we do not include this weight concept in our basic model, we use it to provide additional flexibility to the end user for generating alternative routing solutions that favor different preferences on the cost terms. This structure also allows us to account for additional cost terms that will be introduced in various extensions of the problem (e.g. time window violations, waiting or idle time) that are discussed in the case studies. The typical form of the weighted objective function becomes

$$F = \alpha_1 f_1 + \alpha_1 f_1 + \alpha_1 f_1 + \cdots$$

where a user may adjust these weights upon the specific business needs and/or geographic characteristics.

The assignment procedure consists of three parts: (1) building initial routes, (2) inserting stops, and (3) improving assignment. Let us now describe these in more detail.

When an initial route is built, a "dummy" route is in fact created containing only three stops: starting location, seed point, and ending location. These stops provide the basis for assigning all unassigned customers. When an unassigned customer is inserted into a route as a stop, the weighted objective value changes and an incremental insertion cost is calculated as follows:

$$\Delta F_{ikt} = \alpha_1 \Delta f_{1,ikt} + \alpha_2 \Delta f_{2,ikt} + \alpha_3 \Delta f_{3,ikt} + \cdots$$

Where $\Delta f_{n,ikt}$ is the change in the corresponding cost term f_n as a result of the insertion of stop i at position t of route k, and ΔF_{ikt} is the total incremental insertion cost. The algorithm proceeds by evaluating the ΔF_{ikt} value for each unassigned stop on each possible route and position. In some cases to be discussed later, this set of insertion possibilities is reduced in size due to some assignments not being feasible. Nevertheless, at each iteration, the stop with the minimal objective function increase (i.e. insertion cost) is picked for assignment to the corresponding route and position. This procedure is repeated until there are no unassigned stops left or no route can further accept any new unassigned stop.

During the stop insertion phase described above, the algorithm considers the insertion cost with a local (i.e. greedy) perspective without looking much further for global cost minimization.

Figure 1. Improvement swaps and exchanges

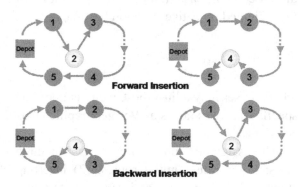

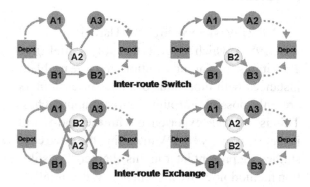

Moreover, the insertion phase may result in routes unbalanced in terms of total route time. To address these issues and improve the assignment result, the algorithm can optionally be asked to execute an improvement procedure. In this improvement step, stops may be transferred from their original routes to different (destination) routes and/or two stops may be exchanged between their respective routes. The main goal of this improvement step is to create more balanced routes while keeping the increase in the weighted objective function at minimum.

We should note here that many extensions of the VRPTW that are not included in the basic model may require the Assignment procedure to handle the insertion of stops differently. For instance, if a customer requires a particular specialty or capability on the part of the vehicle, driver or technician, only eligible routes will be considered by the Assignment procedure for insertion purposes. Similarly, if certain customers have priority of service over the others, these customers may be inserted before the others. Whenever applicable, the Assignment procedure adjusts the insertion cost so that different rules can effectively be addressed. We leave the discussion of such variations to the next section where different operational rules are justified according to the needs of the business.

Improvement

After initial routes are built, that is all unassigned stops get assigned or no route can accept any more unassigned stops, the assignment result can be improved further. This is done via intra-route and inter-route improvement moves. An intra-route move means modifying the position of a single stop within its route to find a better position and hence improve the objective function. An inter-route move means moving a stop to a different route or exchanging two stops between their respective routes, again to find a better solution in terms of total cost. Figure 1 shows an illustration of these two concepts. Please note that even though in Figure 1 a location is represented by a node, it may as well be a group of sequential nodes in a route; that is one or two groups of nodes can be involved in the improvement procedure.

Similar to the improvement steps in the stop insertion procedure, inter-route improvement consists of two major components: stop transfer and stop exchange. While the algorithm seeks for possibilities to implement these, all feasibility rules must be enforced at all times. In other words, such improvement operations may not produce infeasible routes. In our basic model, feasibility means respecting capacity, time windows and route time limits, but additional rules like specialty-matching, preferred vehicle assignment among others may have to be additionally considered in other extensions of the model.

The intra-route and inter-route improvement moves described above are executed in a heuristic fashion, and the execution continues as long as there is room for improvement. Here improvement means that the corresponding weighted objective function value can be reduced. It is known that this technique of local search may occasionally get the algorithm trapped in local optimum solutions. To avoid this, the Improvement procedure also executes a tabu search (TS) logic. Our TS implementation utilizes short-term based memory to declare some candidate moves tabu for a number of iterations, which hopefully causes the algorithm to escape local optima and explore new parts of the solution space. According to our computational experiments, the tabu search add-on can bring us on average an additional 10% improvement on final solution quality compared to those yielded merely by traditional heuristics.

As mentioned above, TS is a *metaheuristic* that guides local search procedures to overcome local optima and reach more satisfactory solutions. Based upon the TS principles, a solution can be accepted even if its objective value is worse than the current one as long as it does not violate the tabu criteria. For the VRPTW discussed here, a solution space consists of routes and stops in each route. The attributes of a solution space that need particular attention are the *route* servicing stops and the *visit sequence* of a stop on a route, and these attributes are defined as *solution space attributes*. Whenever an inter- or intra-route improvement procedure (move) mentioned above is applied to the current solution space, the solution space is changed due to the solution space attribute change caused by the move. A new (neighboring) solution space and its attributes are formed.

It is clear that a cycle of repeating solutions can be avoided if the solution space attributes of each solution at each improvement iteration are different. Keeping track these solution space attributes, however, can be costly and inefficient.

To overcome this difficulty, in our implementation we adapt a more coarse evaluation strategy. At each improvement move, we keep track of the changes in the solution space attributes of a stop involved in the move. A move is called *tabu*, i.e., it might not be accepted for execution, if the solution space attributes of the involved stops yield the same solution space attribute values found in one of last t iterations, where t is called *tabu list size* or *tabu tenure*. Particularly for:

- Inter-route improvement moves: stop returns to the previous assigned route and visit sequence;
- Intra-route improvement moves: stop returns to the previous visit sequence.

Nevertheless, a tabu move can be overridden if one or more certain aspiration criteria are met, which adds more flexibility to the search process; here we accept a tabu move if the value of the objective function is better than the current best one. Furthermore, we incorporate some hard constraints such as route capacities into the objective function with penalty. If the value of this penalty is very high, then this constraint cannot be violated at all. This allows exploring more of the solution space by relaxing some constraints. Oscillation strategy (changing the penalty periodically according to a predefined logic) is employed to accept infeasible solutions. The outcome of applying this strategy is highly satisfactory.

TS stops when a stopping criterion is met: that is, when either the predefined total number of improvement iterations or the number of non-improvement iterations is executed.

Algorithm 1 summarizes the two-phase algorithm described above:

TS implementation may include Intensification and Diversification strategies to guide the search process for exploring the solution space more thoroughly. Intensification strategy records the best n solutions, where n is a solver parameter and can be adjusted by the user. The solution

Algorithm 1.

```
    Step 0. Read input data, initialize data structures and initialize all
routes to dummy.
    Step 1. (Assignment) - Repeat until no more stops can be inserted:
        1.1 Evaluate each possible feasible insertion of a stop into an avail-
able route.
Pick the insertion that has the lowest value of ΔF_{ikt}.
        1.2 Execute the insertion found in Step 1.2
    Step 2. (Sequencing)
        2.1 Initialize tabu lists and tabu tenures.
        2.2 Repeat until total number of iterations are executed:
            2.2.1 Evaluate all feasible intra-route improvement possibilities
            2.2.2 Evaluate all feasible inter-route improvement possibilities
            2.2.3 Select the best improving tabu or non-tabu move. If there
is no such move, select the best non-improving non-tabu move.
            2.2.4 Execute the move found in Step 2.2.3
            2.2.5 Update the tabu lists.
            2.2.6 If new solution is better than the best known solution, re-
cord it as the new best solution.
        2.3 Report the best known solution.
```

procedure will record stop solution space attributes. The intensification procedure will restart the search process from the current best solution and fix the stop solution space attributes (i.e., routes servicing them and visit sequences) that look more promising. A stop solution space attribute is considered promising if this attribute appears in the collected good solutions most of the time.

The second strategy, known as *diversification*, attempts to explore some unexplored part of the solution space. Under this strategy, the algorithm restarts the search process from a solution in which the stop solution space attributes rarely appear based on the records. That is, a route rarely services a certain set of stops and/or rarely contains certain stop visit sequences.

Although it is shown that intensification and diversification strategies in a TS implementation are able to obtain better solutions than those obtained by simple implementations of TS, our experience in various VRPTW cases in the service industry suggests that a TS implementation using only short-term memory is able to yield very high-quality solutions. Therefore, we exclude intensification and diversification strategies from our TS implementation in order to speed up the solution procedure as the computational time is a critical factor for the end user to accept the application systems deployed.

CASE STUDIES

In this section, we present case studies for three real implementations of the VRPTW in the service sector. These include home appliance/furniture delivery and maintenance, gas service maintenance, and finally packaged bread distribution sectors. While the nature of the VRPTW is somewhat different in each case study, the general characteristics of the problems are very similar, and each problem

Table 2. SLS and SPS business

	Sears Logistics Services	Sears Product Services
Vehicles or Personnel	1,000+ consisting of contracted carriers and Sears-owned trucks	12,500 service technicians
Annual Stops	4+ million	15 million
Service Area	Regional delivery center based	Regional service center based
Business Objective	Deliver furniture and appliances	Provide repair, installation, home improvement and homeowner services
System Objectives	Improve customer satisfaction Reduce operational costs Consolidate delivery operations Plan consistent routes	Increase completed service calls on first attempt Improve customer service Provide same day service Reduce operational costs Consolidate dispatch operations
Algorithm Objectives	Automatically build routes that reduce travel time while honoring side constraints.	Automatically build routes that reduce travel time while honoring side constraints.

is solved using a heuristic optimization approach coupled with GIS data processing techniques.

Case Study 1: Sears Home Delivery and Home Services

Sears is the one of largest retailers in the U.S., and its stores offer variety of products from appliances to garden furniture. When a customer buys a merchandise from Sears, he/she can enjoy the friendly home delivery service offered by Sears. Sears also offers additional services for fixing various products such as refrigerators and TVs as well as for improving homes. These two kinds of services are carried by Sears Logistics Services (SLS) and Sears Product Services (SPS). When delivery routes are built in a SLS office, one tries to:

- Provide customers with accurate and most convenient time windows for deliveries;
- Provide truck drivers with consistent routes, and
- Minimize total delivery costs

A dispatcher at a SPS service center attempts to achieve the following while he/she builds home service routes:

- To maximize the completion of the service calls on the first attempt;
- To enhance the customer services, and
- To minimize overall service costs.

Although the problems to be solved here can be modeled as VRPTW, the size of the problems and their practical complexity make them of both theoretical and practical interest. SLS manages a national fleet of more than 1,000 delivery vehicles that includes contracted carriers and Sears-owned vehicles. Sears provides the largest home delivery service of furniture and appliances in the U.S., with over 4 million deliveries a year of 21,000 unique items. SLS home delivery serves 70 percent of the U.S. population. Sears product services (SPS) operates another national fleet of more than 12,500 service vehicles and associated technicians who repair and install appliances, and provide home improvement and homeowner services. SPS call center receives 15 million calls for on-site service annually. Table 2 summarizes the businesses for SLS and SPS:

In order to solve these problems more effectively and provide more realistic solutions to the users, we have developed a system that combines a geographic information system (GIS) with optimization techniques. The system possesses a user friendly graphic interface that allows users to:

- Display all underlying streets and their attributes
- Display all delivery/service areas or territories
- Zoom in to a route extent
- List driving directions for routes
- View all routes and their desired delivery/ service area (seed points)
- Manually adjust a route, for instance, select a route and change the stop sequences or reassign stop(s) from one route to another
- Manually assign a delivery/service area (seed point) to a driver or service technician

While solving the corresponding VRPTW, besides the factors mentioned above, we take into account other business logic or constraints, which may include:

- The skill of service technician matching the one required by the service order
- The start and end locations of a route being different (a service route can start at a job location and end at another job location)
- For some service routes, parts store being included so that proper parts for the service job can be picked up
- For some delivery routes, considering the stop precedence; for instance, a delivery truck may have to go to a store to pick up a product before delivering it to the customer location
- Taking into account customer route preference
- Honoring the maximum number of service/delivery stops based on a contract
- Visiting certain areas only within certain periods of time during the day; for instance, a mountain area may not be visited after 5:00 PM or before 7:00 AM due to limited road conditions

These additional considerations increase the complexity of the problem to be solved. In order to cope with the complexity of the problem and still complete the solution process in a reasonable computational time, we have developed a series of algorithms based upon heuristic/metaheuristic strategies, as described in more detail in the previous section. With the combination of GIS and optimization techniques, where the GIS is employed to provide necessary information for modeling VRPTW properly and implementing the solvers more efficiently, the problems were solved quite effectively in practice.

Our solution procedure can be viewed as a *cluster-first, route-second* approach with three major phases: (1) building an OD matrix, (2) assigning orders to routes, and (3) performing improvement steps. The solving techniques involved in these phases have been previously discussed in detail. Here we outline some special considerations related to the VRPTW found in SLS and SPS.

Building an Origin: Destination Matrix

An Origin-Destination (OD) matrix contains the travel times and distances between each pair of stops in the VRPTW, and is a basis to solve the problem. For providing more realistic solutions in a real application, we need to consider various geographic conditions or barriers while building an OD matrix, such as mountains, water bodies, coastal areas, areas with no road access. GIS is the most suitable system to extract this type of information to assist building an OD matrix. Hereby we employ ESRI ArcGIS to build the network data structure that supports OD matrix building. While the number of stops we deal with for SLS's VRPTTW problem is relatively small (less than a thousand), we build an OD matrix with several thousands of stops for SPS's problem, which may not be completed in a timely fashion. Although it is possible to find a shortest path between any pair of stops quickly, building an OD matrix for thousands of stops, particularly when the underlying geographic area is large and/or the stops are spread out to several states, takes a long time (at times longer than 20 minutes). The main reason is the fact that the road network includes millions of features (arcs and nodes). One must find a better and faster way to construct an OD matrix. Based on the business characteristics of SPS, we incorporate the following factors into the OD matrix building procedure:

- Technician skills: this parameter forces stops to be included in the OD matrix for a technician to match the technician skill set.
- Maximum travel time/distance (between any pair of stops): also known as the cutoff distance, the OD matrix for a technician will not include any travel time/distance entries larger than this value.
- Minimum candidates: the OD matrix for a technician cannot contain fewer stops specified by this value whenever possible.
- Maximum candidates: the number of stops in the OD matrix for a technician cannot be larger than this value.

By incorporating these into the OD matrix building process, we are able to provide sufficient travel times/distances for assignment and route improvement procedures while avoiding some unnecessary OD calculations. If a stop does not have a travel time/distance included in the OD matrix for a route, then this stop will not be put on that route. This strategy adopted for OD matrix creation proves to be very effective, which significantly cuts down the computational time needed to build an OD matrix.

Assigning Orders to Routes

This is the step to assign delivery or service orders to drivers or service technicians. In the previous section, we have described this assignment algorithm in detail. Here we illustrate how we apply the assignment algorithm to the problems encountered in SLS and SPS. Here we use the term *stop* to represent a customer location requesting delivery or service.

During the assignment procedure, some constraints such as technician skills, vehicle capacities (weights and/or volumes), and stop visiting precedence are treated as "hard" rules, i.e., they cannot be violated at any time. Other constraints such as time windows and overtime are treated as "soft" rules, and their violations are penalized. As discussed above, the assignment procedure attempts to minimize such violation penalties plus the operational costs (mainly the travel costs) when assigning stops to routes. Our objective function for the VRPTW is a weighted one containing several cost factors (operational and penalty costs). For a route r, we can compute the travel time (or distance) t_r, the amount of time window violation v_r, and waiting (or idle) time w_r. The value of the weighted objective function for the entire problem is then calculated as:

$$\alpha_1 \Sigma t_r + \alpha_2 \Sigma v_r + \alpha_3 \Sigma w_r$$

where α_1, α_2, and α_3 are adjustable weights for travel time (or distance), total time-window violation and total waiting (or idle) time, respectively. After we build the initial routes, this function provides the basis for assigning all unassigned stops. We apply the stop assignment (insertion) procedure described above.

Clearly if a route does not have the specialty required by a stop, it will not be a candidate for insertion. A stop with the minimal objective function change is selected for assignment to the corresponding route and position, and the procedure is repeated until all stops are assigned or no route can accept any new stop.

Optionally, the inter-route improvement procedure can be executed to improve the solution after the stop insertion process is completed.

When unassigned stops are inserted into various routes, further business logic specific to SPS

Table 3. Economic benefits for SLS and SPS

	SLS		SPS	
	Before	**After**	**Before**	**After**
Geocoding accuracy	55%	**95%**	55%	**95%**
Arrival time window	4 Hour	**2 Hour**	2 Hour	**2 Hour**
On-time performance	78%	**95%**	84%	**95%**
Time spent routing	5 Hours	**20 Minutes**	8 Hours	**1-2 Hours**
Miles per stop	1.6	**1.2**		
Stops per vehicle	16	**20**		
Dispatch facilities	46	**22**	92	**6**
Completed calls	N/A	**N/A**	---	**+3%**
Overtime				**-15%**
Drive time				**-6%**

must be taken into account. A technician may have primary and secondary specialties. The insertion cost of an unassigned stop is therefore adjusted based on the technician's primary or secondary specialty. The adjustment favors a technician in getting stops that require his/her primary specialty. Technicians may be also categorized as full-time, part-time, or flexible-time. The insertion step adjusts the insertion cost so that the routes corresponding to full-time technicians get as many stops as possible (considering the maximum duration of the route and the technician's schedule).

Improvement

The improvement phase consists of intra-route and inter-route improvements embedded in the tabu search metaheuristic procedure. During the improvement process, the feasibility of performing an improvement step is validated. Except those considered in the oscillation strategy, no hard rules can be violated during improvement. These include specialty, stop visit precedence constraint, and pre-assignment of stops to routes.

Economic Benefits

The systems we built for SLS and SPS have been out in use for several years and have yielded im-

pressive economic outcomes. Table 3 summarizes the major achievements obtained for SLS and SPS:

Because of the reduction in travel mileage, SLS is able to deliver more stops per truck and hence increase the utilization of its resources. Both systems eliminate the need for dispatchers to have local knowledge since the underlying GIS provides all necessary geographic data, together with embedded optimization techniques for the VRPTW which helps dispatchers make good decisions in response to regular as well as emergency orders. In the SPS case, the on-time performance was increased from 84% to 95%, and the overtime was reduced by 15%. Due to the arrival time accuracy, customer service level and satisfaction are increased. The total savings achieved through the implementation is more than $15 million annually.

Case Study 2: On-Site Gas Maintenance Services by a Large Energy Distributor Company

Our second case study is from the energy sector where a leading energy services provider company in California, U.S.A. provides natural gas to millions of residential customers. Gas utility companies such as this one face an everyday challenge of bringing and maintaining gas service to the residents of their service area. These services range from routine ones such as connecting or disconnecting gas service, installing or maintaining gas appliances and collecting unpaid accounts, to emergency services such as responding to gas leaks. This company for which we have developed a GIS-based VRPTW solution implementation serves most of central and southern California, with a geographical coverage of over 23,000 square miles. The company is the largest natural gas distribution utility in the U.S., providing gas service to approximately 19 million people through more than five million gas meters. Field technicians complete roughly four million service orders every year. The size and scope of this business clearly suggests that higher operational efficiency may be achieved by using optimization techniques in the context of the VRPTW.

The main problem faced by the company is how to deploy its fleet of hundreds of vehicles and service technicians most efficiently to serve approximately 10,000 daily calls received at its call center. The goal is to build routes on a daily basis to visit each and every one of the customers requesting service, while:

a.   minimizing total operational costs
b.   maximizing customer satisfaction by completing the service within the quoted time-window
c.   respecting all operational rules of the company

The business problem of interest in this study requires, based on pre-defined company rules, assignment of each service request to an eligible technician and scheduling an on-site visit for the actual work. Since requests arrive over time and they are collected in the company database for "next-day routing" purposes, a cut-off time is used to select the set of requests that will be subject to routing optimization. Emergency service requests, such as those due to gas leaks, are excluded from this implementation as they must be attended as soon as they are received and hence clearly cannot be made subject to next-day-routing. The company has a policy of offering a 4-hour time window to any customer for the on-site visit, in an attempt to provide flexibility and convenience as the customers will be expected to stay at home before and during the service encounter. Furthermore, the following additional rules apply:

a.   each vehicle is operated by a single technician
b.   all technicians in a particular district start and end their day at their district office
c.   on-site service time depends on the type of service call but is fixed once the type of service is known
d.   each technician has a "specialty" meaning he/she has the capability of one or more pre-defined types of service operation
e.   a customer may request a specific technician to visit on-site (e.g. a Spanish speaking technician)
f.   it is extremely undesirable to not visit a customer on the promised day
g.   it is possible but undesirable to visit a customer outside the quoted time window.

With these characteristics, the problem we deal with is a variant of the VRPTW. One complicating factor, though, is the size of the problem. Clearly, no VRP optimization algorithm (exact or heuristic) known to date can handle, in reasonable time, 10,000 visit points with hundreds of (service) routes, so one must take actions to reduce the size of the problem instance. We have taken a divide-and-conquer approach, effectively using the district structure the company itself employs in organizing its operations. We describe this in more detail below along with other details on the solution methodology we have adopted. But first, let us describe the modifications that are needed on the basic VRPTW model.

Modifications to the Basic Model

The first three business rules a), b) and c) listed above require no modification in our basic model. This is due to the fact that in our model, vehicles and technicians are used interchangeably and each route starts and ends its day at a single "depot" location (similar to the district office). Furthermore, our basic model assumes a constant service time p_i for each customer i.

Business rule d) requires that each technician/vehicle is associated with zero, one or more specialty and each customer request requires zero or more specialty. We model this by introducing a binary decision variable y_{ik} that indicates the assignment of customer i to vehicle/technician k, and a binary compatibility index q_{ik} as follows:

y_{ik}: 1, if customer i is assigned to vehicle k, 0 otherwise

q_{ik}: 1, if customer i *can* be assigned to vehicle k (i.e. the specialty requirements of customer i do match the capabilities of technician k), 0 otherwise

Then we add the following constraints to our model to handle business rule d):

$$\sum_{j \in I^+} x_{ijk} \leq y_{ik}$$

$$\forall i \in I, \forall k \in K \quad (15)$$

$$y_{ik} \leq q_{ik}$$

$$\forall i \in I, \forall k \in K \quad (16)$$

$$y_{ik} \in \{0,1\}$$

$$\forall i \in I, \forall k \in K \quad (17)$$

Note that as a result of this business rule, there may not exist, generally speaking, a vehicle with the required specialty/capability to serve a customer, so we must relax constraint (1) as follows:

$$\sum_{k \in K} \sum_{j \in I^+} x_{ijk} \leq 1$$

$$\forall i \in I \quad (1B)$$

which allows leaving some customers unassigned. This might be necessary to avoid an infeasible model.

To handle business rule e), it is sufficient to add a new constraint to the model:

$$y_{i^* k^*} = 1 \quad (18)$$

for each customer i^* requiring a particular vehicle k^*

The two remaining business rules are slightly more complicated to model. Rule f) suggests that some customers may be left unassigned even though this is very undesirable. Although the original goal of the model is to assign all customers to a route, this may not be possible due to several reasons: a) total capacity of all vehicles may not be sufficient, b) total route time and overtime available may not be sufficient to serve all customers, and c) there may not be enough specialty/capability within the vehicle/technician set to serve all customers. Therefore, we introduce a penalty-based approach to handle the case of unassigned customers. Let

c_i^p : "priority" cost of customer i

meaning that for each different priority level p, there is a fixed cost of leaving customer i unassigned. Then the following cost term is added to the objective function for penalizing instances of unassigned customers.

$$\sum_{i \in I} c_i^p \left(1 - \sum_{k \in K} y_{ik}\right)$$

In our implementation, we have assumed a total of 10 priority levels, where $p = 1$ is the highest priority level that has the highest c_i^p cost value, where $p = 10$ is the lowest.

Finally, rule g) suggests that the hard time windows imposed by the constraint (11) in our basic model must be relaxed and converted into soft time windows. But since this is undesirable from a customer satisfaction point of view, we introduce another set of penalty costs for violating the hard time window. The penalty costs we implement come in two flavors: one, a fixed cost c^f for each violation of a hard time window; and second, a variable penalty cost c^v for each violation proportional to the total number of minutes violated. To accomplish these, we introduce the following three additional decision variables:

z_i : 1, if customer i has its (single) time window violated, 0 otherwise

v_i : total time window violation amount (in minutes) of customer i

u_i : dummy variable for keeping track of time window violations

Then, we add the following cost term to the objective function to keep track of the total fixed and variable costs of time window violations:

$$\sum_{i \in I}(c^f z_i + c^v v_i)$$

and the following, to replace constraint (11) in the basic model:

$$v_i \geq a_i - s_{ik} \qquad \forall i \in I, \forall k \in K \qquad (19)$$

$$v_i \geq s_{ik} - b_i \qquad \forall i \in I, \forall k \in K \qquad (20)$$

$$z_i \geq 1 - M u_i \qquad \forall i \in I \qquad (21)$$

$$v_i \leq M(1 - u_i) \qquad \forall i \in I \qquad (22)$$

$$z_i, u_i \in \{0, 1\} \qquad \forall i \in I \qquad (23)$$

$$v_i \geq 0 \qquad \forall i \in I \qquad (24)$$

The user can set the fixed or variable cost parameters (or both) to zero to adjust the behavior of time window violations as they appear in the optimal solution.

Although the above model can handle all the business rules of the company, the size of the problem still dictates us to solve it using a heuristic solution approach, which we describe below:

Solution Approach

The company's problem requires solving VRPTW instance(s) in a very large region with hundreds of vehicles. As mentioned above, we have chosen to use the district structure of the company in reducing the one large VRPTW instance to a number of manageable instances. The company is organized into 32 geographical districts, which means on average there are about 312 service calls per district received daily. This approach works well for the company because it requires no additional restructuring or data manipulation, and more importantly reduces the problem size to within the limits of our implementation.

Since cost minimization is the main objective of our implementation, the heuristic algorithm we have implemented continuously seeks to minimize the sum of the following cost terms:

a.   Travel cost (dollars per mile × total miles driven)
b.   Technician cost (dollars per hour × total route time)
c.   Cost of customers left unassigned (dollars per customer as a function of service priority), if any
d.   Time window violation penalties, if any

The solution methodology we have implemented to solve the extended VRPTW problem detailed above is along the same lines with the heuristic approach we have discussed previously. The heuristic algorithm consists of two main phases: Assignment and Improvement. In the Assignment phase, the algorithm strives to assign each customer to an eligible technician in a sequential manner, while satisfying the business rules of specialties, capacities, route time and overtime limits, and specific technician requests of customers. In each iteration, all possible customer-vehicle assignments are evaluated for the resulting increase in the objective function and the one with the minimum cost increase is selected. The iterations continue as long as there is room in any one of the routes to assign a new customer. This approach treats the time windows as soft constraints (meaning time windows can be violated) with the proper inclusion of time window violation penalty terms in the incremental cost of each assignment. The assignment algorithm, hence, starts out as a constructive heuristic and ends when it creates a partial initial solution, where some customers may be left unassigned. Because of the order priority mentioned above, the assignment algorithm will attempt to service those "VIP" service orders first whenever it is possible.

The Improvement phase takes the initial solution created in the previous phase and executes steps to reduce the total cost of the incumbent solution. These steps are the same as those described in our Algorithm section, namely the intra-route and inter-route improvement moves. Tabu Search memory structures are again employed to avoid local optima. The result of the Improvement phase is one route per technician with a full visit schedule for each.

One of the important features of the GIS implementation we developed for the company was to provide a visit schedule to the end-user and allow him/her to make the following type of edits on the visit schedule:

a.   move customers between routes
b.   delete customers who had a last-minute cancellation
c.   distribute the entire work of a technician to fellow technician(s) if the technician calls in sick

In such cases, the end-user typically requests a re-calculation of the visit sequence of one (or few) technicians. When such a computation is requested, the system independently calls the Improvement module as a standalone execution for each technician and improves, if possible, the visit sequence of customers assigned to that technician.

Implementation and Benefits

The system we have built for the company can be characterized as a GIS-based decision support system that has tightly integrated vehicle routing and scheduling optimization routines. This is essentially a 3-tier system with a client-server type architecture: end-users employ the client mapping application and its graphical interface in the top tier to view routing results and send route optimization requests over the intranet to the main server (middle tier) where routing optimization solver resides. The bottom tier is the corporate database level where all data required for optimization as well as map-making are stored and maintained. The requests are sent either in *batch* optimization mode for routing all districts sequentially at a designated time of the day before the actual customer visits, or in *manual* optimization mode,

Figure 2. GIS implementation interface for gas maintenance technician routing optimization

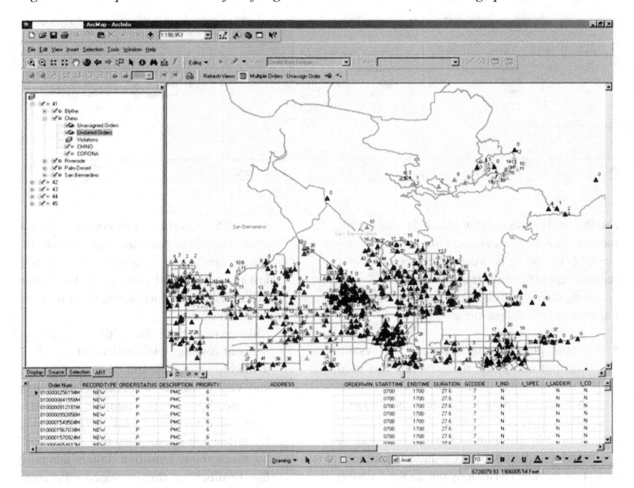

where individual routes are re-optimized for better visit sequence.

The graphical user interface (GUI) for the system not only shows the basemap, district hierarchy and customers with daily visit requests (see Figure 2), but also presents the user with a series of screens to set up the parameters of routing optimization (Figure 3). Once the user completes the input settings for optimization, the information is stored in a configuration file accessed by a Scheduler service.

The Scheduler essentially runs as a continuous process or service at the Operating System level and it constantly monitors input changes and launches different modules of the optimization engine as necessary at designated times in a daily routine. For instance, at noon, the Scheduler downloads all service request and fleet availability data and starts building an OD matrix. Next, it runs the Assignment followed by the Improvement module to assign all requests received up to that point in time to a technician route. Later during the day, the same modules are launched again to insert any additional requests that may have been received in the meantime. Later in the evening, the routes are reviewed and manually revised (if necessary, using the interface shown in Figure 2) by a route planning personnel

Figure 3. Routing parameter configuration screens

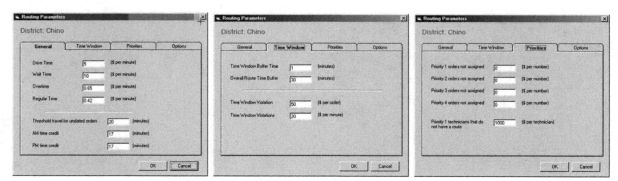

and the final routes are downloaded to field technicians' handheld devices. This routine is repeated every day of the year and customer service requests are efficiently routed.

Using this system on a daily basis, the company has realized the following savings:

- Route planning time: before the system was put into place, the company had used a semi-manual system for building routes. A route planning personnel would manually assign service requests for a specific district to different technician routes as he or she finds suitable. A sequence optimization module (written by one of the authors) would then be executed to find a near-optimal point visit sequence for each route. After the DSS implementation, all route-building became automatic, with manual intervention only required to handle exceptions (e.g. last minute changes in the service request or technician data). This has significantly reduced the amount of time of the personnel needed to complete the routing task. Furthermore, the user-friendly interface has also made it much easier for the users to effectively complete the task.
- Route planning personnel: before the system was put into the place, a route planning personnel would typically be dedicated to 3 or 4 districts, meaning a total of approxi-

mately 15-16 personnel responsible for the entire operation. After the implementation, 3 personnel were sufficient to handle any last minute manual changes on the routes that may be necessary before the routes are sent to the field.

- Mileage reduction: One of the main advantages of routing optimization is to pool all available resources and service requests, and visit customer locations using routes that are shorter, more compact and better allocated (in terms of total cost) to service technicians. It is estimated that the company saves about 2 million dollars annually that results from this increased efficiency. Considering the investment put into implementing such a large real system, one can safely say that the payback period is less than one year.

It is also possible, of course, to restructure the district hierarchy and the service technician fleets to perhaps reduce the fleet sizes instead of or in addition to mileage. At the time of implementation, the company chose to leave its district structure unchanged due to organizational reasons. The top management thought it would be too much and beyond the scope of the project to change the districts as well, since they already expected some amount of resistance from the route planners as well as field technicians. This is clearly an important issue in any optimization-based solution implementation, since optimization may drastically change the normal way of performing tasks for most people in an organization (especially the service technicians in the field who execute the routes). Therefore it is of utmost importance to set the expectations early and get all stakeholders of the project outputs involved to eliminate such resistance and have full cooperation of the entire organization.

Case Study 3: Packaged Bread Distribution in Turkey

Our third case study is on distributing packaged bread in Turkey, a country that spans a large geographical region in part of Europe and Asia, with approximately 780,000 sq. kilometers of area, 1600 kilometers from east to west and 700 kilometers from north to south. The company that produces and distributes packaged bread, which we have worked with, was established in the early1990s in Istanbul. Within a decade, it became the biggest packaged bread producer and distributor company and achieved an approximate 70% market share in Turkey with $100 million of sales turnover. During this period, the company has moved its production plant three times from the European side of Istanbul to the Asian side for growth purposes. During this expansion, the organization also started to get more complex. At the very beginning, there were only sales and production departments which were managed by the shareholders. After several years, the Company's sales boomed due to a shift in consumer behavior towards industrial bread. This situation forced the top management to change the layers and create a modern organization for a controlled process management.

The first improvement was made in production planning. A separate department was established. The main purpose of this was to have the sales force take next day orders in a systematic way and pass them to the production department. The

second improvement was made in the accounting department. The department was divided into two as sales accounting and accounting. The daily transaction paperwork of the sales force started to be recorded in sales accounting along with the responsibility to create new customer accounts.

Within ten years, the visited points of sales of the company have increased from 1,000 per day to 4,000 per day. The new millennium brought prosperity to Turkey's population and the consumption of packaged bread increased exponentially. This situation forced the company to increase its distribution fleet size to execute more efficient delivery to the increased number of sales points. In the beginning of year 2003, the company had only 109 trucks. This number tripled only in six years and reached 306 by the end of year 2009 (Figure 4), with a total of 14,000 sales points on average visited daily by 300+ truck drivers. The increased capacity of the distribution system demanded new abilities from the sales force. Handheld terminals entered the sales systems with the ERP modules in accounting departments. At that time, such technology was only capable of invoicing and recording the sales details such as time, sales point address and the sales amount in terms of units and currency.

In its first years of operation, the company sales were mostly to the national key accounts who were the country's biggest retailers such as Migros, Carrefour, Gima (merged with Carrefour in 2005) and Tansaş (acquired by Migros in 2005). On the other hand, the company was also selling to the local markets and the groceries. In 2009, the distribution of sales according to the channels consisted of 48% to the national key accounts, 8% to the groceries, 20% to the local markets and 24% as B2B.

Operational Rules

Industrial bread production needs great efforts for several reasons. First of all, the average shelf life of the product is approximately 5 days. This

Figure 4. The increase in distribution fleet size of the company

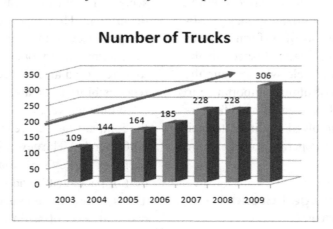

means that there is no possibility to work with stocks especially since the company is working with more than 100 SKUs. The production planning department has to be very systematic to make the correct calculations for the next day's market demand. For this reason, the company sales force collects every day each sales point's next day order with the help of handheld terminals. The system then delivers this information in the afternoon to the production planning department to organize the next day's production.

The complexity of the system results from the number of combinations between the warehouses and the order amounts of more than 100 SKUs. The company has five warehouses, in addition to Istanbul, in five different territories: Ankara, Bursa, Izmir, Antalya, Bodrum. Every warehouse has to inform the order collection department in the headquarters before 5pm. After receiving the orders, the orders collection department forwards this information to the production planning department.

The logistics department has to organize the produced SKUs according to the customer order lists and loads the trucks with the current day's distribution. To organize this complex workflow, the company has created a vertical hierarchy within its sales force organization. A sales director, who controls the nationwide actions, gives instructions

to his three sales channel managers who control the local markets, groceries and the key accounts, respectively. Assistant managers and the supervisors are all organized to control the truck drivers under their channel managers.

The distribution system is built on the performance of the truck drivers and their supervisors. Every driver has a route plan which is programmed by the managers and their assistants. The supervisors who are managed by the channel managers inform the truck drivers about the daily plans. Every driver has to load his truck approximately at 5am and visit an average of 40 sales points per day. The driver has to carry the bread cases, keep the truck clean and visit every point on the route plan. Besides these obligations, the driver has to make invoicing during the route and collect the receivables if any. At the end of the day he has to come to the warehouse and give a daily report to the sales accounting department.

Constraints of the Distribution System

The company's complex distribution system started to face problems with the increasing number of sales points during the twelve month period spanning second half of 2008 and first half of 2009. The differences of the product acceptance time between the sales points forced the company to divide the organization according to the sales channels. This way the trucks could be organized according to the sales points' product acceptance time intervals, but it also resulted in less efficient and optimal distribution plans.

Besides the market rules, managing 300+ drivers was not an easy task for management. To meet the legal working hours for drivers and trying to keep the cost of gasoline consumed by trucks as low as possible were some other challenges for the company. The driver behavior in the market was getting more important than ever with the increased sales of the company.

The focus of the Finance department was on the increased cost of the distribution system. Top management meeting agendas were always prioritized by the actions needed to decrease the distribution costs and keeping the sales turnover stable.

The Need for Optimization

In March 2009, the authors and their project team met with the Company officials to solve its distribution problems via optimization of the route plans of truck drivers. The top management believed that if the sales managers could provide the drivers with route plans containing the best way to visit delivery points, the cost of the logistics system would be in a better shape. During the meetings, we have realized that the management would not be satisfied only with the optimization of route planning. In fact, this was the very first step of a long journey for the company; to optimize every single route with the help of a software program which has the capability of modeling the constraints of the delivery system, such as meeting the legal working hours, sales points product acceptance time, driving distance, the cost of the gasoline consumption etc. which were all calculated manually beforehand.

After the initial considerations, the company decided to give it a try with the ArcLogistics™

routing optimization software. This software, the development of which two authors of this chapter have contributed, is a commercial off-the-shelf product offered by a leading GIS software company based in the U.S.A. The two authors' main contribution was to help this GIS company's software development team incorporate the VRPTW algorithm discussed in this chapter into the product. With such kind of a software system, the aim of the company was not only to figure out the best options for route plans of the company, but also to manage the drivers' daily schedule online through a web application. Mapping and optimizing the routes, and monitoring them online were quite new concepts for the company.

ArcLogistics Implementation and Expected Benefits

The company decided to implement the ArcLogistics routing optimization solution in a three-step approach. At the very beginning, top management requested to see real numbers to test the capabilities of the optimization system. As a result, we have worked with the company officials on two actual routes. These routes were chosen from the Anatolian side of the local market channels. This selection was based on the number of visited points and the cost structure of the channel. Compared to the national key accounts channel, the local markets channel was more costly in terms of the distribution sales amount and the times spent for sales activity in the route.

To create an optimized version of these two routes, first we have gathered the detailed address of each sales point from the sales manager. Afterwards, we have geocoded the addresses by the help of handheld terminals the drivers use on their routes. This was made possible by the coordination of three departments. IT management, risk management and the sales management teams worked together to supply the necessary data to upload to ArcLogistics, whose core solvers are similar to the one described in the algorithm section of this

Table 4. Benchmark results with 15 routes at different levels of optimization

Scenario	Distance (km)	% Savings	Duration (hr.)	% Savings	Cost ($)	% Savings
1	11077		923		15527	
2	8364	24.5%	849	8.0%	14098	9.2%
3	7798	29.6%	837	9.4%	13825	11.0%
4	7103	35.9%	815	11.7%	13437	13.5%

chapter. The content of the data that were loaded in ArcLogistics included the addresses of the visiting points, the constraints of the sales points such as the delivery time to the points, minimum sales amounts related to the customer, drivers' legal driving time (i.e. limits on route time), and the gasoline consumption amount per truck. With these settings, the problem we were faced with was clearly another instance of the VRPTW.

After we have worked on the delivery points and a number of optimization scenarios, we have presented the results to top management. The overall savings of 32% on total route time and 24% on total route length was found quite impressive by the management, considering the potential savings on gasoline costs that can be achieved by the company through the use of a route optimization system. But this was only the first phase of our study. The management team, especially the risk department, was impressed with the results and wanted to have a better understanding of the capabilities of the system. A second benchmark study was carried out for an additional set of 15 routes, this time on a different part of the city of Istanbul. Six of these routes were selected from the national key accounts channel, another six routes were selected from the local markets channel and the last three were chosen from the grocery channel. The same process was applied to these fifteen routes and the results were presented to top management. Table 4 shows the savings that were projected at various levels of optimization.

This table shows the potential savings of route optimization according to three performance measures: total distance traveled by 15 routes, total duration and total cost, including fixed and variable costs of the vehicles as well as the labor costs of drivers. The scenarios listed above indicate the increasing level of optimization going from no optimization at all (i.e. current routes) with Scenario 1 to global optimization (all visit points for all channels shuffled) with Scenario 4. The intermediate scenarios correspond to the case where only route visit sequences are optimized within each existing route (Scenario 2) and visit points are optimized within each channel (Scenario 3). These performance measures and scenarios were formed in advance by the risk management department at the company. The outputs of the analysis display that the total saving in the route management was closed to 40% in terms of hard currency (with mileage costs). After these results, top management decided to buy the software and implement the system.

The kick-off meeting for the implementation of the route optimization system was conveyed as a strong message to the sales force of the company. The field people were informed that this program was not only capable of optimizing the routes but was also able to track online the real movements of the truck drivers on the road. Teams from both sides were formed and the responsibilities were distributed among the team members so that the system is well-perceived at all levels of the organization.

Going Online with ArcLogistics

When the company decided to lunch the entire system, the main concern was to make it widely acceptable across the organization. Top management thought this could be achieved by first implementing it in a region where employees and field people were more open to such changes and also the reasonable size of the region allows tractability. Therefore the management team has chosen Antalya region warehouse for the pilot implementation. Another reason for choosing Antalya was because it was a small enough operation (only 5 routes) so that the company can understand and solve potential problems during the live implementation. To organize the whole team for data collection in Antalya routes was much easier than applying the same process in Istanbul.

When the pilot implementation started, the addresses of the sales points were requested from local sales management. After the data were gathered, the IT department completed the geocoding and transferred all the information directly to the ArcLogistics team and the system itself. After testing various different optimization scenarios and configuration parameters, the management determined the best routing solution for the Antalya region. The results revealed that the operation was possible with one route less which meant an improvement of approximately 20% in the cost structure.

To summarize, cost-effective distribution systems constitute the main competitive advantage for the contemporary companies who are acting both in the B2C and B2B markets, as demonstrated in this route optimization project. Without efficient executions in the processes, the differentiation strategies do not always bring the expected returns to a company.

In today's complex market competition, companies make higher profits not only by selling more but also by efficient and cost effective operations. As it can be observed from this case, the company achieved more than 20% cost reduction in its distribution operations by optimizing its route plans. In order to achieve such a success, the management of the company clearly has to be aware of the improvement areas, and moreover has

to have qualifications and knowledge on how the problems can be solved. Without an open-minded approach to similar operational problems and the contributions of a highly-motivated project team, achieving significant improvements is almost impossible, even if there is a good sponsor to back up the project.

Each of the three case studies described in detail in this section provides a significant practical perspective on the vehicle routing problem with time windows. They not only show that these types of routing problems are diversely encountered in the service industry, but also show that they are indeed solvable using certain optimization techniques from the literature. In each case, we as the authors of this chapter were together or individually involved, and acted as system analysts, architects, algorithm designers and developers. We take pride in the fact that these successful implementations of GIS-based optimization systems have provided their respective companies significant cost and time savings, and transformed them in many different ways. We believe these solution techniques and approaches can be applied in yet a larger number of contexts in the service industry.

CONCLUSION

Many logistics problems found in the service industry can be modeled as VRPTW instances, a type of vehicle routing problem which have been studied widely in the operations research literature. To solve real instances of VRPTW, however, poses a significant challenge for both researchers and practitioners. A real VRPTW includes many business rules and logic that are beyond those addressed in mathematical models in the literature, and some business logic cannot even be modeled mathematically. Because of the characteristics of a VRPTW, it is also challenging to solve it within a reasonable computational time or even real-time based various business requirements. Furthermore, the field people who are going to deploy a VRPTW solution in the service industry may have to pay more attention to the feasibility of the solution in practice than the pure mathematical "mileage savings". Without a significant support from the user who is going to deploy the solution of a VRPTW, a project that attempts to apply VRPTW solutions to increase operational efficiency and customer satisfaction usually fails.

In this chapter, with real applications from the service industry, we present the basic VRPTW model and its extensions to some of the problems encountered in the industry. The algorithms that combine GIS and optimization techniques (heuristics and metaheuristics) to solve these real problems more effectively are discussed in detail.

Three case studies are presented based on real applications from the service industry. The VRPTW problems in these studies possess certain special needs and challenges. We discussed in detail how to adapt the basic VRPTW model to these problems and revise the algorithms to accommodate the particular business requirements. The outcomes demonstrate the effectiveness and economic benefits of the proposed enhanced models and algorithms. These algorithms are capable of solving large-scale VRPTW instances from the real world, and the results are closer to real practice and accepted by the user or field people. The proposed algorithms not only address the difficulties embedded in these VRPTW instances but also the concerns of those users about the feasibility of the solutions produced.

REFERENCES

Ahmmed, A. Rana, Md.A.A., Haque, A.A.Md., & Mamun, Md.A. (2008). A Multiple Ant Colony System for Dynamic Vehicle Routing Problem with Time Window. In *Proceedings of International Conference on Convergence and Hybrid Information Technology* (pp. 182-187). IEEE.

Azi, N., Gendreau, M., & Potvin, J. Y. (2010). An Exact Algorithm for a Vehicle Routing Problem with Time Windows and Multiple Use of Vehicles. *European Journal of Operational Research, 202,* 757–763. doi:10.1016/j.ejor.2009.06.034

Bent, R., & van Hentenryck, P. (2004). A Two-Stage Hybrid Local Search for the Vehicle Routing Probşem. *Transportation Science, 38*(11), 515–530. doi:10.1287/trsc.1030.0049

Blakeley, F., Bozkaya, B., Cao, B., Hall, W., & Knolmajer, J. (2003). Optimizing Periodic Maintenance Operations for Schindler Elevator Corporation. *Interfaces, 33*(1), 67–79. doi:10.1287/inte.33.1.67.12722

Bodin, L., Golden, B., Assad, A., & Ball, M. (1983). Routing and Scheduling of Vehicles and Crews: the State of the Art. *Computers & Operations Research, 10,* 104–106.

Braysy, O., & Gendreau, M. (2005). Vehicle Routing Problem with Time Windows, Part I: Routing Construction and Local Search Algorithms. *Transportation Science, 39*(1), 104–118. doi:10.1287/trsc.1030.0056

Braysy, O., & Gendreau, M. (2005). Vehicle Routing Problem with Time Windows, Part II: Metaheuristics. *Transportation Science, 39*(1), 119–139. doi:10.1287/trsc.1030.0057

Clarke, G., & Wright, J. (1964). Scheduling of Vehicles from a Central Depot to a Number of Delivery Points. *Operations Research, 12,* 568–581. doi:10.1287/opre.12.4.568

Dantzig, G. B., & Ramser, J. H. (1959). The Truck Dispatching Problem. *Management Science, 6,* 80–91. doi:10.1287/mnsc.6.1.80

Francis, P., Smilowitz, K., & Tzur, M. (2006). The Period Vehicle Routing Problem with Service Choice. *Transportation Science, 40*(4), 439–454. doi:10.1287/trsc.1050.0140

Garaix, T., Artigues, C., Feillet, D., & Josselin, D. (2010). Vehicle Routing Problems with Alternative Paths: An Application to On-Demand Transportation. *European Journal of Operational Research*, *204*, 62–75. doi:10.1016/j.ejor.2009.10.002

Glover, F. (1986). Future Paths for Integer Programming and Links to Artificial Intelligence. *Computers & Operations Research*, *13*, 533–549. doi:10.1016/0305-0548(86)90048-1

Goel, A., & Gruhn, V. (2008). A General Vehicle Routing Problem. *European Journal of Operational Research*, *191*, 650–660. doi:10.1016/j.ejor.2006.12.065

Gutierrez, G., Desaulniers, G., Laporte, G., & Marianov, D. (2010). A Branch-and-Price Algorithm for the Vehicle Routing Problem with Deliveries, Selective Pickups and Time Windows. *European Journal of Operational Research*, *206*, 341–349. doi:10.1016/j.ejor.2010.02.037

Holland, J. H. (1975). *Adaption in Natural and Artificial System*. Ann Arbor, MI: University of Michigan Press.

Ibaraki, T., Imahori, S., Kubo, M., Masuda, T., Uno, T., & Yagiura, M. (2005). Effective Local Search Algorithms for Routing and Scheduling Problems with General Time-Window Constraints. *Transportation Science*, *30*(2), 206–232. doi:10.1287/trsc.1030.0085

Kalcsics, J., Nickel, S., & Schröder, M. (2005). Towards a Unified Territorial Design Approach: Applications, Algorithms, and GIS Integration. *Top (Madrid)*, *13*(1), 1–56. doi:10.1007/BF02578982

Kallenhauge, B. (2008). Formulation and Exact Algorithms for the Vehicle Routing Problem with Time Windows. *Computers & Operations Research*, *35*, 2307–2330. doi:10.1016/j.cor.2006.11.006

Kim, B.-I., Kim, S., & Sahoo, S. (2006). Waste Collection Vehicle Routing Problem with Time Windows. *Computers & Operations Research*, *33*, 3624–3642. doi:10.1016/j.cor.2005.02.045

Kirkpatrick, S., Gelatt, C. D., & Vecchi, P. M. (1983). Optimization by Simulated Annealing. *Science*, *220*, 671–680. doi:10.1126/science.220.4598.671

Kohl, N., & Madsen, O. B. G. (1997). An Optimization Algorithm for the Vehicle Routing Problem with Time Windows based on Lagrangian Relaxation. *Operations Research*, *45*(3), 395–406. doi:10.1287/opre.45.3.395

Laporte, G. (2009). Fifty Years of Vehicle Routing. *Transportation Science*, *43*(4), 408–416. doi:10.1287/trsc.1090.0301

Lenstra, J., & Kan, A. R. (1981). Complexity of Vehicle Routing and Scheduling Problems. *Networks*, *11*, 221–227. doi:10.1002/net.3230110211

Mendoza, J., Medaglia, A. L., & Velasco, N. (2009). An Evolutionary-Based Decision Support System for Vehicle Routing: The Case of a Public Utility. *Decision Support Systems*, *46*, 730–742. doi:10.1016/j.dss.2008.11.019

Muller, J. (2010). Approximative Solutions to the Bicriterion Vehicle Routing Problem with Time Windows. *European Journal of Operational Research*, *202*, 223–231. doi:10.1016/j.ejor.2009.04.029

Rios-Mercado, R. Z., & Fernandez, E. A. (2009). A Reactive GRASP for a Commercial Territory Design Problem with Multiple Balancing Requirements. *Computers & Operations Research*, *36*(3), 755–776. doi:10.1016/j.cor.2007.10.024

Ropke, S., & Cordeau, J. F. (2009). Branch and Cut and Price for the Pickup and Delivery Problem with Time Windows. *Transportation Science*, *43*, 267–286. doi:10.1287/trsc.1090.0272

Russell, R., & Chiang, W. C. (2006). Scatter Search for the Vehicle Routing Problem with Time Windows. *European Journal of Operational Research, 169*, 606–622. doi:10.1016/j.ejor.2004.08.018

Solomon, M. M. (1987). Algorithms for the Vehicle Routing and Scheduling Problems with Time Window Constraints. *Operations Research, 35*, 254–265. doi:10.1287/opre.35.2.254

Spada, M., Bierlaire, M., & Liebling, Th. M. (2005). Decision-Aiding Methodology for the School Bus Routing and Scheduling Problem. *Transportation Science, 39*, 477–490. doi:10.1287/trsc.1040.0096

Taillard, E. D., Badeau, P., Gendreau, M., Guertin, F., & Potvin, J. Y. (1997). A Tabu Search Heuristic for the Vehicle Routing Problem with Soft Time Windows. *Transportation Science, 31*, 170–186. doi:10.1287/trsc.31.2.170

Weigel, D., & Cao, B. (1999). Applying GIS and OR Techniques to Solve Sears Technician-Dispatching and Home Delivery Problems. *Interfaces, 29*(1), 112–130. doi:10.1287/inte.29.1.112

Yu, B., Yang, Z. Z., & Yao, B. Z. (2009). An Improved Ant Colony Optimization for Vehicle Routing Problem. *European Journal of Operational Research, 196*, 171–176. doi:10.1016/j.ejor.2008.02.028

Zheng, T., & Zhang, Q. (2009). A Hybrid Meta-heuristic Algorithm for the Multi-depot Vehicle Routing Problem with Time Windows. In: *Proceedings of International Conference on Networks Security, Wireless Communications and Trusted Computing* (pp. 798-801), IEEE.

KEY TERMS AND DEFINITIONS

Geographic Information System: Computer-based system for collecting, storing, editing, mapping and visualizing, and analyzing spatial data.

Local Search: A heuristic search technique where the algorithm attempt to improve an incumbent solution by searching the neighborhood

Metaheuristics: Advanced heuristic optimization techniques that serve as guidelines for various search procedures and attempt to perform a more effective search over the solution space of the problem of interest.

Vehicle Routing Problem: A generic mathematical problem that seeks the most cost-effective routing of a fleet of vehicles, under various settings such as single vs. multiple depot, capacitated vs. uncapacitated, single delivery vs. split delivery, to serve a number of customer pickup or delivery locations within allowable time limits.

Vehicle Routing Problem with Time Windows: The version of the problem where customers can accept a delivery or pickup visit only within certain time limits due to operational reasons.

Chapter 4
A Hybrid Genetic Algorithm–Simulated Annealing Approach for the Multi–Objective Vehicle Routing Problem with Time Windows

Gülfem Tuzkaya
Yildiz Technical University, Turkey

Bahadır Gülsün
Yildiz Technical University, Turkey

Ender Bildik
Yildiz Technical University, Turkey

E. Gözde Çağlar
Yildiz Technical University, Turkey

ABSTRACT

In this study, the vehicle routing problem with time windows (VRPTW) is investigated and formulated as a multi-objective model. As a solution approach, a hybrid meta-heuristic algorithm is proposed. Proposed algorithm consists of two meta-heuristics: Genetic Algorithm (GA) and Simulated Annealing (SA). In this algorithm, SA is used as an improvement operator in GA. Besides, a hypothetical application is presented to foster the better understanding of the proposed model and algorithm. The validity of the algorithm is tested via some well-known benchmark problems from the literature.

DOI: 10.4018/978-1-61350-086-6.ch004

INTRODUCTION

Vehicle routing problems (VRP) are concerned with the delivery of some commodities from one or more depots to a number of customer locations with known demand. Such problems arise in many physical systems dealing with distribution, for example, delivery of commodities such as mail, food, newspapers, etc. The specific problem which arises is dependent upon the type of constraints and management objectives. The constraints of the problem may arise from particular factors such as the vehicle capacity, distance/time restriction, number of customers to be serviced by a vehicle, and other practical requirements. The management objectives usually relate to the minimization of cost/distance or fleet size (Achuthan *et al.*, 1997). Among variants of VRP, the VRP with capacity and time window constraints is called vehicle routing problem with time windows (VRPTW) (Hashimoto *et al.*, 2006). VRPTW is a non polynomial-hard (NP-hard) problem, which is encountered very frequently in making decisions about the distribution of goods and services. The problem involves a fleet of vehicles set off from a depot to serve a number of customers, at different geographic locations, with various demands and within specific time windows before returning to the depot. The objective of the problem is to find routes for the vehicles to serve all the customers at a minimal cost (in terms of travel, distance, etc.) without violating the capacity and travel time constraints of the vehicles and the time window constraints set by the customers (Tan *et al.*, 2001). Although cost minimization function is the mostly used function in the VRPTW literature, there may be a need to consider more than one objective in some cases. When the related literature is investigated, Garcia-Najera and Bullinaria (2009), Tang *et al.* (2009), Müller (2010), Jeon *et al.* (2007) are some of the papers in which multiple objectives are considered for VRPTW. For a comprehensive literature review for multi-objective VRPTW concept, Jozefowiez *et al.* (2008) can be reviewed.

The methodologies for solving VRPTW can be classified as given below. This classification is referenced from Badeu *et al.* (1997) and the literature review is updated:

- Exact algorithms (Az, *et al.*, 2007; Kallehauge, 2008; Desrochers *et al.*, 1992),
- Route construction heuristics (Thangiah *et al.*, 1996; Potvin and Robillard, 1995; Russell, 1995; Potvin and Rousseau, 1995; Solomon, 1987),
- Route improvement heuristics (Dror and Levy, 1986; Solomon *et al.*, 1998),
- Composite heuristics that include both route construction and route improvement procedures (Chen *et al.*, 2006; Du *et al.*, 2005; Du *et al.*, 2007; Kontroravdis and Bard, 1995),
- Metaheuristics (Scatter Search (Russell and Chiang, 2006); Tabu Search (Ho and Haugland 2004; Rochat and Taillard, 1995; Taillard *et al.*, 1995; Potvin and Rousseau, 1995); Simulated Annealing (Tavakkoli *et al.*, 2006; Breedam, 1995); Ant Colony (Cheng and Mao, 2007; Mazzeo and Loiseau, 2004; Bell and McMullen, 2004); Genetic Algorithms (Osman *et al.*, 2005; Prins, 2004; Baker and Ayechew, 2003; Hwang, 2002)).

Since the VRPTW belongs to NP-hard combinatorial optimization problems, some heuristic procedures are suggested for the VRPTW as can be seen from literature survey above. Also, quite good results have been achieved for the VRPTW with meta-heuristics (Homberger and Gehring, 2005). Additionally, hybridization of certain meta-heuristics with the other meta-heuristics can be considered for more effective algorithms. For example, as one of the evolutionary algorithms, genetic algorithms (GA) can be combined with a local search technique, for example, with simulated annealing (SA). GA and SA are both popular techniques for combinatorial optimization problems, however, they have some weaknesses and strengths independently. GA can find the region of the optimal values quickly, but, the probability of accurate search in this region is not satisfactory for complex systems. On the other hand, SA can search accurately in certain region, but, it is difficult to explore the whole solution space (Yao *et al.*, 2003). In the literature, there is a large body of study that combines GA and SA to increase their pure performances. One of these studies was prepared by Jwo et al (1999). In this study, the authors proposed a hybrid GA/SA algorithm for optimal planning of large-scale reactive power sources. They used SA to create a quasi-population to a randomly generated population, and the quasi population is genetically evolved to the population of next generation by the genetic operators. This methodology decreases the solution time comparing to the pure SA methodology. Another study is prepared by Yao *et al.* (2003) in the chemical research area. In this study, the normal GA was modified with adaptive multi-annealing crossover and mutation strategies instead of simple strategies. In the scheduling literature, Yoo and Gen (2007) tried to improve the convergence of GA by introducing the probability of SA as a criterion for acceptance of new trial solutions. He and Hwang (2006) presented a hybrid GA/SA methodology to detect damage occurrence in beam-type structures. In that study, they used SA after GA's mutation phase. M'Hallah (2007) proposed a hybrid GA/SA methodology to minimize total earliness and tardiness on a single machine. Yu *et al.* (2000) utilized a hybrid GA/SA algorithm for large scale system energy integration to avoid the common defect of early convergence.

As previously mentioned, GA and SA were combined in different ways for various problems. However, considering the hybrid GA/SA literature, there is no evidence of existence of a hybrid GA/SA algorithm for VRPTW. In this study, we proposed a hybrid GA and SA (HGASA) methodology for multi-objective vehicle routing problem with time windows. Also, the proposed methodology is com-

pared with the pure SA and pure GA algorithms. Additionally, proposed HGASA methodology is tested by means of some well known benchmark problems from the literature. Remaining part of the paper is organized as follows. In the second section, problem formulation for multi-objective VRPTW is given. In the third section, a brief overview of GA and SA is presented. In the fourth section, solution approach is presented. The fifth section is the computational analyses section and the final section is the conclusions section.

THE MULTI-OBJECTIVE VEHICLE ROUTING PROBLEM WITH TIME WINDOWS (VRPTW): PROBLEM FORMULATION

In this study, a modified version of Tan *et al.*'s VRPTW model is used (Tan *et al.*, 2001). In Tan *et al.*'s model, only one objective was considered, in this study, additional three objectives, which are explained below, are considered. The components of VRPTW model are a number of vehicles, a central depot, a number of customer nodes and a network that connects the customers and the depot. There exist $N+1$ nodes and K vehicles. The depot node is defined as the 0. node. Each travel inside the network represents the junction of two nodes and the travel directions. Each route starts from the depot and visits the customer nodes and returns the depot. The number of the routes is equal to the number of vehicles utilized. Each vehicle is allocated only one route. Each travel in the network generates a cost, c_{ij}, and a traveling time, t_{ij}. The distances between customers are calculated as Euclidean distances; and the distance and the cost generated from the travel from i^{th} node to j^{th} node is equal to the distance and cost generated from the travel from j^{th} node to i^{th} node (Tan *et al.*, 2001).

Each customer is served by only one vehicle, each vehicle has equal capacity and the customers have various demand levels. The total amount of the demands of the customers on the one route cannot exceed the vehicle capacity that is assigned to this route. The time constraint is defined as a time window. According to this time window, if a vehicle arrives to the customer before the customer's early time, this situation contributes to a waiting time. Besides, the vehicle cannot go to the customer after the customer's late time. Also, there exist a service time for each customer's load/unload activities. Depending on above mentioned conditions, using Tan *et al.* (2001)'s model, the problem can be formulated as follows.

The Notation

The Decision Variables

t_i arrival time to i^{th} node

w_i waiting time on the ith node

$x_{ijk} \in \{0,1\}$ if there exist a travel from i^{th} node to j^{th} node, 1, otherwise, 0. $i \neq j; i, j \in \{0, 1, 2, ..., N\}$.

Parameters

K total number of vehicles

N total number of customers

d_{ij} the Euclidean distance between i^{th} node to j^{th} node

c_{ij} the cost generated from the travel between i^{th} node to j^{th} node

t_{ij} the traveling time between i^{th} node to j^{th} node

m_i the demand of ith node

q_k the capacity of kth vehicle

e_i the early arrival time of the ith node

l_i the late arrival time of the ith node

f_i the service time of the ith node

r_k the maximum route time allowable for k^{th} route

The Model

The Objective Functions

First objective function (OF1- Total cost minimization incurred on arc from node i to j):

$$\min \sum_{i=0}^{N} \sum_{j=0, j\neq i}^{N} \sum_{k=1}^{K} c_{ij} x_{ijk} \qquad (1)$$

Second objective function (OF2- Minimization of number of routes):

$$\min \sum_{k=1}^{K} \sum_{j=1}^{N} x_{ijk} \qquad i = 0 \qquad (2)$$

Fourth objective function (OF4- Minimization of empty capacities):

$$\min \left(q_k - \sum_{i=1}^{N} m_i \sum_{j=0, j\neq i}^{N} x_{ijk} \right) \qquad k \in \{1, ..., K\} \qquad (3)$$

Fifth objective function (OF5- Minimization of waiting times):

$$\min \sum_{i=0}^{N} w_i \qquad (4)$$

The Constraints

The first constraint tries to ensure that the vehicles in the depot that can serve to the customers not to exceed the maximum number available.

$$\sum_{k=1}^{K} \sum_{j=1}^{N} x_{ijk} \leq K \qquad i = 0 \qquad (5)$$

The second constraint tries to ensure that each vehicle's starting node and returning node be the depot.

$$\sum_{j=1}^{N} x_{ijk} = \sum_{j=1}^{N} x_{jik} \leq 1 \qquad i = 0 \quad ve \quad k \in \{1, ..., K\} \tag{6}$$

The third and the fourth constraints try to ensure that each customer is served by only one vehicle.

$$\sum_{k=1}^{K} \sum_{j=0, j \neq i}^{N} x_{ijk} = 1 \qquad i \in \{1, ..., N\} \tag{7}$$

$$\sum_{k=1}^{K} \sum_{i=0, i \neq j}^{N} x_{ijk} = 1 \qquad j \in \{1, ..., N\} \tag{8}$$

The fifth constraint tries to ensure that the capacity constraint of the vehicles is not exceeded.

$$\sum_{i=1}^{N} m_i \sum_{j=0, j \neq i}^{N} x_{ijk} \leq q_k \qquad k \in \{1, ..., K\} \tag{9}$$

The sixth constraint tries to ensure that the maximum traveling time available is not exceeded.

$$\sum_{i=0}^{N} \sum_{j=0, j \neq i}^{N} x_{ijk}(t_{ij} + f_i + w_i) \leq r_k \qquad k \in \{1, ..., K\} \tag{10}$$

The ninth, tenth, eleventh constraints define the time windows.

$$t_0 = w_0 = f_0 = 0 \tag{11}$$

$$\sum_{k=1}^{K} \sum_{i=0, i \neq j}^{N} x_{ijk}(t_i + t_{ij} + f_i + w_i) \leq t_j \qquad j \in \{1, ..., N\} \tag{12}$$

$$e_i \leq (t_i + w_i) \leq l_i \qquad i \in \{1, ..., N\} \tag{13}$$

Since, VRPTW is a non polynomial-hard (NP-hard) problem, the usage of classical optimization algorithms is not convenient as a solution tool.

So, meta-heuristics are preferred as solution approaches and the model is solved through a HGASA methodology.

GENETIC ALGORTIHMS (GA) AND SIMULATED ANNEALING (SA): AN OVERVIEW

GAs are stochastic search techniques based on the mechanism of natural selection and natural genetics. GAs, differing from conventional search techniques, start with an initial set of random solutions called *population*. Each individual in the population is called a chromosome, representing a solution to the problem at hand. A chromosome is a string of symbols; it is usually, but not necessarily, a binary bit string. The chromosome evolves through successive iterations, called generations. During each generation, the chromosomes are evaluated, using some measures of fitness. To create the next generation, new chromosomes, called offspring, are formed by either, (a) merging two chromosomes from current generation using a crossover operator or (b) modifying a chromosome using a mutation operator. A new generation is formed by (a) selecting, according to fitness values, some of parents and offspring and (b) rejecting others so as to keep the population size constant. Fitter chromosomes have higher probabilities of being selected. After several generations, the algorithms converge to the best chromosome, which hopefully represents the optimum or sub optimal solution to the problem (Gen and Cheng, 1997; Tuzkaya *et al.*, 2011; Tuzkaya *et al.*, in press). As a type of evolutionary algorithms, GAs' general scheme in pseudo code can be given as in Table 1 (Eiben and Smith, 2003).

SA was firstly proposed by Kirkpatrick *et al.* (1983) to solve combinatorial problems in early 1980s. It has the capability of jumping out of the local optima for global optimization. The capability is achieved by accepting with probability neighboring solutions worse than the current

Table 1. General scheme of GAs in pseudo code (Eiben and Smith, 2003)

```
Start
Initialize population with random candidate solutions
Evaluate each candidate
Repeat until (Termination conditions is satisfied)
        Select parents
        Recombine pair of parents
        Mutate the resulting offspring
        Evaluate new candidates
        Select individuals for the next generations
Stop
```

Table 2. General scheme of SA in pseudo code (Dowsland, 1993)

SA for a minimization problem with solution space S, objective function f and neighbourhood structure N

Select an initial solution s_0;
Select an intial temperature $t_0 > 0$;
Select a temperature reduction function $f(t)$;
Repeat
  Repeat
      Randomly select $s \in N(s_0)$;
      $? = f(s)-f(s_0)$;
      If $? < 0$
      then $s_0 = s$
      else
      generate random x uniformly in the range $(0,1)$;
          If $x < e^{-k\frac{\Delta}{T}}$
          then $s_0 = s$;
    Until iteration_count = n_{rep}
    $t = f(t)$;
Until stopping condition = true
s_0 is the approximation to the optimal solution

solution. The acceptance probability is determined by a control parameter (temperature) which decreases during the SA procedure (Seckiner and Kurt, 2007; Tuzkaya *et al.*, 2011; Tuzkaya *et al.*, in press). SA's general scheme in pseudo code can be given as in Table 2 (Dowsland, 1993).

HYBRID GENETIC ALGORITHM-SIMULATED ANNEALING APPROACH (HGASA) FOR THE MULTI-OBJECTIVE VEHICLE ROUTING PROBLEM WITH TIME WINDOWS (VRPTW)

The proposed approach, HGASA, is basically represented in Figure 1. In this approach, SA is

Figure 1. The general structure of HGASA approach

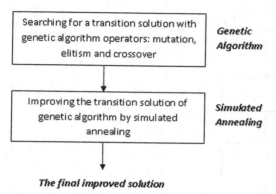

used as an operator of the GA. Firstly, a population is searched by GA and then the best individual of this process is improved by SA.

Details of the HGASA methodology can be given as follows:

Step 1- Initialization: First of all, chromosome representation of the solution is determined. A chromosome consists of a number of genes representing the customers. The customer numbers are assigned to the genes randomly. Here, permutation decoding is used.

Each chromosome has some embedded information which is related with the fitness values of alternative solutions (chromosomes): customers of each route, waiting times of vehicles, transportation times of each route and remaining vehicle capacity at the end of each route. Also considering the time and capacity constraints, each chromosome is divided into parts which represent the routes (or the vehicles). Route determination phase can be explained as in Figure 2.

Fitness value of a chromosome is the weighted sum of the objective values for this solution alternative. As mentioned in the model development section, objective functions are the minimization of the cost (OF1), number of routes (OF2), empty capacities of the vehicles (OF3) and waiting times of the vehicles (OF4). To obtain the best values of the objective functions, the model solved

via HGASA for each objective function separately, for example, for the first time, the model is solved for OF1 and the best value of OF1 (BOF1) is obtained. Same procedure is applied for the other objective functions and the best values of them are obtained (BOF2, BOF3, and BOF4). Here, it should be noted that, meta-heuristics don't guarantee obtaining the global optimal solutions and best values are the best found values after the implementation of HGASA. After determination of best values, expert opinions are used to find the objective function weights: WOF1 (weight of OF1), WOF2 (weight of OF2), WOF3 (weight of OF3), and WOF4 (weight of OF4). Then an integrated objective function (IOF) is obtained as in Eq. (14). Here all the objective functions are the minimization functions.

$$IOF = WOF1*OF1/BOF1+WOF2*OF2/BOF2+WOF3*OF3/BOF3+WOF4*OF4/BOF4 \quad (14)$$

Step 2- Population generation: Generation of a population is replication of the new member generation procedure which is explained in the first step until the determined population size is reached.

Step 3- Parent selection: For the parent selection, tournament parent selection methodology is used. In tournament selection, first of all, a number of members are selected from the population randomly. Then, the best one is selected among these members. The procedure is repeated until the needed number of parents reached. Details of tournament selection can be found in Eiben and Smith (2003).

Step 4- Crossover: In the crossover process, since permutation decoding was used, order crossover operator is selected as a convenient crossover methodology. Details of the order crossover operator can be found in Eiben and Smith (2003).

Step 5- Mutation: For the effectiveness of the proposed methodology, a novel mutation operator which is proposed for this study is used. This

Figure 2. The general structure of the routes constructing process

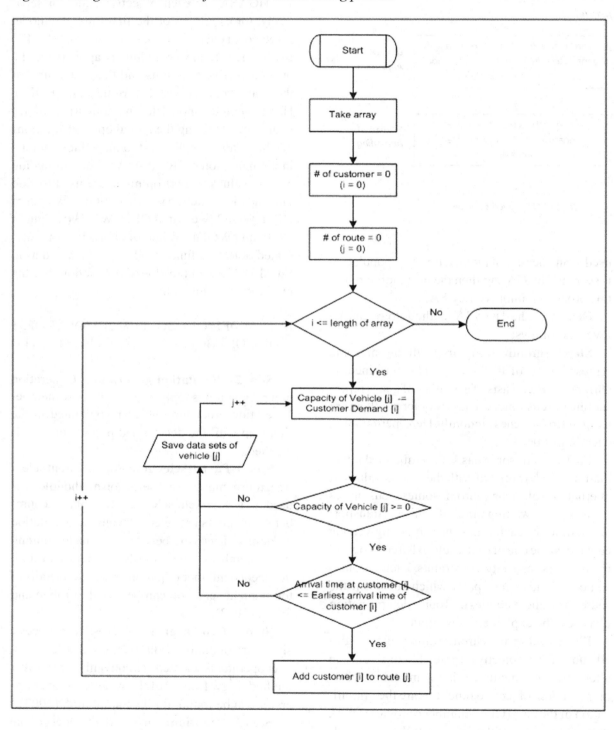

Table 3. Mutation operator of GA and neighborhood searching mechanism of SA

```
Start
Select a route from the solution (chromosome)
For all customers of the route
        Try to change the customer location in the chromosome starting from
the beginning node to the end (With the consideration of time and capacity
constraints)
        If a change can be possible in a route, stop trying and add this cus-
tomer to this route.
Stop
```

study specific operator can be summarized as in the Table 3.

Step 6- Elitism: A certain part of the current generation is transferred to the next generation. Elitism does not provide a variation to the next generation, but it prevents deceiving the better fitness valued members (Tuzkaya *et al.*, in press).

Step 7- Solution improvement via SA: For a certain number of iterations, GA is applied to the initial population. After obtaining a potential solution via GA, this solution is tried to be improved via the SA algorithm as given in Table 2. In SA, for the neighborhood generation procedure, same steps, which are given in Table 3, of the GA's mutation operator is used.

Step 8- End.

COMPUTATIONAL STUDY

An Illustrative Example

To foster the better understanding of the problem, the HGASA approach is solved for a hypothetical example. In this example, the problem is solved for 50 customers. The coordinates of the customers and depot are presented in the Figure 3. The vehicle speed is 50 km/hour and the vehicle capacity is 100 units.

A part of the coordinates of the customers and the depot, demands, early time, service time and late time data can be seen from the Table 4.

The parameter values of the HGASA approach are presented in the Table 5. These parameter values are obtained via a number of experiments.

Using the obtained data to integrate the objective functions, the model is solved by considering only one objective function for each run as explained in the previous section to find the best possible value for each objective. According to the results, minimum number of routes, minimum distance, minimum waiting time, minimum total empty vehicle capacity are obtained as 14; 1812; 411; and 505 units respectively. These values are used for the normalization and integration of the

Figure 3. Coordinates of the customers and the depot

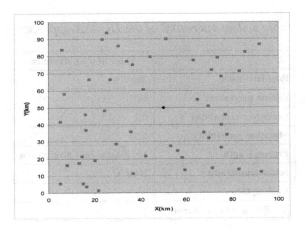

Table 4. Input data for the hypothetical VRPTW

Location	X(km)	Y(km)	Demand	Early Time	Service Time	Late Time
Depot	50	50	-	-	-	-
Customer 0	17,9	66,27	14	136	12,6	175
Customer 1	30,35	85,93	46	55	41,4	79
Customer 2	76,94	45,64	11	108	9,9	132
Customer 3	42,29	21,53	17	150	15,3	186
...	...	...	...	...	...	...
Customer 45	41,4	60,5	26	32	23,4	63
Customer 46	77,7	34	28	153	25,2	199
Customer 47	25,4	93,5	47	134	42,3	153
Customer 48	5,94	83,7	39	147	35,1	196
Customer 49	85,7	82,4	23	116	20,7	157

objective functions (Equation 14). Also objective function weights are determined by the experts as being equal, i.e. 0.25 each.

Following the objective functions integration phase, the problem is solved via HGASA approach. The graphical representation of the solution process of HGASA approach is represented in the Figure 4. In this solution, the chromosome representation is found as (30, 35, 49, 43, 42, 12, 36, 34, 6, 2, 9, 18, 20, 32, 3, 13, 40, 0, 48, 23, 22, 8, 4, 28, 25, 37, 21, 29, 15, 7, 26, 1, 47, 19, 10, 27, 24, 14, 46, 33, 17, 41, 5, 38, 31, 16, 11, 45, 39, 44). For this chromosome, the fitness value is calculated as 1564.72 units. Total route distance

Table 5. The operators of the HGASA approach

	Value of the parameter
Population size	200/1
Elitism percentage	%5
Crossover probability	0.2
Mutation probability	0.08
Process length	100 generations + 50 iterations
İnitial temperature	2000 °C
Cooling factor	0.95
K Adjustment Coefficient	1

is calculated as 2129.49 units and the number of routes is obtained as 14 vehicles.

The routes, the customers of the routes, the total vehicle freight of the routes and the total time consumed in each route is presented in Table 6 and the routes are graphically represented in Figure 4.

In this study, multiple objectives which conflicts with each others are considered. As a result, different solutions are found, like as a solution with less route numbers and more waiting times which cannot be acceptable with our weight combination. However, it can be changed with weight changes of the criteria of the fitness value. In this case study, the weights of the criteria – the route numbers, traveling distances, empty capacities and waiting time's minimization- are assumed to be equal.

Analyzing the Results

For comparison purposes, the model is solved via pure SA and pure GA methodologies. The operators and the related values of these methodologies are presented in the Table 7.

The three algorithms are run for a hundred times each. The solutions obtained with GA, SA, HGASA are compared via paired t-tests. Accord-

Figure 4. Routes and the customers allocated to the routes

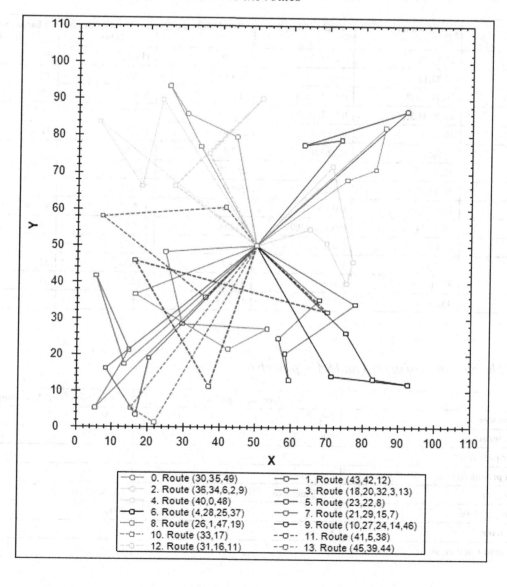

ingly, the null hypothesis, "the mean difference between GAs' solution population's fitness values and SA's solution population's fitness values is not zero" and "the mean difference between GAs' solution population's fitness values and HGASA's solution population's fitness values is not zero" can be rejected with a probability less than one in a ten hundred. However, the null hypothesis

about "the mean difference between HGASA's solution population's fitness values and SA's population's fitness values is not zero" can be rejected according to the tests. Also, standard deviations, mean values and confidence intervals are calculated (Table 8). These results support the superiority of HGASA in terms of time requirements and fitness values.

Table 6. The solution of the hypothetical VRPTW

Routes	Customers	Total waiting time	Total route time	Total route distance	Empty vehicle capacity
0	30,35,49	0,0,8,0	192.86	119.16	49
1	43,42,12	0,0,0	226.47	153.57	49
2	36,34,6,2,9	0,1,54,0,0,0	201.29	116.95	38
3	18,20,32,3,13	0,8,05,0,0,0	266.08	177.93	41
4	40,0,48	0,3,69,0	270.91	178.12	31
5	23,22,8	0,2,63,0	237.95	160.62	47
6	4,28,25,37	0,0,0,0	255.79	146.89	9
7	21,29,15,7	0,0,0,0	295.35	214.35	40
8	26,1,47,19	0,0,4,43,0	238.69	125.36	9
9	10,27,24,14,46	0,0,11,72,0,0	252.96	135.94	13
10	33,17	0,0	214.95	144.75	52
11	41,5,38	0,0,0	284.73	196.53	32
12	31,16,11	0,0,0	211.19	133.79	44
13	45,39,44	0,0,0	196.63	125.53	51

Table 7. The operators of the GA and SA approaches

	Genetic Algorithms	Simulated Annealing
Population size	200	-
Elitism percentage	%5	-
Crossover probability	0.2	-
Mutation probability	0.8	-
Process length	200 generations	100 iterations
İnitial temperature	-	2000 °C
Cooling factor	-	0.95
K Adjustment Coefficient	-	1

Table 8. GA, SA and HGASA results' mean values, standard deviation and confidence interval values in terms of time requirements and fitness values

	Time requirements			Fitness values		
	GA	SA	HGASA	GA	SA	HGASA
Mean value	14.3234	16.4505	12.5374	0.8752	0.8202	0.8181
Standard deviation	2.2032	0.2745	0.2716	0.054	0.026	0.0247
Confidence interval (α=0.5)	14.1748-14.4720	16.4320-16.4690	12.5190-12.5557	0.8715-0.8788	0.8184-0.8219	0.8165-0.8198

Figure 5. % Deviations from the best known route (vehicle) numbers for the Solomon's benchmark problems

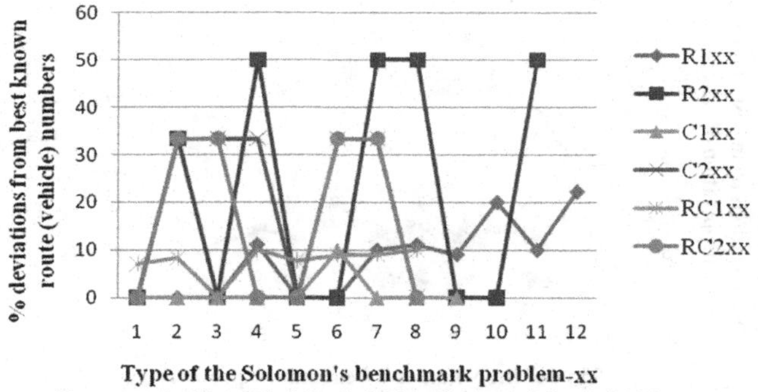

Type of the Solomon's benchmark problem-xx
For example, if xx=01, R1xx is R101; if xx=11, R1xx is R111

Analyzing the Validation of the Proposed Methodology

The proposed HGASA methodology is adapted to solve the well-known benchmark problems of Solomon (http://w.cba.neu.edu/~msolomon/problems.htm). For these test problems, two objectives are considered: minimization of number of vehicles (routes) and minimization of the distances. Solomon proposed six groups of test problems (R1, R2, C1, C2, RC1, and RC2) with different features. The customers of the classes R1 and R2 are uniformly distributed, whereas the customers of classes C1 and C2 are arranged in clusters. The problem sets RC1 and RC2 constitute a mixture of the classes R and C. The classes contain 8–12 different problem instances. The instances within each problem class differ only with respect to the customers' time windows. The customers' coordinates within one class are the same. R1, C1 and RC1 problems have short scheduling horizons and the vehicles have only small capacities. Therefore, each vehicle serves only a few customers. In contrast, R2, C2 and RC2 instances have longer scheduling horizons and the vehicles have higher capacities. Each vehicle supplies more customers and therefore, compared to the type 1 problems, fewer vehicles are needed (Muller, 2010).

For the validation of the proposed HGASA algorithm, Solomon's 56 benchmark problems are solved via the model's adapted version. For the adaptation, the number of objective functions is decreased as it contains only the number of routes and the total route distances minimization objective. General features of the algorithm remain same, i.e. the operators and parameter values are valid for the test process. Number of routes minimization objective is the primary goal of the model and weighted more than the total distance minimization objective. When the tests are realized, for the 26 of the problems, best value for the number of routes can be obtained. For the 6 of the problems, deviations less than 10% are obtained. For the remaining problems there are deviations from the best values between 10%-50% (Figure 5).

As can be expected, for the less weighted objective, total route distance minimization objective, the observed deviations are more than the first objective's deviations from the best known values. As can be seen from Figure 6, deviations from the best known values are observed between 0% and 242.36%.

In general, it can be concluded that proposed HGASA algorithm is more successful for the R1, C1 and RC1 problem classes from the point of route numbers and R1, RC1 problem classes from the point of route distances. In conclusion, it can be said that, proposed algorithm is more success-

Figure 6. % Deviations from the best known route distances for the Solomon's benchmark problems

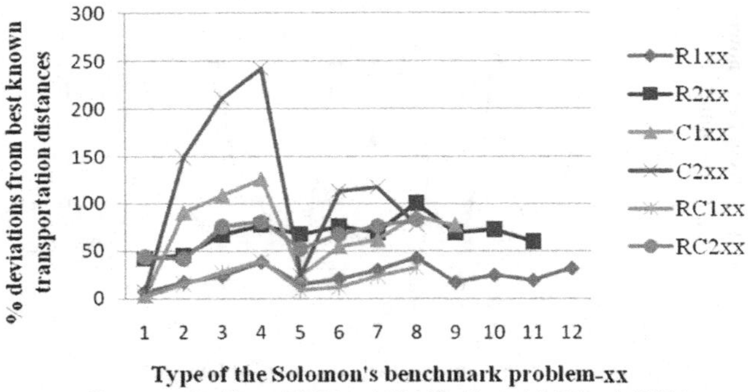

ful for the problems which have short scheduling horizons and the vehicles with relatively small capacities.

FUTURE RESEARCH DIRECTIONS

As a future research direction, utilized techniques can be compared with the other meta-heuristics, such as Tabu Search, Scatter Search, Lagrangean Heuristics etc. Also, more effective hybrid approaches can be investigated. The hybridization of GA with other meta-heuristics, especially with the memory based techniques -Tabu Search, Scatter Search, etc. - may be considered. These techniques' memory advantages may increase the achievement level to get better solutions.

CONCLUSION

In this paper, a HGASA approach for the VRPTW is presented in order to decrease the level of possible weaknesses of the pure GA and pure SA strategies. Some small improvements may be overlooked with GA approach. On the other hand, SA's solution is highly dependent on the initial solution and if the initial solution is not good enough, the convergence to the optimum solution may be a time consuming process. For this reason, in this study, the HGASA approach is proposed and firstly, an initial solution for SA is found via GA with the random searches in the solution space, then, this initial solution is improved via SA with little but effective improvements. According to the statistical analysis, the HGASA approach proves its effectiveness in terms of time consumption and fitness values. Also proposed methodology is tested with Solomon's benchmark problems and proves its effectiveness for the problems which have short scheduling horizons and the vehicles with small capacities.

REFERENCES

Achuthan, N. R., Caccetta, L., & Hill, S. P. (1997). On the Vehicle Routing Problem. *Nonlinear Analysis, Theory. Methods & Applications, 30*(7), 4277–4288.

Azi, N., Gendreau, M., & Potvin, J. Y. (2007). An exact algorithm for a single-vehicle routing problem with time windows and multiple routes. *European Journal of Operational Research, 178*(3), 755–766. doi:10.1016/j.ejor.2006.02.019

Badeu, P., Guertin, F., Gendreau, M., Potvin, J. Y., & Taillard, E. (1997). A Parallel Tabu Search Heuristic for the Vehicle Routing Problem with Time Windows. *Transportation Research Part C, Emerging Technologies, 5*(2), 109–122. doi:10.1016/S0968-090X(97)00005-3

Baker, B. M., & Ayechew, M. A. (2003). A genetic algorithm for the vehicle routing problem. *Computers & Operations Research, 30*(5), 787–800. doi:10.1016/S0305-0548(02)00051-5

Bell, J. E., & McMullen, P. R. (2004). Ant colony optimization techniques for the vehicle routing problem. *Advanced Engineering Informatics, 18*(1), 41–48. doi:10.1016/j.aei.2004.07.001

Breedam, A. V. (1995). Improvement heuristics for the Vehicle Routing Problem based on simulated annealing. *European Journal of Operational Research, 36*(3), 480–490. doi:10.1016/0377-2217(94)00064-J

Chen, H. K., Hsueh, C. F., & Chang, M. S. (2006). The real-time dependent vehicle routing problem. *Transportation Research Part E, Logistics and Transportation Review, 42*(5), 383–408. doi:10.1016/j.tre.2005.01.003

Cheng, C. B., & Mao, C. P. (2007). A modified ant colony system for solving the travelling salesman problem with time windows. *Mathematical and Computer Modelling, 46*(9-10), 1225–1235. doi:10.1016/j.mcm.2006.11.035

Desrochers, M., Desrosiers, J., & Solomon, M. M. (1992). A new optimization algorithm for the vehicle routing problem with time Windows. *Operations Research, 40*(2), 342–354. doi:10.1287/opre.40.2.342

Dowsland, K. (1993). Simulated annealing. In *Modern Heuristic Techniques for Combinatorial Problems*. New York: John Wiley & Sons.

Dror, M., & Levy, L. (1986). A vehicle routing improvement algorithm comparison of a "greedy" and a matching implementation for inventory routin. *Computers & Operations Research, 13*(1), 33–45. doi:10.1016/0305-0548(86)90062-6

Du, T., Wang, F. K., & Lu, P. Y. (2007). A real-time vehicle-dispatching system for consolidating milk runs. *Transportation Research Part E, Logistics and Transportation Review, 45*(5), 565–577. doi:10.1016/j.tre.2006.03.001

Du, T. C., Li, E. Y., & Chou, D. (2005). Dynamic vehicle routing for online B2C delivery. *Omega, 33*(1), 33–45. doi:10.1016/j.omega.2004.03.005

Eiben, A. E., & Smith, J. E. (2003). *Introduction to Evolutionary Computing*. New York: Springer.

Garcia-Najera, A., & Bullinaria, J. A. (2009). Bi-objective Optimization for the Vehicle Routing Problem with Time Windows: Using Route Similarity to Enhance Performance. *Lecture Notes in Computer Science, 5467*, 275–289. doi:10.1007/978-3-642-01020-0_24

Gen, M., & Cheng, R. (1997). *Genetic Algorithms and Engineering Design*. New York: John Wiley & Sons, Inc.

Hashimoto, H., Ibaraki, T., Imahori, S., & Yagiura, M. (2006). The vehicle routing problem with flexible time windows and traveling times. *Discrete Applied Mathematics, 154*(16), 2271–2290. doi:10.1016/j.dam.2006.04.009

He, R. S., & Hwang, S. E. (2006). Damage detection by an adaptive real-parameter simulated annealing genetic algorithms. *Computers & Structures, 84*(31-32), 2231–2243. doi:10.1016/j.compstruc.2006.08.031

Ho, S. C., & Haugland, D. (2004). A Tabu search heuristic for the vehicle routing problem with time windows and split deliveries. *Computers & Operations Research, 31*(12), 1947–1964. doi:10.1016/S0305-0548(03)00155-2

Homberger, J., & Gehring, H. (2005). A two-phase hybrid metaheuristic for the vehicle routing problem with time windows. *European Journal of Operational Research, 162*(1), 220–238. doi:10.1016/j.ejor.2004.01.027

Hwang, H. S. (2002). An improved model for vehicle routing problem with time constraints based on genetic algorithms. *Computers & Industrial Engineering, 42*(2-4), 361–369. doi:10.1016/S0360-8352(02)00033-5

Jeon, G., Leep, H. R., & Shim, J. Y. (2007). A vehicle routing problem solved by using a hybrid genetic algorithm. *Computers & Industrial Engineering, 53*(4), 680–692. doi:10.1016/j.cie.2007.06.031

Jozefowiez, N., Semet, F., & Talbi, E.-G. (2008). Multi-objective vehicle routing problems. *European Journal of Operational Research, 189*(2), 293–309. doi:10.1016/j.ejor.2007.05.055

Jwo, W. S., Liu, C. W., & Liu, C. C. (1999). Large-scale optimal VAR planning by hybrid simulated annealing/genetic algorithm. *Electrical Power and Energy Systems, 21*, 39–44. doi:10.1016/S0142-0615(98)00020-9

Kallehauge, B. (2008). Formulations and exact algorithms for the vehicle routing problem with time windows. *Computers & Operations Research, 35*(7), 2307–2330. doi:10.1016/j.cor.2006.11.006

Kirkpatrick, S., Gelatt, C. D., & Vecchi, M. P. (1983). Optimization by Simulated Annealing. *Science, 220*(4598), 671–680. doi:10.1126/science.220.4598.671

Kontroravdis, G., & Bard, J. (1995). A GRASP for the vehicle routing problem with time windows. *ORSA Journal on Computing, 7*(1), 10–23.

M'Hallah, R. (2007). Minimizing total earliness and tardiness on a single machine using a hybrid heuristic. *Computers & Operations Research, 34*(10), 3126–3142. doi:10.1016/j.cor.2005.11.021

Mazzeo, S., & Loiseau, I. (2004). An Ant Colony Algorithm for the Capacitated Vehicle Routing. *Electronic Notes in Discrete Mathematics, 18*, 181–186. doi:10.1016/j.endm.2004.06.029

Muller, J. (2010). Approximative solutions to the bicriterion Vehicle Routing Problem with Time Windows. *European Journal of Operational Research, 202*(1), 223–231. doi:10.1016/j.ejor.2009.04.029

Osman, M. S., Abo-Sinna, M. A., & Mousa, A. A. (2005). A effective genetic algorithm approach to multiobjective routing problems (MORPs). *Applied Mathematics and Computation, 163*(2), 769–781. doi:10.1016/j.amc.2003.10.058

Potvin, J. Y., & Robillard, C. (1995). Clustering for vehicle routing with a competitive neural network. *Neurocomputing, 8*(2), 125–139. doi:10.1016/0925-2312(94)00012-H

Potvin, J. Y., & Rousseau, J. M. (1995). A parallel route building algorithm for the vehicle routing and scheduling problem with time Windows. *European Journal of Operational Research, 66*(3), 331–340. doi:10.1016/0377-2217(93)90221-8

Potvin, J. Y., & Rousseau, J. M. (1995). An Exchange heuristic for routing problems with time windows. *The Journal of the Operational Research Society, 46*(12), 1433–1446.

Prins, C. (2004). A simple and effective evolutionary algorithm for the vehicle routing problem. *Computers & Operations Research, 31*(12), 1985–2002. doi:10.1016/S0305-0548(03)00158-8

Rochat, Y., & Taillard, E. (1995). Probabilistic diversification and intensification in local search for vehicle routing. *Journal of Heuristics, 1*, 147–167. doi:10.1007/BF02430370

Russell, R. A. (1995). Hybrid heuristics for the vehicle routing problem with time windows. *Transportation Science, 29*(2), 156–166. doi:10.1287/trsc.29.2.156

Russell, R. A., & Chiang, W. C. (2006). Scatter search for the vehicle routing problem with time Windows. *European Journal of Operational Research, 169*(2), 606–622. doi:10.1016/j.ejor.2004.08.018

Seckiner, A. U., & Kurt, M. (2007). A Simulated annealing approach to the solution of job rotation scheduling problems. *Applied Mathematics and Computation, 188*(1), 31–45. doi:10.1016/j.amc.2006.09.082

Solomon, M. M. (1987). Algorithms for the vehicle routing and scheduling problems with time window constraints. *Operations Research, 35*(2), 254–265. doi:10.1287/opre.35.2.254

Solomon, M. M., Baker, E. K., & Schaffer, J. R. (1998). Vehicle routing and scheduling problems with time window constraints: Efficient implementations of solution improvement procedures. In Golden, B. L., & Assad, A. A. (Eds.), *Vehicle Routing: Methods and Studies* (pp. 85–105). Amsterdam: North Holand.

Taillard, E., Badeau, P., Gendreau, M., Guertin, F., & Potvin, J. Y. (1995). A new neighborhood structure for the vehicle routing problem with time windows. *Technical report CRT-95-66. Center de recherche sur les transport*, Universite de Montreal, Montreal, Canada

Tan, K. C., Lee, L. H., Zhu, Q. L., & Ou, K. (2001). Heuristic methods for vehicle routing problem with time windows. *Artificial Intelligence in Engineering, 15*, 281–295. doi:10.1016/S0954-1810(01)00005-X

Tang, J., Pan, Z., Fung, R. Y. K., & Lau, H. (2009). Vehicle routing problem with fuzzy time windows. *Fuzzy Sets and Systems, 160*(5), 683–695. doi:10.1016/j.fss.2008.09.016

Tavakkoli-Moghaddam, R., Safaei, N., & Gholipour, Y. (2006). A hybrid simulated annealing for capacitated vehicle routing problems with the independent route length. *Applied Mathematics and Computation, 176*(2), 445–454. doi:10.1016/j.amc.2005.09.040

Thangiah, S. R., Potvin, J. Y., & Sun, T. (1996). Heuristic approaches to vehicle routing with backhauls and time windows. *Computers & Operations Research, 23*(11), 1043–1057. doi:10.1016/0305-0548(96)00018-4

Tuzkaya, G., Gülsün, B., & Bildik, E. (2011). Reverse logistics network design using a hybrid genetic algorithm and simulated annealing methodology. In Mahdavi, I., Mohebbi, S., Cho, N. (Editors), Electronic *Supply Network Coordination in Intelligent and Dynamic Environment: Modeling and Implementation* (pp. 168-186). Hershey, PA:IGI Global, USA.

Tuzkaya, G., Gülsün, B., & Onsel, S. (in press). A methodology for the strategic design of reverse logistics networks and its application in Turkish white goods industry. *International Journal of Production Research.* doi:.doi:10.1080/00207543.2010.492804

Yao, R., Yang, B., Cheng, G., Tao, X., & Meng, F. (2003). Kinetics research for the synthesis of branch ether using genetic-simulated annealing algorithm with multi-pattern evolution. *Chemical Engineering Journal, 94*(2), 113–119. doi:10.1016/S1385-8947(03)00025-1

Yoo, M., & Gen, M. (2007). Scheduling algorithm for real-time tasks using multiobjective hybrid genetic algorithm in heterogeneous multiprocessors system. *Computers & Operations Research, 34*(10), 3084–3098. doi:10.1016/j.cor.2005.11.016

Yu, H., Fang, H., Yao, P., & Yuan, Y. (2000). A combined genetic algorithm/simulated annealing algorithm for large scale system energy integration. *Computers & Chemical Engineering*, *24*(8), 2023–2035. doi:10.1016/S0098-1354(00)00601-3

ADDITIONAL READING

Dan, Z., Cai, L., & Zheng, L. (2009). Improved multi-agent system for the vehicle routing problem with time windows. *Tsinghua Science and Technology*, *14*(3), 407–412. doi:10.1016/S1007-0214(09)70058-6

Eksioglu, B., Vural, A. V., & Reisman, A. (2009). The vehicle routing problem: A taxonomic review. *Computers & Industrial Engineering*, *57*(4), 1472–1483. doi:10.1016/j.cie.2009.05.009

El-Sherbeny, N. (2010). Vehicle routing with time windows: An overview of exact, heuristic and metaheuristic methods. *Journal of King Saud University-Science*, *22*(3), 123–131. doi:10.1016/j.jksus.2010.03.002

Garcia-Najera, A., & Buillinaria, J. A. (2011). An improved multi-objective evolutionary algoritghm for the vehicle routing problem with time windows. *Computers & Operations Research*, *38*(1), 287–300. doi:10.1016/j.cor.2010.05.004

Ghoseiri, K., & Ghannadpour, S. F. (2010). Multi-objective vehicle routing problem with time windows using goal programming and genetic algorithms. *Applied Soft Computing*, *10*(4), 1096–1107. doi:10.1016/j.asoc.2010.04.001

Kuo, Y. (2010). Using simulated annealing to minimize fuel consumption for the time-dependent vehicle routing problem. *Computers & Industrial Engineering*, *59*(1), 157–165. doi:10.1016/j.cie.2010.03.012

Marinakis, Y., & Marinaki, M. (2010). A hybrid genetic-particle swarm optimization algorithm for the vehicle routing problem. *Expert Systems with Applications*, *37*(2), 1446–1455. doi:10.1016/j.eswa.2009.06.085

Nagata, Y., Brasysy, O., & Dullaert, W. (2010). A penalty-based edge assembly memetic algorithm for the vehicle routing problem with time windows. *Computers & Operations Research*, *37*(4), 724–737. doi:10.1016/j.cor.2009.06.022

Ngueveu, S. U., Prins, C., & Calvo, R. W. (2010). A effective mememtic algorithm for the cumulative capacitated vehicle routing problem. *Computers & Operations Research*, *37*(11), 1877–1885. doi:10.1016/j.cor.2009.06.014

Tang, J., Pan, Z., Fung, R. Y. K., & Lau, H. (2009). Vehicle routing problem with fuzzy time windows. *Fuzzy Sets and Systems*, *160*(5), 683–695. doi:10.1016/j.fss.2008.09.016

Yu, B., Yang, Z. Z., & Yao, B. Z. (2011). A hybrid algorithm for vehicle routing problem with time windows. *Expert Systems with Applications*, *38*(1), 435–441. doi:10.1016/j.eswa.2010.06.082

KEY TERMS AND DEFINITIONS

Genetic Algorithms: GA is an evolutionary algorithm technique which uses a number of technique specific operators such as mutation, crossover, elitism, etc. (Tuzkaya *et al.*, 2011).

Hybrid Meta-Heuristics: Hybrid meta-heuristics are the integration of two or more meta-heuristics for the utilization from their advantages which are coming from different features of each (Tuzkaya *et al.*, 2011).

Meta-Heuristics: Meta-heuristics are solution methods that orchestrate an interaction between local improvement procedures and higher level strategies to create a process capable of escaping from local optima and performing a robust search of a solution space (Glover and Kochenberger, 2003).

Simulated Annealing: SA is a search technique for the combinatorial optimization problems with the capability of jumping out of the local optima (Tuzkaya *et al.*, 2011).

Vehicle Routing Problem (VRP): VRPs are concerned with the delivery of some commodities from one or more depots to a number of customer locations with known demand (Achuthan *et al.*, 1997).

Vehicle Routing Problem with Time Windows (VRPTW): VRPTW is a kind of VRP in which the customers must be served within time windows considering the capacity constraints of the vehicles.

Chapter 5
Strategies for an Integrated Distribution Problem

Helena R. Lourenço
Universitat Pompeu Fabra, Spain

Rita Ribeiro
Catholic University of Portugal (Porto), Portugal

ABSTRACT

Problems arising in the logistics of commercial distribution are complex and involve several players and decision levels. One of the most important decisions is the design of the routes to distribute the products in an efficient and inexpensive way but also satisfying marketing objectives such as customer loyalty. This chapter explores three different distribution routing strategies. The first strategy corresponds to the classical vehicle routing problem where total distance or cost is minimized. This one is usually an objective of the Logistics department. The second strategy is a master route strategy with daily adaptations where customer loyalty is maximized, which is one of the objectives of the Marketing department. The authors propose a third strategy which takes into account the cross-functional planning between the Logistics and the Marketing department through a multi-objective model. All strategies are analyzed in a multi-period scenario. A metaheuristic algorithm based on the Iterated Local Search is proposed and applied to optimize each strategy. An analysis and comparison of the three strategies is presented through a computational experiment. The cross-functional planning strategy leads to solutions that put in practice the coordination between the two functional areas of Marketing and Logistics and better meet business objectives in general.

DOI: 10.4018/978-1-61350-086-6.ch005

INTRODUCTION

The growing number of problems that firms are facing nowadays in relation to the distribution of their products and services has lead Logistics and Marketing to be of primary concern to many industries. An important aspect of the logistics management task is to coordinate the activities of the traditional distribution functions together with purchasing, materials planning, manufacturing, marketing and often R&D. One important aspect of the integration process is cross-functional planning, which consists of coordinating different areas inside the firm, allowing for cost reductions and service improvement (Christopher, 1998).

The motivation of our work arises in the context of integration of logistics functions with other functions of the firm. In our case, we will focus our study on two key areas: Distribution and Logistics management and Marketing management. One source of competitive advantage for many firms is the development of an integrated relationship between the firm's marketing and logistics functions, as this integration has the ability to further enhance the firm's customer focus. This integration can be obtained by doing an integrated and coordinated planning of the logistics operations. In our case we focus on the distribution strategies. On one hand, the importance of good distribution strategies in today's competitive markets cannot be overstressed. In many industries, an important component of distribution systems is the design of the routes of vehicles to serve their customers' demand. On the other hand, as pointed out by some industry leaders, new trends in supply-chain management include, "…better customer service… greater customer sophistication" (Partyka & Hall, 2000). Customer service is becoming more important. Customers demand more than a product. They demand a product arriving on time via an easy ordering system or just-in-time distribution.

In this work, we will study integrated distribution management from a strategic point of view. The logistics distribution problem consists of deciding how to assign customers to vehicles and how to design the routes made by each vehicle minimizing a transportation cost function. This is the well-known Vehicle Routing Problem (**VRP**) (Toth & Vigo, 2002b). The transportation cost represents a large percentage of the total logistics costs, so it makes sense to try to reduce this cost. Having the products arrive on time is also an important objective of the logistics department when planning distribution.

However, after interviews with several retailing companies, we realized that many of them do not consider minimizing transportation cost as the prime objective, but rather place greater importance on the customer relationship and customer service in the designing of distribution routes (Ribeiro, 2004). Marketing and Sales departments argue that drivers also perform sales activities and have responsibilities for promotion and the introduction of new products. So, if a driver is assigned always to the same customers this creates a good relationship and it leads to a sales increase.

We thus identified the two different primary strategies in the design of distribution routes: the Logistics department wants to minimize transportation costs and the Marketing and Sales department wants to maximize customer relationships, i.e. assign the same driver to each customer every day or most days.

This led us to the following question: What is the best strategy for an efficient distribution? On the one hand we have the classical VRP minimizing a transportation cost function. On the other hand, we have the strategy to always assign the same driver to the same customer to maximize customer loyalty. Beyond evaluating these two strategies, we propose a third one based on a bi-objective approach that tries to balance the two previous ones. This last strategy involves the implementation of integrated distribution processes.

The motivation for the present work arose from distribution problems faced by the food and beverage industry. In these industries, the tendency is to have lower inventories and higher delivery frequencies. Please note that the objective of this work is not to provide a system to optimize a particular distribution problem, but to study and analyze what is the best planning strategy for the distribution of a product among a set of customers.

In the next section, we present in detail the different distribution strategies proposed:

1. the classical VRP strategy, where the objective is to minimize the transportation costs;
2. the master routes strategy, where the main objective is maximizing the number of customers assigned to the same driver for a set period of time;
3. the new bi-objective strategy we propose that considers the integration between the marketing and logistics departments.

In third section, we present a brief literature review, followed by a section where we present the mathematical models for the three strategies proposed. Next section presents the tool designed to optimize the routes. This tool is based on Iterated Local Search Heuristics, and we use the same tool to optimize the routes in order to be able to make a fair comparison. In the results section, we analyze the results and, in particular, the impact on integrated decision-making between the logistics and marketing departments. Finally, in the last section, we present the conclusions of the work.

THE DISTRIBUTION STRATEGIES

Distribution strategy has a great impact on the firm's performance, in particular in the retailing area. Frequently, this strategy is defined by the Logistics department, but sometimes the decision is made by the Marketing department. The objectives when defining this distribution strategy can be very different depending on the department involved. In this work, we will define and analyze three different distribution strategies that

reflect different potential distribution policies in an organization.

The first strategy (Strategy 1) has a distribution policy that minimizes distance or transport costs. The objective consists in minimizing total routing cost, measured in distance units as in the classical VRP. This is a well-known problem and there exist a very large number of articles published on this subject. However, the objective function of this problem is often an object of criticism by users and planners, since it does not take into consideration other concerns of the company, for example, customer service and customer loyalty. The second strategy (Strategy 2) tries to implement a marketing policy based on customer service and loyalty. In an increasingly competitive environment, many firms adopt strategies of tight relationships with their customers where loyalty and friendship play a key role, through the delivering agents (Baker, Cronin, & Hopkins, 2009). By this strategy, routes are predefined so that each delivering agent or driver is associated with a specific set of customers. The third strategy (Strategy 3) is the one that considers marketing and distribution objectives at the same time, in an integrated manner.

The distribution strategies correspond to different situations and concerns inside the firm. By comparing them, we can analyze the effect that integrating two areas can have on the distribution policies. The objective of this analysis is to provide a set of possible alternative solutions to the decision maker, who, with the use of additional information on each particular distribution problem, can then make a good choice.

The strategies are evaluated for a planning horizon of a week, five working days. The choice of this period is based on the need for a strategic perspective; we want to study the impact of a sequence of decisions on different objectives. As a consequence, we need several periods to analyze the marketing effect and a week seems to be a reasonable choice since in many industries, the behavior of the orders for a customer follows a weekly pattern (examples are the Beverage & Food industry). In any case, this assumption could be relaxed and the problem could be extended to a larger number of periods.

Strategy 1: Distance Minimization

In this strategy, the distribution policy is constructed based on routing cost or distance. Cost reduction is one of the biggest concerns in transportation and distribution management, but not the only one as we will see later. We want to find the route for each of the vehicles that will pass through the demand points in such a way as to satisfy all the demand with the smallest transport cost or distance. The classical VRP considers only one period at a time and chooses the optimal routes for that period. Strategy 1 corresponds to the classical Vehicle Routing Problem (VRP) repeated for each day of the planning horizon.

Strategy 2: Master Routes

The second strategy is based on marketing principles, and the distribution strategy is based on service measures. An important source of value to the firm can be obtained from a close relationship between the firm and its customers. Drivers see customers regularly, and perform sales activities and have responsibilities for promotions and the introduction of new products. Therefore, it is believed by the Marketing department that if the same driver is assigned always to the same customer this can create a good relationship and leads to increased sales.

This marketing policy is giving emphasis to the personal relationship between drivers and customers as a way to improve customer service. One of the identified advantages of this customer relationship management policy is that it makes it more difficult for a customer to switch to another provider. It is known that relationships require a time investment from both the customer and the provider (Simchi-Levi, Kaminsky, & Simchi-Levi, 2003). These marketing strategies allow the firm to obtain more information on customer needs. And, at the same time, it becomes easier to introduce new products, define promotions and even speeds up the delivery process due to experience effects on both sides. In the marketing literature, we can find several studies of relationships between firm employees and customers that lead to an improvement in customer satisfaction and loyalty, see for example (Baker et al., 2009), (Guenzi & Pelloni, 2004), (Chao, Fu, & Lu, 2007) and (Barroso-Castro, Armario, & Marin-Ruiz, 2004). These authors mention that maintaining a long term relationship between employees (in our case drivers) and customers may improve customer perceptions of the quality of services received, and consequent company performance.

In this strategy, each driver will serve always the same customers. So, master routes are designed considering all customers and an average daily demand, and then these routes are adapted daily so the driver always visits the same customers and he or she only visits customers with demand. Capacity constraints are also taken into account.

Strategy 3: Multi-Objective

The third strategy is the integrated distribution management model, which consists of taking into account in the decision process the concerns of the Logistics department and Marketing department i.e. the reduction of transportation costs and the emphasis on the personal relationship between driver and customer. We propose a multi-objective model with two objectives, each objective corresponds to a different function. The first is the transportation cost and the second a marketing function. This strategy tries to include in the same model the objectives of the two previous strategies. The best solution for the transportation problem might not always be the best solution for the marketing objective. In some cases, these two objectives may conflict and that is the main justification for a trade-off analysis between these two objectives. We need to find a solution (or several solutions) that integrate marketing and logistics objectives.

In the next section, we will present a brief literature review. In following section, we will present the well-known mathematical model for the VRP that serves as the basis for the models of the different strategies, and also present the mathematical model for each strategy.

LITERATURE REVIEW ON VRP

The classical VRP model is behind the models for the three distribution strategies. This problem is an NP-hard problem, which implies a non-polynomial increase in the size of the solutions space when the number of nodes is increased. A significant amount of research effort has been dedicated to VRP. See the survey articles on VRP by (Laporte & Osman, 1995), (Laporte, 1992), (Bodin, Golden, Assad, & Ball, 1983), (Christofides, Mingozzi, & Toth, 1981), (Fisher, 1995), (Crainic & Laporte, 1998), (Cordeau, Gendreau, Laporte, Potvin, & Semet, 2002), (Laporte, 2007), (Golden, Raghavan, & Wasil, 2008) and (Juan, Faulin, Ruiz, Barrios, & Caballé, 2010). An extensive list of VRP research papers can be found on http://www.imm.dtu. dk/~orgroup/VRP_ref/. Although this problem has been studied for decades, (Laporte, 2009), it still gets the attention of many researchers.

Although the VRP is an important problem, the main contribution of this chapter is not regarding the VRP but rather Strategic Distribution Decisions. After several interviews with different Food & Beverages Companies we realized that in decision making about distribution routes, it was not only cost that was important, but also customer service and customer loyalty. We found that the Operations Research literature focuses mainly on minimizing transportation cost or distance, whereas Marketing literature has continuously emphasized the importance of human interactions and relationships in the process of delivery goods.

Several studies indicate that good relationships between firm employees and customers lead to greater customer satisfaction and loyalty. Baker, Cronin & Hopkins (2009) conclude that higher levels of involvement lead to greater levels of consumer loyalty. Guenzi & Pelloni (2004) mention that building customer loyalty is increasingly a major goal for a large number of companies and, also that a strong relationship between front-line employees and customers positively affects customer satisfaction and loyalty to the company. Chao, Fu & Lu (2007) say that customer orientation and interpersonal relationships may reinforce the quality-loyalty linkage. Barroso-Castro, Armario & Marin-Ruiz (2004) analyzes the effect that service company employee behavior has on customer perceptions of the quality of service received, and consequent company performance.

Therefore the proposed distribution strategies are based not only on the classical VRP, but also on a multi-period and multi-objective vehicle-routing problem. As far as we know there are no studies on routing problems with multiple periods and this type of marketing oriented objective function. There are some multi-objective VRP that consider other types of objectives. Hong & Park (1999) consider the minimization of customer waiting time as the second objective function, in a VRP with time windows constraints. Lee & Ueng (1999) developed an integer linear model that searches for the shortest travel path and balances driver's load simultaneously. The objectives are related to travel and loading time. Pasia, Doerner, Hartl, & Reimann (2007) present a population-based local search for solving a bi-objective vehicle routing problem. The objectives of the problem are minimization of the tour length and balancing the routes. Muller (2010) presents an approximate method to the bi-criterion Vehicle Routing Problem with soft time-windows. Jozefowiez, Semet, & Talbi (2008) surveys the existing research related to multi-objective optimization in routing problems. It examines routing problems in terms of their definitions, their objectives, and the multi-objective algorithms proposed for solving them.

Also, some work on periodic VRP has been done. Baptista, Oliveira, & Zúquete (2002) present a period vehicle routing problem based on the assignment problem and the vehicle routing problem. Collection days have to be assigned to each customer and vehicle routes have to be designed for each day of the period (time horizon) so that the total distribution cost is minimized. Francis, Smilowitz, & Tzur (2006) present a variation of the periodic VRP in which service frequency is a decision of the model. Mourgaya & Vanderbeck (2007) propose a column generation-based heuristic for the periodic VRP. Hemmelmayr, Doerner, & Hartl (2009) propose a new heuristic for the Periodic Vehicle Routing Problem (PVRP) based on variable neighborhood search.

The main contribution of this work is to present a new model and new method to solve a multi-period and multi-objective vehicle-routing problem, but the most important contribution is to analyze three different alternative distribution strategies that can be adopted in a firm when planning their routing and evaluate the consequences of adopting each one of them.

THE MODELS FOR THE DISTRIBUTION STRATEGIES

The most well known model for routing is a basic VRP. This model considers a set of nodes, representing retailers or customers, at a known location, that must be served by one depot. Each node has a known demand. A set of vehicles, with equal capacity is available to serve the customers. The routes must start and finish at the depot. The objective is to define the set of routes to serve all customers with minimal cost.

For each pair of nodes, a fixed known cost is associated. We assume this cost matrix is symmetric and can represent a real cost, distance or time. The main constraints of the problem are that

all the demand must be satisfied and the vehicles' capacity cannot be exceeded.

The basic VRP is a generalization of the Traveling Salesman Problem, where more than one vehicle is available, for TSP references see for example (Lawler, Lenstra, Rinnooy Kan, & Shmoys, 1985). There are several formulations of the classical VRP in the literature, for some of these formulations see (Fisher & Jaikumar, 1978), (Fisher & Jaikumar, 1981), (Kulkarni & Bhave, 1985), (Gouveia, 1995) and (Toth & Vigo, 2002a).

The classical model of the VRP can be formulated as an integer linear programming and this is the formulation we will use throughout later chapters.

Consider the following data:

$I = 1,..., n$, set of nodes, that correspond to the different locations of the customers, node 1 corresponds to the depot.

$K = 1,..., m$, set of vehicles;

Q, capacity of each vehicle;

q_i, demand of customer i, $i = 1,...,n$;

c_{ij} cost of going from i to j, $i = 1,...,n$; $j = 1,...,n$.

This formulation considers two types of variables:

$$x_{ijk} = \begin{cases} 1, & \text{if vehicle } k \text{ visits customer } j \\ & \text{immediatly after customer } i \\ 0, & \text{otherwise} \end{cases}$$

The formulation of the problem is:

Objective Function: $Min \sum_{i=1}^{n} \sum_{j=1}^{n} c_{ij} \sum_{k=1}^{m} x_{ijk}$ (1)

Subject to:

$$\sum_{k=1}^{m} y_{ik} = 1, \quad \forall \ i = 2,...,n \qquad (2)$$

$$\sum_{k=1}^{m} y_{1k} = m \tag{3}$$

$$\sum_{i=2}^{n} q_i y_{ik} \leq Q, \quad \forall \ k = 1, ..., m \tag{4}$$

$$\sum_{j=1}^{n} x_{ijk} = \sum_{j=1}^{n} x_{ijk} = y_{ik}, \quad \forall \ i = 2, ..., n; k = 1, ..., m \tag{5}$$

$$\sum_{j,i \in S} x_{ijk} \leq |S| - 1, \quad \forall S \text{ non-empty subset of } \{2, ..., n\}; k = 1, ..., m \tag{6}$$

$$x_{ijk} \in \{0, 1\}; y_{ik} \in \{0, 1\}, \quad \forall i = 1, ..., n; k = 1, ..., m \tag{7}$$

Constraint (2) ensures that each customer is visited by one vehicle only. Constraint (3) guarantees that all vehicles visit the depot. Constraint (4) represents the vehicle capacity constraint. For each vehicle k, we guarantee that the sum of the demand of the nodes that the vehicle covers is less than or equal to its maximum capacity. Here we assume that none of the customers has a daily demand that exceeds Q. The constraint (5) ensures that if a vehicle visits a customer it also has to leave that customer. Constraint (6) is the sub-tour elimination constraint. This constraint implies that the arcs selected contain no sub-cycles. It states that for every vehicle, the following holds: for every non-empty subset S of {2,..,n}, the number of arcs that are in the route of this vehicle, with both nodes belonging to S, has to be less than or equal to the number of elements of S minus 1. The last constraint (7) defines the variables x and y as binary. The objective function is minimizing the total cost of the routes.

The TSP is a sub-problem of the VRP, the TSP belongs to the class of NP-hard (non-deterministic polynomial time) problems, and so do the basic VRP and extensions. This means that the compu-

tational complexity of the problem grows exponentially with its size, i.e., it grows exponentially with the number of customers.

In this section we will present the mathematical models associated with the three strategies. First of all, we describe the assumptions of the model.

We assume that the firm is responsible for the distribution of its own products. Therefore, there are no questions of outsourcing to be handled. These firms face the pressures of a competitive market making them concerned about both consumer satisfaction and internal efficiency.

The classical VRP considers only one period and chooses the optimal routes for that period. Here we will introduce more periods by considering a week-long analysis. Each day we have a different set of customers to serve and different corresponding quantities to deliver. Reduction of inventory levels and increasing frequency of orders are tendencies in many businesses to lower stock handling costs.

Other assumptions of the model are:

- All the demand is satisfied on the same day that it is required and not on any other day of the week.
- Only unloading is done at each customer.
- The number of vehicles is fixed and there are no fixed costs associated with the use of the vehicles. They all have the same capacity. Moreover, the number of vehicles available is enough to satisfy all the demand.
- Each vehicle is assigned to a driver. We consider that each driver works every day of the period in question.
- One vehicle can only be used once a day and the time it takes to deliver the full capacity is less than a working day.

Next, we will present the model in detail. The following data is considered in the mathematical formulation:

$i, I,$ index and set of nodes, $I=1,...,n$ where 1 is the depot and 2 to n are the customers locations;

$k, K,$ index and set of vehicles, $K=1,...,m;$

$t, T,$ index and set of days which represent the period, $T=1,...,p;$

$T_i,$ set of days where customer i has a demand that is greater than zero, i = 2,...,n;

$q_i^t,$ demand of customer i on day t, i = 1,...,n and $t = 1,...,p;$

$c_{ij},$ the cost of going from i to j, this is a fixed matrix , $i=1,...,n$ and $j=1,...,n;$

$Q,$ capacity of a vehicle.

The variables of the model are:

$$x_{ijk}^t = \begin{cases} 1, & \text{if vehicle } k \text{ visits customer } j \\ & \text{immediatly after customer } i \text{ on day } t \\ 0, & \text{otherwise} \end{cases}$$

$$y_{ik}^t = \begin{cases} 1, & \text{if customer } i \text{ is visited by vehicle } k \text{ on day } t \\ 0, & \text{otherwise} \end{cases}$$

Strategy 1: Distance Minimization

The objective function minimizes routing costs, for all customers during the week period. This strategy corresponds to repeating a classical VRP for each day of the week.

The formulation of this objective will be the same as the one used for the classical model but with a new parameter, t, representing the day of the week.

Objective function:

$$Min \sum_{t=1}^{p} \sum_{i=1}^{n} \sum_{j=1}^{n} \sum_{k=1}^{m} c_{ij} x_{ijk}^t \qquad (8)$$

Strategy 2: Master Routes

This strategy and the associated model are very close to common practice in many companies. It consists of: first defining "master routes" and,

afterwards performing daily adjustments depending on the demand of the customer and on the capacity of the vehicle. To obtain the "master routes" we consider a VRP model, where all customers are in the input data and the demand of each customer depends on the average daily demand. To adjust the daily routes we consider other constraints such as capacity and number of vehicles. The requirement that a customer will always be served by the same driver may have to be sacrificed but we will try to enforce this at least for the best customers. Therefore, the idea is: the better the customer, the more interest we have in maintaining the same driver.

The mathematical formulation for this strategy is identical to the one for the classical VRP for one period, but in this case all customers are considered for the "master routes".

Strategy 3: Multi-Objective

In this strategy, we propose a multi-objective model with two objectives: minimization of routing costs and maximization of service levels that reflect an integration of the strategies of the Logistics and Marketing departments.

In most cases of multiple objectives it is unlikely that the problem is optimized by the same alternative parameter choices. Hence, some trade-off between the criteria is needed to ensure a satisfactory design.

In the multi-objective optimization an important relation is the dominance relation. Let (z_1) and (z_2) be two solutions of a multi-objective minimization problem with R objectives. We say that: Solution (z_1) **dominates** (z_2) if $z_{1r} \le z_{2r}$ for all objectives r in $\{1,...,R\}$ and $z_{1r} < z_{2r}$ for at least one r and $(z_{1r}) \neq (z_{2r})$. A feasible solution is **efficient** if it is non-dominated. Based on this concept we will optimize the two objective functions to find non-dominated solutions.

Ideally, we would like to find the solution that would be optimal for both objectives at the same time. In multi-objective programming, this solution point rarely exists. So, we would like to find solutions that are close to this ideal point.

Mathematically, all non-dominated solutions are equally acceptable. It is the decision maker who is responsible for choosing the final solution. The decision maker is someone who has a deep knowledge of the problems, the relationships and the implications of each solution. The choice among these non-dominated solutions is determined by the decision maker's preferences among the multiple objectives.

The two objective functions considered within the integrated strategy are:

Objective A: Minimizing Cost

The formulation of this objective will be the same as in equation (8), the one used for the model of strategy 1.

$$Min \sum_{t=1}^{p} \sum_{i=1}^{n} \sum_{j=1}^{n} \sum_{k=1}^{m} c_{ij} x_{ijk}^{t}$$

Objective B: Marketing Objective

In terms of mathematical formulation, the second objective works as follows: For each customer we have a set of pairs of days with positive demand, T_i, for each pair of days *(g, h)* in T_i (with $g \neq h$) we want to minimize the difference in the assignment to a vehicle k. The objective is to minimize $\left| y_{ik}^{g} - y_{ik}^{h} \right|$.

The importance is given by the total demand for the period, therefore a weight is introduced: the total amount ordered by each customer. The objective function becomes:

$$Min \sum_{i=1}^{n} \sum_{k=1}^{m} \sum_{\substack{g,h \in T_i \\ g<h}} \left[\left(\sum_{t=1}^{p} q_i \right) \times \left| y^{g}_{ik} - y^{h}_{ik} \right| \right]$$

The importance of a customer is measured in terms of sales. In some cases other measures could be used to classify the goodness of a customer, for example, frequency of orders, credit history, etc. This function is non linear.

Considering a multi-period model is an essential aspect of our study. Since objective B is not static but measures decisions across more than one period, it only makes sense to consider a multi-period base.

In the integrated strategy the objective is to find a set of non-dominated solutions and give the decision maker the possibility to choose not only between strategies but also between solutions.

The constraints of the model for strategy 1 and 3 are:

$$\sum_{k=1}^{m} y_{ik}^{t} = 1, \quad \forall \; i = 2,...,n; t \in T_i \qquad (9)$$

$$\sum_{k=1}^{m} y_{ik}^{t} = m, \quad \forall \; t \in T_i; i = 1 \qquad (10)$$

$$\sum_{i=2}^{n} q_i^{t} y_{ik}^{t} \leq Q, \quad \forall \; k = 1,...,m; t = 1,...,p \qquad (11)$$

$$\sum_{j=1}^{n} x_{ijk}^{t} = \sum_{j=1}^{n} x_{jik}^{t} = y_{ik}^{t}, \quad \forall \; i = 2,...,n; k = 1,..,m; t = 1,...,p \qquad (12)$$

$$\sum_{k=1}^{m} y_{ik}^{t} = 0, \quad \forall \; i = 2,...,n; t \notin T_i \qquad (13)$$

$$\sum_{j,i \in S} x_{ijk}^{t} \leq |S| - 1, \quad \forall \; S \; \text{nonempty subset of} \; \{2,...,n\}; k = 1,..,m; t = 1,...,p \qquad (14)$$

$$x_{ijk}^{t} \in \{0,1\}; y_{ik}^{t} \in \{0,1\}, \quad \forall \; i = 1,...,n; k = 1,..,m; t = 1,...,p \qquad (15)$$

Constraints (9) to (15) are similar to the ones in the basic model, but for each day of the period in question. Constraint (9) ensures that on the days where a customer has a positive demand, that customer is visited by only one vehicle. Constraint (10) imposes that each day all vehicles go to the depot. Constraint (11) ensures that, the daily loading of a vehicle does not exceed its capacity. Constraint (12) guarantees that if the vehicle enters a node, on day t, it also has to leave that node, on the same day. Constraint (13) prohibits a vehicle from visiting a customer on a day where that customer has zero demand. Finally constraint (14) avoids sub-tours, but now not only for each vehicle but also for each day. The sub-tour elimination constraint represents an exponential number of constraints. The last constraint (15) defines all variables as binary.

SOLUTION APPROACH

The main objective of this work is to make a fair comparison of the three distribution strategies therefore we will use the same solution technique to optimize each strategy. As mentioned, the proposed problems are NP-hard, so they require an heuristic methodology in order to solve large instances. A heuristic algorithm is a solution method that does not guarantee an optimal solution, but in general has a good level of performance in terms of solution quality and convergence. Heuristics may be constructive (producing a single solution), local search (starting from one given random solution and moving iteratively to other nearby solutions) or a combination of the two. Heuristics for VRP have been extensively studied. Cordeau et al. (2002) summarize the most important classical and modern heuristics for the VRP.

Local search is the most powerful general approach for finding high quality solutions to hard combinatorial optimization problem in reasonable time. It is based on the iterative exploration of neighborhoods of solutions trying to improve the current solution by local changes. The type of local search that may be applied to a solution is defined by a neighborhood structure.

Our proposal is to use a metaheuristic algorithm that has proven to give quite good results for other problems and that is easy to implement, modify and adapt to different strategies: the Iterated Local Search (ILS).

The Iterated Local Search for the VRP

ILS is a simple and generally applicable metaheuristic which iteratively applies local search to modifications of the current search point. For more detailed information on ILS see (Lourenço, Martin, & Stützle, 2003), (Lourenço, Martin, & Stützle, 2010) and (Stützle, 1998). At the start of the algorithm a local search is applied to some initial solution. Then, a main loop is repeated until a stopping criterion is satisfied. This main loop consists of a modification step ("perturbation"), which returns an intermediate solution corresponding to a modification of a previously found locally optimal solution.

Next, local search is applied to yielding a locally optimal solution. An "acceptance criterion" then decides from which solution the search is continued by applying the next "perturbation". Both, the perturbation step and the acceptance test may be influenced by the search history. ILS is expected to perform better than if we just restart local search from a new randomly generated solution.

The architecture of the ILS is shown in Example 1.

The proposed ILS heuristics is based on the ILS metaheuristic developed by (Stützle, 1998) and (Kunz, 2000) to solve the classical VRP. The ILS used for the VRP is shown in Example 2.

We will now present the implementation of each step of the above algorithm in more detail.

Savings Heuristic

This is a greedy heuristic to construct an initial solution, (Clarke & Wright, 1964). It has been

Example 1. Architecture of the ILS Algorithm

Procedure ILS:
s^0 = GenerateInitialSolution
s^* = LocalSearch(s^0)
Repeat
s' = Perturbation(s^*, history)
$s^{*\prime}$ = Local search(s')
s^* = Acceptance Criterion(s^*, $s^{*\prime}$, history)
Until termination condition met
End

Example 2. ILS for the VRP

Step 1. Savings Heuristic - Initial Solution
Step 2. ILS for TSP on each tour:
Step 2.1. Local Search for TSP
Step 2.2. Perturbation for TSP
Step 2.3. Acceptance criterion
Step 3. ILS for the VRP
Step 3.1. LS for the Assignment Problem
Step 3.2. Perturbation for VRP
Step 3.3 Acceptance Criterion
Step 4. ILS for the TSP on the new routes

proved that starting from a random solution gives worse results (Stützle, 1998)). This savings heuristic obtains the initial solution.

ILS for the TSP

On each of the tours obtained in the savings heuristic, we apply an ILS. At this step of the algorithm, we ignore any relation between routes.

LS for TSP: The LS used was a 2-opt local search. The 2-opt move can be defined as follows: on one tour, 2 connections are removed and two others are included, since there is only one possibility for reconstructing the tour. We tested for all combinations. Only when a complete run without improvements finishes has one reached a 2-opt solution.

Searching in a complete 2-opt would not be efficient. So, to reduce the search space, some techniques are introduced that quicken the process whilst still generating good quality solutions: a list of candidates and "don't look bits". One "don't look bit" is associated with each node. Initially, all "don't look bits" =0, if for a node no improving move can be found, then "don't look bit" is turned on (set to 1) and is not considered as a starting node in the next iteration. If an edge incident to a node is changed by a move, the node's "don't look bit" is turned off again - reduces to $O(n)$.

Perturbation (Kick-move) for TSP: On the local minimum that has been reached, we apply the kick-move and arrive at a new start solution. The goal here is to escape from local optima by applying perturbations to the current local minimum.

For the LS on the TSP we use a "double bridge" move. This perturbation cuts four edges and introduces 4 new ones.

Figure 1. Example of a 2-opt move for the TSP

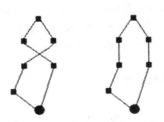

Figure 2. Example of a Double Bridge move

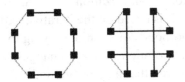

Figure 3. Example of a 2-opt move for the VRP

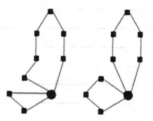

Acceptance criterion: The acceptance criterion used at this step is 'better'; this means that the new tour is accepted if it has a lower cost.

ILS for the VRP

The ILS for the VRP is implemented considering the initial solution for the routes obtained from the ILS of the TSP.

LS for the assignment problem: The local search for the VRP is a 2-opt and again a list of candidates and "don't look bits" techniques are applied to restrict the search.

We have two possibilities for a 2-opt: A customer of a tour is postponed until a later tour or a customer trades with another customer from another tour. First, if capacity restrictions allow and it reduces costs, a city is inserted in the tour. Only if it cannot be inserted do we check if an exchange with another tour improves the solution.

The same techniques as those used in LS for the TSP are used: "don't look bit" and list of candidates.

Kick-moves: "Numb-crosser": This perturbation consists of exchanging a group of customers from 2 tours. In this case, 1/3 of the customers of the tour are exchanged.

Acceptance criterion: 'Best', the same as the acceptance criterion for the TSP.

Example 3. Structure of the algorithm for Strategy 1

Step 1: Set loop = 0
Step 2: Set day = 1
Step 3. Savings Heuristic - Initial Solution
Step 4. ILS for TSP on each tour
Step 5. ILS for the VRP
Step 6. ILS for the TSP on the new routes
Step 7. Set day = day + 1; Repeat Step 3 to 6 until day = 5;
Step 8. Set loop = loop + 1
Step 9. Repeat Step 2 to 8 until loop = L

ILS for the TSP on the New Routes

Repeats the ILS procedure for the TSP.

The ILS for Each Strategy

The ILS for the VRP is now adapted to solve the 3 models for the different strategies. Next we will describe in detail the ILS for each of them.

Strategy 1: Since in this strategy we have a classical VRP model, for each day we apply the ILS to find the best daily routes, according to the capacity of the vehicle and the daily demand (see Example 3). The algorithm is repeated for several runs and chooses the best solution for each day.

Let L be the total number of loops

Strategy 2: In this strategy, we have considered a classical VRP model to obtain the "master routes", where all customers are taken into account based on average demand (see Example 4). Therefore, to obtain the master routes we apply an ILS. Afterwards, the routes for each day of the week are obtained in the following way: consider the master routes for each day and eliminate from these the customers that have no demand on that day. If on any of the routes the capacity constraint is violated, we identify the least important customer, and we delete it from this tour and insert it on another tour. This tour is chosen in such a

Example 4. Structure of the algorithm for Strategy 2

Step 1: For all customers do
Step 1.1. Savings Heuristic - Initial Solution
Step 1.2. ILS for TSP on each tour
Step 1.3. ILS for the VRP
Step 1.4. ILS for the TSP on the new routes
Step 2: Set day = 1
Step 3: For each tour eliminate customers with zero demand
Step 4: For each tour, if capacity constraints are violated remove customer with lowest total demand
Step 5: ILS for the TSP on the new routes
Step 6: Set day = day + 1
Step 7: Repeat Step 3 to 6 until day = 5;

way as to minimize routing costs within capacity constraints.

Strategy 3: In this strategy we face a multi-objective combinatorial optimization problem (MOCOP). Ehrgott & Gandibleux (2002) provide an annotated bibliography on MOCOP (see Example 5).

Two main approaches can be found in the metaheuristics for the MOCOP: methods of local search (LS) in object space and population based methods. In the LS methods, we start from an initial solution and the procedure approximates a part of the non-dominated frontier corresponding to the given search direction. A local aggregation mechanism of the objectives, based on the weighted sum, produces the effect to focus the search on a part of the non-dominated frontier. The principle is repeated for several search directions. In the population-based methods, the whole population contributes to the evolution process toward the non-dominated frontier. Here we will use the first approach, i.e. methods based on local search.

In this case, after having decided the routes for the first day, the program takes into consideration objective B, through a weighted function of both objectives. To do this, we calculate the effect of a move in the weighted function of the objectives. Then, the acceptance criterion determines that a new solution is accepted if the weighted function has improved. The algorithm is repeated for several different sets of weights. All the non-dominated solutions are retained during the run of the algorithm.

An objective function Z is used as the weighted function. Z is the weighted sum of the single objectives A and B.

Let f_r be the single objective function of objective r,

$$Z = \sum_{r=1}^{2} w_r f_r \text{ and } \sum_{r=1}^{2} w_r = 1$$

The solution is very sensitive to the weights that have been defined. The problem lies also in having objectives with different variables and scales. In our case, for example, we are adding costs and quantities. Notation:

w_a = weight for *Objective A*, with $0 \leq w_a \leq 1$;
w_b = weight for *Objective B*, with $0 \leq w_b \leq 1$;

and
$w_a + w_b = 1$

$$Z = w_a(ObjectiveA) + w_b(ObjectiveB)$$

Example 5. Structure of the algorithm for Strategy 3

Step 1: Set $w_a = 1$ and $w_b = 0$
Step 2: Set day = 1
Step 3. Savings Heuristic - Initial Solution
Step 4. ILS for TSP on each tour
Step 5. ILS for the VRP
Step 5.1. LS for the Assignment Problem
Step 5.1.1. For each move calculate the effect on objective A and B
Step 5.1.1.1. Accept only if the new z is smaller
Step 5.2. Perturbation for VRP
Step 5.3. Repeat Step 3.1
Step 5.4 Acceptance Criterion
Step 6. ILS for the TSP on the new routes
Step 7. Set day = day + 1; Repeat Step 3 to 6 until day = 5;
Step 8. Set $w_a = w_a - 0.1$ and $w_b = w_b + 0.1$
Step 9. Repeat Step 2 to 8 until $w_a =1$ and $w_b =0$

ANALYSIS OF THE RESULTS

The main objective of this experiment is to evaluate the three strategies and analyze the effect of each objective on the solutions. With this purpose, we applied the above algorithms to several sets of randomly generated examples. The results are expressed in terms of the values of the objectives and total number of vehicles needed. For each strategy two values were calculated: the Routing Cost and the Marketing (or service) Value. The first is measured in distance and the second can be interpreted as the unit cost for the distributor for not serving a customer with the same driver, working in a similar way as a penalty cost. Next we will explain the data used and analyze some important results of this experiment.

The Data

For the computational experiment, we have generated several sets of examples concerning the total number of customers (50,100,200,400). Also, we have examples with two types of demand (low variation and high variation) and two types of vehicles capacity, high and low.

To obtain the demand, we have used a normal distribution with mean 50 and standard deviation 20 for the case where demand has a high variation and a standard deviation of 5 for the examples with low variation. The probability to obtain a negative value is very small, and we have never found one. On each day, on average, 25% of the customers have zero demand. This implies that for a problem with 100 customers, there will be about 375 deliveries to make during the 5 day week. The customer locations are uniformly generated in a 100×100 square with the depot located in the centre with the coordinates (50, 50).

Truck capacity is 300 for problems with 50, 100 and 200 customers and 700 for problems with 400 customers. We also run cases with 200 customers and a truck capacity of 500. In total, we have studied 30 examples for each strategy; therefore we will consider 90 problems per run.

All data is available at the first author's web page: http://www.econ.upf.edu/~ramalhin/. A standard personal computer, Intel ® Core™ 2 Duo CPU T9300 @ 2.50 GHz and 3 GB RAM, was used to solve all instances.

Analysis of the Results

In this section, we will present the results obtained for each example in terms of the objective function values, the number of vehicles used, the non-dominated solutions and the run times.

We can illustrate the aim of the different strategies by looking at a small example with 2 days and a few customers: in Figure 4 we have the routes for two days, for strategies 1, 2 and 3. Strategy 1 has fewer and more efficient routes in terms of distance, Strategy 2 has more routes, but the routes are the same for each day. And, Strategy 3 has solutions that are not completely efficient in terms of distance, but allowing for a better service level.

Figure 4. Routes for Strategies 1, 2 and 3

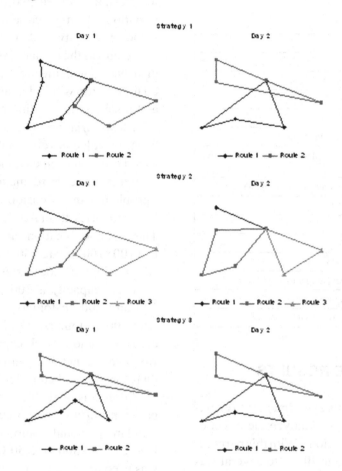

Table 1 shows the results for each example and for each strategy. Strategy 1 tries to find lowest cost, strategy 2 the best service level and strategy 3 the set of non-dominated solutions with respect to the integrated strategy. Note that objective (a) can be decimal due to the calculation of the distance based on the coordinates, however objective (b) is always an integer value. We can observe that, as expected, strategy 1 will always give us the solution with the lowest objective A and the highest objective B when compared with strategy 2. For strategy 2, we have much lower marketing values but the cost of routes increases significantly.

Concerning Strategy 3, we can say that, in almost every example, we can find more than one

non-dominated solution. In case 4, for example, we have 4 non-dominated solutions and it would be the responsibility of the decision maker to decide between the alternatives.

In Figures 5 and 6 we can see the set of all solutions obtained after 22 iterations of the strategy 3 heuristic for examples 4 and 30 with 50 customers. The diamonds correspond to the dominated solutions and the squares correspond to non-dominated solutions.

The number of vehicles needed for each solution strategy also varies and this is reflected in the total distance cost. In Table 2, we can observe these differences. The master routes approach always requires a much higher number of vehicles each week. This is due to the route design proce-

Table 1. Routing Cost (a) and Marketing Level (b) for Strategies 1, 2 and 3

N	Example	Strategy 1			Strategy 2		Strategy 3	
		a	b		a	b	a	b
50	1	14,344.15	36,840		17,018.93	3,306	14,510.34	32,327
							14,344.15	36,840
	2	13,589.47	38,538		16,304.18	4,590	13,755.11	35,826
							13,697.92	38,148
							13,589.47	38,538
							13,680.72	38,278
	3	13,225.97	40,284		15,744.37	4,997	13,289.63	36,178
							13,228.96	40,284
							13,278.06	40,140
	4	11,710.86	32,341		15,597.20	5,950	11,850.30	25,753
							11,811.55	31,776
							11,710.86	32,341
							11,788.70	32,289
	5	13,452.19	38,084		16,832.34	3,012	13,541.62	30,733
							13,462.15	38,426
							13,473.14	38,198
							13,485.40	37,925
							13,534.13	37,952
100	6	22,970.35	75,096		28,356.94	8,368	23,240.29	64,967
							23,033.35	75,012
							22,971.54	75,096
							23,162.88	74,404
							23,153.66	74,601
	7	21,999.94	73,497		27,755.47	7,209	22,045.08	61,244
							22,041.77	73,416
							21,999.94	73,497
	8	21,839.25	74,834		26,873.79	10,264	21,907.99	63,623
							21,839.25	74,834
	9	20,638.13	70,492		24,874.82	5,045	20,836.26	59,365
							20,820.51	69,385
							20,612.55	69,987
	10	22,383.01	76,252		27,892.60	5,987	22,632.56	63,871
							22,467.32	76,110
							22,493.46	75,632
							22,462.16	76,252
200	11	40,438.90	152,536		52,738.09	19,418	40,682.92	132,320

continued on following page

Table 1. Continued

N	Example	Strategy 1			Strategy 2		Strategy 3	
		a	b		a	b	a	b
							40,438.90	152,536
							40,484.58	152,292
	12	40,420.19	152,564		52,089.76	9,967	40,757.39	134,118
							40,420.19	152,564
	13	38,484.12	151,187		49,881.28	19,803	38,498.67	131,916
							38,423.14	150,677
	14	38,481.27	148,056		47,837.33	9,999	38,681.92	129,944
							38,601.73	148,056
							38,502.60	148,186
							38,581.57	148,113
							38,624.36	147,863
							38,457.64	148,254
							38,649.81	147,718
	15	40,047.94	130,399		50,744.95	15,778	40,047.94	130,399
							40,028.26	151,554
200*	16	28,589.23	152,040		35,849.68	8,375	28,883.37	132,744
							28,782.42	151,361
							28,780.13	151,569
							28,686.55	151,883
							28,551.03	152,164
							28,630.92	152,040
	17	28,675.59	150,844		34,171.20	2,096	28,814.46	130,891
							28,711.49	150,542
							28,704.59	150,844
	18	27,350.06	149,576		33,919.54	9,715	27,511.87	130,867
							27,474.54	149,315
							27,255.56	150,108
							27,503.72	149,261
							27,397.52	149,435
							27,371.86	149,576
	19	27,674.99	147,608		33,632.54	9,637	27,676.81	128579
							27,613.74	147754
	20	27,836.23	152,388		34,002.28	9,320	28,035.45	130,763
							27,896.09	151,456
							27,824.33	151,509
							27,990.09	151,355
400	21	40,013.36	304,388		49,637.55	9,607	40,120.90	260,814
							40,101.29	304,184

continued on following page

Table 1. Continued

N	Example	Strategy 1			Strategy 2		Strategy 3	
		a	b		a	b	a	b
							40,023.38	304,388
	22	39,758.16	308,956		47,691.43	9,401	39,961.71	270,449
							39,845.07	308,604
							39,842.23	308,956
	23	39,576.78	300,057		47,635.00	6,954	39,658.17	255,775
							39,584.53	299,568
							39,579.08	300,084
	24	39,949.22	302,980		47,978.58	9,525	40,022.79	266,906
							39,956.93	303,057
							39,970.21	302,980
	25	39,552.16	299,976		46,682.14	9,538	39,593.30	264,664
							39,583.25	299,976
50	26	12,606.09	37,756		15,118.07	2,396	12,870.39	33,258
(low stdev)							12,716.23	37,124
							12,606.09	37756
							12,867.78	36802
	27	13,752.04	37,759		16,724.64	3,329	13,861.01	34,403
							13,715.64	37,757
							13,855.72	37,428
	28	12,723.78	39,888		14,507.04	777	12,820.79	33,940
							12,781.62	39,888
	29	12,468.30	32,983		14,737.70	1,335	12,571.04	25,854
							12,489.20	32,330
	30	12,687.26	36,396		15,024.22	1,894	12,765.22	31,287
							12,657.08	36,504
							12,685.23	36,352
							12,747.45	36,043

* Truck capacity =500

dure. The routes are constructed considering all customers, and then for each day eliminating the ones with no demand. When constructing the "master routes" we have used the daily average demand of each customer. The higher the values used for the demand associated with each customer, the higher the number of vehicles used in the "master routes" and the lower the marketing values.

Comparing the number of vehicles for Strategy 1 and Strategy 3 we observe that, on average, Strategy 3 has the same or a higher number of vehicles. This is due to the existence of the second objective, which introduces a preference for service rather than just distance. To achieve better service we need to sacrifice the routing efficiency and this can require the use of an additional vehicle.

Figure 5. Example 4 - set of dominated and non-dominated solutions for Strategy 3

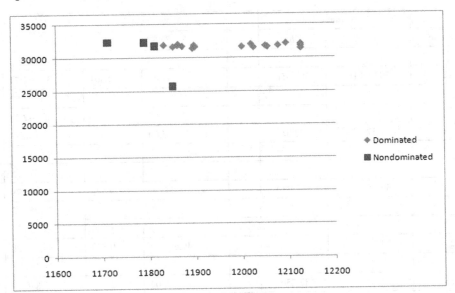

Figure 6. Example 30 - set of dominated and non-dominated solutions for Strategy 3

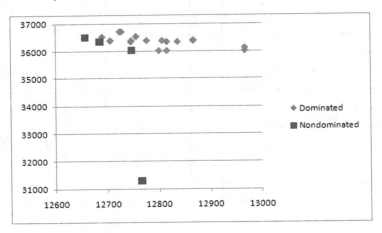

Table 2. Average number of vehicles needed per week, for Strategies 1, 2 and 3

N	Strategy 1	Strategy 2	Strategy 3
50	36	44	36
100	68	84	68
200	135	167	135
200(cap=500)	81	99	81
400	114	141	114
50 (low stdev)	36	43	36

The running time should not be overemphasized. The first and third strategies are the ones that take more time to compute. But, since we are referring to strategic planning, it does not seem impractical for a firm with a network of 400 customers to spend one hour run prior to strategic decision making each week. Table 3 summarizes running times. For Strategies 1 and 3 we have done the same number of iterations. The magnitude of the difference in running time for strategy 2 is due to the fact that we only run the VRP once for the master case. For the other two strategies we have to run the VRP for each day of the planning period several times.

Finally, in Table 4 we show the results of the other versions of the algorithm for strategy 3. In version 2 we have introduced more iterations for each weight. And, in version 3 we have done more iterations for the ILS for each day, and kept the same number of iterations per weight. From the results we can conclude that by allowing more running time, the algorithm of version 2, on average, gives more non-dominated solutions in 3 of the 5 problems. In version 3, on average the number of non-dominated solutions is smaller than in the other versions but we are able to improve the solutions, when comparing with version 1 and 2.

SUMMARY AND CONCLUSION

In this chapter, we have explored different distribution strategies to analyze an integrated distribution problem. The strategies cover a week-long planning horizon and reflect different ways of looking at the distribution problem. The first strategy is the classical VRP approach, which reflects only transportation cost: For each day of the planning horizon the routes are designed minimizing routing costs. The second strategy is a more customer oriented strategy based on customer relationship management principles, where master routes are constructed to ensure a marketing policy where each customer is always served by the same driver. The third strategy is a multi-objective combinatorial optimization problem with two objectives: minimizing cost and improving customer service. This third strategy results from the integration of the two other strategies and brings together two areas of great importance in many industries: Distribution and Marketing. The idea was to compare this new approach with the other two strategies.

For each of the above strategies we have presented a mathematical model and a heuristic procedure, based on the ILS, to solve the problems. Then, the three algorithms were applied to a set of randomly generated instances.

The main conclusion is that the multi-objective model gives several non-dominated solutions that can be seen as a good balance between optimizing the transportation cost or customer service and loyalty. The decision maker has to choose the solution that best meets business needs, since cost minimization is not the only concern in distribution management.

There are several possible extensions of this work, one is in the area of the metaheuristics and here it would be interesting to develop multi-objective population based metaheuristic to solve the multi-objective model and to perform a comparison with the current approach. The second extension would be to include other objectives that would reflect different business needs, as for example, the one of balancing the routes. This is particularly interesting if we assume that driver's remuneration can be related to truck loading. In this case, we would be studying the integration of decisions of the Human Resources department.

ACKNOWLEDGMENT

Thanks are due to the Ministerio de Ciencia e Innovación, Spain. (ECO2009-11307) for providing funding to support the work of Helena R. Lourenço.

Table 3. Average run time in seconds, per problem size, for Strategies 1, 2 and 3

N	Strategy 1	Strategy 2	Strategy 3
50	39.62	0.69	39.68
100	106.98	1.97	104.16
200	294.63	4.53	290.01
200(cap=500)	394.25	5.60	388.28
400	899.01	7.70	746.59
50 (low stdev)	42.42	0.67	0.67

Table 4. Routing Cost (a) and Marketing Level (b) for the non dominated solutions of Strategy 3, for 3 different versions of the algorithm

N	Example	Strategy 3, version 1		Strategy 3, version 2		Strategy 3, version 3	
		a	b	a	b	a	b
50	1	14,510.34	32,327	14,510.34	32,327	14,372.34	32,327
		14,344.15	36,840	14,376.34	36,570	14,251.39	36,840
				14,318.05	36,840		
	Run Time	40.59		103.29		110.75	
	2	13,755.11	35,826	13,589.45	38,538	13,631.61	38148
		13,697.92	38,148	13,644.05	38,376	13,657.49	35826
		13,589.47	38,538	13,680.72	38,278	13,629.26	39450
		13,680.72	38,278	13,697.92	38,148		
				13,755.11	35,826		
	Run Time	40.92		99.03		105.43	
	3	13,289.63	36,178	13,289.63	36,178	13,235.85	35,668
		13,228.96	40,284	13,224.70	40,284	13,229.69	40,148
		13,278.06	40,140			13,183.31	40,284
	Run Time	41.75		106		112.48	
	4	11,850.30	25,753	11710.85523	32,341	11812.68164	25,393
		11,811.55	31,776	11751.11426	32,062	11676.1062	31,848
		11,710.86	32,341	11805.80127	31,416	11641.05762	32,182
		11,788.70	32,289	11850.29736	25,753		
	Run Time	34.46		88.04		93.06	
	5	13,541.62	30,733	13,452.19	38,084	13,515.69141	30,336
		13,462.15	38,426	13,485.39	37,925	13,411.3667	37,662
		13,473.14	38,198	13,541.62	30,733	13,364.65	38,084
		13,485.40	37,925			13,441.13	36,998
		13,534.13	37,952				
	Run Time	40.69		103.7		109.28	

REFERENCES

Baker, T. L., Cronin, J. J., & Hopkins, C. D. (2009). The impact of involvement on key service relationships. *Journal of Services Marketing*, *23*(2-3), 115–124.

Baptista, S., Oliveira, R. C., & Zúquete, E. (2002). A period vehicle routing case study. *European Journal of Operational Research, 139*(2), 220–229. doi:10.1016/S0377-2217(01)00363-0

Barroso-Castro, C., Armario, E. M., & Marin-Ruiz, D. (2004). The influence of employee organizational citizenship behavior on customer royalty. *International Journal of Service Industry Management, 15*(1), 27–53. doi:10.1108/09564230410523321

Bodin, L., Golden, B., Assad, A., & Ball, M. (1983). Routing and Scheduling of Vehicles and Crews - The state of the art. *Computers & Operations Research, 10*(2), 105–121.

Chao, P., Fu, H. P., & Lu, I. Y. (2007). Strengthening the quality loyalty linkage: The role of customer orientation and interpersonal relationship. *Service Industries Journal, 27*(4), 471–494. doi:10.1080/02642060701346425

Christofides, N., Mingozzi, A., & Toth, P. (1981). Exact Algorithms for the Vehicle-Routing Problem, based on Spanning Tree and Shortest Path Relaxations. *Mathematical Programming, 20*(3), 255–282. doi:10.1007/BF01589353

Christopher, M. (1998). *Logistics and Supply Chain Management: Strategies for reducing cost and improving service.* London: Financial Times Pitman Publishing.

Clarke, G., & Wright, J. (1964). Scheduling of vehicles from a central depot to a number of delivering points. *Operations Research, 12*, 568–581. doi:10.1287/opre.12.4.568

Cordeau, J. F., Gendreau, M., Laporte, G., Potvin, J. Y., & Semet, F. (2002). A guide to vehicle routing heuristics. *The Journal of the Operational Research Society, 53*(5), 512–522. doi:10.1057/palgrave.jors.2601319

Crainic, T. G., & Laporte, G. (1998). *Fleet Management and Logistics.* Boston: Kluwer Academic Publishers. doi:10.1007/978-1-4615-5755-5

Ehrgott, M., & Gandibleux, X. (2002). *Multiple Criteria Optimization: State of the Art Annotated Bibliographic Surveys (Vol. 52).* New York: Springer.

Fisher, L. M. (1995). Vehicle routing. In M. O. Ball & T. L. Magnanti & C. L. Monma & G. L. Nemhauser (Eds.), *Network Routing* (Vol. Handbooks in Operations Research and Management Science, pp. 1-33). Amsterdam: NorthHolland.

Fisher, L. M., & Jaikumar, R. (1978). *Handbooks in Operations Research and Management Science (report 78-11-05).* Philadelphia, Pennsylvania: Department of Decision Sciences, The Wharton School, University of Pennsylvania.

Fisher, M. L., & Jaikumar, R. (1981). A Generalized Assignment heuristics for Vehicle-Routing. *Networks, 11*(2), 109–124. doi:10.1002/net.3230110205

Francis, P., Smilowitz, K., & Tzur, M. (2006). The Period Vehicle Routing Problem with Service Choice. *Transportation Science, 40*(4), 439–454. doi:10.1287/trsc.1050.0140

Golden, B., Raghavan, S., & Wasil, E. E. (2008). *The Vehicle Routing Problem: Latest Advances and New Challenges.* New York: Springer. doi:10.1007/978-0-387-77778-8

Gouveia, L. (1995). A Result on Projection for the Vehicle-Routing Problem. *European Journal of Operational Research, 85*(3), 610–624. doi:10.1016/0377-2217(94)00025-8

Guenzi, P., & Pelloni, O. (2004). The impact of interpersonal realtionships on customer satisfaction and loyalty to the service provider. *International Journal of Service Industry Management, 15*(3-4), 365–384. doi:10.1108/09564230410552059

Hemmelmayr, V. C., Doerner, K. F., & Hartl, R. F. (2009). A variable neighborhood search heuristic for periodic routing problems. *European Journal of Operational Research, 195*(3), 791–802. doi:10.1016/j.ejor.2007.08.048

Hong, S. C., & Park, Y. B. (1999). A heuristic for bi-objective vehicle routing with time window constraints. *International Journal of Production Economics, 62*(3), 249–258. doi:10.1016/S0925-5273(98)00250-3

Jozefowiez, N., Semet, F., & Talbi, E.-G. (2008). Multi-objective vehicle routing problems. *European Journal of Operational Research, 189*(2), 293–309. doi:10.1016/j.ejor.2007.05.055

Juan, A. A., Faulin, J., Ruiz, R., Barrios, B., & Caballé, S. (2010). The SR-GCWS hybrid algorithm for solving the capacitated vehicle routing problem. *Applied Soft Computing, 10*, 215–224. doi:10.1016/j.asoc.2009.07.003

Kulkarni, R. V., & Bhave, P. R. (1985). Integer Programming Formulations of Vehicle-Routing Problems. *European Journal of Operational Research, 20*(1), 58–67. doi:10.1016/0377-2217(85)90284-X

Kunz, C. (2000). *Iterierte Lokale Suche ur das Vehicle-Routing Problem*. Germany: TU Damstadt.

Laporte, G. (1992). The Vehicle-Routing Problem - An Overview of Exact and Approximate Algorithms. *European Journal of Operational Research, 59*(3), 345–358. doi:10.1016/0377-2217(92)90192-C

Laporte, G. (2007). What you should know about the vehicle routing problem. *Naval Research Logistics, 54*(8), 811–819. doi:10.1002/nav.20261

Laporte, G. (2009). Fifty Years of Vehicle Routing. *Transportation Science, 43*(4), 408–416. doi:10.1287/trsc.1090.0301

Laporte, G., & Osman, I. H. (1995). Routing problems: A bibliography. *Annals of Operations Research, 61*, 227–262. doi:10.1007/BF02098290

Lawler, E. L., Lenstra, J. K., Rinnooy Kan, A. H. G., & Shmoys, D. B. (1985). *The Traveling Salesman Problem*. New York: Wiley & Sons.

Lee, T., & Ueng, J. (1999). A study of vehicle routing problems with load-balancing. *International Journal of Physical Distribution & Logistics Management, 29*(10), 646–658. doi:10.1108/09600039910300019

Lourenço, H. R., Martin, O., & Stützle, T. (2003). Iterated local search. In Glover, F., & Kochenberger, G. (Eds.), *Handbook of Metaheuristics* (*Vol. 57*, pp. 321–353). Norwell, MA: Kluwer Academic Publishers.

Lourenço, H. R., Martin, O., & Stützle, T. (2010). Iterated Local Search: Framework and Applications. In Gendreau, M., & Potvin, J. Y. (Eds.), *Handbook in Metaheuristics* (2nd ed., *Vol. 146*, pp. 363–397). New York: Springer. doi:10.1007/978-1-4419-1665-5_12

Mourgaya, M., & Vanderbeck, F. (2007). Column generation based heuristic for tactical planning in multi-period vehicle routing. *European Journal of Operational Research, 183*(3), 1028–1041. doi:10.1016/j.ejor.2006.02.030

Muller, J. (2010). Approximative solutions to the bicriterion Vehicle Routing Problem with Time Windows. *European Journal of Operational Research, 202*(1), 223–231. doi:10.1016/j.ejor.2009.04.029

Partyka, J. G., & Hall, R. W. (2000, August). On the Road to Service. *OR/MS Today* 26-35.

Pasia, J. M., Doerner, K. F., Hartl, R. F., & Reimann, M. (2007). A population-based local search for solving a bi-objective vehicle routing problem. *Evolutionary Computation in Combinatorial Optimization. Proceedings, 4446*, 166–175.

Ribeiro, R. (2004). *Integrated distribution management problems: an optimization approach*. Barcelona, Spain: Universitat Pompeu Fabra.

Simchi-Levi, D., Kaminsky, P., & Simchi-Levi, E. (2003). *Designing and Managing the Supply Chain: Concepts, Strategies and Case Studies*. Irwin: MacGraw-Hill.

Stützle, T. (1998). *Local Search Algorithms for Combinatorial Problems - Analysis, Improvements, and New Applications*. Department of Computer Science, Darmstadt University of Technology.

Toth, P., & Vigo, D. (2002a). Models, relaxations and exact approaches for the capacitated vehicle routing problem. *Discrete Applied Mathematics, 123*(1-3), 487–512. doi:10.1016/S0166-218X(01)00351-1

Toth, P., & Vigo, D. (2002b). An overview of vehicle routing problems. In Toth, P., & Vigo, D. (Eds.), *Vehicle Routing Problem* (pp. 1–26). Philadelphia, PA: Society for Industrial and Applied Mathematics. doi:10.1137/1.9780898718515.ch1

KEY TERMS AND DEFINITIONS

Cross-Functional Planning at Distribution: consists of coordinating different areas inside the firm, as marketing and logistics for example, allowing for cost reductions and service improvement.

Iterated Local Search (ILS): ILS is a simple and generally applicable meta-heuristic which iteratively applies local search to modifications of the current search point. At the start of the algorithm a local search is applied to some initial solution. Then, a main loop is repeated until a stopping criterion is satisfied. This main loop consists of a modification step ("perturbation"), which returns an intermediate solution corresponding to a modification of a previously found locally optimal solution.

Local Search Methods (LS): Local search is the most powerful general approach for finding high quality solutions to hard combinatorial optimization problem in reasonable time. It is based on the iterative exploration of neighborhoods of solutions trying to improve the current solution by local changes. The type of local search that may be applied to a solution is defined by a neighborhood structure.

Multi-Objective Combinatorial Optimization Problem (MOCOP): Combinatorial problems are characterized by the consideration of a selection or permutation of a *discrete* set of "items" or by an assignment among these. The MOCOP are combinatorial optimization problems with several objective functions.

Savings Heuristic: This is a greedy heuristic to construct an initial solution based on the saving calculations and tour construction. This savings heuristic (Clarke & Wright, 1964), obtains the initial tour for the VRP problem.

Traveling Salesman Problem (TSP): Given a collection of cities (or points) and the cost (or distance) of travel between each pair of them, the traveling salesman problem is to find the cheapest way of visiting all of the cities and returning to your starting point.

Vehicle Routing Problem (VRP): This problem considers a set of nodes, representing retailers or customers, at a known location, that must be served by one depot. Each node has a known demand. A set of vehicles K, with equal capacity is available to serve the customers. The routes must start and finish at the depot. The objective is to define the set of routes to serve all customers with minimal cost.

Chapter 6

A Hybrid Algorithm Based on Monte–Carlo Simulation for the Vehicle Routing Problem with Route Length Restrictions

Angel A. Juan
Open University of Catalonia, Spain

Javier Faulin
Public University of Navarre, Spain

Tolga Bektaş
University of Southampton, UK

Scott E. Grasman
Missouri University of Science and Technology, USA

ABSTRACT

This chapter describes an approach based on Monte Carlo Simulation (MCS) to solve the Capacitated Vehicle Routing Problem (CVRP) with route length restrictions and customer service times. The additional restriction introduces further challenges to the classical CVRP. The basic idea behind our approach is to combine direct MCS with an efficient heuristic, namely the Clarke and Wright Savings (CWS) algorithm, and a decomposition technique. The CWS heuristic provides a constructive methodology which is improved in two ways: (i) a special random behavior is introduced in the methodology using a geometric distribution; and (ii) a divide-and-conquer technique is used to decompose the original problem in smaller sub-problems that are easier to deal with. The method is tested using a set of well-known benchmarks. The chapter discusses the advantages and disadvantages of the proposed procedure in relation to other approaches for solving the same problem.

DOI: 10.4018/978-1-61350-086-6.ch006

INTRODUCTION

The Capacitated Vehicle Routing Problem (CVRP) is probably one of the most popular routing problems in Combinatorial Optimization. The objective is to find an 'optimal' set of routes for a fleet of homogeneous vehicles so that demands of a set of customers are satisfied. All routes begin and end at one or several depots, where all resources are initially located. Typically each vehicle has a maximum loading capacity, each customer is supplied by a single vehicle, and a vehicle cannot visit the same customer twice. Therefore, the objective function consists in minimizing total delivery costs, which are typically related to distances traveled by vehicles.

Known to be an NP-hard problem (Laporte and Semet 2001, Prins 2004), the CVRP has been studied for decades. Even so, it is still attracting a great amount of attention from researchers worldwide due to its potential applications, both in real-life scenarios situations as well as for the development of new algorithms, optimization methods and meta-heuristics for solving other combinatorial problems (Toth and Vigo 2002, Golden et al. 2008). Various approaches to the CVRP have been proposed during the past decades, ranging from the use of pure optimization methods such as linear programming –mainly used for solving small- to medium-size problems with relatively simple constraints–, to the use of heuristics and meta-heuristics that provide near-optimal solutions for medium and large-size problems with more complex constraints (Laporte 2007).

This chapter considers the CVRP with additional restrictions, in particular: (a) there is a route length restriction per vehicle, i.e., no route can exceed a given cost (assuming that cost is related to length), and (b) a service time restriction, which forms a part of a given tour's duration, needs to be considered for each customer being served. This service time is usually transformed into a penalty cost per service that must also be added to the distance-based costs associated with each route.

All in all, the main goal of this chapter is threefold. First, it aims to illustrate the use of simulation-based heuristic approaches to deal with the CVRP with additional constraints such as those defined above. Second, it aims to show that simulation-based approaches can be competitive with existing heuristic approaches, in terms of the quality of the solutions obtained, in solving a combinatorial problem. Finally, it aims to highlight some interesting benefits that simulation-based approaches might offer.

PREVIOUS RELATED WORK

The CVRP has been studied extensively in the literature. The problem can be solved by exact methods (mathematical models and branch and bound algorithms) or heuristic approaches. Exact methods are able to prove optimal solutions, but their computational time requirements grow exponentially when the problem size increases. Heuristic approaches, on the other hand, include classical heuristics and metaheuristics. Among the former, Clarke and Wright's Savings (CWS) constructive algorithm (Clarke and Wright 1964) is probably the most cited heuristic to solve the CVRP. The CWS first generates an initial feasible solution by assigning one vehicle to each node. Every pair of nodes defines an edge, so a list of possible edges can be constructed and then sorted according to the 'savings' associated with each edge –that is, the reduction in costs that would be attained if the respective routes containing both edge extremes were merged into a single route. The initial solution is then improved by an iterative route-merging process in which edges are sequentially selected from the sorted list and the corresponding routes merged if possible –i.e., if the resulting route does not violate any constraint and if the nodes are both directly connected to the depot so that the merge is feasible. The

CWS algorithm usually provides relatively good solutions, especially for small and medium-size problems. Many variants and improvements of the CWS have been proposed in the literature. For instance, Mole and Jameson (1976) generalized the definition of the savings function, introducing two parameters for controlling the savings behavior. Similarly, Holmes and Parker (1976) developed a procedure based upon the CWS algorithm, using the same savings function but introducing a solution perturbation scheme in order to avoid poor quality routes. Beasley (1981) adapted the CWS method in order to use it to optimize inter-customer travel times. Dror and Trudeau (1986) developed a version of the CWS method for the Stochastic VRP. Paessens (1988) analyzed the main characteristics of the CWS method and its performance in generic VRP. Recently, the CWS heuristic has been finely tuned by means of genetic algorithms experimentation by Battarra et al. (2008) and Doyuran and Çatay (2010).

Using constructive heuristics as a basis, metaheuristics became popular for the solution of the CVRP during the nineties. These procedures are able to find (but unable to prove) near-optimal and even global optimum solutions for combinatorial problems. Some early examples applied to solve the CVRP are the Tabu Route method by Gendreau et al. (1994) or the BoneRoute method of Tarantilis and Kiranoudis (2002). Tabu search (TS) algorithms, like those proposed by Taillard (1993) or Toth and Vigo (2003) are among the most popular metaheuristics. Genetic algorithms (GA) have also played a major role in the development of effective approaches for the VRP. Some examples are the studies of Berger and Barkaoui (2003) and Mester and Bräysy (2007). Other important meta-heuristic approaches to the VRP are Simulated Annealing (SA) (Alfa et al. 1991), Greedy Randomized Adaptive Search Procedure (GRASP) (Resende 2008, Festa and Resende 2009), Ant Colony Optimization (AC) (Bell and McMullen 2004) and Evolutionary Algorithms (EA) (Prins 2004).

While the CVRP has been extensively studied in the literature, we believe this is not the case for the CVRP with route length restrictions and service time requirements, and that more flexible and simpler methods should be proposed to deal with these realistic constraints. Following these ideas, the approach presented in this chapter combines Monte Carlo Simulation (MCS) with the CWS heuristic and some divide-and-conquer techniques to reduce the problem complexity. MCS can be defined as a set of techniques that makes use of random numbers and statistical distributions to solve certain stochastic and deterministic optimization problems (Law 2007). MCS has proved to be extremely useful for obtaining numerical solutions to complex problems which cannot be efficiently solved by using analytical approaches. To the best of our knowledge, Buxey (1979) was the first author to combine MCS with the CWS algorithm to develop a procedure for solving the CVRP. This method was revisited by Faulin and Juan (2008), who introduced an entropy function to guide the random selection of nodes. MCS has also been used by Fernandez et al. (2000) and Juan et al. (2009) to solve the basic CVRP. This chapter goes one step beyond and discusses how to combine MCS and the CWS heuristic to solve the CVRP with restrictions on route length and service time considerations. Thus, one of the main contributions of this chapter is to discuss to which degree simulation-based approaches can be a viable alternative to the previously cited approaches for the CVRP variants with the aforementioned additional constraints.

The next section presents a formal description of the problem studied in this chapter and an integer linear programming formulation of the same.

FORMAL PROBLEM DESCRIPTION AND MATHEMATICAL MODELING

The problem studied in this chapter can be formally described as follows. Given a graph $G =$

(V, A) where $V = \{1, 2, ..., n\}$ is the set of *nodes* (*vertices*), 0 is the *depot* (*origin, home city*) and the remaining nodes are customer nodes denoted by the set V_0, i.e., $V_0 = V \setminus \{0\}$. The set $A = \{(i, j): i, j \in V, i \neq j\}$ is an *arc* (or *edge*) set. Traversal of each arc (i, j) induces a travel cost c_{ij} that is equal to the length of the shortest path between nodes i and j (which may be symmetric, asymmetric, Euclidean, deterministic, random, etc.). Here, "length" may be defined in terms of physical travel distance, travel time, fuel cost or any other measure. In this chapter, we will consider the case where "length" corresponds to the fixed travel time between two nodes. The matrix $\mathbf{C} = [c_{ij}]_{nxn}$ is said to be *symmetric* if $c_{ij} = c_{ji}$ for all $(i, j) \in A$, and *asymmetric* otherwise. If $c_{ij} + c_{jk} \geq c_{ik}$ for all $i, j, k \in V$, $\mathbf{C}$ is said to satisfy the *triangle inequality*. There are at most m homogeneous *vehicles* that are available for use, each able to carry commodities of up to Q units. Each customer $i \in V_0$ has a predefined service time denoted by s_i and a demand of q_i units. We assume the problem is that of a collection, i.e., each customer has q_i units of demand to be picked-up by the serving vehicle. The problem consists of finding a set of at most m vehicle routes where (i) each route starts and ends at the depot node, (ii) each customer is visited (thus its demand is served) exactly once by any vehicle, (iii) the distance of each route does not exceed a route length denoted T, and (iv) the total demand served in each route does not exceed Q. The objective is to minimize the total length traversed by all the vehicles.

In this section, we describe a mathematical formulation of the problem. We note that Lin et al. (2009) also present a mixed integer programming formulation for the same problem using three-index variables. The one proposed below makes use of two-index variables, hence is smaller in size in terms of the number of binary variables involved. The model described uses a binary variable x_{ij} that takes the value 1 if arc (i, j) is traversed in the solution, and the value 0 otherwise. The model also uses two continuous variables, u_i denoting the cumulative amount of goods the vehicle has collected as soon as it leaves node $i \in V_0$, and v_i showing the cumulative time the vehicle has spent in traveling from the depot until it arrives to node $i \in V_0$. Based on these definitions, the formulation is presented below.

Minimize

$$\sum_{(i,j) \in V} c_{ij} x_{ij} \tag{1}$$

Subject to

$$\sum_{j \in V} x_{ij} = 1 \qquad i \in V_0 \tag{2}$$

$$\sum_{j \in V} x_{ji} = 1 \qquad i \in V_0 \tag{3}$$

$$\sum_{j \in V} x_{0i} \leq m \tag{4}$$

$$\sum_{i \in V} x_{i0} \leq m \tag{5}$$

$$u_i - u_j + Q x_{ij} + (Q - q_i - q_j) x_{ji} \leq Q - q_j \qquad i, j \in V_0, i \neq j \tag{6}$$

$$u_i \geq q_i + \sum_{j \in V_0} q_j x_{ji} \qquad i \in V_0 \tag{7}$$

$$u_i \leq Q - (Q - \max_{j \neq i}\{q_j\} - q_i) x_{0i} - \sum_{j \in V_0} q_j x_{ij} \qquad i \in V_0 \tag{8}$$

$$v_i - v_j + (T - c_{0j} - c_{i0} + c_{ij} + s_i) x_{ij} + (T - c_{0j} - c_{i0} - c_{ji} - s_j) x_{ji} \leq T - c_{0j} - c_{i0} \qquad i, j \in V_0, i \neq j \tag{9}$$

$$v_i \geq c_{0i}x_{0i} + \sum_{j \in V_0}(c_{0j} + c_{ji} + s_j)x_{ji} \qquad (10)$$
$$i \in V_0$$

$$v_i \leq T - c_{i0} - (T - c_{i0} - c_{0i})x_{0i} \qquad (11)$$
$$i \in V_0$$

$$x_{ij} \in \{0,1\} \qquad (12)$$
$$(i,j) \in A$$

The formulation (1)–(12) presented above minimizes the total length of all tours through the objective function (1). Constraints (2) and (3) are used to ensure each customer $i \in V_0$ is visited exactly once, whereas constraints (4) and (5) are used to limit the total number of vehicles used in the solution by m. Capacity limitations on each tour are modeled through (6)–(8), which also serve as prohibiting possible formation of subtours, which are tours forming amongst customer nodes only and are not connected to the depot. These constraints are due to Desrochers and Laporte (1991) and Kara *et al.* (2004). Similarly, constraints (9)–(11) model route length restrictions. More specifically, these constraints ensure that a tour's length which is composed of the total travel time between nodes and the service times at each node cannot exceed T. These constraints are initially due to Kulkarni and Bhave (1985), with corrections, liftings and refinements being suggested by Achutan and Caccetta (1991), Desrochers and Laporte (1991), Naddef (1994) and Kara and Bektaş (2005).

SOME FUNDAMENTAL IDEAS OF OUR APPROACH

Recent advances in the development of high-quality pseudo-random number generators (RNGs) (L'Ecuyer 2006) may have opened new perspectives in the use of Monte Carlo simulation in combinatorial problems. To test how state-of-the-art random number generators can be used to improve existing heuristics and even push them to new efficiency levels, we combine MCS techniques with one of the best-known classical heuristics for the CVRP, namely the CWS heuristic. In particular, we selected the parallel version of this heuristic since it usually offers better results than the sequential version.

One of the main ideas of our approach is to introduce some random behavior within the CWS heuristic so that a random feasible solution is obtained each time the randomized CWS is executed. Then, just by iterating this random construction process, a set of different feasible solutions are generated and the best ones are saved into a solutions database. Each of these feasible solutions will consist of a set of roundtrip routes from the depot that, altogether, satisfy all problem constraints and node demands. Sometimes, though, the lowest-costs solution is not the best choice in practice due to factors such as existence of intersecting or unbalanced routes –i.e., some routes cover large distances while others cover short distances (Figure 1). Of course, the key question here is how to randomize the CWS so that the resulting solutions will also be competitive in terms of associated costs. As stated in the literature review section, at each step of the solution-construction process the CWS algorithm always chooses the edge with the highest savings value. Our approach, instead, assigns a selection probability to each edge in the savings list. This probability will reflect the savings value associated with each edge, i.e., edges with higher savings are more likely to be selected from the list than those with lower savings. Finally, this selection process should be done without introducing too many parameters in the algorithm –otherwise, it would be necessary to perform fine-tuning, which usually is a non-trivial and time-consuming process.

To reach all these goals, we employ a single-parameter geometric distribution during the randomized CWS solution-construction process. That way, edges with higher savings values are always more likely to be selected from the list,

Figure 1. Examples of solutions showing typical problems

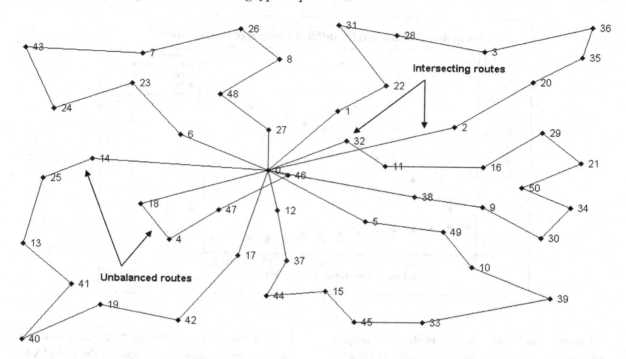

but the exact probabilities assigned will depend on the specific value assigned to the distribution parameter, α, being 0 < α < 1. Figure 2 shows a comparison of two probability functions (PD) and cumulative distribution functions (CDF) related to geometric distributions with different values of α. Notice that using relatively low values of this parameter (e.g.: α = 0.10) implies that more edges in the savings list are potentially eligible –i.e., the corresponding cumulative distribution function shows a relatively low increasing rate. On the contrary, using relatively high values for this parameter (e.g.: α = 0.40) implies that only a few edges from the sorted saving list are potentially eligible in practice –i.e., the corresponding cumulative distribution function shows a relatively high increasing rate.

Another fundamental idea behind our approach is the use of splitting or divide-and-conquer techniques to reduce the original problem size. The goal here is to divide the original set of nodes into two disjoint subsets and then solve each of these subsets by applying the same randomized CWS approach described before. Different splitting policies can be used, but the basic principle should always be the same: once a randomized CWS solution has been found, use a proximity criterion to select a subset of routes and their corresponding nodes; then, in order to look for a better way to travel those nodes around, apply the iterative randomized CWS construction process to them. The proximity criterion employed in this work is based on the position of the geometric center of each route with respect to the position of the global solution geometric centre –i.e., with respect to all nodes geometric center. The geometric center of a given set of nodes is the average of the x and y coordinates of these nodes. Note that the geometric center is considered as the reference point instead of the depot. This allows obtaining balanced splitting even for those VRP instances where the depot is located in an extreme position with respect to the rest of the nodes.

Figure 2. Probabilities associated with two different geometric distributions

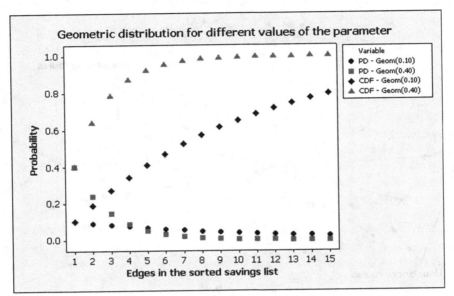

Figure 3 illustrates how the divide-and-conquer technique works for a given solution: (1) a subset of routes from the given solution is selected according to a geometric criterion (in this case, routes located below the line x = y are selected, but many other criteria can be used instead); (2) then, the selected routes are dissolved and the corresponding nodes are considered to be a new vehicle routing problem to which the iterative randomized CWS process is applied; (3) finally, the best solution obtained for the sub-problem is used together with the non-selected routes to build a new improved solution for the initial VRP instance.

A HIGH-LEVEL DESCRIPTION OF OUR ALGORITHM

The approach described in this chapter can be summarized in the following six-step algorithm, which is also represented in Figure 4:

Figure 3. Divide-and-conquer process

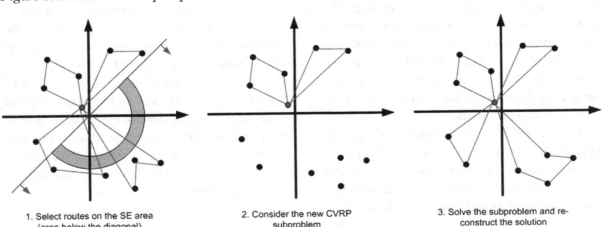

Figure 4. Scheme of our simulation-based methodology

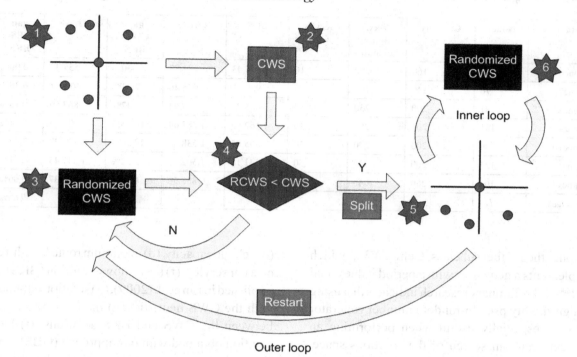

1. Initially, a CVRP instance is given.
2. The corresponding CWS solution is obtained.
3. A random solution is obtained by executing the randomized CWS procedure.
4. The resulting random solution is compared against the CWS one, which is used as a permanent reference to classify each new solution as a promising one or as a non-promising one. If the randomized solution does not outperform the current one, then the randomized solution is not a promising one and the process starts again from step 3.
5. Otherwise, the randomized CWS solution is divided into two sets of routes, the front set and the back set. Each of these sets is then considered as a new CVRP problem with the same initial constraints but with fewer nodes –which significantly reduces the dimension of the solution space with respect to the original problem.
6. Now, an inner loop starts. At each iteration of this loop, a new sub-problem is solved by using the randomized CWS algorithm. Once this inner loop has finished, the resulting solution is sorted and saved in a database, and the process restarts from step 3 (outer loop). Notice that this restarting factor is decisive in order to avoid that the methodology gets trapped into a local minimum.

VERIFICATION AND VALIDATION

The methodology described in this chapter has been implemented as a Java application. Being an interpreted language, Java-based programs do not execute as fast as other compiled programs such as those developed in C, but Java allows for rapid development of object-oriented prototypes that can be used to test the potential of an algorithm. At the core of our Java application, some state-of-the-art pseudo-random number generators are employed. In particular, we have used some classes from the SSJ library (L'Ecuyer 2002),

Table 1. Comparison between our simulation-based approach and the best-known solution

Instance	Nodes	Capacity	Max. Route Length	Service Cost	BKS	CWS	gap CWS-BKS	OBS	gap OBS-BKS
vrpnc6	51	160	200	10	555.43	584.87	5.30%	555.43	0.00%
vrpnc7	76	140	160	10	909.68	975.46	7.23%	912.91	0.36%
vrpnc8	101	200	230	10	865.94	973.94	12.47%	867.50	0.18%
vrpnc9	151	200	200	10	1,162.55	1,287.64	10.76%	1,178.65	1.38%
vrpnc10	200	200	200	10	1,395.85	1,538.66	10.23%	1,428.29	2.32%
vrpnc13	121	200	720	50	1,541.14	1,592.26	3.32%	1,547.45	0.41%
vrpnc14	101	200	1040	90	866.37	868.50	0.25%	866.37	0.00%
Averages	*114*						7.08%		*0.66%*

among them, the subclass GenF2W32, which implements a generator with a period value equal to $2^{800}-1$. Preliminary research indicates that using a high-quality pseudo-random number generator may be especially useful when performing an in-depth random search of the solutions space. Moreover, the use of such a long-period RNG has other important advantages: the algorithm can be easily parallelized by splitting the RNG sequence in different streams and using each stream in different processors.

As explained in the Introduction, our main goal was to develop a simulation-based approach that was able to efficiently deal with the CVRP with a restriction on the route length and considering customer service times. In order to test the effectiveness of our approach and its efficiency as compared with other existing approaches, we used the classical CVRP benchmark instances from Christofides, Mingozzi and Toth (1979) which feature the special constraints of the problem considered here, namely vrpnc6, vrpnc7, vrpnc8, vrpnc9, vrpnc10, vrpnc13 and vrpnc14.

A standard personal computer, with an Intel® Core™2 Duo CPU processor at 2.4 GHz and a 2 GB RAM, was used to perform all tests. Results of these tests are summarized in Table 1, which contains the following information for each instance: (a) name of instance, (b) number of nodes,

(c) vehicle capacity, (d) maximum route length, (e) cost per service, (f) best-known solution (BKS) as published in Lin et al. (2009), (g) solution obtained with the CWS heuristic, (h) the percentage gap between the CWS and BKS solutions, (i) best solution obtained with our approach (OBS), and (j) gap between the OBS and BKS solutions. In the table, the percentage gap between solution value v_Δ produced by a given heuristic Δ and the known best solution value v^* of the instance is calculated as $100(v_\Delta - v^*)/v^*$.

Table 2 shows the best solutions obtained with different well-known meta-heuristics, as well as their corresponding gaps with respect to the best-known solution. This data has also been obtained from Lin et al. (2009). In particular, the meta-heuristics considered are: Simulated Annealing (SA), Granular Tabu Search (GTS), Genetic Algorithms (GA), Ant Colony (AC) and Evolutionary Algorithms (EA).

Tables 1 and 2 indicated that our simulation-based approach seems to be competitive, in terms of quality of the solutions, with the other meta-heuristic approaches shown in Table 2, with the exception of EA. In effect, EAs seem to perform significantly better than the rest of the meta-heuristics for the analyzed instances. The promising performance of our algorithm is particularly interesting if we consider its relative simplicity

Table 2. Comparison with other well-known meta-heuristics

Instance	SA	gap SA-BKS	GTS	gap GTS-BKS	GA	gap GA-BKS	AC	gap AC-BKS	EA	gap EA-BKS
vrpnc6	555.43	0.00%	555.43	0.00%	559.04	0.65%	560.24	0.87%	555.43	0.00%
vrpnc7	909.68	0.00%	920.72	1.21%	909.94	0.03%	916.21	0.72%	909.68	0.00%
vrpnc8	866.75	0.09%	868.48	0.29%	872.82	0.79%	866.74	0.09%	865.94	0.00%
vrpnc9	1,164.12	0.14%	1,173.12	0.91%	1,188.22	2.21%	1,195.99	2.88%	1,162.55	0.00%
vrpnc10	1,417.85	1.58%	1,435.74	2.86%	1,451.63	4.00%	1,451.65	4.00%	1,402.75	0.49%
vrpnc13	1,545.98	0.31%	1,545.51	0.28%	1,560.79	1.28%	1,559.92	1.22%	1,542.86	0.11%
vrpnc14	890.00	2.73%	866.37	0.00%	872.34	0.69%	867.07	0.08%	866.37	0.00%
Averages		*0.69%*		*0.79%*		*1.38%*		*1.41%*		*0.09%*

and the fact that it does not require complex fine-tuning processes, a process which most EA algorithms require

BENEFITS AND LIMITATIONS OF OUR APPROACH

As previously described, our approach makes use of an iterative process to generate a set of random feasible solutions based on the CWS heuristic. According to the experimental tests carried out, each iteration only requires a few milliseconds on a standard computer. Since we are introducing a 'tiny' biased randomness in the edge-selection process, odds are than the generated solution outperforms the one given by the CWS heuristics. This means that our approach is able to provide, in real-time, a feasible solution that outperforms the CWS heuristics. Moreover, as verified by testing, several alternative solutions outperforming the CWS can be obtained after a few seconds of computation, each of them having different attributes regarding intangible costs, workload balance, visual attractiveness, etc. By doing so, a list of alternative solutions can be constructed, thus allowing the decision-maker to filter this solutions list according to his/her utility function, which might be difficult or impossible to model

in the initial objective function. Furthermore, as it has been already discussed, by adding a local search process based on a divide-and-conquer technique, our algorithm is capable to provide – with more computational time– feasible solutions that maintain a low average gap with respect to the best-known solution for every tested instance.

Another important point to consider here is the relative simplicity of the presented methodology. In effect, our approach is relatively simple to implement in code and it needs little fine-tuning –there is just one parameter, α, which usually can be considered to be between 0.15 and 0.25. This is quite interesting in our opinion, since according to (Kant et al. 2008) some of the most efficient heuristics and meta-heuristics are not used in practice because of the difficulties they present when dealing with real-life problems and restrictions. On the contrary, simple approaches like the one introduced here tend to be more flexible and, therefore, they seem more appropriate to deal with real restrictions and dynamic work conditions. From Tables 1 and 2, notice also that our approach seems to be quite competitive with regards other existing approaches, particularly in the small- and medium-size instances.

Moreover, our methodology is designed to be easily implemented/executed in parallel, that is: by simply changing the values of α or even the seed of the random number generator, several instances of the algorithm can be run in parallel. This can be an interesting field to explore in future work, given the current trend in multi-core CPUs and distributed computing.

At this point, it is also import to discuss some potential limitations of our approach. First of all, even when we have been able to reach low-gap solutions in all tested instances, we are not completely sure that by employing more computational time –or, alternatively, more processing power– we are able to match all best-known solutions. Secondly, convergence times are variable –from seconds to hours– and might depend upon the right choice of the parameter α –so the algorithm is not completely free of fine-tuning if performance is a requirement. Notice, however, that both drawbacks of our approach are also common drawbacks in most other approaches such as SA, GA, TS, GRASP, etc., since they all are eventually based on some kind of random behavior. Hopefully, as discussed before, the combined use of long-period RNGs, processing power, and parallel programming can speed-up convergence rates to a matter of a few seconds for most medium-size CVRP problems.

Finally, it is convenient to highlight that our simulation-based approach can be used beyond the CVRP scenario: with little effort, similar methodologies based on the combination of Monte Carlo simulation with already existing heuristics can be developed for other routing problems and, in general, for other combinatorial optimization problems. In our opinion, this opens a new range of potential applications that could be explored in future works.

CONCLUSION

In this chapter we have shown that it is possible to develop simulation-based approaches to solve the Capacitated Vehicle Routing Problem with route length restrictions and service time requirements. Our approach uses Monte Carlo Simulation to introduce randomness in a classical constructive heuristic. Then, an iterative process generates a set of feasible solutions from which the best ones are saved. The approach also benefits from divide-and-conquer techniques, which contribute to reduce the difficulty of the original instance. Some initial tests show that our approach is competitive, in terms of quality of the generated solution, with other well-known approaches. Some potential advantages and limitations of our approach are also discussed. Finally, the chapter proposes several future research lines, including the use of parallel programming and also the development of similar simulation-based methodologies to solve other combinatorial problems.

ACKNOWLEDGMENT

This work has been partially supported by the CYTED IN3-HAROSA Network, by the Spanish Ministry of Science and Technology under grants TRA2006-10639/TRA2010-21644-C03 and by the Government of Navarre under the research network "Sustainable TransMET".

REFERENCES

Achuthan, N. R., & Caccetta, L. (1991). Integer linear programming formulation for vehicle routing problem. *European Journal of Operational Research*, *52*, 86–89. doi:10.1016/0377-2217(91)90338-V

Alfa, A., Heragu, S., & Chen, M. (1991). A 3-opt based simulated annealing algorithm for the vehicle routing problem. *Computers & Industrial Engineering*, *21*, 635–639. doi:10.1016/0360-8352(91)90165-3

Battarra, M., Golden, B., & Vigo, D. (2008). Tuning a parametric Clarke-Wright heuristic via a genetic algorithm. *The Journal of the Operational Research Society, 59,* 1568–1572. doi:10.1057/palgrave.jors.2602488

Beasley, J. (1981). Adapting the Savings Algorithm for Varying Inter-Customer Travel Times. *Omega, 9,* 658–659. doi:10.1016/0305-0483(81)90055-4

Bell, J., & McMullen, P. (2004). Ant Colony Optimization Techniques for the Vehicle Routing Problem. *Advanced Engineering Informatics, 18,* 41–48. doi:10.1016/j.aei.2004.07.001

Berger, J., & Barkaoui, M. (2003). A Hybrid Genetic Algorithm for the Capacitated Vehicle Routing Problem. In E. Cantó-Paz (ed) *Proceedings of the International Genetic and Evolutionary Computation Conference,* 646–656. Illinois, Chicago: Springer-Verlag.

Buxey, G. (1979). The Vehicle Scheduling Problem and Monte Carlo Simulation. *The Journal of the Operational Research Society, 30,* 563–573.

Christofides, N., Mingozzi, A., & Toth, P. (1979). *The vehicle routing problem.* In N. Christofides, A. Mingozzi, P. Toth, and L. Sandi. (ed). Combinatorial Optimization, 315–338, Chichester, UK: Wiley.

Clarke, G., & Wright, J. (1964). Scheduling of Vehicles from a central Depot to a Number of Delivering Points. *Operations Research, 12,* 568–581. doi:10.1287/opre.12.4.568

Desrochers, M., & Laporte, G. (1991). Improvements and extensions to the Miller-Tucker-Zemlin subtour elimination constraints. *Operations Research Letters, 10,* 27–36. doi:10.1016/0167-6377(91)90083-2

Doyuran, T., & Çatay, B. (2010). A robust enhancement to the Clarke-Wright savings algorithm. *The Journal of the Operational Research Society, 62,* 223–231. doi:10.1057/jors.2009.176

Dror, M., & Trudeau, P. (1986). Stochastic Vehicle Routing with Modified Savings Algorithm. *European Journal of Operational Research, 23,* 228–235. doi:10.1016/0377-2217(86)90242-0

Faulin, J., & Juan, A. (2008). The ALGACEA-1 Method for the Capacitated Vehicle Routing Problem. *International Transactions in Operational Research, 15,* 1–23. doi:10.1111/j.1475-3995.2008.00640.x

Fernandez, P., Garcia, L., Mayado, A., & Sanchis, J. (2000). A Real Delivery Problem Dealt with Monte Carlo Techniques. *Top (Madrid), 8,* 57–71. doi:10.1007/BF02564828

Festa, P., & Resende, M. G. C. (2009). An Annotated Bibliography of GRASP- Part I: Algorithms. *International Transactions in Operational Research, 16,* 1–24. doi:10.1111/j.1475-3995.2009.00663.x

Gendreau, M., Hertz, A., & Laporte, G. (1994). A Tabu Search Heuristic for the Vehicle Routing Problem. *Management Science, 40,* 1276–1290. doi:10.1287/mnsc.40.10.1276

Golden, B., Raghavan, S., & Wasil, E. (2008). *The Vehicle Routing Problem: Latest Advances and New Challenges.* New York: Springer. doi:10.1007/978-0-387-77778-8

Holmes, R., & Parker, R. (1976). A Vehicle Scheduling Procedure Based Upon Savings and a Solution Perturbation Scheme. *Operational Research Quarterly, 27,* 83–92.

Juan, A., Faulin, J., Ruiz, R., Barrios, B., Gilibert, M., & Vilajosana, X. (2009). Using oriented random search to provide a set of alternative solutions to the capacitated vehicle routing problem. In J. Chinneck, B. Kristjansson, M. Saltzman (ed). *Operations Research and Cyber-Infrastructure,* 331–346. New York: Springer.

Kant, G., Jacks, M., & Aantjes, C. (2008). Coca-Cola Enterprises Optimizes Vehicle Routes for Efficient Product Delivery. *Interfaces, 38,* 40–50. doi:10.1287/inte.1070.0331

Kara, I., & Bektaş, T. (2005). *Integer Linear Programming Formulations of Distance Constrained Vehicle Routing Problems*. Technical Report, Baskent University, Department of Industrial Engineering.

Kara, I., Laporte, G., & Bektaş, T. (2004). A note on the lifted Miller-Tucker-Zemlin subtour elimination constraints for the capacitated vehicle routing problem. *European Journal of Operational Research, 158*, 793–795. doi:10.1016/S0377-2217(03)00377-1

Kulkarni, R. V., & Bhave, P. R. (1985). Integer programming formulations of vehicle routing problems. *European Journal of Operational Research, 20*, 58–67. doi:10.1016/0377-2217(85)90284-X

L'Ecuyer, P. (2002). SSJ: A Framework for Stochastic Simulation in Java. In *Proceedings of the 2002 Winter Simulation Conference* 234–242.

L'Ecuyer, P. (2006). Random Number Generation. In S. Henderson and B. Nelson (eds) *Handbooks in Operations Research and Management Science: Simulation*, 55–81. Amsterdam: Elsevier Science.

Laporte, G. (2007). What you should know about the Vehicle Routing Problem. *Naval Research Logistics, 54*, 811–819. doi:10.1002/nav.20261

Laporte, G., & Semet, F. (2001). *The vehicle routing problem*. In P. Toth and D. Vigo (eds.) SIAM monographs on discrete mathematics and application, 109–125.

Law, A. (2007). *Simulation Modeling & Analysis*. New York: McGraw-Hill.

Lin, S., Lee, Z., Ying, K., & Lee, C. (2009). Applying hybrid meta-heuristics for capacitated vehicle routing problem. *Expert Systems with Applications, 36*(2), 1505–1512. doi:10.1016/j.eswa.2007.11.060

Mester, D., & Bräysy, O. (2007). Active-guided evolution strategies for the large-scale capacitated vehicle routing problems. *Computers & Operations Research, 34*, 2964–2975. doi:10.1016/j.cor.2005.11.006

Mole, R., & Jameson, S. (1976). A Sequential Route-building Algorithm Employing a Generalised Savings Criterion. *Operational Research Quarterly, 27*, 503–511.

Naddef, D. (1994). A remark on "Integer linear programming formulation for a vehicle routing problem" by N.R. Achutan and L. Caccetta, or how to use Clark and Wright savings to write such integer linear programming formulations. *European Journal of Operational Research, 75*, 238–241. doi:10.1016/0377-2217(94)90198-8

Paessens, H. (1988). The Savings Algorithm for the Vehicle Routing Problem. *European Journal of Operational Research, 34*, 336–344. doi:10.1016/0377-2217(88)90154-3

Prins, C. (2004). A Simple and Effective Evolutionary Algorithm for the Vehicle Routing Problem. *Computers & Operations Research, 31*, 1985–2002. doi:10.1016/S0305-0548(03)00158-8

Resende, M. (2008). Metaheuristic hybridization with Greedy Randomized Adaptive Search Procedures. In Z. Chen and S. Raghavan, (ed), *TutORials in Operations Research*, 295–319.

Taillard, E. (1993). Parallel Iterative Search Methods for Vehicle Routing Problems. *Networks, 23*, 661–673. doi:10.1002/net.3230230804

Tarantilis, C., & Kiranoudis, C. (2002). BoneRoute: an Adaptative Memory-Based Method for Effective Fleet Management. *Annals of Operations Research, 115*, 227–241. doi:10.1023/A:1021157406318

Toth, P., & Vigo, D. (2002). *The Vehicle Routing Problem. SIAM Monographs on Discrete Mathematics and Applications.* SIAM.

Toth, P., & Vigo, D. (2003). The Granular Tabu Search and its Application to the Vehicle Routing Problem. *INFORMS Journal on Computing, 15,* 333–346. doi:10.1287/ijoc.15.4.333.24890

Section 2
Hybrid Algorithms for Scheduling Problems

Chapter 7
A Hybrid Particle Swarm Algorithm for Resource-Constrained Project Scheduling

Jens Czogalla
Helmut-Schmidt-University Hamburg, Germany

Andreas Fink
Helmut-Schmidt-University Hamburg, Germany

ABSTRACT

The authors present and analyze a particle swarm optimization (PSO) approach for the resource-constrained project scheduling problem (RCPSP). It incorporates well-known procedures such as the serial schedule generation scheme and it is hybridized with forward-backward improvement. The authors investigate the application of PSO in comparison to state-of-the-art methods from the literature. They conduct extensive computational experiments using a benchmark set of problem instances. The reported results demonstrate that the proposed hybrid particle swarm optimization approach is competitive. They significantly improve previous results of PSO for the RCPSP and provide new overall best average results for the medium size data set. Furthermore, the authors provide insights into the importance of crucial components for achieving high-quality results.

1 INTRODUCTION

The problem considered in this chapter is the non-preemptive single mode resource-constrained project scheduling problem (RCPSP). It consists in scheduling a set of activities with deterministic processing times, resource requirements, and precedence relations between activities. The aim is to find a schedule with minimum makespan (total project duration) respecting both precedence relations and resource limits. The RCPSP is a classical problem in project scheduling. It is related to and subsumes many other scheduling problems (e.g., the job shop scheduling problem as a special case

DOI: 10.4018/978-1-61350-086-6.ch007

(Brucker et al., 1999)). The RCPSP is encountered in diverse application areas, including production, service industry, software development, and civil engineering. For a recent survey of variants and extensions of the RCPSP we refer to Hartmann and Briskorn (2010).

Various exact methods for the RCPSP have been proposed – e.g., implicit enumeration with branch and bound, zero-one programming, and dynamic programming (for a survey see Kolisch & Padman (2001)). The currently best known exact method is described by Schutt et al. (2009); it is based on the constrained programming approach.

Since the RCPSP is NP-hard (Blazewicz et al., 1983), exact methods may be time consuming and inefficient for solving large problems and real-world applications. Hence, the majority of state-of-the-art algorithms are based on metaheuristics. Kolisch & Hartmann (2006) present a comprehensive experimental evaluation of heuristic approaches for the RCPSP. In their tests the best performing heuristics are population-based metaheuristics that use the activity-list representation and the serial schedule generation scheme. In addition, the forward-backward improvement method is noted as an effective component of most state-of-the-art algorithms.

Evolutionary computation (EC) algorithms manipulate a population of solutions rather than a single solution. A prominent subclass of these algorithms is based on ideas recently derived from swarm intelligence. To the best of our knowledge almost no research has been devoted on using and investigating the paradigm of swarm intelligence, in particular particle swarm optimization (PSO), for the RCPSP with comprehensive computational experiments following the test design used by Kolisch & Hartmann (2006). Zhang et al. (2005) propose a PSO approach for the RCPSP and compare the effectiveness of different solution representations; computational results are provided only for small problem instances.

The aim of this chapter is to develop and investigate a robust evolutionary computation

algorithm which combines concepts from swarm intelligence and well-known procedures for the RCPSP that is competitive to state-of-the-art algorithms. Via computational experiments we analyze the importance of algorithm components that are crucial for achieving high-quality results. The remainder of this chapter is organized as follows: We provide a formal description of the RCPSP and a review of related literature in Section 2. In Section 3 we present a general framework for EC algorithms and describe the incorporation of swarm intelligence features and procedures for the RCPSP. The computational experiments will be subject of Section 4. Finally we draw conclusions in Section 5.

2 BACKGROUND

In this section we formally introduce the RCPSP and briefly review the related literature.

2.1 Formal Problem Description

A project consists of a set J of N activities, $J = \{1, ..., N\}$ and a set R of K renewable resources, $R = \{1, ..., K\}$. In general the dummy start activity 1 and the dummy termination activity N are added to the project and act as source and sink of the project, respectively. The duration or processing time of activity $j \in J$ is d_j with $d_1 = d_N = 0$. Each activity has to be processed without interruption. Precedence constraints force activity j not to be started before all its immediate predecessors in the set $P_j \subset J$ have been finished. The structure of a project can be represented by an activity-on-node network $G = (V, A)$, where V is the set of activities J and A is the set of precedence relationships (Valls & Ballestin, 2004). While being processed, activity j requires $r_{j,k}$ units of resource $k \in R$ in every time unit of its duration (with $r_{1,k} = r_{N,k} = 0$, $k = 1, ..., K$). For each renewable resource k there is a limited capacity of R_k at any point in time. The values d_j, R_k, and $r_{j,k}$ (duration of activities, availability of resources, and resource requirements of activities) are assumed to be nonnegative and deterministic.

A schedule can be presented as $S = (s_1, \ldots, s_N)$, where s_j denotes the start time of activity j with $s_1 = 0$. The objective is to determine the start time of each activity, so that the project makespan (total project duration, s_N) is minimized, and both the precedence and the resource constraints are satisfied.

As a generalization of the classical job shop scheduling problem the RCPSP belongs to the class of NP-hard optimization problems (Blazewicz et al., 1983) and it is noted as $PS \mid prec \mid C_{max}$ according to the common classification and notation described by Brucker et al. (1999).

2.2 Literature Review

For the RCPSP comprehensive surveys are available in the literature. Ozdamar & Ulusoy (1995) classify research on the RCPSP according to the considered objectives and constraints. Herroelen et al. (1998) discuss the research on exact solution procedures for the RCPSP and related problems. Brucker et al. (1999) provide a classification scheme which is compatible with machine scheduling, propose a unifying notation, and review exact and heuristic algorithms for the RCPSP. Kolisch & Hartmann (1999) give a survey of heuristic approaches for the RCPSP, including priority rules and metaheuristics; based on extensive computational experiments they evaluate the performance of the reviewed approaches. Kolisch & Padman (2001) survey the literature with a perspective towards integrating models, data, and optimal and heuristic algorithms; a comparison of commercial project scheduling systems is presented as well as an overview of web-based decision support systems. Hartmann & Kolisch (2000) and Kolisch & Hartmann (2006) present basic components of heuristic approaches and evaluate the state-of-the-art of the design and application of metaheuristics for the RCPSP on a benchmark set of test instances.

Heuristic methods for the RCPSP are mainly based on the application of schedule generation schemes (SGS). Activity lists (permutations of the activities) represent the activities' priorities within a SGS, which determines the start times of the activities. Thus, the solution space of the RCPSP is indirectly represented by the set of all permutations of the activities. The application of metaheuristics for the RCPSP provides guidance for search processes within such a solution space – with the aim of balancing intensification (exploitation of solutions within promising regions of the search space) and diversification (exploration within the global search space). Metaheuristics can be broadly classified into local search methods and population-based approaches. These approaches may be hybridized; often local search is used as an intensification mechanism within a population-based procedure.

Boctor (1996) presents a simulated annealing algorithm using the serial SGS and one neighborhood operator. Bouffard & Ferland (2007) improve the simulated annealing algorithm presented by Jeffcoat & Bulfin (1993); the algorithm works directly on schedules and is enhanced with a variable neighborhood search using four neighborhood operators. Nonobe & Ibaraki (2002) describe a tabu search approach based on the activity list representation and the serial SGS; a random neighborhood reduction mechanism is introduced in order to reduce the size of the neighborhoods. Thomas & Salhi (1998) propose a tabu search that operates directly on schedules; they define three neighborhoods and present a repair method since schedules obtained by applying a neighborhood move may be infeasible.

Hartmann (1998) proposes a genetic algorithm using a permutation-based genetic encoding containing problem-specific knowledge. In Hartmann (2002) a self-adapting genetic algorithm is described, which employs a genetic encoding where a gene decides if a serial or a parallel SGS is used.

Hindi et al. (2002) propose a genetic algorithm based on the activity list representation and the serial SGS. Alcaraz & Maroto (2001) propose a genetic algorithm using novel crossover techniques and a new solution representation, which is based on the standard activity list representation where an additional gene decides if forward or backward scheduling is used. Alcaraz et al. (2004) and Alcaraz & Maroto (2006) further develop the solution representation proposed in Alcaraz & Maroto (2001) and employ an additional gene to encode if a serial or a parallel SGS is used (as in Hartmann, 2002).

Debels et al. (2006) propose a scatter search algorithm employing a recombination operator based on ideas from electromagnetism theory; forward-backward improvement is integrated in order to enhance single solutions. Kochetov & Stolyar (2003) describe an evolutionary algorithm which is based on a path relinking strategy and tabu search combined with a variable neighborhood local search. Merkle et al. (2002) propose an ant colony optimization algorithm where the ants use a combination of two pheromone evaluation methods to find new solutions. During the search process the relative influence of the heuristic on the decisions of the ants is changed. Additional features are the decreasing influence of elitist solutions by forgetting them at regular intervals as well as a 2-opt-based local search phase.

Valls & Ballestin (2004) propose a population-based approach with two phases; in the first phase elements of scatter search and path relinking and an alternative application of an improving procedure create promising solutions; in the second phase the search space around those high-quality solutions is explored. Valls et al. (2005) propose the so-called double justification technique and show its efficiency by incorporating it in several heuristic algorithms. Valls et al. (2008) present a hybrid genetic algorithm employing a novel crossover operator (peak crossover) and a new selection operator; a local improvement operator

(double justification) is applied to all generated schedules.

The recent literature includes only very few descriptions of the use of PSO for the RCPSP and related problems. Zhang et al. (2005) propose a PSO for the RCPSP and compare the effectiveness of priority-based representation and permutation-based representation. The serial schedule generation scheme is employed. Computational results for the standard set of small instances indicate the superiority of the permutation-based solution representation. Zhang et al. (2006) employ the random key representation to transform real valued particle positions in permutations of activities and modes to solve the multimode resource-constrained project scheduling problem (MRCPSP). The serial SGS is used to generate a schedule. A repair mechanism is introduced which handles constraint violations of nonrenewable resources. Linyi & Yan (2007) propose a PSO for the resource-constrained multi-project scheduling problem (RCMPSP). The serial SGS is used to transform an activity list into a schedule. As genetic operators a one-point crossover and a mutation called activity search are employed. Jarboui et al. (2008) propose an approach to solve the MRCPSP where a PSO is employed to select the mode for each activity. The activities are then ordered by a local search procedure.

3 ALGORITHM

In this section we first present a framework for EC algorithms and give a brief description of the main features of the general algorithm. Then we review the particle swarm optimization (PSO) approach and present our approach of adapting it to the RCPSP. That is, we describe the design of swarm intelligence features and heuristic methods for the RCPSP within the general framework for EC algorithms.

Algorithm 1. The used general framework for EC algorithms

```
 1:    initialize parameters
 2:    P:= CreatePopulation ()
 3:    repeat
 4:        repeat
 5:                parents:= Selection (P)
 6:                offspring:= Recombination (parents)
 7:                offspring:= Mutation (offspring)
 8:                offspring:= Improvement (offspring)
 9:                P:= Include (P, offspring)
10:            until iteration completed
11:    until stop criterion met
```

3.1 Evolutionary Computation Algorithms

The basic idea of EC algorithms is that individuals of a population, which represent solutions, interact with one another in order to create new individuals (solutions) containing information inherited from the parents. Probabilistic operators such as selection, recombination, and mutation are employed to guide the evolution process with the aim to transform the population towards better fitness values (i.e., better objective function values). Algorithm 1 shows a general framework for EC algorithms, which defines the template for our design of a specific PSO approach for the RCPSP. That is, in Section 3.3 we describe the solution representation and the definition of the procedures employed in Algorithm 1.

First, the *CreatePopulation*() method initializes the population. Randomly created individuals may be inserted into the population until a predefined population size is reached. More sophisticated techniques (e.g., special construction heuristics) may be employed to generate improved individuals for the initial population. Additionally, acceptance criteria (e.g., with respect to the diversity within the population) may be defined for the inclusion of individuals (e.g., a lower bound

for the minimum distance to all other individuals that are already included in the population).

The population evolves iteratively until some termination criterion is met (e.g., with respect to the elapsed computation time or the number of generated (evaluated) schedules). In each iteration a number of individuals are created (e.g., depending on the population size). In the *Selection*() method a number of individuals are selected as parents. Since some of the individuals may be selected more than once parents constitutes a multiset. In the *Recombination*() method new individuals, called offspring, are created by combining two or more solutions from parents. The *Mutation*() method applies unary operators to offspring individuals with the aim to introduce variability. In the *Improvement*() method individuals may be enhanced by means of problem-specific operators. Finally the offspring solutions may be included into the population according to the *Include*() method, which may implement different strategies, e.g., replacement of all individuals contained in parents, replacement of some of the worst solutions of the population, or simply adding new solutions (thus increasing the population size). Again additional acceptance criteria may be defined, e.g., the included solutions may have to improve the average fitness of the population or they must not already be contained in the population.

Most of the state-of-the-art algorithms reported in Kolisch & Hartmann (2006) fit within the general framework presented in Algorithm 1. Classical genetic algorithms (GA), which are inspired by the mechanism of natural evolution combining survival of the fittest and randomized information exchange (Holland, 1975), are the most prominent example of EC algorithms. Genetic algorithms for the RCPSP are proposed by Alcaraz & Maroto (2001), Alcaraz et al. (2004), Hartmann (1998, 2002), Kochetov & Stolyar (2003), and Valls et al. (2005, 2008). Scatter search (Glover et al., 2003) generally operates on a relatively small number of solutions, called reference set. Some combination of two or more candidates from the reference set creates new solutions, which may be improved by means of local search. Some of the obtained solutions may be inserted into the population according to some rule with the aim to guarantee both high solution quality and high diversity among the solutions in the reference set. Debels et al. (2006) propose a scatter search algorithm for the RCPSP.

3.2 Particle Swarm Optimization

Particle swarm optimization (PSO) is a metaheuristic based on swarm intelligence ideas, originally introduced and applied for the optimization of continuous nonlinear functions by Kennedy & Eberhart in 1995 (Kennedy & Eberhart, 1995; Eberhart & Kennedy, 1995). Merkle & Middendorf (2005) provide an introduction to PSO and the related literature. Kennedy & Eberhart (2001) present a more detailed introduction to PSO within the scope of swarm intelligence.

The basic idea of PSO is that a swarm of particles (i.e., individuals), which represent search (solution) space locations (positions), moves through the search space, thus exploring it and finding new solutions. The position $x_i \in R^n$ of each particle i is updated depending on the current location and locations where good solutions have already been found by the particle itself (individual memory) or other particles in the swarm (social memory). The velocity v_i of a particle i is canonically updated as follows:

$$v_i := w * v_i + c_1 * U(0,1) * (p_i - x_i) + c_2 * U(0,1) * (g - x_i)$$

where p_i is the best previous position of the particle and g is the best found position within the swarm so far. The parameter w is called the inertia weight and represents the influence of the previous velocity. The parameters c_1 and c_2 are acceleration coefficients which determine the impact of p_i and g, i.e., the individual and social memory, respectively. Randomness is introduced by weighting the influence of the individual and social memory by random values uniformly drawn from [0,1]. After updating the velocity, the new position of the particle is calculated as

$$x_i := x_i + v_i.$$

There are different approaches for applying PSO to combinatorial optimization problems. On the one hand one may use, e.g., a random key representation (Bean, 1994) and convert real-valued position values into an activity permutation by ordering them according to ascending position values (see the priority-based representation in Zhang et al. (2005)). On the other hand the solution representation and the position update may be adapted for the considered combinatorial optimization problem. Allahverdi & Al-Anzi (2006) present an approach where particles are associated with permutations of elements and two velocities that correspond to probabilities of changing elements. Hu et al. (2003) introduce a modified PSO were the velocity update is redefined based on the similarity of two particles. Particles change their permutations with a random rate defined by their velocity. Moraglio et al. (2007) introduce geometric particle swarm optimization (GPSO) as a generalization of the original PSO for combinatorial optimization problems. This approach is based on the definition of geometric crossover operators depending on a distance function (metric) for the search space and a related neighborhood structure. While GPSO provides a general framework to be applied for any combinatorial optimization problem on the basis of some solution space and neighborhood structure, discrete particle swarm optimization (DPSO) as described by Pan et al. (2006) is based on problem-specific solution spaces and operators (see also Czogalla & Fink, 2008). Using a binary operator $\oplus$ with the meaning that the first operand defines the probability that the operator given as second operand is applied, the update of a particle position is defined as

$$X_i := c_2 \oplus F_3 (c_1 \oplus F_2 (w \oplus F_1 (X_i), P_i), G).$$

The first term of this equation is $\lambda_i = w \oplus F_1 (X_i)$ which represents the "velocity" of the particle. F_1 is a swap operator which swaps two randomly chosen activities within the permutation X_i of the i-th particle. The second part $\delta_i = c_1 \oplus F_2 (\lambda_i, P_i)$ represents the individual memory of the particle and F_2 is a crossover operator applying a one-cut crossover on λ_i and the best position of the particle so far. The social part is represented by $X_i = c_2 \oplus F_3 (\delta_i, G)$ with F_3 as a crossover operator using a two-cut crossover on δ_i and the best position of the swarm G. The parameters w, c_1, and c_2 determine the probabilities of the application of swap and crossover operators, respectively.

3.3 Discrete PSO for the RCPSP

In this section we incorporate swarm intelligence concepts from PSO, as described earlier in this section, into the general framework for EC algorithms (Algorithm 1) and we design the problem-specific features for the RCPSP.

SOLUTION REPRESENTATION AND SCHEDULE GENERATION SCHEME

A solution (particle) is represented as an activity list which is assumed to be a precedence feasible permutation of the set of activities J. The position in the activity list defines the activities' priorities (highest priority for the first position). In order to derive a schedule (i.e., to determine start times of the activities) from the activity list a schedule generation scheme (SGS) is used as decoding procedure. For a detailed description of the serial and parallel generation scheme see Kolisch (1996). In this chapter we use the serial SGS, which proceeds in N stages. At each stage one activity, with every predecessor activity scheduled, is selected according to the priorities and is scheduled at its earliest precedence and resource feasible start time. The algorithm terminates when all activities are scheduled.

In addition to this forward scheduling technique backward scheduling can be applied. Starting with the last activity in the activity list, an activity can be scheduled at its latest feasible start time such that all precedence constraints are observed. Applying different scheduling modes to the same activity list may result in different schedules with different makespans (Alcaraz & Maroto, 2001).

The result of the serial SSG is an active schedule, i.e., no activity can be started earlier without delaying some other activity (Hartmann and Kolisch, 2000). For a formal definition of active schedules see Sprecher et al. (1995). The set of active schedules will always contain an optimal solution, i.e., the serial SGS does not exclude optimal schedules a priori (Hartmann and Kolisch, 2000). There is some redundancy in the search space since different activity lists (individuals or solutions within the search space) may be related to the same schedule.

Since the solution representation is assumed to be a precedence feasible permutation, list scheduling, a more efficient variant of the serial SGS, can be used. Given a precedence feasible activity list, the activities can be scheduled in the order of the list at the earliest precedence and resource feasible start time. As a special case of the serial SGS, list scheduling has the same properties as the serial SGS. That is, it generates active schedules and hence there is always an activity list for which list scheduling will generate an optimal schedule (Hartmann & Kolisch, 2000).

As in Alcaraz & Maroto (2001) we add an additional gene (forward-backward gene) to the solution to indicate which scheduling mode is used to generate the schedule.

Creation of the Initial Population

We make use of two ways to create the initial swarm population: random and biased sampling. In the random approach the list of activities is constructed such that each activity appears in the list in a random position after all its predecessors. In addition to this random approach, we employ a method which determines the initial population using the *regret-based biased random sampling procedure* as described in Kolisch (1996). As priority rule we use the *latest finish time rule* (LFT) in order to derive probabilities which are used to select the next activity for the activity list.

In order to determine the value of the forward-backward gene two schedules are generated for each individual using both scheduling modes. If the better schedule is obtained with the forward scheduling the forward-backward gene is set to "forward". Otherwise it is set to "backward" (as in Alcaraz & Maroto, 2001).

Selection and Include

The selection mechanism employed by the DPSO algorithm selects the current solution (position) of the particle, the best solution found by the particle, and the best solution found by the swarm so far (i.e., the *Selection*() method is deterministic). The *Include*() method replaces the current position of the particle with the generated offspring.

Recombination

In the *Recombination*() method a crossover operator is applied to parents with the probability p_{rec} in order to create a new solution.

In Hartmann (1998) the *two-point crossover* was proposed along with the proof that it produces only precedence feasible offspring when applied to two precedence feasible parents. Since in our PSO approach *parents* consists of three elements, we extend the design of the crossover operator to create one offspring individual from three parent solutions. First, two integers q_1 and q_2 with $1 \leq q_1 < q_2 \leq N$ are chosen as cut points. The offspring O is determined by first taking the list of activities at the positions $i = 1, ..., q_1$ from the first parent P_1:

$$j_i^O := j_i^{P1}.$$

Then the activities at positions $i = q_1 + 1, ..., q_2$ are taken from the second parent P_2:

$$j_i^O := j_k^{P2}$$

where k is the lowest index such that

$$j_k^{P2} \notin \{ j_1^O, ..., j_{i-1}^O \}.$$

The remaining activities $i = q_2 + 1, ..., N$ are taken from the third parent P_3:

$$j_i^O := j_k^{P3}$$

where k is the lowest index such that

$$j_k^{P3} \notin \{ j_1^O, ..., j_{i-1}^O \}.$$

As an example we consider the (precedence feasible) individuals

$$P_1 = \{ 1, 2, 5, 6, 3, 7, 4, 8, 10, 9, 11 \},$$

$$P_2 = \{ 1, 3, 4, 2, 8, 7, 6, 5, 9, 10, 11 \},$$

and

$$P_3 = \{ 1, 4, 8, 2, 6, 5, 9, 3, 7, 10, 11 \}.$$

With the cut points chosen as $q_1 = 2$ and $q_2 = 7$ the offspring results in

$$O = \{ 1, 2 \mid 3, 4, 8, 7, 6 \mid 5, 9, 10, 11 \}.$$

The acceleration coefficients c_1 and c_2 determine the impact of the parents on the offspring and thus influence the balance between exploration and exploitation. In our design the cut points q_1 and q_2 reflect the influence of the parent solutions on the offspring. In order to design a robust algorithm and to reduce the number of parameters we randomly chose values for q_1 and q_2 prior to each application of the crossover operator. Furthermore we decide randomly how the actual particle solution, the best particle solution, and the best solution found by the swarm are assigned as parents P_1, P_2, and P_3.

The decision which scheduling mode is used to interpret the generated activity list is also part of the evolutionary process. The probability of choosing forward or backward scheduling is proportional to the frequency of the scheduling modes in the three parents. In order to enable diversity with respect to the scheduling mode the inverse scheduling mode is selected with a probability of 0.10 if all three parents are interpreted by the same scheduling mode.

Mutation

The mutation operator applied in the *Mutation*() method is a restricted shift or insertion operator, which is well-known for permutation-based representations (see, e.g., Alcaraz & Maroto, 2001; Boctor, 1996). A neighbor is generated by choosing an activity and randomly changing its position in the list. In order to generate a precedence feasible solution, the selected activity must be moved to a position that neither precedes any of its predecessors nor succeeds any of its successors. Formally,

let r_i denote the position of the i-th activity in the current list, P_i the set of its immediate predecessors, S_i the set of its immediate successors, $L_i = \max \{ r_j, \forall j \in P_i \}$, and $H_i = \min \{ r_j, \forall j \in S_i \}$. If i is to be moved to a new position it has to be placed in a position between (and including) the position $L_i + 1$ and the position $H_i - 1$. Scanning the activity list each activity will be subject to the described mutation operator with probability p_{mut}. Note that the mutation probability is usually quite small (see Section 4).

Improvement

Current research generally shows the usefulness of the hybridization of evolutionary algorithms with problem-specific improvement operators in order to obtain high-quality results. Consequently, most effective evolutionary methods use some kind of hybridization to improve individual solutions; see, e.g., Ruiz et al. (2006). Resulting algorithms are also called memetic algorithms (Krasnogor & Smith, 2005; Moscato, 1989), termed in relation to the concept of a meme (coined by Richard Dawkins), which describes the acquisition and propagation of learned features (beyond genes). Scatter search (Glover, 1997; Glover et al., 2003) is an example for an EC algorithm which emphasizes local search as a crucial element of the search process.

As shown by Kolisch & Hartmann (2006) most state-of-the-art algorithms for the RCPSP use a local improvement method called forward-backward improvement (FBI). This multi-pass heuristic scheduling procedure was proposed by Li & Willis (1992) and used by Ozdamar & Ulusoy (1996). We employ FBI in the *Improvement*() method to the solutions generated in the evolutionary process with probability p_{imp}. The FBI method employs a SGS, in our case the serial variant, in order to iteratively schedule the project by alternating between forward and backward scheduling. The backward and forward passes are based on free slack of activities. The forward free slack and backward free slack of an activity in a feasible schedule is the amount of time that the activity can be shifted right or left, respectively, allowing the remaining activities to start on their scheduled dates (Tormos & Lova, 2001). A feasible schedule is improved by a backward-forward pass. In the backward pass, the activities are considered from right to left and scheduled at the latest feasible time (i.e., they are shifted to the right). Subsequently, in the forward pass, they are considered form left to right and scheduled at the earliest feasible time (i.e., they are shifted back to the left) (Kolisch & Hartmann, 2006). In every pass two schedules are generated. This method is repeated until no further improvement can be achieved. Depending on the scheduling mode the procedure's sequence may be reversed. A similar procedure (called double justification) is proposed and generalized by Valls et al. (2005, 2006).

4 COMPUTATIONAL RESULTS

We implemented the DPSO for the RCPSP in C#, pursuing an object-oriented approach, thus allowing easy combination of different heuristic components. The DPSO was run on an Intel Core 2 Duo processor with 3.0 GHz and 2 GB RAM.

We employ the test sets J30, J60, J90, and J120 which have been constructed by the problem instance generator ProGen (Kolisch et al., 1995; Kolisch & Sprecher, 1996). The projects consist of 30, 60, 90 and 120 activities, respectively. In total there are 480 instances with 30, 60, and 90 activities and 600 instances with 120 activities. The instances, as well as the best known solutions, are available from the project scheduling library PSPLIB (available at http://129.187.106.231/psplib/).

The design of the experiments is in line with Kolisch and Hartmann (2006) in order to compare our approach with state-of-the-art methods for the RCPSP. We use a specified number of generated

schedules as termination criterion. Each configuration is evaluated by 5 runs for each problem instance. The quality of the results is reported as the percentage relative deviation

$$\Delta_{avg} = (F_A - F_{ref}) / F_{ref} * 100$$

where F_A is the makespan generated by the examined algorithm A and F_{ref} is the optimal makespan for the test set J30 and the critical path lower bound (obtained by computing the length of a critical path in the resource relaxation of the problem) for the instances with 60, 90, and 120 activities.

4.1 Parameter Selection

In order to determine accurate values for the parameters *popsize* (number of particles), p_{rec} (recombination/crossover probability), p_{mut} (mutation probability), and p_{imp} (probability for application of FBI) a full factorial design might be desirable, which would test all combinations of parameters from specific sets of reasonable values. However, such a strategy is impractical because of the large number of experiments to be carried out. Therefore, we utilize ParamILS, a local search approach for algorithm configuration proposed by Hutter et al. (2007) (see also Hutter, 2007). Based on some preliminary experiments the parameters were discretized as shown in Table 1. (A full factorial design would consist of 10 * 11 * 14 * 11 = 16940 parameter configurations.) ParamILS was run using FocusedILS with the objective of maximizing the average approximation quality relative to the best known solutions with 1000 generated schedules as termination criterion. The obtained parameter values are presented in Table 2. Note that we use the same parameter configuration for the runs with 1000, 5000, and 50000 schedules as termination criterion (unlike some other papers).

Table 1. Considered parameter values

Parameter	Values considered for tuning
popsize	10, 20, 30, 40, 50, 60, 70, 80, 90, 100
p_{rec}	0, 0.1, 0.2, 0.3, 0.4, 0.5, 0.6, 0.7, 0.8, 0.9, 1
p_{mut}	0, 0.01, 0.02, 0.03, 0.04, 0.05, 0.06, 0.07, 0.08, 0.09, 0.1, 0.15, 0.2, 0.3
p_{imp}	0, 0.1, 0.2, 0.3, 0.4, 0.5, 0.6, 0.7, 0.8, 0.9, 1

Table 2. Determined parameter values

Parameter	J30	J60	J90	J120
popsize	70	30	20	20
p_{rec}	0.80	1.00	1.00	1.00
p_{mut}	0.20	0.05	0.05	0.03
p_{imp}	0.60	1.00	1.00	1.00

4.2 Basic Results

Computational results of our approach are presented in Table 3. In addition to the average deviation (Δ_{avg}) we report the standard deviation (S.D.), the minimum (Min.) and the maximum (Max.) of the average deviation, and the average CPU time (CPU) in seconds.

Tables 4, 5, and 6 compare the DPSO approach to state-of-the-art methods for the instance sets J30, J60, and J120, respectively. The tables extend tables taken from Kolisch & Hartmann (2006): We add our results (DPSO, in bold) as well as

results reported by Alcaraz & Maroto (2006) and Jedrzejowicz & Ratajczak (2006) (in italics). The results for Alcaraz & Maroto (2001) are supplemented with the average deviations for 50,000 schedules and reordered accordingly. The used procedures are described by keywords, the used SGS, and the reference to the literature. The methods are ordered with respect to the results for 50,000 evaluated schedules.

The results show that our algorithm is competitive compared to state-of-the-art methods and even performs best on the instance set J60. The small standard deviations reported in Table 3 indicate the robustness of the algorithm.

We note that the results are by far better than those of Zhang et al. (2005). This may be explained through the absence of a mutation operator that limits the effectiveness of the PMX crossover operator. Additionally no improvement method is used to enhance single solutions.

Table 3. Results for DPSO

Instance set	Schedules	Δ_{avg}	S.D.	Min.	Max.	CPU
J30	1,000	**0.358**	0.013	0.343	0.371	0.05
	5,000	**0.143**	0.019	0.141	0.184	0.22
	50,000	**0.049**	0.011	0.032	0.060	2.07
J60	1,000	**11.558**	0.034	11.513	11.605	0.09
	5,000	**11.008**	0.022	10.982	11.042	0.45
	50,000	**10.681**	0.023	10.657	10.712	4.40
J90	1,000	**11.319**	0.035	11.269	11.362	0.15
	5,000	**10.768**	0.019	10.734	10.779	0.70
	50,000	**10.345**	0.017	10.326	10.369	6.88
J120	1,000	**34.945**	0.068	34.853	35.022	0.25
	5,000	**33.335**	0.047	33.260	33.382	1.11
	50,000	**32.192**	0.059	32.108	32.250	10.60

Table 4. Average deviations (%) from optimal makespan (J30) (extension of Kolisch and Hartmann (2006))

Algorithm	SGS	Reference	Schedules		
			1,000	5,000	50,000
GA,TS – path relinking	both	*Kochetov and Stolyar (2003)*	0.10	0.04	0.00
GA – *hybrid, FBI*	*both*	*Alcaraz and Maroto (2006)*	*0.15*	*0.06*	*0.01*
Scatter Search – FBI	serial	*Debels et al. (2006)*	0.27	0.11	0.01
GA – hybrid, FBI	serial	*Valls et al.(2008)*	0.27	0.06	0.02
GA – FBI	serial	*Valls et al. (2005)*	0.34	0.20	0.02
GA – forw.-backw., FBI	both	*Alcaraz et al. (2004)*	0.25	0.06	0.03
sampling – LFT, FBI	both	*Tormos and Lova (2003b)*	0.25	0.13	0.05
DPSO – FBI	**serial**	**Czogalla and Fink**	**0.36**	**0.14**	**0.05**
TS – activity list	serial	*Nonobe and Ibaraki (2002)*	0.46	0.16	0.05
sampling LFT, FBI	both	*Tormos and Lova (2001)*	0.30	0.16	0.07
PLA	*serial*	*Jedrzejowicz and Ratajczak (2006)*	*0.45*	*0.13*	*0.08*
GA – self-adapting	both	*Hartmann (2002)*	0.38	0.22	0.08
GA – activity list	serial	*Hartmann (1998)*	0.54	0.25	0.08
sampling – LFT, FBI	both	*Tormos and Lova (2003a)*	0.30	0.17	0.09
GA – forw.-backward	serial	*Alcaraz and Maroto (2001)*	0.33	0.12	*0.10*
PSO – activity list	serial	*Zhang et al. (2005)*	0.69	0.61	-

Table 5. Average deviations (%) from critical path lower bound (J60) (extension of Kolisch and Hartmann (2006))

Algorithm	SGS	Reference	Schedules		
			1,000	5,000	50,000
DPSO – FBI	**serial**	**Czogalla and Fink**	**11.56**	**11.00**	**10.68**
Scatter Search – FBI	serial	*Debels et al. (2006)*	11.73	11.10	10.71
GA – hybrid, FBI	serial	*Valls et al.(2008)*	11.56	11.10	10.73
GA,TS – path relinking	both	*Kochetov and Stolyar (2003)*	11.71	11.17	10.74
GA – FBI	serial	*Valls et al. (2005)*	12.21	11.27	10.74
GA – *hybrid, FBI*	*both*	*Alcaraz and Maroto (2006)*	*11.67*	*11.05*	*10.80*
GA – forw.-backw., FBI	both	*Alcaraz et al. (2004)*	11.89	11.19	10.84
GA – self-adapting	both	*Hartmann (2002)*	12.21	11.70	11.21
GA – activity list	serial	*Hartmann (1998)*	12.68	11.89	11.23
sampling – LFT, FBI	both	*Tormos and Lova (2003b)*	11.88	11.62	11.36
sampling LFT, FBI	both	*Tormos and Lova (2003a)*	12.14	11.82	11.47
PLA	*serial*	*Jedrzejowicz and Ratajczak (2006)*	*13.33*	*12.86*	*11.52*
sampling – LFT, FBI	both	*Tormos and Lova (2001)*	12.18	11.87	11.54
GA – forw.-backward	serial	*Alcaraz and Maroto (2001)*	12.57	11.86	*11.70*

4.3 Analysis

In order to examine the importance of the different heuristic components incorporated in the proposed DPSO approach we perform a number of experiments with different configurations and analyze the results by means of *analysis of variance* (ANOVA, see, e.g., Howell, 2002). In the experiments we consider four factors: swarm intelligence ideas (interaction by means of multi-parent recombination, i.e. crossover operator),

mutation, forward/backward improvement, and the creation of the initial population (*IP*). In the design of the experiments we consider two levels for each factor. In case a component is used in a certain configuration the corresponding parameter is set to the value presented in Table 2. The factorial design, which includes all combinations of levels of the factors, consists of 16 experiments. The experiments are in line with the description earlier in this section.

Table 6. Average deviations (%) from critical path lower bound (J120) (extension of Kolisch and Hartmann (2006))

Algorithm	SGS	Reference	Schedules 1,000	5,000	50,000
GA – hybrid, FBI	serial	*Valls et al.(2008)*	34.07	32.54	31.24
GA – *hybrid, FBI*	*both*	*Alcaraz and Maroto (2006)*	*34.97*	*33.51*	*31.38*
GA – forw.-backw., FBI	both	*Alcaraz et al. (2004)*	36.53	33.91	31.49
Scatter Search – FBI	serial	*Debels et al. (2006)*	35.22	33.10	31.57
GA – FBI	serial	*Valls et al. (2005)*	35.39	33.24	31.58
GA,TS – path relinking	both	*Kochetov and Stolyar (2003)*	34.74	33.36	32.06
DPSO – FBI	**serial**	**Czogalla and Fink**	**34.95**	**33.34**	**32.19**
population-based - FBI	serial	*Valls et al. (2005)*	35.18	34.02	32.81
GA – self-adapting	both	*Hartmann (2002)*	37.19	35.39	33.21
sampling – LFT, FBI	both	*Tormos and Lova (2003b)*	35.01	34.41	33.71
PLA	*serial*	*Jedrzejowicz and Ratajczak (2006)*	*35.83*	*35.12*	*33.88*
ant system	serial	*Merkle et al. (2002)*	-	35.43	-
GA – activity list	serial	*Hartmann (1998)*	39.37	36.74	34.03
GA – forw.-backward	serial	*Alcaraz and Maroto (2001)*	39.36	36.57	*34.40*
sampling LFT, FBI	both	*Tormos and Lova (2003a)*	36.24	35.56	34.77
sampling LFT, FBI	both	*Tormos and Lova (2001)*	36.49	35.81	35.01
TS – activity list	serial	*Nonobe and Ibaraki (2002)*	40.86	37.88	35.85

Tables 7–10 show the average deviations for the four test sets. An "x" indicates that the parameter value is set according to Table 2 (0.00 otherwise). The configurations are ordered with respect to the results for 50,000 evaluated schedules. We use the Ryan procedure in combination with the studentized range distribution (REQWQ, see Howell (2002) for details) with a significance level of $\alpha =$ 0.05 to classify the average deviations into groups that are homogeneous in the sense that there is no significant difference among group members. The groups are indicated by the small numbers. The results show that there are differences among the configurations that cannot be attributed to error. Therefore we calculate eta-squared (η^2) to measure the magnitude of effect associated witch

Table 7. Average deviations (%) from optimal makespan (J30) for different parameter configurations

p_{rec}	p_{mut}	p_{imp}	IP	Schedules 1,000		5,000		50.000	
x	x	x	LFT	0.358	1	0.143	1	0.049	1
x	x	x	random	0.386	1	0.163	1	0.049	1
x	x	-	LFT	0.616	3	0.293	2	0.157	2
x	x	-	random	0.629	3	0.333	2/3	0.166	2
x	-	x	random	0.510	2	0.391	3	0.329	3
x	-	x	LFT	0.486	2	0.369	3	0.343	3
x	-	-	LFT	0.918	4	0.867	4	0.834	4
-	-	x	LFT	0.930	4	0.871	4	0.894	4/5
-	x	x	LFT	0.978	4/5	0.918	4/5	0.897	4/5
x	-	-	random	1.018	5	0.923	4/5	0.904	5
-	x	x	random	1.019	5	0.989	5	0.928	5/6
-	-	x	random	1.026	5	0.958	5	0.985	6
-	x	-	LFT	1.822	6	1.656	6	1.597	7
-	-	-	LFT	1.771	6	1.771	7	1.771	8
-	x	-	random	1.985	7	1.837	7	1.802	8
-	-	-	random	2.050	7	2.050	8	2.050	9

Table 8. Average deviations (%) from critical path lower bound (J60) for different parameter configurations

p_{rec}	p_{mut}	p_{imp}	IP	Schedules					
				1,000		5,000		50.000	
x	x	x	LFT	11.559	1	11.008	1	10.682	1
x	x	x	random	11.614	1/2	11.082	1	10.748	1
x	-	x	LFT	11.673	2	11.312	2	11.212	2
x	-	x	random	11.842	3	11.477	3	11.353	3
x	x	-	LFT	12.516	4	11.982	4	11.557	4
x	x	-	random	13.609	4/5/6	12.092	4	11.670	5
-	-	x	LFT	12.665	5/6	12.417	5	12.319	6
-	x	x	random	12.714	6	12.473	5	12.395	6
-	x	x	LFT	12.587	4/5	12.415	5	12.406	6
-	-	x	random	12.932	7	12.652	6	12.625	7
x	-	-	LFT	13.261	8	13.127	7	13.107	8
x	-	-	random	13.450	9	13.372	8	13.359	9
-	x	-	LFT	15.523	11	15.008	9	14.880	10
-	-	-	LFT	14.998	10	14.998	9	14.998	11
-	x	-	random	15.681	12	15.371	10	15.328	12
-	-	-	random	15.592	11/12	15.592	11	15.592	13

each factor (see Levine and Hullett (2002) for a discussion on eta-squared vs. partial eta-squared). The results are reported in Tables 11–14. Effects that are not significant at a significance level of $\alpha = 0.05$ are marked with an asterisk.

The largest effect can be attributed to swarm intelligence ideas and to forward/backward improvement. With increasing instance size the balance between these two factors shifts from swarm intelligence towards forward/backward improvement. The reverse effect can be observed with an increasing number of generated schedules.

The factor mutation has a much smaller effect which increases with the number of generated schedules. Mutation helps to add diversity to the population when the crossover operator alone might not be able to create new permutations due to the similarity of the particles.

The way the initial population is created has the smallest effect even for small numbers of

Table 9. Average deviations (%) from critical path lower bound (J90) for different parameter configurations

p_{rec}	p_{mut}	p_{imp}	IP	Schedules					
				1,000		5,000		50.000	
x	x	x	LFT	11.319	1	10.768	1	10.345	1
x	x	x	random	11.482	2	10.853	1	10.422	1
x	-	x	LFT	11.330	1	11.014	2	10.857	2
x	-	x	random	11.591	3	11.196	3	11.064	3
x	x	-	LFT	12.666	6	12.060	4	11.541	4
x	x	-	random	12.867	7	12.256	5/6	11.768	5
-	-	x	LFT	12.324	4	11.996	4	11.786	5
-	-	x	random	12.630	6	12.285	6	12.042	6
-	x	x	LFT	12.331	4	12.195	5	12.160	7
-	x	x	random	12.529	5	12.223	5/6	12.184	7
x	-	-	LFT	13.553	8	13.482	7	13.372	8
x	-	-	random	13.800	9	13.757	8	13.696	9
-	-	-	LFT	15.404	10	15.404	9	15.404	10
-	x	-	LFT	16.053	11	15.637	10	15.428	10
-	x	-	random	16.059	11	15.952	11	15.853	11
-	-	-	random	15.982	11	15.982	11	15.982	12

Table 10. Average deviations (%) from critical path lower bound (J120) for different parameter configurations

p_{rec}	p_{mut}	p_{imp}	IP	Schedules 1,000		5,000		50.000	
x	x	x	LFT	34.945	1	33.335	1	32.192	1
x	x	x	random	35.470	2	33.694	2	32.447	2
x	-	x	LFT	35.050	1	33.888	3	33.450	3
x	-	x	random	35.706	3	34.481	4	34.035	4
-	-	x	LFT	37.430	4	36.500	5	38.809	5
x	x	-	random	39.229	7	37.616	9	36.305	6
-	-	x	LFT	38.352	6	37.285	8	34.411	6
-	x	x	random	38.002	5	37.027	7	36.682	7
-	x	x	LFT	37.368	4	36.840	6	36.726	7
-	x	-	random	39.639	8	38.136	10	36.873	8
x	-	-	LFT	41.336	9	41.049	11	41.001	9
x	-	-	random	41.792	10	41.633	12	41.570	10
-	-	-	LFT	45.795	11	45.795	13	45.795	11
-	x	-	LFT	47.117	13	46.383	14	45.904	11
-	x	-	random	47.225	13	46.886	15	46.947	12
-	-	-	random	46.988	12	46.988	15	46.988	12

created schedules. This may be caused by the small sample size used for the construction of the initial population or it may be an indicator of the effectiveness of the other factors.

In general, in order to achieve best results all components have to be included in the algorithm.

5 CONCLUSION AND FUTURE RESEARCH DIRECTIONS

In this chapter we present a robust evolutionary computation algorithm which uses ideas derived from swarm intelligence in combination with well-known procedures for the RCPSP. The computa-

Table 11. Eta-squared (η^2) for test set J30

Source	Schedules 1,000	5,000	50,000
Main effects			
Swarm intelligence (SI)	0.564	0.608	0.626
Mutation (M)	0.011	0.037	0.058
Forward-backward improvement	0.332	0.258	0.221
Intial population	0.007	0.006	0.004
Interaction effects			
SI, M	0.012	0.020	0.022
SI, FBI	0.063	0.053	0.047
SI, IP	0.002	0.002	0.003
M, FBI	0.003	0.013	0.014
M, IP	0.001	0.000 *	0.000
FBI, IP	0.002	0.001	0.002
SI, M, FBI	0.002	0.001	0.002
SI, M, IP	0.000 *	0.000 *	0.000 *
SI, FBI, IP	0.001	0.001	0.001
M, FBI, IP	0.000 *	0.000 *	0.000 *
SI, M, FBI IP	0.000 *	0.000 *	0.000 *

Table 12. Eta-squared (η^2) for test set J60

Source	Schedules		
	1,000	5,000	50,000
Main effects			
Swarm intelligence (SI)	0.395	0.414	0.439
Mutation (M)	0.005	0.021	0.037
Forward-backward improvement	0.507	0.483	0.434
Intial population	0.005	0.006	0.006
Interaction effects			
SI, M	0.010	0.013	0.023
SI, FBI	0.065	0.049	0.044
SI, IP	0.001	0.001	0.001
M, FBI	0.000	0.005	0.008
M, IP	0.001	0.001	0.001
FBI, IP	0.000	0.001	0.001
SI, M, FBI	0.009	0.005	0.005
SI, M, IP	0.000	0.000 *	0.000
SI, FBI, IP	0.000	0.001	0.001
M, FBI, IP	0.000	0.000 *	0.000 *
SI, M, FBI IP	0.000	0.000 *	0.000

Table 13. Eta-squared (η^2) for test set J90

Source	Schedules		
	1,000	5,000	50,000
Main effects			
Swarm intelligence (SI)	0.303	0.318	0.342
Mutation (M)	0.002	0.012	0.022
Forward-backward improvement	0.608	0.581	0.533
Intial population	0.005	0.005	0.005
Interaction effects			
SI, M	0.009	0.018	0.031
SI, FBI	0.060	0.051	0.050
SI, IP	0.000	0.000	0.000
M, FBI	0.001	0.006	0.011
M, IP	0.001	0.001	0.000
FBI, IP	0.000 *	0.001	0.001
SI, M, FBI	0.009	0.007	0.004
SI, M, IP	0.000	0.000	0.000 *
SI, FBI, IP	0.000 *	0.000	0.000
M, FBI, IP	0.000	0.000 *	0.000 *
SI, M, FBI IP	0.000	0.000 *	0.000 *

Table 14. Eta-squared (η^2) for test set J120

Source	Schedules		
	1,000	5,000	50,000
Main effects			
Swarm intelligence (SI)	0.257	0.273	0.284
Mutation (M)	0.002	0.010	0.018
Forward-backward improvement	0.672	0.648	0.611
Intial population	0.005	0.004	0.003
Interaction effects			
SI, M	0.007	0.013	0.027
SI, FBI	0.048	0.040	0.041
SI, IP	0.000	0.000	0.000
M, FBI	0.001	0.008	0.009
M, IP	0.000	0.000	0.000
FBI, IP	0.000	0.000	0.001
SI, M, FBI	0.007	0.006	0.004
SI, M, IP	0.000	0.000	0.000
SI, FBI, IP	0.000 *	0.000	0.000
M, FBI, IP	0.000	0.000 *	0.000
SI, M, FBI IP	0.000	0.000	0.000 *

tional experiments serve to analyze the importance of crucial algorithm components for achieving high-quality results. The proposed algorithm is competitive with state-of-the-art methods for the RCPSP. We provide new overall best average results for the medium size data set. Moreover, we significantly improve previous results of PSO for the RCPSP. The good performance can mainly be attributed to swarm intelligence ideas and the forward/backward improvement heuristic. Those findings are in line with Kolisch & Hartmann (2006) who noted, based on a literature survey, the effectiveness of population-based metaheuristics and the FBI procedure.

In subsequent work we will investigate if premature convergence, a well-known problem for evolutionary computation algorithms, may have prevented better results. The balance between exploration and exploitation may be improved by controlling the influence of the actual particle solution, the best particle solution, and the best solution found by the swarm. The use of different neighborhood relations between particles (swarm topologies) can be beneficial as well; see Czogalla & Fink (2009). Furthermore it might be interesting to investigate different strategies for the application of FBI with respect to which particle will be subject to FBI.

REFERENCES

Alcaraz, J., & Maroto, C. (2001). A robust genetic algorithm for resource allocation in project scheduling. *Annals of Operations Research, 102*, 83–109. doi:10.1023/A:1010949931021

Alcaraz, J., & Maroto, C. (2006). *Perspectives in Modern Project Scheduling*, chap. A Hybrid Genetic Algorithm Based on Intelligent Encoding for Project Scheduling. International Series in Operations Research & Management Science (pp. 249–274). Berlin: Springer.

Alcaraz, J., Maroto, C., & Ruiz, R. (2004). Improving the performance of genetic algorithms for the RCPS problem. In *Proceedings of the Ninth International Workshop on Project Management and Scheduling* (pp. 40–43). Nancy.

Allahverdi, A., & Al-Anzi, F. S. (2006). A PSO and a tabu search heuristic for the assembly scheduling problem of the two-stage distributed database application. *Computers & Operations Research, 33*, 1056–1080. doi:10.1016/j.cor.2004.09.002

Bean, J. C. (1994). Genetic algorithms and random keys for sequencing and optimization. *ORSA Journal on Computing, 6*, 154–160.

Blazewicz, J., Lenstra, J. K., & Rinnooy Kan, A. H. G. (1983). Scheduling subject to resource constraints: Classification and complexity. *Discrete Applied Mathematics, 5*, 11–24. doi:10.1016/0166-218X(83)90012-4

Boctor, F. F. (1996). Resource-constrained project scheduling by simulated annealing. *International Journal of Production Research, 34*, 2335–2351. doi:10.1080/00207549608905028

Bouffard, V., & Ferland, J. A. (2007). Improving simulated annealing with variable neighborhood search to solve the resource-constrained scheduling problem. *Journal of Scheduling, 10*, 375–386. doi:10.1007/s10951-007-0043-7

Brucker, P., Drexl, A., Möhring, R., Neumann, K., & Pesch, E. (1999). Resource-constrained project scheduling: Notation, classification, models, and methods. *European Journal of Operational Research, 112*, 3–41. doi:10.1016/S0377-2217(98)00204-5

Czogalla, J., & Fink, A. (2008). On the effectiveness of particle swarm optimization and variable neighborhood descent for the continuous flow-shop scheduling problem. In Xhafa, F., & Abraham, A. (Eds.), *Metaheuristics for Scheduling in Industrial and Manufacturing Applications, Studies in Computational Intelligence (Vol. 128*, pp. 61–90). Berlin: Springer. doi:10.1007/978-3-540-78985-7_3

Czogalla, J., & Fink, A. (2009). Particle swarm topologies for resource constrained project scheduling. In N. Krasnogor, M. B. Melin-Batista, J. A. Moreno-Prez, J. M. Moreno-Vega, & D. A. Pelta (Eds.), *Nature Inspired Cooperative Strategies for Optimization (NICSO 2008), Studies in Computational Intelligence*, vol. 236, (pp. 61–73). Berlin: Springer.

Debels, D., De Reyck, B., Leus, R., & Vanhoucke, M. (2006). A hybrid scatter search/electromagnetism meta-heuristic for project scheduling. *European Journal of Operational Research, 169*, 638–653. doi:10.1016/j.ejor.2004.08.020

Eberhart, R. C., & Kennedy, J. (1995). A new optimizer using particle swarm theory. In *Sixth International Symposium on Micro Machine and Human Science* (pp. 39–43). IEEE.

Glover, F. (1997). A template for scatter search and path relinking. In Hao, J. K., Lutton, E., Ronald, E., Schoenauer, M., & Snyers, D. (Eds.), *Artificial Evolution, Lecture Notes in Computer Science (Vol. 1363*, pp. 13–54). Berlin: Springer.

Glover, F., Laguna, M., & Marti, R. (2003). Scatter search. In Ghosh, A., & Tsutsui, S. (Eds.), *Advances in Evolutionary Computing: Theory and Applications* (pp. 519–538). Berlin: Springer.

Hartmann, S. (1998). A competitive genetic algorithm for resource-constrained project scheduling. *Naval Research Logistics, 45*, 733–750. doi:10.1002/(SICI)1520-6750(199810)45:7<733::AID-NAV5>3.0.CO;2-C

Hartmann, S. (2002). A self-adapting genetic algorithm for project scheduling under resource constraints. *Naval Research Logistics, 49*, 433–448. doi:10.1002/nav.10029

Hartmann, S., & Briskorn, D. (2010). A survey of variants and extensions of the resource-constrained project scheduling problem. *European Journal of Operational Research, 207*, 1–14. doi:10.1016/j.ejor.2009.11.005

Hartmann, S., & Kolisch, R. (2000). Experimental evaluation of state-of-the-art heuristics for the resource-constrained project scheduling problem. *European Journal of Operational Research, 127,* 394–407. doi:10.1016/S0377-2217(99)00485-3

Herroelen, W., De Reyck, B., & Demeulemeester, E. (1998). Resource-constrained project scheduling: A survey of recent developments. *Computers & Operations Research, 25,* 279–302. doi:10.1016/S0305-0548(97)00055-5

Hindi, K. S., Yang, H., & Fleszar, K. (2002). An evolutionary algorithm for resource-constrained project scheduling. *IEEE Transactions on Evolutionary Computation, 6,* 512–518. doi:10.1109/TEVC.2002.804914

Holland, J. H. (1975). *Adaption in Natural and Artificial Systems.* Ann Arbor: University of Michigan Press.

Howell, D. C. (2002). *Statistical Methods for Psychology* (5th ed.). Pacific Grove, CA: Duxbury.

Hu, X., Eberhart, R. C., & Shi, Y. (2003). Swarm intelligence for permutation optimization: A case study of n-queens problem. In *Proceedings of the 2003 IEEE Swarm Intelligence Symposium* (pp. 243–246). IEEE.

Hutter, F. (2007). *Quick start guide for ParamILS. Department of Computer Science.* University of British Columbia.

Hutter, F., Hoos, H., & Stützle, T. (2007). Automatic algorithm configuration based on local search. In *Proceedings of the Twenty-Second AAAI Conference on Artificial Intelligence* (pp. 1147–1152). Menlo Park, CA: AAAI Press.

Jarboui, B., Damak, N., Siarry, P., & Rebai, A. (2008). A combinatorial particle swarm optimization for solving multi-mode resource-constrained project scheduling problems. *Applied Mathematics and Computation, 195,* 299–308. doi:10.1016/j.amc.2007.04.096

Jedrzejowicz, P., & Ratajczak, E. (2006). *Perspectives in Modern Project Scheduling, chap. Population Learning Algorithm for the Resource-Constrained Project Scheduling. International Series in Operations Research & Management Science* (pp. 275–297). Berlin: Springer.

Jeffcoat, D. E., & Bulfin, R. L. (1993). Simulated annealing for resource-constrained scheduling. *European Journal of Operational Research, 70,* 43–51. doi:10.1016/0377-2217(93)90231-B

Kennedy, J., & Eberhart, R. C. (1995). Particle swarm optimization. In *Proceedings of the 1995 IEEE International Conference on Neural Networks* (pp. 1942–1948). IEEE.

Kennedy, J., & Eberhart, R. C. (2001). *Swarm Intelligence.* San Francisco, CA: Morgan Kaufmann Publishers.

Kochetov, Y. A., & Stolyar, A. A. (2003). Evolutionary local search with variable neighborhood for the resource constrained project scheduling problem. In *Proceedings of the 3rd International Workshop of Computer Science and Information Technologies.* Ufa, Russia.

Kolisch, R. (1996). Serial and parallel resource-constrained project scheduling methods revisited: Theory and computation. *European Journal of Operational Research, 90,* 320–333. doi:10.1016/0377-2217(95)00357-6

Kolisch, R., & Hartmann, S. (1999). *Project scheduling: Recent models, algorithms and applications, chap. Heuristic Algorithms for Solving the Resource-Constrained Project Scheduling Problem: Classification and Computational Analysis* (pp. 147–178). Amsterdam: Kluwer Academic Publishers.

Kolisch, R., & Hartmann, S. (2006). Experimental investigation of heuristics for resource-constrained project scheduling: An update. *European Journal of Operational Research, 174,* 23–37. doi:10.1016/j.ejor.2005.01.065

Kolisch, R., & Padman, R. (2001). An integrated survey of deterministic project scheduling. *Omega, 29,* 249–272. doi:10.1016/S0305-0483(00)00046-3

Kolisch, R., & Sprecher, A. (1996). PSPLIB – A project scheduling problem library. *European Journal of Operational Research, 96,* 205–216. doi:10.1016/S0377-2217(96)00170-1

Kolisch, R., Sprecher, A., & Drexl, A. (1995). Characterization and generation of a general class of resource-constrained project scheduling problems. *Management Science, 41,* 1693–1703. doi:10.1287/mnsc.41.10.1693

Krasnogor, N., & Smith, J. E. (2005). A tutorial for competent memetic algorithms: model, taxonomy, and design issues. *IEEE Transactions on Evolutionary Computation, 9,* 474–488. doi:10.1109/TEVC.2005.850260

Levine, T. R., & Hullett, C. R. (2002). Eta squared, partial eta squared, and misreporting of effect size in communication research. *Human Communication Research, 28,* 612–625. doi:10.1111/j.1468-2958.2002.tb00828.x

Li, K. Y., & Willis, R. J. (1992). An iterative scheduling technique for resource-constrained project scheduling. *European Journal of Operational Research, 56,* 370–379. doi:10.1016/0377-2217(92)90320-9

Linyi, D., & Yan, L. (2007). A particle swarm optimization for resource-constrained multi-project scheduling problem. In *Proceedings of the 2007 International Conference on Computational Intelligence and Security* (pp. 1010–1014).

Merkle, D., & Middendorf, M. (2005). Swarm intelligence. In Burke, E. K., & Kendall, G. (Eds.), *Search Methodologies – Introductory Tutorials in Optimization and Decision Support Techniques* (pp. 401–435). New York, NY: Springer.

Merkle, D., Middendorf, M., & Schmeck, H. (2002). Ant colony optimization for resource-constrained project scheduling. *IEEE Transactions on Evolutionary Computation, 6,* 333–346. doi:10.1109/TEVC.2002.802450

Moraglio, A., Di Chio, C., & Poli, R. (2007). Geometric particle swarm optimization. In M. Ebner, M. O'Neill, A. Ekart, L. Vanneschi, & A. I. Esparcia-Alcazar (Eds.), *Proceedings of the 10th European Conference on Genetic Programming, Lecture Notes in Computer Science,* vol. 4445 (pp. 125–136). Berlin: Springer.

Moscato, P. (1989). *On evolution, search, optimization, genetic algorithms and martial arts: Towards memetic algorithms. Technical Report Report 826.* Pasadena: Caltech Concurrent Computation Program, California Institute of Technology.

Nonobe, K., & Ibaraki, T. (2002). *Essays and Surveys in Metaheuristics, chap. Formulation and Tabu Search Algorithm for the Resource Constrained Project Scheduling Problem. Operations Research/Computer Science Interfaces Series* (pp. 557–588). Boston: Kluwer Academic Publishers.

Ozdamar, L., & Ulusoy, G. (1995). A survey on the resource-constrained project scheduling problem. *IIE Transactions, 27,* 574–586. doi:10.1080/07408179508936773

Ozdamar, L., & Ulusoy, G. (1996). A note on an iterative forward/backward scheduling technique with reference to a procedure by Li and Willis. *European Journal of Operational Research, 89,* 400–407. doi:10.1016/0377-2217(94)00272-X

Pan, Q.-K., Tasgetiren, M. F., & Liang, Y.-C. (2006). A discrete particle swarm optimization algorithm for single machine total earliness and tardiness problem with a common due date. In *IEEE Congress on Evolutionary Computation 2006* (pp. 3281–3288). IEEE.

Ruiz, R., Maroto, C., & Alcaraz, J. (2006). Two new robust genetic algorithms for the flowshop scheduling problem. *Omega, 34,* 461–476. doi:10.1016/j.omega.2004.12.006

Schutt, A., Feydy, T., Stuckey, P. J., & Wallace, M. G. (2009). Why cumulative decomposition is not as bad as it sounds. In Gent, I. P. (Ed.), *Principles and Practice of Constraint Programming – CP 2009, Lecture Notes in Computer Science* (*Vol. 5732*, pp. 746–761). Berlin: Springer. doi:10.1007/978-3-642-04244-7_58

Sprecher, A., Kolisch, R., & Drexl, A. (1995). Semi-active, active, and non-delay schedules for the resource-constrained project scheduling problem. *European Journal of Operational Research, 80,* 94–102. doi:10.1016/0377-2217(93)E0294-8

Thomas, P. R., & Salhi, S. (1998). A tabu search approach for the resource constrained project scheduling problem. *Journal of Heuristics, 4,* 123–139. doi:10.1023/A:1009673512884

Tormos, P., & Lova, A. (2001). A competitive heuristic solution technique for resource-constrained project scheduling. *Annals of Operations Research, 102,* 65–81. doi:10.1023/A:1010997814183

Tormos, P., & Lova, A. (2003a). An efficient multi-pass heuristic for project scheduling with constrained resources. *International Journal of Production Research, 41,* 1071–1086. doi:10.1080/0020754021000033904

Tormos, P., & Lova, A. (2003b). *Integrating heuristics for resource constrained project scheduling: One step forward. Technical Report.* Department of Applied Statistics, Operations Research and Quality, Polytechnic University of Valencia.

Valls, V., & Ballestin, F. (2004). A population-based approach to the resource-constrained project scheduling problem. *Annals of Operations Research, 131,* 305–324. doi:10.1023/B:ANOR.0000039524.09792.c9

Valls, V., Ballestin, F., & Quintanilla, S. (2005). Justification and RCPSP: A technique that pays. *European Journal of Operational Research, 165,* 375–386. doi:10.1016/j.ejor.2004.04.008

Valls, V., Ballestin, F., & Quintanilla, S. (2006). *Perspectives in Modern Project Scheduling,* chap. Justification Technique Generalizations. In *International Series in Operations Research & Management Science* (pp. 205–223). Berlin: Springer. doi:10.1007/978-0-387-33768-5_8

Valls, V., Ballestin, F., & Quintanilla, S. (2008). A hybrid genetic algorithm for the resource-constrained project scheduling problem. *European Journal of Operational Research, 185,* 495–508. doi:10.1016/j.ejor.2006.12.033

Zhang, H., Li, X., Li, H., & Huang, F. (2005). Particle swarm optimization-based schemes for resource-constrained project scheduling. *Automation in Construction, 14,* 393–404. doi:10.1016/j.autcon.2004.08.006

Zhang, H., Tam, C. M., & Li, H. (2006). Multimode project scheduling based on particle swarm optimization. *Computer-Aided Civil and Infrastructure Engineering, 21,* 93–103. doi:10.1111/j.1467-8667.2005.00420.x

Chapter 8
Marriage in Honeybee Optimization to Scheduling Problems

Pedro Palominos
University of Santiago of Chile, Chile

Victor Parada
University of Santiago of Chile, Chile

Gustavo Gatica
University of Santiago of Chile, Chile

Andrés Véjar
Université de Nancy, France

ABSTRACT

The biological inspired optimization techniques have proven to be powerful tools for solving scheduling problems. Marriage in Honeybee Optimization is a recent biological technique that attempts to emulate the social behavior in a bee colony and although has been applied to only a limited number of problems, it has delivered promising results. By means of this technique in this chapter the authors explore the solution space of scheduling problems by identifying an appropriate representation for each studied case. Two cases were considered: the minimization of earliness-tardiness penalties in a single machine scheduling and the permutation flow shop problem. The performance was evaluated for the first case with 280 instances from the literature. The technique performed quite well for a wide range of instances and achieved an average improvement of 1.4% for all instances. They obtained better solutions than the available upper bound for 141 instances. In the second case, they achieved an average error of 3.5% for the set of 120 test instances.

DOI: 10.4018/978-1-61350-086-6.ch008

INTRODUCTION

Methods for solving optimization problems related to productive, administrative, or logistic processes have become particularly important in the globalized world, where intensified competition has made optimization necessary for the survival of all types of organizations. Modeling the scheduling problems that arise in production and logistics management can be quite complex. For example, a manufacturing company may need to determine the order in which machines should process jobs. Assuming that the Master Production Schedule already exits, the start and end times for the production operations must be set based on the available capacity. These kinds of problems belong to the NP-hard class (Garey & Johnson, 1979) and have been studied extensively by Pinedo(2008).

Swarm Intelligence (SI) is an area of artificial intelligence that focuses on modeling the behaviors of social insects like ants and bees (Bonabeau, Dorigo, & Theraulaz, 1999). Ant Colony Optimization (ACO) is a well-known SI Metaheuristic (MH) in which optimization algorithms are inspired by the decentralized, collective behavior of ant colonies (Dorigo & Gambardella, 1997; Dorigo & Caro, 1999). Another SI MH is Marriage in Honeybee Optimization (MBO), which analyzes the mating flight of honey-making bees; MBO was originally proposed by H. Abbass (Abbass, 2001a, 2001b, 2001c) to solve the SAT problem (Garey & Johnson, 1979).

The original MBO algorithm is a hybrid MH based on Simulated Annealing (SA) (Kirkpatrick, Gelatt, & Vecchi, 1983), Genetic Algorithms (GA) (Goldberg, 1989), and Local Search (LS) (Talbi, 2009). It incorporates a mating function similar to SA and provides the advantages of GA and LS for generating and improving the broods by the worker bees. However, MBO also has a large number of distinguishing characteristics.

The literature includes two approaches based on the mating behavior of bees: MBO and Honeybee Mating Optimization (HBMO), the second is a modified version of MBO that considers bee populations. Chang (2006) demonstrated the theoretical capacity of MBO for solving combinatorial optimization problems and pointed out that the algorithm converges. A. Baykasoğlu et al. (2007) reviewed the literature on bee MH approaches. Both methods have been applied to a variety of problems, including SAT, data mining (Amiri & Fathian, 2007; Benatchba, Admane, & Koudil, 2005; Fathian, Amiri, & Maroosi, 2007), water resource management (A. Afshar, Bozorg Haddad, Marino, & Adams, 2007; Bozorg Haddad & A. Afshar, 2004; Bozorg Haddad, Abbas Afshar, & Mariño, 2006), constrained and unconstrained nonlinear optimization (Bozorg Haddad et al., 2006), the traveling salesman (C. Yang, Tu, & Chen, 2007), the traveling salesman with vehicle routing (Marinakis, Marinaki, & Dounias, 2007, 2008), dynamic stochastic scheduling (Bozorg Haddad et al., 2006), the reconfiguration of a radial energy distribution system (Niknam, 2009; Niknam, Olamaie, & Khorshidi, 2008), state estimation of a power distribution network system (Niknam, 2008), and the sales forecast problem (Pai, S. Yang, & P. Chang, 2009).

This chapter provides an exploratory analysis of MBO application for scheduling problems and evaluates the potential utility and adaptability of this method. Two scheduling problems are considered: minimization of earliness-tardiness penalties under single machine scheduling with a common due date constraint and the permutation flow shop problem.

MARRIAGE IN HONEYBEE OPTIMIZATION

Fundamentally, Marriage in Honeybee Optimization is a biological inspired algorithm that attempts to emulate the social behavior related to marriage in a bee colony. The MBO strategy is based on a search for neighboring solutions. The

Figure 1. Representation of the Marriage Bee Optimization

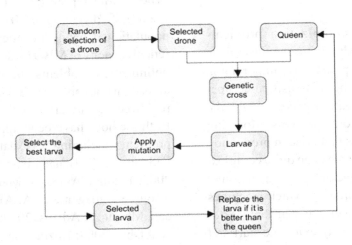

natural coupling process in a bee colony, which is composed of a queen bee, drones, workers, and broods, begins when the queen bee and the drones complete a nuptial flight. In each effective coupling between the queen and a drone, the queen stores the drone's material in a "spermatheca", which forms the genetic reserve of the hive. Every egg laid by the queen bee is fertilized by a random mixture of the material accumulated in the spermatheca. These eggs generate the broods, which are cared for by the worker bees. A schematic diagram is presented in Figure 1.

In MBO, the mating flight of the queen bee is represented by a set of state transitions. The queen moves between different states and selects drones probabilistically. The algorithm randomly initializes the queen's genotype and then improves it using heuristics that represent worker bees. A series of mating flights occur in which the queen's energy and speed are initialized randomly. Thus, in each flight, the queen moves among the different states (solutions) in the space according to its speed and mates with drones that have randomly generated genotypes. The probability of successful mating is high when the queen is at the beginning of its flight and therefore has high speed or when the fitness (the value of the objective func-

tion) of the drone is as good as that of the queen. If a drone mates successfully with the queen, its genetic material is added to the queen's spermatheca (list of partial solutions), and the queen's speed and energy are immediately reduced. After the queen completes its mating flight, it returns to the hive, randomly chooses material from the spermatheca, and then generates the broods through crossover and mutation operations between its genetic material and that of the drones. The broods created through the crossover are improved by local search heuristics, which represent the role of workers. Finally, the queen is replaced by the larva with the best fitness if the larva is more fit than the queen. The rest of the broods are eliminated, and a new flight begins; the algorithm ends when a certain number of mating flights have been completed.

MBO includes three main processes: a) the mating flight of the queen, which selects the parents of the future broods; b) the crossover between the genetic material of the queen bee and the drones selected in the mating flight, which generates the broods; and c) the care and improvement of the broods carried out by the workers, which corresponds to the process of solution mutation through the application of heuristics (Teo & Abbass, 2001).

All of these processes are equally relevant in the algorithm because each step or change is significant in the structure of the final solution.

The Mating Flight of the Queen

At the beginning of the flight (and therefore of the algorithm), the queen has an initial energy E0 and an initial speed S0; these values are initialized randomly in the [0.5, 1] interval to ensure a reasonable number of mating events per flight. Initial values are sufficient for mating with between 7 and 17 drones per flight. Both the energy and speed of the queen decrease according to the rules defined by Equations (1) and (2), respectively:

$$E(t+1) = E(t) - g \qquad (1)$$

$$S(t+1) = \alpha S(t) \qquad (2)$$

Parameters g and α correspond to the reduction factors for the queen's energy and speed at instant t, respectively; g is defined by Equation (3), and M is the capacity of the spermatheca.

$$g = 0.5 \, E(t)/M \qquad (3)$$

The energy and speed specifications for the queen logically emulate the behavior observed in nature; the queen's energy specification is directly related to the duration of each flight because the queen can search for drones in the neighborhood of the solution space until either its energy is zero or its spermatheca is full. Similarly, the queen's speed specification is related to the probability of successfully mating with each drone. Thus, when the queen's speed is high (at the beginning of its flight), there is a higher probability of successful mating. In contrast, when the queen's speed is low, the probability of successful mating is lower.

The success of the random mating flight of the queen depends on the route followed by the drones due to drones that are closer to the queen are more likely to successfully mate.

Although the drones are also initialized randomly, they mutate in the solution space before mating with a probability that depends on the queen's speed.

After the generation of the initial trajectories of the queen (q) and drones (d), the drones with which the crossover of genetic material will take place are selected. This process is conducted by considering the crossover probability of each drone with the queen, as defined by Equation (4).

$$p(q, d) = \exp\{- \, l(q,d)/s(q) \} \qquad (4)$$

Where $l(q,d) = diff(f(q), f(d))$ is the difference between the evaluations of the fitness functions; if f is defined in R, then $l(q,d) = |(f(q) - f(d)|$. The function $p(q, d)$ represents the probability of successful mating (the probability that the genetic material of the drone will be added to the spermatheca of the queen). The function $s(q)$ is the speed of queen q at instant t. The probability of a successful mating is high when the difference between the fitness of the queen and of the drone is small or when the speed of the queen is sufficiently high.

In MBO, the queen accepts the drones as parents by a random process. To emulate that behavior a random number in the [0, 1] interval is generated for each queen and is then compared with the highest mating probability of a certain drone with respect to each queen. If the mating probability is greater than the generated number, the queen accepts the drone as a parent and utilizes one-half of the drone's genetic material.

After each state transition in a flight, the queen's energy and speed are updated according to Equations (1) and (2). The mating flight ends when the queen's energy is zero ($E(t) = 0$) or when its spermatheca (M) is full.

Crossover

Once the queen's flight has ended, the reproduction stage takes place by generating the larvae. During reproduction, a drone's sperm that was previously deposited in the spermatheca is selected randomly; the crossover creates a new larva.

The Care and Improvement of Broods

Once the larvae have been created, the workers improve them by mutation. The workers are modeled as local search algorithms that improve the larvae obtained from the queen-drone crossover. Once the broods have been improved, if there is a larva with better fitness than the queen, it replaces the queen. The remaining broods are eliminated, and a new mating flight begins. This is repeated until all of the mating flights have been completed or until the end condition is satisfied.

Abbass (2001b) describes a variant of MBO that considers the mating flight of several queens. In the main loop, the algorithm initializes the speed and energy of each queen, which then moves between different states and chooses drones probabilistically. In the final stage, the weakest queen is replaced by the best brood.

APPLYING MBO TO SCHEDULING PROBLEMS

The purpose of this section is to apply MBO to two types of scheduling problems: the minimization of earliness-tardiness penalties in a single machine scheduling problem with a common tight due date and the permutation flow shop problem (Pinedo, 2008).

Minimizing Earliness: Tardiness Penalties in a Single Machine Scheduling Problem with Common Tight Due Dates

In a single machine scheduling problem, optimization techniques are used to minimize the total penalties accrued due to early or tardy job

completion time with respect to a common due date (SMWET). Each job $j, j = \{1,2,\ldots, n\}$ has a processing time p_j, and the due date d is shared by all of the jobs within the set. A job is considered early if its completion time C_j is less than the time between the start time and the common due date. On the other hand, a job is considered tardy if it is completed after the due date. Therefore, if the time for completing the job j is longer or shorter than the period between the start time and the due date, a penalty is incurred.

Earliness and tardiness are obtained as $E_j = \max \{ 0, -L_j \} = \max \{ 0, d - C_j \}$ and $T_j = \max \{ 0, L_j \} = \max \{ 0, C_j - d \}$, respectively, for each job j. The unit penalties per unit time of job j for being early or tardy are α_j and β_j, respectively. The objective is to find a feasible schedule, S, that minimizes the total penalties for earliness and tardiness (Equation 5).

$$f(S) = \sum_{j=1}^{n} \alpha_j \left(d - C_j \right) + \sum_{j=1}^{n} \beta_j \left(C_j - d \right) = \sum_{j=1}^{n} \left(\alpha_j E_j + \beta_j T_j \right)$$

(5)

In general, problems that involve common due dates can be classified into two categories: Tight and Loose Due Dates. If the common due date has no influence on the optimum sequence of the jobs, the problem is said to be a Loose Due Date case. On the other hand, if the given common due date influences the optimum job sequence, the problem is said to be a Tight Due Date (M. Feldmann & D. Biskup, 2003). Equation (5) refers to the Tight Due Date case.

The minimization problem for total job earliness and tardiness penalties with respect to a common due date has been studied by multiple authors (Gordon, V. et al., 2002, Baker & Scudder, 1989, 1990). Hall et al. (1991) showed that the problem is NP-Hard.

Due to the complexity of the problem, several authors have used heuristic approaches. For ex-

Table 1. Parameters for Marriage Bees Optimization

Parameter	Source	Value
Number of queen bees	Preliminary Experiments	4
Number of drones	Preliminary Experiments	100
Initial speed of the queen bees	Teo & Abbass (2003)	0.9
Energy reduction factor of the queen bees	Teo & Abbass (2001)	g
Speed reduction factor of the queen bees	Preliminary Experiments	0.98
Spermatheca capacity	Abbass (2001a, 2001b, 2001c)	10
Number of flights	Preliminary Experiments	20

ample, Lee and Kim (1995) solved SMWET by means of a parallel genetic algorithm, and James (1997) used a tabu search algorithm. However, until Biskup and Feldmann (2001), no authors had accounted for the third property mentioned by these authors: an optimum sequence of jobs does not necessarily start at time zero. Biskup and Feldmann (2001) prepared a set of test instances and solved them by two specific heuristic methods. They presented the values obtained for the upper bounds of the solution and established a point of comparison for future approaches. Biskup and Feldmann (2001) studied SMWET with five different MH approaches: evolutionary strategy, simulated annealing, algorithms based on threshold-accepting, evolutionary strategy with a destabilizing phase, and algorithms based on threshold-accepting strategy with search process stabilization. Later, Hino et al. (2005), Pan, Q-K. et al.(2006), Shih-Wei Lin et al. (2007), Liao C. and Cheng C. (2007), Pham D.T. et al. (2007), and Nearchou (2008) utilized the comparison points proposed by Biskup and Feldmann (2001) during their studies of SMWET.

In order to present a generic solution for SMWET (Nearchou, 2008), we use a permutation chain that represents a physical sequence of jobs. Thus, for an instance that considers n jobs, the solution space contains $n!$ different permutations.

Defining the Set of Parameters

Each genotype (queen, drone and larva) is represented by a sequence of jobs of equal length n. The first job in an optimum schedule may not start at time zero. Fixed parameters are used to solve all of the instances (Dirk Biskup & Martin Feldmann, 2001).

Three general parameters are employed in the proposed algorithm. The number of queens (Q) was set at four, and a different solution was delivered for each of the queens at each iteration. The number of drones (D), the maximum number of drones with which the queen will mate in a flight, was set experimentally at $D = 10$ drones per flight. The capacity of the spermatheca (M), the amount of drone genetic material that the queen can store after each flight, was defined as $M = 10$ (Abbas, 2001b). The other parameters are shown in Table 1.

Determining the Initial Population

To provide greater diversity in the algorithm, the initial solution was randomly generated for two of the four queens and was obtained from the LPT and SPT rules for the other two (A. Afshar et al., 2007; Pinedo, 2008; Teo & Abbass, 2003).

The initial queens were improved by local search algorithms, which represent the workers.

Figure 2. "Genotype Marker" operator

Genotype	2	4	9	5	8	7	1	6	3	10
Genotype marker	m	n/m	n/m	m	m	m	n/m	n/m	n/m	m
Marked genotype	2	*	*	5	8	7	*	*	*	10
Disordered marked genotype	*	8	7	*	2	*	5	10	*	*

The initial population of drones was also randomly generated, and each drone mutated randomly at the time of coupling.

Mutations were completed with a genotype marker that randomly marks exactly one-half of the genes in the drone's genotype. These marked genes, which correspond to those used in the crossover, are disordered after the marking operation. Figure 2 depicts a drone's genotype, the genotype marker operator, and the mutation operator; m corresponds to a marked gene, n/m indicates that the genotype has not been marked, and * represents a nonexistent gene.

Through this process, the original drone genotype denoted by SD becomes the mutated drone genotype denoted by $S'D$ at each transition. If $f(S'D) < f(SD)$, the mutated drone replaces the original one: $SD = S'D$.

Selecting the Drones' Genetic Material

In the application of the algorithm to SMWET, the queen randomly adds the drone's material to its spermatheca according to Equation (4). A random number in the interval [0, 1] is generated for each queen and is then compared to the highest mating probability of a certain drone with respect to each queen. If the mating probability is greater than the generated number, the queen accepts the drone as a parent and accepts half of the drone's genetic material. Finally, if the fitness of a drone is better than the fitness of a queen, the latter is replaced by the former.

Obtaining Broods

The drone genetic material is chosen randomly from the available material stored in the spermatheca and is combined with randomly chosen queen genetic material to generate broods by applying the crossover operator.

A new larva is generated from the genotypes of parent 1 and parent 2. Genes from parents 1 and 2 are used as the tail and head of the new larva, respectively, as depicted in Figure 3.

Experimentally, it was decided to consider the drone to be parent 1 in 70% of the cases and the queen to parent 1 in 30% of the cases. This is justified because the genotype of the queen is generally better than of the drone.

Improvement of the Larvae

Three heuristics were applied to model the process by which workers improve both the initial queen population and the larvae obtained from the crossover. The heuristics corresponded to hill climbing (Haouari & M'Hallah, 1997), simulated annealing (Kirkpatrick et al., 1983), and a local search operator of Biskup and Feldmann ((2001). The heuristic was selected from the three candidates probabilistically. Each heuristic candidate was associated with a choice probability, and the heuristic with the highest probability was chosen. At the beginning of the iterations, the probability was 1/w, where w represents the total number of workers.

The average improvement i_h obtained by each heuristic, which corresponds to the average im-

Figure 3. Crossover operators

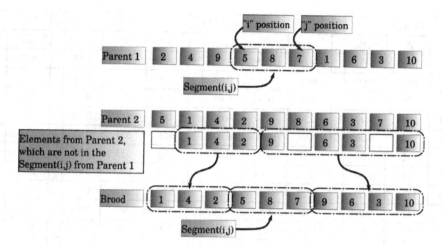

provement of the solution (larva), was updated and saved on a list. The choice probability was updated to consider the impact of the heuristic that provided the greatest average improvement. The new choice probability p' is defined as the previous probability p plus the fraction of total improvement due to h, corrected by the number of workers w. The new choice probability is given by Equation (6):

$$p' = p + i_h / \sum w \, i_h \qquad (6)$$

The choice rule shown in Equation (6) was used after each iteration of the heuristics to identify the heuristic with the highest choice probability. After the method of improvement was chosen, it was executed multiple times: 200 iterations for simulated annealing, 50 for hill climbing, and 40 for the local search operator. The numbers of iterations were obtained experimentally.

Test Instances Used for Experiments

The MBO proposed for SMWET was implemented in the Python language on Linux and was executed on a personal computer with an AMD Athlon 64 3000+, 1 GB RAM. The algorithm was tested by solving a set of test instances available in OR-

Library (Beasley, 1990). This set of instances includes a total of 280 benchmarks covering seven problem categories, with $n = 10, 20, 50, 100, 200, 500$ and 1000 jobs with ten instances each. Tight due date values were $r = 0.2, 0.4, 0.6$ and 0.8. The common due date value was generated by $d = r \cdot \sum p_j$; in other words, for each instance, the common due date value was estimated by multiplying the value of the tight factor by the sum of the processing times p_j of the n jobs. Thus, smaller values of r indicate tighter problems.

Numerical Results

MBO performance was measured by comparing the percent error e (Equation 7) of the solutions obtained (f^*) related to the upper bound values u, which were taken from Biskup and Feldmann (2001).

$$e = 100(f^* - u)/u \qquad (7)$$

Tables 2 and 3 detail the results obtained for the 280 instances. Table 2 shows the results for the small instances with 10, 20 and 50 jobs, and Table 3 shows the results for the large instances with 100, 200, 500 and 1000 jobs. For each set of instances, the two tables include the problem

Table 2. Result for SMWET, with n = 10, 20 and 50

n	k	r = 0.2 u	f*	e (%)	r = 0.4 u	f*	e (%)	r = 0.6 u	f*	e(%)	r = 0.8 u	f*	e(%)
10	1	1936	1936	0.00	1025	1025	0.00	841	841	0.00	818	818	0.00
	2	1042	1042	0.00	615	615	0.00	615	615	0.00	615	615	0.00
	3	1586	1586	0.00	917	917	0.00	793	793	0.00	793	793	0.00
	4	2139	2139	0.00	1230	1230	0.00	815	815	0.00	803	803	0.00
	5	1187	1187	0.00	630	630	0.00	521	521	0.00	521	521	0.00
	6	1521	1521	0.00	908	908	0.00	755	755	0.00	755	755	0.00
	7	2170	2170	0.00	1374	1374	0.00	1101	1101	0.00	1083	1083	0.00
	8	1720	1720	0.00	1020	1020	0.00	610	610	0.00	540	540	0.00
	9	1574	1574	0.00	876	876	0.00	582	582	0.00	554	554	0.00
	10	1869	1869	0.00	1136	1136	0.00	710	710	0.00	671	671	0.00
20	1	4431	4394	-0.01	3066	3066	0.00	2986	2986	0.00	2986	2986	0.00
	2	8567	8430	-0.02	4897	4847	-0.01	3260	3206	-0.02	2980	2980	0.00
	3	6331	6210	-0.02	3883	3838	-0.01	3600	3583	-0.01	3600	3583	-0.01
	4	9478	9188	-0.03	5122	5118	-0.01	3336	3317	-0.01	3040	3040	0.00
	5	4340	4215	-0.03	2571	2495	-0.03	2206	2173	-0.02	2206	2173	-0.02
	6	6766	6527	-0.04	3601	3582	-0.01	3016	3010	0.00	3016	3010	0.00
	7	11101	10455	-0.06	6357	6238	-0.02	4175	4126	-0.01	3900	3878	-0.01
	8	4203	3920	-0.07	2151	2145	0.00	1638	1638	0.00	1638	1638	0.00
	9	3530	3465	-0.02	2097	2096	0.00	1992	1965	-0.01	1992	1965	-0.01
	10	5545	4979	-0.10	3192	2925	-0.08	2116	2110	0.00	1995	1995	0.00
50	1	42363	40697	-0.04	24868	23792	-0.04	17990	17969	0.00	17990	17937	0.00
	2	33637	30624	-0.09	19279	17920	-0.07	14231	14054	-0.01	14132	14200	0.01
	3	37641	34425	-0.09	21353	20502	-0.04	16497	16509	0.00	16497	16591	0.01
	4	30166	27755	-0.08	17495	16657	-0.05	14105	14121	0.00	14105	14215	0.01
	5	32604	32307	-0.01	18441	18007	-0.02	14650	14612	0.00	14650	14618	0.00
	6	36920	34969	-0.05	21497	20385	-0.05	14251	14274	0.00	14075	14116	0.00
	7	44277	43134	-0.03	23883	23038	-0.04	17715	17637	0.00	17715	17682	0.00
	8	46065	43859	-0.05	25402	24892	-0.02	21367	21403	0.00	21367	21435	0.00
	9	36397	34234	-0.06	21929	19986	-0.09	14298	14202	-0.01	13952	14056	0.01
	10	35797	32960	-0.08	20048	19167	-0.04	14377	14409	0.00	14377	14416	0.00

size n, the instance number k, the tight due date factor r, the upper bound u found by Bector *et al.* (1988), the value found by the MBO f^*, and the error e according to Equation (7).

For all 120 small instances, the solution found is better or equal to the best known solution. On average, the solution improved the previously best known solution by 1.40% (Table 2). Simi-

Table 3. Result for SMWET, with n = 100, 200, 500 and 1000

N	k	r = 0.2			r = 0.4			r = 0.8		
		u	f*	e (%)	u	f*	e (%)	u	f*	e(%)
100	1	156103	145623	-6.71	89588	86380	-3.58	72019	73183	1.62
	2	132605	124972	5.76	74854	73486	-1.83	59351	60362	1.70
	3	137463	129911	-5.49	85363	79763	-6.56	68537	69697	1.69
	4	137265	129749	-5.48	87730	79589	-9.28	69231	70262	1.49
	5	136761	124436	-9.01	76424	71627	-6.28	55277	55973	1.26
	6	151930	139321	-8.30	86724	78067	-9.98	62519	63146	1.00
	7	141613	135181	-4.54	79854	78597	-1.57	62213	63453	1.99
	8	168086	160158	-4.72	95361	94629	-0.77	80844	81370	0.65
	9	125153	116653	-6.79	73605	69916	-5.01	58771	58996	0.38
	10	124446	119120	-4.28	72399	72133	-0.37	61419	62285	1.41
200	1	526666	499408	-5.18	301449	298952	-0.83	254268	264365	3.97
	2	566643	543008	-4.17	335714	320699	-4.47	266028	274201	3.07
	3	529919	490462	-7.45	308278	298587	-3.14	254647	268894	5.59
	4	603709	587741	-2.64	360852	353113	-2.14	297269	307182	3.33
	5	547953	515285	-5.96	322268	305632	-5.16	260455	269743	3.57
	6	502276	479853	-4.46	292453	280955	-3.93	236160	247641	4.86
	7	479651	456839	-4.76	279576	278022	-0.56	247555	256231	3.50
	8	530896	496257	-6.52	288746	280299	-2.93	225572	233697	3.60
	9	575353	530693	-7.76	331107	316412	-4.44	255029	265234	4.00
	10	572866	540116	-5.72	332808	326195	-1.99	269236	279286	3.73
500	1	3113088	2975034	-4.43	1839902	1789511	-2.74	1581233	1640983	3.78
	2	3569058	3393446	-4.92	2064998	1999487	-3.17	1715332	1810535	5.55
	3	3300744	3121429	-5.43	1909304	1900634	-0.45	1644947	1698452	3.25
	4	3408867	3255505	-4.50	1930829	1888910	-2.17	1640942	1703427	3.81
	5	3377547	3132862	-7.24	1881221	1809312	-3.82	1468325	1519876	3.51
	6	3024082	2811235	-7.04	1658411	1632663	-1.55	1413345	1489321	5.38
	7	3381166	3199398	-5.38	1971176	1904756	-3.37	1634912	1698743	3.90
	8	3376678	3154755	-6.57	1924191	1843914	-4.17	1542090	1602894	3.94
	9	3617807	3391379	-6.26	2065647	1979537	-4.17	1684055	1772641	5.26
	10	3315019	3163870	-4.56	1928579	1840624	-4.56	1520515	1601720	5.34
1000	1	15190371	14099474	-7.18	8570154	8149624	-4.91	6411581	6685430	4.27
	2	13356727	12454682	-6.75	7592040	7327215	-3.49	6112598	6365740	4.14
	3	12919259	12061237	-6.64	7313736	7116546	-2.70	5985538	6250910	4.43
	4	12705259	11903382	-6.31	7300217	7105489	-2.67	6096729	6354634	4.23
	5	13276868	12556618	-5.42	7738367	7398453	-4.39	6348242	6672924	5.11

continued on following page

Table 3. Continued

N	k	r = 0.2				r = 0.4				r = 0.8		
		u	f*	e (%)		u	f*	e (%)		u	f*	e(%)
	6	12236080	11749705	-3.97		7144491	6987842	-2.19		6082142	6415273	5.48
	7	14160773	13354947	-5.69		8426024	7982541	-5.26		6575879	6903158	4.98
	8	13314723	12324002	-7.44		7508507	7289547	-2.92		6069658	6360704	4.80
	9	12433821	11865221	-4.57		7299271	7284531	-0.20		6188416	6468270	4.52
	10	13395234	12485997	-6.79		7617658	7322548	-3.87		6147295	6493815	5.64

larly, for instances with 100 or more jobs, MBO achieved better solutions for all instances with tight factors of 0.2 and 0.4 (Table 3). For the tight instances ($r = 0.2$), average improvements were 3.84% for instances with 20 jobs, 5.69% for instances with 50 jobs, 6.11% for instances with 100 jobs, and 5.46% for 200 jobs. For instances with 20 jobs and $r = 0.6$ or 0.8, the average improvements obtained were 0.72% and 0.41%, respectively. For instances with 50 jobs, average improvements obtained were 0.20% for $r = 0.6$ and 0.28% for $r = 0.8$ (Table 2). For problems with $r = 0.8$ and $n =$ more than 100 jobs, MBO solutions were worse than the previously best known solutions.

The experiment shows the potential of using MBO to minimize the total penalties due to earliness and tardiness in a single machines scheduling problem. Performance was evaluated with a set of 280 standard instances from the SMWET literature. It was found that MBO performed quite well for a wide range of instances and achieved an average improvement of 1.4% for all instances. We obtained better solutions than the available upper bound for 141 instances. Additionally, for 193 instances, MBO yielded solutions that were better than or equal to the previously best known solution, demonstrating that MBO is an effective tool for SMWET.

Permutation Flow-Shop Problem

The permutation flow-shop problem (PFSP) is a particular case of the flow-shop problem in which there are m machines in series and each job has to be processed sequentially by every machine. The objective is to determine an optimal schedule (Pinedo, 2008). In PFSP, the sequence of jobs is the same for every machine. In other words, if a job is at the ith position on one machine, then it is at the ith position on all machines. As a consequence, optimization is used to minimize the makespan: the finishing time for n jobs on m machines. This problem has been widely studied because it has many real applications and because it continues to pose a challenge due to its computational complexity (Amiri & Fathian, 2007; Framinan, J. N. Gupta, & Leisten, 2004; Ribas, Companys, & Tort-Martorell, 2010).

Structure of Solution and Parameters

The genotypes of the drones, queens and larvae are represented by a permutational sequence of jobs of equal length for all the individuals. For example, Figure 4 depicts representations of a queen, a drone and a larva when seven jobs are available.

MBO parameters for PFSP are shown in Table 4. Most of these parameters were obtained experimentally, and the others were obtained from the literature.

Obtaining the Initial Population

The best queen was generated by Palmer's heuristic (1965), and the rest of the queens were obtained by a random procedure. The drone population was

Figure 4. Structure of individual genotypes

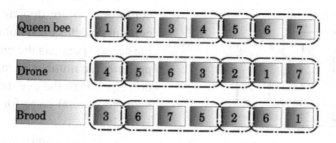

Table 4. Parameters for the Permutation Flow Shop Problem with MBO

Parameters	Source	Value
Number of Queens	Preliminary Experiments	3
Drones population	Preliminary Experiments	100
Spermatheca capacity	Preliminary Experiments	100
Initial speed of Queen Bees	Preliminary Experiments	10
Initial energy of Queen Bees	Random	[0, 1]
Lost energy of Queen Bees	Abbass (2001a)	0.1

obtained by a random procedure that is designed to generate only feasible solutions. Because the drones cannot have the same genetic material, different drones were created for different flights to increase the number of explored permutations.

Selecting the Drone's Genetic Material

Energy and speed are defined as uniform random variables in the interval [0, 1], and both parameters decrease according to α and g, respectively (Equations 1 and 2). When a particular mating takes place, the queen chooses randomly whether to open its spermatheca for the selected drone; a number between 0 and 1 is generated to represent the queen's decision. If this number is smaller than the drone's mating probability, the queen will open its spermatheca, allowing the algorithm to choose among the different solutions provided by the drones. Finally, once all of the selected drone's

sperm has entered the spermatheca, the drone is immediately removed from the search space.

Obtaining Broods

Crossover is achieved by randomly selecting a cutting point in the genetic material for each of the queens within the sequence of jobs. Specifically, we used the crossover developed by Davis (1991) called OX. In Figure 5, five jobs are used to describe a crossover between queen $R1$ and drone $Z1$ to produce two larvae.

Mutation involves the random alteration of each component in the sequence of jobs. The mutation used is illustrated in Figure 6.

Evaluating the Larvae and Updating the Population

The evaluation function determines whether an individual fits in the configuration space based on its cost. The function attempts to obtain the best makespan for each individual. The population is updated by replacing the least adapted queen with the best larvae that was obtained from the crossover between a queen and a drone.

Stopping Criteria

During the iteration process, the objective function is always reduced. Therefore, the number of flights (iterations) initialized and input to the computer program controls the extent of the evaluation of

Figure 5. OX crossover between a queen bee and a drone

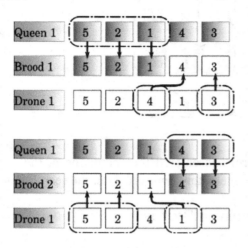

MBO efficiency. In this case, the stopping criterion was 1000 iterations.

Numerical Results

A computer with an AMD Athlon 64 3000+, 1 GB RAM, Linux and the Python 2.5 programming language was used for the experiment. Instances were taken from OR-Library (Beasley, 1990) and 120 instances from Taillard (1990).

Each instance was executed ten times with its corresponding parameters to assess the average error and efficiency of the algorithm. The error in the best solution (e) is determined by Equation (8), where f^* is best solution found and u is the best known solution.

$$e = 100f^*/u \qquad (8)$$

The results obtained for each evaluated configuration are depicted in Table 5; the first column presents the number of the configuration, the second presents the number of jobs, the third presents the number of machines and the fourth corresponds to the average error. In Table 5, the average general error for the 120 test instances is 4.93%.

The first set of ten instances, which considered twenty jobs and five machines, yielded an average error of 1.24% and a standard deviation of 0.56%.

As given in the last column of Table 6, running time averaged 46.3 seconds. Additionally, Table 7 shows other results with different numbers of jobs.

A comparison of running times (Table 6) demonstrates that run times tend to increase as the number of jobs and the number of machines in the test instances increase.

Table 8 shows the results for Taillard's instances (1990), which are larger and tend to require a greater amount of computation time. Nevertheless, the percent error with respect to the best value available in the OR-Library did not necessarily increase.

The MBO used in this work achieved an efficiency of 96.5% and an average error of 3.5% for the set of 120 test instances. The running time was affected more by the number of jobs to be scheduled than by the number of machines used. We believe that this is primarily due to the time required to handle more extensive genotypes.

Figure 6. Transposed mutation for a larva

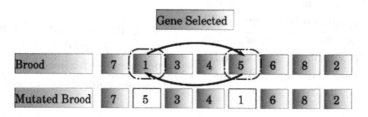

Table 5. Instances used for the Permutation Flow Shop Problem

Configuration Number	Number of Jobs	Number of Machines	e [%]
1	20	5	3.60
2	20	10	4.80
3	20	20	4.70
4	50	5	3.30
5	50	10	7.30
6	50	20	9.10
7	100	5	2.30
8	100	10	4.60
9	100	20	9.10
10	200	10	4.10
11	200	20	8.90
12	500	20	6.30

Table 6. Results for the Permutation Flow Shop Problem with 20 jobs and 5 machines

Problem	u	f^*	e [%]	Running Time [s]
1	1278	1288	0.78	45.78
2	1359	1368	0.66	46.89
3	1081	1102	1.94	46.51
4	1293	1309	1.24	44.79
5	1235	1243	0.65	46.12
6	1195	1222	2.26	48.38
7	1234	1253	1.54	46.77
8	1206	1215	0.75	46.95
9	1230	1247	1.38	44.16
10	1108	1121	1.17	46.69

CONCLUSION

In this chapter, we apply an MBO-based approach to solve two scheduling optimization problems: the minimization of earliness-tardiness penalties on single machine scheduling and the permutation flow shop. This method yielded solutions that were equal to or better than the best known solutions for most of the instances studied.

State-of-the-art evolutionary techniques have proven to be powerful tools for solving scheduling problems; their results are competitive with those produced by traditional techniques. Although MBO is a recent technique that has been applied to only a limited number of problems, it has delivered promising results. Additional experimental work will provide interesting information on its potential, adaptability and results for other scheduling problems.

By appropriately combining parameters and adequately representing the solution, competitive results are obtained for both running time and solution quality.

Table 7. Computational results with MBO for the Permutation Flow Shop Problem

Number, Instance size (*m.n*)	*u*	*f**	*e* [%]	Running Time [s]	Number Instance size (*m.n*)	*u*	*f**	*e* [%]	Running Time [s]
1(20.10)	1582	1631	3.10	54.14	1(50.10)	2991	3065	2.47	85.4
2	1659	1715	3.38	54.47	2	2867	3023	5.44	85.2
3	1496	1513	1.14	53.89	3	2839	2982	5.04	83.6
4	1377	1414	2.69	55.86	4	3063	3138	2.45	84.5
5	1419	1458	2.75	54.54	5	2976	3121	4.87	85.2
6	1397	1428	2.22	54.34	6	3006	3178	5.72	82.4
7	1484	1511	1.82	53.47	7	3093	3261	5.43	83.2
8	1538	1593	3.58	54.27	8	3037	3163	4.15	85.1
9	1593	1651	3.64	54.59	9	2897	3030	4.59	86.0
10	1591	1643	3.27	54.64	10	3065	3229	5.35	84.1
1(20.20)	2297	2345	2.09	71.9	1(50.20)	3847	4031	4.78	120.8
2	2099	2135	1.72	69.6	2	3704	3874	4.59	123.4
3	2326	2394	2.92	70.4	3	3640	3818	4.89	120.2
4	2223	2294	3.19	70.2	4	3719	3903	4.95	122.1
5	2291	2361	3.06	71.3	5	3610	3759	4.13	122.0
6	2226	2275	2.20	69.7	6	3679	3853	4.73	123.1
7	2273	2357	3.70	70.8	7	3704	3871	4.51	121.3
8	2200	2258	2.64	70.2	8	3691	3841	4.06	120.2
9	2237	2310	3.26	69.9	9	3741	3915	4.65	121.2
10	2178	2263	3.90	70.4	10	3756	3939	4.87	122.6
1(50.5)	2724	2770	1.69	66.3	1(100.5)	5493	5604	2.02	99.4
2	2834	2921	3.07	67.1	2	5268	5311	0.82	99.7
3	2621	2687	2.52	69.3	3	5175	5305	2.51	101.2
4	2751	2848	3.53	68.2	4	5014	5058	0.88	100.4
5	2863	2961	3.42	68.4	5	5250	5326	1.45	101.3
6	2829	2832	0.11	69.4	6	5135	5259	2.41	98.6
7	2725	2812	3.19	67.3	7	5246	5370	2.36	100.4
8	2683	2702	0.71	67.0	8	5094	5242	2.91	101.8
9	2552	2634	3.21	68.8	9	5448	5598	2.75	101.3
10	2782	2846	2.30	66.7	10	5322	5414	1.73	100.5

Table 8. Computational results of MBO for Taillard's instances

Number Instance size (m,n)	Taillard's value	f*	e [%]	Running Time [s]	Number Instance size (m,n)	Taillard's value	f*	e [%]	Running Time [s]
1 (100.10)	5770	5963	3.34	133.9	6	10329	10735	3.93	233.7
2	5349	5547	3.70	130.6	7	10854	11273	3.86	235.3
3	5676	5852	3.10	137.6	8	10730	11130	3.73	238.6
4	5781	6030	4.31	136.0	9	10438	10804	3.51	233.6
5	5467	5644	3.24	135.5	10	10675	11001	3.05	235.0
6	5303	5441	2.60	137.1					
7	5595	5820	4.02	131.5	1(200.20)	11181	11733	4.94	346.1
8	5617	5836	3.90	132.2	2	11203	11847	5.75	372.0
9	5871	6079	3.54	135.7	3	11281	11860	5.13	356.1
10	5845	6074	3.92	138.6	4	11275	11921	5.73	358.3
					5	11259	11835	5.12	366.1
1 (100.20)	6202	6512	5.00	206.4	6	11195	11782	5.24	369.5
2	6183	6527	5.56	201.6	7	11360	12013	5.75	364.1
3	6271	6616	5.50	206.7	8	11334	11942	5.36	373.1
4	6269	6545	4.40	205.0	9	11192	11826	5.66	358.1
5	6314	6594	4.43	209.6	10	11288	11942	5.79	357.9
6	6364	6730	5.75	201.0					
7	6268	6621	5.63	207.0	1(500.20)	26059	27224	4.47	658.8
8	6401	6718	4.95	208.0	2	26520	27610	4.11	643.8
9	6275	6615	5.42	211.0	3	26371	27466	4.15	653.1
10	6434	6773	5.27	207.0	4	26456	27505	3.97	647.3
					5	26334	27414	4.10	653.1
1(200.10)	10862	11103	2.22	239.4	6	26477	27481	3.79	642.2
2	10480	10876	3.78	236.7	7	26389	27378	3.75	655.2
3	10922	11321	3.65	230.4	8	26560	27669	4.18	648.4
4	10889	11232	3.15	234.6	9	26005	27020	3.90	646.3
5	10524	10890	3.48	236.5	10	26457	27400	3.56	653.5

ACKNOWLEDGMENT

The second and third authors thanks to the Complex Engineering Systems Institute (ICM: P-05-004-F, CONICYT: FBO16)

REFERENCES

Abbass, H. A. (2001a). A monogenous MBO approach to satisfiability. In M. Mohammadian (Ed.), *The International Conference on Computational Intelligence for Modelling, Control and Automation*, (pp. CD-ROM). Las Vegas: University of Canberra.

Abbass, H. A. (2001b). A single queen single worker honey–bees approach to 3-SAT. *In L. Spector et al. (Ed.), Proceedings of the Genetic and Evolutionary Computation Conference*, (pp. 807-814). San Francisco: Morgan Kaufmann.

Abbass, H. A. (2001c). MBO: marriage in honey bees optimization a Haplometrosis polygynous swarming approach. In J. Kim (Ed.). *Proceedings of the 2001 Congress on Evolutionary Computation*, (pp. 207-214). Seoul: IEEE, Inc.

Afshar, A., Bozorg Haddad, O., Marino, M. A., & Adams, B. J. (2007). Honey-bee mating optimization (HBMO) algorithm for optimal reservoir operation. *Journal of the Franklin Institute, 344*(5), 452–462. doi:10.1016/j.jfranklin.2006.06.001

Amiri, B., & Fathian, M. (2007). Integration of self organizing feature maps and honey bee mating optimization algorithm for market segmentation. *Journal of Theoretical and Applied Information Technology, 3*(3), 70–86.

Baker, K. R., & Scudder, G. D. (1989). On the assignment of optimal due dates. *The Journal of the Operational Research Society, 40*(1), 93–95.

Baker, K. R., & Scudder, G. D. (1990). Sequencing with earliness and tardiness penalties: a review. *Operations Research, 38*(1), 22–36. doi:10.1287/opre.38.1.22

Baykasoglu, A., Özbakir, L., & Tapkan, P. (2007). Artificial bee colony algorithm and its application to generalized assignment problem. In Chan, F., & Tiwari, M. (Eds.), *Swarm Intelligence: Focus on Ant and Particle Swarm Optimization* (pp. 115–144). Vienna: Itech Education and Publishing.

Beasley, J. E. (1990). OR-Library: Distributing test problems by electronic mail. *The Journal of the Operational Research Society, 41*(11), 1069–1072.

Bector, C. R., Gupta, Y. P., & Gupta, M. C. (1988). Determination of an optimal common due date and optimal sequence in a single machine job shop. *International Journal of Production Research, 26*(4), 613–628. doi:10.1080/00207548808947888

Benatchba, K., Admane, L., & Koudil, M. (2005). Using bees to solve a data mining problem expressed as a max-sat one. In Mira, José; Álvarez, José R. (Eds.), *Artificial Intelligence and Knowledge Engineering Applications: A Bioinspired Approach*. (pp. 212-220). Madrid, SP: Lecture Notes in Computer Science, Vol 3562/2005, Springer Verlag.

Biskup, D., & Feldmann, M. (2001). Benchmarks for scheduling on a single machine against restrictive and unrestrictive common due dates. *Computers & Operations Research, 28*(8), 787–801. doi:10.1016/S0305-0548(00)00008-3

Bonabeau, E., Dorigo, M., & Theraulaz, G. (1999). *Swarm intelligence: from natural to artificial systems*. New York: Oxford University Press.

Bozorg Haddad, O., & Afshar, A. (2004). MBO (Marriage Bees Optimization): A new heuristic approach in hydro systems design and operation. *In Proceedings of the 1st International Conference on Managing Rivers in the 21st Century: Issues and Challenges*. (pp. 499-504). Penang.

Bozorg Haddad, O., Afshar, A., & Mariño, M. (2006). Honey-Bees Mating Optimization (HBMO) algorithm: A new heuristic approach for water resources optimization. *Water Resources Management, 20*(5), 661–680. doi:10.1007/s11269-005-9001-3

Chang, H. S. (2006). Converging marriage in honey-bees optimization and application to stochastic dynamic programming. *Journal of Global Optimization, 35*(3), 423–441. doi:10.1007/s10898-005-5608-4

Davis, L. (1991). *Handbook of genetic algorithms*. New York, NY: Van Nostrand Reinhold.

Dorigo, M., & Caro, G. (1999). The ant colony optimization meta-heuristic. In Corne, D., Glover, F., & Dorigo, M. (Eds.), *New Ideas in Optimization* (pp. 11–32). USA: McGraw-Hill Ltd.

Dorigo, M., & Gambardella, L. (1997). Ant colony system: a cooperative learning approach to the traveling salesman problem. *IEEE Transactions on Evolutionary Computation, 1*(1), 53–66. doi:10.1109/4235.585892

Fathian, M., Amiri, B., & Maroosi, A. (2007). Application of honey-bee mating optimization algorithm on clustering. *Applied Mathematics and Computation, 190*(2), 1502–1513. doi:10.1016/j.amc.2007.02.029

Feldmann, M., & Biskup, D. (2003). Single-machine scheduling for minimizing earliness and tardiness penalties by meta-heuristic approaches. *Computers & Industrial Engineering, 44*(2), 307–323. doi:10.1016/S0360-8352(02)00181-X

Framinan, J. M., Gupta, J. N., & Leisten, R. (2004). A review and classification of heuristics for permutation flow-shop scheduling with makespan objective. *The Journal of the Operational Research Society, 55*(12), 1243–1255. doi:10.1057/palgrave.jors.2601784

Garey, M., & Johnson, D. (1979). *Computers and Intractability: A Guide to the Theory of NP-completeness*. New York: W. H. Freeman & Co.

Goldberg, D. E. (1989). *Genetic Algorithms in Search, Optimization, and Machine Learning* (1st ed.). Boston: Addison-Wesley Professional.

Gordon, V., Proth, J. M., & Chu, C. (2002). A survey of the state-of-the-art of common due date assignment and scheduling research. *European Journal of Operational Research, 139*(1), 1–25. doi:10.1016/S0377-2217(01)00181-3

Hall, N. G., & Posner, M. E. (1991). Earliness-tardiness scheduling problems, I: weighted deviation of completion times about a common due date. *Operations Research, 39*(5), 836–846. doi:10.1287/opre.39.5.836

Haouari, M., & M'Hallah, R. (1997). Heuristic algorithms for the two-stage hybrid flowshop problem. *Operations Research Letters, 21*(1), 43–53. doi:10.1016/S0167-6377(97)00004-7

Hino, C. M., Ronconi, D. P., & Mendes, A. B. (2005). Minimizing earliness and tardiness penalties in a single-machine problem with a common due date. *European Journal of Operational Research, 160*(1), 190–201. doi:10.1016/j.ejor.2004.03.006

James, R. J. W. (1997). Using Tabu Search to solve the common due date early/tardy machine Scheduling Problem. *Computers & Operations Research, 24*(3), 199–208. doi:10.1016/S0305-0548(96)00052-4

Kirkpatrick, S., Gelatt, C. D., & Vecchi, M. P. (1983). Optimization by Simulated Annealing. *Science, 220*(4598), 671–680. doi:10.1126/science.220.4598.671

Lee, C. Y., & Kim, S. J. (1995). Parallel genetic algorithms for the earliness-tardiness job scheduling problem with general penalty weights. *Computers & Industrial Engineering, 28*(2), 231–243. doi:10.1016/0360-8352(94)00197-U

Liao, C. J., & Cheng, C. C. (2007). A variable neighborhood search for minimizing single machine weighted earliness and tardiness with common due date. *Computers & Industrial Engineering, 52*(4), 404–413. doi:10.1016/j.cie.2007.01.004

Lin, S. W., Chou, S. Y., & Ying, K. C. (2007). A sequential exchange approach for minimizing earliness-tardiness penalties of single-machine scheduling with a common due date. *European Journal of Operational Research, 177*(2), 1294–1301. doi:10.1016/j.ejor.2005.11.015

Marinakis, Y., Marinaki, M., & Dounias, G. (2007). Honey bees mating optimization algorithm for the vehicle routing problem. In N. Krasnogor; V. Nicosia; M. Pavone; D.A. Pelta (Eds.). Nature Inspired Cooperative Strategies for Optimization, (pp. 139-148*). Studies in Computational Intelligence*, Vol 129/2007. Berlin: Springer Verlag.

Marinakis, Y., Marinaki, M., & Dounias, G. (2008). Honey Bees Mating Optimization algorithm for large scale vehicle routing problems. *Natural Computing, 9*(1), 5–27. doi:10.1007/s11047-009-9136-x

Nearchou, A. C. (2008). A differential evolution approach for the common due date early/tardy job scheduling problem. *Computers & Operations Research, 35*(4), 1329–1343. doi:10.1016/j.cor.2006.08.013

Niknam, T. (2008). Application of honey-bee mating optimization on state estimation of a power distribution system including distributed generators. *Journal of Zhejiang University-Science A, 9*(12), 1753–1764. doi:10.1631/jzus.A0820047

Niknam, T. (2009). An efficient hybrid evolutionary algorithm based on PSO and HBMO algorithms for multi-objective Distribution Feeder Reconfiguration. *Energy Conversion and Management, 50*(8), 2074–2082. doi:10.1016/j.enconman.2009.03.029

Niknam, T., Olamaie, J., & Khorshidi, R. (2008). A hybrid algorithm based on HBMO and fuzzy set for multiobjective distribution feeder reconfiguration. *World Applied Sciences Journal, 4*(2), 308–315.

Pai, P., Yang, S., & Chang, P. (2009). Forecasting output of integrated circuit industry by support vector regression models with marriage honeybees optimization algorithms. *Expert Systems with Applications, 36*(7), 10746–10751. doi:10.1016/j.eswa.2009.02.035

Palmer, D. S. (1965). Sequencing jobs through a multi-stage process in the minimum total time -A quick method of obtaining a near optimum. *The Journal of the Operational Research Society, 16*(1), 101–107. doi:10.1057/jors.1965.8

Pan, Q. K., Tasgetiren, M., & Liang, Y. C. (2006). Minimizing total earliness and tardiness penalties with a common due date on a single-machine using a discrete particle swarm optimization algorithm. In M. Dorigo; L.M. Gambardella; M. Birattari; A. Martinoli; R. Poli; Th. Stützle (Eds.). *Ant Colony Optimization and Swarm Intelligence.* (LNCS vol 4150-2005, pp. 460-467). Brussels: Springer Verlag.

Pham, D. T., Koç, E., Lee, J. Y., & Phrueksanant, J. (2007). Using the Bees Algorithm to schedule jobs for a machine. *In Proc. of the 8th Int. Conf. and Exhibition on Laser Metrology, Machine Tool, CMM & Robotic Performance* (pp. 430-439). Wales.

Pinedo, M. (2008). *Scheduling: theory, algorithms, and systems.* New York: Springer Verlag.

Ribas, I., Companys, R., & Tort-Martorell, X. (2010). Comparing three-step heuristics for the permutation flow shop problem. *Computers & Operations Research, 37*(12), 2062–2070. doi:10.1016/j.cor.2010.02.006

Taillard, E. (1990). Some efficient heuristic methods for the flow shop sequencing problem. *European Journal of Operational Research, 47*(1), 65–74. doi:10.1016/0377-2217(90)90090-X

Talbi, E. (2009). *Metaheuristics: From Design to Implementation.* Hoboken, NJ: Wiley & Sons.

Teo, J., & Abbass, H. (2003). A true annealing approach to the marriage in honey-bees optimization a algorithm. *International Journal of Computational Intelligence and Applications*, *3*(2), 199–211. doi:10.1142/S146902680300094X

Teo, J., & Abbass, H. A. (2001). *An annealing approach to the mating-flight trajectories in the marriage in honey bees optimization algorithm*. Technical Report CS04/01. Academic Press, School of Computer Science, University of New South Wales at ADFA.

Yang, C., Tu, X., & Chen, J. (2007). Algorithm of marriage in honey bees optimization based on the Wolf Pack Search. *In International Conference on Intelligent Pervasive Computing* (pp. 462-467). Los Alamitos.

ADDITIONAL READING

Anderson, J. H. (2004). *Handbook of Scheduling: Algorithms, Models, and Performance Analysis* (1° ed.). Boca Ratón, FL: Chapman and Hall/CRC.

Baker, K. R., & Trietsch, D. (2009). *Principles of Sequencing and Scheduling*. Hoboken, NJ: Wiley. doi:10.1002/9780470451793

Bonabeau, E., Dorigo, M., & Theraulaz, G. (1999). *Swarm Intelligence: From Natural to Artificial Systems*. New York, NY: Oxford University Press.

Chen, D., Batson, R. G., & Dang, Y. (2010). *Applied Integer Programming: Modeling and Solution*. Hoboken, NJ: Wiley.

Clerc, M. (2006). *Particle Swarm Optimization*. New Port Beach, CA: ISTE USA. doi:10.1002/9780470612163

Davis, L. (1991). *Handbook of Genetic Algorithms*. New York, NY: Van Nostrand Reinhold.

Dorigo, M., & Stützle, T. (2004). *Ant Colony Optimization*. Cambridge, MA: The MIT Press.

Garey, M. R., & Johnson, D. S. (1979). *Computers and Intractability. A guide to the Theory of NP-completeness*. New York, NY: W.H. Freeman and Company.

Goldberg, D. E. (1989*). Genetic Algorithms in Search, Optimization, and Machine Learning* (1° ed). Boston: Addison-Wesley Professional.

Menon, A. (2004). *Frontiers of Evolutionary Computation* (1° ed.). Norwell, MA: Kluwer Academic Publishers.

Michalewicz, Z. (1996). *Genetic Algorithms + Data Structures = Evolution Programs*. Charlotte, NC: Springer Verlag.

Michalewicz, Z. (2010). *Advances in Metaheuristics for Hard Optimization* (1° ed.). New York, NY: Springer-Verlag.

Michalewicz, Z., & Fogel, D. B. (2004). *How to solve it: modern heuristics*. New York, NY: Springer-Verlag.

Michener, C. D. (1974). *The Social Behavior of the Bees: A Comparative Study*. Belknap Press.

Papadimitriou, C. H., & Stieglitz, K. (1982). *Combinatorial Optimization: Algorithms and Complexity*. Englewood Cliffs, NJ: Prentice-Hall.

Rothlauf, F. (2006). *Representations for Genetic and Evolutionary Algorithms* (2° ed.). Berlin: Berlin, Springer Berlin Heildelberg.

Steiner, R. (1998). *Bees. Gt.* Barrington, MA: Anthroposophic Press.

Winston, M. (1987). *The Biology of the Honey Bee*. Boston: Harvard University Press.

Wolsey, L. A., & Nemhauser, G. L. (1999). *Integer and Combinatorial Optimization* (1° ed.). Princeton, NJ: Wiley-Interscience.

Yang, X. (2008). *Nature-Inspired Metaheuristic Algorithms*. United Kingdom

Chapter 9
Global Bacteria Optimization Meta-Heuristic:
Performance Analysis and Application to Shop Scheduling Problems

Elyn L. Solano-Charris
Universidad de La Sabana, Colombia

Libardo S. Gómez-Vizcaíno
Universidad Autónoma del Caribe, Colombia

Jairo R. Montoya-Torres
Universidad de La Sabana, Colombia

Carlos D. Paternina-Arboleda
Universidad del Norte, Colombia

ABSTRACT

A large number of real-life optimization problems in economics and business are complex and difficult to solve. Hence, using approximate algorithms is a very good alternative to solve this class of problems. Meta-heuristics solution procedures represent general approximate algorithms applicable to a large variety of optimization problems. Most of the meta-heuristics mimic natural metaphors to solve complex optimization problems. This chapter presents a novel procedure based on Bacterial Phototaxis, called Global Bacteria Optimization (GBO) algorithm, to solve combinatorial optimization problems. The algorithm emulates the movement of an organism in response to stimulus from light. The effectiveness of the proposed meta-heuristic algorithm is first compared with the well-known meta-heuristic MOEA (Multi-Objective Evolutionary Algorithm) using mathematical functions. The performance of GBO is also analyzed by solving some single- and multi-objective classical jobshop scheduling problems against state-of-the-art algorithms. Experimental results on well-known instances show that GBO algorithm performs very well and even outperforms existing meta-heuristics in terms of computational time and quality of solution.

DOI: 10.4018/978-1-61350-086-6.ch009

INTRODUCTION

A large number of real-life optimization problems in economics and business are complex and difficult to solve. They cannot be solved in an exact manner within a reasonable amount of time (Talbi, 2009). Using approximate algorithms is the main alternative to solve this class of problems. According to Talbi (2009), approximate algorithms can be classified in two classes: dedicated heuristics and meta-heuristics. The former are problem-dependent and are designed and applicable to a particular problem. The latter are called meta-heuristics procedures and represent more general approximate algorithms applicable to a large variety of optimization problems. Meta-heuristics solve instances of problems that are believed to be hard in general, by exploring the usually large solution search space of these instances. Those algorithms achieve this by reducing the effective size of the space and by exploring that space efficiently. With the improvement of computing performance, the past 20 years have witnessed the development of numerous meta-heuristic algorithms in various communities that sit at the intersection of several fields, including artificial intelligence, computational intelligence, soft computing, mathematical programming, and operations research. Most of the meta-heuristics mimic natural metaphors to solve complex optimization problems (e.g., evolution of species, annealing process, ant colony, particle swarm, immune system, bee colony, and wasp swarm). Meta-heuristics are more and more popular in different research areas and industries.

In this chapter, we present a novel meta-heuristic to solve hard combinatorial optimization problems. The meta-heuristic is inspired from biology, and in particular from the bacterial phototaxis, which is a kind of taxis that occurs when an organism reacts to light stimulation. This is advantageous for phototrophic organisms as they can orient themselves most efficiently to receive light for photosynthesis. The effectiveness of the proposed meta-heuristic algorithm is compared with the well-known meta-heuristic MOEA (Multi-Objective Evolutionary Algorithm) using a set of mathematical functions. Its performance is also analyzed by solving mono-criterion and multi-criteria jobshop scheduling problems against well known state-of-the-art procedures.

GLOBAL BACTERIA OPTIMIZATION META-HEURISTIC

Preliminaries: What is a Bacterium?

A bacterium is a prokaryotic unicellular organism. Its structure is basically conformed by a central body of microscopic size that can take many different forms (Young, 2006) and whose size can vary from 0.01 μm^3 to a volume 10^{10} times bigger (Angert et al., 1993; Rappe et al., 2002). Many bacteria are endowed with a series of rotating flagella in its cell surface that act as propellants, allowing them to swim at a speed of 10-35 $\mu m/s$ (Guzmán et al., 2010). In addition to the appropriate structure to move in an autonomous way, bacteria have potential receivers (chemoreceptors and photoreceptors) capable of detecting temporal-space changes in the environment that surrounds them. In this way, when an external perturbation is detected, bacteria use their memory to make a temporal-space comparison of the gradients found. Depending on the external conditions sensed, bacteria change their movements from a random walk to a biased walk (Guzmán et al., 2010).

Preliminaries: Bacterial Behavior to Solve Optimization Problems

When using this behavior to solve optimization problems, works in literature have only applied the artificial chemotaxis optimization process (Sierakowski & dos Santos Coelho, 2006; Guzmán et al., 2010; Chen et al., 2010). The chemotaxis algorithm (CA) is pioneered by Bremermann and (1974), proposed by analogy to the way bacteria react to chemo-attractants in concentration gradients. Müller et al. (2000,2002) and Passino (2002) proposed the bacterial chemotaxis (BC) algorithm based on the chemotaxis algorithm (CA). The simplicity and robustness of BC algorithm have been verified, however, the bacteria are considered as individuals and social interaction is not used in the models. As pointed out by Kuo et al. (2011), these models differ from the interaction models for the behavior of social insects (such as ants, bees, wasps, or termites) that are viewed as systems with collective intelligence and the performance of the basic BC algorithm is just equivalent to the basic genetic algorithm (GA) and is even poorer than the improved GA (Coelho, 2006). The bacterial colony chemotaxis (BCC) algorithm, proposed by Li et al. (2005), is a swarm intelligent algorithm and is developed from the bacterial chemotaxis (BC) algorithm. In this model, both the reaction response to the chemo-attractants of the individuals and their social interaction are considered, and the performance is improved greatly. BCC algorithm is an excellent swarm intelligent algorithm with the capabilities of global search, fast convergence speed and high precision and has been applied to the structure optimization of neural network (Zhao et al., 2007) and the reactive power optimization in power system (Huang et al., 2007).

To the best of our knowledge, the emulation of the bacteria phototaxis process has been very little applied to solve combinatorial optimization problem: some preliminary works have been presented by Montoya-Torres et al. (2010) who tested the algorithm on the solution of the makespan jobshop scheduling problem. The proposed meta-heuristic procedure, called Global Bacterial Optimization (GBO), emulates the biological process known as "bacterial phototaxis". This is a kind of taxis that occurs when a whole organism moves in response to the stimulus from light. This is advantageous for phototrophic organisms as they can orient themselves most efficiently to receive light for photosynthesis. Phototaxis is called positive if the movement is in the direction of light and negative if the direction is opposite.

Two types of positive phototaxis are observed in prokaryotes (i.e., bacteria). The first is called scotophobotaxis (from the word "scotophobia"), which is observed only under a microscope. This occurs when a bacterium swims by chance out of the area illuminated by the microscope. Entering darkness signals the cell to reverse direction and re-enter the light. The second type of phototaxis is true phototaxis, which is a directed movement up a gradient to an increasing amount of light. This is analogous to positive chemotaxis (i.e., oriented movement toward or away from a chemical stimulus) except that the attractant is light rather than a chemical.

As stated before, we propose the design of an effective (in terms of quality of solution) meta-heuristic algorithm based on bacteria phototaxis to solve hard combinatorial optimization problems. Algorithm's performance is first validated on multi-objective mathematical functions and then on two jobshop scheduling problems with single and multiple objectives. The next subsection presents the algorithm in detail.

Algorithm Description

The pseudo-code of the bacterial algorithm is presented in figure 1. In order to solve any combinatorial optimization problem using this meta-heuristic, an object-oriented programming model can be used. It is mandatory to define a class, named "Colony" that is composed of an array of bacteria and the number of bacteria, and a class named "Bacterium" which is represented by a class with the attribute "energy". Depending on the problem under study, many other classes have to be defined. For example, for the case of jobshop scheduling problems, as proposed later in this chapter, three classes of objects are to be defined: a class called "Processing routes" that contains the execution order of operations on machines; a class named "Machines" which is a

Figure 1. Pseudo-code of the bacterial algorithm

```
Procedure Bacteria Phototaxis
        Colony_of_Initial_bacteria ();
        A := Bacterium_Cycle;

        While (A > 1)
            Bacterial_Spin ();
            Race_to_Light ();
            Binary_Fission ();
            Spontaneous_Mutation ();
            Reverse_Mutation ();
            Bacterium_Discharge ();
            Photosynthesis ();
            A = A – 1;
        End_While
    Select_Best_Solution ();
End
```

class that contains the number of machines, their identification codes and the set of jobs that has to be processed on each one; and finally, a class named "Jobs" containing the identification code of jobs, their processing times on machines, their due dates, and their starting dates of processing.

The complexity of this algorithm is $O(A \times |C|)$, where A is the number of bacterium cycles (iterations), and $|C|$ is the number of initial bacteria in the Colony (Montoya-Torres et al., 2010). Subroutines of the algorithm are presented next.

- **Colony_of_Initial_Bacteria**. This subroutine builds the initial solution for the particular problem under study. It is necessary to define an object class named "Colony" with a set of feasible bacteria, which represents a set of feasible solutions. It is hence necessary to define how these feasible solutions (bacteria) will be built to start running the algorithm (initial solution).

- **Bacterial_Spin**. Each bacterium with energy level higher than the lost caused by rotation can implement the "cartwheel" (term used in biology that refers to a bacterial turnaround). This creates an array of best solutions, which are evaluated using equation (1):

$$GLS_i = \frac{\prod_{r=1}^{\frac{nobj}{2}} e^{\left(\frac{-f_{2 \times r-1}(B_i)}{max\{f_{2 \times r-1}(C)\}} \right)}}{\prod_{r=1}^{\frac{nobj}{2}} e^{\left(\frac{-f_{2 \times r-1}(B_i)}{max\{f_{2 \times r}(C)\}} \right)}} \qquad (1)$$

Where *nobj* is the total number of objectives for the given optimization problem, f_r is the *r*-th objective function, C is the colony of bacteria, and B_i is the *i*-th bacterium. The size of the colony (number of bacteria) is a parameter of the algorithm that has be defined set. The actual value recommended for the problems under study in this chapter will be presented later under the computational experiments section.

- **Race_to_Light**. This subprocedure allows each bacterium to move following the intensity of light. For the algorithm here, one of the best fourth bacteria is randomly selected from the vector of best solutions.

- **Binary_Fission**. The binary fission method consists on duplicating a bacterium in order to generate a new bacterium with energy equal to that of the initial bacterium and located at the position of this initial bacterium. If such initial bacterium has enough energy, it hence moves to the light.

- **Spontaneous_Mutation**. A bacterium changes its structure and position with reference to the light, which may improve or not the current solution. This mutation is made only over some bacteria selected according to a certain probability. Those bacteria must have enough energy to be mutated.

- **Reverse_Mutation**. This process is made over a given percentage of mutated bacteria. It consists on relocating mutated bacteria to their initial position if the solution obtained after the Spontaneous Mutation procedure did not improve the current solution.

- **Bacterium_Discharge**. Bacteria having lower energy than a given lower bond level are eliminated from the Colony because they are far away from the light and do not have the energy required to change the position or to mutate. New bacteria generated during binary fission process are included in the Colony.

- **Photosynthesis**. As explained previously, in the natural process, bacteria need energy to survive. Using chemical processes, phototrophic bacteria transform light in energy. In order to emulate this natural process in the algorithm, a mathematical formula was developed to assign energy (ATP) depending on the closeness of the bacterium to the simulated light, as shown by:

$$ATP_i = Energy\ from\ photosynthesis \times \sum_{r=1}^{nobj} e^{\left[\frac{-f_r(B_i)}{\max\{f_r(C)\}}\right]} \tag{2}$$

Where ATP_i is the energy that bacterium i obtains after the photosynthesis process, *nobj* is the total number of objectives for the given optimization problem, f_r is the r-th objective function, C is the colony of bacteria, and B_i is the i-th bacterium.

- **Select_Best_Solution**. At the end of each bacterium cycle (iteration), a colony of bacteria is obtained, representing the set of solutions. In order to obtain the final solution of the iteration, only the best solution is useful for the final colony.

It is to note that GBO can be seen as belonging to the family of evolutionary algorithms.

PERFORMANCE ANALYSIS: EXPERIMENTS ON MATHEMATICAL FUNCTIONS

This section presents a first experimental analysis on the proposed algorithm. The purpose of these experiments is to study its behavior on generic mathematical functions which may act as representations of an objective function of a hard combinatorial optimization problem (Deb et al., 2002; Guzmán et al., 2010). Two functions have been chosen according to previous works in the literature. We first present the experimental design and then the analysis of results.

Description of Experiments

As considered in several works in the literature (see for example Deb et al., 2002; Guzmán et al., 2010), one of the most interesting experiments that allow a rigorous comparison about the performance of heuristic algorithms for hard optimization problems consists on using mathematical functions. In order to analyze the efficiency and effectiveness of the algorithm, an experimental study was conducted using the same multiple objective mathematical functions presented by Donoso and Fabregat (2007). The experiment aimed to analyze the behavior of the GBO algorithm against the well-known meta-heuristic procedure called MOEA (Multi-Objective Evolutionary Algorithm). The experiments were run on a PC bi-processor Intel[R] Pentium[R] Dual CPU T2370 at 1.73 GHz with 2.00 GB RAM and was programmed on C++ language. Simple mathematical functions are considered:

$$f_1(x, y) = x^2 + y^2 \tag{3}$$

$$f_2(x, y) = (x - 2)^2 + (y - 2)^2 \tag{4}$$

Figure 2. Results for the Pareto-front: GBO versus MOEA

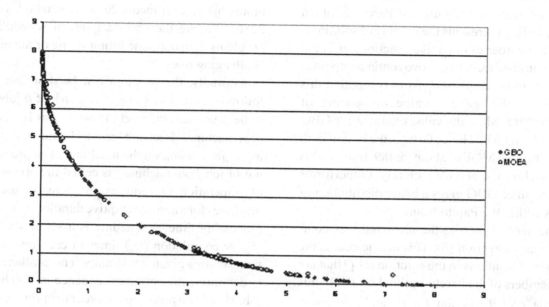

In order to run the algorithm for a comparative computational experiment, some parameters have to be well defined. For the purpose of this experiment, the spin radius was defined to be 5. The Race large was set to be 13, 16, and 19. The probability of spontaneous mutation was defined to be 0.7. The probability of reverse mutation was defined to be 0.3. The initial energy was defined to be 30, while the photosynthesis energy was defined to be 8. The waste for mutation was defined to be 1. The waste for fission was defined to be 3. The waste for spin was defined to be 4. The number of the initial bacteria was set to be 20, 30, and 40. Finally, the bacterial cycle was set to be 6 and 12. These parameters were used to perform the experiments whose results are presented next.

Results

Figure 2 presents a comparison of the Pareto-front obtained using both GBO and MOEA procedures over the mathematical function considered in this experiment. When generating the combined Pareto-front of GBO versus MOEA procedures,

we can see that algorithms overlap, except the maximum and minimum of the function in which the GBO dominates completely. At the first endpoint, function f_1 has been increased by 6.4811%, while function f_2 decreases over a 97.7701%. Besides, in the second endpoint the function f_1 decreases a 99.9686% and the function f_2 increases by 5.2621%.

Two performance metrics were also computed so as to obtain numerical values of the effectiveness of the GBO procedure. These metrics were spacing and the error ratio. The spacing metric evaluates the distribution of points in the non-dominated Pareto front calculated by the algorithm. Original presented by Schott (1995), the equation presented here is the one reproduced by Deb (2001) and Coello et al. (2002). The spacing metric was computed as:

$$Spacing = \sqrt{\frac{1}{q-1}\sum_{i=1}^{m}(\bar{d} - d_i)^2} \qquad (5)$$

This metric intends to evaluate the distribution of points in the non-dominated Pareto-front. In the formula, q represents the number of solutions, m is the number of objective functions, d_i is the Euclidean distance between two continuous points, and $\bar{d}$ is the average of d_i. After computing this metric, MOEA gave a value of spacing of 0.327562988 while the value obtained for GBO was 0.059675638. Hence GBO is the best of both outperformed MOEA about 5.489 times. This results shows that GBO clearly outperforms MOEA, since GBO gives a better distribution of points within the Pareto front.

The second metric, the error ratio, is computed using equation (6). This metric counts the number of solutions in the solution set Q that are not members of the Pareto-optimal set $P*$. In this formula, $e_i=1$ if solution $i \notin P^*$ and $e_i=0$ otherwise. For this analysis, since MOEA and GBO overlap and are on the same face, the true error rate is 0. This means that GBO performs as well as MOEA, according to the value of the true error.

$$ER = \frac{\sum_{i=1}^{|Q|} e_i}{Q} \qquad (6)$$

APPLICATION TO SOLVE SHOP SCHEDULING PROBLEMS

This section aims to analyze the performance of the Global Bacteria Optimization algorithm on hard single- and multi-criteria combinatorial optimization problems. In Scheduling Theory, the jobshop problem is a hard optimization problem found in real industrial contexts for which several meta-heuristics procedures have been successfully applied (Jourdan et al., 2009). Generally speaking, scheduling is a form of decision-making that plays a crucial role in manufacturing and service industries. It deals with the allocation of limited resources (machines) to tasks (jobs) over given time periods and its goal is to optimize one or more objectives (Pinedo, 2008; Montoya-Torres, 2010). Among the various types of scheduling problems, jobshop scheduling is one of the most challenging ones.

Formally, the problem can be described as follows. A set $J = \{j \mid j = 1,...,n\}$ of n jobs is to be processed on a set $M = \{i \mid i = 1,...,m\}$ of m machines. Each job has a technological routing of processing on the machines. The processing of job j on machine i is called the operation O_{ij}. Operation O_{ij} requires an exclusive use of machine i for a non-preemptive duration p_{ij}, called processing time. A schedule is a set of starting (S_{ij}) or completion (C_{ij}) times of each operation that satisfies given constraints. The challenge is to determine the optimum sequence in which the jobs should be processed in order to optimize one or more performance measures, such as the total duration of the schedule (or makespan), the mean flowtime, the total tardiness, the number of late jobs, etc. In this chapter, we consider both the makespan, computed as $C_{max} = \max\{C_j\}$ where C_j is the completion time of job j, and the total tardiness of jobs, computed as $T = \sum_{j=1}^{n} \max\{0, L_j\}$ where $L_j = C_j - d_j$ is the lateness of job j.

The classical jobshop scheduling problem with minimization of the makespan is known to be NP-hard (Garey et al., 1976). This means that it is not possible to find exact (optimal) solutions for large-sized instances in reasonable computational time, except for some strongly restricted special cases. For the standard jobshop scheduling problem, the size of the solution search space is $(n!)^m$ and it is computationally unfeasible to try every possible solution since the required computation time increases exponentially with the size of the instance (i.e., the number of jobs). In practice, many real-life jobshop scheduling problems have larger number of jobs and machines as well as additional constraints, which in turn further increase its complexity.

In the literature, comprehensive surveys of solution approaches for the general jobshop scheduling problem are proposed by Blazewicz et al. (1996) or Jain and Meeran (1998). Exact approaches, such as mathematical programming, branch-and-bound techniques have been proposed. Because of its complexity, heuristic and meta-heuristic algorithms have also been considered by researchers. For instance, for the single objective case, Tabu Search (TS) has revealed to be an effective local search algorithm for the jobshop scheduling problem (Nowick and Smutnicki, 1996). However, the best solution found by TS may depend on the initial solution used. Simulated Annealing (SA) is the most popular technique in threshold algorithm category. It has been applied extensively to jobshop scheduling (Aarts et al., 1994; Yamada, 2003) and can avoid local optima. However, as SA is a generic technique, it is unable to achieve good solutions quickly. The Shifting Bottleneck (SB) heuristic (Pinedo, 2008) has had the greatest influence on approximation methods. The primary weakness of this algorithm, however, is the high computing effort required and many re-optimizations are necessary to achieve good results. In addition, best solutions are achieved from several different parameter settings. Another fundamental problem is the difficulty in performing re-optimization and the generation of unfeasible solutions.

Inspired by the principles of behavior found in real ant colonies, the Ant Colony Optimization (ACO) meta-heuristic has been applied to a variety of scheduling problems with promising results. However, the available results are quite poor and have yet to prove with currents state-of-art algorithms (Hart et al., 2005). Greedy Randomized Adaptive Search Procedure (GRASP) is a problem-space-based method that consists of a constructive phase and an iterative phase (Feo and Resende, 1989, 1995). It generates many different starting solutions using fast problem-

specific constructive procedures, which are then used by local search. Even though GRASP has been applied successfully to several NP-complete problems, the limited results available so far for jobshop scheduling are quite poor (Jain and Meeran, 1998). Genetic algorithms have also been proposed in literature for the jobshop scheduling problem (Cheng et al., 1996).

In real-life jobshop scheduling, it is necessary to optimize several criteria, such as the length of the schedule (makespan) or the utilization of different resources simultaneously. In general, the minimization of the makespan is used as the optimization criterion in single-objective jobshop scheduling. However, the minimization of tardiness, flowtime, machine idle time, etc, are also important criteria in jobshop scheduling. As discussed in Hart et al. (2005), makespan may not be the only commercial interest in scheduling. It is desirable to generate many near-optimal schedules considering multiple (often conflicting) objectives, according to the requirements of the production order or customer demand.

During the past decades, attention from researchers has been given to solve jobshop scheduling with multiple criteria. Sakawa and Kubota (2000) presented a genetic algorithm incorporating the concept of similarity among individuals by using Gantt charts with fuzzy processing times and fuzzy due dates. The objective is to maximize the minimum agreement index, to maximize the average agreement index and to minimize the maximum fuzzy completion time. Werner et al. (2000) proposed to associate a genetic algorithm with genetic programming to evolve the genetic algorithm. Ponnambalam et al. (2001) proposed a multi-objective genetic algorithm to derive the optimal machine-wise priority dispatching rules to resolve the conflict among the contending jobs in the Giffler-Thompson procedure (Giffler and Thompson, 1960) applied in jobshop scheduling. The objective was to minimize the weighted sum of completion times, the total idle time of machines and the total tardiness. Esquivel et al. (2002) proposed an evolutionary algorithm for single and multi-objective jobshop scheduling. Kacem et al. (2002) presented a hybrid approach based on the fusion of fuzzy logic and multi-objective evolutionary algorithm. Xia and Wu (2005) proposed a hybrid particle swarm optimization (PSO) and simulated annealing algorithm to multi-objective flexible job shop scheduling problems. Those mentioned approaches optimize the weighted sum of objective functions and can produce one or several optimal solutions.

Some studies have attempted to simultaneously optimize all objectives and obtain a group of Pareto optimal solutions. Lei and Wu (2006) developed a crowding measure-based multi-objective evolutionary algorithm. Ripon (2007) also proposed a genetic algorithm using jumping genes with the objective of simultaneous minimizing the makespan and the total tardiness, named JGGA. Lei (2008) proposed a particle swarm optimization (PSO) for multi-objective job shop scheduling problem with simultaneous minimization of makespan and total tardiness of jobs. The jobshop scheduling is converted into a continuous optimization problem and then Pareto-archive particle swarm optimization is designed, in which the global best position selection is combined with the crowding measure-based archive maintenance. Other works on solving jobshop scheduling problems with multiple objectives are those of Ponnambalam et al. (2001), Wang and Zheng (2001), Xia and Wu (2005), Liang et al. (2005), Suresh and Mohanasndaram (2006), Lei (2008) or Sha and Lin (2010),

In this section, we consider two applications of GBO procedure to solve jobshop scheduling problems. The first study is as single-objective jobshop problem in which the aim is to minimize the total tardiness, while the second application concerns the resolution of the jobshop scheduling problem when both makespan and total tardiness are minimized.

Solving the Minimum Tardiness Jobshop Scheduling Problem

This subsection considers the minimization of the total tardiness of jobs, that is $\sum_{j=1}^{n} T_j$, where $T_j = \max_{j \in \{1,...,n\}} \{0, L_j\}$ with $L_j = C_j - d_j$, and C_j and d_j being, respectively, the completion time and due date of job j. Using the classical notation, the problem considered here is noted as $Jm \parallel \sum T_j$. This problem is known to be NP-hard (Garey et al., 1976), which means that it is not possible to find exact (optimal) solutions for large-sized instances in reasonable computational time. In order to evaluate the performance of the meta-heuristic in terms of solution quality, we run the algorithm on various benchmark instances. These instances were selected taken into account the selection of previous works from literature (Ripon et al., 2006), and (Ripon, 2007). The first set of instances considered was the well-known data sets named *mt06*, *mt10*, and *mt20* formulated by Muth and Thomson (1963); the second set of instances are those proposed by Adams et al. (1988), which consists on sets *abz7*, *abz8*, *abz9*; and the last set of instances were proposed by Lawrence (1984) and consists of sets named as *la21*, *la24*, *la25*, *la27*, *la29*, *la38*, and *la40*. The full description of all those instances is available on the Internet at the OR-Library webpage at http://people.brunel.ac.uk/~mastjjb/jeb/info.html. Since we consider the minimization of the total tardiness, due dates for all jobs have to be defined. Due dates values considered in this chapter are the same employed by Ripon (2007) and Ripon et al. (2006), which are based on the work of Ponnambalam et al. (2001) and Lei and Wu (2006).

In order to run the algorithm, some parameters need to be defined. Some preliminary runs were performed to define those parameters (Montoya-Torres et al., 2010). The final values are presented

Table 1. Comparison of results for the total tardiness jobshop problem

Instance	JGGA	NSGA II	GBO	%dev(JGGA)	%dev(NSGA II)
mt06	0	0	0	0%	0%
mt10	625	630	645	3%	2%
mt20	8359	7997	7989*	-4%	0%
abz7	531	553	531	0%	-4%
abz8	654	757	654	0%	-14%
abz9	1009	1213	763*	-24%	-37%
la21	1299	1316	1297	0%	-1%
la24	1216	1206	1205*	-1%	0%
la25	1070	1225	1089	2%	-11%
la27	3300	3436	3342	1%	-3%
la29	4311	4419	4357	1%	-1%
la38	1339	1343	1345	0%	0%
la40	551	535	570	3%	7%

next. The initial colony of bacteria representing the initial feasible solutions for the problem is generated randomly. The size of the colony is a $m \times n$, where m is the number of machines in the jobshop and n is the number of jobs to be scheduled. The initial energy level was set to be 30; the photosynthesis energy was set to be 8; the spin radius was 5 and the race large was set to be 13, 16 and 19. The probabilities of spontaneous and reverse mutation were respectively defined as 0.7 and 0.3. The energy levels were 1 for energy waste due to mutation, 3 for energy waste due to fission, and 4 for energy waste due to spin.

Table 1 shows the comparison of our algorithms with procedures JGGA and NSGAII reported by Ripon (2007). The last two columns of this table correspond to the improvement obtained using our algorithm against those from literature, computed using equation (7), where Z is either procedure JGGA or procedure NSGAII:

$$\%dev(Z) = \frac{\sum T_j(GBO) - \sum T_j(Z)}{\sum T_j(Z)} \qquad (7)$$

It is to note that if $\%imp(Z)=0\%$, then our algorithm obtains the same value of the total tardiness than the corresponding Z procedure. Also, if $\%imp(Z)>0\%$, then GBO algorithm outperforms previous results from literature. Among the instances considered, we can observe that our procedure always outperformed algorithm NSGA-II. Also, when the solution given by our algorithm was not better than JGGA, the solution of the bacteria phototaxis algorithm was never worse than -3% of the solution given by JGGA (this occurred for instances *mt10* and *la40*). For the other instances (except *la25, la27, la29*) GBO algorithm outperformed or obtained the same solution value given by JGGA. In comparison with algorithm NSGA II, the bacterial procedure GBO obtained a better value (except for instances *mt10* and *la40*).

Solving a Bi-Criteria Jobshop Scheduling Problem

As stated before, extraordinary research efforts have been done in the scientific community to solve mono-objective jobshop scheduling problems. In order to have more realistic models, multiple criteria can be considered when solving scheduling problems. In this part of the chapter, we consider again the jobshop scheduling problem described before, but this time we seek to simultaneously optimize the makespan and the total tardiness. The first criterion is computed as $C_{max} = \max_{j \in \{1,...,n\}} C_j$, where C_j is the completion time of job j. We recall that the total tardiness of jobs is computed as $\sum_{j=1}^{n} T_j = \sum_{j=1}^{n} \max_{j \in \{1,...,n\}} \{0, L_j\}$, with $L_j = C_j - d_j$, and C_j and d_j being, respectively, the completion time and due date of job j. Attention from researchers has been given to solve jobshop scheduling with multiple criteria, as explained before.

In order to evaluate the performance of the GBO meta-heuristic in the context of multi-objective jobshop scheduling problem described here, we run the algorithm on various benchmark instances. We again considered the same experimental design already proposed in literature by Ripon (2007), who solved the same problem studied in this section. The first sets of instances are the well-known data sets considered previously in the previous section. The parameters of the GBO algorithm were set to be the same as in the experiments of the previous section.

Table 2 shows the best results of the experimental comparison of our procedure with multi-objective procedures JGGA and NSGAII reported by Ripon (2007). The last two columns of this table corresponds to the deviation of each objective value (i.e. makespan and total tardiness) given by our procedure against the values reported in literature. This percentage deviation is computed using equation (8), where F is the objective function either the makespan (C_{max}) or the total tardiness ($\sum T_j$). It is to note that if $\%dev<0\%$, then GBO algorithm outperforms previous results from literature.

$$\%dev(F) = \frac{(GBO) - (F)}{(F)} \qquad (8)$$

As it is possible to observe in Table 2, among the instances considered, our proposed procedure obtained a makespan value never higher than 0.1% and a total tardiness never higher than 6.5% of previous results from literature. It is to note that our algorithm equals (*%dev*=0) or outperformed (*%dev*<0) previous results in 92.3% of the cases tested (12 of a total of 13 instances) for the makespan value, and in 69.2% of the cases tested (9 of a total of 13 instances) for the total tardiness value. In this last situation, the total tardiness was even improved in more than 37% (instance *abz*9).

In order to illustrate the convergence and diversity of the solutions, the non-dominated solutions (i.e., the Pareto-front) of the final generation produced by procedures JGGA (Ripon, 2007) and the GBO based on bacterial phototaxis proposed in this chapter, for the test instances *la*21 and *la*38, are presented in Figures 3 and 4, respectively. From these, we can observe that the final solutions are well spread and converged. In particular, the solutions produced by our proposed meta-heuristic procedure are as well spread as that of JGGA, which was shown by Ripon (2007) to be a capable to find extreme solutions. This means that our procedure is also able to find extreme solutions. It can be further justified that our algorithm performs well in terms of diversity of solutions.

CONCLUDING REMARKS

This chapter presented a novel meta-heuristic algorithm inspired from the behavior of bacteria and their reaction to the stimulus of light and is called global bacteria optimization (GBO). The performance of this procedure was first studied on mathematical functions. Afterwards, two NP-hard combinatorial optimization problems from Scheduling Theory were considered: the

Table 2. Results for the multi-objective jobshop problem

Instance	Procedure	%dev(C_{max})	%dev(ΣJ)
mt06	JGGA	0.0%	0.0%
	NSGA II	0.0%	0.0%
mt10	JGGA	0.0%	3.2%
	NSGA II	-1.3%	2.4%
mt20	JGGA	-1.6%	-4.4%
	NSGA II	-0.5%	-0.1%
abz7	JGGA	-0.7%	0.0%
	NSGA II	0.0%	-4.0%
abz8	JGGA	-0.1%	0.0%
	NSGA II	-1.0%	-13.6%
abz9	JGGA	-0.4%	-24.4%
	NSGA II	0.0%	-37.1%
la21	JGGA	0.0%	-0.2%
	NSGA II	0.0%	-1.4%
la24	JGGA	0.0%	-0.9%
	NSGA II	0.0%	-0.1%
la25	JGGA	0.0%	1.8%
	NSGA II	0.0%	-11.1%
la27	JGGA	0.1%	1.3%
	NSGA II	0.1%	-2.7%
la29	JGGA	-3.1%	1.1%
	NSGA II	-3.4%	-1.4%
la38	JGGA	-0.1%	0.4%
	NSGA II	0.0%	0.1%
la40	JGGA	-0.2%	3.4%
	NSGA II	-0.5%	6.5%

Figure 3. Comparison of final Pareto-front for instance la21

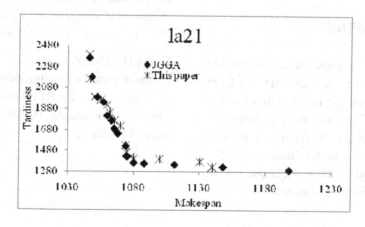

Figure 4. Comparison of final Pareto-front for instance la38

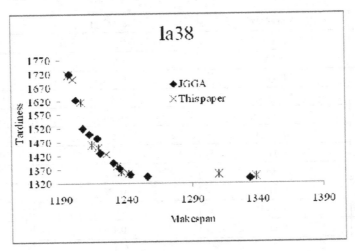

single-objective jobshop problem with total tardiness minimization and the bi-objective jobshop problem with makespan and total tardiness minimization. Results are very interesting and show that the proposed procedure can obtain very good solutions and even betters solutions compared against those procedures.

In further research, our algorithm may be implemented to solve other complex scheduling problems, such as flowshops or flexible jobshops, or even other combinatorial optimization problems. The hybridization of this algorithm can also be considered, as for example obtaining the initial solution by applying some efficient heuristic algorithm.

ACKNOWLEDGMENT

Authors want to acknowledge the comments and suggestions of the three reviewers and those from the editors that allowed the improvement of the chapter. The work of first and third authors was supported by Research Funds from Universidad de La Sabana, Colombia, under Grants CEA-53-2010 and CEA-24-2008. This work is also part of the HAROSA Knowledge Community.

REFERENCES

Aarts, E. H., Van Laarhoven, P. J. M., Lenstra, J. K., & Ulder, N. J. (1994). A computational study of local search algorithms for job shop scheduling. *ORSA Journal on Computing, 6*(2), 118–125.

Angert, E. R., Clements, K., & Pace, N. (1993). The largest bacterium. *Nature, 362,* 239–241. doi:10.1038/362239a0

Blazewicz, J., Domschke, W., & Pesch, E. (1996). The jobshop scheduling problem: Conventional and new solution techniques. *European Journal of Operational Research, 93*(1), 1–33. doi:10.1016/0377-2217(95)00362-2

Bremermann, H. J. (1974). Chemotaxis and optimization. *Journal of the Franklin Institute, 297,* 397–404. doi:10.1016/0016-0032(74)90041-6

Chen, H., Zhu, Y., & Hu, K. (2010). Multi-colony bacteria foraging optimization with cell-to-cell communication for RFID network planning. *Applied Soft Computing, 10,* 539–547. doi:10.1016/j.asoc.2009.08.023

Cheng, R., Gen, M., & Tsujimura, Y. (1996). A tutorial survey of job-shop scheduling problems using genetic algorithms – I: Representation. *Computers & Industrial Engineering, 30*(4), 983–997. doi:10.1016/0360-8352(96)00047-2

Coelho, L. D. S., & Sierakowski, C. A. (2006). Bacteria colony approaches with variable velocity applied to path optimization of mobile robots. In: *ABCM Symposium Series in Mechatronics, 2,* 297-304.

Coello Coello, C. A., Van Veldhuizen, D. A., & Lamont, G. B. (2002). *Evolutionary algorithms for solving multi-objective problems.* New York, NY: Kluwer Academic Publishers.

Deb, K. (2001). *Multi-objective optimization using evolutionary algorithms.* Chichester, UK: John Wiley & Sons, Inc.

Deb, K., Pratap, A., Agarwal, S., & Meyarivan, T. (2002). A fast and elitist multiobjective genetic algorithm: NSGA II. *IEEE Transactions on Evolutionary Computation, 6*(2), 182–197. doi:10.1109/4235.996017

Donoso, Y., & Fabregat, R. (2007). *Multi-Objective Optimization in Computer Networks Using Metaheuristics.* Boca Raton, FL: Taylor & Francis.

Esquivel, S., Ferrero, S., Gallard, R., Salto, C., Alfonso, H., & Schütz, M. (2002). Enhanced evolutionary algorithm for single and multi-objective optimization in job shop scheduling problem. *Knowledge-Based Systems, 15,* 13–25. doi:10.1016/S0950-7051(01)00117-4

Feo, T. A., & Resende, M. G. C. (1989). A probabilistic heuristic for a computationally difficult set covering problem. *Operations Research Letters, 8,* 67–71. doi:10.1016/0167-6377(89)90002-3

Feo, T. A., & Resende, M. G. C. (1995). Greedy randomized adaptive search procedures. *Journal of Global Optimization, 6,* 109–133. doi:10.1007/BF01096763

Garey, M., Johnson, D., & Sethi, R. (1976). The complexity of flow shop and job shop scheduling. *Mathematics of Operations Research, 1,* 117–129. doi:10.1287/moor.1.2.117

Giffler, B., & Thompson, G. L. (1960). Algorithm for solving production scheduling problems. *Operations Research, 8,* 487–503. doi:10.1287/opre.8.4.487

Guzmán, M. A., Delgado, A., & De Carvalho, J. (2010). A novel multiobjective optimization algorithm based on bacterial chemotaxis. *Engineering Applications of Artificial Intelligence, 23*(3), 292–301. doi:10.1016/j.engappai.2009.09.010

Hart, E., Ross, P., & Corne, D. (2005). Evolutionary scheduling: A review. *Genetic Programming and Evolvable Machines, 6,* 191–220. doi:10.1007/s10710-005-7580-7

Huang, W., Zhang, J. H., & Zhang, C. (2007). Reactive power optimization in power system based on bacterial colony chemotaxis algorithm. [in Chinese]. *Automation of Electric Power Systems, 31*(7), 29–33.

Jain, A. S., & Meeran, S. (1998). *A state-of-the-art review of job-shop scheduling techniques. Technical Report, Department of Applied Physics, Electronic and Mechanical Engineering.* Scotland: University of Dundee.

Jourdan, L., Basseur, M., & Talbi, E. G. (2009). Hybridizing exact methods and metaheuristics: a taxonomy. *European Journal of Operational Research, 199,* 620–629. doi:10.1016/j.ejor.2007.07.035

Kacem, I., Hammadi, S., & Borne, P. (2002). Approach by localization and multi-objective evolutionary optimization for flexible job shop scheduling problems. *IEEE Transactions on Systems. Man and Cybernetics Part C, 32*(1), 1–13. doi:10.1109/TSMCC.2002.1009117

Kuo, W., Chen, L., Sun, F., & Yan, L. (2011). Application of bacterial colony chemotaxis optimization algorithm and RBF neural network in thermal NDT/E for the identification of defect parameters. *Applied Mathematical Modelling, 35*, 1483–1491. doi:10.1016/j.apm.2010.09.024

Lei, D. (2008). A Pareto archive particle swarm optimization for multi-objective job shop scheduling. *Computers & Industrial Engineering, 54*, 960–971. doi:10.1016/j.cie.2007.11.007

Lei, D., & Wu, Z. (2006). Crowding-measure-based multiobjective evolutionary algorithm for job shop scheduling. *International Journal of Advanced Manufacturing Technology, 30*(1-2), 112–117. doi:10.1007/s00170-005-0029-6

Li, W. W., Wang, H., & Zou, Z. J. (2005). Function optimization method based on bacterial colony chemotaxis. [in Chinese]. *Chinese Journal of Circuits Systems, 10*(1), 58–63.

Liang, Y. C., Ge, H. W., Zho, Y., & Guo, X. C. (2005). A particle swarm optimization-based algorithm for job-shop scheduling problems. *International Journal of Computational Methods, 2*(3), 419–430. doi:10.1142/S0219876205000569

Montoya-Torres, J. R. (2010). *Scheduling Models and Methods*. Bogota, Colombia: Mac Graw Hill-Lulu. (in Spanish)

Montoya-Torres, J. R., Gómez-Vizcaíno, L. S., Solano-Charris, E. L., & Paternina-Arboleda, C. D. (2010). (Accepted). Global Bacteria Optimization Meta-heuristic Algorithm for Jobshop Scheduling. *International Journal of Operations Research and Information Systems*, (January): 2010.

Müller, S., Airaghi, S., & Marchetto, J. (2000). Optimization algorithms based on a model of bacterial chemotaxis, In: *Proceedings of 6th International Conference on Simulation of Adaptive Behavior: From Animals to Animats*, pp. 375–384.

Müller, S., Airaghi, S., & Marchetto, J. (2002). Optimization based on bacterial chemotaxis. *IEEE Transactions on Evolutionary Computation, 6*(1), 16–29. doi:10.1109/4235.985689

Nowicki, E., & Smutnicki, C. (1996). A fast tabu search algorithm for the job-shop scheduling problem. *Management Science, 42*, 797–813. doi:10.1287/mnsc.42.6.797

Passino, K. M. (2002). Biomimicry of bacterial foraging for distributed optimization and control. *IEEE Control Systems Magazine, 6*, 52–67. doi:10.1109/MCS.2002.1004010

Pinedo, M. (2008). *Scheduling: Theory, Algorithms, and Systems*. New York, NY: Springer.

Ponnamambalam, S. G., Ramkumar, V., & Jawahar, N. (2001). A multiobjective evolutionary algorithm for job shop scheduling. *Production Planning and Control, 12*(8), 764–774. doi:10.1080/09537280110040424

Ramesh, R., & Cary, J. M. (1989). Multicriteria jobshop scheduling. *Computers & Industrial Engineering, 17*(1-4), 597–602. doi:10.1016/0360-8352(89)90132-0

Rappe, R. S. (2002). Cultivation of the ubiquitous SAR11 marine bacterioplankton clade. *Nature, 418*, 630–633. doi:10.1038/nature00917

Ripon, K. S. N. (2007). Hybrid evolutionary approach for multi-objective job-shop scheduling problem. *Malaysan Journal of Computer Science, 20*(2), 183–198.

Ripon, K. S. N., Tsang, C. H., & Kwong, S. (2006). Multi-objective evolutionary job-shop scheduling using jumping genes genetic algorithm. *Proceedings of the 2006 International Conference on Neural Network*. July 16-21. pp. 3100-3107

Sakawa, M., & Kubota, R. (2000). Fuzzy programming for multi-objective job shop scheduling with fuzzy processing time and fuzzy due date through genetic algorithm. *European Journal of Operational Research, 120,* 393–407. doi:10.1016/S0377-2217(99)00094-6

Sha, D. Y., & Lin, H. H. (2010). A multi-objective PSO for job-shop scheduling problems. *Expert Systems with Applications, 37,* 1065–1070. doi:10.1016/j.eswa.2009.06.041

Sierakowski, C. A., & dos Santos Coelho, L. (2006). Path planning optimization for mobile robots based on bacteria colony approach. In Abraham, A., Baets, B., Köppen, M., & Nickolay, B. (Eds.), *Applied Soft Computing Technologies: The Challenge of Complexity* (pp. 187–198). Berlin, Heidelberg: Springer-Verlag. doi:10.1007/3-540-31662-0_15

Suresh, R. K., & Mohanasndaram, K. M. (2006). Pareto archived simulated annealing for job shop scheduling with multiple objectives. *International Journal of Advanced Manufacturing Technology, 29,* 184–196. doi:10.1007/s00170-004-2492-x

Talbi, E. G. (2009). *Metaheuristics: from design to implementation.* Hoboken, NJ: John Wiley & Sons, Inc.

Wang, L., & Zheng, D.-Z. (2001). An effective hybrid optimization strategy for job shop scheduling problems. *Computers & Operations Research, 28,* 585–596. doi:10.1016/S0305-0548(99)00137-9

Werner, J. C., Aydin, M. E., & Fogarty, T. C. (2000). Evolving genetic algorithm for job shop scheduling problem. *Proceedings of the Fourth International Conference on Adaptive Computing in Design and Manufacture (ACDM'2000).* I.C. Parmee (ed.). Springer. Available on-line at: www.geocities.com/ jamwer2002/rep1.pdf

Xia, W., & Wu, Z. (2005). An effective hybridization approach for multi-objective flexible job-shop scheduling. *Computers & Industrial Engineering, 48*(2), 409–425. doi:10.1016/j.cie.2005.01.018

Yamada, T. (2003). *Studies on meta-heuristics for jobshop and flowshop scheduling problems.* PhD Thesis, Kyoto University, Japan.

Young, K. (2006). The selective value of bacterial shape. *Microbiology and Molecular Biology Reviews, 70,* 660–703. doi:10.1128/MMBR.00001-06

Zhao, Z. G., Miao, K., & Lv, H. X. (2007). Hybrid structure optimization algorithm of radial basis function neural network. *Chinese Journal of Scientific Instrument, 28*(4), 650–656.

ADDITIONAL READING

Askin, R. G., & Goldberg, J. B. (2002). *Design and Management of Lean Production Systems.* New York, NY: John Wiley & Sons, Inc.

Bagchi, T. (1999). *Multiobjective Scheduling by Genetic Algorithms.* Dordrecht, The Netherlands: Kluwer Academic Publisher. doi:10.1007/978-1-4615-5237-6

Chinyao Low, C., Yip, Y., & Wu, T. H. (2006). Modelling and heuristics of FMS scheduling with multiple objectives. *Computers & Operations Research, 33*(3), 674–694. doi:10.1016/j.cor.2004.07.013

Jaszkiewicz, A. (2002). Genetic local search for multi-objective combinatorial optimization. *European Journal of Operational Research, 137*(1), 50–71. doi:10.1016/S0377-2217(01)00104-7

Montoya-Torres, J. R. (2010). *Scheduling Models and Methods.* Bogota, Colombia: Mac Graw Hill-Lulu. (in Spanish)

Nagara, A., Haddocka, J., & Heragu, S. (1995). Multiple and bicriteria scheduling: A literature survey. *European Journal of Operational Research*, *81*(1), 88–104. doi:10.1016/0377-2217(93)E0140-S

Pinedo, M. (2008). *Scheduling: Theory, Algorithms, and Systems*. New York, NY: Springer.

T'Kindt. V., Billaut, J.C., & Scott, H. (2002). *Multicriteria Scheduling: Theory, Models and Algorithms*. Berlin Heidelberg: Springer-Verlag.

Talbi, E. G. (2009). *Metaheuristics: from design to implementation*. Hoboken, NJ: John Wiley & Sons, Inc.

KEY TERMS AND DEFINITIONS

Approximate Algorithm: Solution procedure that runs in polynomial time used to find approximate solutions for hard optimization problems without guaranteeing the optimum value of the objective function.

Job Shop: Shop configuration in which jobs has to visits a set of machines with a predefined processing route that may not be the same as the one of other jobs.

Meta-Heuristic: A kind of approximate algorithm that iteratively tries to improve a candidate solution with regard to a given measure of quality, by making few or no assumptions about the problem being optimized and can search very large spaces of candidate solutions.

Scheduling: Decision-making process consisting on the allocation of a set of jobs to a set of machines in order to optimize one or several objective functions.

Chapter 10
Hybrid Algorithms for Manufacturing Rescheduling:
Customised vs. Commodity Production

Luisa Huaccho Huatuco
University of Leeds, UK

Ani Calinescu
University of Oxford, UK

ABSTRACT

This chapter investigates manufacturing rescheduling of customised production and compares the results with those found for commodity production in earlier research by the authors. The hybrid rescheduling algorithms presented in this chapter were obtained by combining two key rescheduling-related elements found in the literature (a) rescheduling criteria (i.e., job priority, machine utilisation and right-shift delay) with (b) level of disruption transmitted to the shop-floor due to rescheduling (i.e., High disruption and Low disruption). The main advantage of hybrid rescheduling algorithms over individual rescheduling algorithms consists of their ability to combine the main features of two different algorithms, in order to achieve enhanced performance, depending on the objective of the organisation. The five hybrid rescheduling algorithms taken into account in this chapter are: Priority High, Priority Low, Utilisation High, Utilisation Low and Right-Shift. The authors' case study research in three manufacturing companies has identified the use of a set of these hybrid algorithms in practice. Each of the case studies is evaluated in terms of time-based performance in three main areas: suppliers' interface, internal production and customers' interface. This evaluation is carried out for both customised and commodity production, using the same hybrid rescheduling algorithms and performance measure the authors used in their previous research work, for comparability purposes (i.e. the entropic-related complexity). The findings show that customised production exhibits a lower entropic-related complexity than commodity production. Although this behaviour may seem unexpected, the entropic-related complexity analysis allows for an

DOI: 10.4018/978-1-61350-086-6.ch010

interpretation / understanding of its underlying reasons. For example, companies making customised products first agreed the specifications of the products with the customer, and then they mutually agreed on a contract which would financially protect manufacturers (should last minute customer changes occur), by specifying analytically determined penalties or premium charges. Furthermore, a set of recommendations were made to the companies involved in this research study based on the analysis presented in this chapter, such as the need for manufacturing organisations of customised products to ensure they have dependable suppliers, and that, internally, they plan for and embed sufficient spare capacity to cope with internal or external disturbances.

INTRODUCTION

This chapter aims to assess the relationship between hybrid rescheduling algorithms, entropic-related complexity, and customised production, by using real-world manufacturing case studies. The paper thus makes a theoretical and applied contribution on these inter-related topics, which (to our knowledge) have not been previously studied in conjunction before.

The main research question explored in this chapter is: *In the context of customised production, how do hybrid rescheduling algorithms impact entropic-related complexity?* The following objectives guide this chapter: (a) To identify the typical hybrid rescheduling algorithms used in the context of customised production, and (b) To explain why and how hybrid rescheduling algorithms vary across organisations.

Given the current climate of increased global competition, manufacturing companies need to focus on customised production. It is important to consider the ever-increasing need for value-adding product design and manufacturing processes (Browning *et al.*, 2002). Tu *et al.* (2001) argue that firms need to move from the internal efficiency maximisation mindset towards the emphasis on customer value. In the same vein, Professor El-Maraghy (ElMaraghy, 2009) states that one of the key challenges that manufacturing organisations face nowadays is "to satisfy the market need for products variations and customization, utilizing new technologies, while reducing the resulting

variations in their manufacturing and associated cost" (p. v).

In order to satisfy the customization need of the market at a competitive price, it is necessary to understand that the above goals are neither straightforward nor easily achievable. Furthermore, the additional complexity that arises in trying to pursue them should be carefully managed. As Griffiths and Margetts (2000) point out: "customers want high quality products and services, at a reasonable cost, and they want them 'now'" (p. 155). Managing the complexity resulting from such a dynamic environment plays a key role in keeping costs under control. If organisations do not manage complexity through rescheduling or other complexity management approaches, they could face some of the following consequences (Huaccho Huatuco, 2003): customer dissatisfaction, which can then lead to losing customer demand and, related to this, less flexibility and product variety.

The type of rescheduling problem tackled in this chapter could be classified as a "stochastic scheduling problem" (Pinedo, 2008) where the disturbances were arbitrarily assigned, but the spare capacity of the original production schedule (processing times, number of jobs and number of loaded machines) varied according to a random probability distribution. These experiments were designed, run and tested in our previous work (Huaccho Hautuco *et al.*, 2009), so their detailed discussion is outside the scope of this chapter. The aim in this chapter is to provide manufacturing organisations that make customised products with recommendations on which hybrid rescheduling algorithms are more likely to be of effective use to them.

The hybrid rescheduling algorithms presented in this chapter combine priority dispatch rules with the disruption effects on the shop floor, namely: *Priority High*, *Priority Low*, *Utilisation High*, *Utilisation Low* and *Right-Shift*. These algorithms were previously studied by the authors (Huaccho Huatuco *et al.*, 2009) for commodity production. The novelty and thus contribution of this chapter consists of the extension of these hybrid algorithms to the context of customised production.

The remainder of this chapter is organised as follows. A literature review follows next, on three inter-related topics: hybrid rescheduling algorithms, entropic-related complexity and customised production. Then, the measurement methodology section gives details on the case-based research carried out. Next, the data analysis section is briefly presented. After that, the section on case studies for customised production covers the following results: entropic-related complexity, hybrid rescheduling algorithms, customised versus commodity production, and recommendations to case study companies. Next, the discussion of results section focuses on implications to Scheduling practice as well as Value-adding (VA) versus non-value adding complexity (NVA). Finally, some conclusions including some implications for theory and practice, together with some future work directions are provided.

LITERATURE REVIEW

This section discusses the links and dependencies among hybrid rescheduling algorithms, entropic-related complexity and customised production. Major, established and more recent publications in these topics include a diverse range of rescheduling methods (Ouelhadj & Petrovic, 2009; Silva *et al.*, 2008), as well as links with customised production (Da Silveira *et al.*, 2001; Smart, 2009).

Hybrid Rescheduling Algorithms

There has been no shortage of hybrid algorithms reported in the literature for manufacturing systems. For example, Bierwirth & Mattfeld (1999) used Genetic Algorithms (GA) together with a tunable parameter (in terms of the length of machine idle time) to carry out hybrid scheduling, whereas Gao *et al.* (2009) also proposed the use of GA in combination with Ant-colony algorithms to determine the order of manufacturing jobs and machine assignment, respectively. Wang *et al.* (2006, 2010) focused on hybrid algorithms for the blocking flow shop scheduling problem, proposing a combination of genetic algorithms with local search algorithms. In relation to rescheduling, the work by Deblaere *et al.* (2010) combined exact reactive scheduling with Tabu search algorithms. Most of the work presented in previous literature uses simulations as a means to test the performance of rescheduling algorithms. This chapter analyses and discusses hybrid rescheduling algorithms using real-world manufacturing case studies, rather than computer simulations.

The hybrid rescheduling algorithms presented in this chapter were obtained by combining two key rescheduling-related elements found in the literature (a) rescheduling criteria (i.e., job priority) (Yamamoto & Nof, 1985; Jain and ElMaraghy, 1997, Smith 2002), machine utilisation (Jain & ElMaraghy, 1997) and right-shift delay (Yamamoto & Nof, 1985; Cheng, 1998; Holthaus, 1999) with (b) level of disruption transmitted to the shop-floor due to rescheduling (i.e., High disruption) (Yamamoto & Nof, 1985) and Low disruption (Smith, 2002). It is worth mentioning that Priority is normally assigned by order / job due date, but it could be also assigned by customer importance, by order value, or by a factor determined at the discretion of the scheduler.

The main advantage of using hybrid rescheduling algorithms is that they provide a better approach to rescheduling than if separate individual rescheduling algorithms were used, such as their ability to combine the best features of two different algorithms in order to achieve an enhanced performance, depending on the objective of the organisation. For example, while some organisations may strive on getting robust schedules (schedules that would remain valid for a long period of time), other organisations could be interested in getting near-optimal schedules which could be generated in a relatively shorter time. As mentioned before, the five hybrid rescheduling algorithms that have been used in our previous research are: *Priority High, Priority Low, Utilisation High, Utilisation Low* and *Right-Shift* (Huaccho Huatuco *et al.*, 2009).

Algorithms Description

Each of these hybrid rescheduling algorithms is briefly described next.

- *Priority High*: This algorithm takes into account the Priority of the jobs (e.g. each job's due date). Additionally, in the case of a disturbance affecting production (e.g., customer changes), the *Priority High* algorithm generates a new schedule (rescheduling) immediately. This causes high disruption to the shop floor (i.e., no threshold condition is used to filter down the disruption transmitted to the production shop floor).
- *Priority Low*: This algorithm includes a threshold condition (added to the *Priority High* algorithm) in order to filter down the disruption to the shop floor (Low disruption). In our previous research on the impact of machine breakdowns on rescheduling, the threshold condition was based on the *downtime* being greater than the *remaining* time of the disrupted job (Huaccho Huatuco, 2009). Once the threshold condition is fulfilled or surpassed (Pfeiffer *et al.*, 2007), rescheduling takes place.
- *Utilisation High*: The algorithm takes into account machine utilisation. In the case of

a disturbance, it chooses the least utilized machine immediately (High disruption) to allocate the affected job.
- *Utilisation Low*: The algorithm includes a threshold condition (added to the *Utilisation High* algorithm), as explained for the *Priority Low* algorithm.
- *Right-Shift*: The algorithm delays the disrupted job until the disturbance has ended, right-shifting (delaying) all the remaining jobs accordingly.

The pseudocode for these hybrid rescheduling algorithms is provided next, where:

- **Active:** The processing time of the job before the occurrence of the disturbance.
- **Affected Jobs Downtime:** The procedure that checks that the arrival times of the jobs affected by the disturbance is right-shifted.
- **Alternatives:** The procedure that looks for alternative machines for the jobs affected by disturbances.
- **Knock-On Effect:** The procedure that right-shifts the jobs both on the affected machine and on the alternative machine, due to the occurrence of a disturbance.
- **Remaining:** The remaining processing time of the job that needs to complete after the occurrence of a disturbance.
- **Disturbances:** The procedure that writes the disturbance effect on the production schedule, in the form of unavailability of the affected machine.
- **Right-Shift:** The procedure that delays the jobs affected by disturbances.

The pseudocode for the main part of the High disruption algorithms (*Priority High* and *Utilisation High*) is given next.

The pseudocode for the Low disruption algorithms (*Priority Low* and *Utilisation Low*) is given next. Note that only Step 7 changes in relation to the High disruption pseudocode.

Algorithm 1.

1.   Process schedule, part data and disturbance data
2.   *Assign Excel data to VBA variables* (This is how Arena 5.0 handles the introduction of the analysts' own logic into the simulation package)
3.   For all jobs (i=1 to n, where n is the number of scheduled jobs)
If Job_i is affected by a disturbance, then
Rewrite arrival time of Job_i
Call 'Knock-on effect' procedure
4.   If disturbance affects a machine that is busy, then
Generate Schedule [Perform Rescheduling]
Go to (6)
5.   *Process* (run jobs) *according to Process Schedule, then go to (10)*
6.   If $active_i>0$, then
7.   If $remaining_i>0$, then
Rewrite Process Time of Part Data
Update schedule
Call 'Alternatives' procedure
Call 'Disturbances' procedure
8.   Else [$remaining_i >0$]
Process according to Process Schedule
Call 'Affected jobs downtime'
Call 'Disturbances'
Call 'Knock-on effect'
9.   Else [$active_i >0$] Call 'Alternatives' procedure
10.   End

Algorithm 2.

7.   If $remaining_i>0$, then
Rewrite Process Time of Part Data
Update schedule
If $Downtime_i>Remaining_i$, then
Call 'Alternatives' procedure
Call 'Disturbances' procedure
Else [$Downtime_i>Remaining_i$]
Call 'Right-shift' procedure
Call 'Disturbances' procedure

Algorithm 3.

7.   If $remaining_i>0$, then
Rewrite Process Time of Part Data
Update schedule
Call 'Right-shift' procedure
Call 'Disturbances' procedure
8.   Else [$remaining_i >0$]
Process according to Process Schedule
Call 'Affected jobs downtime'
Call 'Disturbances'
Call 'Knock-on effect'
9.   End

The pseudocode for the *Right-shift* algorithm is given next. Note that Steps 7, 8 and 9 change in relation to the High disruption pseudo code.

Although disturbances can affect both customised and commodity production, the analysis of the performance needs to focus on the type of disturbance that is more relevant to the problem under study. Thus, the analysis in this chapter focuses on customer changes, which are more relevant to customised production than machine breakdowns (as studied previously). Customer satisfaction is one of the main targets of manufacturing organisations, which can be achieved by accommodating customer changes requests in their production schedule. As stated by Efstathiou (1996), schedules should retain flexibility (which could be achieved by allowing spare capacity in the production schedule, for example) in order to allow manufacturing companies attending to those requests, while at the same time companies should be able to estimate the inconvenience and the possible disruption to other orders. Customer changes include: changes in order specifications (e.g. quantity ordered [more or less], delivery times [earlier or later], cancellations, inserting new—ordinary or rush—orders) or in terms of customisation changes, modifying the product specifications. However, satisfying the customer has to be carefully balanced with production schedule stability. For example, in the case of rush orders (also called Fast Turn Around or FTA orders), Krajewski *et al.* (2005) suggested that suppliers can use their contracts to their advantage (e.g. charging a premium for them).

The decision element of the rescheduling model will be whether to satisfy a customer that requires a rescheduling action or not and, if so, to what extent (this is determined by the disruption threshold conditions). The threshold conditions are taken into consideration by the level of disruption to the shop floor (High or Low disruption) that the scheduler would prefer / allow to accommodate. As Monostori *et al.* (2007) expressed, finding the appropriate threshold, which ideally should

be an informed and quantitative-based decision, may imply that there is a compromise between schedule stability and schedule quality. In another paper, Pfeifer *et al.* (2007) tested different levels of thresholds before rescheduling took place by evaluating the performance in terms of schedule efficiency and schedule stability. It is worth mentioning that the level of threshold can be determined either statically or dynamically (at run time). Examples of criteria which could be used for deciding which type of threshold to use include: the type of manufacturing environment, performance objectives, information availability and information processing costs.

With reference to customer changes, the following disturbances were derived from Jain & ElMaraghy (1997): (a) Increasing the priority of existing orders (as noted earlier, also known as rush orders or Fast turn around or FTA), (b) Decreasing the priority of existing orders, (c) Introducing new orders, which could be either rush orders or standard duration orders, and (d) Cancelling already placed orders. Each of these is explained in turn below. Assuming that a customer's order corresponds to a single machine job, then:

A. ***Increasing the priority of existing orders (rush orders or Fast Turn around or FTA)***: This disturbance involves finding the job corresponding to the order for which the priority is increased. If the job has not been loaded to any machine, and if the machine required to process it is free, then assign the job to start immediately on it. Otherwise, pre-empt the machine and start the job immediately, all the other jobs on that machine are right-shifted accordingly.

B. ***Decreasing the priority of existing orders:*** This disturbance involves finding the job corresponding to the order for which the priority is decreased. If the job has not been loaded to any machine, and if the machine required to process it is free, then recalculate the priority of the jobs and assign a lower priority to the job, depending on the revised due date. Otherwise, pre-empt the machine and start the next higher priority job on it, the remaining part of the job gets right-shifted accordingly.

C. ***Introducing new orders, which could be either rush orders or standard duration orders:*** If it is a rush order the highest priority is assigned to its corresponding job, then the new job is treated as in part (a) above. If it is a standard duration order, then priority is assigned accordingly, and the job is inserted into the current schedule.

D. ***Cancelling already placed orders***: This disturbance involves finding the job corresponding to the cancelled order. If the job has not been loaded to any machine and if the machine required to process it is free, then do not load it. Otherwise, pre-empt the machine and cancel the remaining completion time of the job from it. Advance any jobs that were due to be processed later on that machine to finish earlier too.

Entropic-Related Complexity

Entropic-related complexity is a measure derived from entropy (Shannon, 1949). This measure was adapted and applied to manufacturing systems in the "Complexity in the Supply Chain" project by Efstathiou & Frizelle (EPSRC Grant No. GR/M57842). This project was run jointly by the University of Oxford and the University of Cambridge, in collaboration with industrial partners including: Unilever, BAE Systems and ALPLA. Complexity, within this context, is defined as the uncertainty and the variety within a system. Hence the two main characteristics of complexity which we consider in this chapter are uncertainty and variety. Variety refers to the many parts of the manufacturing system that need to be managed, whereas uncertainty refers to the unpredictability of the behaviour of each of those parts (probability of occurrence).

Entropic-related complexity is quantified into indices that highlight high complexity areas and help focus management attention to examine their causes. The higher the index the greater the complexity displayed by the system. This can be measured in different areas or levels, for example in this chapter we focus on three areas: at the suppliers' interface, internal production, and at the customers' interface. The complexity index is evaluated based on Equation 1, which gives the fundamental form for describing entropy. Here, the entropy (H) is defined as the uncertainty and variety of the system associated with a set of n events (states), where p_i is the probability of the ith event occurring. The complexity index units are given in bits per state (bps).

$$H = -\sum_{i=1}^{n} p_i \log_2(p_i) \qquad (1)$$

For example, a machine can be in one of three states: "idle," "making product" or "broken down." Each state occurs with certain frequency in a given period of time, which can then be used to obtain its probability of occurrence. Assuming the machine is "idle" for 10% of the time, "making product" for 85% of the time and "broken down" for the remaining 5% of the time, then the Complexity index is calculated as follows:

$$H = -0.1 \times \log_2 0.1 - 0.85 \times \log_2 0.85 - 0.05 \times \log_2 0.05$$

$$H = 0.75 bps$$

Several practical considerations need to be taken into account when taking the entropic-related complexity measurements. First, a series of observations are made of the production processes relevant to the research study. These observations include both qualitative and quantitative behaviour, in the form of managing information flows, applying formal and informal methods, such as generating production schedules, taking

/ making customer phone calls, or carrying out procedures in case of unexpected events. Counting the variations and weighting each by the likelihood of occurrence gives rise to the probability of each state. The overall complexity index is calculated using Equation 1, and represents the entropic-related complexity of the system or subsystems investigated.

The level of unexpected variation (which corresponds to the uncertainty) within a system, indicates the level of "out of control." A system that behaves totally predictably can be assumed to be completely "in control." As the uncertainty and thus unpredictability of the system increases, the level of control decreases. A greater understanding of the behaviour and level of controllability of a system can be achieved through measuring the deviations from what was expected to happen. The aim of the measurements is to record these variations, and to identify their causes. This method of measuring the variations can be applied to information, to material flows, and/or to monetary values. The variations can be analysed by employing a time-, quantity- or reason-based analysis, or a combination of these.

Entropic-related complexity methods can be used for analysing and understanding how manufacturing organisations behave within their supply chain. The main idea is that the delivery performance of suppliers impacts upon the manufacturing organisation, which in turn could affect its delivery performance towards its customers. In this connection, it is hypothesised that rescheduling plays a key role in managing complexity.

Customised Production

As stated by Duray *et al.* (2000), without some degree of customer involvement in the design process, a product cannot be called customised. At the customised end of the spectrum the following customisation levels are considered: Build-to-order and Make-to-order manufacturers (Gunasekaran & Ngai, 2005). They considered

that responsiveness and flexibility were both the key objectives and enablers in the customised production environment.

Four quadrants were presented in Huaccho Huatuco (2003), which resulted from the combination of the X-axes: "functional product" and "innovative product" and the Y-axes: "efficient scheduling objective" and "responsive scheduling objective." The two quadrants of interest to the work presented in this chapter are: "functional product, responsive scheduling" and "innovative product, responsive scheduling." The former refers to commodity production, whereas the latter refers to customised production. In terms of managing complexity, companies belonging to either of these two quadrants were identified to manage complexity using "rescheduling." However, in the search for an alternative way of managing complexity, the emphasis shifts from using "decision-making," for commodity production, towards the use of "spare capacity" in customised production. So, ideally, the production schedules in customised production should embed higher spare capacity levels than the production schedules in commodity production. "Responsive scheduling" is related to the Just-in-Time (JIT) Operations Management philosophy by its aim to satisfy the customer by delivering the right product, in the right quantity and at the right time.

Duray *et al.* (2000) built upon Mintzberg's work (1988), and stated that customization can be pure (from the conception stage), tailored (at the fabrication stage) or standardised (at the assembly stage).

Summary of the Literature Review

This section has covered the three inter-related topics of interest for this chapter: hybrid rescheduling algorithms, entropic-related complexity and customised production. Hybrid rescheduling algorithms have been extensively used in the manufacturing context, since they are robust in providing solutions that could take the best features of each algorithm. The rescheduling algorithms considered in this chapter are: *Priority High, Priority Low, Utilisation High, Utilisation Low* and *Right-shift*. Entropic-related complexity has been presented as a holistic, comparable and useful measure to managers. They can use it to prioritise and direct their efforts in an informed and objective manner. Customised production was discussed in the light of the level of customisation, and the need to enable organisations to achieve flexibility and responsiveness. This can be done through a combination of "rescheduling" and "spare capacity" approaches to managing complexity.

MEASUREMENT METHODOLOGY

The measurement methodology used in this research was case-based research, with individual-companies case study analyses followed by a cross-case analysis. The case study protocol was followed (Voss *et al.*, 2002) with particular application of the stages proposed in Sivadasan *et al.* (2002), which are diagrammatically represented in Figure 1.

Company A, Company B and Company C participated in the "Rescheduling and complexity for customised products" project. The information flow complexity within these companies was evaluated by measuring the entropic-related complexity (i.e., the uncertainty and variety of the information transfers between suppliers and customers), for example. Data was triangulated using: (a) semi-structured interviews, (b) observations of the shop floor and (c) documents in electronic or hard copy form.

Familiarisation

Prior to conducting the actual complexity measurements, between two and three days were spent within each company for collecting preliminary information with people, information flows and processes. This involved an interactive process of semi-structured interviews with key personnel, to understand the operations and to map out the key material and information flows. In terms of plant familiarisation a tour of the plant sites was given by the companies, which provided a better understanding of the manufacturing processes such as process layout, and additional information

Figure 1. The case study methodology

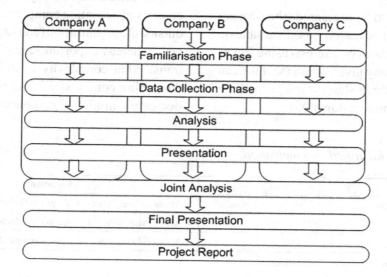

Figure 2. Information flows investigated

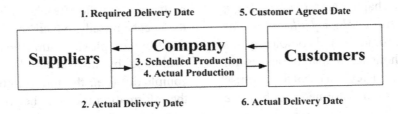

about types of resources and their capabilities, at each organisation.

Key Information Flows and Variations

The diagrammatic representation of the information flows studied is given in Figure 2, where the arrows represent the information flows.

The variations identified and investigated in this research are given in Table 1.

The Parameters Considered Prior to Data Collection

To ensure the effectiveness and accuracy of data collection, and the applicability of the complexity measurement method, the following parameters were determined prior to taking measurements:

- The variables to be measured (time-based, quantity-based or reason-based variables).
- The possible states of interest (using Equation 1) (e.g. at any given time a machine can be in one of three states: "idle," "making product" or "broken down").

- Frequency and duration of observations (e.g. once every hour, shift or day, for two weeks).
- Key information flows and variations (e.g. despatch notes and delivery requirements for the last three months).

The Variables to be Measured

For example, in the case of deliveries at the supplier interface, goods may not arrive on time and / or in full (OTIF) (i.e., time and quantity variations). The variables we chose were: time-based deliveries—for the suppliers' and customers' interfaces, and time-based production—for the internal production.

Additionally, the reasons for time and quantity variations were identified and recorded, in order to detect the instances of importing, exporting and absorbing complexity. Briefly, importing complexity consists of accepting complexity from elsewhere outside the organisation (e.g. suppliers or customers), whereas exporting complexity consists of transferring complexity to those organisations. Absorbing complexity is the way organisations decrease / minimise complexity internally. For

Table 1. Variations identified and measured

Area	Variation*
Suppliers' interface: Procurement	2. Actual Delivery Date – 1. Required Delivery Date
Company: Internal Production	4. Actual Production – 3. Scheduled Production
Customers' interface: Delivery	6. Actual delivery Date – 5. Customer agreed date

*Note: the symbol "–" refers to arithmetic difference.

a full discussion on complexity transfers please refer to Sivadasan *et al.* (2004). Also, the reasons for variations are useful in order to facilitate the understanding, interpretation and meaningfulness of the entropic-related complexity.

The Possible States of Interest

The results of this study focused on time-based analysis (i.e. the variations stated in Table 1). States were defined so as to accurately capture the investigated processes. They were kept the same across all case studies, whenever possible, for comparability purposes. The following states of interest were taken into account at the suppliers' and customers' interface:

- on time or early.
- < 1 week late.
- 1-2 weeks late.
- 2-4 weeks late.
- 4-8 weeks late.
- > 8 weeks late.

Frequency and Duration of Observations

The frequency of the information and material transfer was used as a guideline for the frequency of measurements. In the case of event-based activities (such as deliveries) the analyses utilise all the available data for each case study, which can be either live or historical. In terms of live data, two weeks were used for carrying out the data collection on site. In terms of historical data, it was determined that at least three months of weekly data would provide sufficient data points for the analysis.

Data Collection

Data collection consists of sampling information and material flows over time. In this study, information variations were investigated and recorded in terms of actual versus expected performance over the data collection period. Thus sufficient data (typically a minimum of 30 data points) should be gathered to ensure each state have been observed to give an estimate of its probability. As mentioned earlier, data consists of: (a) semi-structured interviews, (b) observations of the shop floor and (c) documents in electronic or hard copy form.

Data Analysis

The data analysis involved the calculation of the complexity indices, for the variations mentioned earlier, and the interpretation of the results thus obtained.

The computation of the complexity indices comprises five steps:

1. Calculate the arithmetic difference between the actual information flows and the scheduled information flows (e.g. if a delivery was expected on the 5th August, but it arrived on the 4th August, then the arithmetic difference would be: 4-5=-1 [a day early]).
2. Classify the difference calculated at step 1 using the pre-defined states (e.g. if a state is defined as "a day early") then, for illustration purposes, suppose 40 deliveries belong to that state.
3. Estimate the probability associated with each state. For the example above, if the total deliveries were 400, therefore 40 deliveries represent 10%, so the probability of "a day early" deliveries is 0.10.
4. With the estimated probabilities at step 3, use Equation 1 to calculate the entropy (e.g. continuing with the calculation from previous step: $-0.1 \log_2 0.1 = 0.33$ bps).
5. Add up all the entropy values to calculate the entropic-related complexity (e.g. $0.33 + \ldots = 2.58$ bps).

The subsequent analysis of the indices involves three more steps:

Table 2. Summary of the case study companies

Company (size)	Product	Main disturbance(s)	Relative level of customisation according to Duray *et al.* (2000)
A (Large, part of a multinational corporation)	Pumps for oil, water or waste	Suppliers do not always deliver on time. Bottlenecks exist in the production shopfloor (as a consequence, queues develop)	Each pump is a project on its own, depending on where the pump is to be installed. The customer determines the specification of the pump. Customisation is tailored (at the fabrication stage).
B (Large, part of a multinational corporation)	Paper chemicals manufacturer	Customers change their orders at the last minute, and innovative products are likely to fail in the shop floor. For example, new chemical products for paper to achieve particular properties, such as: allowing the quick drying of the ink printed on them.	Innovative paper chemicals with improved properties. Customer needs are gathered by the company's own dedicated customer service staff who work closely with customers. Customisation is pure (at the conception stage).
C (SME)	Industrial doors	None apparent	Each door is a project on its own, depending on where the door is to be installed. There is a limited range of door types on offer (four types), but the overall specifications such as size and location characteristics are unique for each door. Customisation is standardised (at the assembly stage).

1. Compare relevant complexity indices calculated for the different areas being analysed, to identify high complexity areas. The rule of thumb used here was: < 1 bps: low; 1 to 2 bps: medium; > 2 bps: high. This rule of thumb results from considering that the maximum entropic complexity for a six-state system is 2.58 bps or bits per state ($=\log_2 6$), and a rough estimation of the low, medium and high values, respectively. It is worth mentioning that the specific state definitions have a direct impact on the results. However, the recommendations derived from the calculations in this chapter are robust, as they hold when tested with slightly different states, as in the case of Company B (Huaccho Huatuco *et al.*, 2010). For more details on the issue of state definitions for the entropic-related complexity, please refer to Sivadasan *et al.* (2001).

2. Identify specific reasons within each complexity area (e.g. suppliers' interface, internal production and customers' interface), and observe their frequency of recurrence throughout the flows, grouping them if necessary. For example, similar reasons can be aggregated into a state, "low materials quality" and "delays in suppliers' delivery" could be grouped into "suppliers-related reasons."

3. Provide recommendations to the manufacturing organisations about managing their entropic-related complexity. The key findings, such as high complexity areas and prioritisation of the areas that require managerial attention, were presented to each participating manufacturing organisation.

CASE STUDIES FOR CUSTOMISED PRODUCTION

This section is based on the "Rescheduling and Complexity for Customised Products" project involving three UK manufacturing companies in customised production (Huaccho Huatuco, 2006). The case studies are summarised in Table 2.

Both material flows (such as the raw materials and work in progress) and information flows (such as the production schedules) are important when

Table 3. Issues identified

Company	Issues identified
Company A	• Difficult for the researchers to see the big picture (i.e. what is happening in other departments and the organisation as a whole). • Not much historical data recording. • Pressure on the scheduler for the individual projects to meet milestones / deadlines.
Company B	• Frequent rescheduling due to customer rush orders • No charge to customers for rush orders • Flexibility: strength or weakness? There is enough spare capacity to accommodate rush orders. However, the scheduler is finding increasingly difficult to manage the complexity associated with them. • Not enough operators – in the short term this is mostly because in the original schedule not many operators are needed, but in practice with the new rush orders coming in, shortage of labour becomes an issue.
Company C	• No extra charge to customers for rush orders or fast turnaround (FTA) deliveries. • Production earliness could become an issue when storage space is limited.

rescheduling manufacturing systems. Details of the companies rescheduling practices were collected from interviews, direct observations of the shop floor and paper / electronic documents. These case studies are used to abstract the characteristics of the hybrid rescheduling algorithms as used in practice.

The following benefits to the participating companies were anticipated:

• Diagnosis and benchmarking of each company's rescheduling practice.

• Evaluation of the amount of entropic-related complexity they are handling when rescheduling.

• Recommendations as how to manage complexity to their advantage.

These companies are based in the UK and were chosen among different candidate companies due to their different levels of customisation. All three companies agreed to participate in the research project by providing access to their management staff in relation to scheduling and production.

The following good practice elements were gathered from all the case studies:

• People involvement and commitment.
• Frequent communications both formal (printed documents) and informal (phone and face-to-face conversations).

• Expertise coming from experience.
• Quality awareness throughout the process.

Some of the issues identified at each manufacturing organisation are given in Table 3.

Table 4 shows the data collection details in terms of time period. It also shows that between 3 and 17 months historical data were collected.

The remainder of this results section is divided into: entropic-related complexity, hybrid rescheduling algorithms, customised versus commodity production, and recommendations to case study companies. These are discussed in turn next.

Table 4. Data collection details

Company	Area of assessment	Time Period
Company A	Suppliers' interface	10 months
	Internal Production	3 months
	Customers' interface	17 months
Company B	Suppliers' interface	3 months
	Internal Production	9 months
	Customers' interface	3 months
Company C	Suppliers' interface	7 months
	Internal Production	4 months
	Customers' interface	4 months

Entropic-Related Complexity Results

The results were shown to each manufacturing organisation by means of a Power Point presentation. Prior to this meeting, hard-copies of the presentation were distributed to the attendees to allow them to assess the confidentiality and sensitivity of the information. The attendees included key people within the organisation, people who had participated in the case study and people to whom the results would be most relevant. The participants provided feedback on their views and agreed with the results of our analysis. The most important point they made was in regards to being able to "quantify" the amount of complexity they were handling. Also, they acknowledged the fact that internal complexity does not exist in isolation and it is influenced by their suppliers' and customers' interfaces.

The results of the analysis have been classified, according to the type of entropic-related complexity handled due to rescheduling: Suppliers' interface, Internal Production, and Customers' interface. Each of these categories is discussed in turn next.

Suppliers' Interface

The complexity indices associated with the procurement or suppliers' performance are plotted in Figure 3. An example of the entropic-related complexity calculation is presented next. Company C's suppliers' interface was observed to be in one of the following states: "on time or early," "< 1 week late" and "2-4 weeks late." There were: 21, 59 and 20 occurrences of each of these states, respectively. Applying Equation 1, they generate: 0.22, 0.39 and 0.15 bps, respectively. Adding these up, the complexity associated with the suppliers' interface at Company C is calculated at 0.76 bps.

In Figure 3, the horizontal axis shows the states of earliness or lateness associated with suppliers' deliveries to Company A, Company B and Company C, whereas the vertical axis shows the complexity index associated with those states. It can be seen that the average complexity associated with deliveries from suppliers to Company A is high at 2.41 bps (>2 bps), it is medium from suppliers to Company B at 1.09 bps (1-2 bps) and it is low from suppliers to Company C at 0.76 bps

Figure 3. Entropic-related complexity at the suppliers' interface

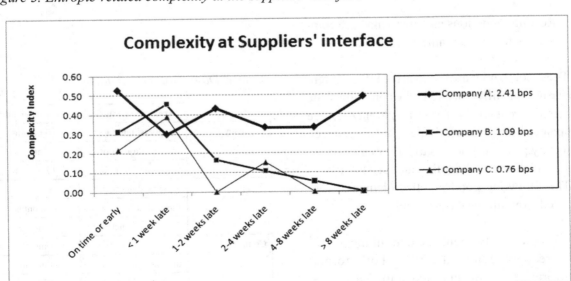

Table 5. Percentage of occurrence of states (suppliers' interface)

State	Company A	Company B	Company C
On time or early	32	75	84
< 1 week late	8	19	13
1-2 weeks late	17	3	0
2-4 weeks late	10	2	3
4-8 weeks late	10	1	0
> 8 weeks late	23	0	0

(<1 bps). All three results are within the limits of manageable complexity (Miller, 1956).

The complexity associated with the state of being "on time or early" could be regarded as value-adding complexity, which is the complexity that is needed to satisfy the end customer. However, early deliveries can cause some problems to companies, in terms of inventory, especially those working in a lean / JIT environment. The states of lateness are regarded as non-value adding complexity. Suppliers to Company A are most complex in the "on time or early" and the ">8 weeks late" states. This could be explained as due to the fact that suppliers' deliveries of common components are not a problem, whereas suppliers' deliveries of critical components such as pump motors are more prone to take longer than estimated. Suppliers to Company B and to Company C show a similar pattern of behaviour, with the highest source of complexity coming from the "<1 week late," and decreasing for the rest of the lateness states. This is because their suppliers are reasonably reliable and, if they missed the requested delivery date, they will deliver sooner rather than later. This is a direct consequence of the percentage of occurrence of states, which is presented in Table 5. As mentioned earlier, states are pre-defined in the analysis, so another way of analysing the data could consider two states: "on time or early" versus "late" deliveries. However, the six states used here have been defined taking into account the scheduler's decision making points as to whether to take action according to

their implications on the shop floor production. For example, lateness of less than a week (i.e. "<1 week late") would not normally prompt as much managerial attention as lateness by a month or so (i.e. "4-8 weeks") would.

Internal Complexity

Although all three companies make customised products, they have their own individual production scheduling characteristics that make them different from one another. For example, their production lead time is 9 to 12 months, 1 to 2 weeks, and 4 weeks for Company A, Company B and Company C, respectively. Thus, the complexity results of their internal production are presented separately, in the next three sections.

Company A

Table 6 shows the percentage of occurrences for each of the areas which can be rescheduled in the order book. It can be observed that the schedule adherence ("OK" state) accounts for 17% of the total. The following processes contribute almost equally: factored, project equipment and materials (between 14% and 15%). Most importantly, it can be observed that rescheduling of the order book due to the assembly area accounts for 22% of the total. This is not surprising, given the nature of the product which is engineer-to-order pumps, and which implies that there is a high level of uncertainty when making one-off products.

Figure 4 shows that the amount of complexity that is handled at Company A accounts for 2.80 bps, which is classified as high in this research. The value-adding complexity (represented by the black bar) accounts for 15% of the total, and the state that contributes the most to the non-value adding complexity is "assembly." Assembly consists of a series of steps, some of which are outsourced, so the performance is highly influenced by the performance of the outsourcees.

Company B.

Table 7 shows that on time or according to the schedule production accounts for 46% of the total. The data used in the table corresponds to the combined live and historical data. Also, it can be seen that the percentages increase with lateness (i.e. once Company B has missed the production scheduled date, the customised product is expected to be made later rather than sooner). This can be due to technical issues, such as the different behaviour of the chemicals in the shop floor compared with the experiments carried out previously in the laboratory.

Table 6. Order book rescheduling by production process at Company A

Production process	%
OK (production according to schedule)	17
Assembly	22
Factored	15
Project equipment	15
Materials	14
Machining	10
Fabrications	7

Table 7. Actual versus scheduled production performance at Company B

State	%
On time	46
<2 days late	6
2-3 days late	6
3-6 days late	12
6-8 days late	12
>8 days late	18

Figure 4. Internal entropic-related complexity at Company A

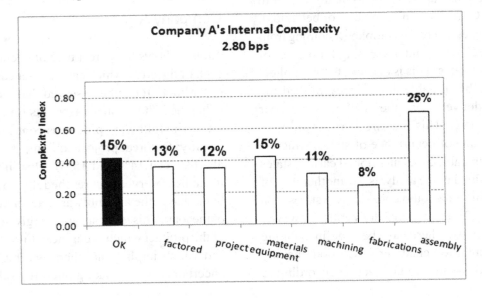

Figure 5. Internal entropic-related complexity at Company B

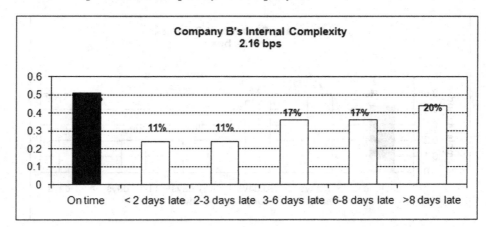

In Figure 5, we observe that Company B manages a high overall amount of complexity, at 2.16 bps, and that the value-adding complexity (represented by the black bar) accounts for 24% of the total. Then the non-value adding complexity states increase with lateness, with the biggest one coming from the ">8 days late" state. This can be attributed to technical errors during production and to knock-on effects in the production schedule.

Company C

During the period for which data were collected, which comprised both live and historical data, Company C's production was always on time or early. This was mainly due to the fact that the standard delivery time had been set to four weeks, which gave plenty of time to account for any unforeseen circumstances that could delay production. So, Company C's way of absorbing complexity consisted of allocating high spare capacity levels in their original production schedule. This also relates to the "spare capacity" identified earlier as another way of managing complexity instead of "rescheduling." It was also noted that Company C placed a strong emphasis on fixed delivery dates with the customer, so once these are agreed with them, deadlines are quite firm,

with the customer potentially bearing the costs for any rescheduling caused by them.

Further analysis was performed regarding the earliness of production, as seen in Table 8. It can be observed from this table that 50% of the doors were finished up to a week early; another observation is that the percentage of finished doors decreased with increased levels of earliness.

The overall amount of complexity handled at Company C, at 1.99 bps is in the medium range (1-2 bps), as seen in Figure 6. The value-adding complexity or "on-time" delivery accounts for 21% of the total. It could be argued that finishing products early is value-adding, since once the doors are completed the resulting spare capacity could be used for accommodating other orders. However, finishing products too early, such as

Table 8. Actual versus scheduled production performance at Company C

State	%
On time	16
<7 days early	50
7-9 days early	19
9-11 days early	5
11-13 days early	5
>13 days early	5

Figure 6. Internal entropic-related complexity at Company C

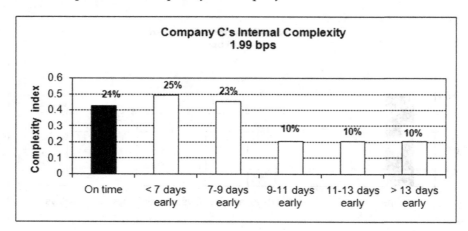

the last three states ("9-11," "11-13" and ">13" days early) may be tying up capital that could be otherwise used, doors could become damaged or lost, and physical space may become an issue if the business were to expand. That is why those early states have been classified as non-value adding. This understanding was communicated to and validated by the company during the presentation of results.

It is worth mentioning that Company C's performance is remarkable, because no instances of late internal production were identified during the analysis period. This case is unusual among the other case studies carried out to date by the authors. The fact that 74% of Company's C requested deliveries were classified as fast turnaround (FTA) or rush orders makes its reliable performance even more surprising.

Customers' Interface

The entropic-related complexity was calculated at the customers' interface too. Table 9 shows the percentage of occurrences for each state at each company. It can be seen in this table that Company A and Company B exhibit about 60% on time or early deliveries to customers, compared with 98% from Company C. It is also shown that the last two lateness states ("4-8" and ">8 weeks" late) are heavily occurring in the case of Company A, but are hardly seen in Company B or Company C.

In this context, Figure 7 shows that Company A and Company B exhibit a medium amount of complexity (1-2 bps), whereas Company C transfers a very low amount (<1 bps). Company B and Company C show a similar pattern in terms of the states, with the highest being "<1 week late,"

Table 9. Percentage of occurrence of states (customers' interface)

State	Company A	Company B	Company C
On time or early	61	62	98
< 1 week late	2	20	2
1-2 weeks late	5	9	0
2-4 weeks late	7	7	0
4-8 weeks late	10	1	0
> 8 weeks late	14	1	0

Figure 7. Entropic-related complexity at the customers' interface

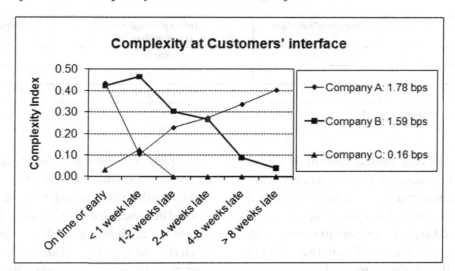

and then decreasing complexity as the lateness increase. This means that once these companies have missed a promised delivery date they will try to deliver sooner rather than later. Company A's deliveries show a different pattern, with a distinctive increase of the complexity as lateness increases (Figure 7). The reason for this behavioural pattern is that, having missed the deadline, efforts are made to deliver as soon as possible, to avoid reaching and surpassing the penalties ceiling. Once this ceiling is surpassed, the efforts are then directed towards other projects (pumps) that may be in danger of becoming late, too.

Summary of Entropic-Related Complexity Results

Table 10 summarises the results presented so far in this chapter. The results indicate that the higher the complexity at the suppliers' interface, the higher the complexity handled internally. As mentioned earlier, the more complexity is imported by suppliers or customers into the organisation, the more complexity the company would need to handle internally. So, not surprisingly, good suppliers enable good internal performance. It was

also noticed that all three companies handled less complexity at their customers' interface than the complexity they handled internally. This can be explained as the case study companies absorbing complexity (i.e., using ways of managing complexity such as "rescheduling" and the use of "spare capacity" in the production schedule to absorb it). It was suggested to companies that they should make their customers aware of this fact. By doing this, customers could become more amenable to pay a Premium (cost of peace of mind), as in the case of Company C; this approach could also help ease some of the pressure from Company A. These understanding and control mechanisms can be linked to the variety and uncertainty of processes, which in the case of customised products were prone to happen more often, as seen in Company B.

Hybrid Rescheduling Algorithms Results

Company A

The emphasis of the production of the pumps at Company A was on the deadlines for achieving

Table 10. Entropic-related complexity in bits per state (bps)

Case study	Suppliers' interface	Internal complexity (value adding %)	Customers' interface
Company A	2.41	2.80 (15%)	1.78
Company B	1.09	2.16 (24%)	1.59
Company C	0.76	1.99 (21%)	0.16

Note: <1:low; 1-2: medium; >2: high

the milestones of each project (pump). If a need for rescheduling occurred, Priority was given according to the importance of the project (dictated by its monetary value). Company A operates in a highly regulated supply chain environment, with contractual clauses which will penalise it for not delivering on time to the customer. In terms of the level of disruption transmitted to the shop floor, the scheduler at Company A would consider the customer requests carefully against all the projects that were in the pipeline, and would just delay the jobs rather than pre-empt and interrupt the course of the jobs already running. So, Low disruption was transmitted to the shopfloor. Therefore, it could be concluded that Company A's preferred hybrid rescheduling algorithm was Priority Low (Figure 4).

Company A's poor performance at the customer interface is mostly the result of a knock-on accumulated effect of its suppliers' failure to deliver on time and in full, and of its own NVA internal complexity.

Company B

In terms of rescheduling strategies, it was observed that Company B was using Utilisation-based rescheduling strategies. This is because it was normally operating with large amounts of spare capacity, in the form of idle vessels. Thus, when a rush order was requested by a customer, Company B could easily accommodate it in its current production schedule by allocating the rush order to one of the vessels that was available. In terms of disruptions transmitted to the shopfloor,

the objective of the scheduler was to satisfy the customer. As a result, the production schedule was updated quite often, on a shift-by-shift basis. So, it could be concluded that Company B's preferred hybrid rescheduling algorithm was Utilisation High (Please note that "High" refers to the high disruption transmitted to the shopfloor and not to high utilisation). See Figure 5.

In terms of the disturbances due to customer requests, Company B showed the following common requests: (a) increasing the priority of existing orders, and (b) introducing new orders, which were mostly rush orders. From the interviews at Company B it was found that it had verbal agreements with suppliers and contractual agreements with customers. This was because, as Company B's customers are a small set of paper mills (who may switch to another supplier if not satisfied), they had to pay extra attention to customer service. This could place Company B in a vulnerable situation in the context of its supply chain, since power can be imbalanced (New & Ramsay, 1997).

Company C

Company C did not need to carry out rescheduling at all (Figure 6) – the reasons for this are explained next. Firstly, at the suppliers' interface, Company C carefully selected its suppliers, such that they were highly dependable. It is worth mentioning that Company C was in a position to do so, as they focussed on a niche in the market, raising issues of costs versus added-value. Internally, spare capacity was built in the production schedule, so it remained mostly unaffected by disturbances (again

Table 11. Rescheduling characteristics: customised vs. commodity production

Rescheduling characteristics	Customised production	Commodity production
Product unit cost (£)	High	Low
Product type	Specialised	Standard
Pace of production	Slow	Fast
Threshold conditions used for production rescheduling	More common	Less common
Spare capacity embedded in the production schedule	Medium to High	Low to Medium
Company protected by contractual agreements with customers	Very common	Not common
Preferred hybrid rescheduling algorithms for reducing entropic-related complexity	*Priority Low* (Company A) and *Utilisation High* (Company B)	*Utilisation High* and *Right-shift* (Huaccho Huatuco *et al.*, 2009)

a way of absorbing complexity). At the customers' interface, Company C used formal contracts with customers to protect itself against last minute changes. As a consequence, Company C did not need to reschedule its production at all during the studied period. This result was due to including spare capacity in its production schedule, and to its careful selection of suppliers and customers. This solution may be more suitable and feasible in the Company's C industry type rather than in other industries.

Customised vs. Commodity Production

Table 11 deals with the comparison between customised and commodity production results. Key differences between these two types of production on observed rescheduling practices are:

- The use of threshold conditions (associated with Low disruption rescheduling algorithms) for carrying out rescheduling is more common in customised production than in commodity production. Threshold conditions mean the use of decision making points in order to filter disruption transmitted to the shop floor due to disturbances (Low disruption). Typically companies of customised production are protected by formal

contracts against customer changes, with attached penalties / premiums for last minute changes or late deliveries.
- Spare capacity in the original production schedule is higher in the customised production than in commodity production.

A key similarity between the two contexts is that *Utilisation High* is a useful hybrid rescheduling algorithm in both customised and commodity production. Additionally, *Priority Low* (as observed in Company A) is better suited for customised production, and *Right-shift* is better suited for commodity production.

RECOMMENDATIONS TO CASE STUDY COMPANIES

The following recommendations were given to the case study companies; these are linked with Table 3, about the issues identified:

Suppliers' Interface (Figure 3)

⇒ Company A (high complexity): Exercise tighter control over suppliers' performance, develop partnerships with key reliable suppliers, and allow the production schedulers to play a more important role in the process of purchasing materials or components. This approach will allow Company A to focus on managing its own internal complexity, by first reducing the uncertainty of suppliers' deliveries. However, it should be kept in mind that changing structures / responsibilities could be difficult in a large company such as this. Change should be driven by the top management with direct involvement of the shopfloor management and operators, and it should be carefully monitored and controlled to ensure that the overall objectives are achieved.

⇒ Company B (medium complexity) and Company C (low complexity): Maintain the good planning of purchasing materials by the production scheduler, and further develop good relationships with reliable suppliers. These were identified through observations / interviews with the productions schedulers at these companies.

Internal Complexity (Figures 4, 5 and 6)

⇒ Company A (high complexity): Synchronise production machining-assembly-test, in order to avoid bottlenecks, and improve forecasting of delivery dates (they were too optimistic) by allowing some slack in the production schedule, to cater for unforeseen problems (this recommendation also applies to Company B). This may allow the schedule to become more robust, therefore reducing the need for rescheduling. However, it is acknowledged that they may find allocating slack time in the schedule is too costly, if there are idle times when many jobs are waiting to be processed.

⇒ Company B (high complexity): Continue monitoring the production system; rescheduling does help towards delivering the products on time.

⇒ Company C (medium complexity): Improve forecast of delivery dates (they were too pessimistic), since most of the complexity is coming from earliness. This is a potential problem, and the company was made aware of this at the result presentation. This may seem to contradict the earlier "slack in the schedule" recommendation. However, it was noticed that Company C was overbuffering itself, and it could easily promise the customer and achieve "on time" deliveries of standard products up to 3 weeks instead of 4 weeks, should they wish to do so.

Customers' Interface (Figure 7)

⇒ Company A (medium complexity): Develop partnerships with customers, with especial review of the contractual agreements and the applied penalties in case of lateness.

⇒ Company B (medium complexity) and Company C (low complexity): Develop threshold conditions regarding rush orders or fast turnaround products (FTA). This will allow Company B to achieve Low disruption transmitted to the shop floor because, during the period of study, the customers were taking for granted that their requests will be taken into account without penalty. For Company C, the threshold is so wide that it could risk becoming uncompetitive, should its competitors offer to provide the same product faster.

Although managers knew that certain areas were more complex than others, entropic-related complexity allowed them to measure and to compare the complexity levels. The ability to integrate and quantify complexity in a single comparable measure was considered useful by managers, and it provided a basis for fruitful discussions between researchers and practitioners.

Table 12. Entropic-related complexity for each hybrid rescheduling algorithm: customised vs. commodity production

Hybrid rescheduling algorithm	Customised production	Commodity production*
Priority High	Not identified	2.731[b]
Priority Low	2.800	3.028[a]
Utilisation High	2.160	2.709 [b]
Utilisation Low	Not identified	2.713 [b]
Right Shift	Not identified	2.712 [b]

*Taken from Huaccho Huatuco *et al.* (2009): (a) The complexity associated with the information content of schedules and (b) The complexity associated with the variation between schedules (bps).

DISCUSSION OF RESULTS

The counter-intuitive result in this chapter is that companies in customised production do not necessarily face high levels of complexity. This is because, as observed in the companies reported in this chapter, in practice companies in customised production ensure that they have formal contractual agreements in place for the delivery of the final products. Also, these companies ensure they have the resources to enable them flexibility, and to cope with the additional process complexity due to customisation. This can work in their favour, such in the case of Company C, which uses spare capacity as a buffer to protect itself from disturbances. Alternatively, it could work against the company, such as in the case of Company A, which tries to avoid the lateness penalties of its tightly arranged schedule. It could be argued that Company C operated in a niche market and could afford to place higher conditions onto its customers, than, for example, Company B, for which competition is more intense.

Table 12 compares the results previously reported in the literature by the authors (Huaccho Huatuco et *al.*, 2009) with the results of the case studies reported in this chapter. It can be seen that *Utilisation High* achieves lower levels of entropic-related complexity than *Priority Low*, in both customised and commodity productions. However, customised production shows, surprisingly, a lower level of complexity than commodity production for both identified hybrid rescheduling algorithms. In order to explain this, it is important to use the case-based research methodology to investigate entropic-related complexity, since it also captures the qualitative aspects through interviews and observations. Direct observations and historical data have been used to obtain meaningful results, by providing explanations from schedulers and managers about the reasons for rescheduling. Historical data can also help to smooth out any unusual performance into a more stable, and thus representative pattern.

Implications for Scheduling Practice

The more threshold conditions are embedded in the hybrid rescheduling algorithm, the less disruption is transmitted to the shop floor. So, this chapter encourages manufacturing organisations to be reactive to disturbances, whilst also taking into account thresholds for deciding when to react. As discussed in the literature review section (Monostori *et al.*, 2007; Pfeiffer *et al.*, 2007), thresholds could be tested at different levels using computer simulations in order to test 'what if' scenarios and taking into account the studied organisation's objectives.

The High disruption algorithms (*Priority High* and *Utilisation High*) monitor the state of the system and react whenever there is a disruption. This is called event-based rescheduling. However, that reaction is constrained sometimes because the alternative machine is busy, but the effort to check alternative machine availability had already been made. Whereas the Low disruption algorithms (*Priority Low* and *Utilisation Low*) monitor the state of the system, they only react if the remaining processing time is greater than a threshold. When executing the *Right-shift* algorithm there is less need to update the schedule, as it only affects the jobs on the affected machine.

Value-Adding (VA) vs. Non-Value Adding Complexity (NVA)

Table 10 depicts the value adding percentage of internal complexity. In this chapter value adding is related to "on time or early" production, as it is assumed that these states will allow a manufacturing company to satisfy its customers. In this respect, Company B and C achieved over 20% VA complexity, whereas Company A achieved a 15% VA complexity.

It is worth mentioning that determining what is VA and NVA complexity depends on the company or industry sector under study. A trade-off of the potential benefits versus losses should be performed in order to give more general insights and to decide the VA and NVA states and complexity.

Even when a company is handling a high amount of VA complexity, this still needs to be managed by the company. However, a different type of action is needed for this. As mentioned in the Appendix: "Key Terms and Definitions," the manager would need to decide on the VA complexity level it could allow into the system depending on the company, sector and wider context.

The NVA complexity, which is the complexity that does not help with satisfying the customers, needs to be both monitored and controlled. NVA complexity could possibly not be entirely eliminated, but it can be reduced. In order to do this, the reasons that cause it in the first place need to be identified and analysed.

CONCLUSION

The conclusions section provides theoretical-based insights for customised versus commodity production, and it derives practical guidelines for production managers / schedulers about the hybrid rescheduling algorithms which are more likely to succeed in practice.

The main research question explored in this chapter was: *In the context of customised production, how do hybrid rescheduling algorithms impact entropic-related complexity?* The following objectives guided this chapter: (a) To identify the typical hybrid rescheduling algorithms used in the context of customised production, and (b) To explain why and how hybrid rescheduling algorithms vary across organisations.

For the research question, it can be seen from the results that *Priority Low* (originated from Company A) generates higher complexity indices than *Utilisation High* (originated from Company B). This can be dependent on the context of the organisations studied, for example production lead times were longer at Company A than Company B. It was also confirmed that the less rescheduling is carried out the lower the complexity, with Company C (SME making customised production) showing a level of complexity management that could serve as a beacon for other companies. As a reminder, Company C embedded flexibility into their manufacturing process by allocating spare capacity in their production schedule.

A counter-intuitive finding was that the entropic-related complexity associated with customised production was lower than that related to commodity production. This could be explained by the fact that commoditised production typically faces tougher competition; the customer could easily switch from one supplier to another and this can happen as late as already placed orders or production set into motion (Sivadasan *et al.,* 2010). By contrast, in the case of customised production, once the customer has made up their mind and agreed to the specification of their product (which had been discussed in order to match its specifications), then the company is protected (or bounded) by contract to provide what has been agreed. This leads to a more stable production schedule in practice.

Regarding the first objective, it could be argued that manufacturing organisations in customised production prefer the two hybrid rescheduling algorithms identified in this chapter: *Priority Low* and *Utilisation High*. However, this is dependent on the companies selected for the case studies, so different companies may use different hybrid rescheduling algorithms. With respect to the second objective, several other factors not included in this chapter could have an influence on the different choices of hybrid rescheduling algorithms by manufacturing companies, production lead times (e.g. weeks or months) or the type of competition (e.g. sheltered or competitive).

Implications for Theory and Practice

This chapter brings a novel and analytically-based insight into the effects of hybrid rescheduling algorithms on entropic-related complexity. An unpredicted result—of customised production leading to lower complexity than mass production—is highlighted and explained. The work presented in this chapter has shown the application of concepts derived from previous research carried out by the authors to real-world manufacturing companies. As stated earlier, the two quadrants of interest to the work presented in this chapter were: "functional product, responsive scheduling" and "innovative product, responsive scheduling" (Huaccho Huatuco, 2003). The former refers to commodity production, whereas the latter refers to customised production.

Organisations that belong to the "functional product, responsive scheduling" quadrant can manage complexity through decision-making and rescheduling. Here the key point is to be responsive to customer requests by adapting the current scheduled quantity. This was observed in previous case studies carried out by the authors (Sivadasan *et al.*, 2010).

Organisations that belong to the "innovative product, responsive scheduling" quadrant, which are made-to-order of customised products, can deal with complexity through spare capacity and rescheduling in order to become responsive. In this chapter it has been found that *Priority Low* and *Utilisation High* are the preferred hybrid rescheduling algorithms used by manufacturing organisations in practice. However, these results should not be taken prescriptively. Each company should identify its main objectives, and design and manage the system consistently with these objectives. The thresholds/ tolerance limits / trade-offs of spare capacity should be analytically investigated and linked with each company's ability to manage the additional complexity, either value- or non-value adding, associated with these decisions. In this line, companies should reserve spare capacity for products at greater risk of mismatch between their supply and demand, since additional spare capacity in the production schedule can be a detriment to internal performance measures and a drain on costs.

Future work should consider the possibility of carrying out extra case studies for customised production to see whether the other rescheduling strategies are used in practice: *Priority High, Utilisation Low* and *Right Shift* in the context of customised production environment. Another future work direction could be to design, set up and run computer simulations, which should include some spare capacity already built-in the Original Schedule (OS), a sign of robust and sound scheduling methods. Then, a comprehensive statistical analysis of results could be performed.

REFERENCES

Bean, J. C., Birge, J. R., Mittenthal, J., & Noon, C. E. (1991). Matchup scheduling with multiple resources, release dates and disruptions. *Operations Research*, *39*(3), 470–483. doi:10.1287/opre.39.3.470

Bierwirth, C., & Mattfeld, D. C. (1999). Production scheduling and rescheduling with genetic algorithms. *Evolutionary Computation*, *7*(1), 1–17. doi:10.1162/evco.1999.7.1.1

Browning, T. R., Deyst, J. J., & Eppinger, S. D. (2002). Adding value in Product Development by Creating Information and Reducing Risk. *IEEE Transactions on Engineering Management*, *49*(4), 443–458. doi:10.1109/TEM.2002.806710

Calinescu, A., Efstathiou, J., Schirn, J., & Bermejo, J. (1998). Applying and Assessing Two Methods for Measuring Complexity in Manufacturing. [JORS]. *The Journal of the Operational Research Society*, *49*(7), 722–733.

Calinescu, A., Efstathiou, J., Sivadasan, S., Schirn, J., & Huaccho Huatuco, L. (2000). Complexity in manufacturing: an information theoretic approach, In I.P. McCarthy & T. Rakotobe-Joel, eds. *Proceedings of the conference on complexity and complex systems in industry*, pp.30-44. Warwick: The University of Warwick.

Cheng, Y. (1998). Hybrid simulation for resolving resource conflicts in train traffic rescheduling. *Computers in Industry*, *35*(3), 233–246. doi:10.1016/S0166-3615(97)00071-7

Da Silveira, G., Borenstein, D., & Fogliatto, F. S. (2001). Mass customization: Literature review and research directions. *International Journal of Production Economics*, *72*(1), 1–13. doi:10.1016/S0925-5273(00)00079-7

Deblaere, F., Demeulemeester, E., & Herroelen, W. (2010). Reactive scheduling in the multi-mode RCPSP. *Computers & Operations Research*. doi:. doi:10.1016/j.cor.2010.01.001

Duray, R., Ward, P. T., Milligan, G. W., & Berry, W. L. (2000). Approaches to mass customisation: configuration and empirical validation. *Journal of Operations Management*, *18*(6), 605–625. doi:10.1016/S0272-6963(00)00043-7

Efstathiou, J. (1996). Anytime heuristic schedule repair in manufacturing industry. *IEE Proceedings. Control Theory and Applications*, *143*(2), 114–124. doi:10.1049/ip-cta:19960277

Efstathiou, J., Tassano, F., Sivadasan, S., Shirazi, R., Alves, J., Frizelle, G., & Calinescu, A. (1999). Information complexity as a driver of emergent phenomena in the business community, *Proceedings of the international workshop on emergent synthesis*, pp. 1-6. Japan: Kobe University.

ElMaragy, H. A. (Ed.). (2009). *Changeable and Reconfigurable Manufacturing Systems*. New York: Springer. doi:10.1007/978-1-84882-067-8

Frizelle, G., & Woodcock, E. (1995). Measuring complexity as an aid to developing operational strategy. *International Journal of Operations & Production Management*, *15*(5), 26–39. doi:10.1108/01443579510083640

Gao, Y., Ding, Y.-S., & Zhang, H.-Y. (2009). Job-shop scheduling considering rescheduling in uncertain dynamic environment. *Proceedings of the 16th International Conference on Management Science & Engineering*. 14th-16th September 2009. Moscow, Russia.

Griffiths, J., & Margetts, D. (2000). Variation in production schedules – implications for both the company and its suppliers. *Journal of Materials Processing Technology*, *103*(1), 155–159. doi:10.1016/S0924-0136(00)00408-8

Gunasekaran, A., & Ngai, E. W. T. (2005). Build-to-order supply chain management: a literature review and framework for development. *Journal of Operations Management*, *23*(5), 423–451. doi:10.1016/j.jom.2004.10.005

Herrmann, J. W. (2001). *Improving manufacturing system performance through rescheduling [online]*. Maryland, University of Maryland. Available from: http://www.isr.umd.edu/~jwh2/papers/rescheduling.html [Accessed 3rd December 2010].

Herrmann, J. W., & Delalio, D. R. (2001). Algorithms for Sheet Metal Nesting. *IEEE Transactions on Robotics and Automation*, *17*(2), 183–190. doi:10.1109/70.928563

Herrmann, J. W., & Pundoor, G. (2002). *Rescheduling frequency and Supply Chain performance*. Institute for Systems Research (ISR). TR 2002-50. 25 p.

Holthaus, O. (1999). Scheduling in job shops with machine breakdowns: an experimental study. *Computers & Industrial Engineering*, *36*, 137–162. doi:10.1016/S0360-8352(99)00006-6

Hornby, A. S. (2000). *Oxford Advanced Learner's Dictionary of Current English*. 6th edition. Wehmeier Sally (Ed). Oxford: Oxford University Press, pp. 29 & 638.

Huaccho Huatuco, L. (2006). *Rescheduling and Complexity for Customised Products. Final report of the Seed corn fund research project. Leeds University Business School* (p. 19). UK: LUBS.

Huaccho Huatuco, L., Burgess, T. F., & Shaw, N. E. (2010). Entropic-related complexity for reengineering a robust supply chain: a case study. *Production Planning & Control*. Advance online publication, 15th July 2010, doi 10.1080/09537281003596185, 12 p.

Huaccho Huatuco, L., Efstathiou, J., Calinescu, A., Sivadasan, S., & Kariuki, S. (2009). Comparing the impact of different rescheduling strategies on the entropic-related complexity of manufacturing systems. *International Journal of Production Research*, *47*(15), 4305–4325. doi:10.1080/00207540701871036

Huaccho Huatuco, L., Efstathiou, J., Sivadasan, S., & Calinescu, A. (2001). The value of dynamic complexity in manufacturing systems. *Proceedings of the International Conference of the Production and Operations Management Society (POMS-Brazil 2001)*. 11th -14th August 2001, Escola de Administração de Empresas de São Paulo (Business Administration School of Sao Paulo), Brazil, 180-188.

Huaccho Huatuco, L. D. (2003). *The role of rescheduling in managing manufacturing systems' complexity*. DPhil thesis. Oxford:University of Oxford, pp. 237.

Jain, A. K., & ElMaraghy, H. A. (1997). Production scheduling/rescheduling in flexible manufacturing. *International Journal of Production Research*, *35*(1), 281–289. doi:10.1080/002075497196082

Krajewski, L., Wei, J. C., & Tang, L.-L. (2005). Responding to schedule changes in build-to-order supply chains. *Journal of Operations Management*, *23*(5), 452–469. doi:10.1016/j.jom.2004.10.006

Miller, G. A. (1956). The magical number seven, plus or minus two: Some limits on our capacity for processing information. *Psychological Review*, *63*(2), 81–97. doi:10.1037/h0043158

Mintzberg, H. (1988). Generic strategies: Toward a comprehensive framework. *Advances in Strategic Management*, *5*(1), 1–67.

Monostori, L., Kadar, B., Pfeiffer, A., & Karnok, D. (2007). Solution approaches to real-time control of customised mass production. *Annals of the CIRP*, *56*(1), 431–434. doi:10.1016/j.cirp.2007.05.103

Morton, T. E., & Pentico, D. W. (1993). *Heuristic Scheduling Systems: with applications to production systems and project management. Wiley Series in Engineering and Technology Management*. New York: John Wiley and Sons.

New, S., & Ramsay, J. (1997). A critical appraisal of aspects of the lean chain approach. *European Journal of Purchasing & Supply Management, 3*(2), 93–102. doi:10.1016/S0969-7012(96)00019-6

Ouelhadj, D., & Petrovic, S. (2009). A survey of dynamic scheduling in manufacturing systems. *Journal of Scheduling, 12*(4), 417–431. doi:10.1007/s10951-008-0090-8

Pfeiffer, A., Kadar, B., & Monostori, L. (2007). Stability-oriented evaluation of rescheduling strategies, by using simulation. *Computers in Industry, 58*(7), 630–643. doi:10.1016/j.compind.2007.05.009

Pinedo, M. (2008). *Scheduling: Theory, Algorithms, and Systems*, 3ʳᵈ Edition. New York: Springer Science+Business Media, LLC.

Shannon, C. E. (1949). The mathematical theory of communication. In Shannon, C. E., & Weaver, W. (Eds.), *The mathematical theory of communication* (pp. 3–91). Illinois: University of Illinois Press.

Silva, C. A., Sousa, J. M. C., & Runkler, T. A. (2008). Rescheduling and optimization of logistic processes using GA and ACO. *Engineering Applications of Artificial Intelligence, 21*(3), 343–352. doi:10.1016/j.engappai.2007.08.006

Sivadasan, S., Efstathiou, J., Calinescu, A., & Huaccho Huatuco, L. (2001). A discussion of the issues of state definition in the entropy-base measure of operational complexity across supplier-customer systems. *Proceedings of the 5th World Multi-Conference on Systemics, Cybernetics and Informatics (SCI 2001), 22*ⁿᵈ – 25ᵗʰ July 2001, Orlando, Florida, USA, Vol. II, 227-232.

Sivadasan, S., Efstathiou, J., Calinescu, A., & Huaccho Huatuco, L. (2004). Supply Chain Complexity. In New, S., & Westbrook, R. (Eds.), *Understanding Supply Chains* (pp. 133–163). Oxford: Oxford University Press.

Sivadasan, S., Efstathiou, J., Calinescu, A., & Huaccho Huatuco, L. (2006). Advances on Measuring the Operational Complexity of Supplier-Customer Systems. *European Journal of Operational Research, 171*(1), 208–226. doi:10.1016/j.ejor.2004.08.032

Sivadasan, S., Efstathiou, J., Frizelle, G., Shirazi, R., & Calinescu, A. (2002). An Information-Theoretic Methodology for Measuring the Operational Complexity of Supplier-Customer Systems. *International Journal of Operations & Production Management, 22*(1), 80–102. doi:10.1108/01443570210412088

Sivadasan, S., Smart, J., Huaccho Huatuco, L., & Calinescu, A. (2010). Operational Complexity and Supplier-Customer Integration: Case studies insights and complexity rebound. [JORS]. *The Journal of the Operational Research Society, 61*(12), 1709–1718. doi:10.1057/jors.2009.138

Smart, J. (2009). Book reviews. *International Journal of Production Research, 47*(6), 1713–1714. doi:10.1080/00207540802316568

Smith, S. F. (2002). Technologies for dynamic scheduling. In Workshop on on-line planning and scheduling of the *6ᵗʰ International Conference on Artificial Intelligence Planning and Scheduling (AIPS'02)*. American Association for Artificial Intelligence / European Association of Excellence in AI Planning (AAAI/PLANET).

Tu, Q., Vonderembse, M. A., & Ragu-Nathan, T. S. (2001). The impact of time-based manufacturing practices on mass customization and value to customer. *Journal of Operations Management, 19*(2), 201–217. doi:10.1016/S0272-6963(00)00056-5

Vieira, G. E., Herrmann, J. W., & Lin, E. (2003). Rescheduling Manufacturing Systems: A Framework of Strategies, Policies, and Methods. *Journal of Scheduling, 6*(1), 39–62. doi:10.1023/A:1022235519958

Voss, C., Tsikriktsis, N., & Frohlich, M. (2002). Case research in operations management. *International Journal of Operations & Production Management, 22*(2), 195–219. doi:10.1108/01443570210414329

Wang, L., Pan, Q.-K., Suganthan, P. N., Wang, W.-H., & Wang, Y.-M. (2010). A novel hybrid discrete differential evolution algorithm for blocking flow shop scheduling problems. *Computers & Operations Research, 37*(3), 509–520. doi:10.1016/j.cor.2008.12.004

Wang, L., Zhang, L., & Zheng, D.-Z. (2006). An effective hybrid genetic algorithm for flow shop scheduling with limited buffers. *Computers & Operations Research, 33*(10), 2960–2971. doi:10.1016/j.cor.2005.02.028

Yamamoto, M., & Nof, Y. (1985). Scheduling/rescheduling in the manufacturing operating system environment. *International Journal of Production Research, 23*(4), 705–722. doi:10.1080/00207548508904739

KEY TERMS AND DEFINITIONS

Commodity Production: Commodity production refers to the production of mass produced, standard or off-the-shelf products.

Customised Production: Customised production refers to the production where the customer's preferences for the configuration of a final product are taken into account.

Entropic-Related Complexity: Entropic-related complexity is defined as the expected amount of information required to describe the state of the system (Calinescu *et al.*, 2000). It is based on "entropy," which was first proposed in the seminal work by Shannon (1949), and was later adapted to manufacturing systems by Frizelle & Woodcock (1995) and Efstathiou *et al.* (1999). As a result, a number of studies about the entropy measure in the context of manufacturing

systems emerged (e.g. Sivadasan *et al.*, 2002, 2004, 2006, 2010 and Huaccho Huatuco *et al.*, 2009). Entropy captures two characteristics of complexity: the variety and uncertainty within the system, corresponding to the structural and operational complexity, respectively (Calinescu *et al.*, 2000).

Hybrid Algorithm: Taking the separate definitions of "hybrid" and "algorithm" from the Oxford Dictionary (Hornby, 2000), and combining them, a "Hybrid algorithm" can be defined as the product of mixing two or more sets of rules that must be followed when solving a particular problem. In this chapter the problem refers to rescheduling manufacturing systems.

Non-Value Adding (NVA) Complexity: Non-value-adding (NVA) complexity is the complexity that is not helping the company achieve the satisfaction of its customers (e.g. in the form of late deliveries). This complexity needs to be both monitored and controlled, in order to reduce it and mitigate its possible consequences. For a paper on VA and NVA complexity, please refer to Huaccho Huatuco *et al.* (2001).

Rescheduling: Rescheduling, also known as "predictive-reactive scheduling" (Vieira *et al.*, 2003; Morton & Pentico, 1993), is defined in this chapter as changing the schedule in terms of time, quantity or product specifications in response to disturbances (Huaccho Huatuco *et al.*, 2009). Disturbances can be of internal or external nature. Internal disturbances are those that occur within the manufacturing system, such as machine breakdowns; whereas external disturbances are those that occur outside the manufacturing system, such as customer changes (Calinescu *et al.*, 1998). Rescheduling affects the performance of manufacturing organisation(s) (Herrmann, 2001; Hermann & Delalio, 2001; Hermann & Pundoor, 2002). Previous research normally uses traditional measures, such as mean tardiness to evaluate the effectiveness of the rescheduling procedure (e.g. Bean *et al.*, 1991).

Value Adding (VA) Complexity: Value adding (VA) complexity is defined in this chapter as the complexity needed to satisfy the customers (e.g. in the form of "on time" delivery). This complex-ity needs to be managed too, with the manager judging the level that is suitable to allow into the system. This decision depends on the company, its industry sector and wider context where it operates.

Section 3
Other Applications of Hybrid Algorithms

Chapter 11
HMIP Model for a Territory Design Problem with Capacity and Contiguity Constraints

Fabian Lopez
Universidad Autónoma de Nuevo León (CEDEEM), México

ABSTRACT

Small geographic basic units (BU) are grouped into larger geographic territories on a Territory Design Problem (TDP). Proposed approach to solve a TDP is presented through a study case developed on a large soft drinks company which operates in the city of Monterrey, México. Each BU of our TDP is defined by three activity measures: (1) number of customers, (2) sales volume and (3) workload. Some geographic issues about contiguity and compactness for the territories to be constructed are considered. An optimal solution is obtained when the constructed territories are well balanced taking into consideration each activity measure simultaneously. In particular, contiguity is hard to be represented mathematically. All previous research work indicates that this NP-Hard problem is not suitable for solving on large-scale instances. A new strategy which is based on a hybrid-mixed integer programming (HMIP) approach is developed. Specifically, our implementation is based on a Cut-Generation Strategy. We take advantage from territory centers obtained through a relaxation of a P-median based model. This model has a very high degree of connectivity. Thus, small number of iterations to find connected solutions is required. The authors detail out their methodology and then they proceed to its computational implementation. Experimental results show the effectiveness of our method in finding near-optimal solutions for very large instances up to 10,000 BU's in short computational times (less than 10 minutes). Nowadays, this model is being used by the firm with important economical benefits.

DOI: 10.4018/978-1-61350-086-6.ch011

INTRODUCTION

A territory design problem (TDP) is defined as the problem of grouping small geographic areas called basic units (e.g. counties, zip codes or customers) into larger geographic clusters called territories in such a way that these territories are acceptable according to relevant planning criterion. Depending on any particular context, these considerations can either be economically motivated (e.g. average sales, workload or number of customers) or have a demographic background (e.g. number of inhabitants, voting population). Moreover some spatial constraints like contiguity and compactness are often required. Note that literature often uses the term Territory Alignment instead of Territory Design.

The model we propose on this work is integrated into an interactive and user-friendly Geographic Information System (GIS) application, named MAPINFO©. This chapter illustrates the potential of the proposed approach as an easy to use decision tool in the context of a study case developed on a large soft drinks company that operates in the city of Monterrey, México. Embotelladoras ARCA (www.e-arca.com.mx) is a company dedicated to production, distribution and sale of soft drinks brands owned by The Coca-Cola Company, some own-labels and third parties. ARCA was formed in 2001 by integrating three of the oldest bottlers in Mexico and become the second largest bottler of Coca-Cola products in Latin America and the fifth in the world. The company distributes its products in the north region of the Mexican Republic and since 2008, in the northeastern region of Argentina. ARCA also produces and distributes branded salty snacks Bokados. Thus, the company has an enormous market that makes us think that it could be better achieved by taking into account an operation research model.

The company faces a commercial TDP. On this work we are going to focus our application in the distribution operation on the city of Monterrey, México. In distribution industry, TDP is motivated by changes on the customers served by a given route. As each territory is serviced by a single resource, it makes sense to use some planning criterion to balance the number of customers, volume of sales and workload required to cover on each territory. It is often required to balance demand among the territories in order to delegate responsibility fairly. For this, the firm wishes to partition the city area into disjoint territories that are suitable for their commercial purposes. In particular, given a set of basic units (BU's), the firm wants to create a specific number of territories according to some planning criterion such as compactness and balancing. The main objective of TDP is to group customers into manageable sized territories in order to guarantee that BU's assigned to a territory are relatively close to each other.

On this work we are proposing a Hybrid Mixed Integer Programming model (HMIP) to find near-optimal solutions for our commercial TDP. This HMIP model heuristically oriented is integrated in an interactive and user friendly Geographic Information Systems (GIS). The algorithm consists of iteratively solving a relaxed MIP model (relaxing contiguity constraints). Then we identify the violated contiguity constraints in order to add a subset of cuts to the model as necessary. The procedure continues until no more contiguity constraints are needed. The model was implemented and tested. We found that this procedure is successful to find near-optimal solutions for very large-scale instances up to 10,000 BU's.

BACKGROUND AND SOME APPLICATIONS FOR TERRITORY DESIGN

The criteria for defining a meaningful territory design lie in the purpose of the studies and depend mainly on each particular case. These criteria are often guided by the problem specifications or even more restricted by the available data. For a sales territory context, well–planned decisions enable an efficient market penetration and lead to decreased costs and improved customer service. By the other hand in terms of political districting, an algorithmic approach protects against politically motivated manipulations during the territory design process. Either way, the most commonly used set of criteria includes contiguity, compactness and balanced territories. We can define Compactness as the spatial property of being close and firmly united (i.e. having the minimum distance between all the entities of a given area). We define Contiguity as a continuous connection of a group of entities throughout an unbroken sequence and sharing a common border. Researchers and practitioners have put diverse opinions on what other design criteria to consider. These include:

- Minimum variation in spatial characteristics among territories (i.e. area, size, shape);
- Territorial homogeneity in economic characteristics like number of customers or level of sales.
- Equal trip generation or workload.
- Maximum compatibility with already existing territories.

TDP is a truly multidisciplinary research which includes several fields like Geography, Political Science, Public Administration and OR as well. We can generalize that TDP is common to all applications that operate within a group of resources that need to be assigned in an optimal way in order to subdivide the work area into balanced regions of responsibility. We can mention pickup and delivery applications, waste collection, school districting, sales workforce territory design and even some others related to geopolitical concerns. Most public services including hospitals, schools, etc., are administered along territorial boundaries. We can mention either economic or demographic issues that may be considered for setup a well balanced territory. TDP is motivated by quite different applications like political districting, design of territories for schools, social facilities,

emergency services, waste collection and sales & service territory design. In what follows we will present several applications which all have in common the task of subdividing the region under inspection into a number of territories, subject to some side constraints.

In political districting applications, a governmental area, such as a city or state, has to be partitioned into a given number of territories. We note that in this context, territories are usually called districts. The problem of determining political territories can be viewed as one of dividing a governmental area, such as a city or a state, into subareas from which political candidates are elected. As each territory elects a single member to a parliamentary assembly, the main planning criterion is to have approximately the same number of voters in each territory (i.e. territories of similar size) in order to respect the principle of "one man–one vote." In general, the process of redistricting has to be periodically undertaken in order to account for population shifts. The length of these periods varies from country to country. For recent books on political districting, the reader is referred to Mehrotra et al. (1998) and Grilli di Cortona et al. (1999).

The other common set of applications is referred as sales and service territory design problems. In general, the task of designing sales territories is common to all companies which operate a sales-force and need to subdivide the market area into regions of responsibility. Typical planning requirements are to design territories which are similar in size, e.g. in terms of sales potentials or workload, or that reduce travel times within the territories needed to attend the customers or service incidents. The TDP applications for attending customers asking for technical facilities are very common and often quite similar criterion is employed. Sales promotions and advertising amongst the retailers is very important in the considered business and is carried out by sales agents, where each agent is in charge of a certain territory. Some cases are motivated mainly because of the uneven distribution of workload. Here, the workload is expressed taking into account sales value and frequency of visits. In general, there are several motivations for aligning existing or designing new territories. First an increase or decrease in the number of sales or service obviously requires some adjustment of the territories. Other reasons are to achieve better coverage with the existing personnel or to evenly balance workload among them. Moreover, customer shifts or the introduction of new products make it necessary to align territories see Zoltners and Sinha (1983).

Besides the most common problems for sales territory design and political districting, several authors report on various other closely related applications. In some cases, it is required to design territories for facilities which provide service at a fixed location. On these cases, customers have to visit a public facility in order to obtain service (e.g. schools or hospitals). Ferland and Guénette (1990) deal with the problem of assigning residential areas to schools. As an outcome of the planning process, all residential areas in the region under consideration are partitioned into a number of territories, one for each school. A criterion generally taken into account is capacity limitations, equal utilization of the schools, maximal or average travel distances for students, good accessibility and racial balance. When planning territories for social facilities, like hospitals or public utilities, administrative units have to be aggregated into territories. As a result, it is determined for every inhabitant to which facility he should go in order to obtain service. Typically the number of inhabitants on each territory has to be within predetermined bounds in order to account for service utilization and a limited capacity of the social facility. Moreover territories should be contiguous and the facilities should be easily accessible for all inhabitants within the respective territory, as public transportation for example.

Several (public) institutions provide their service not at a fixed location but distributed over a geographic region or on–site where the service incident occurs. Muyldermans et al. (2002) deal with the planning of winter gritting and salt spreading services. Thus, the region under consideration has to be partitioned into territories, where each territory contains at least one vehicle depot. Afterwards, vehicle routes for providing service are planned for each territory separately. The main design criterion for the territories is balance in terms of travel distance, compactness and contiguity. Closely related is the problem of waste or garbage collection. In a first step, so-called sectors are determined, where each sectors consists of a set of streets or street segments in which waste has to be collected on a certain day. Afterwards, routes for the garbage trucks within the sectors are computed. According to Hanafi et al. (1999), the overall time for collecting garbage should be minimized (i.e. compactness). In other words, the time for collecting garbage should be approximately the same for all sectors (i.e. balance) and the sectors should be contiguous. Whereas in the case study of Muyldermans et al. (2002), territories are required to be non–overlapping, Hanafi et al. (1999) reports that, depending on how often per week waste has to be collected, certain streets can belong to more than one territory. Thus, in this special case, the BU's are not mutually exclusively assigned to territories. D'Amico et al. (2002) report a case study for police district design. Here the police departments have to partition their jurisdiction into so-called command districts. After the districts have been fixed, an optimal number of patrol cars that should be on duty are assigned to each command district. The "goodness" of the districts in terms of several different performance measures is assessed.

There are many ways of assigning small geographic BU's to larger territories. Territory design has the spatial constraint which accounts for contiguity which is important for all BU's contained within each territory. This constraint limits the set of acceptable solutions to the problem. The main difficulty with this feature is that a typical mixed integer programming (MIP) model has an exponential number of contiguity constraints. It is impossible to write all these constraints explicitly. Thus, the problem grows exponentially with additional individual BU's. This feature increases considerably the complexity of our problem. Indeed, one of the reasons TDP for being especially difficult is the size of the solution space. The dimension of a common real world problem makes unfeasible any attempt to explicitly enumerate all the possible solutions. The total number of possible solutions for a TDP is very large and is given by the Stirling number of the second kind (Altman, 1998). For large, complex sets, the problem is immense. Indeed, in terms of computational complexity, the TDP has been shown to be NP-Complete (Crescenzi, & Kann, 1998). Due to legal regulations, shifting markets or the introduction of new products, territory design decisions have to be frequently re–evaluated. Especially for a large number of BU's and territories this is a lengthy task and therefore an algorithmic optimization approach for expediting the process is often required. Thus, hybrid techniques seem to be the best available option to produce solutions to the problem in reasonable computational time.

PREVIOUS SOLUTION APPROACHES FOR TERRITORY DESIGN

The TDP has been largely studied since the 60's and several models and techniques have been proposed to solve it. In Operations Research the first work about TDP can be traced back to Forrest (1964) and to Garfinkel's (1968). Some of these approaches are based on set covering or set partitioning formulations. In general for solving large scale problems, the allocation phase can be tackled by relaxing the integrality constraints on the assignment variables (i.e. binary variables). However, this procedure usually assigns portions of BU's to more than one territory center which is

not desired. Hess et al. (1971) propose a simple rule, which exclusively assigns the so-called split areas to the territory center that "owns" the largest share of the split area. Zoltners and Sinha (1983) model the allocation problem assigning BU's to the closest territory center. This procedure yields compact and often connected territories, however, usually not well balanced. Moreover, Fleischmann and Paraschis (1988) report poor results with this heuristic based on a two phase Location-allocation approach. They find that about 50% of the balancing activity constraints for the territories obtained were violated.

It is interesting to note that only a few authors consider more than one criterion simultaneously for a balanced TDP (Zoltners and Sinha, 1983). By the other hand, very few works provide optimal solutions for the problem with connectivity constraints. Particularly, Hojati (1996) show that a good selection for the territory centers may impact on the resulting territories. Mehrotra, et al. (1998) use an exact method based on a Brach and Price structure to find optimal solutions for a political districting problem with connectivity constraints. In their empirical work, they are able to solve instances with up to 39 BU's. Among the last works we find on exact methods for TDP we have Caro et al. (2004), Lorena & Senne (2004) and Senne, Lorena, & Pereira (2005). These models have been based on Column generation strategies and Branch-and-price. Size instances up to 1000 BU's are reported here.

Some metaheuristics have been developed extensively to solve TDP. Algorithms based on simulated annealing are proposed by Browdy (1990), and D'Amico et al. (2002). Ricca (1997) develop a Tabu-search algorithm. Tabu-search algorithm has been applied in Bozkaya et al. (2003), Blais et al. (2003) and Taillard (2003). Genetic algorithms for solving territory design problems have been introduced by Forman and Yue (2003) and Bergey et al. (2003). They encode the solution in a similar way as is used to solve the Traveling Salesman Problem (i.e. TSP). The encoding is a path representation through each BU. As the BU's are traversed, territories are built on this sequence. In Genetic Algorithms we find some more recently works on Kirkizoglu (2005) and Bacao et.al (2005). Vargas-Suarez, Ríos-Mercado, and López–Perez (2005) address a related commercial TDP with a variable number of territories *P*, using as an objective a weighted function of the activity deviations from a given goal. No compactness is considered here. A basic GRASP is developed and tested for a few instances obtaining relatively good results. Haugland et al. (2007) work with stochastic data which they argue is frequently present in territory design decisions. They deal with uncertain demand for BU's. In Segura and Ríos-Mercado (2007), they model the dispersion as a p-median (p-MP) objective function.

Among the most important applications for the TDP we find Ríos-Mercado and Fernandez (2009). They study the problem considering compactness and contiguity but without joint assignment constraints. They model TDP as a p-center problem (p-CP). This scheme consists of a two-stage iterative process where territory centers are first located and then customers are allocated to centers. However this technique has been designed to solve problems involving just one single balancing constraint. In this work, the authors propose and develop a reactive GRASP algorithm for instances up to 500 BU's. They test with some instances of different sizes and find that solutions obtained from the relaxation of the p-MP based models have a very high degree of connectivity. When p-CP is used as dispersion measure, the number of instances that require additional cuts on its relaxed problem is larger than when p-MP is used as dispersion. Particularly this p-MP feature has a good impact on computational efficiency since very few iterations are needed, to find connected solutions as opposed to the center-based models. As a consequence, they conclude that models with a p-MP objective function are solved faster than the ones using a p-CP objective. On Table 1 we present a brief list of previous research works applied to TDP. The paper by Kalcsics, Nickel, and Schröder (2005) is an extensive survey of approaches to TDP that gives an up to date state of the art and unifying approach to the topic. For a more extensive review related to TDP solution approaches see Zoltners and Sinha (2005).

TERRITORY DESIGN APPLICATION AT EMBOTELLADORAS ARCA

TDP solutions are case-specific, since each one of them has its own constraints and objectives, making it virtually impossible to create an algorithm that can be applied to all types of instances. When reviewing the literature, one can observe that only few papers consider territory design problems independently from a concrete practical background. Hence the tendency in operations research to separate the model from the application and establish the model itself as a self-contained topic of research cannot be observed. Therefore, we will introduce a real business model applied for territory design and present our approach for solving the problem in detail.

Territory Design Problem (TDP) groups small geographic areas, into territories. Every basic unit (BU) should be assigned to just one territory. We require compactness and contiguity for territories to be constructed. Contiguity can be defined as a territory that is undistorted geographically. In order to obtain contiguous territories, explicit neighborhood information for the BU's is required. Our problem definition includes some prescribed and/or forbidden territories. This modeling feature can be applied to take into account geographical obstacles like rivers and mountains. As can be verified, prescribed and/or forbidden features can be easily extended to consider some territories that may already exist at the start of the planning process. The TDP for Embotelladoras ARCA is stated as follows:

Table 1. List of previous research work applied to TDP

Reference	Year	Comments	Solution Method
Garfinkel	1968	Set Covering & Set Partitioning	Implicit enumeration
Hess & Samuels	1971	Split Resolution technique	Heuristic
Fleischmann & Paraschis	1988	Two phase location-allocation method	Heuristic
Hojati	1996	How territory centers impact on BU's Allocation	Centers: Relaxation. Splitting: Capacitated Transp
Ricca & Simeone	1997	Tabu Search	Meta-Heuristics
Mehrotra et al.	1998	Up to 39 BU's	Exact MIP, Branch-and-price
D'Amico et al.	2002	Simulated Annealing	Meta-Heuristics
Bozkaya et al.	2003	P-median, Tabu Search and Adaptive memory	Meta-Heuristics
Forman and Yue	2003	Genetic Algorithms	Meta-Heuristics
Blais et al.	2003	Tabu Search	Meta-Heuristics
Taillard	2003	Tabu Search	Heuristic methods
Caro et al.	2004	Column generation and Branch-and-price	Integer programming
Lorena & Senne	2004	Size up to 900 BU's	Capacitated p-median, Column generation
Klose and Drexl	2005	Column generation and Branch-and-price	Branch and Bound
Zolterns and Sinha	2005, 1983	Several approaches. Alignment of sales territories.	Meta-Heuristics
Bacao et al.	2005	Genetic Algorithms	Meta-Heuristics
Kalcsics et al.	2005	From 100 up to 1000 BU's	Heuristic & Metaheuristics
Senne et al.	2005	Up to 818 BU's	P-median, Branch-and-price
Haugland et al.	2007	Stochastic	Meta-Heuristics
Ríos-Mercado & Fernández	2009	Up to 500 BU's	Meta-Heuristics: GRASP

a. Given a set V of BU's (city blocks or individual customers) for delivery of goods, we need to assign each BU to just one territory for delivery tasks. The firm wants to partition these BU's into a specific number of disjoint territories. The number of territories P is fixed and given as a parameter. These territories define a partition of V, which is represented by a subset of BU's $V_T \subset V$.

b. All BU's must be assigned fully to just one territory. It is not allowed to split BU's. For all BU's the route that delivers products type 1 should be the same as the one that is responsible for delivery of products type 2, 3, etc.

c. Each $BU\, i$ (where $i \in V$) has associated location coordinates $(X_i,\ Y_i)$. In addition, there are three quantifiable activity measures for each BU. We define $A=\{1,2,3\}$ as the set of activities measures for each BU. Let W^m_i be the value of activity m at the BU i, where $m \in A$. We define $m=1$ (number of customers), $m=2$ (sales volume), and $m=3$ (workload). The total activity measure for a territory is the sum up of the total BU's contained on that territory.

d. The firm wants to design territories that are balanced (similar in size). This balancing requirement exists to each of the three different activity measures individually and

Table 2. MHIP procedure for TDP

HMIP procedure for TDP
Input: Instance of the TDP
    Graph of adjacent (BU's contiguity) $\rightarrow G = (V, L)$
    Total set of network arcs. Euclidean distance between BU i and BU $j \rightarrow Dij$.
    Set of activity measures. Activity measure m for each BU $j \rightarrow W^m$
    Tolerance for territory balance on each activity measure $m \rightarrow T^m$
    Number of territories to be constructed $\rightarrow p$
(a) Pre-Processing Heuristic for Network Simplification:
Input: set heuristic parameter $F1$ for network simplification
Output: reduced set $R \rightarrow$ binary variables Xij, where $i,j \in V$, $Xij \in R$ and $R \subset D$
(b) MIP Model for Territory Centers Location:
Input: set heuristic parameter $F2$ for territory center strategy
    Output 1: subset P of BU's selected for territory centers (where $P \subset V$)
Output 2: reduced set $S \rightarrow$ variables Xij, where $i \in P \subset V, j \in V$, $Xij \in S$ and $S \subset R \subset D$
(c) MIP Model for BU's Allocation to Territory Centers:
Input: set heuristic parameter $F3$ for territory kernels
Integral assignments $\rightarrow$ binary variables Xij, where $i \in P \subset V, j \in V$, $Xij \in S$ and $S \subset R \subset D$
        $\Rightarrow$ **(1) if BU j is assigned to territory center i, (0) otherwise**
(d) Pre-assigned and forbidden BU's constraints
(e) Territory contiguity constraints
(f) Heuristic for fast convergence: set heuristic parameter $F4$.

---

simultaneously. In other words, the number of customers, volume of sales and workload of the BU's assigned to each territory should be evenly distributed among the workforce (i.e. territories).

e. An important feature is that all the customers (i.e. BU's) assigned to each territory should be contained totally within the territory. This is territory contiguity.

f. We have some pre-defined and/or forbidden joint assignments of BU's, so that specified pairs of BU's must (or must not) be assigned to the same territory. It means that from the beginning of the planning process we already have some BU's that require (or do not require) to be assigned to a specific territory.

g. The objective function is to minimize the territory dispersion. Formally we have as follows: *make an optimal and feasible partition of a set of BU's V into a number of P territories which satisfy the specified planning criterion of balance, compactness and contiguity.*

HMIP MODEL FOR TERRITORY DESIGN PROBLEM

We develop a new strategy based on a Hybrid-Mixed Integer Programming method (HMIP). From previous research work found in Ríos-Mercado and Fernandez (2009), we decided to model our TDP as a P-Median (i.e. p-MP) distance objective function. The p-MP objective is a good alternative to be used in TDP that have compact-ness as performance criterion. Before we detail out each step, we present our solution approach as follows on Table 2:

A. Pre-Processing Heuristic for Network Simplification

For explanation purposes, we start here from a quantity of 5000 BU's *(set V)* which constitutes the entire Monterrey metropolitan area. Each BU is represented by a node i. The problem is modeled by a graph. Let $G = (V, L)$ be an adjacent graph. An arc connecting nodes (i,j) exists in set L if BU's i and j are adjacent BU's (where $i,j \in V$). Each BU i is defined by a geographic location with coordinates *(Xi, Yi)*. Let's define *Dij* as the entire set of arcs that represents the distance between BU *i* and BU *j*. All BU's can be used as candidate location for final territories centers. We need to model the network *Dij* in order to identify a subset *P* of BU's (where $P \subset V$) that will be selected for territory centers. This is done by assigning each BU *j* to only one BU *i*. We can define that the total activity measure for a territory with center at BU *i* is the sum up of the total contained BU's *j* assigned to that territory (i.e. assigned to BU *i*). Ideally each territory *i* should have an average size for each activity measure *m*. The average of each activity measure *m* is defined as:

$$\mu^m = \sum_{j \in V} \frac{W_j^m}{p}, \forall m \in A, W_j^m = \text{activity measure}$$

of *m* of BU *j*, *p* = # of territories to construct

(1.1)

As an integer assignment problem, it is easy to verify that each arc on *Dij* would require a binary decision variable. We proceed now to reduce the complexity of our problem by limiting the number of relevant arcs on the original set *Dij*. For each BU *i* we identify a reduced sub set of *l* neighbor BU's with minimal Euclidean distance. We have now a reduced set of arcs *R* with size *i*l* (where $R \subset D$). The basic idea of our heuristic is to select a sub set of arcs from the network *Dij* in such a way that each element will not be greater than a certain upper bound. With this in mind, the problem can be solved more efficiently. We must assure that each relevant BU *j* has at least one arc on set *R* connecting to the entire network. If there is any BU without this connectivity feature, a subset of arcs should be added to set *R* if required. However, in our implementation we find that it is quite problematic to estimate in advance an appropriate set of arcs *R* that are required in order to keep the problem feasible. For that reason, we propose a special strategy for the upper bound used to define the set *R*. We implement in the model a

parameter *F1* that define an upper bound for each activity measure. Thus, the subset of BU's *l* that are considered for each BU *i* on set *R* depends not only on a minimal Euclidean distance but also considering an upper bound for each activity measure as well. Formally we define elements of set *R* as follows:

Define X_{ij} binary $\in R \subset D$, such that
$$\sum_{j \in V} X_{ij} W_j^m \cong F1 \mu^m, \forall i \in V, \forall m \in A\{1,2,3\} \quad (H1)$$

On the heuristic expression (H1), we define binary variables *Xij* until we reach the upper bound on the three activity measures. However the BU's *j* must be first sorted according to their Euclidean distance to the candidate territory center *i*. Thus, parameter *F1* can be defined in terms of the number of times we allocate BU's *j* to a given territory with center at BU *i*. Our problem definition considers three activity measures. For that reason, three upper bounds must be reached on each BU *i* before we stop to add arcs on set *R*. As a result we obtain a reduced set of decision variables *Xij*, where BU's *i,j* $\in V$, arcs *Xij* $\in R$ and $R \subset D$. Now, we introduce a new parameter *F2* that accounts for the *territory center strategy*. Parameter *F2* is the strategy that the model uses to calculate the optimal centers on the location stage. Parameter *F2=1* assures integral constraints on binary variable *Yi* only. Parameter *F2=2* assures integral constraints on binary variables *Yi* and *Xij* as well. Taking in mind that our initial instance has 5000 BU's, we can show now the following information on Table 3 for nonzero elements and binary variables that result from different combinations on values for parameter *F1* and *F2*. The last column is a ratio that indicates how many elements from original set *Dij* has being considered on the reduced subset *R*.

We can verify on Table 3 that the number of binary variables grows exponentially as long as we increase the value of parameter *F1*. If we set

Table. 3 Non-zero elements and binary variables as a function of parameters F1 and F2 for network simplification heuristic

F2 Territory center strategy 1 Int. Yi 2 Int. Yi, Xij	F1 Network Simplification	Nonzero Elements (Constraints and Variables)	Number of Binary Variables	Network Simplification Ratio: R / D
1	2.0	538,507	5,000	0.02%
1	4.0	1,062,085	5,000	0.02%
1	8.0	2,030,480	5,000	0.02%
2	2.0	538,507	92,628	0.37%
2	4.0	1,062,085	182,868	0.73%
2	8.0	2,030,480	350,941	1.40%

the parameter $F1$ equal to 4, this means that each BU i candidate for a territory center, will allocate BU's j in such a way that all activity measures sum up to 4 times the activity average defined for each territory on equation (1.1). In summary, the strategy we adopt is to decrease the solution search space into a new and less complex problem that can be solved more efficiently without a significant lost on optimality. This strategy reduces the search space because it decreases the number of possible candidates for territory centers selection. This trade-off on optimality is going to be detailed on the next section.

B. MIP Model for Territory Centers Location

We have a parameter p that defines the number of territories to be constructed. We proceed now to identify the subset P of BU's (where $P \subset V$) that will be selected for territory centers. We implement and solve a relaxed assignment MIP model in order to identify the BU's i to be selected as territory center. We use the subset R defined on the previous section to model this optimal location problem. Constraint (1.2) assures that each BU j is assigned to only one BU i. Constraint (1.3) assures that each BU j can be assigned to a BU i if and only if the BU i is selected as a territory center. Constraint (1.4) assures the creation of

exactly p territories. BU's j should be assigned to the territories centers i in such a way that all p territories constructed must be balanced. As can be verified, due to the discrete structure of the problem and the unique assignment constraint, it is practically impossible to have perfectly balanced territories with respect to each activity measure m. To overcome this difficulty we measure a balance degree by computing the *relative deviation* of each territory from its average size μ^m. Indeed, we consider a tolerance T^m for each activity measure m. Thus, parameter T^m on constraint (1.5) defines a lower bound that must be fully covered for each territory that is constructed. Upper bound for territorial balance is not considered on this stage since this MIP model is implemented just to find the optimal territory centers only. Integral assignments of BU j to BU i can be considered at this stage. As we mention before, parameter $F2=1$ assures integral constraints on binary variable Yi only. By the other hand, parameter $F2=2$ assures integral constraints on binary variables Yi and Xij as well.

Compact territories usually have geographically concentrated operation, therefore we can expect less travel and better service levels because we have more time available to attend the customers. Therefore, we model compactness as an objective function. In particular, we implement a P-median location model as the objective function on equation (1.6). Territory dispersity represents

Table 4. Trade-off on optimality as a function of parameters F1 and F2 for the territory centers location MIP model

F2 Territory center strategy 1 Int. Yi 2 Int. Yi, Xij	F1 Factor for Network Simplification	Number of Binary Variables	Simplex LP Relaxed Solution	Computational Minutes	Branch & Bound Solution	% Gap to Optimality	% Lost on Optimality
1	2.0	5,000	61.0747	10	61.3021	0.1977%	0.13%
1	4.0	5,000	61.0747	20	61.2212	0.2333%	0%
1	8.0	5,000	61.0747	20	61.2212	0.23%	0%
2	2.0	92,628	61.0747	10	62.9642	2.669%	1.08%
2	4.0	182,868	61.0747	20	62.2926	0.8998%	0%
2	8.0	350,941	61.0747	not finish	not finish	not finish	not finish

the sum of the Euclidean distances between each BU j and its center BU i. In this sense, minimizing dispersion is equivalent to maximizing compactness. Our territory centers location MIP model is presented as follows:

Parameters:

Dij = set of network arcs. Euclidean distance between BU i and BU j.

T^m = territorial tolerance (i.e. *lower bound*) for each activity measure m.

Decision Variables:

Yi binary $\Rightarrow$ (1) if BU i is defined as territory center, (0) otherwise. $\forall$ i $\in$ V

Xij binary $\Rightarrow$ (1) if BU j is assigned to BU i, (0) otherwise. $\forall$ i,j $\in$ V, $Xij \in R$, $R \subset D$

Subject to:

$$\sum_{i \in V} Xij = 1, \forall j \in V, Xij \in R, R \subset D \quad (1.2)$$

$$Xij \le Yi, \forall ij \in V, Xij \in R, R \subset D \quad (1.3)$$

$$\sum_{i \in V} Yi = p, \text{where } p = \text{number of territories to}$$
construct $\quad (1.4)$

$$\sum_{j \in V} Xij W_j^m \ge Yi \mu^m (1 - T^m), \forall i \in V, Xij \in R, R \subset D, \forall m \in A$$
$$(1.5)$$

$$\text{F.OBJ min} \sum_{i \in V} \sum_{j \in V} Xij Dij, Xij \in R, R \subset D$$
$$(1.6)$$

Taking in mind that our initial instance has 5000 BU's, we can show now the following information on Table 4. This table shows different combinations on values for parameter *F1* (network simplification) and parameter *F2* (territory center strategy). This table is useful to figure out how much optimality is lost as a trade-off of parameters *F1* and *F2*.

We can verify that the best solution found for *F1* = 2 is not very different from obtained for *F1* = 4. Even, if we assume integral assignments on variable *Xij* we obtain similar values on the objective function. Thus for gap optimality we have (62.9642 / 62.2926 − 1) equal to 1.08%. So, there is no significant lost on optimality. For integrality constrains applied just for variable *Yi* (parameter *F2* = 1), the lost on optimality is even much lower (0.13%). In Table 4, it is interesting to compare solution results depending if integral assignments for *Xij* are constrained or not. This is particularly true when we compare results obtained for *F1* = 4. We have 61.2212 on the objective function for not constrained case versus

62.2926 for integral constrained case. There is no significant difference on the gap to optimality reported on both cases and computational effort is comparable. However, it is plausible to determine that BU's selection for territory centers would be better when we set integral assignments on variables Xij. This comparison is going to be developed on the next section.

C. MIP Model for BUs Allocation to Territory Centers

For this allocation MIP model, we take only the BU's i that were defined as territory centers on the previous model. Let's define this subset of BU's i selected for territory centers as P, where $P \subset V$. It is easy to verify that set R can be simplified again filtering the partition of territory centers that were found on the previous model. Let's name this new reduced set as S, where $Xij \in S, S \subset R \subset D$. Moreover, as we have now a set of fixed territory centers P, thus we can heuristically assign a partition of geographic BU's j to the nearest territory center i where $i \in P$. This heuristic is implemented with a new parameter $F3$. Thus parameters $F1$ and $F3$, both are expressed in terms of the average of each activity measure defined on equation (1.1) for each territory. Particularly, parameter $F3$ is used as an upper bound to pre-assign (e.g. with a value of 1) a partial subset of binary arcs Xij of subset S. In other words, a partition of BU's j will be fixed as a kernel for a territory i. For example, if we set parameter $F3 = 0.5$, it means that each territory center i, will have some BU's j fixed assigned in such a way that each territory activity measure sum up to 0.5 times the average defined on equation (1.1). We test several values for the parameter $F3$. These results are shown afterwards on the next sections. Use of parameter $F3$ can be formally presented as follows:

Let $(Xij = 1) \subset S \subset R \subset D$, such that
$$\sum_{j \in V} Xij W_j^m \cong F3\mu^m, \forall i \in P, \forall m \in A\{1,2,3\} \quad (H2)$$

On the heuristic expression (H2), we set *(Xij = 1)* until we reach the upper bound for the three activity measures on each territory center i. However the BU's j must be first sorted according to their Euclidean distance to the territory center i. All BU's j should be integrally assigned to territories centers i in such a way that all p territories constructed must be well balanced. A set of constraints are defined on (2.2) to ensure that each territory is within a maximal deviation from the average target μ^m defined for each activity measure. These constraints assure that each activity measure is within predefined lower and upper bounds. Thus, the size of each territory must lie within a range (measured by tolerance T^m) around its average size μ^m. In particular, the upper bound on constraint (2.2) assures that if no territory center is placed at i, no BU j can be assigned to it. Constraint (2.1) assures that each BU j is assigned to one territory only. Formally we have our BU's allocation MIP model presented as follows:

Decision Variables:

Xij binary $\Rightarrow$ (1) if BU j is assigned to BU i, (0) otherwise. $\forall i \in P, j \in V, Xij \in S, S \subset R \subset D$

Subject to:

$$\sum_{i \in P} Xij = 1, \forall j \in V, Xij \in S, S \subset R \subset D$$
$$(2.1)$$

$$\mu^m(1-T^m) \leq \sum_{j \in V} Xij W_j^m \leq \mu^m(1+T^m), \forall i \in P, Xij \in S, \forall m \in A\{1,2,3\}$$
$$(2.2)$$

F. OBJ min $\sum_{i \in P} \sum_{j \in V} Xij Dij, Xij \in S, S \subset R \subset D$
$$(2.3)$$

D. Pre-Assigned and Forbidden BU's Constraints Modeling

As we point out before, we have some pre-defined and/or forbidden joint assignments of BU's, so that specified pairs of BU's must (or must not) be assigned to the same territory. It means that from the beginning of the planning process we already have some BU's that require (or do not require) to be assigned to a specific territory. Depending on the context of the requirement we can model it as a hard constraint or as an objective function. Geographical issues like rivers or mountains are modeled explicitly as hard constraints. We explicitly enumerate into a subset F all pairs of BU's that cannot be assigned on the same territory. Formally we have:

$$Xij + Xih \leq 1, \forall i \in P, \forall jh \in F \subset V, Xij \in S \subset D$$
$$(2.4)$$

By the other hand, pre-assigned or forbidden requirements that arise from business issues like territory realignment, we model it in the objective function. From the practical standpoint, the issue of territory realignment for the daily basis is an important area of opportunity for the company. The basic idea about any given current territory design is on how the model could efficiently accommodate for changes like customer's additions or dropouts trying not to disrupt the previous design considerably. Something similar happens for customers that may require to be visited on a specific day of the week or even on a different frequency per week. In all those cases specific information is input to the model as predefined assignments. Some of these pre-assignments may come from the actual territory design. Some others come from changes on customers demand. Let's define a subset E for all BU's with pre-assigned information. It is important to point out that in our implementation only a small proportion of the BU's is set up in this special subset E. This subset E never exceeds from 15% of the total

BU's. Subset E is implemented as a second component on the objective function. Moreover, we weight all BU's assignments on subset E with a parameter Mij. This parameter Mij is different from case to case and depends on how important is each pre-assigned BU j to a territory center i. We modeled as follows:

F. OBJ min

$$\sum_{i \in P} \sum_{j \in V} XijDij - \sum_{i \in P} \sum_{j \in V} MijXij, Xij \in S \subset D, Mij \in E$$
$$(2.5)$$

It is easy to verify that this formulation is not hard enough to prevent that some pre-assigned BU's may change. However, we formulate a hard constraint to assure that at least a proportion of these pre-assigned BU's can be assured (in this example we set a 10%). We modeled as follows:

$$\sum_{i \in P} \sum_{j \in V} Xij \geq 10\% \cdot |E|, Xij \in E \subset S \qquad (2.6)$$

E. Territory Contiguity Constraints Modeling

In order to obtain contiguous territories, explicit neighborhood information for the BU's is required to be considered on the MIP allocation model. The main difficulty we have here is that our problem has an exponential number of contiguity constraints, which makes it impossible to write them explicitly. Instead, our computational implementation incorporates this graph information based on a cut generation strategy. That is, iteratively we add some relevant cuts on the primal problem. The basic idea of our method is to recursively check for the contiguity constraints that are required to impose on each territory. For each iteration, the procedure evaluates if all the territories obtained satisfy the contiguity constraint. For each territory that violates this condition, we formulate additional geographic constraints in order to setup a new incremental model. This procedure iterates until no additional contiguity constraints are needed and therefore territory design problem is finally solved. Note that, a feasible solution to the relaxed previous model may yield unconnected territories. One way to reinforce the formulation of the relaxed model is by introducing the following constraint:

$$\sum_{q \in N^j} X_{iq} \geq X_{ij}, \forall i \in P, \forall j \in V, X_{ij} \in S \quad (2.7)$$

These valid inequalities can be interpreted as follows. If BU j is assigned to territory i at least one of the neighbors of BU j ($q \in N^j$) needs to be assigned to the same territory as BU j. These constraints avoid territories with just one single BU unconnected. The motivation for this constraint (2.7) comes from previous research work in Ríos-Mercado and Fernandez (2009). They show that optimal solutions of the relaxed model contain most of the unconnected subsets with cardinality equal to 1, that is where $|C| = 1$. In fact, we have a polynomial number of these constraints. So, we don't have to implement constraints (2.7) within a cut generation stage, instead these can be easily written from the beginning of the primal model. This strategy is chosen in order to speed up the procedure and converge on feasible solutions for most of the contiguity constraints. However our cut generation strategy, consider all the unconnected subsets with cardinality $|C| > 1$. Thus, we can model our cut generation strategy as follows:

$$\sum_{q \in N^c} X_{iq} - \sum_{j \in C} X_{ij} = 1 \mid C \mid, \forall i \in P, C_i \subset \{X_{ij} = 1\}, N^c = \bigcup_{j \in C} N^j, X_{ij} \in S \quad (2.8)$$

Constraints (2.8) guarantee the connectivity of the territories. It evaluates if a subset C contains a partition of BU's that are assigned to a territory center i but are disconnected from the rest of BU's assigned to the same territory. Cardinality of subset C ranges from 1 up to $H/2$, where H is the number of BU's assigned to the territory.

Subset N^c represents the union set of all BU's that are adjacent to any member of C. Constraint (2.8) operates very similar as constraint (2.7). At least one of the BU's q that are adjacent to any of the member of C must be assigned to the same territory i as it is with all the members of C. These constraints were proposed by Drexl and Haase in 1999 and are similar to the constraints used in routing problems to guarantee routes connectivity. Note that there are an exponential number of such constraints. For that reason this constraints are implemented within a cut generation stage. In summary, our model can be viewed as a P-median problem with multiple capacity and side constraints. Given that even the incapacitated vertex p-center problem is *NP*-hard, it follows that our TDP is also *NP*-hard. All the computational experiments we perform from here are done taking in consideration a value of *0.1%* for our solver *MIP optimality tolerance*. This optimality tolerance is set in the solver engine in order to identify a true near-optimal solution for each instance tested. Finally, it is important to point out about the territory tolerance for each activity measure (i.e. parameter T^m) that will be used for the solution preference. We set equal criterion on lower and upper bounds for the three activity measures around +10% and -10%.

We test the efficiency of our model with two values on parameter *F2* which accounts for the strategy that the model uses to calculate the optimal centers on the MIP model. Parameter *F2 = 1* assures integral constraints on variable *Yi* only. Parameter *F2 = 2* assures integral constraints on variables *Yi* and *Xij* as well. In order to compare the results for different values on parameter *F1* for territory centers location MIP model, we deploy the information in two tables. Specifically, table 5 corresponds to our results obtained for territory centers location MIP model with parameter *F1 = 2*. Table 6 results are for territory centers location MIP model with parameter *F1 = 4*. It is important to point out here that the effect of the parameter *F1* for territory centers location MIP

Table 5. Trade-off on optimality as a function of F1, F2 and F3 heuristic parameters at the BU's allocation MIP model (territory centers location MIP model with F1 = 2)

F2 Territory center strategy 1 Int. Yi 2 Int. Yi, Xij	F1 for Allocation BU's to Territory Centers	F3 Kernel for Territories	# of Iterations	Computational seconds	Branch & Bound Solution	% Lost on Optimality
1	3.0	0.55	49	121	63.0545	0.06%
1	3.0	0.25	33	116	63.0146	0.00%
1	3.0	0.10	51	195	63.017	0.00%
1	3.0	0.0	52	212	63.0165	0.00%
1	4.0	0.55	36	127	63.0592	0.07%
1	4.0	0.25	27	118	63.0209	0.01%
1	4.0	0.10	79	447	63.0195	0.01%
1	4.0	0.0	56	319	63.0209	0.01%
1	5.0	0.55	35	136	63.0512	0.06%
1	5.0	0.25	70	354	63.0188	0.01%
1	5.0	0.10	46	309	63.0164	0.00%
1	5.0	0.0	64	485	63.0191	0.01%
2	3.0	0.55	40	105	63.1659	0.24%
2	3.0	0.25	51	170	63.1541	0.22%
2	3.0	0.10	33	121	63.1501	0.22%
2	3.0	0.0	48	194	63.1555	0.22%
2	4.0	0.55	42	147	63.1723	0.25%
2	4.0	0.25	34	155	63.155	0.22%
2	4.0	0.10	47	236	63.1593	0.23%
2	4.0	0.0	82	584	63.1554	0.22%
2	5.0	0.55	49	194	63.1696	0.25%
2	5.0	0.25	36	191	63.1553	0.22%
2	5.0	0.10	39	239	63.1471	0.21%
2	5.0	0.0	64	471	63.16	0.23%

model is different from the effect on parameter *F1* for BU's allocation MIP model. Territory centers location MIP model does not consider all the side and contiguity constraints. By the other hand, BU's allocation MIP model takes a full consideration about all the required constraints including contiguity. We report now on Table 5 and Table 6, our results obtained with different values on parameters *F1*, *F2* and *F3*. As we can verify, depending on the setting we use for parameters *F1* and *F2* for the territory centers location

MIP model we can obtain different results on the optimality of BU's allocation MIP model. In the following we will analyze this impact.

Thus, with our results we can be able now to analyze some questions:

• How the parameter *F1* for territory centers location MIP model impacts on the BU's allocation optimality? Do we lose some optimality if we set a smaller value on *F1* for territory centers location MIP model?

Table 6. Trade-off on optimality as a function of F1, F2 and F3 heuristic parameters at the BU's allocation MIP model (territory centers location MIP model with F1 = 4)

F2 Territory center strategy 1 Int. Yi 2 Int. Yi, Xij	F1 for Allocation BU's to Territory Centers	F3 Kernel for Territories	# of Iterations	Computational seconds	Branch & Bound Solution	% Lost on Optimality
1	3.0	0.55	25	56	62.5027	0.01%
1	3.0	0.25	38	116	62.5056	0.02%
1	3.0	0.10	46	155	62.4972	0.00%
1	3.0	0.0	50	181	62.4978	0.00%
1	4.0	0.55	44	144	62.5011	0.01%
1	4.0	0.25	60	241	62.4986	0.00%
1	4.0	0.10	48	195	62.4972	0.00%
1	4.0	0.0	54	264	62.4957	0.00%
2	3.0	0.55	36	95	62.7553	0.42%
2	3.0	0.25	52	157	62.732	0.38%
2	3.0	0.10	110	396	62.7302	0.38%
2	3.0	0.0	35	123	62.7367	0.39%
2	4.0	0.55	41	142	62.7563	0.42%
2	4.0	0.25	52	218	62.7349	0.38%
2	4.0	0.10	53	239	62.7391	0.39%
2	4.0	0.0	53	251	62.7345	0.38%

- How much the parameter $F2$ for territory center strategy on the MIP location model impacts on the BU's allocation optimality? Do we gain some optimality on BU's allocation if we constraint variables Xij for integrality on the territory centers location MIP model?

- Do we lose some optimality on BU's allocation MIP model if we make a network simplification (parameter $F1$) and relax the integrality constraints (parameter $F2$) on the territory centers location MIP model?

From Tables 3 and 4 we can make some measures to synthesize our results. We average each indicator assuming that parameter $F3$ for kernel on territories affects in the same manner for the rest of the parameters. On Table 7 we present the average indicators for different combinations on parameters as following:

Finally from results indicated on Table 7 we can make the following assumptions:

- The parameter $F1$ for territory centers location impacts on the BU's allocation optimality. We can gain some optimality if we set a larger value on $F1$ for territory centers location (e.g. $F1 = 4$).

- The parameter $F2$ for territory center strategy impacts on the BU's allocation optimality. The territory centers location model can be relaxed on integrality constraints for variables Xij without any lost on optimality. In other words, we can set parameter $F2 = 1$.

Table 7. Average indicators on optimality for different combinations on heuristic parameters F1 and F2 at the BU's allocation MIP model (territory centers location MIP model with F1 = 2 and F1 = 4)

F1 for Territory Centers Location	F2 Territory center strategy 1 Int. Yi 2 Int. Yi, Xij	F1 for Allocation BU's to Territory Centers	# of Iterations	Computational seconds	Branch & Bound Solution	% Lost on Optimality
2	1	3	46.3	161.0	63.0257	0.84%
2	1	4	49.5	252.8	63.0301	0.85%
2	2	3	43.0	147.5	63.1564	1.05%
2	2	4	51.3	280.5	63.1605	1.06%
4	1	3	39.8	127.0	62.5008	0.00%
4	1	4	51.5	211.0	62.4982	0.00%
4	2	3	58.3	192.8	62.7386	0.38%
4	2	4	49.8	212.5	62.7412	0.39%

F. Heuristic for Fast Convergence

Our model presented on previous section with valid inequalities for contiguity constraints works fine in terms of processing time for instances up to 5000 BU's. Our model converges on feasible near-optimal solutions on less than 3 minutes in average and in some cases in less than 2 minutes. However, for larger instances up to 10,000 BU's we have computational times very large that are not practical for a business user application (more than an hour). Thus, we proceed to implement a new heuristic as part of the whole Hybrid MIP model. As was explained on previous section, for each iteration, our algorithm identifies violated contiguity constraints and adds these cuts to the model. After cuts are added to the basis and just before the algorithm iterates to solve the new basis of the problem, we implement some changes on the objective function. In fact, we add some penalize terms to the objective function. Two aspects must be analyzed for each BU in order to add a penalize term on the objective function: (1) contiguity and (2) compactness. Contiguity is easy to implement because was already evaluated for each BU on previous section. Indeed constraints (2.8) are added at each iteration for all the BU's that are disconnected. Let's define a dynamical parameter

Z_t as the number of BU's that are disconnected at each iteration t. This parameter is dynamical because the number of BU's disconnected changes at each iteration. In fact, it is expected that this parameter Z_t will reduce at each iteration as a result of constraints (2.8) which are added to the problem basis.

We add now a penalize term for all the BU's which are already connected. The basic idea of this heuristic is to feedback to the MIP objective function about which BU's j are already connected to a territory center i and no further changes are expected. Let's name this sub set of BU's already connected to territory center i as U, where $U \subset Xij$. Subset U is redefined at each iteration as well. Thus, subset U_{ij}^t is used to indicate to the MIP objective function about which BU's j are expected to maintain assigned to the actual territory center i with no further changes. Parameter Z_t is used to weight U_{ij}^t criterion on the objective function. As can be verified on equation (2.9), if we have a smaller value on parameter Z_t, the weight of U_{ij}^t criterion on the objective function will be larger. In other words, at any given iteration if we have a smaller number of BU's that are disconnected, the *current connected assignments* criterion on the objective function will be larger in order to rapidly converge. On this way, our objective function is now suffixed at each iteration as well (i.e. FO_t).

About compactness issue, the penalize term on the objective function for each BU j is inversely proportional to Dij. That is, as closer we have the distance of the BU j to the territory center i, larger will be the penalize term on the objective function in order to avoid any change on this assignment for the decision variable Xij. In other words, this pursuit to hold BU j assigned to the actual territory center i. The new objective function includes now a third component that is modeled as follows:

F. OBJ $_{(t)}$ min

$$\sum_{i \in P} \sum_{j \in V} Dij Xij - \sum_{i \in P} \sum_{j \in V} Mij Xij - F4 \sum_{i \in P} \sum_{j \in V} Uij^t Dij \, / \, Z_t$$

where: $Xij \in S, Mij \in E, Uij^t \subset Xij$ (2.9)

As can be verified on equation (2.9), our heuristic is implemented as a penalized function added to the MIP objective function just for U_{ij}^t *current connected assignments where $i \in P$ and $j \in V$.* This penalized function is redefined on each iteration t. It is easy to verify that subsets U_{ij}^t and Z_t are dynamic in nature and they are a function of the current connected BU's assignments to territory centers on the MIP problem. By the other hand, the parameter $F4$ weights the U_{ij}^t criterion on the objective function in a static mode. As we have a larger value in parameter $F4$ we enforce the MIP objective function to procure no different assignments on BU's to territory centers. This heuristic is true cost effective because we reduce the computational time for a feasible near-optimal solution. Obviously, if we set a value of zero for parameter $F4$ means that we cancel at all this special heuristic for fast convergence. No further cuts are added to the model as part of our heuristics. Thus, there is no space solution omitted on the branch & bound search tree.

We report now on Table 8, our results obtained with different values on $F1$, $F3$ and $F4$ parameters. We use the territory centers obtained from MIP location model with parameter $F1 = 4$ (network simplification) and parameter $F2 = 1$ (territory center strategy) as was pointed out from results of Table 7. Due to comparison reasons our results on Table 8 corresponds to the same set of instances of 5000 BU's that were considered on Tables 3, 4 and 5. Once again, optimality tolerance is set to 0.1% on the solver engine in order to identify a true near-optimal solution for each instance. The territory tolerance for each activity measure (i.e. parameter T^m) is set equally on lower and upper bounds for the three activity measures around +10% and -10%. It is important to let it know that our new dynamical objective function (see equation 2.9) has changed and for that reason cannot be directly compared with the original model (see equation 2.5). Thus, for gap optimality analysis we need to separate the fast convergence heuristic from the objective function. From here now, we will report all our results without the heuristic element on the objective function. With this in mind, we can make an appropriate comparison versus the original model.

From results on Table 8, it is very interesting to verify how fast a near-optimal solution can be found. The optimal solution is obtained in 264 seconds when we set the parameter $F4 = 0$ (i.e. no heuristic for fast convergence). The fastest solution time is found in 7 seconds. Combinations on parameters offer very short computational times that range from 7 to 45 seconds with an average of 17 seconds. All these computational times are very far away from the ones obtained on Tables 3, 4 and 5. Besides that and much more important we can verify that the problem can be solved more efficiently without a significant lost on optimality. Thus, our lost on optimality is less than 0.13% in average. On the next section we are going to deploy our full model including the fast convergence heuristic in order to solve a very large real world instance of 10000 BU's.

Table 8. Heuristic parameters F1, F3 and F4 for BU's allocation MIP model. Territory centers location obtained from MIP model with parameter F1 = 4 and parameter F2 = 1. Instance = 5000 BU's

F1 for Allocation BU's to Territory Centers	F3 Kernel for Territories	F4 for Fast Convergence	# of Iterations	Computational seconds	Branch & Bound Solution	% Lost on Optimality
3.0	0.55	10	8	10	62.5605	0.10%
3.0	0.25	10	9	11	62.628	0.21%
3.0	0.10	10	15	18	62.5937	0.16%
3.0	0.0	10	13	15	62.6166	0.19%
4.0	0.55	10	12	19	62.5409	0.07%
4.0	0.25	10	5	7	62.5454	0.08%
4.0	0.10	10	5	7	62.5454	0.08%
4.0	0.0	15	23	33	62.5951	0.16%
4.0	0.0	12	17	24	62.6067	0.18%
4.0	0.0	10	5	7	62.5454	0.08%
4.0	0.0	7	7	11	62.5499	0.09%
4.0	0.0	5	9	13	62.5682	0.12%
4.0	0.0	3	29	45	62.5682	0.12%
4.0	0.0	0 (optimal)	54	264	62.4957	0.00%

IMPLEMENTATION AND RESULTS

According to our H-MIP solution procedure previously presented, some input data is required to feed to the model. Thus, some tasks are necessary to consider:

- A Geo-database layer with the set of points representing the customers to group into territories. To develop this database was necessary to locate all customers using a GPS device. This data collection was accomplished by sales people thru hand held equipments. All the customers on the city of Monterrey (about 65000) were visited and points to every one of them were marked using a GPS device that received latitude and longitude coordinates.
- Eventually thru a very simple GIS application, all these customers were aggregated into a number of 10000 BU's. Each of these BU's corresponds to a physical block on the city of Monterrey.
- An Info-database layer containing the three activity measures (attributes) for each BU. As we mention before we have: (1) number of customers, (2) sales volume and (3) workload.
- Territory tolerance T^m for each activity measure used for the solution preference. We use equal criterion bounds for the three activity measures around +10% and -10%.
- The number of territories the end-user requires to construct.

We present now on Table 9 the computational results of our method for solving a very large scale instance of 10,000 BU's. For each combination with different values for parameters we measure the computational time required to optimize or at least achieve a feasible, near-optimal solution. CPU configuration used in our implementation was Win X32, 2 Intel Cores at 1.4GHz. We imple-

Table 9. Results for a 10000 BU's instance: heuristic parameters for the allocation MIP model. Territory centers location obtained from MIP model with parameter F1 set to 4 and parameter F2 set to

F1 for Allocation BU's to Territory Centers	F3 Kernel for Territories	F4 for Fast Convergence	# of Iterations	Computational seconds	Branch & Bound Solution	% Lost on Optimality
3	0.0	15	64	200	124.295	0.13%
3	0.0	10	53	182	124.222	0.07%
3	0.0	7	84	288	124.189	0.04%
3	0.0	5	54	237	124.15	0.01%
3	0.0	2 (optimal)	135	870	124.139	0.00%
3	0.10	20	136	413	124.297	0.13%
3	0.10	15	47	169	124.256	0.09%
3	0.10	12	75	242	124.372	0.19%
3	0.10	10	33	110	124.225	0.07%
3	0.10	9	41	143	124.209	0.06%
3	0.10	7	52	194	124.169	0.02%
3	0.10	5	47	203	124.171	0.03%
3	0.10	2	181	1242	124.146	0.01%
3	0.25	20	50	164	124.294	0.12%
3	0.25	15	25	83	124.226	0.07%
3	0.25	12	30	114	124.255	0.09%
3	0.25	10	29	113	124.248	0.09%
3	0.25	7	49	173	124.227	0.07%
3	0.25	5	60	233	124.185	0.04%
3	0.25	2	138	752	124.169	0.02%
3	0.50	50	305	891	124.732	0.48%
3	0.50	40	21	78	124.558	0.34%
3	0.50	20	61	189	124.473	0.27%
3	0.50	15	49	173	124.386	0.20%
3	0.50	12	48	152	124.442	0.24%
3	0.50	10	76	243	124.443	0.24%
3	0.50	7	79	284	124.312	0.14%
3	0.50	5	97	404	124.373	0.19%
3	0.50	3	107	502	124.318	0.14%
3	0.50	2	135	805	124.302	0.13%
3	0.50	1	193	2496	124.274	0.11%
4	0.0	10	33	168	124.232	0.07%
4	0.10	10	114	561	124.328	0.15%
4	0.25	10	57	244	124.256	0.09%
4	0.50	10	54	264	124.401	0.19%

ment our model on X-PRESS © MIP Solver from FICO™ (i.e. Fair Isaac, formerly Dash Optimization). The number of territories we use on this test is $P = 50$. Optimality tolerance is set to 0.1% on the solver engine in order to identify a true near-optimal solution for each instance. For this BU's allocation MIP model we use the territory centers obtained from the MIP location model with parameter $F1 = 4$ and parameter $F2 = 1$. The territory tolerance for each activity measure (i.e. parameter T^m) is set equally on lower and upper bounds for the three activity measures around +10% and -10%. We test some combinations for different values on heuristic parameters $F1$ (network simplification), $F3$ (kernel for territories) and $F4$ (fast convergence). Results are presented as following:

As we can verify on Table 9, large values for parameter $F4$ results on short computational times. We obtain computational times around 206 seconds in average for instances with parameter $F4 \geq 7$. By the other hand, we have computational times around 583 seconds in average for $1 < F4 < 7$. Particularly when we set the parameter $F4 = 1$ (i.e. a small value), we observe a very large computational time (up to 2496 seconds). However, we can verify that all branch & bound solutions obtained are very similar. We obtain branch & bound solutions around 124.3048 in average for instances with parameter $F4 \geq 7$. By the other hand, we have branch & bound solutions around 124.2227 in average for $1 \leq F4 < 7$. Thus, our lost on optimality is less than 0.07% in aver-

age. In other words, practically there is no optimality lost when the parameter $F4$ is used to speed up the solution time for a feasible near-optimal solution. In order to show the behavior of our model in terms of solution quality versus computational time we graph the following measures: (1) unconnected BU's, (2) unconnected territories, (3) cuts added and (4) objective function value. Several instances are graphed as is indicated on Table 10.

As it can be verified on figures 1-2, the first two runs with a very high value on parameter $F4$ have a similar behavior. The number of unconnected BU's, unconnected territories and cuts added on the MIP model are reducing as the computational time is in progress. Something similar happens with the objective function value but in a growing sense. We average here 124.7965 in the objective value. On the other two cases (figures 3-4) with a lower value on parameter $F4$, we have a very different behavior. Particularly, the objective function value moves slowly as the computational time take place. Indeed, this is the reason why we average here a lower value (124.2395) in the objective function. In this comparison analysis we have up to 0.62% on the optimality lost. Either way, it is important to point out that our methodology presents a MIP model that ensures integral assignments at each iteration all the time. Thus, it is interesting to verify how rapidly our heuristic implemented on the allocation MIP model can evolve and converge on cuasi-connected solutions (see Figures 1-4). How-

Table 10. Cross-reference figures for a 10000 BU's instance. Parameter T^m defined equally on lower and upper bounds for the three activity measures around +10% and -10%

Figure No.	F1 for Allocation BU's to Territory Centers	F3 Kernel for Territories	F4 for Fast Convergence	Computational seconds	Branch & Bound Solution	% Lost on Optimality
1	3	0.25	50	138	124.688	0.44%
2	3	0.25	35	226	124.905	0.62%
3	3	0.25	25	258	124.310	0.14%
4	3	0.10	7	191	124.169	0.02%

ever, a future research opportunity exists in order to prove the viability of this paradigm when gap optimality is required to confirm.

We test now the efficiency of our model with a smaller territory tolerance. Parameter T^m is now defined equally on lower and upper bounds for the three activity measures around +5% and -5%.

This new value for parameter T^m is much narrower than the previous one. Thus, we have a very large scale instance with a very narrow territory tolerance. This makes the problem extraordinarily difficult to solve. Our results are presented on Table 11 as follows.

Figure 1. Model's behavior in terms of solution quality versus computational time. F3 = 0.25, F4 = 50.

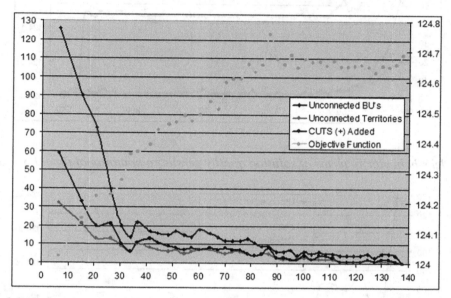

Figure 2. Model's behavior in terms of solution quality versus computational time. F3 = 0.25, F4 = 35.

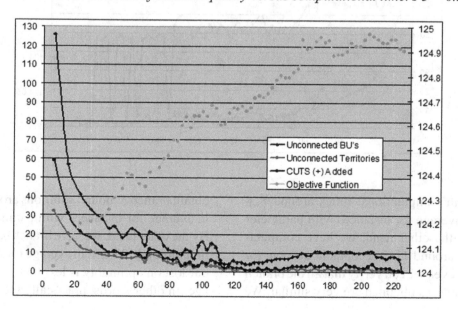

Figure 3. Model's behavior in terms of solution quality versus computational time. F3 = 0.25, F4 = 25.

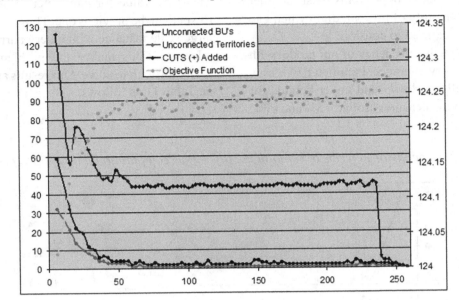

Figure 4. Model's behavior in terms of solution quality versus computational time. F3 = 0.10, F4 = 7.

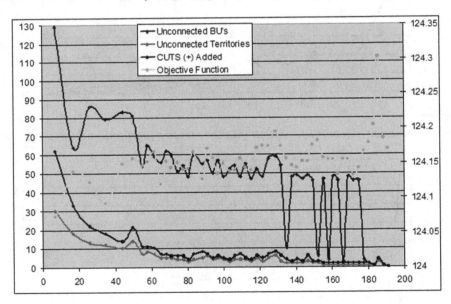

We obtain computational times around 828 seconds in average for instances with parameter $F4 \geq 7$. By the other hand, we have computational times around 1112 seconds in average for $F4 < 7$. However, we can verify that all the branch & bound solutions obtained are very similar. We obtain branch & bound solutions around 127.709 in average for instances with parameter $F4 \geq 7$. By the other hand, we have branch & bound solutions around 127.572 in average for $F4 < 7$. Thus, our lost on optimality is less than 0.11% in average. In other words, practically there is no opti-

Table 11. Results for a 10000 BU's instance with parameter T^m defined equally on lower and upper bounds for the three activity measures around +5% and -5%

F1 for Allocation BU's to Territory Centers	F3 Kernel for Territories	F4 for Fast Convergence	# of Iterations	Computational seconds	Branch & Bound Solution	% Lost on Optimality
3	0.10	15	478	1697	127.929	0.31%
3	0.10	10	154	812	127.698	0.13%
3	0.10	7	100	545	127.626	0.07%
3	0.10	5	61	694	127.532	0.00%
3	0.10	3	75	2261	127.543	0.01%
3	0.25	15	55	424	127.633	0.08%
3	0.25	10	54	689	127.77	0.19%
3	0.25	7	45	800	127.595	0.05%
3	0.25	5	35	615	127.587	0.04%
3	0.25	3	54	874	127.626	0.07%

mality lost when the parameter *F4* is used to speed up the solution time for a feasible near-optimal solution.

After the solution generation, the proposed solution and its compactness measurements can be visually displayed on MAPINFO © GIS application. Due to clearness convenience, we report the geographical output for our 5000 BU's instance of Monterrey metropolitan area. On figure 5 we graph 50 Territories. Each territory complies within (+/-) 5% tolerance for the parameter T^m (i.e. from 95% up to 105%). This is in reference to the μ^m target that we define for each activity measure. Contiguity and compactness properties can be verified for each territory obtained.

The legend besides the graph indicates the number of BU's contained on each territory. As expected, we don't find any balancing representation regarding this measure because it was not considered an activity measure in our problem definition.

ACHIEVEMENTS AND SAVINGS

We integrate our model into an advanced interactive tool based on MAPINFO © application.

Thus, we achieve a practical functionality to the end-users. This GIS environment can be used in different contexts. At the operational level, it represents a valuable tool to quickly produce and deploy different solutions. At the tactical level it can be used to simulate alternative scenarios and evaluate the impact of changes in territories. It is important to point out the interest of the end users about how our model can easily take the already existing territories into account. Particularly, the model is ready prepared to consider any prescribed and forbidden territory centers. This means that one can impose some fixed territory centers or BU's allocations to territory centers, which have to be taken into account, or, in the other way, that cannot be allowed to be selected. Thus all these features can be extended for any case when some territory information is present at the beginning of the planning process. The issue of territory realignment is an important area of opportunity because it is crucial for customer's satisfaction of the firm. Thus, the company evaluates how our model efficiently accommodates for system changes like customer's additions or dropouts trying not to disrupt the previous design considerably.

From business standpoint, our TDP application was developed and implemented at Embotellado-

Figure 5. Geographic results for a Territory Design Problem applied on Monterrey city with 5000 BU's

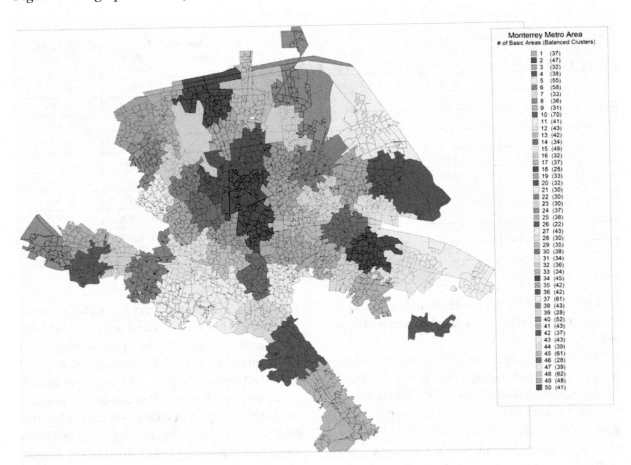

ras ARCA in order to optimize the distribution operation to the end customers. During the last years, the firm was interested in developing a better territory and routing plan for the distribution operation to end customers. In fact, this is the first operation research (OR) application that has been implemented in ARCA. The company point out that the overall results have been very positive. The firm's top management recognize that features included in the OR model implemented are truly outstanding. The project was a major undertaking, requiring a great deal of thought and effort. The first plans for territory design suggested by the optimization model were implemented eight months ago. Throughout the ramp-up and launch

of the project, those plans for distribution operation were analyzed. Sometime after, the project has resulted in a significant increase in productivity and direct savings to the firm. We can list some of the benefits that the company has achieved within this project:

- The firm identifies now a rational set of activity measures to target and balance on each truck resource. This results on an optimal fleet of trucks, drivers and sales people.
- An increase in efficiency and effectiveness on the planning process required to set up territory and route designs. The typical fully-manual planning process time was

reduced from 2 weeks to less than an hour using the new OR application. This permitted the company to refine its capacity each season on a dynamic basis. As a result the company achieves an optimal capacity to attend demand on each territory with an optimization of 30 delivery routes on the Monterrey metropolitan area. This represents a 15% reduction from the original number of routes.

- Streamline truck capacity to align it to a new end customer distribution strategy. The added throughput allows the firm to defer investments on trucks and other equipments that were originally allocated. The save on investments for trucks was about 8% of the entire fleet.

- Identify and implement an optimal cost of service depending on each route model type. This allowed the firm to set an optimal frequency for customer delivery operations. This means less travel time between customers and 5% increase in volume delivered per route per day.

- As a result of our contiguity constraining featured model, there are no more territory overlaps and the territories are now better geographically defined. It is now easy to decide which sales worker would be responsible when new customers appears (and for dropouts too). They have been able to better define areas of responsibility and loading.

- As a result of our compactness objective featured model, the territories are more compact so the total travel time decreased, improving the productivity of the distribution people. According to the compactness measurement, the managers decided to rationalize the number of trucks available to the distribution people.

- Our model deals with a small territory tolerance on lower and upper bounds for the three activity measures around +/-5%. The

"after alignment" structure is much better balanced than the former one. The standard deviation of the "number of customers per territory" or the "level of workload for each salesman" decreased 24% in average. This alignment allows making an increase in the level of service to the end customers on the marketplace. An increase on sales at the 3% is estimated as direct benefit of the new territory alignment.

Besides all these business benefits, the new OR model will allow the company to speed up some others "Route to Market" initiatives which are of special interest among Coca Cola bottlers around the world. The proposed model approach can extend the basic problem to address different specific business rules or additional planning criterion. This can easily be modeled as activity measures on the BU's. Overall, we have provided a very valuable tool for a more efficient territory design planning according to the company business requirements. Our model is ready prepared to deal with very large instances, even larger than 10000 BU's. Nowadays, our model is being used by the firm to obtain a business solution with significant benefits.

MODEL APPROACH CONTRIBUTION AND APPLICABILITY

We think that districting problems are multi-criteria in nature, thus we avoided to state a single holistic model. As can been seen in our background section, there are a lot of applications, each being slightly different from the other, requiring a different model. The same argumentation applies to the objective(s). The solutions are case-specific, since each one of them has its own constraints and objectives, making it virtually impossible to create an algorithm that can be applied to all TDP applications. Rather, we present building blocks of a broad applicability. In TDP is very application related to identify which criteria are viewed as a (hard) constraints and which should be optimized. Hence, we don't want to restrict to a specific objective. Moreover, the model we present is flexible enough to cope with different combinations of objectives and constraints that are very common to find on typical TDP problems. Particularly, our method is not focused on minimize the total activity measure deviation for each territory. Instead, our P-median objective function is focused to minimize the total geographic distance that exists on each territory (i.e. maximizes compactness). The model we present try to achieve the different goals in a heuristic fashion. The novelty of our model approach presented in this chapter is the combination of 3 basic components that interact in order to solve effectively the TDP. The three components are:

- A pre-processing heuristic to create a network simplification for the TDP that reduce the search space. We prove that this heuristic has a minimal impact on the optimal solution.
- A MIP model to define near optimal location for territory centers. Here we relax some side and contiguity constraints.
- A hybrid MIP model to define near optimal BU's allocation to territory centers. Contiguity constraints are fully considered within an iterative cut strategy framework. Some heuristics are considered within this model in order to speed up the MIP search for a feasible near optimal solution.

We are aware that working with a point–representation of the BU's could lead to problems with the compactness of the territories. For that reason we prefer to work from the beginning with BU's represented by polygons (see figure 5). The idea to include only a small percentage of the possible links (subset $X_{ij} \in S$ and $S \subset R \subset D$) as decision variables in the MIP allocation model is based on a distance criterion. However this heuristic is not robust at all to handle all the cases. Indeed,

it is quite problematic to estimate in advance the number of links necessary for each BU in order to assure the allocation model feasibility. For arbitrarily chosen territory center locations any type of assumptions cannot be made. Thus, one of the main contributions of our work is to develop a model that is stable on input data in order to find a way to dismiss enough links to make the solution of the MIP allocation model very efficient. In order to accomplish that goal some heuristics are developed (see expressions *H1* and *H2*). Both heuristics are implemented very successfully for our territory centers location model and also for the BU's allocation model.

A main contribution of our work is the implementation of contiguity constraints. Particularly our implementation is based on a cut generation strategy. Empirical results show the efficiency of these valid inequalities to constraint connected territories. To the best of our knowledge, this is the first time that these valid constraints are implemented for instances of comparable size. In addition, we take advantage that solutions obtained from the relaxation of the P-median based model have a very high degree of connectivity. Thus, a very few iterations are needed to find connected solutions as opposed to the P-center based models. In addition, our model is suitable to handle different values on lower and upper tolerances for each activity measure (i.e. parameter T^m) which is very common in real world TDP applications. Our implementation indicates that the considered model provides with an appropriate trade-off for the various activity measures that are considered. All these features are very important if we consider how easy this model could be extended to other cases.

The proposed model not only addresses the difficulties embedded in the TDP problem but also some practical concerns about pre-defined and/or forbidden joint assignments of BU's. Pre-assigned or forbidden requirements arise from business issues like territory realignment. From the practical standpoint, the issue of territory realignment is as how the model could efficiently accommodate for changes like customer's additions or dropouts trying not to disrupt the previous design considerably. Moreover, geographic obstacles can be easily handled in our approach by delivering neighboring information of incumbent BU's to the allocation MIP model. With respect to our industrial experience as well as the end-users thoughts at Embotelladoras ARCA, we believe that our model can be applied in quite different settings like sales territories, locations of new stores in a chain and delivery areas for distribution.

We believe that our main contribution in present work is the incorporation of the special heuristic for fast convergence on the BU's allocation MIP model (see equation 2.9). This dynamic objective function approach is crucial to solve very large scale instances beyond 10,000 BU's when solution time is critical. To the best of our knowledge, there is no previous work on heuristics or meta-heuristics that can handle efficiently this scale of instances. Either way, it is important to point out that our methodology presents a MIP model that ensures integral assignments at each iteration all the time. Thus, it is interesting to verify how rapidly this heuristic implemented on the allocation MIP model can evolve and converge on quasi-connected solutions (see figures 1-4). However, a future research opportunity exists in order to prove the viability of this paradigm when gap optimality is required to confirm. Our computational results are only to give some evidence to our arguments. They are not intended to be an in-depth comparison of available methods for TDP. Finally, it is true the convenience we achieve when we integrate our OR model into a GIS environment application in order to complete a territory design framework. Clearly territory design process cannot be completely automated, but GIS is an appropriate tool to help in this process. However, a pure GIS does not offer much support for the design and optimization of the territories. Therefore a hybrid combination of heuristics and MIP exact models for optimization are required. We think that this

kind of optimization featured applications will be the future trend on GIS industry.

CONCLUSION

This chapter has addressed the territory design problem as a critical component of the operational planning process in sales and services companies. Many logistics problems found in service industry can be modeled as a TDP problem. TDP problems are multidisciplinary and have been widely studied in the operations research literature. However, solving a real world TDP possesses a significant challenge for both researchers and practitioners. A real world TDP problem includes many business rules and logic that are beyond those addressed in mathematical models in literature. In particular, there are some business rules like contiguity that cannot be easily modeled. A particular emphasis is given to a business application case at Embotelladoras ARCA. With a real world application from the service industry, we present a rich featured TDP model. We include some extensions that are very common to some of the problems encountered in industry. Because of the characteristics of a TDP, it is also challenging to solve it within a reasonable computational time based upon the concrete business requirement. Furthermore, field people who are going to deploy the solution of a TDP may have to pay more attention to the feasibility of the solution in practice than a pure optimal solution in terms of mathematics.

TDP is NP-hard since we can reduce the well-known Partition Problem to it. Within OR various algorithmic approaches have been proposed, some based on integer linear programming, others on classical heuristics and, more recently, on some meta-heuristics. Real-world instances of this NP-hard combinatorial optimization problem are very large, so exact methods have failed even for relatively medium-size instances. In fact, demand points are first aggregated into small groups (i.e. BU's) that serve as the basis for the construction of final territories. As a result, depending on the level of detail or aggregation, we can reduce the mathematical complexity of the problem.

Our TDP instance is motivated by a real world application in the soft drink industry. In particular, it is of interest to deal with very large scale instances. Several different objectives and constraints in the territory design process are identified and discussed. In order to tackle these simultaneous and conflicting objectives, a hybrid approach has been developed to accommodate to the particular business requirements. Some heuristics and optimization techniques we use to solve the TDP more effectively are discussed in detail. We present the components of the model and a step-by-step description of the solution procedure. In particular, we implement a minimal dispersion TDP based on a P-Median objective function. We extend some previous approaches and propose a new adaptation to handle multiple balancing constraints. An important contribution of our work is the implementation of contiguity constraints. Particularly our implementation is based on a cut generation strategy. Empirical results show the efficiency of these valid inequalities to constraint connected territories.

The main contribution for the present work is the incorporation of a special heuristic for fast convergence on the BU's allocation MIP model. Without this heuristic we can solve to optimality only instances not greater than 5000 BU's. For gap optimality comparison we implement this heuristic first on instances of 5000 BU's. The optimal solution is obtained in 264 seconds when we set the parameter $F4 = 0$ (i.e. no heuristic for fast convergence). The fastest solution time is found in 7 seconds. All combinations on parameters offer very short computational times that range from 7 to 45 seconds with an average of 17 seconds. Thus, it is very interesting to verify how fast a near-optimal solution is found with this heuristic. We verify that the problem is solved more efficiently without a significant lost on optimality; less than 0.13% in average.

This heuristic approach is crucial to solve very large scale instances beyond 10000 BU's. Experimental results show the effectiveness of this heuristic in finding good-quality solutions in reasonably short computation times. We implement this heuristic first for a deviation tolerance $T^m = 10\%$. We obtain solution times around 206 seconds in average for instances with parameter $F4 \geq 7$ and 583 seconds in average for $1 < F4 < 7$. Branch & bound solutions obtained are very similar, 124.3048 in average for the first case and 124.2227 in average for the second case. Thus, our lost on optimality is less than 0.07% in average. Practically there is no lost on optimality when the parameter $F4$ is used to speed up the solution time for a feasible near-optimal solution. Latter on we implemented this heuristic for a deviation tolerance $T^m = 5\%$. We obtained similar results for a lost on optimality less than 0.11% in average.

In summary, our model is capable of solving very large-scale real world TDP problems, and results are closer to real practice and accepted by user people. We solve instances of 10000 BU's in 222 seconds in average for parameter $T^m = 10\%$ and 684 seconds in average for parameter $T^m = 5\%$. Practically there is no lost on optimality when the parameter $F4$ is used to speed up the solution time for a feasible near-optimal solution. The outcomes demonstrate the effectiveness and economic benefits of the proposed model. The potential of the proposed approach as a practical and readily implementable tool decision is also demonstrated. To the best of our knowledge, no hybrid MIP schemes have been ever developed for instances of comparable size. However, a future research opportunity exists in order to prove the viability of this paradigm when gap optimality is required to confirm. Finally, we conclude that all districting problems are multi-objective in nature. Depending on the specific application we can define which attributes may be modeled as hard constraints and which should be optimized.

REFERENCES

Altman, M. (1998). *Districting Principles and Democratic Representation.* Pasadena, California: PhD, California Institute of Technology.

Bacao, F., Lobo, V., & Painho, M. (2005). Applying genetic algorithms to zone design. *Soft Computing, 9*(5), 341–348. doi:10.1007/s00500-004-0413-4

Bergey, P.K., & Ragsdale, C.T. and Hoskote. (2003). M.: A simulated annealing genetic algorithm for the electrical power districting problem. *Annals of Operations Research, 121,* 33–55. doi:10.1023/A:1023347000978

Blais, M., Lapierre, S. D., & Laporte, G. (2003). Solving a Home-Care Districting Problem in an Urban Setting. *The Journal of the Operational Research Society, 54,* 1141–1147..doi:10.1057/palgrave.jors.2601625

Bozkaya, B., Erkut, E., & Laporte, G. (2003). A tabu search heuristic and adaptive memory procedure for political districting. *European Journal of Operational Research, 144*(1), 12–26. doi:10.1016/S0377-2217(01)00380-0

Browdy, M. H. (1990). Simulated Annealing: An Improved Computer Model for Political Redistricting. *Yale Law & Policy Review, 8*(1), 163–179. Retrieved from http://www.jstor.org/stable/40239326.

Caro, F., Shirabe, T., Guignard, M., & Weintraub, A. (2004). School redistricting: embedding GIS tools with integer programming. *The Journal of the Operational Research Society, 55*(8), 836–849. doi:10.1057/palgrave.jors.2601729

Crescenzi, P., & Kann, V. (1998). *A compendium of NP optimization problems: Dipartimento di Scienze della Informazione.* Uinversita di Roma La Sapienza.

D'Amico, S. J., Wang, S.-J., Batta, R., & Rump, C. M. (2002). A Simulated Annealing Approach to Police District Design. *Computers & Operations Research, 29*(6), 667–684. doi:10.1016/S0305-0548(01)00056-9

Ferland, J. A., & Gu'enette, G. (1990). Decision Support System for a School Districting Problem. *Operations Research, 38,* 15–21. doi:10.1287/opre.38.1.15

Fleischmann, B., & Paraschis, J. N. (1988). Solving a Large Scale Districting Problem: A Case Report. *Computers & Operations Research, 15*(6), 521–533..doi:10.1016/0305-0548(88)90048-2

Forman, S., & Yue, Y. (2003). Congressional districting using a TSP-based genetic algorithm. In E. Cantú-Paz et al., (ed), *Genetic and evolutionary computation – GECCO 2003. Genetic and evolutionary computation conference,* Chicago, IL, USA, July 12-16, Proceedings, Part II. Berlin: Springer. (LNCS, Vol. 2724 (2003) 2072-2083).

Forrest, E. (1964). Apportionment by computer. *The American Behavioral Scientist, 8*(4), 23–25.. doi:10.1177/000276426400800407

Garfinkel, R. (1968). *Optimal Political Districting.* Ph.D. Thesis, John Hopkins University.

Grilli di Cortona, P., Manzi, C., Pennisi, A., Ricca, F., & Simeone, B. (1999). *Evaluation and Optimization of Electoral Systems.* SIAM Monographs on Discrete Mathematics and Applications. doi:10.1137/1.9780898719819

Hanafi, S., Freville, A., & Vaca, P. (1999). Municipal Solid Waste Collection: An Effective Data Structure for Solving the Sectorization Problem with Local Search Methods. *INFOR, 37,* 236–254.

Haugland, D., Ho, S. C., & Laporte, G. (2007). Designing delivery districts for the vehicle routing problem with stochastic demands. *European Journal of Operational Research, 180,* 997–1010. doi:10.1016/j.ejor.2005.11.070

Hess, S.W. and Samuels, S.A. (1971). Experiences with a sales districting model: criteria and implementation. *Management Science, 18,* (4-Part II), 41-54. Doi: 10.1287/mnsc.18.4.P41

Hojati, M. (1996). Optimal political districting. *Computers & Operations Research,* 23(12), 1147-1161. Doi: doi:10.1016/S0305-0548(96)00029-9

Kalcsics, J., Nickel, S., & Schröder, M. (2005). Towards a unified territorial design approach - Applications, algorithms and GIS integration. *Sociedad de Estadística e Investigación Operativa TOP, 13*(1), 1–74. doi:.doi:10.1007/BF02578982

Kirkizoglu, Z. (2005). *A Genetic Algorithm Approach for Sales Territory Alignment Problem.* Paper presented at the 35th International Conference on Computers and Industrial Engineering, Istanbul.

Klose, A., & Drexl, A. (2005). Facility location models for distribution system design. *European Journal of Operational Research, 162*(1), 4–29. doi:10.1016/j.ejor.2003.10.031

Lorena, L. A. N., & Senne, E. L. F. (2004). A column generation approach to capacitated p-median problems. *Computers & Operations Research, 31*(6), 863–876. doi:10.1016/S0305-0548(03)00039-X

Mehrotra, A., Johnson, E. L., & Nemhauser, G. L. (1998). An Optimization Based Heuristic for Political Districting. *Management Science, 44*(8), 1100–1114..doi:10.1287/mnsc.44.8.1100

Muyldermans, L., Cattrysse, D., van Oudheusden, D., & Lotan, T. (2002). Districting for Salt Spreading Operations. *European Journal of Operational Research, 139,* 521–532. doi:10.1016/S0377-2217(01)00184-9

Ricca, F., & Simeone, B. (1997). Political Districting: Traps, Criteria, Algorithms and Tradeoffs. *Ricerca Operativa AIRO, 27,* 81–119.

Ríos-Mercado & Fernández. (2009). A reactive GRASP for a commercial territory design problem with multiple balancing requirements. *Computers & Operations Research, 36*(3), 755–776. doi:10.1016/j.cor.2007.10.024

Senne, E. L. F., Lorena, L. A. N., & Pereira, M. A. (2005). A branch-and-price approach to p-median location problems. *Computers & Operations Research, 32*(6), 1655–1664. doi:10.1016/j.cor.2003.11.024

Taillard, É. D. (2003). Heuristic Methods for Large Centroid Clustering Problems. *Journal of Heuristics, 9*(1), 51–73. doi:10.1023/A:1021841728075

Vargas-Suarez. Rios-Mercado, & López-Perez. (2005). Usando GRASP para resolver un problema de definición de territorios de atención comercial. In M. G. Arenas, F. Herrera, M. Lozano, J. J. Merelo, G. Romero, & A. M. Sánchez, (eds). *Proceedings of the IV Spanish Conference on Metaheuristics, Evolutionary and Bioinspired Algorithms (MAEB),* pages 609-617,Granada, Spain, September 2005.

Zoltners, A. A., & Shinha, P. (2005). Sales Territory Design: Thirty Years of Modeling and Implementation. *Marketing Science, 24*(3), 313–331.. doi:10.1287/mksc.1050.0133

Zoltners, A. A., & Sinha, P. (1983). Toward a unified territory alignment: a review and model. *Management Science, 29*(11), 1237–1256. doi:10.1287/mnsc.29.11.1237

KEY TERMS AND DEFINITIONS

Compactness: The spatial property of being closes and firmly united (i.e. having the minimum distance between all the entities of a given area).

Contiguity: Continuous connection of a series of entities, a grouping of parts connected throughout an unbroken sequence and sharing a common border.

Geographic Information System: Computer-based system for collecting, storing, editing, mapping, visualizing and analyzing spatial data.

Meta-Heuristic: Advanced heuristic optimization techniques that serve as guidelines for various searchprocedures and attempt to perform a more effective search over the solution space of the problem of interest.

Sales-Force: Company people who execute several activities related to the marketing function and are a crucial connection between the companies and their customers.

Territory Alignment: The process of shaping and balancing small geographic units and grouping them in such a way that they completely cover a given territory under analysis, based on criteria important to a business or activity.

Territory Design: Planning of territories, measuring and allocating resources to each of them, so as to completely cover a region, in the most efficient and effective manner, according to criteria related to the type of activity in question.

Chapter 12
Hybrid Heuristics for the Territory Alignment Problem

Jorge Freire de Sousa
Universidade do Porto, Portugal

José A. Barros-Basto
Universidade do Porto, Portugal

Paulo Lima Júnior
Universidade do Vale do São Francisco, Brazil

ABSTRACT

The territory alignment problem is part of a bigger procedure, the territory design, which consists of assigning small geographic regions to larger areas following the most relevant criteria for planning. This chapter aims to briefly update the review of the existing literature on the territory alignment problem, its applications and solution approaches, and to illustrate the most recent tendencies by means of a hybrid meta-heuristic developed by the authors.

The approach is based in GRASP and Tabu Search meta-heuristics. The algorithm was integrated in an interactive and user-friendly Geographic Information System application, named MultiACE, also developed in the context of this study. This application was embedded in the ArcGIS software.

This chapter also illustrates the potential of the proposed approach as a practical and readily implementable management decision aid in the context of a current case that involved the maintenance team of a Portuguese regional office of a worldwide equipment company.

DOI: 10.4018/978-1-61350-086-6.ch012

1 INTRODUCTION

The territory alignment problem (TAP) is part of a bigger procedure, the territory design, which consists of assigning small geographical regions to larger areas following the most relevant criteria for planning.

The territory design problem, that also has been referred to in the literature as the territory project, the automatic zoning design, the land allocation, the (re)districting, the region partitioning and the geographic deployment, is an important problem that is present in a great number of geographic projects and has potential application in various subjects, for instance, the establishment of political districts, location of schools, trash collection, social services (health centers, hospitals, etc.), emergency services, sales and distribution of products and maintenance teams. A quite interesting evaluation of the several areas of application of the territory design can be found in (Kalcsics, Nickel, & Schroder, 2005).

There are many ways of assigning small geographic regions to larger areas or, in other words, of defining a zoning system. The criteria for defining a meaningful zoning system lie in the purpose of the studies and depend on the experience of the zone designer. The zoning criteria are often guided by the problem specifications or restricted by the available data. Depending on the problem context, a careful partition of a territory may represent an increase of efficiency of an activity, a better workload balance or a shorter distance covered.

In the problem of electoral districting, probably the most well known case of the TAP, aside from its obviously political aspect, the process must be evaluated against specified redistricting criteria. For instance, some of the criteria are constitutionally required while other geographical and political concerns may be advocated. Electoral districting consists of the partitioning of administrative units into a predetermined number of zones (districts) such that the units in each zone are contiguous, each zone is geographically compact and the sum of the populations of the units in any district are as similar as possible or lies within a predetermined range.

According to (Bacao, Lobo, & Painho, 2005a), the constraints of the zone design problem are similar to the ones that characterize the clustering problem. Let the set of initial areal units be $X = \{x_1, x_2 \ldots, x_n\}$, where x_i is the i-th areal unit. Let the number of zones be K. Let Z_i be the set of all the areal units that belong to zone Z_i. Then:

$$Z_i \neq 0, \text{ for } i = 1, \ldots, K,$$

$$Z_i \cap Z_j = 0, \text{ for } i \neq j,$$

$$\bigcup_{i=1}^{K} Z_i = X \qquad (1)$$

These constitute the set of constraints that can be applied equally in clustering and in zone design. Nevertheless, in zone design an additional constraint has to be included, which accounts for contiguity and creates a more complex problem. This constraint limits the set of acceptable solutions to the problem and consists in assuring contiguity between all the areal units that build up a zone. Contiguity is defined as a continuous connection of a series of entities, a grouping of parts connected throughout an unbroken sequence and sharing a common border. In other words, it means that each areal unit in a zone is connected to every other areal unit via areal units that are also in the zone (Cloonan, 1972; Niemi et al., 1990; Shirabe, 2005a; Shirabe, 2005b).

One of the reasons for the zone design problem being especially difficult is the size of the solution space. The dimension of a usual real world problem makes unfeasible any attempt to explicitly enumerate all the possible solutions. The calculation of the total number of possible solutions for a zone design problem is similar to the clustering problem and is given by the Stirling number of the second kind (Altman, 1998). If we have "n"

unit blocks and want to create "*k*" districts, the number S of possible districts is:

$$S(n,k) = \frac{1}{k!}\sum_{i=0}^{k}(-1)^i\left(\frac{k!}{(k-i)!\,i!}\right)(k-i)^n$$

(2)

Additionally, in terms of computational complexity, the zone design problem has been shown to be NP-Complete (Crescenzi, & Kann, 1998). Thus, heuristic techniques seem to be the best available option to produce solutions to the problem in a reasonable computational time. This is certainly a compromise, but guaranteed optimality seems at this stage merely a mirage.

The knowledge about this kind of algorithm, heuristically oriented, and integrated in interactive and user friendly Geographic Information Systems (GIS), is the core of this chapter.

Another purpose of this chapter is to demonstrate the potential of the proposed approach as a practical and readily implementable management decision aid in the context of a real case involving the maintenance team of a Portuguese regional office of a worldwide equipment company (called "Company A" for confidentiality reasons). The regional managers at Company A were interested in learning how our approach could be used to evaluate and possibly improve their territories structure.

According to (Zoltners, 2004), the TAP is a question that most companies face at least once a year, because it depends on the changes that may occur in the territories, and, frequently, these changes are most relevant on a yearly basis.

The algorithm presented in this chapter was developed to attend only the balancing of territories. Once the boundaries of the territories are defined, a routing solver or algorithm can be applied to each territory in order to provide a route or optimized sequence that has to be followed.

The remainder of this chapter is organized as follows:

Section 2 outlines the main concepts regarding territory design; discusses some of the traditional approaches to the territories alignment problem; and presents a literature review on the main subjects used to implement the solution proposed in this chapter. Sections 3 and 4 introduce the innovative approach to the TAP and present the main characteristics of the implementation of the MultiACE algorithm. Sections 5 and 6 present some remarks regarding the efficiency of the algorithm and discusses the results obtained applying the MultiACE algorithm to a real case. Section 7 proposes subjects for future research. Finally, in Section 8, we highlight some conclusions to this chapter.

2 BACKGROUND OF TERRITORY DESIGN

2.1 Approaches and Areas of Application in the Literature

The TAP has been largely studied since the 60's and several models and techniques have been proposed to solve it. Most of these approaches are based on set covering or set partitioning formulations, where the objective function consists in the minimization of the sum of the distances. In most cases, these models are solved using integer programming techniques often supported by column generation methods. More recently, several meta-heuristics have been applied to the set covering and the set partitioning problems with very promising results. The reader who wants to further review the basic concepts of TAP approaches and algorithms is referred to the research papers in Table 1.

In more recent years, there has been a growing interest in hybrid meta-heuristic algorithms applied to combinatorial optimization problems, but only a very low number of approaches are related to the territory alignment problem (Ehrgott, & Gandibleux, 2000). In Table 2 is a quite interesting list of papers, mainly regarding heuristics and

Table 1. Selected operations research studies for the TAP

Reference	Application
Hess et al., 1965	Political redistricting
Hess, & Samuels, 1971	Sales districts of a pharmaceutical and a computer company
Zoltners, 1976	Sales territory alignment
Parasuraman, 1977	Profitability of territories and sales resource allocation decision making
Zoltners, 1980	Modeling of a structure for the sales resource allocation
Lodish, 1980	Sales force sizing and products and markets allocation
Zoltners, & Lorimer, 1983	Sales force sizing of a pharmaceutical company
Lodish et al., 1988	Sales force sizing
Howick, & Pidd, 1990	Models for sales force sizing, sales people's time allocation and sales territory alignment
Mehrotra, Johnson, & Nemhauser, 1998	Political districting
Barker, 2001	Territory design and sales organization performance
Kalcsics et al., 2001	Sales territory design
Scaparra, & Scutella, 2001	Building blocks of location models
Sinha, & Zoltners, 2001	Activities and decisions of a sales force changes implementation process
Zoltners, Sinha, & Lorimer, 2004	Sales territories and their impact on the profitability of the companies
Pereira et al., 2004	Dividing territories in "homogeneous" areas
Zoltners, & Sinha, 2005	Alignment of sales territories.

meta-heuristics applied to TAP and related location problems.

According to the literature, one can notice that the early papers regarding TAP were related to the pharmaceutical industry representatives' territories and school and political districting, and there was a tendency of migration from solutions based on set-covering and enumeration techniques to solutions based on heuristics and meta-heuristics. Another interesting consideration is that the authors developed several algorithms based on p-median formulations, adapting them to their specific problem and available data.

Two additional remarks:

- There is a tendency to use heuristic-based solutions, especially hybrid solutions, which apply concepts of meta-heuristics as GRASP, Tabu Search and Genetic Algorithms, among others;

- The solutions are case-specific, since each one of them has its own constraints and objectives, making it virtually impossible to create an algorithm that can be applied to all TAP.

In the context of our work, we developed a new algorithm that applies the core ideas of two meta-heuristics, GRASP and Tabu Search, in conjunction with a technique of spatial division based on Voronoi diagrams. Additionally, we implemented a partition strategy that reduces the solution space, inserting characteristics in the MultiACE algorithm that are still lacking in the literature.

2.2 Software and Companies for Territory Alignment

The territory optimization software packages use algorithms that evaluate millions of potential align-

Table 2. Selected papers regarding different solution approaches for TAP and location problems

Number	Reference	Application	Solution Approach or Tool
1	Garfinkel, & Nemhauser, 1969	Set-Partitioning	Set-covering with equality constraints
2	Garfinkel, & Nemhauser, 1970	Political districting	Implicit enumeration
3	Helbig, Orr, & Roediger, 1972	Political districting	Computer method (heuristic)
4	Shanker, Turner, & Zoltners, 1975	Sales territory design	Set-partitioning
5	Ross, & Zoltners, 1979	Various applications	Weighted Assignment Models
6	Fleischmann, & Paraschis, 1988	Districting	Location-allocation approach
7	Leach, & Kandel, 1990	Redistricting	PC-based expert system
8	Beasley, 1993	Location	Lagrangean heuristic
9	Leach, & Kandel, 1993	Redistricting	Knowledge-based expert system
10	Rolland, Schilling, & Current, 1996	P-median	Tabu Search
11	Bozkaya, Zhang, & Erkut, 1997	P-median	Tabu Search
12	Resende, 1998	Maximum Covering	GRASP
13	Klose, 1998	Facility Location	Branch and Bound
14	Mehrotra, Johnson, & Nemhauser, 1998	Political districting	Branch-and-price
15	Delmaire et al., 1999	Capacitated plant location	Tabu Search and GRASP
16	Pirkul, Gupta, & Rolland, 1999	P-median	Visual interactive tool
17	Drexl, & Haase, 1999	Sales force deployment	Fast approximation methods
18	Lorena et al., 1999	P-median	Column generation and GIS
19	Cano et al., 2000	Clustering	GRASP
20	Guo, Trinidad, & Smith, 2001	Zoning	Graph partitioning
21	Macmillian, 2001	Redistricting	Switching points
22	D'Amico et al., 2002	Police district design	Simulated annealing
23	Zhou, Min, & Gen, 2002	Balanced allocation of customers	Genetic algorithm
24	Bozkaya, Erkut, & Laporte 2003	Political districting	Tabu Search and Adaptive memory
25	Taillard, 2003	Clustering	Heuristic methods
26	Bergey, Ragsdale, & Hoskote, 2003	Electrical power districting	Simulated Annealing and Genetic Algorithm
27	Wei, & Chai, 2004	Spatial zoning	Hybrid meta-heuristic (tabu search and scatter search)
28	Pereira et al., 2004	Districting	Evolutionary algorithm with local search
29	Caro et al., 2004	School redistricting	Integer programming
30	Lorena, & Senne, 2004	Capacitated p-median	Column generation
31	Senne, Lorena, & Pereira, 2005	P-median	Branch-and-price
32	Ahmadi, & Osman, 2005	Capacitated clustering	Greedy random adaptive memory programming search
33	Kirkizoglu, 2005	Sales territory alignment	Genetic algorithm
34	Bacao, Lobo, & Painho, 2005	Zone design	Genetic algorithm
35	Batun, 2005	Sales Territory Alignment	Tabu Search
36	Marianov, & Fresard, 2005	Locations, capacities and districting of jails	Minimum regret procedure
37	Reese, 2005	P-median	Annotated bibliography

continued on following page

Table 2. Continued

Number	Reference	Application	Solution Approach or Tool
38	Galvao et al., 2006	Logistics districting	Multiplicatively-weighted Voronoi diagram
39	Negreiros, & Palhano, 2006	Capacitated centred clustering	Polynomial heuristic algorithm
40	Resende, & Werneck, 2006	Uncapacitated facility location	Multistart heuristic
41	Diaz, & Fernandez, 2006	Capacitated p-median	Hybrid scatter search
42	Jackson, Rouskas, & Stallmann, 2007	P-median	Specific heuristic
43	Ricca, Scozzari, & Simeone, 2008	Political districting	Weighted Voronoi diagram
44	Ríos-Mercado, & Fernández, 2009	Territory alignment	GRASP
45	Novaes et al., 2009	Location-districting	Voronoi diagrams
46	Hu, Ding, & Shao, 2009	Partition balancing	Evolutionary algorithm
47	Yamada, 2009	Political districting	Mini-max spanning forest
48	Gonzalez-Ramirez et al., 2010	Logistics districting (tobacco distribution)	Tabu Search and GRASP
49	Hu, Yang, & Huang, 2010	Distribution partition	Evolutionary algorithm

ments to find one that best meets specified criteria regarding territory profitability, workload, sales potential, size, travel, and/or disruption (Zoltners, Sinha, & Lorimer, 2004).

There are several products on the market that intend to treat the problem of alignment and optimization of territories. With the sole purpose of informing the reader, we present in Table 3 a list of some of these commercial systems and their websites. In general, such systems have some characteristics in common, as listed below:

- Import data from several types of sources (ODBC, TXT, Access, DBF, etc.);
- Use georeferenced digital maps with automatic updating possibilities;
- Possess a support to assist the customers and a good group of tutorials;
- Use tools for map manipulation and for thematic map creation;
- The optimization algorithms work with real street networks data and can optimize trip time;
- Create compact and contiguous territories;

- Present the capacity to produce reports in text files and electronic spreadsheet formats;
- Do not provide many details about their territory alignment algorithm and the applied techniques.

This last issue - coupled with the high cost of the listed software and the lack of a set of "benchmark" problems - complicates a comparative analysis of the performance of the available solvers.

The interested reader may find in (Junior, 2008) a comparison between the results achieved by the MultiACE algorithm and the optimal solutions obtained by CPLEX, when solving a set of small to medium instances of "laboratory" problems, which may be obtained from the authors upon request. A sample of these results can be found in Section 5 of this chapter.

3 THE MULTIACE ALGORITHM

The novelty of the new algebraic approach presented in this chapter is the combination of five

Table 3. Software and companies for territory alignment

Software/Company	Website
AlignPlus	http://www.advantagems.com/
AlignStar	http://www.alignstar.com/optimizer.html
Analytics In Focus, LLC	http://www.salesterritoryalignment.com/
ArcGIS/ESRI	http://www.esri.com
Arcus	http://www.arcusgroup.ca/
Bayser Consulting	http://www.bayser.com/
Empower Geographics	http://www.empower.com/
IncentAlign	http://incentalign.com/products/salesalign-territory/
Maponics	http://www.maponics.com/
Mapping Analytics – Proalign	http://www.mappinganalytics.com/ProAlign/index.html
MarketRx	http://www.marketrx.com/Solutions/smo.asp
Synygy	http://www.synygy.com/
TerrAlign	http://www.terralign.com/about/leadership.html
TransCAD	http://www.caliper.com/tcovu.htm
ZS Associates/MAPS	http://www.zsassociates.com/

basic components that interact in order to solve the TAP. The five components are:

- A Voronoi Diagram based strategy, to create solutions;
- A 2-sets partitioning strategy, to decrease the search space;
- A GRASP based candidates list;
- Tabu Search (TS) based short-term and long-term memories;
- An optimization technique to define the best solutions.

Moreover, the algorithm was integrated into an advanced interactive tool (ArcGIS Geographic Information System (GIS) environment) which can be used in different contexts. At the operational level, it represents a valuable tool to quickly produce alternative solutions. At the tactical level it can be used to simulate different operating scenarios and evaluate the impact of changes in territories. Furthermore, it can be also applied by planners to support the testing of new prerequisites and new criteria can be easily incorporated.

Figure 1 shows the flowchart for the algorithm and how these five components interact to create the solutions and manipulate the data. The reader who wants to further review the details and main concepts regarding the basic components of the MultiACE algorithm is referred to (Júnior, 2008; Júnior, Sousa, & Basto, 2008).

3.1 Voronoi Diagram Based Solutions

A Voronoi Diagram is a special kind of decomposition of a metric space determined by distances to a specified discrete set of objects in the space (e.g., determined by a discrete set of points) (Aurenhammer, & Klein, 2000).

Let S be a set of points in an Euclidean space of dimension d and with cardinality equal to P. Let T be the number of territories in which we want to divide the set S. For each point c (the centers of the territories) of S, the Voronoi cell $V(c)$ (the territory of c) is the set of points that are closer to c than to other centers of S. The Voronoi

Figure 1. The MultiACE algorithm overall flowchart

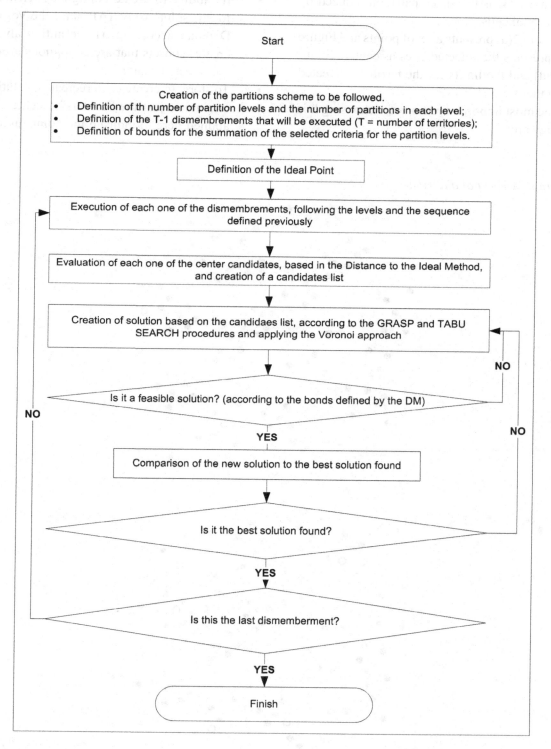

Diagram *V(S)* is the space partition induced by the Voronoi cells.

Figure 2(a) presents a set of points and Figure 2(b) presents the selected ones as centers (highlighted) and the limits for the territories created using them.

The most important reasons for choosing this strategy are:

- Its ability to create contiguous territories for the solutions of TAP, since the Voronoi Diagram, according to its definition, always creates subsets that are contiguous around the selected centers;

- To store, to create or to recreate a solution, one needs just the "centers" ("centers" is applied here to indicate the points used to

Figure 2. A Voronoi diagram

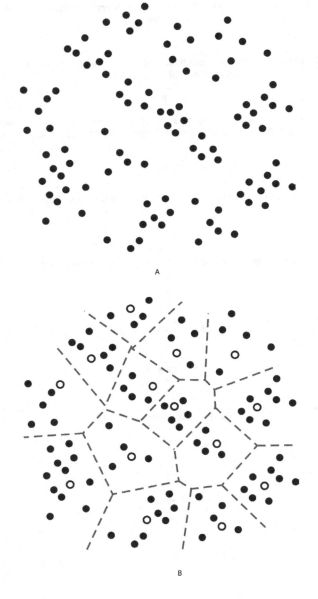

generate the territories, not in the geometric sense). This advantage is very useful when dealing with big sets of points and there is the need to make many calculations based on the "centers" positions.

3.2 2-Sets Partitioning Strategy to Decrease the Search Space

The strategy adopted to decrease the solutions search space divides the problem into some minor problems that can be solved more efficiently. It basically dismembers the original problem into new, smaller and less complex problems, starting with the original set of points and dividing it into two parts as follows:

Proportional to $\dfrac{T-1}{2}$ and $\dfrac{T+1}{2}$, if T is odd,

both proportional to $\dfrac{T}{2}$, if T is even.

where T is the number of territories. Then, this procedure is repeated until it generates T different territories. This procedure is represented in the Algorithm 1.

The number of dismemberments is always *T-1* and, in the end, T subparts are obtained, which will be the balanced territories, according to the balancing bounds. If one tries to divide 100 points into 4 territories using 4 centers at a time, there are 8214570 possible solutions. If one uses the 2-sets partition strategy, the total number of solutions needed to evaluate is equal to 10680 (i.e., it is only 0.13% of the total amount for the first strategy).

For each one of the levels of partitions defined in Algorithm 1, the summation bounds of the selected criteria for the partitions are also defined. The higher level receives the bounds defined by the decision-maker (DM) and the other levels receive bounds according to the number of the level, as follows:

$$UpperBound_{i+1} = 2 \times UpperBound_i$$
$$LowerBound_{i+1} = 2 \times LowerBound_i$$

where:

- i is the index of the level of partition;
- ***UpperBound***$_i$ and ***LowerBound***$_i$ are the upper and lower bounds for the summation of the selected criteria for the partitions of the level *i*;
- ***UpperBound***$_{i+1}$ and ***LowerBound***$_{i+1}$ are the upper and lower bounds for the summation of the selected criteria for the partitions of the level *i+1*.

This strategy reduces the search space because it decreases the number of possible candidates for the centers selection (Voronoi Diagram). Since each set is divided into two and only two subsets, the algorithm always selects two points as centers and allocates all the others to one, and only one, of these centers. This is a very fast way to generate and test solutions, because there is no need to improve the created solution in any way; it is just created and tested.

For all the dismemberments, the main objective is to create two balanced sub-sets. The algorithm tries to keep all the subsets balanced, when considering the attributes selected by the DM. If, in a given level, the algorithm does not find a feasible solution, it takes the closest solution obtained and continues executing the other dismemberments in order to obtain partial solutions that can be manually adjusted later. These manual adjustments are very easy to accomplish, because the data can be manipulated inside the GIS environment. Some of these manual adjustments can be used, after obtaining a solution, as an easy way to make its fine tuning. Section 6 provides a real case application of the algorithm and explains how these manual adjustments can be done and the importance of the DM's will in this process.

Algorithm 1. The Partition Scheme Algorithm Structure

```
1.  Initialize the number of territories (NumberOfTerritories)
2.  NumberOfPartitions = NumberOfTerritories -1
3.
4.  for i = 1 To 10 (2 ^ i is the maximum number of territories the algorithm can create)
5.      TerritoriesLimit = 2 ^ i
6.          If (NumberOfTerritories <= TerritoriesLimit) Then
7.              NumberOfPartitionLevels = i
8.              Exit for
9.          end if
10. end for
11.
12. for Level=1 to NumberOfPartitionLevels
13.       if Level = 1 then
14.             NumberToDivide = NumberOfTerritories
15.           if NumberToDivide is even then
16.             PartitionsMatrix(1, 1) = NumberToDivide / 2
17.               PartitionsMatrix(2, 1) = NumberToDivide / 2
18.           else
19.               PartitionsMatrix(1, 1) = (NumberToDivide - 1) / 2
20.               PartitionsMatrix(2, 1) = (NumberToDivide + 1) / 2
21.           end if
22.       else
23.           for j=1 to 2^(Level-1)
24.               NumberToDivide = PartitionsMatrix(j, Level - 1)
25.               if NumberToDivide = 1 then
26.                   PartitionsMatrix(2 * j - 1, Level) = 0
27.                   PartitionsMatrix(2 * j, Level) = 0
28.               end if
29.               if NumberToDivide > 1 And NumberToDivide is even then
30.                   PartitionsMatrix(2 * j - 1, Level) = NumberToDivide / 2
31.                   PartitionsMatrix(2 * j, Level) = NumberToDivide / 2
32.               end if
33.               if NumberToDivide > 1 And NumberToDivide is odd then
34.                   PartitionsMatrix(2 * j - 1, Level) = (NumberToDivide - 1) / 2
35.                   PartitionsMatrix(2 * j, Level) = (NumberToDivide + 1) / 2
36.               end if
37.           end for
38.       end if
39. end for
```

3.3 GRASP Based Candidates List

The greedy randomized adaptive search procedure (GRASP) is a meta-heuristic algorithm commonly applied to combinatorial optimization problems. GRASP typically consists of iterations made up of successive constructions of a greedy randomized solution and subsequent iterative improvements of it through a local search. The greedy randomized solutions are generated by adding elements to the problem's solution set from a list of elements ranked by a greedy function according to the quality of the solution they will achieve. To obtain variability in the candidate set of greedy solutions, well-ranked candidate elements are often placed on a restricted candidate list (also known as RCL), and chosen at random when building up the solution. (Feo, & Resende, 1995; Resende, 1998; Festa, & Resende, 2002; Festa, & Resende, 2004).

In the MultiACE algorithm, the ideal point is defined, for each one of the sub-partitions, as the most desirable, weighted, hypothetical alternative (decision outcome) and, for optimization problems, the closest alternative to the ideal point is the best alternative (the separation is measured in terms of metric distance (Lorena et al., 1999)).

For the TAP problem, the location (L_I) of the ideal point in the Euclidean space of dimension *d* can be described in Eq. 3:

$$L_I = (a_1, a_2, \ldots, a_d) \tag{3}$$

These numbers $a_1, \ldots, a_d$ are called the coordinates of the ideal point and each one of them represents the summation of one specific attribute of the points of an ideal territory.

The calculation of the location of the ideal point is important for the evaluation of the possible centers and the creation of the candidate list that will be used in the solution search.

When one wants to divide a set of points into two subsets, the first step, according to the algorithm, is to select the centers from a candidate list using a greedy strategy. The alternatives are ranked according to their distance from the ideal point and are sorted to create the candidate list.

Since a wide exploration of the solution space is important to effectively force the algorithm to navigate into the various regions of the search domain, one important step in the current approach is to create solutions with a diversification purpose in order to encourage the search process to examine random regions of the solution space.

The algorithm generates a solution using the candidates list, but it includes randomness in this process. The centers ranking defines a probability ranking as well. This probability ranking is defined in Eq. 4.

$$\Pr(c) = \frac{i_c - N}{1 - N}(\delta) + \varphi \tag{4}$$

where, *Pr(c)* is the probability of the point *c* to be selected as a center, i_c is the position of the point in the candidates list, *N* is the number of sites, φ is the lowest probability value and $\delta + \varphi$ is the highest probability value.

If one chooses $\delta=0.8$ and $\varphi=0.1$, the best center will have the probability of 90% and the worst center the probability of 10%. The range 90% − 10% is used by the algorithm to select the centers. These values permit the choice of the best centers as the inclusion of randomness can help to search a wider space and to avoid local optima at the same time.

The complete process to select two points as centers of a solution consists of these steps:

- The algorithm starts at the top of the candidates list and randomly generates a number in the range of 0 to 1 (normally distributed);
- If the random number is equal or smaller than the *Pr(c)* defined to this point, it will be selected as a center;

- If the random number is larger than the *Pr(c)* defined to this point, it will not be selected as a center and the algorithm will go down the candidates list repeating this process;
- If the algorithm reaches the end of the candidates list, it will start again at the top of the list and will repeat the search process until it finds two points to be used to create a solution.

3.4 Tabu Search Based Memories

Tabu search (TS) is a mathematical optimization method, belonging to the class of local search techniques. TS enhances the performance of a local search method by using memory structures: once a potential solution has been determined, it is marked as "taboo" ("tabu" being a different spelling of the same word) so that the algorithm will not visit that possibility repeatedly. TS is attributed to Fred W. Glover (Glover 1989; Glover 1990a; Glover 1990b; Glover, & Laguna, 1993; Glover, Taillard, & Werra, 1993; Hertz, Taillard, & Werra, 1995; Laguna, & Glover, 1996).

The algorithm we propose uses a short-term memory and a long-term memory. The long-term memory lists the set of solutions that have been tested. Complementarily, the short-term memory leads the way by which our algorithm tries to explore the search space.

When a point is selected as a center to generate a territory and the result is not feasible, given the bounds in one or more criteria, this aspirant center enters the TS list with a number equal to the number of rounds that this point will be denied to enter in the solutions creation process.

Once this "quarantine" expires, the point can eventually be chosen again as a center. We need to define the quarantine's size as a function of the number of points being divided at the current stage of the algorithm. As can be imagined, the quarantine size for a large set must be bigger than for a small set of points, given the need for a "rejected" center to stay away from the solution candidates during an extra period of time in order to allow the exploration of a larger search space.

3.5 Optimization Criteria

We adopted the *Distance to the Ideal Point Technique* as the objective function to be minimized in our algorithm. This measurement was chosen given that:

- It is easy to understand and to implement;
- It is easy to incorporate the DM's choices;
- It is efficient, in terms of the computational requirements.

During the course of the algorithm, we proceed to the division of the current set of points. For each one of the divisions, an Ideal Point is calculated. Then, the territories of the solutions are compared to the bounds for each one of their attributes, and, if both the territories are feasible (a feasible territory is a territory whose attributes satisfy the constraints defined by the DM, in relation to the Ideal Point and the error bounds), the solution is considered valid.

Next, if a solution is valid, it is then compared to the "so far" best found solution. We continue to use the same concept of Ideal Point, but trying to achieve an Ideal Point that is "perfectly balanced": achieving smaller differences between the attributes of the solution's territories will give us a better solution.

The MultiACE algorithm tries to minimize the grade shown in Eq. 5.

$$SG = \sum_j w_j (\sum_{i=1}^{F} a_{ji} - \sum_{l=1}^{G} a_{jl}) \qquad (5)$$

where:

- *SG* is the solution grade;
- *F* is the number of points in the first subset;

- G is the number of points in the second subset;
- i is the index of the point in the first subset;
- l is the index of the point in the second subset;
- j is the index of the attribute selected by the DM;
- w_j is the weight of the attribute j defined by the DM;
- a_{ji} is the value of the attribute j to the i point of the first subset;
- a_{jl} is the value of the attribute j to the l point of the second subset.

4 IMPLEMENTATION AND APPLICATION

The algorithm was built on top of ArcGIS, a powerful GIS software.

The main reasons for choosing the ArcGIS package as the environment for implementing the MultiACE algorithm were:

- The 9.2 release of ArcGIS includes some scripting languages allowing the user to customize or extend the software in order to suit his/her particular needs;
- It also offers a geo-environment that allows the execution of traditional GIS processing tools (such as clipping, overlay, and spatial analysis) either interactively or from any scripting language that supports COM standards;
- The graphical functionality in ArcGIS provides the user means to visualize the solutions and, hence, speed up the feedback loop. Furthermore, ArcGIS provides a mechanism for the user to make a manual edition of the solutions, a task that would be difficult without a GIS.

We have chosen Visual Basic Application (VBA) to code the MultiACE embedded in the GIS package. The input data for the TAP was stored in proprietary formats of ArcGIS. Each feature layer contains a set of objects considered as elements of alternative solutions. Since it was not possible to use the GIS standard operations alone to generate the solutions, the proposed algorithm was specifically designed, coded and aggregated in the VBA code to deal with the TAP.

4.1 Data

To input the necessary data to feed the algorithm, the user (DM) must build:

- A personal geo-database layer with points representing the units to aggregate into territories. The authors are aware that working with a point-representation of the basic units could lead to problems with the compactness of territories, but the geographic obstacles, on the other hand, can be easily handled in this approach by delivering to the algorithm the network distances between points;
- A database containing all the attributes of each unit (point).

The finding of solutions is done by ArcGIS and the MultiACE algorithm. The user must guide the software by supplying a few parameters and choosing some basic options. After the solution generation, the proposed solution and its measurements of compactness can be visually controlled.

4.2 Constraints

In our problem, constraints may be classified as hard or soft.

Soft constraints are the ones defined by the DM and consider criteria faced as requirements in the objective function or in the constraints of the mathematical model.

Hard constraints are the natural bounds such as rivers or one-way streets. To avoid splitting a territory with respect to natural boundaries such as major rivers or bodies of water, the DM must choose the network distances option. The algorithm will read a file containing all the distances between each pair of points and shall use these distances during the computations. The tool "Network Analyst", that is part of the ArcGIS package, can be used to easily obtain the required file of distances.

4.3 Objectives

The MultiACE algorithm tries to cover two main objectives:

The first objective is that the territories should be contiguous and as compact as achievable. There are many proposed ways to measure compactness and the MultiACE uses the summation of the Euclidean distances of all points to the geometric center of the territories. This objective is achieved using the Voronoi Diagram based strategy.

The second objective is that the territories must be balanced by one or more criteria. This means that the summation of the attributes for every territory must lie within the defined bounds. These constraints can be formulated as shown in Eq. 6.

$$(1 - \beta_j)(Ideal_{j1}) \leq (\sum_{i=1}^{F} a_{ji}) \leq (1 + \varphi_j)(Ideal_{j1})$$

$$and$$

$$(1 - \beta_j)(Ideal_{j2}) \leq (\sum_{l=1}^{G} a_{jl}) \leq (1 + \varphi_j)(Ideal_{j2})$$

$$(6)$$

where:

- j is the index of the criteria selected by the DM;
- F is the number of points in the first subset;
- G is the number of points in the second subset;
- i is the index of the point in the first subset;
- l is the index of the point in the second subset;
- $Ideal_{j1}$ is the value of the attribute j to the Ideal Point 1; (each subset is compared to a

different Ideal Point, since the subsets can be of different sizes; if the subsets are of the same size, the Ideal Point 1 is equal to the Ideal Point 2.);
- $Ideal_{j2}$ is the value of the attribute j to the Ideal Point 2;
- a_{ji} is the value of the attribute j to the i point of the first subset;
- a_{jl} is the value of the attribute j to the l point of the second subset;
- β_j is the lower bound for the attribute j of the subsets;
- φ_j is the upper bound for the attribute j of the subsets.

According to Eq. 6, one can notice that the greater the number of points, the harder it will be to solve the system, because the number of constraints increases. It can also be noticed that the smaller the attribute bounds, the harder it will be for the algorithm to find feasible solutions, because this will decrease the size of the area in the search space where the feasible solutions can be found. Finally, the bigger the number of attributes, the harder it will be to determine the solutions for the problem, also because it increases the number of equations in the set of constraints.

4.4 Algorithm's Parameters

The algorithm's parameters are:

- Number of territories to generate;
- Set of points to process (in the GIS environment, the layer of points);
- Criteria (attributes of the points) to use in the multi-criteria analysis;
- Weights of each criterion used in the analysis and the solution preferences;
- Stopping rules;
- The type of measurement for the geographical distance between points.

The number of territories to generate is the first and the easiest parameter to choose and understand. According to this number, the algorithm will elaborate the scheme of partitions to follow until the final solution.

The set (layer) of points to process is the layer of information that will be used in the analysis. The user has to choose not only the layer, but the key field, the field where the solution will be stored, and, if it is necessary, a field that indicates a subgroup selection. The subgroup selection is used to generate territories using only a selected set of units that are in the selected layer.

The criteria (up to three) are the fields where the values of the attributes for each unit are stored. First, the DM selects how many criteria he will use and then he selects each field separately. The last definition about criteria is the weight definition. These weights will guide the algorithm through the solutions search.

The stopping rules are the criteria that the algorithm will use to stop the solutions search. The options are: a time limit; a limit for the number of tested solutions; the finding of the first feasible solution, or the DM will.

In order to measure the physical (geographical) distance between points, four options may be used: Euclidean distances, Chebyshev distances, Manhattan distances and Network distances; in this latter one there are still two options, considering two-way or one-way streets. The option selected will impact the shape of the territories and it has to be done according to:

- the existence of any specific geographical constraint for the area under analysis (rivers, lakes, etc.);
- the availability of data concerning the direction of the flow in each link of the network.

There are three important decisions that influence the way the algorithm works.

The first one is to choose if the algorithm will look for solutions in a heuristic way or if it will make an exhaustive search. The exhaustive search is indicated when one have small sets of points, because the algorithm can be more efficient. One has to define the size of the sets that will make the algorithm use the exhaustive search procedure. The DM also defines the maximum number of analyzed solutions to keep in memory (long-term memory) and the percentage of the number of points that will define the short-term memory.

The next decision to make is related to the objective function. The DM must decide if the algorithm will look for:

- the most compact solutions, or;
- the most well-balanced (with the least deviation from the Ideal Point) solutions, according to the criteria selected.

This is an important question, because it influences the shape of the territories and the final results. Figure 3 shows two different territory solutions for the same problem. The first one shows a set of territories optimized for the DM preferences (weights), while the second shows a set of territories more compact than the ones of the first solution.

The third decision to make is optional and related to the bounds defined for each of the partitions carried out by the algorithm. If it is necessary, the DM may allow the algorithm to increase the bounds considered for the partition until it finds a feasible solution for that partition. This option is useful in helping to find solutions when the DM defines very narrow bounds for the balancing of the territory criteria.

Regarding to the checking of the proposed solutions, there is still another parameter to define, namely the territory Compactness Measurement. It can be calculated in one, and only one, of these four ways:

- Average distance from the points to the center of the territory;

Figure 3. Two different solutions for the same problem

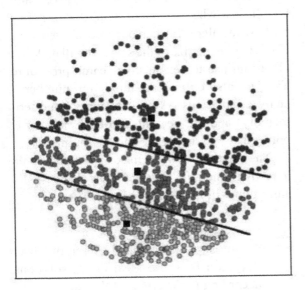 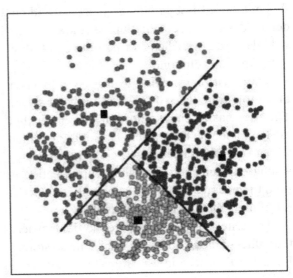

- Summation of the distances from the points to the center of the territory;
- Maximum radius from the territory centroid (MRTC) (i.e. the distance from the center of the territory to the most distant point);
- Maximum distance between two points of a territory.

The compactness measurement used by the DM to analyze the quality of the solution is directly connected to a specific operational objective. Its choice can influence the final solution because it can affect the shape of the territories. Section 6 presents a real case where the operational objective was to create territories with a minimum MRTC because the company had an operational objective properly explained in Section 6.6.

4.5 Algorithm Structure

The MultiACE algorithm can be summarized in the structure listed in Algorithm 2.

5 ALGORITHM'S EFFICIENCY

In order to present the algorithm's efficiency, Table 4 summarizes the results obtained applying the MultiACE algorithm and the CPLEX optimization package. In this set of experiments we decided to show that the strategy to create solutions (Voronoi based strategy) and the strategy to decrease the search space (Two-set partitioning strategy) work well and can generate high-quality solutions in a set of "laboratory" problems. We carried out the experiments varying the parameters of our problems and a more complete explanation can be found in (Júnior, 2008).

We can notice that the difference between MultiACE results and CPLEX results (DIST. SUMM) is not greater than 5% and the amount of time to find the solutions, for these datasets, is always greater when we use the CPLEX formulation. The mean of the differences is 1,3% and the greatest value is 19,9%, but it occurred just once. The greatest differences appeared when we set the values for the number of territories close to the maximum number for each dataset and when

Algorithm 2. MultiACE algorithm structure

```
1.  Initialize the number of territories
2.  Calculate the Number of Partition Levels (NumLev)
3.  Calculate the Number of Partitions in each Level (NumPartOfLev)
4.  Generate the Partitions Scheme
5.  for Level=1 to NumLev do
6.          for Partition=1 to NumPartOfLev
7.                  Calculate the Proportion Between the Territories
8.                  Read the points attributes
9.                  Calculate the Ideal Point
10.                 Read or Calculate the distances between points
11.                 Evaluate each point as a possible center
12.                 Generate the candidates list
13.                 while (Keep calculating solutions = TRUE)
14.                         Define the centers to generate a solution
15.                         Generate the solution
16.                         Calculate the statistics of the solution
17.                         Evaluate the solution
18.                         Test the Stopping Criteria
19.                 end while
20.         end for
21. end for
```

we tried to balance three criteria at the same time, increasing the complexity of the partition problem.

For all runs, CPLEX is the most time-consuming method. For this set of experiments, the required computation times for the smallest datasets (100 and 200 points) are not significantly larger than the ones of MultiACE but, as the size of problems grows, the required computation times become much larger, compared to MultiACE.

6 SOLVING REAL PROBLEMS

6.1 Company A Case Background

The company sells new equipment and provides maintenance to new and old equipment. There is a specific division responsible for the maintenance tasks, and, in Portugal, the operation is divided into sub-areas. The area in which this study was accomplished is a sub-area in the North of Portugal and is shown in Figure 4. The area under study is almost restricted to the district of Porto, with just a few equipment out of this district.

Company A designs, manufactures, installs, maintains, and modernizes equipment for almost every type of building requirement worldwide. The company is dedicated to latest-technology engineering, and mechanical and microprocessor-technology products designed and rigorously tested for comfort, efficiency, and reliability.

In the area under analysis, the company maintains approximately six thousand equipmentsupported by a team of technical experts and solution providers. In the office, ten supervisors coordinate and lead various crews that maintain and repair customers' equipment.

Table 4. CLEX vs MultiACE efficiency comparison

Dataset	Number of territories	Bounds for the Criteria: +/- 5%			
		CPLEX TIME (s)	MultiACE TIME (s)	CPLEX DIST. SUMM. (m)	MultiACE DIST. SUMM. (m)
100	2	8	2	7306	7306
200	2	108	20	14333	14335
	3	109	26	11575	11697
300	2	874	64	21389	21390
	3	1352	83	16977	17416
	4	535	81	14128	14140
400	2	3569	150	29848	29875
	3	2571	195	23868	24297
	4	3084	191	19535	19538
	5	1798	205	17659	17901
	6	1415	212	15761	16373
500	2	8326	287	35664	35664
	3	5720	372	28583	29040
	4	4495	364	24023	24161
	5	4975	390	21963	22418
	6	12137	388	19852	20549
	7	3589	392	18223	18636

There are two special supervisors: one that takes care of a special group of equipment and another one that takes care of a special type of clients' equipment. The other eight supervisors take care of the remaining equipment, approximately five thousand and two hundred.

Each technician has a list of equipment for which to provide maintenance. This list is what we define as the technician's territory. The supervisor is responsible for all equipment of the technicians of his group and he manages all the back-office work related to the equipment.

The technicians are supposed to visit each of the equipment on his list once a month to perform both preventive maintenance (adjusting, examining and repairing or replacing worn components, lubricating and cleaning parts) and services for customer trouble calls (callbacks). Customer callbacks are usually assigned to the responsible maintenance technician, if available.

6.2 The Territory Assignment Process

A territory assignment process according to (Zoltners, Sinha, & Lorimer, 2004), was implemented: a central alignment that acts as a benchmark, with local adjustments. The central benchmark alignment parameters (criteria) were defined by the Company A managers and were based on objective business criteria.

In the first step, the managers determined the main objectives and the alignment criteria as follows:

- To distribute equipment equitably. First, define the supervisors' territories and then subdivide these territories into technicians' territories. The number of supervisors' territories should change to 7 territories, instead of 8, and the technicians' territories should

Figure 4. Company A: equipments of the area under study

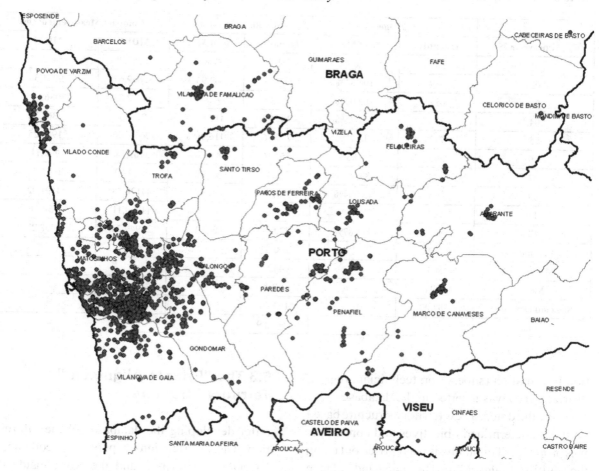

be in the range of 108 to 132 pieces of equipment (120 pieces of equipment ±10%);

- To distribute workload equitably and, since there is a calculated maintenance time (based on characteristics of the equipment such as: age, size, technology, etc.) for each piece of equipment, the total sum of a territory's maintenance time should never be more than 136 maintenance hours per month;
- To merge the Company A territories and the territories of the small companies subcontracted by Company A;
- To create contiguous territories;
- To create territories as compact as possible.

These criteria were defined after some brainstorming sessions and after some scenarios proposed using the MultiACE algorithm. Here, only the final group of criteria is listed.

In the second step, a database was developed. This database included all the equipment locations and alignment attributes (workload). The first step to developing this database was to locate all equipment using a GPS device and this data collection was accomplished with the help of the maintenance team. All the equipment of their territories were visited and points to every one of them were marked using a GPS device (each equipment received latitude and longitude coordinates). The current hierarchical organiza-

Table 5. "Prior to alignment" supervisor territories data

Supervisor	Equipment		Workload (hours)		Compact Measurement (m)	
	Quantity	% of Mean	Quantity	% of Mean	MDBP	MDTC
01	581	96,87%	651,59	97,82%	26667,29	5493,97
02	639	106,54%	685,71	102,95%	35869,67	9251,38
03	612	102,03%	652,05	97,89%	64062,85	10865,15
04	736	122,71%	782,99	117,55%	27446	8365,32
05	712	118,71%	779,06	116,96%	7683,58	1985,25
06	545	90,86%	556,36	83,53%	3769,54	767,11
07	524	87,36%	588,47	88,35%	5279,69	1355,53
09	804	134,04%	943,66	141,67%	44128,78	4191,92
11	162	27,01%	290,87	43,67%	11219,11	1391,1
12	683	113,87%	730,12	109,61%	29949,24	7458,22
Minimum	162		290,87			
Maximum	804		943,66			
Mean	599,8		666,09			
Standard Deviation	167,99		163,46			
Total	5998		6660,89			

tion information (supervisor, technician, region, districts, etc.) was inserted in the database too.

In the third step, a new territory structure based on the predetermined objectives and constraints was proposed. This analysis was carried out using the MultiACE algorithm. The shape and balance of the proposed territories were based on the combination of the criteria. The result of this step was an optimized territory alignment.

In the fourth step, the real-world factors and organizational uniqueness that shapes the maintenance team environment were taken into account. The management team audited and adjusted the territories. The audit group included the regional and district managers.

In the fifth step, the optimal territory alignments were developed. After this, a personnel assignment was proposed and adjusted, since the specific geography and account assignments for each territory were known.

In the sixth step, the alignments and personnel assignments were audited and finalized with the help of the management team.

6.3 The "Prior to Alignment" Territory Structure

After developing the database, all the information was inserted into a personal geodatabase (ArcGIS file format) and the work inside the GIS environment began. The first task was to analyze the current situation of the territories. This evaluation was very important to define the regions or subgroups of equipment that needed more attention or were less balanced.

The "prior to alignment" supervisor areas presented some problems, unbalanced situations and different shapes and geographical distributions. Table 5 shows, for each territory, its number of equipment, its workload (summation of the theoretical work mean-time of each piece of equipment in the territory), its maximum distance between points (MDBP), and its mean sum of Euclidean distances to the center of the territory (MDTC).

Table 6 shows the "prior to alignment" supervisors' territories balance situation for the area under study.

Table 6. Supervisors' territories: "prior to alignment" balance

Supervisor	Equipment		Workload (hours)	
	Quantity	% of Mean	Quantity	% of Mean
01	578	101,05%	645,67	105,23%
02	633	110,66%	673,09	109,69%
03	375	65,56%	403,55	65,77%
04	736	128,67%	782,99	127,60%
05	691	120,80%	747,39	121,80%
06	545	95,28%	541,92	88,32%
07	507	88,64%	562,79	91,72%
09	400	69,93%	436,1	71,07%
12	683	119,41%	729,01	118,81%
Minimum	375		403,55	
Maximum	736		782,99	
Mean	572		613,61	
Standard Deviation	120,40		128,16	
Total	5148		5522,51	

For the final analysis, we excluded, from the 5998 equipment set, the supervisor 11 territory (special client equipment), some equipment transferred to other regional office and some equipment assigned to the special equipment supervisor. In Table 6 one can see the distance between the minimum and maximum number of equipment in the territories and notice their unbalanced state.

Besides the different sizes and shapes, the supervisors' territories have a contiguity problem. There are overlaps in some areas, as shown in Figure 5. The same problem occurs to several territories of the maintenance team and it is an important factor that decreases the productivity of the teams and increases the company costs.

Table 7 shows the summary of the "prior to alignment" territories balance situation for the study area. One can notice the distance between the minimum and maximum number of equipment in the maintenance team territories and their unbalanced state.

After the analysis of the "prior to alignment" supervisors and maintenance team territories, we noticed that the area under analysis needed to be subdivided before we start to generate the new territory structure. The reason for this procedure is that the study area was very large and had a heterogeneous distribution of equipment. So, the managers decided to divide the equipment into 3 areas (see Figure 6): the first one, a very compact and central area; the second one, bigger than the first area and around it; and the third one, a very big and dispersed area in the outskirts.

To divide these areas we used only the ArcGIS tools (selection and database tools), according to the managers' will. We carried out this partition trying to use the geographical characteristics of the areas, either visually or using the database tools.

To confirm the differences between these areas we used the Network Analyst to create minimum distance routes passing in every point of the areas and we used the total distance of the routes to calculate the mean distance between equipment (MDBE) and the mean distance between stops (MDBS), shown in Table 8.

According to the comparative analysis of the 3 areas, the managers decided to change the bounds

Figure 5. Overlap of the territories of supervisors 01, 02, 03, and 12

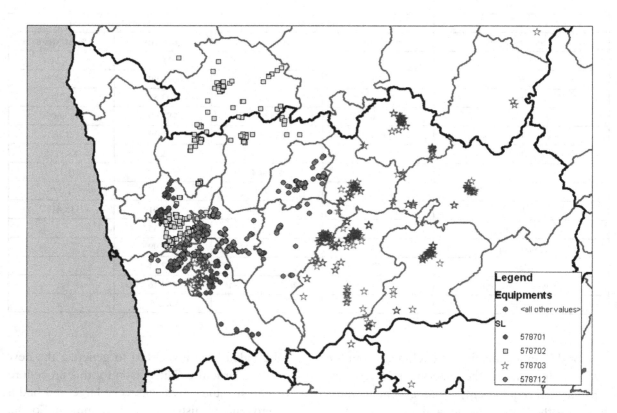

of the number of equipment for the areas 2 and 3. They did not set new values for the bounds but decided that areas 2 and 3 could have territories 5-10% smaller than the territories in area 1. The reason for this change is that the mean distances between equipment in these areas are very large, increasing the travel time between equipment.

Table 7. "Prior to alignment" maintenance team territories balance summary

Statistics	Number of Equipment	Workload (hours)
Minimum	55	55,88
Maximum	433	451,64
Mean	122,58	131,49
Standard Deviation	79,08	84,27
Total	5148	5522,51

6.4 "After Alignment" Territory Structure

After the evaluation of the "prior to alignment" situation, the next step was to project the new territories for the supervisors. We divided the 5148 (pieces of) equipment into 7 territories using some different strategies to create them, but, to run the MultiACE algorithm we used the following options:

- Number of supervisors territories: 3;
- First criterion: Number of equipment;
- First criterion bounds: +10% and -10%;
- First criterion weight: 1;
- Second criterion: Workload;
- Second criterion bounds: +10% and -10%;

Figure 6. The 3 different areas obtained during the analysis of the "prior to alignment" territories structure and definition of the "after alignment" territories structure

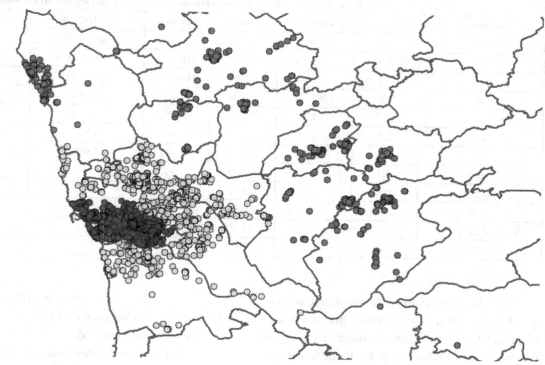

- Second criterion weight: 1;
- Processing time limit: 10 minutes;
- Ideal point distance measurement: Euclidean distances;
- Physical distance measurement: Network distances;
- Streets type: two-way distances;
- Short term memory: 30% of the number of points;
- Long term memory: 200000 solutions.

The first supervisor territory was obtained manually using the ArcGIS selection tools and the MultiACE to generate a summary of the criteria values of this territory. We used this approach to create the first territory because it covered a very sparse area and the algorithm aims to solve problems in homogeneous areas. After this, we selected part of the Area 3 to create the supervisor territory 01.

The remaining points of Area 3 points and all the points of Area 2 were used to generate 3 territories and, finally, Area 1 was used to generate the last 3 territories, with the help of the Multi-ACE algorithm.

Table 8. A comparative analysis of the data related to the 3 generated areas

Area	Equipment	Stops	Total Distance (m)	MDBE (m)	MDBS (m)
1	2160	1248	211919,4	98,11	169,80
2	2007	1015	474507,8	236,42	467,49
3	981	559	455099,4	463,91	814,13

Table 9. Supervisors' territories: "after alignment" balance

Supervisor	Equipment		Workload (hours)		Compactness Measurement (m)	
	Quantity	% of Mean	Quantity	% of Mean	MDBP	MDTC
01	762	103,61%	807,32	102,33%	60354,13	10765,61
02	794	107,96%	869,02	110,15%	24870,64	7910,59
03	752	102,25%	817,01	103,56%	23291,99	5681,51
04	798	108,51%	851,98	107,99%	11704,06	3226,56
05	697	94,77%	762,16	96,61%	7015,9	1947,96
06	723	98,31%	785,58	99,58%	6128,06	1539,69
07	622	84,58%	629,43	79,78%	5730,88	951,03
Minimum	622		629,43			
Maximum	798		869,02			
Mean	735,43		788,93			
Standard Deviation	57,10		73,37			
Total	5148		5522,51			

After the generation of the solutions, we analyzed them and did some small manual adjustments. The proposed solutions were very good and we just changed some points from one territory to another to adjust the shape of the territories. The last adjustment in the supervisors' territories was carried out only after we calculated the Technicians territories, but, at this time, we did just the whole technician territory changes, moving from one Supervisor territory to another. The final supervisors' territories are shown in Table 9.

The next step consisted of matching the supervisors' territories and the new maintenance teams' territories. At this time, we used the MultiACE algorithm to create all the territories. For each one of the supervisors' territories we applied the MultiACE algorithm and, since we did not have very large sets of points, we used the exhaustive method to create better solutions. The MultiACE parameters used are:

- Number of territories: 5 or 6;
- First criterion: Number of equipment;
- First criterion bounds: +10% and -10%;
- First criterion weight: 1;
- Second criterion: Workload;

- Second criterion bounds: +10% and -10%;
- Second criterion weight: 1;
- Exhaustive method;
- Ideal point distance measurement: Euclidean distances;
- Physical distance measurement: Network distances;
- Streets type: two-way distances.

The final maintenance team territories summary is shown in Table 10. The territory with the minimum number of equipment and workload is beyond the bounds determined by the managers because it is located in the most dispersed area.

6.5 Achievements and Savings

The "after alignment" territory structure implemented and the main achievements and savings obtained with it were:

- Comparing Table 6 to Table 9, the standard deviation of the "Number of Equipment" decreased from 79,08 to 8,00 (90% reduction) and the standard deviation for the "Workload" decreased from 84,27 to 9,03

Table 10. "After alignment" maintenance team territories balance summary

Statistics	Number of Equipment	Workload (hours)
Minimum	89	92,54
Maximum	130	137,18
Mean	114,4	122,72
Standard Deviation	8,00	9,03
Total	5148	5522,51

(89% reduction). This demonstrates that the "after alignment" structure is much better balanced than the former one;

- The managers were able to quickly get an overview of where all the territories were and where there was some overlap in the structure. There are no more territory overlaps and the territories are now better geographically defined. It was easy to decide which maintenance worker would take care of new equipment. They have been able to better define areas of responsibility and loading;

- The maintenance team territories were more compact, so the total travel time decreased, improving the productivity of the maintenance team;

- According to the MRTC compactness measurement, the managers decided to decrease the number of cars available to the maintenance team. They decided that the territories with MRTC smaller than 1700 meters would not have a car. The result was a decreasing of eight cars from the maintenance fleet, with direct and indirect cost reduction of approximately eighty thousands Euros per year.

6.6 Improving the Solution

The solution represented by the "after alignment" structure is one of the six scenarios studied dur-ing the whole study. The managers could explain their ideas, including the constraints that we must respect and their subjective goals for the new structure.

Some of these constraints and subjective goals influenced the final result and we believed that we could improve this solution. So, we decided to create a different structure to compare to the selected one and show some improvements that could be made.

The changes we decided to make are:

- **Number of supervisors:** instead of seven supervisors, we decided to use eight;

- **Number of technicians:** instead of forty-five, we decided to use forty-six;

One may think that these changes would increase the direct and indirect costs, but we intend to show that the selection of a structure (scenario) in a territory design is a trade-off among the several objectives the managers have to achieve.

To create the territories for the supervisors, we used the three Areas defined previously, but this time we divided Area 3 into two territories, Area 2 into three territories and Area 1 into three territories.

The next step was to divide the supervisors' territories into maintenance team territories. We used the same criteria and MultiACE parameters defined previously, but this time we changed the number of territories according to Table 11. The improved "new aligned" territory structure is shown in Table 12.

The main remark we would like to make about the data of the "new aligned" structure (Table 12) is that the number of territories with MRTC smaller than 1700 meters (in bold) increased from 15 to 20, decreasing thirteen cars from the maintenance fleet, with direct and indirect cost reduction of approximately ninety-six thousand Euros per year, including the costs of one more supervisor, one more maintenance worker and one more vehicle for the supervisor. This kind of trade-off

Table 11. Improving the solution: number of territories

Supervisor	Maintenance Territories
11	6
12	6
13	6
21	6
22	6
23	6
31	5
32	5
Total	46

between the size of the maintenance team and the cost reduction can be made easily and many scenarios can be analyzed in a very short time.

7 FUTURE RESEARCH DIRECTIONS

A research work such as the one described in this chapter is never fully closed. Several issues do clearly deserve further research. In the following points we briefly present some of these issues:

- The heuristic can be tested handling several other activity measures. In this case while examining a partition, one could take different activity measures into account when determining the best territory structure;
- The algorithm can be prepared to consider prescribed and forbidden territory centers. This means that one can impose some fixed territory centers at the beginning, which have to be taken into account, or, the other way around, some basic entities that cannot be allowed to be selected as centers;
- In the case in which some territories are already given at the beginning of the planning process the algorithm can be adapted to take the already existing territories into account and possibly add additional clients to them;

- The heuristic can be incorporated into a larger framework in order to apply it to different practical planning problems. For example, scenarios where a limit on the maximal allowed geographic extent of the territories has to be taken into account;
- One can avoid the number of territories to be fixed in advance. Instead, the algorithm can choose the appropriate number of territories in such a way that the planning criteria would be best fulfilled. For example, the partition of the basic areas in the region under consideration into as few as possible territories such that the size of all territories should be below a certain maximal bound;
- The heuristic can be incorporated into an open source framework in order to allow it to be used and tested by several planners, decision-makers and developers around the world. This can be a good way to spread the utility of the GIS in the field of territory planning. This action can also encourage other developers to solve different kinds of alignment problems, with different kinds of criteria and in different situations. This open source implementation can be the cornerstone of a promising field of applied research.

8 CONCLUSION

This chapter has addressed the territory alignment problem as a critical component of the operational planning process in sales/services companies. A particular emphasis was given to the case of a Portuguese company and the tool developed and used in this context has been described in more detail.

A new perspective on approaching TAP that is closer to the real problems and to the planners' work has been proposed and several different objectives and constraints used by companies in their alignment process were identified and

Table 12. Improved "new aligned" territory structure: maintenance team

Territory	Equipments		Workload (hours)		MRTC
	Quantity	% of Mean	Quantity	% of Mean	
111	14	99,65%	126,17	110,29%	1686,66
112	21	105,77%	128,04	111,93%	1683,41
113	13	98,78%	124,61	108,93%	1552,41
114	20	104,90%	125,09	109,34%	1521,71
115	19	104,02%	129,20	112,94%	1355,31
116	10	96,15%	129,97	113,61%	845,86
121	17	102,27%	132,27	115,62%	1980,00
122	18	103,15%	120,71	105,51%	1765,94
123	15	100,52%	120,88	105,66%	1488,59
124	18	103,15%	137,18	119,92%	1170,32
125	26	110,14%	134,78	117,82%	1139,13
126	22	106,64%	136,24	119,09%	1055,98
131	30	113,64%	132,87	116,14%	2537,08
132	18	103,15%	123,72	108,15%	950,21
133	21	105,77%	126,47	110,55%	940,12
134	23	107,52%	122,93	107,46%	841,27
135	27	111,01%	122,77	107,32%	746,70
136	28	111,89%	131,39	114,85%	740,78
211	20	104,90%	128,32	112,17%	5532,80
212	16	101,40%	129,30	113,03%	3071,89
213	18	103,15%	127,06	111,07%	2522,92
214	08	94,41%	116,51	101,84%	2008,93
215	08	94,41%	120,86	105,65%	1631,53
216	14	99,65%	136,46	119,28%	920,67
221	9	86,54%	104,23	91,11%	4403,48
222	10	96,15%	109,57	95,78%	3609,37
223	11	97,03%	115,91	101,32%	2780,20
224	14	99,65%	124,45	108,79%	2299,70
225	20	104,90%	134,74	117,78%	2024,33
226	17	102,27%	126,66	110,72%	1673,83
231	01	88,29%	106,24	92,87%	9427,35
232	08	94,41%	115,88	101,29%	8531,43
233	16	101,40%	125,54	109,74%	3101,91
234	16	101,40%	130,05	113,68%	2856,50
235	01	88,29%	113,46	99,18%	2292,30
236	10	96,15%	122,49	107,07%	1942,48
311	02	89,16%	113,99	99,64%	10719,57
312	8	76,92%	84,22	73,62%	10638,55
313	10	96,15%	117,38	102,61%	6240,20

continued on following page

Table 12. Continued

Territory	Equipments		Workload (hours)		MRTC
	Quantity	% of Mean	Quantity	% of Mean	
314	6	75,17%	93,87	82,06%	4217,79
315	**04**	**90,91%**	**109,53**	**95,74%**	**1665,10**
321	8	76,92%	91,84	80,28%	22203,75
322	00	87,41%	102,51	89,61%	11274,06
323	08	94,41%	119,20	104,19%	4670,80
324	3	81,29%	98,58	86,17%	4331,88
325	**02**	**89,16%**	**110,41**	**96,51%**	**1304,93**
Minimum	6		84,22		
Maximum	30		137,18		
Mean	11,91		120,31		
Standard Deviation	0,40		12,26		
Total	148		5534,56		

discussed. In order to tackle these simultaneous and conflicting objectives, an approach based on GRASP and TS has been developed.

This new hybrid meta-heuristic lies on a combination of a Voronoi Diagram based strategy, to create solutions; a two-sets partitioning strategy, to decrease the search space; a GRASP based candidates list; Tabu Search based short and long term memories; and an optimization technique to define the best solutions. We presented and discussed these components and a step-by-step description of the meta-heuristic solution procedure, its basic structure, initialization, subset generation and combination, dominance comparison, quality measurement and adaptive memory structure used.

Finally, the potential of the proposed approach as a practical and readily implementable management decision aid in the context of a current case that involved the maintenance team attached to the Portuguese regional office of a worldwide equipment company was also demonstrated.

REFERENCES

Ahmadi, S., & Osman, I. H. (2005). Greedy random adaptive memory programming search for the capacitated clustering problem. *European Journal of Operational Research, 162*(1), 30–44. doi:10.1016/j.ejor.2003.08.066

Altman, M. (1998). *Districting Principles and Democratic Representation*. Pasadena, California: PhD, California Institute of Technology.

Amorim, S. G. d., Barthélemy, J.-P., & Ribeiro, C. C. (1992). Clustering and Clique Partitioning: Simulated Annealing and Tabu Search Approaches. *CLASSIF: Journal of Classification, 9*(1), 17–41. doi:10.1007/BF02618466

Aurenhammer, F., & Klein, R. (2000). Voronoi Diagrams. In Sack, J.-R., & Urrutia, J. (Eds.), *Handbook of Computational Geometry* (pp. 201–290). Amsterdam, Netherlands: North-Holland. doi:10.1016/B978-044482537-7/50006-1

Bacao, F., Lobo, V., & Painho, M. (2005). Applying genetic algorithms to zone design. *Soft Computing, 9*(5), 341–348. doi:10.1007/s00500-004-0413-4

Barker, A. T. (2001). Salespeople characteristics, sales managers' activities and territory design as antecedents of sales organization performance. *Marketing Intelligence & Planning, 19*(1), 21–28. doi:10.1108/02634500110363772

Batun, S. (2005). *A Tabu Search Algorithm for Sales Territory Alignment Problem*. Paper presented at the 35th International Conference on Computers and Industrial Engineering, Istanbul, Turkey.

Beasley, J. E. (1993). Lagrangean heuristics for location problems. *European Journal of Operational Research, 65*(3), 383–399. doi:10.1016/0377-2217(93)90118-7

Bergey, P., Ragsdale, C., & Hoskote, M. (2003). A Simulated Annealing Genetic Algorithm for the Electrical Power Districting Problem. *Annals of Operations Research, 121*(1-4), 33–55. doi:10.1023/A:1023347000978

Bozkaya, B., Erkut, E., & Laporte, G. (2003). A tabu search heuristic and adaptive memory procedure for political districting. *European Journal of Operational Research,* (144): 12–26. doi:10.1016/S0377-2217(01)00380-0

Bozkaya, B., Zhang, J., & Erkut, E. (1997). *An Effective Genetic Algorithm for the P-Median Problem* (p. 32). Edmonton, Alberta: University of Alberta - Falculty of Business - Department of Finance and Management Science.

Cano, J. R., Cordon, O., Herrera, F., & Sanchez, L. (2000). *A Greedy Randomized Adaptive Search Procedure to the Clustering Problem* (p. 9). Granada, Spain: ETS de Ingenieria Informatica. University of Granada.

Caro, F., Shirabe, T., Guignard, M., & Weintraub, A. (2004). School redistricting: embedding GIS tools with integer programming. *The Journal of the Operational Research Society, 55*(8), 836–849. doi:10.1057/palgrave.jors.2601729

Cloonan, J. B. (1972). A Note on the Compactness of Sales Territories. *Management Science, 19*(4), 469.

Crescenzi, P., & Kann, V. (1998). *A compendium of NP optimization problems: Dipartimento di Scienze della Informazione*. Uinversita di Roma La Sapienza.

D'Amico, S. J., Wang, S.-J., Batta, R., & Rump, C. M. (2002). A simulated annealing approach to police district design. *Computers & Operations Research, 29*(6), 667–684. doi:10.1016/S0305-0548(01)00056-9

Delmaire, H., Diaz, J. A., Fernandez, E., & Ortega, M. (1999). Reactive GRASP and tabu search based heuristics for the single source capacitated plant location problem. *INFOR, 37*, 194–225.

Diaz, J. A., & Fernandez, E. (2006). Hybrid scatter search and path relinking for the capacitated p-median problem. *European Journal of Operational Research, 169*(2), 570–585. doi:10.1016/j.ejor.2004.08.016

Drexl, A., & Haase, K. (1999). Fast Approximation Methods for Sales Force Deployment. *Management Science, 45*(10), 1307–1323. doi:10.1287/mnsc.45.10.1307

Ehrgott, M., & Gandibleux, X. (2000). A survey and annotated bibliography of multiobjective combinatorial optimization. *OR-Spektrum, 22*(4), 425–460. doi:10.1007/s002910000046

Feo, T. A., & Resende, M. G. C. (1995). Greedy randomized adaptive search procedures. *Journal of Global Optimization, 6*, 109–133. doi:10.1007/BF01096763

Festa, P., & Resende, M. G. C. (2002). *GRASP: An annotated bibliography* (pp. 325–367). Essays and Surveys on Metaheuristics.

Festa, P., & Resende, M. G. C. (2004). An Annotated Bibliography of GRASP: AT&T Labs Research Technical Report.

Fleischmann, B., & Paraschis, J. N. (1988). Solving a large scale districting problem: a case report. *Computers & Operations Research, 15*(6), 521–533. doi:10.1016/0305-0548(88)90048-2

Galvao, L. C., Novaes, A. G. N., Souza de Cursi, J. E., & Souza, J. C. (2006). A multiplicatively-weighted Voronoi diagram approach to logistics districting. *Computers & Operations Research, 33*(1), 93–114. doi:10.1016/j.cor.2004.07.001

Garfinkel, R. S., & Nemhauser, G. L. (1969). The Set-Partitioning Problem: Set Covering with Equality Constraints. *Operations Research, 17*(5), 848–856. doi:10.1287/opre.17.5.848

Garfinkel, R. S., & Nemhauser, G. L. (1970). Optimal Political Districting by Implicit Enumeration Techniques. *Management Science, 16*(8), B-495–B-508. doi:10.1287/mnsc.16.8.B495

Glover, F. (1989). Tabu Search - Part I. *ORSA Journal on Computing, 1*(3), 190-206.

Glover, F. (1990a). Tabu Search - Part II. *ORSA Journal on Computing, 2*(1), 4–32.

Glover, F. (1990b). Tabu search: A tutorial. *Interfaces, 20*(4), 74. doi:10.1287/inte.20.4.74

Glover, F., & Laguna, M. (1993). *Tabu Search*. Paper presented at the Modern Heuristic Techniques for Combinatorial Problems, Oxford, England.

Glover, F., Taillard, E., & Werra, D. d. (1993). A user's guide to tabu search. *Annals of Operations Research, 41*, 3–28. doi:10.1007/BF02078647

Gonzalez-Ramirez, R. G., Smith, N. R., Askin, R. G., & Kalashinkov, V. (2010). A Heuristic Approach for a Logistics Districtiong Problem. *International Journal of Innovative Computing. Information and Control, 6*(8), 3551–3562.

Guo, J., Trinidad, G., & Smith, N. (2001, February, 21). *MOZART: A Multi-Objective Zoning and AggRegation Tool*.

Helbig, R. E., Orr, P. K., & Roediger, R. R. (1972). Political redistricting by computer. *Communications of the ACM, 15*(8), 735–741. doi:10.1145/361532.361543

Hertz, A., Taillard, E., & Werra, D. d. (1995). *A Tutorial on Tabu Search*. Paper presented at the Proc. of Giornate di Lavoro AIRO'95 (Enterprise Systems: Management of Technological and Organizational Changes), Italy.

Hess, S. W., & Samuels, S. A. (1971). Experiences with a Sales Districting Model: Criteria and Implementation. *Management Science, 18*(4), 41–54. doi:10.1287/mnsc.18.4.P41

Hess, S. W., Weaver, J. B., Siegfeldt, H. J., Whelan, J. N., & Zitlau, P. A. (1965). Nonpartisan Political Redistricting by Computer. *Operations Research, 13*(6), 998–1006. doi:10.1287/opre.13.6.998

Howick, R. S., & Pidd, M. (1990). Sales force deployment models. *European Journal of Operational Research, 48*(2), 295–310. doi:10.1016/0377-2217(90)90413-6

Hu, Z., Ding, Y., & Shao, Q. (2009). Immune co-evolutionary algorithm based partition balancing optimization for tobacco distribution system. *Expert Systems with Applications: An International Journal, 36*(3), 5248–5255. doi:10.1016/j.eswa.2008.06.074

Hu, Z.-H., Yang, B., & Huang, Y.-F. (2010). A Decision Support System for Tobacco Distribution Partition Optimization Based on Immune Co-Evolutionary Algorithm. *Journal of Computers, 5*(3), 432–439. doi:10.4304/jcp.5.3.432-439

Jackson, L. E., Rouskas, G. N., & Stallmann, M. F. M. (2007). The directional p-median problem: Definition, complexity, and algorithms. *European Journal of Operational Research, 179*(3), 1097–1108. doi:10.1016/j.ejor.2005.06.080

Júnior, P. C. R. de L. (2008). *Integration of Geographic Information Systems, Meta-Heuristics and Multi-Criteria Analysis for Territories Alignment.* PhD, University of Porto, Porto.

Júnior, P. L., de Sousa, J. F., & Basto, J. B. (2008, July 1st-4th 2008). *Integration of GIS, Meta-Heuristics and Multi-Criteria Analysis for Territories Alignment.* Paper presented at the International Conference on Collaborative Decision Making, Toulouse, France.

Kalcsics, J., Melo, T., Nickel, S., & Gundra, H. (2001). *Planning Sales Territories - A Facility Location Approach.* Paper presented at the Operations Research 2001, Springer Verlag Berlin.

Kalcsics, J., Nickel, S., & Schroder, M. (2005). Towards a Unified Territory Design Approach. Applications, Algorithms and GIS Integration. *Sociedad de Estadística e Investigación Operativa. Top (Madrid)*, *13*(1), 1–74. doi:10.1007/BF02578982

Kirkizoglu, Z. (2005, June). *A Genetic Algorithm Approach for Sales Territory Alignment Problem.* Paper presented at the 35th International Conference on Computers and Industrial Engineering, Istanbul.

Klose, A. (1998). A Branch and Bound Algorithm for An Uncapacitated Facility Location Problem with a Side Constraint. *International Transactions in Operational Research*, *5*(2), 155–168. doi:10.1111/j.1475-3995.1998.tb00111.x

Klose, A., & Drexl, A. (2005). Facility location models for distribution system design. *European Journal of Operational Research*, *162*(1), 4–29. doi:10.1016/j.ejor.2003.10.031

Laguna, M., & Glover, F. (1996). What is Tabu Search? *Colorado Business Review, LXI*(5).

Leach, S. P., & Kandel, A. (1990). *Grouper: an expert system for redistricting.* Paper presented at the ACM SIGSMALL/PC symposium on Small systems, Crystal City, Virginia, United States.

Leach, S. P., & Kandel, A. (1993). Expert systems in government: a look at the redistricting problem. *SIGAPP Appl. Comput. Rev.*, *1*(1), 2–9. doi:10.1145/152535.152536

Lodish, L. M., Curtis, E., Ness, M., & Simpson, M. K. (1988). Sales Force Sizing and Deployment Using a Decision Calculus Model at Syntex Laboratories. *Interfaces*, (18): 5–20. doi:10.1287/inte.18.1.5

Lorena, L. A. N., & Senne, E. L. F. (2004). A column generation approach to capacitated p-median problems. *Computers & Operations Research*, *31*(6), 863–876. doi:10.1016/S0305-0548(03)00039-X

Lorena, L. A. N., Senne, E. L. F., Paiva, J. A. C., & Marcondes, S. P. B. (1999). Integração de Um Modelo de P-Medianas a Sistemas de Informações Geográficas. In *31° Simpósio Brasileiro de Pesquisa Operacional, Juiz de Fora, MG. Anais.* Rio de Janeiro, RJ: SOBRAPO, 1999. P. 635-647.

Macmillian, W. (2001). Redistricting in a GIS Environment: An Optimisation Algorithm Using Swithcing-Points. *Journal of Geographical Systems*, (3): 167–180. doi:10.1007/PL00011473

Marianov, V., & Fresard, F. (2005). A procedure for the strategic planning of locations, capacities and districting of jails: Application to Chile. *The Journal of the Operational Research Society*, *56*(3), 244–251. doi:10.1057/palgrave.jors.2601790

Mehrotra, A., Johnson, E. L., & Nemhauser, G. L. (1998). An Optimization Based Heuristic for Political Districting. *Management Science*, *44*(8), 1100–1114. doi:10.1287/mnsc.44.8.1100

Negreiros, M., & Palhano, A. (2006). The capacitated centred clustering problem. *Computers & Operations Research, 33*(6), 1639–1663. doi:10.1016/j.cor.2004.11.011

Niemi, R. G., Grofman, B., Carlucci, C., & Hofeller, T. (1990). Measuring Compactness and the Role of a Compactness Standard in a Test for Partisan and Racial Gerrymandering. *The Journal of Politics, 52*(4), 1155–1179. doi:10.2307/2131686

Novaes, A., Cursi, J. S., Silva, A., & Souza, J. (2009). Solving continuous location-districting problems with Voronoi diagrams. *Computers & Operations Research, 36*, 40–59. doi:10.1016/j.cor.2007.07.004

Parasuraman, A. (1977). A Management-Oriented Model for Allocating Sales Effort. *JMR, Journal of Marketing Research, 14*(1), 22. doi:10.2307/3151051

Pereira, F. T., Figueira, J., Mousseaux, V., & Roy, B. (2004). Multiple Criteria Districting Problems, Models, Algorithms, and Applications: The Public Transportation Paris Region Pricing System. *Annals of Operations Research, 154*(1), 69–92.

Pirkul, H., Gupta, R., & Rolland, E. (1999). VisOpt: a visual interactive optimization tool for P-median problems. *Decision Support Systems*, (26): 209–223. doi:10.1016/S0167-9236(99)00032-9

Reese, J. (2005). *Methods for Solving the p-Median Problem: An Annotated Bibliography*. Technical Report, Department of Mathematics, Trinity University.

Resende, M. G. C. (1998). Computing approximate solutions of the maximum covering problem using GRASP. *Journal of Heuristics, 4*, 161–171. doi:10.1023/A:1009677613792

Resende, M. G. C., & Werneck, R. F. (2006). A hybrid multistart heuristic for the uncapacitated facility location problem. *European Journal of Operational Research, 174*(1), 54–68. doi:10.1016/j.ejor.2005.02.046

Ricca, F., Scozzari, A., & Simeone, B. (2008). Weighted Voronoi region algorithms for political districting. *Mathematical and Computer Modelling, 48*, 1468–1477. doi:10.1016/j.mcm.2008.05.041

Ríos-Mercado, R. Z., & Fernández, E. (2009). A reactive GRASP for a commercial territory design problem with multiple balancing requirements. *Computers & Operations Research, 36*(3), 755–776. doi:10.1016/j.cor.2007.10.024

Rolland, E., Schilling, D. A., & Current, J. R. (1996). An efficient tabu search procedure for the p-Median Problem. *European Journal of Operational Research*, (96): 329–342.

Ross, G. T., & Zoltners, A. A. (1979). Weighted Assignment Models and Their Application. *Management Science, 25*(7), 683–696. doi:10.1287/mnsc.25.7.683

Scaparra, M. P., & Scutella, M. G. (2001). *Facilities, Locations, Customers: Building Blocks of Location Models. A Survey. Technical Report, TR-01-18*. Universitá di Pisa, Dipartimento di Informatica.

Senne, E. L. F., Lorena, L. A. N., & Pereira, M. A. (2005). A branch-and-price approach to p-median location problems. *Computers & Operations Research, 32*(6), 1655–1664. doi:10.1016/j.cor.2003.11.024

Shanker, R. J., Turner, R. E., & Zoltners, A. A. (1975). Sales Territory Design: An Integrated Approach. *Management Science, 22*(3), 309–320. doi:10.1287/mnsc.22.3.309

Shirabe, T. (2005a). Classification of Spatial Properties for Spatial Allocation Modeling. *GeoInformatica, V9*(3), 269–287. doi:10.1007/s10707-005-1285-1

Shirabe, T. (2005b). A Model of Contiguity for Spatial Unit Allocation. *Geographical Analysis, 37*(1), 2–16. doi:10.1111/j.1538-4632.2005.00605.x

Sinha, P., & Zoltners, A. A. (2001). Sales-Force Decision Models: Insights from 25 Years of Implementation. *Interfaces, 3*(31), S8 - S44. doi: 1526-548X

Taillard, É. D. (2003). Heuristic Methods for Large Centroid Clustering Problems. *Journal of Heuristics, 9*(1), 51–73. doi:10.1023/A:1021841728075

Wei, B. C., & Chai, W. Y. (2004). A Multiobjective Hybrid Metaheuristic Approach for GIS-based Spatial Zoning Model. *Journal of Mathematical Modelling and Algorithms*, (3): 245–261. doi:10.1023/B:JMMA.0000038615.32559.af

Yamada, T. (2009). A mini-max spanning forest approach to the political districting problem. *International Journal of Systems Science, 40*(5), 471–477. doi:10.1080/00207720802645246

Zhou, G., Min, H., & Gen, M. (2002). The balanced allocation of customers to multiple distribution centers in the supply chain network: a genetic algorithm approach. *Computers & Industrial Engineering, 43*(1-2), 251–261. doi:10.1016/S0360-8352(02)00067-0

Zoltners, A. A. (1976). Integer Programming Models for Sales Territory Alignment to Maximize Profit. *JMR, Journal of Marketing Research, 13*(4), 426–430. doi:10.2307/3151035

Zoltners, A. A. (1980). Integer Programming Models for Sales Resource Allocation. *Management Science, 26*(3), 242–260. doi:10.1287/mnsc.26.3.242

Zoltners, A. A. (1983). Sales Territory Alignment: A Review and Model. *Management Science, 29*(11), 1237–1256. doi:10.1287/mnsc.29.11.1237

Zoltners, A. A., & Sinha, P. (2005). Sales Territory Design: Thirty Years of Modeling and Implementation. *Marketing Science, 24*(3), 313–331. doi:10.1287/mksc.1050.0133

Zoltners, A. A., Sinha, P., & Lorimer, S. E. (2004). *Sales Force Design for Strategic Advance*. New York: Palgrave Macmillan. doi:10.1057/9780230514928

ADDITIONAL READING

Blais, M., Lapierre, S. D., & Laporte, G. (2003). Solving a home-care districting problem in an urban setting. *The Journal of the Operational Research Society, 54*(11), 1141–1147. doi:10.1057/palgrave.jors.2601625

Bong, C. W., Chai, W. Y., & Wong, C. W. (2004). State-of-the-art multiobjective metaheuristic for redistricting. *OCEANS '04. MTTS/IEEE TECHNO-OCEAN '04*, vol. 2, 763-769.

Boots, B., & South, R. (1997). Modeling retail trade areas using higher-order, multiplicatively weighted Voronoi diagrams. *Journal of Retailing, 73*(4), 519–536. doi:10.1016/S0022-4359(97)90033-6

Chiou, Y. C., & Lan, L. W. (2001). Genetic clustering algorithms. *European Journal of Operational Research, 135*(2), 413–427. doi:10.1016/S0377-2217(00)00320-9

Dominguez, E., & Munoz, J. (2008). A neural model for the p-median problem. *Computers & Operations Research, 35*(2), 404–416. doi:10.1016/j.cor.2006.03.005

Ganley, J. L., & Heath, L. S. (1998). An Experimental Evaluation of Local Search Heuristics for Graph Partitioning. *Computing, 60*(2), 121–132. doi:10.1007/BF02684361

George, J. A., Lamar, B. W., & Wallace, C. A. (1997). Political district determination using large-scale network optimization. *Socio-Economic Planning Sciences, 31*(1), 11–28. doi:10.1016/S0038-0121(96)00016-X

Hertz, A., Jaumard, B., Ribeiro, C. C., & Filho, W. P. F. (1994). A multi-criteria tabu search approach to cell formation problems in group technology with multiple objectives. *RAIRO. Operations Research, 28*(3), 303–328.

Hojati, M. (1996). Optimal political districting. *Computers & Operations Research, 23*(12), 1147–1161. doi:10.1016/S0305-0548(96)00029-9

Horn, M. E. T. (1995). Solution techniques for large regional partitioning problems. *Geographical Analysis, 27*(3), 230–248. doi:10.1111/j.1538-4632.1995.tb00907.x

Muyldermans, L., Cattrysse, D., van Oudheusden, D., & Lotan, T. (2002). Districting for salt spreading operations. *European Journal of Operational Research, 139*(3), 521–532. doi:10.1016/S0377-2217(01)00184-9

Okabe, A., Boots, B., & Sugihara, K. (1994). Nearest neighborhood operations with generalized Voronoi diagrams: a review. *International Journal of Geographical Information System, 8*(1), 43–71. doi:10.1080/02693799408901986

Okabe, A., & Suzuki, A. (1997). Locational optimization problems solved through Voronoi diagrams. *European Journal of Operational Research, 98*, 445–456. doi:10.1016/S0377-2217(97)80001-X

Piercy, N. F., Cravens, D. W., & Morgan, N. A. (1999). Relationships between Sales Management Control, Territory Design, Salesforce Performance and Sales Organization Effectiveness. *British Journal of Management, 10*, 95–111. doi:10.1111/1467-8551.00113

Skiera, B., & Albers, S. (1998). COSTA: Contribution Optimizing Sales Territory Alignment. *Marketing Science, 17*(3), 196–213. doi:10.1287/mksc.17.3.196

Trejos, J., Piza, E., & Murillo, A. (1999, March). *A Tabu Search Algorithm for Partitioning.* Preprint. Preprint 1-1999 CIMPA, University of Costa Rica. San Jose, Costa Rica.

Williams, J. C. Jr. (1995). Political redistricting: a review. *Papers in Regional Science, 74*, 13–40. doi:10.1111/j.1435-5597.1995.tb00626.x

Zoltners, A., Sinha, P., & Lorimer, S. (2008). Sales Force Effectiveness: A Framework for Researchers and Practitioners. *Journal of Personal Selling & Sales Management, 28*(2), 115–131. doi:10.2753/PSS0885-3134280201

KEY TERMS AND DEFINITIONS

Case Study: collection and presentation of detailed information and analysis about a particular entity (person, organization, business, etc.), that constitutes a form of qualitative descriptive research.

Compactness: the spatial property of being close and firmly united (i.e. having the minimum distance between all the entities of a given area).

Contiguity: continuous connection of a series of entities, a grouping of parts connected throughout an unbroken sequence and sharing a common border.

Decision Support System: a class of computer-based systems dedicated to supporting decision-making activities.

Geographic Information System: any system that captures, stores, analyzes, manages, and presents data that are linked to location.

Salesforce/Maintenance Team: company people who execute several activities related to the marketing/maintenance function and are a crucial connection between the companies and their customers.

Territory Alignment: the process of shaping and balancing small geographic units and grouping them in such a way that they completely cover a given territory under analysis, based on criteria important to a business or activity.

Territory Design: planning of territories, measuring and allocating resources to each of them, so as to completely cover a region, in the most efficient and effective manner, according to criteria related to the type of activity in question.

Chapter 13
A Hybrid Lagrangian Relaxation and Tabu Search Method for Interdependent–Choice Network Design Problems

Chi Xie
The University of Texas at Austin, USA

Mark A. Turnquist
Cornell University, USA

S. Travis Waller
The University of Texas at Austin, USA

ABSTRACT

Hybridization offers a promising approach in designing and developing improved metaheuristic methods for a variety of complex combinatorial optimization problems. This chapter presents a hybrid Lagrangian relaxation and tabu search method for a class of discrete network design problems with complex interdependent-choice constraints. This method takes advantage of Lagrangian relaxation for problem decomposition and complexity reduction while its algorithmic logic is designed based on the principles of tabu search. The algorithmic advance and solution performance of the method are illustrated by implementing it for solving a network design problem with lane reversal and crossing elimination strategies, arising from urban evacuation planning.

DOI: 10.4018/978-1-61350-086-6.ch013

INTRODUCTION

The interest about hybrid optimization methods has grown rapidly for last few years (Talbi, 2002; Jourdan *et al.*, 2009). Hybridization has become a pervasive trend and a very promising strategy in designing and developing improved metaheuristic solution methods, in view of their heuristic nature, greater flexibility and less strict mathematical property. A hybrid metaheuristic method combines structure and efficiency advantages from different principles and approaches and often provides a highly flexible and efficient tool in solving difficult combinatorial optimization problems.

A large number of production, communication, distribution and transportation infrastructure investment and planning problems can be characterized as network design problems. The common goal of a generic network design problem is to seek an optimal cost-effective network topology and capacity expansion solution with taking into account the infrastructure investment cost and the resulting network operation efficiency. Discrete network design problems, which deal with selecting (and deselecting) facility location and capacity at nodes or on arcs from a discrete choice set, are typically formulated as integer or mixed integer programming models (Wong, 1985). Many of these network design problems cause very difficult combinatorial issues, depending on the interrelationship between individual discrete choice components and the underlying network flow routing behaviors. Even in their simplest form, discrete network design problems pose the NP-hard computational complexity. Johnson *et al.* (1978) establishes its NP-completeness by showing that the classic knapsack problem is reducible to the simplest discrete network design problem; Wong (1980) showed that even finding an approximate discrete network solution is NP-hard.

Exact solution methods, such as branch and bound and Benders decomposition, are limited to solving discrete network design problems of small size (see, for example, Boyce *et al.*, 1973; Hoang,

1973, 1982; LeBlanc, 1975; Dionne and Florian, 1979; Geoffrion and Graves, 1974; Magnanti and Wong, 1984; Magnanti *et al.*, 1986; Sherali *et al.*, 1991; Cordeau *et al.*, 2006). In contrast, for large-scale applications, more research efforts have been devoted in the past two decades to developing heuristic and metaheuristic solution methods, including genetic algorithms (e.g., Xiong and Schneider, 1992; Jeon *et al.*, 2006), memetic algorithms (Baños *et al.*, 2007), simulated annealing (e.g., Lee and Yang, 1994; Drezner and Wesolowsky, 1997, 2003; Cantarella *et al.*, 2006), tabu search (e.g., Mouskos, 1991; Crainic *et al.*, 2000; Berger *et al.*, 2000), and ant colony optimization (e.g., Poorzahedy and Abulghasemi, 2005), among others.

This chapter discusses a hybrid metaheuristic solution strategy for a class of network design problems that contain complex topological or temporal restrictions (or flexibilities) between discrete arc selection decisions subject to a limited amount of resources (i.e., budget, space, time, etc.). Specifically, given a network $G = (N, A)$, where N is the node set and $A = A_f \cup A_v$ is the arc set (where A_f and A_v are the subsets of fixed arcs and variable arcs, respectively), such a generic form of network design problems is considered as below. For discussion convenience, the notation used in the problem formulation is presented first in Table 1.

Now the generic form of network design problems with discrete arc selections can be written as:

$$\min \ \mathbf{t}^\mathsf{T} \mathbf{x} \tag{1.1}$$

$$\text{subject to } 0 \le \mathbf{x} \le \mathbf{c}\left(\mathbf{y}\right) \tag{1.2}$$

$$\mathbf{y}_v \in \mathbf{Y}_v \tag{1.3}$$

$$\Delta \mathbf{x} = \mathbf{b} \tag{1.4}$$

Table 1. The notation used in the generic form of network design problems

Notation	Definition
N	Set of nodes
A	Set of arcs
A_f	Set of fixed arcs
A_v	Set of variable arcs
b	Vector of net node flow rates: $\mathbf{b} = [b_i]$, $\forall i \in N$
c	Vector of arc capacities: $\mathbf{c} = [c_{js}]$, $\forall (j,s) \in A$
x	Vector of arc flow rates: $\mathbf{x} = [x_{js}]$, $\forall (j,s) \in A$
y	Vector of arc presence: $\mathbf{y} = [y_{js}]$, $\forall (j,s) \in A$, where $\mathbf{y} = (\mathbf{y}_f, \mathbf{y}_v)$
$\mathbf{y}_f$	Vector of presence of fixed arcs: $\mathbf{y}_f = [y_{js}]$, where $y_{js} = 1$, $\forall (j,s) \in A_f$
$\mathbf{y}_v$	Vector of presence of variable arcs: $\mathbf{y}_v = [y_{js}]$, where $y_{js} = \{0,1\}$, $\forall (j,s) \in A_v$
t	Vector of arc costs: $\mathbf{t} = [t_{js}]$, $\forall (j,s) \in A$
Δ	Matrix of node-arc incidence indicators: $\Delta = [\delta_{i,js}]$, $\forall i \in N$, $(j,s) \in A$ where $\delta_{i,js} = 1$, if $i = j$; $\delta_{i,js} = -1$, if $i = s$; $\delta_{i,js} = 0$, if $i \neq j$ and $i \neq s$

$$\mathbf{g}(\mathbf{x}) \leq 0 \qquad (1.5)$$

$$\mathbf{h}(\mathbf{y}_v) \leq 0 \qquad (1.6)$$

$$\text{where} \quad \mathbf{t} = \mathbf{t}(\mathbf{x}, \mathbf{y}) \qquad (1.7)$$

This network design problem has two sets of decision variables: namely, arc flow rates $\mathbf{x} = [x_{js}]_{|A| \times 1}$, $\forall (j,s) \in A$ and arc design choices $\mathbf{y}_v = [y_{js}]_{|A_v| \times 1}$, $\forall (j,s) \in A_v$, where $\mathbf{y}_v$ denotes the variable part of the arc presence vector. The constraint set of the problem includes the flow bounding constraints (1.2), discrete choice constraints (1.3), flow conservation constraints (1.4), flow routing constraints (1.5), and interdependent design constraints (1.6), as well as a definitional constraint (1.7) for arc costs. In constraints (1.5) and (1.6), $\mathbf{g}(\mathbf{x})$ and $\mathbf{h}(\mathbf{y}_v)$ respectively represent an aggregate set of functions specifying the flow routing in the network and defining the interdependent choice relationships among discrete decision variables; these functions may be linear or nonlinear. The flow conservation constraints

reserve the net rate of flows emanating from and arriving at any node[1]. The arc bounding constraints simply set the lower and upper bounds on arc flow rates: $0 \leq x_{js} \leq c_{js}(y_{js})$. If the upper bound is simply determined by a $0-1$ design choice (i.e., $0 \leq x_{js} \leq c_{js}y_{js}$, where $y_{js} = \{0,1\}$), an all-or-nothing capacity assignment scheme is resulted: if $y_{js} = 1$, $x_{js} \leq c_{js}$; if $y_{js} = 0$, $x_{js} = 0$. The flow routing constraints specify the spatial distribution pattern of flows over the network. When traffic congestion is considered, some equilibrium-based routing principles are often employed to describe the network flow distribution. This is the case that will be discussed in this chapter.

The interdependent design constraints define an interdependent-choice relationship on the arc design variables. In its simplest form, a frequently encountered interdependent-choice constraint is the budget or resource constraint (Ohlmann and Bean, 2009), such as $\sum_{(j,s) \in A_v} d_{js} y_{js} - B \leq 0$, where d_{js} is the design cost or resource associated with selecting candidate arc (j,s) and B is the total available budget or resource for network expansion. Another simple example of interdependent-choice constraints appears in the so-called multi-level or multi-facility network design problem (Balakrishnan *et al.*, 1994; Gouveia and Telhada, 2001; Randazzo *et al.*, 2001), in which each variable arc has multiple candidate facilities but only at most one of them can be selected. However, many real-world network design problems are subject to a much more complex spatial and temporal interdependent-choice constraint set, which significantly increases the model complexity and reduces the solution tractability.

As for the definitional constraint, it simply specifies the travel cost on any arc (j,s), t_{js}, as a function of the flow rate on this arc: $t_{js} = t_{js}(x_{js})$, $\forall (j,s) \in A$. In a more general setting, the travel cost on an arc may be a function of flow rates of both this arc and some other arcs in the network. For simplicity, this more general case is not considered in this text. Finally, the objective function of the problem is considered, which simply represents the total travel cost in the network. Given that the total travel cost is the only term in the objective function, if the interdependent-choice constraint is a design budget constraint, as mentioned above, the resulting network design problem becomes the so-called budget design problem (Magnanti and Wong, 1984).

This type of discrete network design problems with a complex interdependent-choice constraint set constitutes an important branch of combinatorial optimization problems. Examples of such network design problems include lane-based traffic network design (Wong and Wong, 2002), route-based transit network design (Guihaire and Hao, 2008), water distribution network design (Baños *et al.*, 2007), and hub-and-spoke logistics network design (O'Kelly and Miller, 1994), to just name a few. In addition to these transportation and logistics problems, many network design problems arising from other fields may have a similar combinatorial difficulty. The common feature of these problems is that the complex logic relationship implied by the problem's interdependent-choice constraints (i.e., the set of constraints (1.6)) makes it very difficult to define and exhaust the prob-

lem's candidate solutions in the solution space, but the problem's constraint set is decomposable or partitionable and the formed smaller problems after decomposition or partition are relatively readily solvable.

A general algorithmic procedure to tackle this type of problems is to start from a feasible solution as an initial point and iteratively update the current solution through a neighborhood search until the optimal solution is found or a certain prespecified stopping criterion is met. Due to the complicated combinatorial relationship on discrete decision variables (as defined by the set of constraints (1.6)), however, implementing this general solution procedure for the above type of network design problems may not be feasible. Specifically, two solution difficulties are often encountered when tackling this class of problems: first, it is difficult to obtain an initial feasible solution; second, it is difficult to define a neighborhood structure. The extensive literature shows that the harder it is to find feasible neighboring solutions, the more ineffective such a search procedure (Boschetti and Maniezzo, 2009). These solution difficulties will be elaborated through an example interdependence-choice network design problem in Section 3.

The focus of this chapter is to present an integrated Lagrangian relaxation and tabu search method and illustrate its effectiveness in tackling the combinatorial complexity of a class of network design problems that contain a complex interdependent-choice relationship (hereafter referred to as the *interdependent-choice network design problem*). The metaheuristic method takes advantage of Lagrangian relaxation for problem decomposition and structure simplification and its algorithmic design is based on the principles of tabu search. By integrated, it means that the updating of Lagrangian multipliers is integrated into the iterative tabu search process, in which Lagrangian multiplier values are reviewed and updated at each iteration in terms of historical and current solutions. This method has been successfully applied to some static and dynamic network design problems of this type, arising from the context of urban evacuation planning (see Xie *et al.*, 2010; Xie and Turnquist, 2011).

This chapter is structured in six sections as follows. Following an introduction above, we give in the next section a brief description about the essential ingredients of Lagrangian relaxation and tabu search techniques and presents the basic idea of the integrated Lagrangian relaxation and tabu search (LR-TS) method. Next, a transportation network design problem with lane reversal (on arcs) and crossing elimination (at nodes) strategies is introduced, which emerges from the urban evacuation planning practice. We use it as an illustrative example to elaborate how the integrated method is designed and implemented. The algorithm effectiveness and computation performance are then evaluated by an example application for an evacuation network of realistic size. Finally, the chapter is concluded in the last section.

INTEGRATION OF LAGRANGIAN RELAXATION AND TABU SEARCH

As the discussion involves both the Lagrangian relaxation and tabu search techniques, this section gets started with a general overview of these two techniques. Following it, the algorithmic idea of combining them for tackling interdependent-choice network design problems is presented.

Lagrangian relaxation is a general mathematical programming method applied for decomposing or relaxing problems to exploit their special structures. It has long been used for discovering theoretical insights and developing solution algorithms for various difficult mathematical programming problems. For discrete and combinatorial optimization problems, Lagrangian relaxation is typically used to relax a set of complicating side constraints and accordingly compensate a penalty term in the objective function (see Geoffrion,

1974, for example). By adjusting the values of Lagrangian multipliers with the penalty term to an appropriate level, the optimal solution may be found by solving the relaxed Lagrangian problem that can often take advantage of various previously developed algorithms.

Tabu search is one of the metaheuristic optimization techniques that are usually used to guide and orient the search of other (local) search procedures. The foundation of tabu search is generally attributed to Glover (1986), in which he described the present form of this technique we use today. Though it belongs to the class of local search techniques, tabu search enhances the performance of a local search method by using memory structures. Tabu search uses a neighborhood search procedure to iteratively move from a solution to another neighboring solution, until some stopping criterion is satisfied. To explore regions of the search space that would be left unexplored and escape local optimality formed by local search, tabu search modifies the neighborhood structure of each solution as the search progresses. The solutions admitted to the new neighborhood are determined through the use of special memory structures.

It is well known that Lagrangian relaxation and tabu search both have been extensively used to construct effective solution methods for difficult discrete and combinatorial optimization problems. The algorithmic idea of combining Lagrangian relaxation and tabu search is not entirely new. Filho and Galvão (1998) discussed and emphasized the effectiveness and efficacy of both Lagrangian relaxation and tabu search techniques in solving computer network design problems (e.g., the capacitated concentrator location problem). Borghetti *et al.* (2001) suggested utilizing these two techniques in an iterative manner to tackle the unit commitment problem (i.e., a specific network design problem arising from electric power system design), by which Lagrangian relaxation is used to obtain good starting solutions and tabu search functions at refining them.

Grünert (2002) proposed a so-called Lagrangian tabu search (LTS) method for linear mixed integer programming problems. In particular, he used a capacitated facility location problem in the context of distribution network design as an example to illustrate the concept and implementation of the LTS method. His LTS procedure is constructed by inserting a Lagrangian relaxation device into a common tabu search framework, in which Lagrangian relaxation performs as defining the solution neighborhood and updating the current solution (with other tabu settings).

In contrast, the hybrid metaheuristic presented in this chapter follows an alternative algorithmic principle to those described above. Given a network design problem or a general combinatorial optimization problem with a complex interdependent-choice relationship on discrete decisions, the most challenging algorithmic barrier is on how to define the neighborhood structure and exhaust the solution evaluations in the neighborhood. To relieve this solution difficulty, a tabu search process is placed into a Lagrangian relaxation framework, by which Lagrangian relaxation decomposes the problem into a relaxation problem and a (or more) penalty term evaluation problem(s) while tabu search is used to tackle the easier relaxation problem and update Lagrangian multipliers.

The integration of Lagrangian relaxation and tabu search for interdependent-choice network design problems is intrigued by the following observation. Suppose that the interdependent-choice constraints of such a network design problem have a special decomposable structure such as,

$$h(y_v) \leq 0 \Rightarrow \begin{cases} h_1(y_v) \leq 0 \\ h_2(y_v) \leq 0 \end{cases}$$

where $h_2(y_v) \leq 0$ is an extra part of the interdependent-choice constraints that complicate the definition of the neighborhood structure of the problem. By the extra part here, it implicitly means that a reduced network design problem, as obtained by removing the $h_2(y_v) \leq 0$ part from the original problem, is relatively readily solvable by using traditional exact or approximate solution methods. This structural feature motivates the use of Lagrangian relaxation.

By relaxing $h_2(y_v) \leq 0$ and compensating this constraint subset by a penalty term into the objective function, the relaxed Lagrangian problem can be written as,

$$\min \quad t^T x + p^T h_2(y_v) \tag{2.1}$$

$$\text{subject to } 0 \leq x \leq c(y) \tag{2.2}$$

$$y_v \in Y_v \tag{2.3}$$

$$\Delta x = b \tag{2.4}$$

$$g(x) \leq 0 \tag{2.5}$$

$$h_1(y_v) \leq 0 \tag{2.6}$$

$$\text{where} \quad t = t(x, y) \tag{2.7}$$

where $p \geq 0$ is the Lagrangian multiplier vector, whose length equals the number of constraints in $h_2(y_v) \leq 0$. Each of the Lagrangian multipliers is used to compensate the violation of one corresponding interdependent-choice constraint in $h_2(y_v) \leq 0$.

Under the Lagrangian relaxation framework, it is well known that the effectiveness of the Lagrangian relaxation method mainly depends on how to determine the values of Lagrangian multipliers. The conventional way to do so is to employ the subgradient method, which is to adjust the Lagrangian multiplier values based on the results of repeatedly solving the Lagrangian problem until the Lagrangian multiplier values converge to a satisfied level. However, given that the relaxed Lagrangian problem is still a difficult combinatorial optimization problem, a procedure that requires solving it repeatedly may not be cost-effective.

Suppose that the relaxed Lagrangian problem can be well tackled by tabu search. Thus, an alternative approach of circumventing the task of determining the optimal values of Lagrangian multipliers is to integrate a multiplier updating mechanism into a tabu search procedure (Gendreau, 2002). Different from the subgradient method that updates Lagrangian multipliers entirely based on the optimal Lagrangian problem solution, the use of iteration-based self-adjusting Lagrangian multipliers is much more efficient and flexible. At any iteration of the tabu search process, the current solution (to the relaxed Lagrangian problem) is examined for the existence of any violation of constraints in $\mathbf{h}_2(\mathbf{y}_v) \leq 0$ and the examination result is recorded into a frequency-based memory, which will then be used to make adjustments to the Lagrangian multiplier values. With the continuously updated Lagrangain multipliers along the search itinerary, the search procedure attempts to find an optimal (or near optimal) solution to the original network design problem by solving the Lagrangian problem (with a set of dynamic Lagrangian multiplier values) once. Such a multiplier self-adjusting mechanism embedded in a tabu search procedure was successfully implemented in Gendreau *et al.* (1994).

It is clear that the tabu search procedure suggested here performs two functions simultaneously, namely, searching for the optimal solution to the Lagrangian problem and updating the Lagrangian multipliers. The implementation of the resulting LR-TS method follows such a rather straight-forward manner: starting with an initial feasible solution to the relaxed Lagrangian problem, the search proceeds with a sequence of local searches and diversification phases until a predetermined stopping criterion is met. Each local search scans all candidate solutions in the neighborhood with evaluating the objective function of the Lagrangian problem for each solution. The objective function evaluation in our case includes two parts: the travel cost term and the penalty cost term. An iteration is finished by accepting the best solution in the neighborhood as the new current solution and updating the Lagrangian multipliers. This scanning and selection process finally stops with the best feasible solution (to the original network design problem) encountered during the search, once a predefined number of diversification phases has been performed. The whole search procedure can be sketched as follows:

Step 0. Choose an initial solution s to the relaxed Lagrangian problem in the search space S. Set $s^* = s$, $i = 0$ and $j = 0$.

Step 1. Set $i = i + 1$ and conduct a diversification move.

Step 2. Set $j = j + 1$ and generate a subset S^* of candidate solutions from the neighborhood of s, $N(s)$, in terms of the recency-based memory and aspiration criterion.

Step 3. Choose an elite subset S^{**} in S^*, and conduct local moves belonging to S^{**} as well as update the recency-based and frequency-based memories, aspiration criterion, current solution s, best solution s^*, and Lagrangian multipliers $\mathbf{p}$.

Step 4. If a stopping criterion for the local search is met, go to the next step; otherwise, go to step 3.

Step 5. If a stopping criterion for the diversification search is met, stop; otherwise, go to step 1.

A LANE-BASED NETWORK DESIGN PROBLEM WITH INTERDEPENDENT-CHOICE CONSTRAINTS

In many cases, the best way to interpret an algorithmic idea is through an example. This text is not an exclusive case. The applicability and effectiveness of the proposed LR-TS method can be better justified and validated by using an example network design problem (in this section) and an application of the method for its solutions (in next section).

The structural complexity of this example problem is mainly caused by the incorporation of two lane-based network design strategies, lane reversal and crossing elimination, which forms the problem's interdependent-choice constraints. Lane reversal has long been used as a traffic control measure to accommodate the unbalanced traffic flows between the two counter driving directions of a congested roadway section. When implemented in evacuation networks, an optimal lane-reversal configuration typically results in the traffic directions of inbound lanes reversed to serve the overwhelming outbound traffic, by which the outbound capacity and network throughput rate are significantly increased. Recent numerical studies (Tuydes and Ziliaskopoulos, 2006; Shekhar and Kim, 2006; Meng *et al.*, 2008; Hamza-Lup *et al.*, 2007) and evacuation practices (Urbina and Wolshon, 2003; Wolshon and Lambert, 2004) proved the effectiveness of lane reversal in traffic delay reduction and evacuation efficiency enhancement. Crossing elimination, on the other hand, is a lane-based capacity reallocation strategy to reduce traffic delays at intersections (Cova and Johnson, 2003). The basic rationale underlying this technique is to convert an intersection with interrupted flow conditions to an uninterrupted flow facility by disabling the existing traffic control device (e.g., a signal or stop/yield sign) and prohibiting some turning movements (through blocking lane entries and limiting flow directions). With removing the stop-and-go traffic control setting, the intersection capacity for those allowable traffic movements is significantly expanded. Recent research has suggested a combination of these two lane-based strategies for evacuation network optimization, which shows greater potential in improving the evacuation efficiency than the application of either of them solely (Kalafaras and Peeta, 2010; Xie *et al.*, 2010; Xie and Turnquist, 2011;). Several

examples of the joint use of lane reversal and crossing elimination are illustrated in Figure 1.

The combination creates a more difficult network design problem than problems relying on either of them solely. To better understand the problem complexity, the problem is defined and analyzed on an expanded traffic network as shown in Figure 2. Given such a network representation, each intersection is represented by an intersection subnetwork and each roadway section represented by a roadway-section subnetwork in the node-arc network. The roadway-section subnetwork between the two intersections includes 6 nodes and 4 arcs, where each traffic direction is represented by a pair of consecutive directed arcs and there are one upstream node, downstream node and intermediate node associated with each traffic direction. The upstream and downstream nodes (i.e., nodes j, k, l, and m) provide connections between the roadway section and its adjacent intersections. The intermediate node is assigned as a traffic source node (i.e., nodes s and t. On the other hand, the intersection subnetwork consists of 8 nodes and 12 arcs, creating 16 potential crossing points if all these arcs are allowed to be present.

The notation used in defining the problem is given in Table 2. The discrete arc design choices of such a network design problem, $\mathbf{y}_v = \left(\mathbf{y}^c, \mathbf{y}^r, \mathbf{n}^r\right) = \left(\left[y_{ij}^c\right], \left[y_{js}^r\right], \left[n_{js}^r\right]\right)$, $\forall (i,j) \in A_c$ $(j,s) \in A_r$, determine the network capacity and connectivity configurations. The connectivity variables, y_{ij}^c, $\forall (i,j) \in A_c$ and y_{js}^r, $\forall (i,j) \in A_r$, are both $0-1$ dummy variables. When $y_{ij}^c = 1$, it indicates that a positive flow rate on intersection arc (i,j) is allowed; when $y_{ij}^c = 0$, it indicates that arc (i,j) is blocked and accordingly $x_{ij} = 0$. When $y_{js}^r = 1$ (or $n_{js}^r \geq 1$), it indicates that at least one lane along roadway-section arc (j,s), is used; when $y_{js}^r = 0$ (or $n_{js}^r = 0$), it indicates that arc (j,s) vanishes in the network (i.e., all lanes originally

Figure 1. Examples of the joint use of lane reversal and crossing elimination

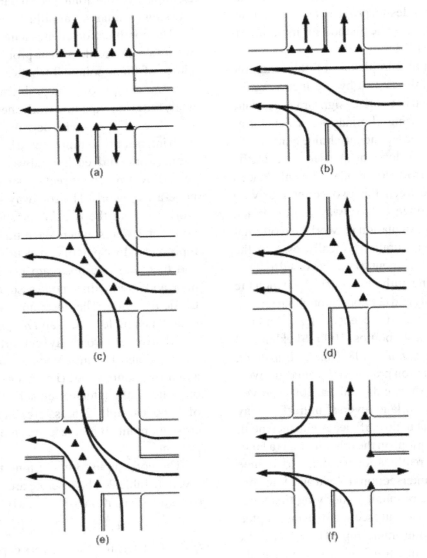

Figure 2. The expanded network representation

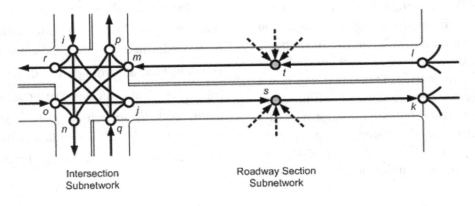

Intersection
Subnetwork

Roadway Section
Subnetwork

Table 2. The notation used in the example network design problem with interdependent-choice constraints

Notation	Definition
N	Set of nodes
N_o	Set of origin nodes
N_d	Set of destination nodes
Γ_j	Set of downstream nodes of node j, $\forall j \in N$
Γ_j^{-1}	Set of upstream nodes of node j, $\forall j \in N$
A	Set of arcs
A_v	Set of variable arcs
A_r	Set of roadway-section arcs, where $A_r \subset A_v$
A_c	Set of intersection arcs, where $A_c \subset A_v$
W_{od}	Set of paths between O-D pair o-d, $\forall o \in N_o$, $d \in N_d$
c_{js}^l	Lane capacity of arc (j,s), $\forall(j,s) \in A_r$
t_{js}^0	Free-flow travel cost on arc (j,s), $\forall(j,s) \in A_r$
b_o	Net flow rate from origin node o, $\forall o \in N_o$
$N_{jk,bn}$	Total number of lanes of two reverse directions of a roadway section, along each of which there is a pair of consecutive roadway-section arcs $[(j,s),(s,k)]$ or $[(l,t),(t,m)]$, $\forall(j,s),(s,k),(l,t),(t,m) \in A_r$
n_{js}^r	Number of lanes on arc (j,s), $\forall(j,s) \in A_r$
n_{jk}^r	Number of lanes on consecutive arc pair $[(j,s),(s,k)]$, $\forall(j,s),(s,k) \in A_r$
c_{js}	Capacity arc (j,s), $\forall(j,s) \in A_r$, where $c_{js} = c_{js}^l n_{js}^r$
x_{js}	Flow rate on arc (j,s), $\forall(j,s) \in A$
t_{js}	Travel cost on arc (j,s), $\forall(j,s) \in A_r$, where t_{js} is a function of x_{js} and n_{js}^r
y_{ij}^c	Connectivity indicator of arc (i,j), $\forall(i,j) \in A_c$, where $y_{ij}^c = 0$ or 1
y_{js}^r	Connectivity indicator of arc (j,s), $\forall(j,s) \in A_r$, where $y_{js}^r = 0$ or 1
v_{od}	Flow rate between O-D pair o-d, $\forall o \in N_o$, $d \in N_d$
f_w^{od}	Flow rate on path w between O-D pair o-d, $\forall o \in N_o$, $d \in N_d$, $w \in W_{od}$
τ_w^{od}	Cumulative individual marginal travel cost on path w between O-D pair o-d, $\forall o \in N_o$, $d \in N_d$, $w \in W_{od}$

continued on following page

Table 2. Continued

Notation	Definition
π_w^{od}	Supplementary travel cost on path w between O-D pair o-d, $\forall o \in N_o$, $d \in N_d$, $w \in W_{od}$
ξ_w^{od}	Travel cost perception error on path w between O-D pair o-d, $\forall o \in N_o$, $d \in N_d$, $w \in W_{od}$
T_w^{od}	Individual perceived travel time on path w between O-D pair o-d, $\forall o \in N_o$, $d \in N_d$, $w \in W_{od}$, where $T_w^{od} = \tau_w^{od} + \pi_w^{od} + \xi_w^{od}$
P_w^{od}	Probability of individuals choosing path w among all paths between O-D pair o-d, $\forall o \in N_o$, $d \in N_d$, $w \in W_{od}$
$\delta_{js,w}^{od}$	Arc-path incidence indicator denoting the relationship between arc (j,s) and path w, where $\delta_{ij,w}^{od} = \{0,1\}$, $\forall (i,j) \in A$, $o \in N_o$, $o \in N_o$, $d \in N_d$, $w \in W_{od}$

designed for this traffic direction are reversed for its counter flows). In summary, the decision variables, y_{ij}^c, $\forall (i,j) \in A_c$, and n_{js}^r and y_{js}^r, $\forall (j,s) \in A_r$, specify the lane-reversal and crossing-elimination settings, respectively.

It is well known that an emergency evacuation is typically caused by one or more unique, one-time events under which, unlike their daily commuting travels, evacuees inevitably have a certain degree of ambiguity and frustration in choosing destinations and routes. In some cases, there are a set of prepared public refuges or shelters by the emergency management authority, while in many other cases, evacuees are only prompted to leave the emergency area as soon as possible. Many evacuees may not affirmatively choose a specific refuge or shelter outside the evacuation network as their destinations before setting out their evacuating trips. Numerous experiences showed that evacuees tend to select their evacuating routes and destinations based on their own perceptions of danger and observations to ongoing traffic conditions (Golding and Kasperson, 1988). To accommodate this ambiguity and uncertainty within travel choices, two specific modeling techniques are applied to describe the traffic distribution and routing process under emergency conditions: 1) the simultaneous destination and route choice concept; 2) the stochastic user-equilibrium traffic routing principle. Without resorting to complex modeling mechanisms, the integrated destination and route choice concept can be readily modeled by a super-destination network representation (see Sheffi, 1985). With this single-destination setting, the destination choice process does not need to be explicitly modeled; instead, all used egress nodes of the evacuation network would be determined as a virtual destination simultaneously when any evacuee chooses a route to the super destination. This setting also simplifies the composition of traffic flows over the network—traffic flows are homogeneous by destination. Stochastic user-equilibrium traffic flows may be described by an equivalent mathematical program, variational inequality, complementarity system, or fixed-point problem. In the problem formulation given below, a mathematical program will be used to define the stochastic user-equilibrium routing.

Problem Formulation

Following the notation list specific to the example problem in Table 2, a detailed mathematical specification of the lane-based network design problem is given, in the modeling framework defined by the generic form of interdependent-choice network design problems. The objective of the problem is to minimize the total travel cost (i.e., the total evacuation time):

$$\min \mathbf{t}^{\mathsf{T}}\mathbf{x} = \sum_{(j,s)\in A_r} t_{js}\left(x_{js}, n_{js}^r\right) x_{js} \tag{3}$$

where the travel cost of arc (j,s), t_{js}, is a function of both the arc flow rate, x_{js}, and the number of traffic lanes, n_{js}^r. The following increasing, convex, continuously differentiable function is used to specify arc travel cost t_{js},

$$t_{js} = t_{js}^0 \left[1 + \alpha_{js}\left(\frac{x_{js}}{c_{js}^l n_{js}^r}\right)^{\beta_{js}}\right] \tag{4.1}$$
$$\forall \left(j,s\right) \in A_r$$

where $\alpha_{js} > 0$ and $\beta_{js} > 0$ are arc-specific function parameters, t_{js}^0 is the free-flow travel cost, and c_{js}^l is the lane capacity. Note that the arc cost function presented above is only applicable to roadway-section arcs. For modeling simplicity, the travel cost associated with any intersection arc is assumed to be zero, because no traffic delay occurs at intersections after crossing elimination:

$$t_{ij} = 0$$
$$\forall \left(i,j\right) \in A_c \tag{4.2}$$

Due to this reason, the objective function of the problem includes the travel cost associated with roadway-section arcs only.

The flow bounding constraints $0 \leq \mathbf{x} \leq \mathbf{c}(\mathbf{y})$ includes two parts: the arc capacity constraints and the flow nonnegativity constraints. By using the discrete design variables, y_{js}^r, and the connectivity indicator of roadway-section arc (j,s), and y_{ij}^c, the connectivity indicator of intersection arc (i,j), the arc capacity and flow nonnegativity constraints for arc (j,s) are,

$$x_{js} \leq N y_{js}^r$$
$$\forall \left(j,s\right) \in A_r \tag{5.1}$$

$$x_{js} \geq 0$$
$$\forall \left(j,s\right) \in A_r \tag{5.2}$$

and the arc capacity and flow nonnegativity constraints for arc (i,j) are,

$$x_{ij} \leq N y_{ij}^c$$
$$\forall \left(i,j\right) \in A_c \tag{5.3}$$

$$x_{ij} \geq 0$$
$$\forall \left(i,j\right) \in A_c \tag{5.4}$$

where N is a sufficiently large number.

The discrete choice constraints for design variables, $\mathbf{y}_v \in \mathbf{Y}_v$, include the 0-1 arc presence settings:

$$y_{ij}^c = \{0,1\}$$
$$\forall \left(i,j\right) \in A_c \tag{6.1}$$

$$y_{js}^r = \{0,1\}$$
$$\forall \left(j,s\right) \in A_r \tag{6.2}$$

and lane-based capacity availability settings:

$n_{js}^r \geq 0$ and integral

$$\forall (j,s) \in A_r \qquad (6.3)$$

The set of flow conservation constraints, $\Delta \mathbf{x} = \mathbf{b}$, have two forms corresponding to two different lane-reversal configurations. Consider the source nodes (i.e., nodes s and t) in the roadway-section subnetwork in Figure 2. When the roadway section allows two-way traffic, the traffic generated from the source node with any direction is accommodated by its corresponding traffic lane(s). The flow conservation constraints for source nodes s and t for the two-way traffic operation are respectively,

$$x_{sk} - x_{js} = b_s$$

$$\forall s \in N_o$$

$$x_{tm} - x_{lt} = b_t$$

$$\forall t \in N_o$$

On the other hand, when one traffic direction (e.g., $[(l,t),(t,m)]$) is fully reversed to serve the other direction (i.e., $[(j,s),(s,k)]$), the traffic originating from the source node (i.e., node s) associated with this direction will be carried by its counter direction. It is equivalent to setting the net flow rate from node t to be 0 and accordingly increasing the net flow rate from node s to $b_s + b_t$. For this one-way traffic operation, the flow conservation constraints for origin nodes s and t are:

$$x_{sk} - x_{js} = b_s + b_t$$

$$\forall s \in N_o$$

$$x_{tm} - x_{lt} = 0$$

$$\forall t \in N_o$$

The above two lane operations can be integrated into the following set of flow conservation constraints, with using the connectivity indicators y_{jk}^r and y_{lm}^r,

$$x_{sk} - x_{js} = b_s y_{jk}^r + b_t \left(1 - y_{lm}^r\right) \qquad (7.1)$$

$$\forall s,t \in N_o$$

$$x_{tm} - x_{lt} = b_t y_{lm}^r + b_s \left(1 - y_{jk}^r\right) \qquad (7.2)$$

$$\forall s,t \in N_o$$

where $y_{jk}^r = y_{js}^r = y_{sk}^r$ and $y_{lm}^r = y_{lt}^r = y_{tm}^r$. The flow conservation constraints for other nodes (except for the destination node) have a standard form with the net flow rate equal to zero. For example, for node j and m in Figure 2, the following flow conservation constraints hold:

$$x_{js} - \sum_{i \in \Gamma_j^{-1}} x_{ij} = 0 \qquad (7.3)$$

$$\forall j \in N \setminus \left(N_o \bigcup N_d\right)$$

$$x_{tm} - \sum_{n \in \Gamma_m} x_{mn} = 0 \qquad (7.4)$$

$$\forall m \in N \setminus \left(N_o \bigcup N_d\right)$$

The arc-based flow conservation constraints given above may be written in the path-based form, by using the following complimentary equations, which favors the expression of the flow routing constraints,

$$v_{od} = \sum_w f_w^{od}$$

$$\forall o \in N_o, d \in N_d$$

$$x_{js} = \sum_{od} \sum_w f_w^{od} \delta_{js,w}^{od}$$

$$\forall (j,s) \in A$$

where the O-D flow rate v_{od} is a function of relevant node flow rates, and arc-path incidence indicator $\delta_{js,w}^{od}$ is determined by relevant arc connectivity indicators.

As aforementioned, the stochastic user-equilibrium principle is adopted to describe traffic flow routing in evacuation networks. In this manner, the flow routing constraints, $\mathbf{g(x)} \leq 0$, can be expressed by the following mathematical program[2]:

$$\min \sum_{od} v_{od} E \left(\min_{w} T_w^{od} | \tau^{od}\left(\mathbf{f}\right) + \pi^{od}\left(\mathbf{f}^{od}\right) \right) - \sum_{od}\sum_{w} \pi_w^{od} f_w^{od} \tag{8}$$

It is important to recognize that the optimal solution of the above mathematical program is equivalent to the stochastic user-equilibrium flow pattern. Due to space limit, only a brief description is provided here. Interested readers are encouraged to refer to Daganzo (1982) and Sheffi (1985) for details about the solution equivalence and uniqueness. In the objective function given above, v_{od} and f_w^{od} are the traffic flow rate from origin o to destination d and the traffic flow rate on path w from origin o to destination d, respectively. The expectation function in the first term, $E \left(\min_{w} T_w^{od} | \tau^{od}\left(\mathbf{f}\right) + \pi^{od}\left(\mathbf{f}^{od}\right) \right)$, denotes the expected perceived travel cost over all the paths connecting O-D pair o-d, where the individual perceived travel cost, T_w^{od}, is a random variable, defined as $T_w^{od} = \tau_w^{od} + \pi_w^{od} + \xi_w^{od}$. The first two parts of T_w^{od} are deterministic: τ_w^{od} is a function related to the traffic flow and travel cost of all arcs on path w, $\sum_{js} \left(\int_0^{x_{js}} t_{js}\left(\omega\right) d\omega / x_{js} \right) \delta_{js,w}^{od}$ and π_w^{od} is defined as such a supplementary path cost in T_w^{od} that the relationship is maintained; the third part, ξ_w^{od}, is the individual stochastic perception error. It is noted that given the flow routing constraints are specified by the mathematical

program given above, the problem formulation has the so-called bi-level structure.

Finally, let us turn to the design choice constraints, $\mathbf{h(y}_v) \leq 0$, which define the interdependent relationship of the discrete decision variables of the problem. First, there exist a set of capacity conservation and continuity constraints for roadway-section subnetworks, which reserves the total capacity of a roadway section that can be used by the two reverse traffic directions and maintains the consistency of number of lanes along either of the traffic directions. Given the fixed lane capacity, the capacity exchange between the two directions of the roadway section is represented by the numbers of their lanes. Referring to the example roadway-section subnetwork in Figure 2, the capacity conservation and continuity constraints can be written as,

$$n_{jk}^r + n_{lm}^r = n_{jk,mn} \\ \forall \left(j,s\right),\left(s,k\right),\left(l,t\right),\left(t,m\right) \in A_r \tag{9.1}$$

$$n_{js}^r = n_{sk}^r = n_{jk}^r \text{ and } n_{lt}^r = n_{tm}^r = n_{lm}^r \\ \forall \left(j,s\right),\left(s,k\right),\left(l,t\right),\left(t,m\right) \in A_r \tag{9.2}$$

where $n_{jk,mn}$ is the total number of lanes of the two reverse traffic directions of a roadway section. This set of constraints regulates the lane-reversal configuration.

There exists an inherent connection between the connectivity indicator of a roadway-section arc and its corresponding number of lanes: for example, given z_{js} and n_{js} in Figure 2, if $y_{js}^r = 1$, then $n_{js} \geq 1$, and vice versa; if $y_{js}^r = 0$, then $n_{js} = 0$, and vice versa. The following set of inequalities is used to describe this relationship:

$$y_{js}^r \leq n_{js}^r \\ \forall \left(j,s\right) \in A_r \tag{10.1}$$

$$y_{js}^r M \geq n_{js}^r$$

$$\forall (j, s) \in A_r \qquad (10.2)$$

where y_{js}^r is a 0-1 binary integer, n_{js}^r is a non-negative integer, and M is a sufficiently large number.

Finally, there are a set of crossing-elimination constraints for intersection arcs. By referring to Figure 2, it can be seen that these constraints have two forms, namely, two-arc constraints and three-arc constraints, as follows,

$$y_{oj}^c + y_{qp}^c \leq 1$$

$$\forall (o, j), (q, p) \in A_c \qquad (11.1)$$

$$y_{ij}^c + y_{mn}^c + y_{qp}^c \leq 1$$

$$\forall (i, j), (m, n), (q, p) \in A_c \qquad (11.2)$$

where these two constraints state that any potential crossing conflict between arc y_{oj} and y_{qp} and between any two of arcs y_{ij}, y_{mn}, and y_{qp}, respectively, is not allowed in an evacuation network. In other words, it means that at most one arc can carry traffic flows and other arcs crossing this one must be disallowed. At a four-leg intersection, there exist 16 potential crossing points, which leads to 4 two-arc constraints and 4 three-arc constraints.

Problem Complexities

Due to the complex relationship among the discrete choice variables confined by the interdependence-choice constraints (see [9] – [11]), a few algorithmic difficulties emerge from implementing a general iterative solution procedure. First, the crossing-elimination constraints define such a strict intersection-arc configuration that no apparent feasible solution is available at hand as an initial solution. The ordinary configuration of a traffic network with intersection controls, as used for daily commuting traffic, does not deliver a feasible solution, because the traffic turning movements at any intersection controlled by traffic signals or stop/yield signs allow crossing points. Therefore, some external procedure, if possible, needs to be developed to obtain an initial feasible solution.

Second, the neighborhood structure of an arbitrary solution is too complex to be defined, given the complementary and conflicting interrelationships between the lane-reversal and crossing-elimination constraint sets. An intuitive definition for a candidate move in a neighborhood region may be an arc addition, reduction, or swap (for intersection arcs) and a lane exchange between the counter arc pairs (for roadway-section arcs). It is not hard to speculate that, to satisfy the network connectivity requirements, implementation of a candidate move typically requires a set of complex network manipulations. Under this situation, extracting an exhaustive candidate list from the neighborhood of a feasible solution becomes a very difficult task.

To tackle these problem difficulties, our focus in the next section is given to how the proposed LR-TS method can be applied for problem decomposition and complexity reduction. In particular, under the Lagrangian relaxation framework, the set of crossing-elimination constraints (i.e., [11]) are relaxed and compensated by a penalty term in the objective function. The relaxed Lagrangian problem is inherently a pure optimal lane-reversal problem (hereafter referred to as the *lane-reversal subproblem*) plus a penalty term. The evaluation of the penalty term becomes a set of optimal intersection crossing-reduction subproblems (hereafter referred to as the *crossing-elimination subproblem*), where it generates one crossing-reduction subproblem for each eligible intersection subnetwork.

IMPLEMENTATION OF THE LR-TS METHOD

The rationale behind the application of the LR-TS method comes from the special structural feature of the proposed model. Note that travel costs are all associated with roadway-section arcs while intersection arcs are merely used for maintaining the network connectivity. In accordance, the intersection crossing-elimination constraints can be regarded as side constraints and the objective function value of the lane-reversal subproblem is actually the system cost with an ignorance of these side constraints. To this end, Lagrangian relaxation offers a convenient tool to decompose the problem and reduce its structural complexity so that the lane-reversal and crossing-elimination subproblems can be dealt with separately.

Lagrangian Relaxation

The Lagrangian problem is generated as follows, after relaxing the crossing-elimination constraints and adding a corresponding penalty term into the objective function,

$$\min \mathbf{t}^{\mathsf{T}}\mathbf{x} =$$

$$\sum_{(j,s)\in A_r} t_{js}\left(x_{js}, n_{js}^r\right)x_{js} + \sum_{(i,j),(m,n)\in A_c} p_{ij,mn}\left(y_{ij}^c + y_{mn}^c - 1\right)^+$$

(12)

subject to (4) – (10), where

$$\left(y_{ij}^c + y_{mn}^c - 1\right)^+ = \max\left(0, y_{ij}^c + y_{mn}^c - 1\right)$$

Note that here *(i,j)* and *(m,n)* are a pair of intersection arcs that have a potential crossing point (refer to Figure 2).

The objective function of the Lagrangian problem consists of two parts. The first part is the objective function of the original problem (i.e., the total travel cost), while the second one is the penalty term supplemented by the Lagrangian relaxation, representing the sum of all penalty costs from the relaxation of the crossing-elimination constraints. In the penalty term, $p_{ij,mn}$ is a Lagrangian multiplier ($p_{ij,mn} \geq 0$), which, in our

case, is also termed as the *unit penalty cost*. The unit penalty cost is used to compensate the violation of a single crossing-elimination constraint $y_{ij}^c + y_{mn}^c - 1$.

With the Lagrangian relaxation action above, the problem is not only benefited from the removal of the crossing-elimination constraints, but also the overall size of the problem is significantly reduced. This can be seen from the observation that with the removal of the crossing-elimination constraints, an intersection subnetwork is reduced to a node, since the lane-reversal manipulation does not take into account and does not need the constraints associated with the crossing-elimination configuration at intersections. The graphical topology with this intersection subnetwork reduction is named *reduced network*. The reduced network from the expanded network in Figure 2 is illustrated in Figure 3, where the intersection subnetwork with 8 nodes and 12 arcs is replaced by a single node. Following the network reduction, network flows can be evaluated much more efficiently on the reduced network than its expanded counterpart.

The complexity reduction is also embodied by the availability of initial feasible solutions. For example, an existing network solution without any lane-reversal and crossing-elimination configuration (e.g., the existing traffic network configuration used for daily commuting traffic) can be used as an initial solution for the Lagrangian problem. Of course, a better initial solution may be obtained by considering reversing lanes on some major eligible roadways. Nevertheless, obtaining an initial feasible solution for the relaxed Lagrangian problem is a relatively easy task compared to that for the original problem.

The relaxed Lagrangian problem is still a complex combinatorial optimization problem. To tackle its combinatorial complexity, a tabu search procedure is implemented below, which functions at searching for the optimal solution of the Lagrangian problem and updating the Lagrangian multipliers simultaneously.

Figure 3. The reduced network representation

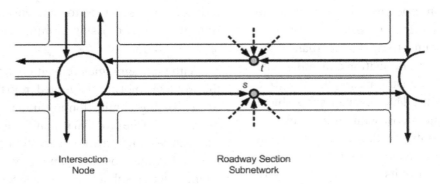

Intersection
Node

Roadway Section
Subnetwork

Tabu Search

The basic elements of the tabu search procedure specific to the example problem are briefly described below, including the neighborhood, moves, elite list, tabu list, aspiration criteria, intensification, diversification, and Lagrangian multiplier updating. More implementation details can be referred to in Xie and Turnquist (2011).

Two types of neighborhoods are used in the proposed tabu search procedure: an *adjacent neighborhood* for the local search phase, and a *distant neighborhood* for the diversification search. A distant neighborhood is used to guide the diversification search to enter an unvisited feasible region and its neighborhood structure and moving mechanism is distinct from an adjacent neighborhood, therefore, the discussion of its implementation will be postponed to a later place in this section.

The adjacent neighborhood for a current network solution is made up of all lane-based network configurations that can be reached by a single lane-reversing transformation from the current solution. The capacity exchange with a lane-reversing operation only occurs between the two adjacent, counter traffic directions of a roadway section. In other words, a move is defined as a lane exchange between the two directions in a roadway-section subnetwork. A single lane reversal may only change the capacity of the two

adjacent arc pairs, or change both the capacity and connectivity of the network, depending on the number of lanes to be reversed and the number of lanes on these two arc pairs before and after the lane reversal. In this regard, three types of moves may be defined to reach a candidate solution in the neighborhood.

The first type of moves only involves a capacity exchange without modifying the network connectivity. The lane-reversing direction of such a move may be ideally determined by comparing the marginal costs to the whole network generated by the two potential directions. Typically, the lane-reversing direction that results in a negative marginal cost should be selected. However, given the discrete requirement, the capacity-reversing amount is quantified by the number of lanes, which in general does not necessarily match the appropriate amount demanded by the desired lane-reversing direction. On the other hand, an accurate estimation of the marginal cost to the whole network with regard to a capacity exchange must be evaluated in terms of some sensitivity analysis technique. Given a stochastic user-equilibrium flow pattern in the network, such a sensitivity analysis is quite complicated. Therefore, an approximation method is used for determining the lane-reversing direction that is to compare the marginal costs with the two potential lane-reversing directions to the local roadway-section subnetwork.

The second type of moves changes the network topology. Specifically, it reduces the number of arcs in the network by reversing all the lanes along a traffic direction in an eligible roadway subnetwork. Suppose the following network configuration and traffic conditions in the roadway-section subnetwork shown in Figure 2: there is one or more lanes on both of the traffic directions (i.e., $n_{jk}^r, n_{lm}^r \geq 1$) but the flow rate on arc pair $[(j,s),(s,k)]$ is equal or close to zero. A direct response to this situation is that the capacity of arc pair $[(j,s),(s,k)]$ is fully or extremely underutilized and hence all of its lanes should be fully reversed to serve the traffic flow on its reverse arc pair $[(l,t),(t,m)]$. This observation defines the second type of moves: a full reversal of lanes on a traffic direction to its reverse direction should be conducted when there is no or ignorable traffic along this direction.

The third type of moves arises subsequent to an iteration that has implemented a move of the second type. In a given network solution, in case that all of the lanes in a roadway subnetwork are used to serve one traffic direction (e.g., $n_{jk}^r = 0$ and $n_{lm}^r = n_{jk,lm}$ in Figure 2), no matter how congested this subnetwork is along the current traffic direction, a candidate move should be suggested that a lane is deducted from the current direction and added to its reverse direction. In our case, if a number of one-way roadway sections exist in the initial network or a large number of full lane reversals emerge in the search itinerary, this type of moves would be frequently encountered. A move of the third type adds an arc pair into the network.

In a local neighborhood search, a scan will exhaust all the eligible roadway subnetworks in the current network solution and choose a candidate move from each roadway subnetwork into a candidate list. In classic tabu search applications, a single best move is selected from this candidate list, in terms of the objective evaluation results as well as subject to the current tabu list and as-

piration criterion. While this best-candidate-only policy provides a precise ordering of potential moves, it may not sufficiently exploit the value of a candidate list, which is determined each time by an exhaustive evaluation of all the eligible lane-reversing operations throughout the whole network and the identification process of which is the most time-consuming computational part of the whole search process. A more efficient method is to select and implement a set of moves in a batch after a candidate list is determined.

A simple heuristic rule is suggested to select a set of moves that may better take advantage of the information implied in a candidate list and accelerate search iterations. An *elite candidate list* is elected from the candidate list, which consists of a given number of best candidate moves based on the sorting result of their corresponding objective function values. The size of this elite candidate list, where it is named *elite capacity*, is an algorithmic parameter, which indicates at most how far a search can move or how many moves a search can convey each time after a move candidate list is presented. An appropriate elite capacity value should be given so as to choose those apparently promising moves in a move candidate list and maintain a good trade-off between the solution quality and search efficiency.

The two most important and essential components used here may be *tabu list* and *aspiration criterion* (in addition to Lagrangian multipliers). These two memory elements are used to record various information (e.g., solution values and attributes) of the solutions encountered in a search history. The purpose of using a tabu list is to avoid cycling traps and hence local optima in a local search procedure. The concept of recency-based memory is used to construct a tabu list that contains a set of recent moves. Whenever a candidate move is identified during the search process, it is compared to the recorded members in the tabu list. If the comparison tells that a member in the tabu list is exactly the counter operation of the candidate move, this candidate move is labeled as a tabu and its candidacy will be canceled unless it satisfies the aspiration criterion. Since a tabu list is built based on the recency-based memory, the general updating mechanism is to put the latest implemented move into the tabu list in place of the oldest member.

Since any lane exchange caused by a move occurs merely between the two counter traffic directions, there is no need of recording both the participating arc pairs, in which one obtains capacity while the other loses. Instead, a more effective tabu-recording rule is to add the arc pair that loses capacity into the tabu list. At each iteration, a tabu examination invokes a comparison between the arc pair that potentially obtains capacity through a candidate move and all the members in the tabu list. If the comparison indicates that this arc pair is equivalent to a member in the current tabu list, this candidate move under consideration is regarded as a tabu move and should be accordingly prohibited in the immediate iteration.

The intensification and diversification strategies realize their functions by using frequency-based memories. A frequency measure, *residence frequency*, is used to evaluate the need for intensification and diversification. Residence frequency is defined as the ratio of the number of iterations where an attribute or element belongs to solutions in a search itinerary (or a section of this itinerary) over the total number of iterations in this itinerary (or the corresponding section of this itinerary). The purpose of using residence frequency is to keep track of how often attributes or elements are members of the historical solutions or how frequently they satisfy some specific status in the search history.

For the lane-reversal subproblem, intensification is useful when a roadway-section subnetwork is set at a specific lane-reversal configuration on a very frequent level, which indicates that a move representing an alternative lane assignment of this subnetwork is seldom selected into the elite list. A frequency threshold is set to determine the qualification of a lane reversal—if the residence

frequency of a full reversal has been greater than the predefined threshold since the first time it appears in the search trajectory, its existence should be fixed in the subsequent solutions until a diversification move is conducted. In other words, this "locked" roadway-section subnetwork will be excluded from the candidate list in succeeding neighborhood searches. In our experiments, it is found that many arcs close to egress nodes or on major routes quickly obtain the intensification qualification for a full reversal assignment for outbound traffic directions.

A high residence frequency with a specific lane reversal in some roadway subnetwork may indicate that this lane-reversal configuration is highly attractive, or may indicate the opposite, if its associated iterations correspond to low-quality solutions. On the other hand, a high residence frequency at which a specific lane reversal exists when there are both high- and low-quality solutions may point to an entrenched attribute that causes the search space to be restricted, and that needs to be jettisoned to allow increased diversity (Glover and Laguna, 1997). Therefore, to judge the necessity of diversifications, it is suggested to investigate both the residence frequency and the solution quality associated with those lane reversals implemented along the search itinerary. The motivation for diversification in our lane-reversal subproblem is, when a large number of iterations have been conducted without any improvement to the objective function value, it may be more attractive to transfer our search into a distant unexplored region than to continue the current local search.

As discussed before, the Lagrangian multiplier updating mechanism is critical to the feasibility and optimality of the solutions derived from the LR-TS procedure. An excessively low value of a Lagrangian multiplier in the penalty term may result in an infeasible solution; an excessively high value may lead to the search process to deviate away from the optimal point (in spite of suboptimal conditions caused by other heuristic factors). A simple but effective iteration-based self-adjusting method for the multiplier updating is set based on the use of another residence frequency that is the number of any specific intersection crossing point existing in solutions during the search process. If a crossing point consecutively exists in the solution itinerary (e.g., 5 times), its corresponding unit penalty cost (i.e., Lagrangian multiplier) is increased; otherwise, the penalty cost is decreased. A unit updating cost is used to specify the increment/decrement amount each time, whose value is dependent on the particular target problem.

Evaluation of the Objective Function

Evaluating the objective function of the Lagrangian problem includes two computational processes: first, a stochastic traffic assignment on the given reduced network; second, an independent traffic crossing-elimination examination for each intersection subject to the network flow pattern obtained from the preceding traffic assignment process.

The stochastic user-equilibrium traffic assignment may be carried out by two network loading methods: logit-based and probit-based methods. The probit-based loading method is preferable to the logit-based because it can properly take into account the overlapping or correlated network proportions when estimating the route cost distributions and route choice probabilities. However, there exists no closed form of exact methods of computing route choice probability for the probit-based network loading. Previous research suggested two approaches of implementing the probit-based network loading: Monte Carlo simulation (Sheffi and Powell, 1982; Sheffi, 1985) and Clark's approximation (Maher, 1992; Maher and Hughes, 1997). The analytical algorithm based on Clark's approximation is employed here to find the stochastic user-equilibrium flow pattern and obtain the corresponding total travel cost over the network.

The traffic flow pattern resulting from the above traffic assignment process on the reduced network does not specify the turning movements at intersections. In fact, the representation of an intersection as a node ignores the crossing-elimination subproblem and regards the intersection as a "black box." To calculate the value of the penalty term of the Lagrangian problem, it is required to check the crossing-elimination violation conditions at all considered intersections subject to the given traffic flow pattern in the reduced network. A mixed integer programming model for the defined intersection crossing-optimization subproblem is suggested for this purpose. The objective of this program is to find the minimum number of crossing points at the given intersection; the constraints include the flow bounding constraints, discrete choice constraints, and flow reservation constraints. For a four-leg intersection such as the one shown in Figure 2, the formulation of this local optimization problem is,

$$\min \sum_{(i,j),(m,n)\in A_c^i} p_{ij,mn} \left(y_{ij}^c + y_{mn}^c - 1 \right)^+ \qquad (13.1)$$

subject to

$$0 \le x_{ij} \le N y_{ij} \qquad \forall (i,j) \in A_c^i \qquad (13.2)$$

$$y_{ij}^c, y_{mn}^c = \{0,1\} \qquad \forall (i,j) \in A_c^i \qquad (13.3)$$

$$\sum_{i\in\Gamma_j^{-1}} x_{ij} = x_{js} \text{ and } \sum_{n\in\Gamma_m} x_{mn} = x_{tm}$$
$$\forall j,m \in N \setminus \left(N_o \bigcup N_d \right) \qquad (13.4)$$

where Γ_j^{-1} is the set of upstream nodes of node j (i.e., $\Gamma_j^{-1} = \{i,o,q\}$) and Γ_m is the set of downstream nodes of node m (i.e. $\Gamma_m = \{n,r,p\}$) and x_{js}

313

and x_{tm} denote the traffic flow rates on roadway-section arcs (j,s) and (t,m), whose values are from the current lane-reversal network solution. This crossing optimization subproblem can be efficiently solved by the branch-and-bound method or a simplex-based pivot method, due to its relative small number of search spaces. The latter method is described and justified in detail in Xie *et al.* (2011).

EXAMPLE APPLICATION AND EVALUATION

Solution quality and efficiency may be the most important indicators for an algorithm's performance. This section evaluates these performance measures of the proposed LR-TS method for the example problem on an evacuation network of realistic size. A couple of simple heuristic methods are used to solve the same problem as comparative alternatives; the solution quality and efficiency of these methods will be discussed and compared.

The Network

The evacuation network is located in Monticello, Minnesota, surrounding the Monticello nuclear power plant. As enacted by the U.S. Nuclear Regulatory Commission (NRC) and Federal Emergency Management Agency (FEMA), an emergency planning zone (EPZ) with a 10-mile radius must be delimited centered at the site of any nuclear power plant in the U.S. If a nuclear accident alarm is triggered, all inhabitants in the EPZ are required to leave the area for one or more designated reception centers, to avoid potential expose to a released radioactive plume. Reception centers can provide evacuees with basic accommodation facilities and medical services. Following the evacuation planning requirement, an evacuation network is extracted from the highways and major arterials in the region, as shown in Figure 4. The reception center for the Monticello

nuclear power plant is located at node 40, which forms the only destination of the network. The evacuation demand generation is estimated based on the demographic data of the region from the U.S. Census 2000 survey. The anticipated number of vehicles leaving the network is about 21,000.

Algorithm Calibration and Implementation

The LR-TS algorithm was coded in C++ and all the numerical experiments was conducted on a PC with a Dual-Core 1.80 GHz CPU and 2 GB RAM. It is well known that the performance of any metaheuristic is highly dependent on the calibration result of its algorithmic parameters. Our LR-TS method is not exclusive. A calibration phase is required prior to the implementation of the algorithmic procedure for large-scale problems and thus it becomes an integral part of the development of the solution procedure. A calibration process on a set of synthetic and realistic networks of small size has been conducted, which suggests the following parameter choices for the example network design problem defined here: tabu tenure = 12, elite capacity = 9, frequency threshold = 0.9, number of allowable unimproved iterations = 50, and number of diversification phases = 3. In addition, the calibration result confirms the initial value of the unit penalty cost = 0 and the use of dynamic increment/decrement penalty costs. As a metaheuristic method, though the solution performance is heavily affected by the parameter calibration result and their relationship is in general not clearly defined, the solution robustness can be appreciated if a set of solutions with a comparable quality level are obtained as long as the parameter values are specified in a reasonable range. In an extensive set of experiments using synthetic and realistic example problems with different sizes, it is found that the largest gap between the best solution and the worst one for any problem instance is 4.2 percent and the average gap is about 1.1 percent. This result indicates the insensitivity

Figure 4. The Monticello evacuation network

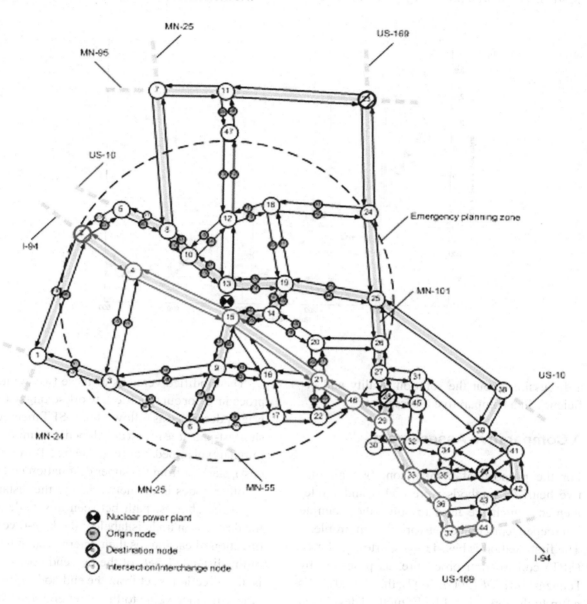

of solution quality with respect to algorithmic parameters in this problem.

The resulting search itinerary and network solution from applying the calibrated LR-TS algorithm to the Monticello network are presented in Figure 5 and Figure 6, respectively. One piece of the computational complexity with this example network design problem can be seen from the search itinerary, in that a larger number of

local optima are encountered during the search process. The optimized solution is identified at iteration 413, and the CPU time for finding this optimized solution is 2.015×10^3 sec. A detailed solution interpretation and policy analysis about this computational result as well as other network scenarios can be referred to in Xie and Turnquist (2011). The remainder of this section focuses on

Figure 5. The search itinerary for the Monticello evacuation network

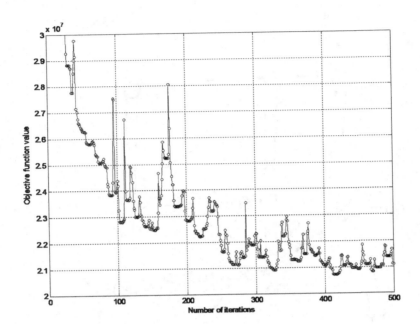

a discussion about the solution quality and efficiency in a comparative assessment.

A Comparative Assessment

For the purpose of comparison, two alternative heuristic methods were coded and implemented, which are used to solve the example interdependent-choice network design problem. The first method is based on a shortest-path tree (SPT) construction procedure, as proposed by Hamza-Lup *et al.* (2004, 2007); the second one is a flip-high-flow-edge (FHFE) method developed by Kim *et al.* (2008), in which the lane-reversal direction on any roadway section is dependent on the congestion conditions of its two traffic directions. Although these two algorithms do not explicitly incorporate the intersection crossing-elimination requirement, the full lane-reversal assumption guarantees an automatic satisfaction of the crossing-elimination constraints and hence the feasibility of optimized solutions.

The modified versions of these two solution procedures for our specific network settings can be briefly described as follows. In the SPT method, a shortest-path tree is first developed in terms of the initial travel impedance (e.g., the free-flow travel cost), starting from the super destination node to all other nodes in the network, and the distance along the shortest path between any node and the destination node is labeled; the lane-reversal direction of each arc is then determined in terms of the distance labels of the two end nodes, that is, the direction is set from the end node with the larger distance value to the other end node with the lower value.

The FHFE method also has a two-stage process. In the first stage, a traffic assignment is carried out in the original network and the traffic flow rate on each arc is recorded; the second stage resorts to a comparison of the congestion level (e.g., volume/capacity (V/C) ratio) of the two traffic directions of each roadway segment, by which the capacity of the traffic direction with the lower V/C value

Figure 6. The optimized solution for the Monticello evacuation network

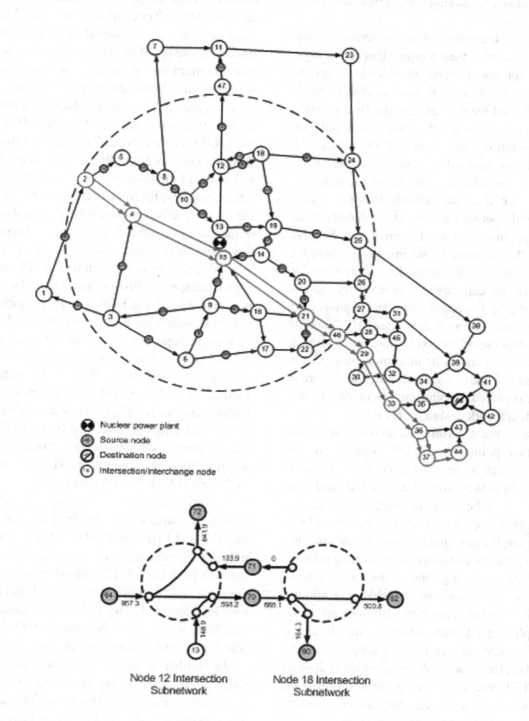

is fully reassigned to supplement its counter traffic direction.

The prominent merit of these alternative solution procedures is their simple algorithmic logic and low computation cost, in which none or only one time of the objective function evaluation needs to be invoked for determining the final solution and no intersection subnetwork manipulation or optimization needs to be actually conducted. However, the optimality condition of these solutions may be subject to the following deficiencies. First, both of the methods do not explicitly consider the network optimization objective such as minimization of the total travel cost. Second, both of the methods do not invoke any iterative process to monitor the network flow variation due to the network capacity and connectivity change, in that the SPT method completely ignores the network congestion effect and the FHFE method only makes use of the congestion information at the local level and in its minimum form. Given these reasons, the two algorithmic procedures can only be regarded as some naïve heuristics for the example network design problem.

Despite these algorithmic deficiencies, from a practical point of view, the simple logic and intuitive solution-deriving principle make these methods to be very attractive candidates and their solutions may be on some degree regarded as a surrogate of evacuation plans that are derived from simple engineering judgments. In contrast, this chapter presents a relatively sophisticated solution procedure. Some algorithm selection questions naturally arise, when we consider the relative performance between these different methods: Is a sophisticated, time-consuming metaheuristic worthwhile, compared to those simple, intuitive heuristics, for the network design problem defined here? If different methods perform on different aspects better than one another, can one combine their merits to form a better hybrid method?

To address these concerns, the two simple heuristics and our hybrid metaheuristic are tested over a set of example synthetic and realistic evacu-ation networks, including the Monticello network described above. The computation results obtained from experiments conducted on the aforementioned PC are listed in Table 3. Solution quality and computation cost are the major performance measures in this comparative assessment. It is apparent that the two simple heuristics run extremely fast, say in one or a few seconds, whilst the LR-TS method typically takes hundreds or thousands of seconds to finish the search process in a range of moderate-size networks. However, when comparing the solution quality, we found that the LR-TS method consistently and significantly outperforms the other two methods: in terms of the objective function value, the SPT and FHFE methods perform worse than the LR-TS method approximately by 40-130 percent and by 20-50 percent, respectively. Evidently, the performance of the two simple methods is far below the LR-TS method in approaching the optimal evacuation network solution with lane reversal and crossing elimination. As shown in Table 3, for example, for the Monticello network, the total travel cost of the SPT solution is 2.92×10^7 vehicle-hours and the FHFE solution gives a total travel cost of 2.52×10^7 vehicle-hours. Compared to the optimized LR-TS solution, these two figures are 41.1 percent and 21.7 percent higher, respectively.

Despite this huge discrepancy on solution quality, the solutions obtained from implementing the SPT and FHFE methods for the Monticello network, for example, are quite similar to the solution from the LR-TS method in terms of the lane-reversal configuration. The SPT and FHFE solutions contain 12 and 5 roadway sections with a different lane-reversal direction from the LR-TS solution, corresponding to merely 16 and 7 percent of the number of reversible roadway sections in the network, respectively. However, similar network solutions do not imply similar network performances, as shown above. This fact exhibits the solution complexity of such an interdependent-choice network design problem, whose objective function is nonlinear and nonconvex to its deci-

Table 3. Comparison of the solution quality and computation cost

Example Network	Number of nodes	Number of arcs	Objective function value[3] (x10³)			Computing time (sec)		
			SPT	FHFE	LR-TS	SPT	FHFE	LR-TS
Synthetic small network	40	60	208.2	133.9	90.4	< 1.0	1.5	250.4
Synthetic grid network	64	96	72.2	58.1	38.0	< 1.0	1.8	538.5
Synthetic urban network	85	128	119.9	89.6	74.2	< 1.0	2.5	1,024.8
Sioux Falls network	100	152	8.6	6.6	5.5	< 1.0	3.9	1,589.3
Monticello network	99	200	29,283.6	25,245.6	20,750.5	< 1.0	3.4	2,015.5

sion variables (if these variables are continuous), due to the nonlinear arc cost function and the network equilibrium requirement. On the other hand, this result justifies, at least empirically, the necessity of applying a sophisticated solution algorithm like the one presented in this chapter to solve these difficult network design problems, as long as an adequate amount of computing time is allowed.

Two suggestions may be drawn with regard to the comparison result between the LR-TS metaheuristic and the two simple heuristics. First, the LR-TS method apparently outperforms the two tested simple heuristics in terms of solution quality. The FHFE method could be regarded as an easy alternative method for the network design problem, considering its relatively good solution quality and low computational cost. Specifically, the gap between the objective function values of the FHFE and LR-TS solutions is around 20 percent while the FHFE method only requires running the time-consuming traffic assignment process once. However, no guarantee can be made on that such a small solution quality gap would be kept with the increasing the network complexity. Second, due to the structural similarity of these solutions, the solutions derived from these simple heuristics could be used as a good initial solution of the sophisticated LR-TS method. With checking the search itinerary of the LR-TS method for

the example problem instance (see Figure 5), it is found that the objective function values of the SPT and FHFE solutions are comparable to that of the LR-TS solutions encountered approximately at its iterations 30 and 150, respectively. If, for example, the FHFE solution is used as the starting point of the LR-TS procedure, a large number of iterations could be eliminated during the search process and the search procedure can focus on more important solution regions more thoroughly.

CONCLUSION

The main body of this chapter is an algorithmic framework of integrating Lagrangian relaxation and tabu search. This hybrid metaheuristic method provides a promising way for solving a class of discrete network design problems with complex interdependent-choice constraints, under which it is very difficult to directly define and search for candidate solutions in the solution space. The basic algorithmic idea of this hybrid method is to decompose the target problem into a relaxed Lagrangian problem and one (or more) penalty evaluation problem(s) and apply tabu search to solve the relaxed Lagrangian problem and update Lagrangian multipliers. Through an example network design problem with lane-reversal and crossing-elimination constraints, it is demonstrated in this chapter how this hybrid method can be applied and implemented and its algorithmic advantages and computational challenges may arise in implementation.

Lagrangian relaxation provides a very flexible problem decomposition paradigm that can accommodate a variety of heuristic and metaheuristic methods. The integration of Lagrangian relaxation and tabu search is only one part of a larger effort in creating new hybrid solution methods for complex combinatorial optimization problems. Other types of Lagrangian-based metaheuristics, such as applying memetic algorithms, simulated annealing, scatter search, or ant colony optimization to tackle relaxed Lagrangian problems and update Lagrangian multipliers, should be investigated and may provide new algorithmic and computational advances. This remains as an important task to algorithm developers in the future.

REFERENCES

Balakrishnan, A., Magnanti, T. L., & Mirchandani, P. (1994). Modeling and heuristic worst-case performance analysis of the two-level network design problem. *Management Science, 40*(7), 846–867. doi:10.1287/mnsc.40.7.846

Baños, R., Gil, C., Agulleiro, J. I., & Rcca, J. (2007). A memetic algorithm for water distribution network design. *Soft Computing in Industrial Applications, 39*(4), 279–289. doi:10.1007/978-3-540-70706-6_26

Berger, D., Gendron, B., Potvin, J. Y., Raghavan, S., & Soriano, P. (2000). Tabu search for a network loading problem with multiple facilities. *Journal of Heuristics, 6*(2), 253–267. doi:10.1023/A:1009679511137

Borghetti, A., Frangioni, A., Lacalandra, F., Lodi, A., Martello, S., Nucci, C. A., & Trebbi, A. (2001). Lagrangian relaxation and tabu search approaches for the unit commitment problem. *Proceedings of IEEE 2001 Power Tech Conference*, Porto, Portugal, 397-413.

Boschetti, M., & Maniezzo, V. (2009). Benders decomposition, Lagrangian relaxation and metaheuristic design. *Journal of Heuristics, 15*(3), 283–312. doi:10.1007/s10732-007-9064-9

Boyce, D. E., Farhi, A., & Weischedel, R. (1973). Optimal network problem: A branch-and-bound algorithm. *Environment and Planning, 5*(4), 519–533. doi:10.1068/a050519

Cantarella, G. E., Pavone, G., & Vitetta, A. (2006). Heuristics for urban road network design: Lane layout and signal settings. *European Journal of Operational Research, 175*(3), 1682–1695. doi:10.1016/j.ejor.2005.02.034

Cordeau, J. F., Pasin, F., & Solomon, M. M. (2006). An integrated model for logistics network design. *Annals of Operations Research, 144*(1), 59–82. doi:10.1007/s10479-006-0001-3

Cova, T. J., & Johnson, J. P. (2003). A network flow model for lane-based evacuation routing. *Transportation Research, 37A*(7), 579–604.

Crainic, T. G., Gendreau, M., & Farvolden, J. M. (2000). A simplex-based tabu search method for capacitated network design. *Journal on Computing, 12*(3), 223–236.

Daganzo, C. F. (1982). Unconstrained extremal formulation of some transportation equilibrium problems. *Transportation Science, 16*(3), 332–360. doi:10.1287/trsc.16.3.332

Dionne, R., & Florian, M. (1979). Exact and approximate algorithms for optimal network design. *Networks, 9*(1), 37–59. doi:10.1002/net.3230090104

Drezner, Z., & Wesolowsky, G. O. (1997). Selecting an optimum configuration of one-way and two-way routes. *Transportation Science, 31*(4), 386–394. doi:10.1287/trsc.31.4.386

Drezner, Z., & Wesolowsky, G. O. (2003). Network design: Selection and design of links and facility location. *Transportation Research, 37A*(3), 241–256.

Filho, V. J. M. F., & Galvão, R. D. (1998). A tabu search heuristic for the concentrator location problem. *Location Science, 6*(1-4), 189–209. doi:10.1016/S0966-8349(98)00046-1

Gendreau, M. (2002). *An Introduction to Tabu Search. Research Report, Centre de recherche sur les transports.* Montréal, Québec, Canada: Université de Montréal.

Gendreau, M., Hertz, A., & Laporte, G. (1994). A tabu search heuristic for the vehicle routing problem. *Management Science, 40*(10), 1276–1290. doi:10.1287/mnsc.40.10.1276

Geoffrion, A. M. (1974). Lagrangian relaxation for integer programming. *Mathematical Programming Study, 2*(1), 82–114.

Geoffrion, A. M., & Graves, G. W. (1974). Multicommodity distribution system design by Benders decomposition. *Management Science, 20*(5), 822–844. doi:10.1287/mnsc.20.5.822

Glover, F. (1986). Future paths for integer programming and links to artificial intelligence. *Computers & Operations Research, 13*(5), 533–549. doi:10.1016/0305-0548(86)90048-1

Glover, F., & Laguna, M. (1997). *Tabu Search.* Norwell, MA: Kluwer Academic Publishers. doi:10.1007/978-1-4615-6089-0

Golding, D., & Kasperson, R. E. (1988). Emergency planning and nuclear power: Looking to the next accident. *Land Use Policy, 5*(1), 19–36. doi:10.1016/0264-8377(88)90004-X

Gouveia, L., & Telhada, J. (2001). An augmented arborescence formulation for the two-level network design problem. *Annals of Operations Research, 106*(1-4), 47–61. doi:10.1023/A:1014553523631

Grünert, T. (2002). Lagrangean tabu search. In C.C. Ribeiro & P. Hansen (Ed.), *Essays and Surveys in Metaheuristics*, 379-397. New York, NY: Springer.

Guihaire, V., & Hao, J. K. (2008). Transit network design and scheduling: A global review. *Transportation Research, 42A*(10), 1251–1273.

Hamza-Lup, G. L., Hua, K. A., Le, M., & Peng, R. (2004). Enhancing intelligent transportation systems to improve and support homeland security. *Proceedings of the 7th IEEE Intelligent Transportation Systems Conference*, Washington, DC, 250-255.

Hamza-Lup, G. L., Hua, K. A., & Peng, R. (2007). Leveraging e-transportation in real-time traffic evacuation management. *Electronic Commerce Research and Applications, 6*(4), 413–424. doi:10.1016/j.elerap.2006.12.002

Hoang, H. H. (1973). A computational approach to the selection of an optimal network. *Management Science, 19*(5), 488–498. doi:10.1287/mnsc.19.5.488

Hoang, H. H. (1982). Topological optimization of networks: A nonlinear mixed integer model employing generalized Benders decomposition. *IEEE Transactions on Automatic Control, 27*(1), 164–169. doi:10.1109/TAC.1982.1102873

Jeon, K., Lee, J. S., Ukkusuri, S., & Waller, S. T. (2006). Selectorecombinative genetic algorithm to relax computational complexity of discrete network design problem. *Transportation Research Record, 1964*, 91–103. doi:10.3141/1964-11

Johnson, D. S., Lenstra, J. K., & Rinnooy Kan, A. H. G. (1978). The complexity of the network design problem. *Networks*, *8*(4), 279–285. doi:10.1002/net.3230080402

Jourdan, L., Basseur, M., & Talbi, E. G. (2009). Hybridizing exact methods and metaheuristics: A taxonomy. *European Journal of Operational Research*, *199*(3), 620–629. doi:10.1016/j.ejor.2007.07.035

Kalafaras, G., & Peeta, S. (2010). Planning for evacuation: Insights from an efficient network design model. *Journal of Infrastructure Systems*, *15*(1), 21–30. doi:10.1061/(ASCE)1076-0342(2009)15:1(21)

Kim, S., Shekhar, S., & Min, M. (2008). Contraflow transportation network reconfiguration for evacuation route planning. *IEEE Transactions on Knowledge and Data Engineering*, *20*(8), 1115–1129. doi:10.1109/TKDE.2007.190722

LeBlanc, L. J. (1975). An algorithm for the discrete network design problem. *Transportation Science*, *9*(3), 183–199. doi:10.1287/trsc.9.3.183

Lee, C. K., & Yang, K. I. (1994). Network design of one-way streets with simulated annealing. *Papers in Regional Science*, *73*(2), 119–134. doi:10.1111/j.1435-5597.1994.tb00606.x

Magnanti, T. L., Mireault, P., & Wong, R. T. (1986). Tailoring Benders decomposition for uncapacitated network design. *Mathematical Programming Study*, *26*(2), 112–154.

Magnanti, T. L., & Wong, R. T. (1984). Network design and transportation planning: Models and algorithms. *Transportation Science*, *18*(1), 1–55. doi:10.1287/trsc.18.1.1

Maher, M. J. (1992). SAM—A stochastic assignment model. In Griffiths, J. D. (Ed.), *Mathematics in Transport Planning and Control*. Oxford, UK: Oxford University Press.

Maher, M. J., & Hughes, P. C. (1997). A probit-based stochastic user equilibrium assignment model. *Transportation Research*, *31B*(4), 341–355.

Meng, Q., Khoo, H. L., & Cheu, R. L. (2008). Microscopic traffic simulation model-based optimization approach for the contraflow lane configuration problem. *Journal of Transportation Engineering*, *134*(1), 41–49. doi:10.1061/(ASCE)0733-947X(2008)134:1(41)

Mouskos, K. C. (1991). *A Tabu-Based Heuristic Search Strategy to Solve a Discrete Transportation Equilibrium Network Design Problem*. Ph.D. Thesis, Department of Civil, Architectural and Environmental Engineering, University of Texas at Austin, Austin, TX.

O'Kelly, M. E., & Miller, H. J. (1994). The hub network design problem: A review and synthesis. *Journal of Transport Geography*, *2*(1), 31–40. doi:10.1016/0966-6923(94)90032-9

Ohlmann, J. W., & Bean, J. C. (2009). Resource-constrained management of heterogeneous assets with stochastic deterioration. *European Journal of Operational Research*, *199*(1), 198–208. doi:10.1016/j.ejor.2008.11.005

Poorzahedy, H., & Abulghasemi, F. (2005). Application of ant system to network design problem. *Transportation*, *32*(3), 251–273. doi:10.1007/s11116-004-8246-7

Randazzo, C. D., Luna, H. P. L., & Mahey, P. (2001). Benders decomposition for local access network design with two technologies. *Discrete Mathematics and Theoretical Computer Science*, *4*(2), 235–246.

Sheffi, Y. (1985). *Urban Transportation Networks: Equilibrium Analysis with Mathematical Programming Methods*. Englewood, NJ: Prentice Hall.

Sheffi, Y., & Powell, W. B. (1982). An algorithm for the equilibrium assignment problem with random link times. *Networks, 12*(2), 191–207. doi:10.1002/net.3230120209

Shekhar, S., & Kim, S. (2006). *Contraflow Transportation Network Reconfiguration for Evacuation Route Planning*. St. Paul, MS: CTS Project Report, Minnesota Department of Transportation.

Sherali, H. D., Carter, T. B., & Hobeika, A. G. (1991). A location-allocation model and algorithm for evacuation planning under hurricane/flood conditions. *Transportation Research, 25B*(6), 439–452.

Talbi, E. G. (2002). A taxonomy of hybrid metaheuristics. *Journal of Heuristics, 8*(5), 541–564. doi:10.1023/A:1016540724870

Tuydes, H., & Ziliaskopoulos, A. K. (2006). Tabu-based heuristic approach for optimization of network evacuation contraflow. *Transportation Research Record, 1964*, 157–168. doi:10.3141/1964-17

Urbina, E., & Wolshon, B. (2003). National review of hurricane evacuation plans and policies: A comparison and contrast of state practices. *Transportation Research, 37A*(3), 257–275.

Wolshon, P. B., & Lambert, L. (2004). *Convertible Roadways and Lanes: A Synthesis of Highway Practice. NCHRP Synthesis 340*. Washington, DC: National Cooperative Highway Research Program, Transportation Research Board.

Wong, C. K., & Wong, S. C. (2002). Lane-based optimization of traffic equilibrium settings for area traffic control. *Journal of Advanced Transportation, 36*(3), 349–386. doi:10.1002/atr.5670360308

Wong, R. T. (1980). Worst-case analysis of network design problem heuristics. *Journal of Algebraic and Discrete Methods, 1*(1), 51–63. doi:10.1137/0601008

Wong, R. T. (1985). Transportation network research: Algorithmic and computational questions. *Transportation Research, 19A*(5/6), 436–438.

Xie, C., Lin, D. Y., & Waller, S. T. (2010). A dynamic evacuation network optimization problem with lane reversal and crossing elimination strategies. *Transportation Research, 46E*(3), 295–316.

Xie, C., & Turnquist, M. A. (2011). Lane-based evacuation network optimization: An integrated Lagrangian relaxation and tabu search approach. *Transportation Research, 19C*(1), 40–63.

Xie, C., Waller, S. T., & Kockelman, K. M. (2011). (in press). An intersection origin-destination flow optimization problem for evacuation network design. *Transportation Research Record*.

Xiong, Y., & Schneider, J. B. (1992). Transportation network design using a cumulative genetic algorithm and neural networks. *Transportation Research Record, 1364*, 37–44.

KEY TERMS AND DEFINITIONS

Combinatorial Optimization: Optimization problems whose space of feasible solutions is discrete.

Crossing Elimination: A traffic control strategy typically used at roadway or highway-rail intersections, which permanently or temporarily removes potential crossings formed by traffic flows of different directions.

Evacuation Planning: A planning process which determines destinations, routes and schedules of moving people threatened by occurring or impending disasters to safe areas or shelters.

Lagrangian Relaxation: A problem relaxation technique which works by moving hard constraints into the objective so as to exact a penalty on the objective if they are not satisfied.

Lane Reversal: A traffic control technique which reverses some or all of the lanes along a traffic direction to its counter direction, to aid in an emergency evacuation or special event, or to facilitate highway widening or reconstruction activities.

Metaheuristic: A general solution strategy which guides other heuristics to search for feasible solutions.

Network Design: A design process which encompasses topological connectivity and capacity setting of a node-arc network.

Tabu Search: A mathematical optimization method, belonging to the class of local search techniques, which enhances the performance of a local search method by using memory structures.

ENDNOTES

[1] It is implicitly assumed here that the underlying network flow problem contains only a single commodity (i.e., network flows have only a single origin or a single destination), so the arc-based flow conservation constraints (1.2) are sufficient to specify a complete origin-destination (O-D) flow pattern.

[2] Note that this is a convex program subject to the flow conservation and nonnegativity constraints. Note that the unconstrained concave program (if multiplied by -1) for the stochastic user-equilibrium problem by Sheffi and Powell (1982) is a Lagrangian dual to this program.

[3] Note that the units of the objective function value associated with different networks are different.

About the Contributors

Jairo R. Montoya-Torres is an Associate Professor of Operations Research and Director of the Master program in Operations Management at the School of Economics and Management Sciences, Universidad de La Sabana, Colombia. He holds a Ph.D. degree from Ecole Nationale Supérieure des Mines de Saint-Étienne, France. He has been Invited Professor at Universidad Nacional Autónoma de Nuevo León, Mexico, in 2009, and Ecole Nationale Supérieure des Mines de Saint-Étienne, France, in 2011 within the Department OMSI. He has been Guest Editor for the *Int. J. of Information Systems and Supply Chain Management* (published by IGI Global), *Annals of Operations Research, Journal of Intelligent Manufacturing and Int. J. of Industrial and Systems Engineering*. Dr. Montoya is currently Associate Editor of the Journal of Modelling and Simulation Systems, and the Journal of Artificial Intelligence: Theory and Application. His research interests include scheduling, applied combinatorial optimization, reverse/sustainable logistics, supply chain management under collaborative and sustainable environments, and modeling and simulation of complex industrial and service systems. His webpage is <http://jrmontoya.wordpress.com>.

Angel A. Juan is an Associate Professor of Simulation and Data Analysis in the Computer Science Department at the Open University of Catalonia (UOC). He is also a Researcher at the Internet Interdisciplinary Institute (IN3-UOC). He holds a Ph.D. in Industrial Engineering, an M.S. in Information Technologies, and a M.S. in Applied Mathematics. His research interests include computer simulation, educational data analysis and mathematical e-learning. He is an editorial board member of the Int. J. of Data Analysis Techniques and Strategies, and a member of the INFORMS society. His web address is <http://ajuanp.wordpress.com>.

Luisa Huaccho Huatuco is a Lecturer in Operations & Business Processes at Leeds University Business School. She obtained her doctorate degree from the Department of Engineering Science, University of Oxford. Before that, she completed a M.Sc. degree at the International Institute for Aerospace Survey and Earth Sciences (ITC), The Netherlands. Her research interests include complexity in manufacturing systems, supply chain management and operations management.

Javier Faulin is an Associate Professor of Statistics and Operations Research at the Public University of Navarre (Pamplona, Spain). He holds a PhD in Economics, a MS in Operations Management, Logistics and Transportation and a MS in Applied Mathematics. His research interests include logistics, vehicle routing problems and simulation modeling and analysis. He is a member of INFORMS and EURO societies and an editorial board member of the International Journal of Applied Management Science and the International Journal of Operational Research and Information Systems. His e-mail address is <javier.faulin@unavarra.es>.

Gloria L. Rodríguez-Verjan graduated with highest honors as industrial engineer from Pontificia Universidad Javeriana, Bogotá, Colombia, and obtained her MSc degree in industrial engineering from Ecole Nationale Supériere des Mines de Saint-Étienne, France. She currently working as Research Engineer at a Franco-Italian semiconductor manufacturer, and working towards a doctoral degree within the Microelectronics Division of Provence (CMP) of Ecole nationale Supérieure des Mines de Saint-Éteinne. She has worked as logistics analyst at P&A Renault, and Demand Manager at Symrise, both enterprises located in Bogotá, Colombia. She has also been part-time lecturer in simulation at Pontificia Universidad Javeriana. Her research work has been focused on coordination and collaboration issues within the supply chains, simulation of logistics operations in maritime ports, and most recently in optimization and statistical analysis of semiconductor manufacturing operations. Results of her researches have been published in various academic journals and presented in various international conferences.

***

Kaan Aktolug has earned his B.S degree at Istanbul University in Economics and his M.B.A & Ph.D. in Marketing at Yeditepe University in Turkey. He is currently working as the financial and risk management director at the leading packaged bread company in Istanbul, Turkey. Dr. Aktolug has worked in several different sectors including banking, shipping and textile. He has extensive experience in enterprise risk management and optimization solutions . He is publishing articles with a specific focus on the successful implementation of risk management in SMEs. Dr. Aktolug's article with Dr. Güngör, "Understanding the Changes in Supply Chain Management: Extensions with a Strategic Marketing Perspective" was presented in the 3rd International Conference on "Economics & Management of Networks" June 2007 Rotterdam – Erasmus University.

José A. Barros-Basto was born in Porto, Portugal, and went to Universidade do Porto (UP), where he studied mechanical engineering and obtained his degree in 1986, staying in the same institution as Lecturer. He passed "Aptitude Tests of Educational and Scientific Capacity" in UP in 1991. He was awarded his Ph.D. in Industrial Engineering from Lehigh University (PA; U.S.A.) in 2000. He is Assistant Professor at UP since 2000, where he teaches Operations Management and leads research in the field of Flexible Manufacturing and Visual Interactive Simulation. Since 1987, he also worked as a consultant and coordinator in several industry projects at INEGI, an interface institute of UP.

Tolga Bektas is a Lecturer in Management Science at the University of Southampton and the Director of the MSc in Business Analytics and Management Sciences at the School of Management. He has a BSc (1998), MSc (2000) and PhD (2005) in Industrial Engineering and postdoctoral research experience at the University of Montreal. His research interests are in discrete optimization with applications to vehicle routing, service network design, and freight transportation and logistics. He is one of the editors of OR Insight and an Associate Editor of Computers & Operations Research. His publications appeared in journals such as Transportation Science, Networks, European Journal of Operational Research, Transportation Research Part C, and the Journal of the Operational Research Society. His e-mail is < tolga.bektas@gmail.com>.

Luca Bertazzi is Associate Professor of Operations Research at the University of Brescia, Italy. His main research interests are: Inventory Routing problems, supply chain optimization, worst-case analysis, exact and heuristic dynamic programming algorithms, reoptimization problems. He has published papers in *Management Science, Transportation Science, Transportation Research, International Journal of Production Economics, Annals of Operations Research, Networks, European Journal of Operational Research, Naval Research Logistics, Computational Management Science, Discrete Applied Mathematics, INFORMS Journal on Computing*. He is Associate Editor of the *Asia Pacific Journal of Operational Research* and *IIE Transactions*.

Ender Bildik, MSc, is currently working as a *Process Engineer* in the Production Engineering Department of Roketsan Missiles Industries Inc. E. Bildik received her MSc. Degree in Mechanical Engineering from Yildiz Technical University (YTU), in 2006, and MSc. Degree in Industrial Engineering from YTU, in 2007 as a double major. Throughout his industrial engineering education, his research interests are meta-heuristic algorithms.

Burcin Bozkaya has earned his B.S. and M.S. degrees in Industrial Engineering at Bilkent University, Turkey, and his Ph.D. in Management Science at the University of Alberta in Canada. He then joined Environmental Systems Research Institute, Inc. of California, U.S.A., and worked as a Senior Operations Research Analyst. In this period, Dr. Bozkaya has participated in many public and private sector projects and acted as an architect, developer and analyst in applications of GIS to routing and delivery optimization. One such project completed for Schindler Elevator Corporation was awarded with 2002 INFORMS Franz Edelman Best Management Science Finalist Award. Currently, Dr. Bozkaya is a professor at Sabanci University, Turkey. His current research interests include routing and location analysis, heuristic optimization, and application of GIS as decision support systems for solving various transportation problems. Dr. Bozkaya is a winner of the 2010 Practice Prize awarded by the Canadian Operational Research Society.

Ani Calinescu holds a 5-year (MSc equivalent) degree in Computer Science Engineering from Technical University of Iasi, Romania (1991), and a DPhil degree from the Department of Engineering of the University of Oxford, United Kingdom (2002). Her DPhil thesis is entitled "Manufacturing complexity: an integrative information-theoretic approach". Since 2002 Dr Ani Calinescu has been a Lecturer at the Oxford University Computing Laboratory. Her research interests include: modelling and reasoning about complex systems; manufacturing systems and supply chains; complexity and performance metrics; ubiquitous and autonomous computing; agent-based modelling; planning, scheduling and control; and the cost and value of information.

James F. Campbell is Professor of Management Science & Information Systems in the College of Business Administration at the University of Missouri – St. Louis. He earned his Ph.D. in Industrial Engineering and Operations Research from the University of California – Berkeley. Dr. Campbell's research centers around modeling and optimization of transportation, logistics and supply chain systems. His current research interests include hub location and transportation network design, logistics for snow removal, barge transportation on the Upper Mississippi River, and deployment of aerial refueling tankers. He has over 60 publications in leading academic and practitioner journals and has editorial positions with *Transportation Research, International Journal of Revenue Management* and *OMEGA: The International Journal of Management Science.*

Buyang Cao has earned his B.S. and M.S. degrees in Operations Research at University of Shanghai for Science and Technology, and his Ph.D. in Operations Research at University of Federal Armed Forces Hamburg, Germany. He is working as an Operations Research team leader at ESRI, Inc. İn California, USA. Currently he is also a guest professor at School of Software Engineering at Tongji Univeristy, Shanghai, China. He has been involved and lead various projects related to solving logistics problems including Sears vehicle routing problems, Schindler Elevator periodic routing problems, a major Southern California Energy technician routing and schedulinig problems, taxi dispatching problems for a luxary taxi company in Boston, etc. He published papers in various international journals on logistics solutions, and he also reviewed scholar papers for several international journals. His main interest is to apply GIS and optimization technologies to solve complicated dicision problems from real world.

Jens Czogalla studied Business Administration and Engineering at the University of the Federal Armed Forces, Hamburg, Germany, and received the Diploma Degree "Wirtschaftsingenieur" (Industrial Engineering) in 2003. He was a Visiting Research Fellow at the Thayer School of Engineering, Dartmouth College, Hanover, NH, USA. As a former member of the Institute of Computer Science, Helmut-Schmidt-University Hamburg, Germany, he received the Doctoral Degree "Dr. rer. pol" in 2010. His research interests include computational and swarm intelligence algorithms for optimization.

Paulo César R. De Lima Jr. was born in Fortaleza, Brazil and went to Universidade Federal do Ceará, where he studied civil engineering and obtained his degree in 1997. He obtained his MSc in Transportation from Instituto Militar de Engenharia, Rio de Janeiro, in 1999 and he was awarded his Ph.D. in Industrial Engineering from Universidade do Porto, Portugal, in 2008. He is Associate Professor at Universidade Federal do Vale do São Francisco, Brazil, since 2008, where he teaches Operations Research, Distribution Logistics and Simulation. He also leads research in the field of Logistics and Visual Interactive Simulation. His e-mail address is: paulo.cesar@univasf.edu.br.

Andreas Fink holds the position of a Full Professor at the Institute of Computer Science at the Helmut-Schmidt-University Hamburg, Germany. He received a diploma degree in Computer Science and Business Administration from the University of Technology Darmstadt in 1995, a doctoral degree in Economics from the University of Technology Braunschweig in 2000, and a habilitation degree from Hamburg University in 2005. He has published in Computers & Operations Research, Computers & Industrial Engineering, European Journal of Operational Research, Transportation Research, Annals of Operations Research, and other journals. His research interests are in decision making and optimization, operations management, and software development.

Gustavo Gatica is a Computer Engineer and currently is a PhD student at the University of Santiago of Chile. His current research interests are on metaheuristic and the automatic generation of heuristic algorithms.

Michel Gendreau is Professor of Operations Research at the Department of Mathematics and Industrial Engineering of École Polytechnique de Montréal (Canada). He received his Ph.D. from Université de Montréal in 1984. From 1999 to 2007, he was the Director of the Centre for Research on Transportation in Montreal.Since September 2009, he is the Chairholder of the NSERC/Hydro-Québec Industrial Chair on the Stochastic Optimization of Electricity Generation. His main research area is the application of operations research to energy, transportation and telecommunication systems planning and management. He has published more than 200 papers on these topics in journals and refereed proceedings. He is also the co-editor of six books dealing with transportation planning and scheduling, as well as with meta-heuristics. Dr. Gendreau is the Editor in chief of *Transportation Science* and member of several other editorial boards. Until December 2009, he was also Vice-President of the International Federation of Operational Research Societies (IFORS) and of The Institute for Operations Research and Management Science (INFORMS). Dr. Gendreau has received several awards including the Merit and the Service Award of the Canadian Operational Research Society. He was elected Fellow of INFORMS in 2011.

Libardo S. Gómez-Vizcaino is full-time professor within the Department of Industrial Engineering at Universidad Autónoma del Caribe, Barranquilla, Colombia and a researcher at the Caribbean Research Center for Enterprise Modeling (FCIMEC). He holds Master of Science and Engineering degrees both from Universidad del Norte, Barranquilla, Colombia. His research interests include computational intelligence applied to complex optimization problems.

Scott E. Grasman is an Associate Professor of Engineering Management and Systems Engineering, as well as Associate Chair for Graduate Studies, at Missouri University of Science and Technology. His research relates to the application of quantitative models to manufacturing and service systems, focusing on the design and development of supply chain and logistics processes. He is the author or co-author of a number of publications and has participated in a variety of research and consulting projects. His email is <grasmans@mst.edu>.

Bahadır Gülsün, Ph.D., is currently working as an *Assistant Professor* at the Department of Industrial Engineering, Yildiz Technical University. His research interests are in the areas of production planning, facility layout design and material handling systems design.

André Langevin is Professor of Operations Research and Logistics at École Polytechnique de Montréal. He earned his Ph.D. in Mathematics for Engineers from École Polytechnique de Montréal. His research interests encompass optimization of logistics and transportation systems, logistics for snow removal, optimization of container terminal operations, and mathematical optimization. He is a member of the Interuniversity Research Centre on Enterprise Networks, Logistics, and Transportation (CIRRELT) and of the Groupe de Recherches en Analyse des Décisions (GERAD). He has over 100 refereed publications. His articles has appeared in *Transportation Science*, *Transportation Research B*, *Annals of Operations Research*, *International Journal of Production Economics*, *International Journal of Production Research*, *European Journal of Operational Research*, and many other journals.

Fabian Lopez is an Associate Professor in the Graduate Program of Management Science at UANL in Monterrey México. He earned his PhD (2004) in Management Science from UANL. He also earned a MBA (1990) and a MSE in Industrial Engineering (1992) at EGADE-Monterrey Tech. He holds BSc in Computer Science (1986) and Electronic Control (1990) at UANL. Dr. Lopez is a SNI Fellow (level 1) a country-wide distinction granted by the "Mexican-National-Council-of-Science-and-Technology" (CONACYT). He has been a SEP-PROMEP Fellow, a country-wide distinction granted by the Secretary for Public Education for excellence in teaching and research. Dr. Lopez is member of the American Production in Inventory Control Society (APICS) and INFORMS Transportation Science and Logistics Section. He has also published articles in several indexed journals. His research work is mainly focused on models for solving difficult optimization problems arising in Production Scheduling, Routing, Transportation and Facility Location. He holds grants from the "Foro-Consultivo-Científico-y-Tecnológico" of CONACYT for research on optimization of Territory Planning. His current research on continuous move transportation is being funded by the CONACYT. Dr. Lopez has been working during the last 20 years at managerial and consulting level in eight different industrial sectors. His professional experience includes Information Technology, Manufacturing, Logistics, Distribution and Supply Chain Planning.

Helena Lourenco has a Bachelors Degree and a Masters in Statistics and Operations Research from the University of Lisbon (Portugal), and a Ph.D. in Operations Research (PhD) from the Cornell University (USA). She is currently Assistant Professor at the Department of Economics and Business at Universitat Pompeu Fabra (Spain). She has participated in several research projects and consulting for public and private companies in the telecommunications, healthcare, transportation, logistics and production industries. She has published several articles in prestigious international scientific journals and has presented several papers at international congresses and conferences. Helena teaches at various masters and postgraduate courses in Spain and Portugal. She is currently a researcher at the Healthcare Research Group, the Business Logistics Research Group (UPF, Spain) and the Centre for Operational Research at the University of Lisbon.

Pedro Palominos is with the Department of Industrial Engineering of the University of Santiago of Chile. He holds a Bachelor Degree and a Professional Degree in Industrial Engineering at the University of Santiago of Chile. He also holds a M.Sc. Degree in Engineering Production at the Federal University of Rio de Janeiro, Brazil and a Dr. Degree in Industrial Engineering at the University of Catalunya, Spain. Dr. Palominos teaches and researches in the use of metaheuristics in operations management.

Victor Parada is a Chemical Engineer; earned a MSc in Industrial Engineering from Catholic University of Rio de Janeiro and his Dr. Sc. in Computer Science and Systems Engineering from the Federal University of Rio de Janeiro, Brazil. He is now Professor at the Informatics Engineering Department of the University of Santiago of Chile. His current research interests are on heuristic methods to solve practical optimization problems.

Carlos D. Paternina-Arboleda is an Associate Professor and former Head of the Department of Industrial Engineering at Universidad del Norte, Barranquilla, Colombia. He is also Director of the Regional Unit of Science and Technology for Logistics & Ports at the Colombian Department of Science and Technology – Colciencias. He received his Ph.D. in Industrial Engineering from the University of South Florida, USA. His research interests are in simulation of production and logistics systems, supply chain management and scheduling.

Nathalie Perrier is a Research Associate in the Mathematics and Industrial Engineering Department at the École Polytechnique of Montreal. She holds a Bachelor of Business Administration and a Master of Science in Administration from HEC Montréal, and a Ph.D. degree in Mathematics for Engineers from the École Polytechnique of Montreal. Her research interests include mathematical modeling and solution of arc routing, winter road maintenance, emergency response logistics and project scheduling problems. She is a member of the Interuniversity Research Centre on Enterprise Networks, Logistics and Transportation (CIRRELT).

Rita Ribeiro Graduate in Management and Business Administration Universidade Católica Portuguesa, MSc in Management at Universitat Pompeu Fabra (Barcelona), PhD in Management (Universitat Pompeu Fabra) completed a thesis in the area of logistics and distribution management entitled "Integrated Distribution Management Problems: an Optimization Approach". Teaching Assistant at Universidade Pompeu Fabra (2000). Collaborators at GREL - Grup de Recerca en Logística Empresarial, Business Logistics research group, from Universitat Pompeu Fabra, www.grel.org . Currently she is Invited Assistant Professor at Universidade Católica Portuguesa and an economic and business consultant.

Elyn L. Solano-Charris is full-time professor within the School of Economics and Management Sciences at Universidad de La Sabana, Colombia. She holds a Master of Science and the Engineering degrees in Industrial Engineering both from Universidad del Norte, Barranquilla, Colombia. Her works have been presented at various academic conferences and published in various international journals. Her research interests include optimization of logistics and production systems and information systems for supply chain management.

Jorge Freire De Sousa got the degree in Electrical Engineering from Universidade do Porto – UP (1978), the M.Sc. in Operations Research from the Technical University of Lisbon (1989) and the Ph.D. in Industrial Engineering from the UP (1996). Since 2006, he is Member of the Board of STCP, the Public Transport Company of Porto, a position he has also occupied between 1998 and 2002. He began his professional career in the industry as a Maintenance Engineer. Since 1987, he worked as consultant and coordinator of several industry projects at INEGI, an interface institute of the UP. He was Head of the Industrial Engineering and Management Unit of the Faculty of Engineering of UP – FEUP (1997-98 and 2003-05). He teaches at FEUP where he is also a research member of IDMEC, a research unit at UP, where his main topics of interest are Transportation, Decision Support Systems and Applied Operations Research.

M.Grazia Speranza is Full Professor of Operations Research at the University of Brescia, Italy. Her main research interests are: Integer programming, combinatorial optimization, routing problems, supply chain optimization, worst-case analysis, exact and heuristic algorithms. She has published more than 100 papers in several international journals such as *Operations Research, Management Science, Transportation Science, Transportation Research, Computers and Operations Research, International Journal of Production Economics, Annals of Operations Research, Networks, European Journal of Operational Research, Naval Research Logistics, Discrete Applied Mathematics, INFORMS Journal on Computing*. She is Associate Editor of *Transportation Science, 4OR, International Transactions in Operational Research*. She is currently President of EURO (Association of European Operational Research Societies).

Mark A. Turnquist is a Professor of Civil & Environmental Engineering at Cornell University, where he has been on the faculty since 1979. He received his Ph.D. in Transportation Systems Analysis from MIT in 1975, and taught at Northwestern University from 1975 to 1979. He specializes in large-scale network optimization models for use in transportation, logistics and manufacturing systems. He has worked extensively with both private industry and the federal government, developing effective analysis methods for problems in these domain areas. His work with both the U.S. Department of Energy and with General Motors has been recognized in the Franz Edelman Award Competition of the Institute for Operations Research and the Management Sciences.

Gülfem Tuzkaya, Ph.D., is currently working as a *Research Assistant* in the Department of Industrial Engineering, Yildiz Technical University. Dr. G. Tuzkaya received her MSc. Degree in Industrial Engineering from Yildiz Technical University, in 2002, MBA degree from Istanbul Technical University, in 2005, and Ph.D. degree in Industrial Engineering from Yildiz Technical University, in 2008. Her research interests are in the areas of reverse-forward logistics systems design, facility layout design and production planning.

Andrés Véjar is a Master of Engineering from the University of Santiago of Chile. Currently he is Ph.D student at the Research Centre for Automatic Control CNRS – Nancy University, France. Today he is in an internship at the Research Centre for Applied Epistemology (CREA) CNRS - École Polytechnique, Paris, France. His research interest lies in Complex Systems Engineering and its Applications.

S. Travis Waller is an Associate Professor of Civil, Architectural and Environmental Engineering at the University of Texas at Austin where he has been on faculty since 2003 and currently holds the Phil M. Ferguson Teaching Fellowship. He was previously an Assistant Professor at the University of Illinois at Urbana-Champaign from 2001 to 2002. In 2000, he received his Ph.D. from Northwestern University in Industrial Engineering and Management Sciences. His work was recognized by MIT's Technology Review Magazine which named him one of the top 100 innovators in science and engineering in the world under 35 years of age in 2003. More recently he received the National Science Foundation CAREER award as well as the Transportation Research Board's Fred Burggraf Award.

Chi Xie obtained his Ph.D. in Transportation Systems Engineering at Cornell University in 2008, with two minor areas of Operations Research and Applied Economics. He has since then been a research fellow of Center for Transportation Research, the University of Texas at Austin. His current research interests include transportation and logistics systems design and analysis, transportation emergency management, travel demand forecasting, and intelligent transportation systems. In addition to academic activities, he also provided consultancy services and developed software tools for a number of federal and state government-sponsored transportation planning projects in the U.S., particularly from the Texas Department of Transportation. His name has been listed in Marquis Who's Who in America and Who's Who in Science and Engineering since 2007.

Index